Field Guide to the

Moths

of Great Britain and Ireland

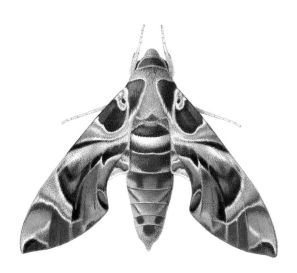

Paul Waring and Martin Townsend

Illustrated by Richard Lewington

British Wildlife Publishing

To my late parents, Doris and Clifford Waring, who encouraged my interest in moths in my formative years and who both died while this guide was in preparation; to my daughter, Kirsty Mae, who was born at the same time as the book, and to my wife, Rachel Thomas, for her support throughout. P.W.

To my late parents, Denis and Barbara Townsend, whose own love and knowledge of the natural world led to my interest in insects and other wildlife. M.T.

First published 2003 by
British Wildlife Publishing
Lower Barn, Rooks Farm
Rotherwick, Hook
Hampshire
RG27 9BG

ISBN 0 9531399 1 3 (paperback)
ISBN 0 9531399 3 × (hardback)

Colour separations by GWP, Kingsclere
Printed in Italy by Printer Trento, S.r.l.

Contents

Introduction

This field guide is written for everyone, from the beginner to the long-term moth enthusiast, from the amateur naturalist with a passing interest to seasoned biological surveyors and professionals responsible for conservation on nature reserves and other land. In order to make the guide more user-friendly, technical terms have been avoided wherever possible in favour of plain English.

One of the major reasons for embarking on this field guide is the difficulty many people have, frequently expressed among the many new moth enthusiasts, in identifying a live moth, with wings folded at rest, from a photograph or painting of a dead cabinet specimen with its wings spread out. The moths in this field guide are shown in their normal resting positions because the emphasis is on identifying live moths.

Moths are often dismissed as drab, night-flying relatives of butterflies. A thumb through the illustrations in this guide shows quite the opposite. In terms of colour, many moths are as brightly patterned and as attractive as any butterflies. In terms of wing shape, body form and size, moths are much more varied than butterflies, and there are so many more species in which to take an interest. The largest resident moth in Britain is the Privet Hawkmoth, which is as big as a mouse, as is the immigrant Death's-head Hawkmoth, which even squeaks like one! This field guide aims to help the reader navigate through this amazing variety of adult moths.

The text covers the latest details on their life cycle, foodplants, habitat, status and distribution. All the larger or so-called 'macro-moths' which have been reported 'in the field' in Great Britain, Ireland and the Channel Isles are covered, from the abundant species you are likely to see in any garden to the rarest of immigrants which have flown to Britain from other parts of the world. The guide also mentions some species that have probably arrived accidentally with imported goods.

How to use this field guide

To identify a moth

In order to identify a moth using the descriptive wing characters given in this guide, position the moth with the body pointing across you, rather than away from you. Some moths have strikingly distinctive wing patterns or other features that enable identification simply by looking through the illustrations to find an exact match. The plates are grouped into families of moths, which share a similar wing shape and body form. With practice, you will be able to recognise the families of moths, and therefore know which block of plates to search.

For other moths, you will find that several of the illustrations provide a fairly good match and you will now need to scrutinise certain details. Turn to the text for the species and use the 'Field characters' section to examine the diagnostic features, which should enable you to finalise your identification. Also take into account variation, habitat, location and time of year, but bear in mind that moths sometimes appear in the 'wrong' place and at the 'wrong' time. Occasionally, species are discovered in parts of Britain where they have never been seen before. Knowledge of geographical distributions is continually being added to, so you may find that you have made an important new discovery, for example, a new county record. The 'Similar species' section of the description draws attention to other species to check. A small minority of species cannot be distinguished reliably by the appearance of the wings and body. In some cases, only small details on the underside of the abdomen or elsewhere enable certain identification, and diagrams of these features are shown or references to other publications are provided. A very few species require examination of the genitalia, at the tip of the abdomen. Moth genitalia are quite complex. Those of the male have a pair of claspers with which he grasps the female, in addition to a penis-like structure, and other associated structures for opening the vagina. The male genitalia are sculptured and have patterns of bristles, all of which fit together with the female genitalia of the same species like a lock and key. Mating with another species, in many cases, is physically impossible. Consequently, the genitalia of a species vary very little, and so are extremely useful in identifying moths and in confirming tentative identifications made using other more variable characters. Where features of the genitalia can be viewed without dissecting the moth, illustrations are given. Where dissection is needed, the reader is referred to more specialist books for diagrams (see Further reading).

Illustrations

Each of the species illustrated is represented by at least one example of the adult, usually a male. Where the female differs substantially in appearance, this is also illustrated. All species are shown at life size unless otherwise indicated. Additional illustrations are provided where a species varies greatly or more than one subspecies occurs. Sometimes additional diagnostic features are shown. Photographs of a number of larvae have also been included. These have been selected to show the great diversity of form between, and even within, family groupings. The selection includes widespread species, and others which are more localised or rare, but of particular interest.

Format of the species accounts

The text accounts contain the following information:

Common name   The English name, exactly as given in the most recent British checklist of moths (Bradley 2000). The English names have the advantage that they have remained largely stable for the last 200 years (compare this guide with those of Newman (1869) and South (1961), for example). For many people the varied English names and their history are part of the charm of studying British moths; see Marren (1998) for a discussion and Salmon (2000) for an insight into the characters that named them. The page numbers here refer to the plate on which the moth is illustrated.

Scientific name   The Latin name follows the British checklist (Bradley 2000), but with the name of the author abbreviated (full names listed on page 414). See page 14 for a full explanation of scientific names.

National status and distribution summary   Every species has been allocated a national status by the Joint Nature Conservation Committee. For resident species, these and their abbreviations are: Red Data Book species (RDB), Nationally Scarce A (Na), Nationally Scarce B (Nb), Local, Common and Uncommon on introduced foodplant. The additional categories are Immigrant, Rare Immigrant, Import, all of which may be qualified with Suspected, and Doubtfully British. See pages 8 and 16 for an explanation of these categories.

There is an abbreviated indication of the geographic distribution within the British Isles, in the form of one or more letters, as follows: T = throughout, S = southern (south of the Wash), C = central (from the Wash northwards to Cumbria and Northumberland), N = northern (from Cumbria and Northumberland to Shetland), E = eastern and W = western (east and west respectively of a north-south line bisecting the Isle of Wight). These may be qualified, so SE means south-east as distinct from S, E meaning south and east. Where the region is shown in parentheses, this means the main part of the distribution is elsewhere but the distribution extends to this area, e.g. S, C, (N). The order of the letters is generally from south to north and west to east, but may differ to indicate the main areas first. The summary is intended to show the general pattern in brief, and the boundaries are not rigid. Used in conjunction with the Status and distribution section, this provides a handy summary for annotating, comparing and analysing moth lists. Species or subspecies occurring only in the Channel Islands, Ireland, Man, the Hebrides, Orkney or Shetland are labelled as such.

Checklist number   The first number is the British checklist number. The second number, in parentheses, is the European checklist number (Euro-number) after Karsholt & Razowski (1996). The order of species, and hence the sequence of numbering, differs greatly between these two checklists. An asterisk by the Euro-number indicates that the scientific name in this checklist differs in some way from that in the British checklist. In both lists the checklist number refers to the entire species, so where two or more subspecies are given in the British list, they share the same number. This guide follows the British sequence, which is slightly different from the original numerical sequence, because a few species have been moved since the numbers were originally allocated in the 1970s. A small number of species on the British checklist are not in the European list, usually because they are immigrants or imports originating from outside Europe.

Field characters This begins with the forewing length, to indicate the size of the moth. Forewing length is given rather than wingspan because the latter can be measured only when the wings are spread. The forewing length is the distance from the forewing-tip to the point where it joins the thorax (see Fig. 1). If necessary, this can be measured using a pair of dividers, assuming the moth is docile. The diagnostic features of the moth are then given, together with a description of its variation. When describing features of the wings, the standard convention is to describe the wing in the singular. When the description states that there are two or more spots, cross-lines or other markings, this is the number on each wing. For species with two or more subspecies or forms, these are also described.

Similar species In this section species, that can easily be confused are listed and diagnostic features are given to separate them.

Flight season Whether the species has one generation or more in a year is specified and if this varies in different parts of the British Isles, this is stated. The approximate period when each generation is on the wing is given. These are the times when you can usually expect to find the adult moth, based on several decades of observations. Note that moths generally emerge earlier in the south than in the north, until late summer, while the onset of autumn and its associated moths is earlier in the north. Also, flight seasons for many species are earlier or later in some years than in others, and many have often been earlier than the long-term average by as much as two weeks since the early 1990s. This correlates with higher than average temperatures, leading to much interest in the use of moths to monitor the effects of climate change. Every year, occasional individuals are reported well outside the usual dates, for reasons that are not always clear.

Other aspects of adult behaviour are also reported in this section. The moths are nocturnal, unless otherwise stated. The extent to which they come to light-traps, other lights and baits is given and this applies to both sexes unless stated. Sugar is used as a shorthand term for sugaring mixture, wine-roping and other sweet baits. See page 16 for more information on light-trapping, baiting and other techniques.

Life cycle The overwintering stage is given first, because much practical habitat management work is done during the winter period, with the intention of minimising the impact on wildlife. It is crucially important to site managers that they know how and where particular moth species spend the winter. Many moths are dormant below ground but others spend the winter as eggs, larvae or pupae on or inside the twigs of both living and dead trees, shrubs and herbaceous plants, and are likely, for example, to be removed by scrub clearance or autumn clearing. Many species pupate in soft earth but remain on the ground surface among plant debris, such as fallen leaves, if the earth is too hard to burrow into. The information on pupation sites is drawn from various sources, in addition to personal experience, but often the only detailed source was Newman & Leeds (1913), in which some of the observations are clearly based on experience in captivity rather than in the field.

Larval foodplants Although this guide is intended for the identification of adult moths, some understanding of the larval requirements is necessary to select appropriate places to search for particular moths and to interpret the results obtained from light-trapping and other monitoring of the adults. The English plant names follow Stace (1997). An effort has been made to specify precise species wherever possible and these begin with capital letters. The scientific names are listed on pages 415-417. In previous works, there has been a tendency to list some foodplants generically, but this can be misleading. For instance, many larvae found on Pedunculate Oak are likely to refuse Evergreen Oak. Also, there is evidence that some moths may prefer either Downy or Silver Birch. Unless stated otherwise, the larva eats the leaves. The most frequently-used foodplants are listed first. If a wide range is involved, closely-related plants appear together. Some species have clear preferences for either mature or scrubby growth in the case of trees, or for plants in the sun or the shade, and this is indicated where known to the authors. There is much work to be done on these subjects and it is hoped this guide will stimulate readers to fill such gaps in our knowledge. Larvae have often been reared in captivity on common and readily available plants such as Dandelion and chickweeds. These are not listed in the accounts, except where the foodplants in the wild are unknown.

Habitat The descriptions used are largely self-explanatory. They are intended to indicate the major habitat type occupied, and whether the species prefers calcareous (e.g. limestone, chalk), acidic (heathland, moorland, bogs), wet or dry (e.g. marshes, sand-dunes), open or sheltered, upland or lowland, and inland or coastal locations. Where certain habitats are preferred, these are presented first, but many species occur equally in a wide range of habitats. Where a species is likely to be found in most gardens within its geographic distribution, this habitat is given first because this is the most accessible habitat for the majority of people. If gardens appear late in the list, you have a fair chance of recording the species in gardens, but the moth is much better represented in other habitats.

Status & distribution All species are described as Resident or Immigrant, or sometimes as both. 'Resident' means breeding and surviving the winter, such that the British or Channel Island populations are not dependent on annual immigration from elsewhere for their survival. The term 'Immigrant' is used where the species has flown or been transported by air-streams from origins outside the British Isles. Some species have been seen flying across the English Channel or arriving from the North Sea and are confirmed immigrants. Others are likely immigrants but are not proven, and are listed as 'Suspected immigrant'. Some have been recorded fewer than ten times, sometimes only once, and these are labelled 'Rare immigrant'.

Other moths are clearly accidental or deliberate imports by man, for example, those that have arrived in association with imported goods. A few have been captured in the field but have origins so far away from Europe that accidental importation is their most likely means of arrival. These are labelled as 'Suspected import'. Whether there is any value or meaning in including known Imports in the British list is debatable, but as this guide aims to cover the entire British list, those that have been admitted are covered separately. Unfortunately, there are also species on the British list that are the result of known or suspected fraud, particularly from the 19th century, and others for which the British data are dubious for other reasons. These are labelled 'Doubtfully British' and the reasons listed. To conserve space, doubtfully British species not reported since 1900 and suspected imports are relegated to the Appendix and are not usually illustrated.

All species recorded in the United Kingdom have been given a national status with the most threatened and scarce species assigned to a conservation category, as listed under National status above and abbreviated in the header of the account. In this part of the text, it is given in full. See pages 15-16 for an explanation of these categories.

There are three main components to the accounts of national distribution. These are the parts of the country in which the species occurs, the density, uniformity or pattern of distribution within these areas, and the frequency with which the species is normally encountered in the field.

For species covering large areas of Britain, terms such as northern and western, upland and lowland are used, sometimes in combination. Note that south-east England is used here to mean Surrey, Kent and Sussex mainly and is not intended to include parts of Essex, except for the Thames Estuary. The Thames Estuary and the London conurbation are major barriers to some species. Essex is generally treated as part of East Anglia. More localised species are described in terms of the counties they occupy. Moth reporting has been based on the Watsonian vice-county system since the 19th century. This is the basis for recent county lists and for reporting first county records and tracking changes in distribution. Generally, this guide uses vice-counties or amalgamations of them (e.g. East and West Sussex into Sussex, Yorkshire to mean its five constituent vice-counties). A noteworthy exception is use of the term Cumbria, which is a readily understood amalgamation of the cumbersomely named vice-county of 'Westmorland with North Lancashire' with the vice-county of Cumberland.

Use of the more recent and transient local government areas such as Strathclyde, Dyfed, Clwyd, Avon and Tyne & Wear has been avoided. These areas in Scotland are frequently too large or not biogeographically useful, and the names and boundaries of some of those in Wales have recently been changed yet again. In many cases, the vice-county boundaries are clearly demarcated on the ground by rivers and other landscape features. In Scotland, many moth distributions follow the valleys of the major rivers and associated lowlands, so it makes more sense to refer to Speyside and Deeside, for instance, than to list the counties. In most cases in England, the text would read the same whether using names of amalgamated vice-counties or modern county names, a notable exception involves those parts of vice-county Berkshire which is now in modern Oxfordshire. Where it is helpful or prevents confusion, the modern county is added. In most cases the distribution is described from south to north and west to east in Great Britain, and then for Man, Ireland and the Channel Islands. National distribution maps have not been included because accurate, up-to-date and properly vetted maps are not currently available for the majority of British moths.

Within these areas, the assessment of the pattern and density of distribution is based on that of the 10km squares from which the species has been recorded. For Nationally Scarce and Red Data Book species, maps are available which gather and show all the records since 1980, or more recently, and the assessment is based on these. The most recently compiled national distribution map, with a date-class of 1960 onwards (see Heath & Emmet 1976-), is the basis for the assessment of other species, considerably augmented by data from recent county lists and journals, and much unpublished information. Unpublished distribution maps for the geometrid moths (not yet covered by the Heath & Emmet series) have been consulted. The following terms are used, the criteria necessarily somewhat loose:

- Very well distributed – records from almost every 10km square
- Well distributed – records from a majority of 10km squares
- Quite well distributed – areas without records not overwhelming
- Local – localised or patchy distribution of records

The distribution of species with relatively few records is described in greater detail. An indication of the usual frequency with which the moth is encountered is also given. Most often this is based on impressions from use of mercury-vapour light-traps, but sometimes species are found to be more numerous using other techniques and this is stated. The number of moths recorded on a site visit depends on the number of traps used and the degree of effort employing other methods. As a very rough guide to what is intended by the following terms, they are based on and explained in terms of the experience of a lone trapper with one to three Robinson light-traps. The categories are:

- Abundant – often 100 or more individuals per light-trap in a single night at peak season (e.g. Large Yellow Underwing)
- Frequent – often seen as more than ten individuals in a visit to an occupied site, or seen on most visits during its flight season
- Fairly frequent – seen on most visits to occupied sites, but seldom as many as ten individuals at one time
- Occasional – unlikely to be seen on most site visits during its flight season and seldom as more than one or two individuals, but likely to be encountered every year.

Species insufficiently numerous to be Occasional are described more specifically, and in cases with few records, these may be listed. Use of these terms for moths on Man, Ireland and in the Channel Islands is according to information supplied by the respective local recorders and not necessarily as above.

Moths in more detail

Moth anatomy

The illustration below shows the Angle Shades moth at rest and with wings spread, as in a cabinet specimen. This shows how some diagnostic features such as resting posture (with furled wings) are lost in the cabinet specimen, while conversely, features of the hindwings are revealed. The difficulty many people have in mentally translating the resting moth into the cabinet specimen is one of the main reasons for producing this guide. This, together with illustrations of Lesser Yellow Underwing and Common Emerald, are used to show the main anatomical terms used in the guide.

Figure 1

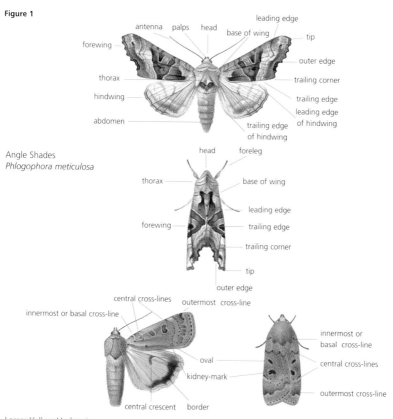

Angle Shades
Phlogophora meticulosa

Lesser Yellow Underwing
Noctua comes

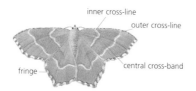

Common Emerald
Hemithea aestivaria

Figure 2 An example of a life cycle of a moth

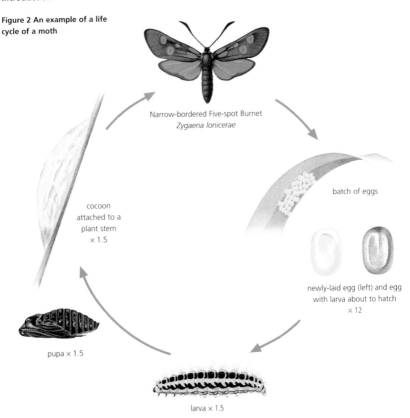

Narrow-bordered Five-spot Burnet
Zygaena lonicerae

cocoon
attached to a
plant stem
× 1.5

batch of eggs

newly-laid egg (left) and egg
with larva about to hatch
× 12

pupa × 1.5

larva × 1.5

The life cycle of the moth
Larvae, larval foodplants and pupation
Moths reproduce by laying eggs, which hatch into caterpillars, commonly known among moth enthusiasts as **larvae** (plural) or **larva** (singular). The larvae are 'feeding machines', which do all the eating and weight-gain necessary to produce an adult moth from a tiny egg. Most moth larvae feed on plant material, usually eating the leaves. Others specialise in eating the flowers, fruits or roots, or bore into the stems or rootstocks. Most specialise in particular plants or plant families, and in many cases will starve rather than feed on anything else.

As the larva grows in size, it sheds its skin in order to enable expansion, revealing a new skin that has formed underneath. This typically happens four times before the larva moults to produce what outwardly looks like a resting stage, the chrysalis, or pupa. For moths, it is generally called the **pupa** (singular) or **pupae** (plural) and the act of forming the pupa is known as **pupation**. The larvae of many species of moths leave the larval foodplant and burrow into the ground before forming the pupa, or pupate among leaf litter. Others attach themselves to the foodplant in various ways, frequently spinning a cocoon of silk, often spun between leaves or in grooves in bark. Some are even spun inside the plant near exit holes made by the larva.

From pupa to adult moth to egg-laying and dispersal
Inside the pupa, the body of the insect reorganises to form the adult moth, which breaks out of the pupa, expands its initially soft wings by pumping fluids into them and allowing them to dry. It is then ready to take flight. For male moths, the main activity is to find females and mate with

them. They do this by following scents released by unmated females, often recognising the females by sight once they are near. Sometimes mating takes place before the female has dried her wings, and there are even species in which the male locates the cocoons of the female and simply waits for her to emerge. Others emerge with the gonads immature and must feed and/or undergo a period of dormancy before mating can occur. The main activities of the female moth are to attract a mate, and to survive long enough to lay as many eggs as she can, which may be over 100, or even 1,000.

Often the females do not move far from the larval foodplants, particularly in the early phase of egg-laying. They may spend much time gluing eggs to particular parts of the foodplant, either singly or in large batches, although others lay them loose and the larvae have to locate the appropriate foodplants. Once some eggs are laid, the females are lighter and may show a greater tendency to wander and seek out new supplies of foodplant. In other species, the males, or both sexes, feed like butterflies, with a tube-like tongue, known as the proboscis. They feed for energy at sugary substances, such as the nectar produced by flowers, honeydew excreted by aphids which often accumulates on leaves, or the sap which oozes from wounds on tree trunks. Many have no requirement to feed and have reduced, non-functional mouthparts, existing on energy stored as fats and carbohydrates when they were larvae.

For many moths, the adult stage is also the main means of dispersal for colonisation of new habitat. Some individuals fly great distances, leaving breeding grounds in the south of Europe and flying north to reach the British Isles as immigrants. Certain species display a strong tendency to migration and arrive in numbers annually from mainland Europe. Others move no more than a few hundred metres during their adult lifespan. Typically, the adult lifespan varies from a few days to two or three weeks in the wild.

For a few species, the larva is the most mobile stage. Tiny caterpillars of tussock moths and some loopers have been found drifting in the upper atmosphere. Eggs and pupae can move hundreds of miles attached to plant material floating on water, or on objects transported by man.

Determining the sex of a moth and examining the genitalia

This is particularly important if you wish to try and breed a species, which is the best start to learning the young stages and finding them more successfully in the wild. Generally, when a wild female moth is found she has already been mated and has received from the male a supply of sperm that will enable her to lay fertile eggs over the next few days. In some species, the size or wing patterns are very different in males and females. Otherwise, the sexes are most easily recognised by examining the antennae and the abdomen.

Antennae – In many species, the antennae of the male are much broader than those of the female. Often they are feathery on one or both sides, while those of the female are single-stranded and thin. The most notable exceptions are those of the burnet moths, which have pointed club ends in both sexes.

Abdomen shape – Features of the abdomen are the best means of sexing these moths. Generally, females have a wider abdomen which does not curve upwards. In geometrids and some hawkmoths, the tip of the male abdomen often curves upwards in an extreme fashion. The abdomen of the female is often fat with eggs, usually tapering to a rather blunt tip, but if all the eggs have been laid it will be slimmer. The rather pointed ovipositor, from which the eggs are laid, is often noticeable, especially after egg-laying has started, when some scales are lost from the end of the abdomen. In male moths of the majority of species, the pair of claspers at the tip of the abdomen are an obvious distinguishing feature and sometimes they also serve to distinguish closely-related species. In other species, the claspers often make the tip of the male's abdomen appear rather squared, sometimes even slightly bulbous, as in the burnet moths.

Genitalia examination

If confirmation of difficult species such as the Marbled Minor group (page 352) or the Grey and Dark Daggers (page 306) is required, it is possible to see the diagnostic differences in the

Common micro-moths that may easily be confused with macro-moths

The reader will find a few common moths which, on the basis of size, could reasonably be expected to be in this book. The following is intended to help beginners recognise what is not a macro-moth and to guide them to sources of information on the larger micro-moths. Most of these belong to the family **Pyralidae**.

Some large and frequent species you will encounter include:

Mother of Pearl *Pleuroptya ruralis* (Scop.), often disturbed from rest by day around Common Nettle, the larval foodplant;

Small Magpie *Eurrhypara hortulata* (L.), also widespread and frequent on Common Nettle;

grass-veneers or **grass-moths** (Sub-family Crambinae) frequent amongst uncut grass, on which the larvae feed;

the various purple-and-gold *Pyrausta* species, which are day-flying, often seen visiting flowers for nectar and feed as larvae on the flowers of labiate plants such as mints, marjorams and thymes, sometimes in herb gardens.

When at rest, most pyralid moths fold the antennae backwards over the wings so that they lie alongside the body. Notable exceptions are the **Bee moth** *Aphomia sociella* (L.) and the **Wax Moth** *Galleria mellonella* (L.), both of which are frequently captured in light-traps. To identify pyralid moths see Goater (1986).

More distinctive than pyralids are the **plume moths** (family Pterophoridae) so named because the wings when spread look like feathers or plumes. The **White Plume** *Pterophorus pentadactyla* (L.) is a widespread and frequent species dependent on bindweeds. Other plumes are generally brown and roll their wings up at rest, in a T-shape, e.g. the **Common Plume** *Emmelina monodactyla* (L.). An exception is the **Twenty-plume moth** *Alucita hexadactyla* L., which looks like a plume moth but belongs in the Alucitidae. It is often encountered hibernating in gardens near the larval foodplant, Honeysuckle. A book on plume moths by Colin Hart is currently in preparation to replace the out of print book by Bryan Beirne (1952).

Tortricoid moths (Super-family Tortricoidea) are widespread, often colourful moths so-named because the larvae twist-up leaves to feed protected within them. They are medium-sized, often bell-shaped moths. The **Green Oak Roller** or **Oak Tortrix** *Tortrix viridana* (L.) is abundant in woodland, the larvae feeding on oak. This species is sometimes confused with the rarer Cream-bordered Green Pea *Earias clorana*. Also illustrated is a typical bell-shaped tortricoid, the **Large Fruit-tree Tortrix** *Achips podana* (Scop.).

The **small ermines**, *Yponomeuta* species (Yponomeutidae), are often confused with macro-moths, both as adult moths and as larvae. The adults are similar in shape to footman moths (Family Arctiidae) and not infrequently have been mistaken for the very rare Speckled Footman *Coscinia cribraria*, because the latter was the only vaguely similar moth in the book that was in use. The small ermines have pin-prick-sized black dots, unlike the smeared streaky spots of the Speckled Footman. The larvae of some of the small ermines defoliate shrubs, which they cover in silk webbing, such as the **Common Hawthorn Ermine** *Y. padella* (L.) on hawthorns, Blackthorn and Cherry Plum and the **Spindle Ermine** *Y. irrorella* (Hb.) on Spindle. The naked greyish larvae with black spots are easy to see in the thin webbing. Touch one on the head and it will wriggle backwards. This 'reverse wriggling test' is a good means of distinguishing larvae of micro-moths from larvae which will produce the macro-moths covered in this book, because the latter will generally not shuffle rapidly backwards, although some, like the larvae of the Buttoned Snout *Hypena rostralis*, wriggle from side to side.

There are many other groups of micro-moths not mentioned above, but in general they really are small (with forewing length 5mm or less), although they are often exceedingly beautiful when examined closely. They have a wider range of life-styles than the macro-moths, including species whose larvae feed on the fur, wool, horns and feathers of mammals and birds, as well as carpets and clothes, such as the familiar brown, black-spotted **Brown House-moth** *Hofmannophila pseudospretella* (Stainton) (Family Oecophoridae). A great many are leaf-miners, living inside a leaf, feeding on the internal tissues. A few have semi- or fully-aquatic larvae, such as the **Brown China-mark** *Elophila nymphaeata* (L.).

genitalia of the males, without dissection, by the following method. We suggest those selected for investigation are placed in a deep-freeze for a minimum of one hour to kill them because examination of genitalia *in situ* may cause internal injuries to live moths. Allow the moth to defrost for several minutes. Lay it on one side to avoid damage to the wings. Gently apply pressure to the central portion of the underside of the abdomen with forceps or a setting needle and work towards the genitalia, which will extrude. The various parts can then be examined with a hand lens or low-power binocular microscope. For species where it is sufficient to examine external spurs and other parts without extrusion, such as the November moth group (page 98), it should be sufficient to anaesthetise the moth with ethyl actetate by leaving it for a few moments in the vapour until it looks asleep. The moth will rouse quickly once back in fresh air.

Small Magpie
Eurrhypara hortulata

Mother of Pearl
Pleuroptya ruralis

Crambus pascuella
a grass-veneer

Pyrausta purpuralis
a purple and gold
pyralid

13

Bee moth
Aphomia sociella

Wax Moth
Galleria mellonella

White Plume
Pterophorus pentadactyla

Twenty-plume moth
Alucita hexadactyla

Green Oak Roller
Tortrix viridana

Large Fruit-tree
Tortrix
Achips podana

Bird-cherry Ermine
*Yponomeuta
evonymella*

Brown House-moth
*Hofmannophila
pseudospretella*

Brown China-mark
Elophila nymphaeata

Adela reaumurella
(Incurvaridae)

Cinnamon Sedge Caddisfly
Limnephilus rhombicus

Figure 3 Some micro-moths that may easily be confused with macro-moths, and a caddisfly.

How to distinguish a moth from a butterfly, and from other insects such as caddisflies

Butterflies and moths are very closely related. Together they comprise the Order Lepidoptera within Class Insecta in the Animal Kingdom. Taxonomically, butterflies are placed in a discrete group of families toward the middle of the moths, implying that they evolved later as a branch of the Lepidoptera 'family tree' rather than early in the history of the group, so the division is somewhat artificial. There are about 165,000 described species of Lepidoptera in the world ,and perhaps as many more awaiting discovery and description. About 2,500 species of moths have been recorded from the British Isles, including some 900 macros. These numbers are constantly changing because new species are colonising Britain from other parts of Europe, others are still being discovered and some species have been lost.

The British butterflies can be distinguished from nearly all British moths by their clubbed antennae. The moths have many types of antennae (see page 11). None, except those of the burnets, are clubbed and the burnets are easily recognised by their slender wings, held close to the body at rest, in marked contrast to all the butterflies.

Caddisflies (Order Trichoptera) are the only other group of insects that are frequently confused with moths, and they often occur in large numbers in light-traps, but they lack the powdery, detachable, overlapping wing-scales after which the moths and butterflies are named (Lepidoptera literally means 'tile-winged', from the Greek). Caddisflies can also be recognised by their long antennae (usually longer than the whole body), which point forward and are held together at rest, and are never moved to lay back along the body or wings, as with many moths. Even moths with very long antennae, such as the members of the Family Incurvariidae, do not generally align the antennae together. Caddisflies are usually brown and the outer wings look coarse and leathery, with few cross-veins.

The division of moths into macro-moths and micro-moths

Like the division into butterflies and moths, the division of moths into macro- and micro-moths is one of convenience rather than science. This field guide covers the macro-moths. The micro-lepidoptera, or 'micros', are in general smaller in size (although there is considerable overlap) with a forewing length of 1cm or less. Macro-moths, being generally larger, are more easily identified and therefore were more widely studied in the early days of entomology, with many people ignoring families of the very small moths. Hence, the convention probably developed over a number of years, rather than being decided upon suddenly. It has anomalies. The micros are considered to be more primitive (indeed, the most primitive have not developed a proboscis for feeding, and, instead, use mandibles) and therefore are placed at the front of the classification. However, a small number of primitive groups have developed quite large species, such as the swifts, goats and clearwings, and these have thus become 'honorary' macros. The placing of the Pyralidae as micros is also puzzling, since they are a diverse group, and even in the British Isles many species are comparable in size to most Geometridae, and are no more difficult to identify than, say, the pugs.

Scientific names

Like all forms of life known to science, from bacteria to bracket fungi to birds, each described species of moth has been given a double-barrelled name in Latin (often mixed with Greek), introduced by Carl von Linné (Linnaeus) around 1758, by convention written in italics. Latin was the internationally understood language of science in the 18th and early 19th century when most European moths were first formally named in print. The name(s) of the author(s) is often given after the name so that it is clear which moth is involved. A list of the abbreviations used in this guide for authors' names is given on page 414.

The scientific names are used throughout the world. So, while the very descriptive English name of the Figure of Eight moth *Diloba caeruleocephala* (Linnaeus, 1758) only means something to a person who speaks English, the scientific name is universal and is useful in all the other places the moth occurs. This is the name first published for the moth using the Linnean system. The first name is the generic name, which is the genus or grouping into which the moth and its close relatives have been put, and this always begins with a capital letter. The second word is the specific or species name and is always written in lower-case. Groupings of moths are likely to change as more is discovered about the evolutionary relationships between them. This results in changes in generic names so the specific name and author(s) are the important identifiers. The name of the author and date of the publication appear in parentheses, unless the moth is still classified in the genus in which it was originally placed. The International Commission on Zoological Nomenclature (ICZN) governs the allocation of scientific names.

It is unfortunate that the majority of people interested in natural history today do not have the benefit of having learned Latin and Greek in school. As a consequence, the scientific names are often perceived as no more than code words which are hard to remember and difficult to pronounce and spell. In fact, they are often as descriptive as the English names. In the case of the Figure of Eight moth, the species name *caeruleocephala* means the 'blue-headed one', and comes from the Latin *caeruleus*, meaning sky-blue, and the Greek *kephale*, meaning head. This refers to the larva, unlike the English name, which refers to the adult moth. Bear in mind that before electric light-traps, many moths were much more easily found as larvae and then reared to adult. The generic name *Diloba* means two lobes in Greek and refers to the same 'figure of eight' marking on the forewing of the moth that inspired the English name.

Subspecies and forms

This guide follows Bradley (2000) in the use of subspecies and forms, in almost all cases. Generally the term subspecies (also synonymous with race, as used in other texts) has been applied to populations of a species in which the individuals are consistently different in form and occur in a different geographical area from other populations, such that they do not generally interbreed, although they are capable of doing so if they encounter one another. If they were unable to interbreed when meeting, they would qualify as separate species. In addition, any population may consist of several recognisable colour forms. Names have been given both to subspecies and forms. Forms are sometimes referred to as aberrations, which automatically implies rarity, but the frequency of a particular form can vary greatly from one population to another, being rare in some, predominating in others, and can change over time!

In scrutinising and comparing cabinet specimens from many locations to prepare this guide, much subtle variation has also been noted. It is clear that intergrading regional differences occur in many species. In practice, this means that species can look somewhat different when you move out of regions you know well into other areas, even though the moths are not recognised as different subspecies or forms. All this variation, and other mutant forms not described here, has been a source of fascination since the earliest days of the study of moths.

National distribution and national recording of moths

The number of people in the British Isles involved in observing and recording moths runs to many thousands. The majority have some contact with the county moth recorders who compile county databases on moths, usually with the aim of producing and updating annotated county lists and atlases, increasingly with local distribution maps. The county recorders are invaluable in quality control – vetting records for accuracy. Most have support and backing from natural history societies, wildlife trusts and other organisations, and have formal or informal groups of moth observers, increasingly supplying data in electronic format. National distribution maps were originally produced by the Biological Records Centre (BRC), Monks Wood, Huntingdonshire, based on returns from all the county recorders and many other individuals. A national recording scheme covering all the macro-moths in the British Isles and the Channel Islands was operated from BRC, co-ordinated by the late John Heath, until his retirement in 1982, when the scheme was formally closed down. Butterfly Conservation are currently exploring ways of re-instating such a scheme. In the interim, national distribution maps have been produced on an *ad hoc* basis, usually by updating existing maps of particular species, for publications such as Heath & Emmet (1976-). Between 1991 and 1996, JNCC set up and co-ordinated the National Scarce Moth Recording Scheme for the 300 rarest species of larger moths. This provided the information and distribution maps for a national review (Waring, in press) and for the UK Biodiversity Action Plan (1999), in which the most recent date class was 1980 onwards. Butterfly Conservation have continued the running of this scheme to date.

National status and conservation categories

The national status and conservation categories of each species of macro-moth are based largely on the most recent national distribution map available from the above sources, modified to take account of more recent published and unpublished information. The categories are as follows:
• Red Data Book species (RDB) – species included in the British Red Data Book for Insects (Shirt, 1987) or meeting Red Data Book criteria subsequently. All species known from 15 or fewer of

the 10km squares in Great Britain. Newly-introduced criteria give greater emphasis to rates of decline, and declining species with recent records (the last 25 years) from more than 15 10km squares can be admitted to this category.

- pRDB species – proposed for inclusion in the next Red Data Book listing because current information indicates the species meets current criteria.
- Nationally Scarce A – recorded from 16-30 10km squares in Great Britain since 1 January 1980.
- Nationally Scarce B – recorded from 31-100 10km squares in Great Britain since 1 January 1980.
- Local – recorded from 101-300 10km squares in Great Britain since 1 January 1960.
- Common – recorded from over 300 10km squares in Great Britain since 1 January 1960.
- Uncommon on introduced foodplant (alien host) – recorded from less than 100 10km squares in Great Britain since 1980 but all known larval foodplants are non-native.
- Immigrant – flown or transported by wind from sources outside the British Isles (and Channel Islands where appropriate). Note that resident populations may be supplemented by immigrants.
- Rare immigrant – immigrants for which ten or fewer individuals reported reaching the British Isles.
- Import – originating outside the British Isles and found with imported goods or in their vicinity, such as in docks and warehouses.
- Doubtfully British – the only records are unsubstantiated, specimens are inadequately labelled, sources uncertain or unreliable, in some cases fraud is suspected. The text accounts include a summary of the available details.

Waring (1994) annotated every species of macro-moth on the British list according to this system. The list was reviewed by Waring (1999b) and some minor changes made to take account of real changes in distribution and additional data. These listings have been widely adopted by moth recorders and in county lists and biological recording packages. This guide follows Waring (1999b) with the following few proposals regarding the Nationally Scarce and Red Data Book species, to take account of recent information: False Mocha Nb (was Local); Slender-striped Rufous Na (was Na, then RDB); Pretty Pinion Local (was Nb); Marsh Pug Nb (was Local); Four-spotted Footman Na as well as Immigrant; Cousin German Na (was Na then RDB); Pale Shining Brown pRDB (was Nb); Bordered Gothic pRDB (was Na); White-spotted Pinion pRDB (was Na); Brighton Wainscot pRDB (was Na).

Field techniques for finding moths

Searching for adult moths

Day-flying moths can be sought as for butterflies, by walking around likely places, inspecting flowers, and tapping vegetation to dislodge resting moths. Some flowers are particularly attractive to moths, such as sallow catkins, ragworts, Hemp-agrimony, Buddleia, heathers, Ivy and the flowerheads of some grasses and sedges, the latter often as a result of infections of ergot fungus which result in sticky, sweet secretions. Success is greater on warm, dry and calm days and a few species require sunshine. Others have dawn or pre-dusk flights. Many species roost on tree trunks, fence posts, rocks or man-made structures by day and, for some species, these objects are well-worth searching, especially early in the morning, as warmth and direct sunlight will often cause the moths to move out of sight later. Places with all-night lighting are worth searching by day, such as hallways, porches, shop windows, street lights, and especially rural telephone boxes and toilet blocks on campsites. As dusk falls, more moths take to the wing. Hedgerows on quiet footpaths are good places at this time. The more species of woody plants in the hedge and the more varied the herbs and grasses in the verge, the greater the variety of moths you can expect. Open woodlands of native trees are the most productive places, but herb-rich, permanent unimproved grassland is also very good. Fens, carr woodland, heathland and moorland all have characteristic species unlikely to be found elsewhere, and for some moths you will need to climb to the very tops of mountains. After dark, you can carry on searching with a torch. You will smell the scent of flowers you never noticed by day and will find moths feeding by searching these, as well as sap runs, over-ripe and fallen fruit and even damp bare ground, animal corpses and dung. Under the cover of darkness you will see many larvae starting to feed more openly, safe from the birds, and you will not be able to resist collecting a few to rear on the same foodplant to find out what they are. Then you will have really become a moth-hunter!

Baiting techniques

Having seen how moths are attracted to fermenting fruit or sap runs, you can provide some attractants of your own. For centuries, moth collectors have mixed up potions based on black treacle or molasses, with various additives, and painted the mixture in vertical strips about 30cm by 2cm on tree-trunks, fence posts or even rocks, to attract moths. This is known as 'sugaring'. The black treacle gives the mixture body and adhesion, but for an effective potion you need to add something to attract the moths from a distance – a dash of rum is traditional and very effective, amyl

Light Crimson Underwing at a wine rope.

acetate is also frequently used, but you only need a drop or two – any more can be repellent. A little beer adds a fermenting smell and can intoxicate the moths and make them easier to catch. Sour chutney and over-ripe bananas are also effective attractants and add substance to the mix. The majority of moths arrive quickly once the 'sugar' has been applied.

Wine-roping is a technique in which approximately 1m lengths of string (the 'ropes') are soaked in a saturated solution of red wine and white sugar and then hung on foliage at dusk. Like sugaring, this can be a very successful means of attracting moths to feed. In this guide, the word 'sugar' is used generically to include all baits based on sugar, including wine-ropes.

Light-trapping

Light-trapping exploits the commonly observed tendency of many moths to approach and become disorientated around bright lights. The types of electric lights which emit part of their output as ultra-violet light have been found to be most effective and two types are favourites among moth-trappers: mercury vapour discharge bulbs and fluorescent (actinic) tubes. Traps are designed around these, operating on the lobster-pot principle. The moths rest in the traps unharmed and can be released again after recording. There are a number of commercially produced designs, chief of which are the Robinson, Skinner and Heath traps. For

A BENHS meeting gathered around a light and sheet.

a complete guide to moth-traps and their use, see Fry & Waring (2001).

Light-trapping is the single most effective technique both for general recording to see what is present and for compiling a site inventory, and for targeted trapping for particular species, both in terms of economy of effort and the wide spectrum of species found.

In the species accounts, the abbreviation 'comes to light' is used to cover all sources of light normally used for light-trapping.

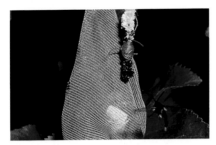

A Red-belted Clearwing attracted to a pheromone lure.

Assembling and pheromone lures

These are techniques that will specifically attract the males of a particular species and provide a wonderful display of how male moths locate females for mating in the wild. Assembling involves rearing a batch of females but keeping them unmated. This can be done by keeping all the pupae in separate containers and determining the sex of the adults when they emerge. However, there are methods of sexing the pupae to sort them into males and females. In many species, female pupae are recognisably larger or fatter than those that will produce males. Generally, if the underside of the pupa is examined, there are four unmarked abdominal segments beyond the tip of the wing cases and a pair of small bumps on the fourth in the male, while the female has only three unmarked segments before grooves and other markings intervene. You may need a hand lens to see this clearly. When rearing for assembling, the larvae and pupae must not be kept too warm, or they will emerge early and fail to coincide with the wild males.

When the virgin females emerge, one or more of them is placed in a netting bag, cage or trap (see below) preferably on the day she emerged from the pupa, or within a day or two thereafter. At some point during the day or night, depending on the species, she will be observed to adopt a hanging position, with the wings slightly parted to expose the hind end of the abdomen (this is known as 'calling'). A small scent gland, which is usually white or yellowish and may glisten, is extruded from the tip of the abdomen. From this a scent known as a pheromone evaporates into the air, to be carried off on the breeze. The males detect this scent using their antennae. The very feathery antennae of the males of some species provide a greater surface area with which to 'comb' the air for the faintest traces of pheromone. Even single molecules touching the antennae have been shown to cause a nervous discharge and recognition behaviour. The males fly upwind towards increasing concentrations of the scent, which brings them to the female. In some species, such as the Emperor moth, Oak Eggar and the clearwings, the females attract the males during the day. These can be seen flying upwind from distances of up to several hundred metres, often adopting a wide zig-zagging behaviour to relocate the scent plume.

For some species, generally those of economic importance as pests, the chemical nature of the scent has been analysed and has been made synthetically in the laboratory, and thus lures are used as part of control and monitoring measures. Often the pheromone has proved to be a blend of more than one chemical. Pheromone lures last for several years if stored in a deep freeze. For assembly or pheromone lures, a trap can be made based on the lobster-pot principle. The virgin female or lure is placed in a small netting bag or box with netting sides (fine enough to prevent mating) inside a trap, which has one or more wide entrances that funnel down into the trap. Once it is in the trap, the chances of the male finding the entrance hole again need to be minimised. This is best achieved by having other parts of the trap made of transparent material to which the males will head when attempting to leave. These assembling traps are particularly useful for the many moths which 'call' during the night, as the traps can be left unattended, like a light-trap.

Searching for eggs, larvae and pupae

Searching for the eggs, larvae or pupae of moths and rearing them to adult to confirm the identification will increase your chances of encountering the full range of species and can provide a great deal of enjoyment, satisfaction and knowledge. This guide includes enough information to enable you to find the larvae and pupae, and in some cases the eggs. Larvae which feed on trees and shrubs can be knocked into an up-turned umbrella or sheet, or a purpose-built beating tray, by jarring the branches with a stick. Those among grasses and herbs can be swept into a heavy-duty net, both methods being most productive at night. See Dickson (1992), Porter (1997) and Tutt (1994) for additional advice.

Conservation of moths

Many moth species are likely to thrive in the British Isles as long as their foodplants and habitat are well represented. For others, the required habitat has been severely reduced in extent or quality, often as a direct result of human activities. Conservation of such species depends largely on preventing further habitat loss and reversing declines by restoration and creation of additional breeding grounds. A small minority of moth species are so restricted and at risk that removal of any individuals from the wild is considered likely to jeopardise the remaining populations. Accordingly, the following are protected by law (Wildlife & Countryside Act 1981, and subsequent amendments) and are labelled as such in the text accounts: New Forest Burnet, Fiery Clearwing, Essex Emerald, Sussex Emerald, Barberry Carpet, Black-veined Moth, Fisher's Estuarine Moth and Reddish Buff. In addition, at the time of press, legal protection is proposed for the following two species via the Fourth Quinquennial Review of the Wildlife & Countryside Act, 1981: Slender Scotch Burnet, Talisker Burnet (= ssp. *jocelynae* of the Narrow-bordered Five-spot Burnet) (for further information, see Parsons *et al.* 2001).

For other species, it is most unlikely that removal of a single specimen, particularly a male, will have any impact on a population, except in the unlikely event of large numbers of people doing so where a population is small and isolated. The population has to be able to withstand much higher losses to predators, parasitoids and inclement weather, or it would not survive. There is a genuine need to collect a voucher specimen of certain species to substantiate the record. For these, a photograph is not an adequate substitute. For most others, however, a series of good photographs, taken from a variety of angles, will enable a specialist to confirm the record. The importance of substantiating and vetting records cannot be emphasised too highly.

Societies and local recording groups

Amateur Entomologists' Society Ideal for beginners, but retains many members for life! Publishes the *AES Bulletin*, many helpful books and leaflets, and holds a large exhibition and trade fair annually. Contact: AES, PO Box 8774, London SW7 5ZG (www.theaes.org)

British Entomological & Natural History Society The national society for the field entomologist. Covers all Orders but contains a large proportion of moth enthusiasts. Publishes *British Journal of Entomology & Natural History*, annual exhibition, lecture space, library and reference collections, indoor lectures and field meetings. Contact: BENHS Secretary, c/o Dinton Pastures Country Park, Davis Street, Hurst, Reading, Berks RG10 0TH (www.benhs.org.uk)

Butterfly Conservation (British Butterfly Conservation Society) Despite the name, involved in conservation of moths as well as butterflies. Has a paid staff and undertakes moth contracts for the government conservation agencies. Lead Partner on moths for UK Biodiversity Action Plan and National Moth Recording Network. Publishes *Butterfly* (formerly *Butterfly Conservation News*), annual members' day, occasional symposia, local branches with meetings and newsletters. Contact: Butterfly Conservation, Manor Yard, East Lulworth, Wareham, Dorset BH20 5QP (www.butterfly-conservation.org)

Royal Entomological Society For professional entomologists and others with special interests in entomology. Various journals, library, international symposia. Contact: 41 Queen's Gate, London SW7 5HR (www.royensoc.co.uk)

Many **moth recording groups** now have their own websites. Check the web for the latest developments.

Hepialidae – Swift moths

The Hepialidae are primitive moths, with five of the 500 or so species occurring in the British Isles. All five have elongated wings which are held almost vertically against the body when at rest. The main flight is from early dusk until full darkness. They come to light-traps, sometimes laying large numbers of eggs which collect in the base. Adults have no func-

Ghost Moth

Common Swift

tional proboscis, so are incapable of feeding, and have very short antennae. The eggs are normally laid in a low flight over the foodplant. The larvae live underground, feeding internally or externally on plant roots, among which they pupate. The life cycle commonly takes two years to complete, with the larvae overwintering twice.

Ghost Moth

page 46

Hepialus humuli humuli (L.)
Common. T   14(80)
ssp. *thulensis* Newm.
Shetland

Field characters FW M 21-29mm F 21-35mm.
Ssp. *humuli* Generally the largest of our swift moths. Male has plain white forewing and hindwing (dark grey underneath); female has unmistakable yellowish-orange forewing.
Ssp. *thulensis* is smaller. Male has creamy white or yellowish forewing, variably marked with brown; those of female are less yellow than in ssp. *humuli*. Hindwing grey in both sexes.
Similar species None.
Flight season One generation. June-early August. Both sexes fly at dusk and after dark, and come to light. Males have a characteristic display or 'lekking' flight at dusk, which can involve up to several dozen moths, each swaying to and fro over one spot as if attached to a pendulum and releasing a goat-like scent. This attracts the female, which sometimes flies directly at a male, and both fall to the ground. Mating pairs are conspicuous on low vegetation by torchlight.
Life cycle Overwinters as a larva, probably twice. Larva July-May. Pupates underground among roots.
Larval foodplants The roots of grasses and many other wild and cultivated herbaceous plants, including Common Nettle, docks, burdocks and Wild Strawberry.
Habitat Grassy or weedy places, both on open ground and in woodland rides and clearings, often where the soil surface has been disturbed and rank vegetation has developed.
Status & distribution Resident. Ssp. *humuli* Common. Throughout Great Britain and Ireland,

including Man, Orkney, Shetland and the Hebrides, but usually at low altitude in the north of Britain. Not as numerous as the Common Swift. No records from the Channel Islands since the 19th century. Ssp. *thulensis* Shetland only. Well distributed and fairly frequent.

Orange Swift

page 46

Hepialus sylvina (L.)
Common. T   15(63*)

Field characters & Similar species FW M 12-18mm F 15-26mm. Male has distinctive bright orange-brown forewing, with two quite narrow, fairly straight, continuous, dark-edged, whitish diagonal lines forming an open V. Duller female is somewhat similar to plainer forms of Map-winged Swift, which has a white dot at base and in centre of forewing, and chequered fringes. Both sexes vary greatly in size, but female is generally larger. See also Common Swift.
Flight season One generation. Late June-early September. Flies from early dusk. Comes to light, sometimes in numbers, and often attracted to house lights.
Life cycle Overwinters twice as a larva. Larva September-May or June. Pupates underground.
Larval foodplants The roots of many herbaceous plants, including Broad-leaved Dock, Dandelion, Bracken and probably grasses.
Habitat Frequent in gardens, on roadside verges, downland, moorland, woodland rides and other rough grassy places.
Status & distribution Resident. Common. Well distributed and fairly frequent from southern England and Wales to the north of mainland Scotland, in the Channel Islands and Man. Rarely in upland areas.

Gold Swift

page 46

Hepialus hecta (L.)

Local. T   16(78*)

Field characters FW M 12-15mm F 13-16mm. The
golden markings on forewing of male are diagnostic.
In particular, the diagonal, sometimes broken band
near base runs roughly parallel to outer markings,
unlike other swift moths. Duller female has broad,
purplish-grey bands on forewing.
Similar species More slender than Common Swift,
banded examples of which have whitish markings,
with that near base angled to almost meet outer
markings near trailing edge, forming an open V.
Flight season One generation. Mid June-mid July.
Males fly at dusk around the larval foodplants,
attracting females with their pineapple-like scent.
Dawn flights are also reported. Both sexes come to
light in small numbers.
Life cycle Overwinters twice as a larva. Larva June-
late May. Pupates underground.
Larval foodplants Bracken is a major foodplant and
larvae have been collected from the roots of young
Bracken shoots in April. The moth also occurs on
sites without Bracken and therefore must also use
herbs or grasses.
Habitat Mainly open woodland, but also scrubby
areas and Bracken-covered slopes on heathland and
rough grassland.
Status & distribution Resident. Local. Most of
mainland Britain but rarely in upland areas. Also Man
and the Hebrides. Recorded from all the counties of
Northern Ireland. There are scattered records from
the Irish Republic, where it is probably under-
recorded.

Common Swift

page 46

Hepialus lupulinus (L.)

Common. T   17(67*)

Field characters FW M 11-16mm F 15-20mm.
Probably the most frequently encountered of the
swifts. Wing markings of male vary greatly in
amount and intensity, ranging from whitish to pale
brown to grey; entirely plain examples occur. Female
is slightly larger, with forewing generally much less
strongly marked, often plain grey.
Similar species Orange Swift is usually found later
in the year; forewing is broader, brighter in male,
with a narrow open V; female browner than
Common Swift, with extensive grey or greyish-white
markings. See also Gold Swift.
Flight season One generation. May-July. Flies mainly
at dusk, and is sometimes attracted to house lights.
Usually caught in light-traps in the first hour of darkness. Male flies swiftly, low over the ground. Mating
pairs may be found after dark, abdomens joined,
with the male hanging head downwards and immo-
bile.
Life cycle Overwinters as a larva. Larva June or July-
April. Pupates underground.
Larval foodplants The roots of grasses and many

Larva of Common Swift.

other wild and cultivated herbaceous plants.
Sometimes a pest of agriculture and horticulture.
Habitat Open grassland, gardens and roadside
verges, including urban sites, and moorland, heathland, fens and grassy woodland rides.
Status & distribution Resident. Common. Most
parts of mainland Britain, Scilly, the Channel Islands
and Man. Sometimes abundant in the south, less so
further north and local in Scotland north to
Caithness, including the Hebrides. Very local and
mainly coastal in Ireland.

Map-winged Swift

page 46

Hepialus fusconebulosa (DeG.)

Local. T   18(69*)

Field characters FW 14-26mm. Sexes have similar
markings. Named after the distinctive, map-like variegated markings on forewing of the most frequent
form. In f. *gallicus* Led., which occurs throughout the
range, forewing is more uniformly yellowish brown
and the whitish markings are limited to two small
dots, one in centre of wing and one at base. Both
forms have chequered fringes, unlike the other swifts.
On the sand-dunes of Orkney the moths are small
and pale. In Shetland some have particularly bright
patterns and have been named f. *shetlandicus* Viette.
Similar species See Orange Swift.
Flight season One generation. Late May-early July
or early August in the north. Flies at dusk, earlier in
Shetland. Comes to light, sometimes in large
numbers.
Life cycle Overwinters twice as a larva. Larva July-
May. Pupates underground.
Larval foodplants Widely associated with Bracken
roots, among which it can be numerous, but has also
been found on the roots of Red Fescue in the
absence of Bracken and probably also uses roots of
broadleaved herbs.
Habitat Moorland, rough pasture, heathland and
open woodland, less often on downland and sand-
dunes.
Status & distribution Resident. Local. In most parts
of mainland Britain, Man, the Hebrides, Orkney and
Shetland, and in Ireland. Most frequent in the north,
and absent from large areas of the south and east of
England.

Cossidae – Leopard and goat moths

This family consists of about 700 species, of which three are found in the British Isles. The wings are elongated and held at a slight angle close to the body when at rest. The antennae are variable and the abdomen is extremely long in some species. The adults are nocturnal, and are incapable of feeding. The females attach the eggs to stems of the host plant. The larvae feed in the wood and stem tissue of trees and other plants, often taking more than one year to complete their growth. Most pupate within the food-plant.

Leopard Moth

Goat Moth

Zeuzerinae

Reed Leopard
Phragmataecia castaneae (Hb.)
RDB. E,S

page 46

160(4178)

Field characters FW 15-23mm. The fine blackish spotting and rounded tip of the slightly transparent straw-white forewing, together with comb-like antennae of male and very long abdomen of female usually extending well beyond wing tips, are diagnostic.
Similar species Several wainscot moths are a similar colour and occur in the same habitat, but none have the combination of features listed above.
Flight season One generation. June-July, sometimes late May or early August. Male comes readily to light soon after dark; female rarely does so but can be found at rest on reed stems at night. They start laying eggs immediately after mating, in batches between the leaf-sheath and stalk.
Life cycle Overwinters twice as a part-grown larva, low down in a reed stem, usually about 20cm or more below the water level. Larva July-May of the third year, feeding in reed stems, moving from one to another, pupating near a prepared exit window through which the pupa breaks to release the adult. Occupied stems tend not to flower.
Larval foodplants The roots and lower stems of Common Reed.
Habitat Fens, marshes and the margins of ponds, both where there is year-round standing water (reedswamp) and only seasonal flooding or waterlogging (reedbed).
Status & distribution Resident. Red Data Book species. Extremely local. Resident only at

Chippenham Fen and Wicken Fen, Cambridgeshire, the Norfolk Broads and a single locality near Wareham, Dorset, where it has been known for over 70 years.

Leopard Moth
Zeuzera pyrina (L.)
Common. S,E,C

page 46

161(4176)

Field characters FW 22-35mm. Six large black spots on big, furry thorax and heavy spotting on whitish wings, along with comb-like antennae of male, are diagnostic. In the rare f. *confluens* Cock., central spots of forewing are joined to form stripes.
Similar species See Puss Moth.
Flight season One generation. Late June-early August. Both sexes come to light and are occasionally found at rest on tree trunks by day.
Life cycle Overwinters two or three times as a larva, feeding in the stems and branches of trees and shrubs, eventually pupating under the bark. Larva August-May. The eggs are attached singly or in small batches to the bark.
Larval foodplants Many woody plants, including willows, Blackthorn, Plum, Cherry, Hawthorn, Apple, Pear, privets, Ash, elms, oaks, Beech, Wayfaring-tree, Honeysuckle, Lilac and Black Currant; sometimes in slender young stems and generally in those less than 10cm in diameter. Occasionally causes economic damage to fruit trees.
Habitat Most frequent in open woodland and scrub, but also found in gardens, orchards and parkland.
Status & distribution Resident. Common. Found widely and frequently in the south of England north to Yorkshire, in the eastern half of Wales, and in the Channel Islands (Jersey only). Only confirmed record for Ireland is one in Co. Mayo on 12 July 1978.

Cossinae

Goat Moth
page 46

Cossus cossus (L.)
Nb. T   162(4151)

Field characters FW 32-42mm. A large, very thicket moth, with silvery grey-brown forewing with many fine, dark, irregular and often branched crosslines, which resemble cracks in bark. It has a distinctive upright resting posture.
Similar species None.
Flight season One generation. June-July. Both sexes occasionally come to light, but are otherwise seldom seen. Female sometimes attracted to sugar bait painted on trees, but since they cannot feed they may in fact mistake the sweet smell for that of oozing sap caused by previous larval damage, a suitable egg-laying site.
Life cycle Overwinters three or four times as a larva, the final time in a cocoon in which it eventually pupates in the spring. Some larvae leave the tree in the autumn to spin a cocoon in rotten wood or soft earth. Eggs are laid in batches in a bark crevice, often near to old larval burrows or other damage.
Larval foodplants Under the bark and in the heartwood of a variety of broadleaved trees, including sallows, willows and poplars, Ash, birches, English Elm, oaks, Alder, Apple and other fruit trees. Trees in low-lying or damp situations which are prone to winter flooding are particularly favoured.
Habitat Riverbanks, fens, marshes, parkland, golf courses, hedgerows and woodland edges.
Status & distribution Resident. Nationally Scarce B. Occurs in widely scattered localities, mainly in eastern England south of the Wash, along the south coast from Devon to Kent, and in the Thames Valley. There are other colonies on the coasts of Wales, Man and north-west England, and in the Great Glen, Invernessshire, and the Nairnshire coast in Scotland. Recorded from a few scattered localities in southern Ireland, annually from Co. Cork. Occasional in the Channel Islands. Has declined in range in recent decades.

23

Zygaenidae – Forester and burnet moths

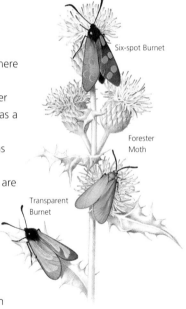

Six-spot Burnet

Forester Moth

Transparent Burnet

This family comprises about 800 species worldwide. There are ten species recorded in Great Britain and Ireland. Typically, these moths live in colonies, sometimes rather isolated from one another for many generations, and as a consequence a number of differences have evolved between populations, some of which are recognised as races or subspecies.

The adults are active mainly by day and their flights are generally rather direct. All have round-tipped, rather narrow forewings which are held at a steep angle quite close to the body when at rest, and stout antennae which are always forward-pointed and in some cases clubbed, rather like those of butterflies. Both adults and larvae are toxic to non-insect predators, releasing poisons such as hydrogen cyanide when attacked. Forester moths are not, in fact, particularly associated with woodland and the name is most probably derived from 'Lincoln green', the colour supposedly worn by medieval foresters in Sherwood Forest.

They regularly visit flowers in open habitats, particularly rough grassland. The larvae feed mainly on herbaceous plants, often members of the pea family. The whitish, tapering, papery cocoons are usually formed low down in the vegetation, but those of some burnet moths are spun high along grass stems, and are rather conspicuous.

Procridinae

Egg laying has been observed on rather small plants in short and fairly sparse sward (up to 5cm tall).

Status & distribution Resident. Nationally Scarce B. Sometimes numerous on breeding sites, but these are very localised. Confined to England and Wales. The distribution extends from Dorset east to Sussex, with old records from Kent, and northwards through Wiltshire and Gloucestershire, following calcareous strata north-eastwards into Bedfordshire and north-wards to the Derbyshire Dales, Yorkshire, Co. Durham on the east coast and the Arnside area of Cumbria on the west. In Wales, it has been recorded from Denbighshire and Caernarvonshire.

Forester
page 47

Adscita statices (L.)

Local. S,C   163(3956)

Field characters & Similar species FW M 12-15mm F 11-13mm. The three British forester moths are superficially almost identical, but can sometimes be separated by careful comparison of individuals of the same sex. Male has slightly larger, broader, feathery antennae than female. When comparing the same sex, Forester and Scarce Forester are about the same size, but Cistus Forester is smaller. Antennae of both sexes of Forester are broader at the tip than in Scarce Forester. See Scarce Forester for further differences.

Flight season One generation. Mid May-July, occasional individuals into August. Flies in sunshine. Both sexes spend much time feeding at flowers such as Ragged Robin, Field and Devil's-bit Scabious, clovers and Viper's-bugloss, even in cloudy weather. Mating pairs are seen in the afternoon. Male sometimes flies again an hour or so before sunset on warm evenings.

Life cycle Overwinters as a part-grown larva, low down among the sward. Larva July-early May, pupating in a cocoon formed near the ground.

Larval foodplants Common Sorrel and Sheep's Sorrel. Will feed on Broad-leaved Dock in captivity; use in wild requires confirmation.

Habitat Open habitats, ranging from damp, neutral grassland to limestone grassland, chalk downland, acid and sandy heathland, mature coastal sand-dunes and woodland rides and clearings.

Status & distribution Resident. Local. Well distributed but local in England and Wales, where many colonies have been lost as a result of agricultural intensification. Very local in western Scotland, in Argyllshire and the islands of Jura, Lismore and Mull. Widespread but local in Ireland. Local and occasional in the Channel Islands.

Cistus Forester
page 47

Adscita geryon (Hb.)

Nb. S,C   164(3948)

Field characters & Similar species FW M 10-12mm F 9-10mm. Both sexes are distinctly smaller than the same sex of Forester and Scarce Forester. See Scarce Forester for differences in antennae.

Flight season One generation. Late May-July, occasionally early August. Active by day. Both sexes visit flowers, including those of Kidney Vetch, Wild Thyme and Common Bird's-foot-trefoil. Male flies in sunshine but female spends much of the time perching on grass stems and other vegetation.

Life cycle Overwinters as a larva, low down among the sward. Larva July-May. Pupates in a cocoon formed close to the ground.

Larval foodplants Common Rock-rose.

Habitat Open grassland on chalk and limestone hills, favouring warm, flower-rich, south-facing slopes.

Scarce Forester
page 47

Jordanita globulariae (Hb.)

Na. S   165(3943)

Field characters & Similar species FW M 12-15mm F 10-12mm. Forewing of both sexes is generally broader and more rounded at tip than in same sex of Forester, and both sexes are larger than those of Cistus Forester. Male antennae are tapering and pointed at tip and lack distinct feather-blade extensions on the last three segments. Those of male Forester and Cistus Forester are not tapering and rather blunt-tipped with ten and seven segments respectively lacking feather-like extensions. Female Scarce Forester's antennae are longer, very slender, and of almost uniform thickness from tip to base, whereas in the other two species they are narrowed towards the base (only seen under a lens or low-power microscope).

Flight season One generation. June-early July. Male flies in sunshine but sits around on flowers and other vegetation in dull weather. Female spends more time perching or resting. Both sexes visit flowers to feed, notably Salad Burnet and knapweeds. Male occasionally captured at night in light-traps away from suitable habitat.

Life cycle Overwinters as a larva, low down amongst vegetation. Larva July-May, feeding until September then again in the spring, pupating in May in a brownish-grey cocoon spun on or just below the ground.

Larval foodplants Common Knapweed and Greater Knapweed.

Habitat Permanent calcareous grassland. The moth and foodplant require quite a rough sward to thrive.

Status & distribution Resident. Nationally Scarce A. Occurs in two main areas of chalk downland. One is centred on Wiltshire, with outlying populations in Gloucestershire and Hampshire. The other is in Sussex, where there are a number of sites, with an outlying, recently rediscovered population near Dover, Kent.

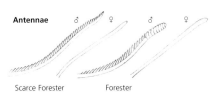

Antennae ♂ ♀ ♂ ♀

Scarce Forester   Forester

Zygaeninae

Scotch Burnet (Mountain Burnet) p. 47

Zygaena exulans (Hohen.)

ssp. *subochracea* White

RDB. N   166(3988)

Field characters & Similar species FW 10-16mm. The thinly-scaled forewing, with five distinct but sometimes very small red spots, distinguishes this burnet from all others except Slender Scotch, in which the spot nearest forewing tip is large and hindwing has a very narrow border. See also Transparent Burnet, which is larger.

Flight season One generation. Mid June-late July. The moths fly strongly in sunshine but drop down among vegetation in bad weather. Both sexes visit flowers, particularly Common Bird's-foot-trefoil, but also Mountain Everlasting and others.

Life cycle Overwinters once or more as a larva. Larva July or August-late May or June. Spins a cocoon low in the vegetation.

Larval foodplants Mainly Crowberry, eating the terminal shoots and unripe berries. Also Cowberry, Bilberry and Heather.

Habitat The higher slopes and summits of mountains, where the vegetation consists mainly of prostrate Crowberry and heathers, lichens and scattered plants of Bilberry, Mountain Everlasting and Trailing Azalea.

Status & distribution Resident. Red Data Book species. Known only from the eastern Cairngorms, near Braemar, Aberdeenshire, where it occurs on mountain slopes at 700-850m and can be numerous very locally. One (probably wind-blown) individual was recorded in 1984 near Loch Builg, to the north. There is also an old unconfirmed record from Lochnagar, to the south-west.

Slender Scotch Burnet   page 47

Zygaena loti ([D. & S.])

ssp. *scotica* (Rowl.-Br.)

RDB (proposed Protected species). NW 167(3983)

Field characters FW 14-16mm. Red spot nearest forewing tip is large, being formed from the merger of two spots. The other four spots are distinct and hindwing has a very narrow black border. Forelegs are yellowish brown in part.

Similar species Six-spot Burnet may have merged spots near wing tip, but is usually larger, has more thickly scaled forewing, a less hairy body, and legs are outwardly black. See also Scotch Burnet and Transparent Burnet.

Flight season One generation. Early June-early July. Male searches out the female, which spends much of her time perching and nectaring, particularly at the flowers of the larval foodplant. Male often visits other flowers, particularly milkworts and Thyme.

Life cycle Overwinters as a larva, sometimes twice.

The eggs are laid in batches on the foodplant. Larva late July-late May or early June. Pupates in a dull white oval-shaped cocoon, spun on or near the ground.

Larval foodplants Common Bird's-foot-trefoil. Most larvae are found on the shorter plants, mostly 2-3cm in height, generally less than 6cm, and often in poor condition.

Habitat Foodplant and moth are most numerous on scree and other areas of slippage, disturbance or moderate grazing (but colonies are vulnerable to overgrazing), on often steep, south or south-west facing slopes by the sea, where the underlying rock is basaltic. Less numerous where other plants have colonised and where the height of the vegetation is greater than 6cm.

Status & distribution Resident. Red Data Book species. Endemic to Scotland, where it is restricted to five or six sites on the Hebridean island of Mull, and on the small adjacent island of Ulva. Formerly found (pre-1945) on the Scottish mainland near Lochaline and Drimnin, Morvern.

New Forest Burnet   page 47

Zygaena viciae ([D. & S.])   168(3992)

ssp. *ytenensis* Briggs
Extinct.

ssp. *argyllensis* Trem.
RDB (Protected species). NW

Field characters FW 12-14mm. A small burnet moth, with very round-tipped forewing and five clearly-defined red spots, with a broad dark area beyond.

Similar species Five-spot Burnet is larger and stouter, with more pointed wings.

Flight season One generation. July. Adults are rather sedentary, especially female. They nectar on Wild Thyme and occasionally other flowers. Male flies only if the weather is warm and calm.

Life cycle Overwinters as a larva, sometimes more than once. Eggs are laid in batches in late July. Larva July-early June. Pupates in a papery cocoon concealed on the underside of leaves and on grass stems low down in the vegetation.

Larval foodplants Meadow Vetchling and Common Bird's-foot-trefoil.

Habitat A herb-rich, steep grassy slope with ledges, facing southwards.

Status & distribution Resident. Red Data Book species; protected by law from collection or disturbance. Ssp. *argyllensis* known only from one site on the coast of western Argyllshire, where it was discovered in 1963. During the late 1980s the slope was heavily grazed and by 1990 breeding was confined to ledges inaccessible to the sheep, with a total adult population estimated at about 15 individuals. Sheep are now excluded, and as a result the sward is taller, herb-rich and, crucially, is allowed to flower. Consequently, the population has increased greatly but it still remains highly vulnerable. Ssp. *ytenensis*

25

formerly occurred in the New Forest, Hampshire, in woodland rides and clearings, but it was last seen there in 1927 and is considered to be extinct.

Six-spot Burnet

Zygaena filipendulae (L.)

ssp. *stephensi* Dupont

Common. T

page 47

169(3998)

Field characters FW 15-19mm. The only British burnet moth with six red spots on each forewing (red patch at base is divided by a vein and counts as two spots). In some forms outermost spots are merged, also sometimes middle pair. Very rarely red colour is replaced by yellow throughout (f. *flava* Robson).
Similar species See Slender Scotch Burnet.
Flight season One generation. Late June-August. Visits flowers such as thistles and knapweeds. Male patrols the area, searching for unmated females.
Life cycle Overwinters as a larva, sometimes twice. Larva August-June. Pupates in a cocoon formed in an exposed position along a grass or other plant stem.
Larval foodplants Mainly Common Bird's-foot-trefoil, but also Greater Bird's-foot-trefoil.
Habitat Flowery grassland, usually on light soils, including roadside verges, downland, permanent pasture, woodland rides, sand-dunes and other grassy coastal habitats.
Status & distribution Resident. Common. Well distributed in England, Wales, Man and Ireland, largely coastal in Scotland, but reaching the northernmost parts of the mainland, and the Outer Hebrides. Local and occasional in the Channel Islands.

Five-spot Burnet

Zygaena trifolii (Esp.)

ssp. *decreta* Ver.

Local. S,WC

ssp. *palustrella* Ver.

Local. S,SE

page 47

170(4000)

Field characters & Similar species FW 14-19mm. Ssp. *decreta* Very difficult to distinguish from the much more widespread Narrow-bordered Five-spot Burnet ssp. *latomarginata* (see also under that species), even using features of genitalia. However, the habitat, time of year and geographical location may help. Only slightly smaller than Narrow-bordered, and colonies found where its foodplant, Greater Bird's-foot-trefoil, is present need careful examination. Examples with the middle pair of spots merged are frequent in Five-spot Burnet, but rare in Narrow-bordered. Also, although flight periods overlap, Narrow-bordered is earlier. Probably the only safe way, in some cases, to ascertain which species are present is to search for larvae or rear them from females. Larva has much shorter hairs than that of Narrow-bordered, which in addition has a wider range of foodplants. Rarely the red is replaced by yellow. Ssp. *palustrella* has thinner scaling and is usually smaller than ssp. *decreta*. Yellow forms are more frequent than in ssp.

decreta, but sill uncommon.
Ssp. *decreta*
Flight season One generation. July-early August.
Life cycle Overwinters as a larva, sometimes twice. Larva August-May or early June. Pupates in a cocoon formed exposed on the stem of a tall herbaceous plant or rush.
Larval foodplants Greater Bird's-foot-trefoil.
Habitat Damp grassland, heathland and wetlands.
Status & distribution Resident. Local. Southern and south-west England, and parts of Wales, usually near the coast, north to Anglesey and Man. Its detailed distribution is imperfectly known because of confusion with Narrow-bordered Five-spot Burnet.
Ssp. *palustrella*
Flight season One generation. Late May-June.
Life cycle Overwinters as a larva, sometimes twice. Larva late June-early May. Pupates in a cocoon formed low down and concealed in the vegetation.
Larval foodplants Common Bird's-foot-trefoil.
Habitat Dry calcareous grassland on chalk and limestone.
Status & distribution Resident. Local. Along the North and South Downs from Hampshire to Kent, Wiltshire (Salisbury Plain) and Gloucestershire (Cotswolds). Widespread and abundant in the Channel Islands.

Narrow-bordered Five-spot Burnet

Zygaena lonicerae (Schev.)

ssp. *latomarginata* Tutt

Common. S,C,(N)

ssp. *jocelynae* Trem.

RDB (Protected species). NW

ssp. *insularis* Trem.

Ireland

page 47

171(3999)

Field characters & Similar species FW 15-19mm. The differences between this species and Five-spot Burnet (especially ssp. *decreta*) are comparative and slight. Generally, in Narrow-bordered forewing is longer and more pointed, leading corner of hindwing is more pointed and black border of hindwing is narrower, but a number of specimens of each are needed in order to see these differences. Ssp. *jocelynae* is larger than ssp. *latomarginata*, with longer, black fur on head, thorax and abdomen, and larger, sometimes suffused and clouded forewing spots. Ssp. *insularis* has larger spots than ssp. *latomarginata*, with a tendency for middle pair to merge. See also Five-spot Burnet.
Flight season One generation. Late June-July. Frequently seen by day, nectaring on many flowers, sometimes in numbers, with others at rest by their white papery cocoons.
Life cycle Overwinters as a larva. Larva July-June. Often sits exposed on the foodplant, especially when fully grown. Pupates in a cocoon spun high on a plant stem.

Larval foodplants Mainly Meadow Vetchling, Red Clover, Sainfoin and Greater Bird's-foot-trefoil. Occasionally Common Bird's-foot-trefoil, White Clover and Bitter-vetch.

Habitat Rough grassland, both on well-drained calcareous ground and on damper clays, uncut roadside verges and embankments, woodland rides and the margins of wetlands. Ssp. *jocelynae* occurs mainly on steep, coastal grassy slopes.

Status & distribution Resident. Common. Ssp. *latomarginata* is well distributed over most of England to Cumbria, Northumberland and the Scottish border counties, and in north and south Wales. Local and occasional on Jersey. Ssp. *jocelynae* Red Data Book species. Confined to Skye, Inner Hebrides. Ssp. *insularis* is widespread in Ireland, mostly in the northern half.

Transparent Burnet — page 47
Zygaena purpuralis (Brünn.) 172(3974*)

ssp. *segontii* Trem.
RDB; presumed extinct. WC

ssp. *caledonensis* Reiss
Na. NW

ssp. *sabulosa* Trem.
Ireland

Field characters & Similar species FW 14-16mm. Distinguished by thinly-scaled forewing with three blunt red streaks, the outermost of which is hatchet-shaped. The red is sometimes inclined to purplish, and in the rare f. *obscura* Tutt is replaced by

blackish. On Skye, and rarely elsewhere, forms occur with red markings replaced by orange or yellow. Scotch and Slender Scotch Burnets also have thinly-scaled forewings, but are smaller and thinner, with distinct spots rather than streaks.

Flight season One generation. Early June-July. Both sexes fly in warm weather, preferring sunshine, and visit nectar flowers such as Wild Thyme. During dull or wet weather they sit about, often fully exposed and wet, on flowerheads or surrounding vegetation, sometimes for days.

Life cycle Overwinters as a larva, sometimes twice. Larva July-May. Pupates in a spun cocoon concealed near the ground.

Larval foodplants Wild Thyme.

Habitat Steep, heathy and grassy, south and south-west facing slopes and under-cliffs on or near the coast, and very locally inland on limestone.

Status & distribution Resident. Great fluctuations in population density have been recorded, sometimes in response to changing grazing levels. The Nationally Scarce A ssp. *caledonensis* occurs on the Hebridean islands of Mull, Ulva, Lismore, Kerrera, Eigg, Rum, Canna and the west coast of Skye. It is also found on the mainland coast of western Argyllshire at Ardnamurchan and Oban, in a limestone area 7km inland of Oban, and on the Mull of Kintyre. Ssp. *segontii* occurred in small colonies along the cliffs near Abersoch on the Lleyn Peninsula, Caernarvonshire. It has not been seen since 1962, in spite of subsequent searches, and could be extinct. Ssp. *sabulosa* occurs in western Ireland, mainly in the Burren district of Cos. Clare and Galway, and on Inishmore in the Aran Islands.

Limacodidae

This family of about 1,000 species is mainly tropical, but has representatives all over the world. There are only two species found in the British Isles, both quite small moths but with the deep, rather rounded forewings and tent-like resting posture characteristic of the group. The proboscis is rudimentary and the adult moths do not feed. The family name derives from *Limax*, the Latin for slug, on account of the distinctive, slug-like larvae.

Festoon   Triangle

Larva of Festoon.

Festoon — page 48
Apoda limacodes (Hufn.)
Nb. S,E,not SW 173(3907)

Field characters FW M 10-12mm F 11-13mm. The curved cross-lines, strongly diverging from leading edge of broad orange-brown forewing, are diagnostic. When fully at rest, forewings are held at a low angle, and are creased so that tips are flattened out. Female is paler than male, which rests with its

abdomen curved upwards. Sometimes the area between cross-lines is darker and occasionally male is as pale as female (f. *ochracea* Seitz). Rare melanic forms of male have forewing lightly or heavy marked with blackish brown (f. *suffusa* Seitz and f. *assella* Esp.).

Similar species None.

Flight season One generation. June-July. Flies mainly at night and comes to light. Occasionally flies in sunshine by day, high in the oak canopy.

27

Life cycle Overwinters as a larva in a cocoon formed on a leaf, which falls to the ground in autumn. Larva late July–early May.

Larval foodplants Usually Pedunculate Oak, but also other oaks and Beech.

Habitat Principally mature lowland broadleaved woodland, but also hedgerows with mature oaks and wooded heathland.

Status & distribution Resident. Nationally Scarce B. Found locally in the southern half of England, mainly in Dorset, Hampshire, the Isle of Wight, Wiltshire, Sussex, Surrey and Kent. Also very locally in Oxfordshire, Berkshire, Buckinghamshire, Essex, East Anglia and Northamptonshire. Has declined in Worcestershire, with recent records from one site only (Trench Wood). One recorded at Usk, Monmouthshire, on 4 June 1967. In Ireland, recorded doubtfully from Co. Galway.

Triangle   page 48
Heterogenea asella ([D. & S.])
RDB. S,E   174(3912)

Field characters FW M 5-7mm F 9-11mm. Small enough to be confused with some microlepidoptera (e.g. Tortricidae). Recognised by the combination of rather triangular forewing with a very curved leading edge, and the tent-like resting posture. Occasionally male is very dark (f. *nigra* Tutt) and female is pale yellow (f. *flavescens* Tutt).

Similar species None.

Flight season One generation. Mid June-late July. Flies mainly at night, coming to light in small numbers, usually only on warm nights. There are a few reports of flight on sunny afternoons.

Life cycle Overwinters as a fully grown larva, in a gall-like cocoon on a leaf or twig. Larva August-May or June, feeding until October.

Larval foodplants Oaks and Beech. Recorded once on poplar.

Habitat Oak and Beech woodland.

Status & distribution Resident. Red Data Book species. Very localised and scarce in the southern half of England. Most records are from the large and ancient oak woodlands of Hampshire, Sussex, south-east Kent and Wiltshire. Also found annually in two Essex woodlands, in Beech woodland near Marlow, Buckinghamshire, prior to 1980, near Looe, Cornwall, in 1960 and 1969, and one was caught in Bardney Forest, Lincolnshire, in 1995. Two larvae were reported from a row of poplars at Seaford, Sussex, in about 1930 and in the 19th century it was recorded from south Devon.

Sesiidae – Clearwing moths

Clearwing moths are fairly closely related to the more familiar burnet moths. There are about 1,000 species worldwide, of which 14 are resident in the British Isles, and one is of uncertain status. They

Hornet Moth   Yellow-legged Clearwing

mimic wasps, which is thought to confer protection from vertebrate predators, but they can in most cases be distinguished from wasps by the dark bar or blotch across the forewings, from which numerous veins radiate. Also, the head and eyes are much smaller. They have very narrow forewings and quite narrow hindwings, both with large transparent areas, and black bodies banded with yellow or red. Species in the genera *Sesia*, *Bembecia* and *Pyropteron* hold their wings quite close to the body when settled, in the position illustrated. *Synanthedon* species settle with their wings extending at a greater angle from the body.

The adults are active by day, particularly in sunny weather, but they are very elusive and until recently those of many species were rarely encountered in the wild. They may be found when freshly emerged by searching the trunks of the larval foodplants from early to mid-morning, but soon disperse when warmed by the sun. Some visit flowers and are occasionally caught when sweep-nets or malaise-traps are used for general invertebrate sampling. The males fly around the larval foodplants, seeking out unmated females. Recently, the use of lures containing synthetic sex pheromones came into use as a recording technique. This has greatly improved the speed and efficiency of detection and some species are proving to be more widespread and frequent than previous records indicated.

Locating the actual breeding sites requires patience, persistence and specialised, yet simple, techniques. Eggs are usually laid singly, often on freshly cut tree-stumps and on callouses and other damaged bark, or on the leaves of herbaceous foodplants. The larvae feed in stems, trunks or roots, boring out tunnels which usually bear traces of silk, distinguishing them from those of other plant-boring insects.

Some betray their presence by issuing brown sawdust-like droppings (frass) from holes in the plant, or by causing a swelling (gall). The life cycle make take up to three years for some species. The pupa is formed in a fibrous cocoon just under the outer layer of the occupied trunk or root, behind a lidded exit hole prepared by the larva, which can be found by careful searching or scraping, and the section containing the insect carefully cut, chiselled or dug out for rearing to adult. In species feeding below ground, a silken tube may be formed leading to the surface of the earth. Breeding sites are best located by searching for empty pupal cases, which are left protuding from exit holes in stems and trunks at the start of the flight season and may remain in place for weeks.

Sesiinae

Hornet Moth page 48
Sesia apiformis (Cl.)
Nb. E,S 370(4030)

Field characters & Similar species FW 17-21mm. As large and bulky as a true Hornet *Vespa crabro*, and even has jerky, wasp-like movements when disturbed. However, it is yellower, and lacks the wasp-waist. Distinguished from Lunar Hornet Moth by bright yellow head and shoulder patches and a black collar.
Flight season One generation. Mid June-July, sometimes to early August. Adults, including mating pairs, can be found at rest on poplar trunks after emergence, usually between 7am and 11am, but are seldom seen when active. A pheromone lure is available but male only infrequently attracted.
Life cycle Overwinters at least twice, as a larva for the first and sometimes second winter, and as a fully grown larva in a cocoon during the second or third winter. Larva September-May of third or fourth year. Females glue the eggs to the base of the trunk. Larva feeds mainly just beneath the bark, near ground level or sometimes just below it. Look for exit holes near the base of the tree. During the flight season, these may have pupal cases projecting from them or lying on the ground nearby.
Larval foodplants The live wood of Black-poplar,

Aspen, Lombardy-poplar and other poplars.
Habitat Includes parks, hedgerows, golf courses, quarries, fens, plantation edges, pond edges and pits. Particular favourites are trees in open habitats, often those planted as wind-breaks, with little vegetation around the base so that the sun warms the trunks. Some trees may be tenanted year after year, and may eventually be killed.
Status & distribution Resident. Nationally Scarce B. Mainly in southern and eastern England, East Anglia and the Midlands. Most frequent in Kent, Essex, Northamptonshire, Huntingdonshire, Oxfordshire and Buckinghamshire. One site only known in Hampshire. Also recorded from Cornwall, Somerset, Gloucestershire and Co. Durham. In Wales, recorded in Denbighshire, Flintshire and Glamorgan, but not recently. Widespread, though apparently very local and infrequent, in the Irish Republic. Local and rare in the Channel Islands.

Lunar Hornet Moth page 48
Sesia bembeciformis (Hb.)
Common. T 371(4032)

Field characters & Similar species FW 15-19mm. Similar to Hornet Moth, but smaller and has black head and shoulders, with a bright yellow collar.
Flight season One generation. July-early August. Adults are very rarely seen, but can be found freshly emerged on willow trunks in the morning. No specific pheromone lure is available.
Life cycle Overwinters, normally twice, as a larva.

Larva August-spring. Feeds close to the ground in the first year. Look for small piles of fine brown frass at the base of the tree. In the second, they move up to 50cm from the tree. Look for old exit holes and rough gashes in the trunks made by woodpeckers trying to reach the larvae. The larval workings are a frequent sight in felled willows.

Larval foodplants The lower trunk and upper roots of sallows and willows, including Goat Willow, Grey Willow and Crack-willow, and reported also from poplars. Mature trees in damp situations seem to be preferred.

Habitat Most situations in which the foodplants occur, particularly fens and carr, open woodland, heaths, moors, hedgerows, old quarries and other scrubby areas.

Status & distribution Resident. Common. The most widespread clearwing in the British Isles, with records from almost every county in England and Wales, southern Scotland, the Inner Hebrides and as far north as Caithness. In Northern Ireland found in Cos. Fermanagh, Down and Armagh. There are scattered records from the Irish Republic, south to Co. Cork. Local and rare in the Channel Islands.

Paranthreninae

Dusky Clearwing   page 48
Paranthrene tabaniformis (Rott.)
Presumed extinct; former resident.   372(4039)

Field characters FW 14mm. Distinguished from all other clearwing moths in Britain and Ireland by dark clouding over most of forewing.

Similar species None.

Flight season One generation. Late May-mid July. Apparently very elusive, and rarely seen in Britain. Males responded well to pheromone lures used recently in Belgium.

Life cycle Not known in Britain, but probably similar to that abroad, where it overwinters twice as a larva. Eggs are laid on a twig of the foodplant or in a bark crevice near the base of the trunk. In the first instance, the small larva overwinters inside the twig gall of the longhorn beetle *Saperda populnea*. It then tunnels along the twig and creates its own gall, more elongated and tapering than that of the beetle, in which it overwinters and pupates in May. Alternatively, the larva feeds under the bark or in the roots and pupates just beneath the surface of the bark.

Larval foodplants In England recorded on Aspen, but possibly also associated with other poplars. In France recorded from poplars, sallows and Sea-buckthorn.

Habitat Generally associated with broadleaved woodland in England, but also in coastal habitats abroad.

Status & distribution Former resident, not seen

since 1924, but given the obscure habits of the adults its rediscovery using pheromone lures is a possibility. In the 19th or early 20th century very small numbers were found in the London area, Middlesex (Colney Hatch), Kent (Bexley), Essex (Epping Forest), Sussex (Brighton), Hampshire (near Portsmouth), Devon (Totnes) and Cornwall (Bodmin). The last record was of an adult found in Tubney Wood, Oxfordshire, in 1924.

Currant Clearwing   page 49
Synanthedon tipuliformis (Cl.)
Nb. S,C,(N)   373(4064)

Field characters FW 8-10mm. Small clearwing with yellow collar. Usually two fine yellow lines running along thorax. Three (female) or four (male) thin yellow cross-bands on abdomen, which is black tipped.

Similar species Sallow Clearwing has no yellow lines on thorax. See also Thrift Clearwing.

Flight season One generation. June-July, usually peaking in late June. Can be seen flying around the larval foodplants in sunny weather, and more inclined to settle on leaves than some other clearwings. Male comes quickly and in numbers (sometimes dozens) to the specific pheromone lure in the afternoon, which is also the main egg-laying time. Recorded visiting the flowers of Ground-elder.

Life cycle Overwinters, usually once, as a larva in the main stem or side stems of the foodplant. Larva August-April or May. In the spring, brownish frass is sometimes found issuing from cut ends of affected shoots, or from cracks in the bark.

Larval foodplants Cultivated and sometimes wild Black and Red Currant, and less frequently on Gooseberry.

Habitat Fruit fields, gardens and allotments, both in rural and urban locations. Neglected Black Currant bushes in sheltered, sunny positions seem to be favoured. Occasionally reported on wild currants in sunny places on the banks of streams in damp woods and the margins of fens.

Status & distribution Resident. Nationally Scarce B, but widespread and under-recorded. It is likely to have declined in recent decades because the foodplants are less frequently grown in gardens and allotments. Recorded from every county in England, and locally in Wales, Scotland and Ireland. Local and rare on Man. Widespread, but occasional in the Channel Islands.

Yellow-legged Clearwing   page 49
Synanthedon vespiformis (L.)
Nb. S,C   374(4059)

Field characters FW 10-12mm. Central cross-bar on forewing is reddish and the easily visible parts of the legs are largely yellow. Four yellow bands on abdomen. Tail fan is yellow above on female (and is conspicuous in flight) whereas that of male is black above, with some yellow underneath. Sometimes leading and trailing edges of forewing are bordered with red (f. *rufimarginata* Spul.).

Similar species Six-belted Clearwing has six yellow bands and holds its wings closer to the body at rest. The reddish central bar on forewing and the yellow legs distinguish this moth from Orange-tailed, Sallow, Currant and Welsh Clearwings.

Flight season One generation. Late May-mid August. Female recorded egg laying on sunny afternoons. Recorded visiting Bramble flowers. Male comes readily to specific pheromone lures near breeding sites, usually between noon and 6pm.

Life cycle Overwinters as a part-grown larva, probably only once. Eggs are laid on recently cut stumps, or in wounds and calluses on the trunk. Larva August-May, feeding between the bark and on stumps cut up to two years previously.

Larval foodplants Usually Pedunculate Oak but also Sweet Chestnut; and recorded on Sessile Oak, Holm Oak, Wych Elm, birches and cherries.

Habitat Open woodland, parkland and hedgerows, especially where felling has taken place in the last three years. One report from a shaded avenue of Wych Elms in London.

Status & distribution Resident. Nationally Scarce B, but probably under-recorded. Found in most counties in England, from Cornwall to Kent, including the Isle of Wight, north to Yorkshire and in south Wales.

White-barred Clearwing   page 49

Synanthedon spheciformis ([D. & S.])

Nb. S,C,not SW   375(4045)

Field characters FW 12-14mm. A relatively large, quite dark species. Diagnostic features are the presence of only one yellowish white band on abdomen, towards the front, together with a whitish band near the tips of antennae.

Similar species Welsh Clearwing has two pale bands on abdomen, a partly or wholly orange tail fan and central band on forewing is broader and more rounded.

Flight season One generation. Mid May-early July, with peak numbers in early June. Once recorded visiting a flower of Guelder-rose. Male is attracted to pheromone lures in the middle of the day.

Life cycle Overwinters as a larva, at least twice. Larva August-May, feeding near the base of the trunk or in the roots. Look for a small pile of frass on the ground beneath the round exit hole, which is about 5mm in diameter.

Larval foodplants Alder and birches.

Habitat Heathland, raised mosses, alder groves, streamsides, woodland edges, glades and way-leaves in damp woods.

Status & distribution Resident. Nationally Scarce B. Recorded widely in south-east England, extending west to the Isle of Wight, Hampshire and Berkshire and northwards into Essex and East Anglia. Also in Gloucestershire, through the West Midlands, north to Cumbria, and in north and south Wales.

Welsh Clearwing   page 49

Synanthedon scoliaeformis (Borkh.)

RDB. N,WC   376(4044)

Field characters FW 12-15mm. The large, broad and roughly heart-shaped central black mark on forewing, pointing towards base of wing, is diagnostic. Antennae are whitish towards tip in female, darker in male, and there are two narrow yellow bands on abdomen. Tail fan is orange in female and brownish orange in male.

Similar species Orange-tailed Clearwing also has two yellow bands on abdomen, but is much smaller with a narrower, squarer central forewing mark, and has black antennae. See also White-barred Clearwing.

Flight season One generation. June-early July. Occasionally found at rest on birch trunks in the morning or seen laying eggs in the afternoon.

Life cycle Overwinters twice as a larva. Larva August-May, feeding on the inner bark of old trees. Look for emergence holes 1-2m above ground and the extruded yellowish-brown pupa which is 15-18mm long.

Larval foodplants Downy Birch.

Habitat Open birch woodland and scrub on hillsides of wet, acidic pasture and moorland.

Status & distribution Resident. Red Data Book species. Found very locally in Wales, in Merionethshire (foothills of Snowdonia) and Montgomeryshire (several sites), and Perthshire (Rannoch and the Trossachs), east Inverness-shire (Glen Affric and Glen Moriston), in Sutherland and in the Irish Republic in the area between Killarney and Kenmare, Co. Kerry. First discovered in Britain in 1854, near Llangollen, Denbighshire. In the 19th and early 20th century it was also found in Glamorgan, Cheshire (Delamere Forest) and Staffordshire, and there are unconfirmed reports from Wiltshire (Ramsbury) and Herefordshire.

Sallow Clearwing   page 49

Synanthedon flaviventris (Stdgr.)

Nb. S   377(4052)

Field characters FW 8-9mm. Small clearwing with a dark thorax and three thin yellow bands on otherwise black abdomen. Occasionally a very faint fourth abdominal band.

Similar species Currant Clearwing is similar in size, but has yellow collar and usually yellow lines on thorax. Yellow-legged Clearwing has largely yellow legs and four distinct yellow bands on abdomen. See also Thrift Clearwing.

Flight season One generation. Mid June-mid July. Seldom seen except when attracted to pheromone lures, mainly in the afternoon.

Life cycle Overwinters twice as a larva in the stem of the foodplant. Larva August-June. The eggs are laid on slender stems and the larva burrows within, causing a pear-shaped gall 25mm in length to form in the second year, in a stem of about 10-15mm in

31

diameter. These can be found mainly in winters from odd to even years, usually on the top-most twigs of old bushes or the young straight stems of those cut back a year or two previously.

Larval foodplants Sallows, particularly Goat Willow and Grey Willow.

Habitat Damp, open woodland and damp heathland.

Status & distribution Resident. Nationally Scarce B. In southern England only, from Devon and Dorset to Kent, including the Isle of Wight, reaching north to Berkshire, Buckinghamshire, Oxfordshire and Gloucestershire.

Orange-tailed Clearwing page 49

Synanthedon andrenaeformis (Lasp.)
Nb. S   378(4053)

Field characters & Similar species FW 9-11mm. Distinctive wide orange and black tail fan on slender abdomen of male is visible even in flight, but see Welsh Clearwing and Yellow-legged Clearwing.

Flight season One generation. Mid May-mid July. Male comes readily to pheromone lures but otherwise the adults are very seldom seen. Recorded in flight around lime blossom. Some populations are reported to produce adults only in alternate years.

Life cycle Overwinters twice as a larva in the stem of the foodplant. Larva July-May, in stems or branches from about 8-25mm or more in diameter, most frequently on bushes growing in sheltered, sunny locations. Look for exit holes up to 6m from the ground. The holes are about 3mm in diameter, covered with a disc of bark about 7mm across, making them quite hard to find. However, the discs are often slightly concave and sometimes fall off, in which case the hole may be plugged with frass.

Larval foodplants Wayfaring-tree and, less often, Guelder-rose.

Habitat Chalk downland, limestone grassland and woodland edges.

Status & distribution Resident. Nationally Scarce B. Found locally in most counties in central southern England, from Dorset and Somerset eastwards to Kent, northwards to Worcestershire and Cambridgeshire. Also reported from Devon (in 1935), and in Wales from Monmouthshire and Glamorgan.

Red-belted Clearwing page 49

Synanthedon myopaeformis (Borkh.)
Nb. S   379(4060)

Field characters FW 9-11mm. Combination of a single broad red band on abdomen with uniformly black forewing markings is diagnostic.

Similar species Large Red-belted Clearwing has a thin scatter of red scales at base of forewing. Red-tipped Clearwing has a dense patch of red scales at tip of forewing.

Flight season One generation. Mid June-early August. Occasionally adults are seen flying around apple trees in the afternoon, when the eggs are laid.

Male can be seen flying around the top-most branches and comes readily to the specific pheromone lure, sometimes in numbers, from mid morning to late afternoon.

Life cycle Overwinters as a larva. Eggs are laid singly on the bark, especially where the main trunk divides to form the largest branches in mature trees. Larva August-May, feeding underneath the bark. Wounded trees are especially favoured, and a tree may be infested for many years. Look for exit holes, empty pupal cases protruding and frass in bark crevices.

Larval foodplants Usually Apple, including native Crab Apple. Also recorded from Hawthorn, Pear, Almond and Rowan.

Habitat Well established orchards and gardens, hedgerows, open woodland and mature scrub.

Status & distribution Resident. Nationally Scarce B, but probably under-recorded. Found locally in most counties in England south of the Humber. Also recorded from Yorkshire, north Wales and Lancashire. Only doubtfully recorded from the Irish Republic. Rare on Jersey.

Red-tipped Clearwing page 49

Synanthedon formicaeformis (Esp.)
Nb. S,C,(N)   380(4051)

Field characters FW 9-11mm. Combination of red forewing tip and a single broad red band on abdomen is diagnostic. On emergence the adults have two bands of powdery yellow scales on abdomen, which are lost during early flights.

Similar species See Red-belted and Large Red-belted Clearwing.

Flight season One generation. Late May-early August, with the peak emergence in mid-June; delayed emergence in cool summers. Adults have been found at rest on trunks in early morning, have been beaten from willow foliage in dull weather and are sometimes seen visiting flowers. Male is attracted to various pheromone lures, usually after noon.

Life cycle Overwinters as a part-grown larva. Larva August-May, living in the trunks, branches and thin stems of the foodplants. Sometimes frass is found where the tree has been damaged in some way.

Larval foodplants Osiers and other willows, including

Empty pupal case of Red-tipped Clearwing.

Goat Willow, Grey Willow and Creeping Willow.
Habitat Sallow carr and swamp, osier or withy beds, riverbanks, flooded gravel pits and ponds, and other places where willows grow, usually in damp or marshy ground.
Status & distribution Resident. Nationally Scarce B. Widespread in England, north to Northumberland, but apparently less frequent in the west. Possibly overlooked in Wales, but reported from Glamorgan in 1893. In Scotland, recorded from Dumfries-shire. In Northern Ireland found in Co. Armagh, where it was first discovered in 1985. Localised and scarce in the Irish Republic, with records from Cos. Kerry, Cork, Sligo and Louth.

Large Red-belted Clearwing   page 49
Synanthedon culiciformis (L.)
Nb. T   381(4048)

Field characters FW 12-14mm. Combination of a single broad red band on abdomen and a scatter of reddish scales at base of forewing is diagnostic.
Similar species See Red-belted Clearwing and Red-tipped Clearwing.
Flight season One generation. Mid May-late June, earlier than most clearwings, but emergence can be delayed by prolonged cool, wet weather. Female sometimes seen in numbers egg laying on freshly cut birch stumps on hot sunny days, but also on intact tree trunks. Recorded visiting flowers, including Wood Spurge, hawthorns and Rhododendron. Male is attracted to pheromone lures.
Life cycle Overwinters as a larva in a cocoon. Larva July-May. Tunnels and pupates under the bark. Look for small holes and frass at the edges of cut stumps, between the bark and the heartwood.
Larval foodplants Downy Birch and Silver Birch, occasionally Alder.
Habitat Birches in light woodland, particularly areas of recent coppicing or felling, and birch and alder scrub on heathlands and other open sunny places, on both light soils and clays.
Status & distribution Resident. Nationally Scarce B. Recorded from most counties in England, from Devon and Kent northwards to Lancashire and Yorkshire, north Wales and Glamorgan. Also from Inverness-shire, Aberdeenshire and Kincardineshire in Scotland. Rare on Jersey.

Six-belted Clearwing   page 49
Bembecia ichneumoniformis ([D. & S.])
Nb. S,C   382(4070)

Field characters FW 9-12mm. The six yellowish bands on abdomen, in combination with a frosting of orange scales on tip and central bar of forewing, distinguish this from all other clearwings. Some males larger and more furry than others.
Similar species Thrift Clearwing is smaller, with fewer, less obvious bands and lacks orange scales on forewing.
Flight season One generation. Late June-mid

August. Adults can be obtained using sweep nets. Male sometimes seen perching on the flowers of Salad Burnet and other vantage points in the afternoon and comes readily to pheromone lures, sometimes in large numbers, from 8am to 7pm. Female sometimes seen laying eggs on the leaves and other parts of the foodplant.
Life cycle Overwinters as a larva. Larva July-May or early June. Can be found only by digging up the foodplant, when frass may be seen along the main root. Look on stressed, rather isolated plants in somewhat disturbed ground, particularly at the edges of paths and tracks, rather than in lush growth.
Larval foodplants Common Bird's-foot-trefoil and Kidney Vetch, and recorded egg laying on Horseshoe Vetch.
Habitat Grassy swards, mainly in areas of chalk or limestone, on downland, coastal grassland and rough upland fields, embankments, quarries, brick-pits and cliffs. Does not thrive under heavy grazing.
Status & distribution Resident. Nationally Scarce B. Recorded from most counties in southern England, from Cornwall to Kent, and north to Staffordshire, Nottinghamshire, Derbyshire and Yorkshire. In south Wales, Pembrokeshire and the Gower. Recorded in north Wales for the first time in 1991. Much over-looked until recently, but may be expanding its range northwards. Rare in the Channel Islands.

Thrift Clearwing   page 49
Synansphecia muscaeformis (Esp.)
Nb. SW,NE   383(4098)

Field characters FW 6-8mm. Our smallest clear-wing, with three (sometimes four) narrow yellowish white bands on abdomen and no orange scales on forewing. When freshly emerged, the wings have a light covering of yellowish-white scales, which are lost on the first flight.
Similar species On Currant Clearwing the dark outer band on forewing is streaked with orange. Sallow Clearwing has a dark thorax. Both are slightly larger, and unlikely to occur in the same habitat as Thrift Clearwing. See also Six-belted Clearwing.
Flight season One generation. Early June-late July. Adults fly rapidly, from late morning until late afternoon, sometimes visiting the flowers of Thrift and Thyme. Male comes readily to pheromone lures.
Life cycle Overwinters as a part-grown larva. Larva August-May, feeding in the roots and stems. The larvae are most frequent in plants growing in rock crevices, often in the splash zone. In occupied plants the part of the cushion of foliage around the larval feeding often dies and turns brown, or there are small piles of reddish-brown frass on the surface.
Larval foodplants Thrift.
Habitat Rocky coastlines and sunken lanes leading to beaches.
Status & distribution Resident. Nationally Scarce B. Mainly restricted to the western coasts of Britain and Ireland, in south Devon, Cornwall and Scilly, Wales,

including Anglesey, Cumbria and Man. In Scotland, in Kirkcudbrightshire, the Moray Firth, Aberdeenshire and Angus. On the coast of the southern half of Ireland, and in Northern Ireland recently discovered in Co. Antrim. Locally frequent in the Channel Islands.

Fiery Clearwing   page 49
Pyropteron chrysidiformis (Esp.)
RDB (Protected species). SE   384(4090)

Field characters FW 9-12mm. The fiery orange-red scales over most of forewing are diagnostic. There are two (female) or three (male) narrow whitish bands on abdomen and the orange-red tail fan is orange centrally. These features are very apparent when the moth is at rest.
Similar species None.
Flight season One generation. Mid June-early July. Adults have been seen flying about the foodplants, egg-laying and visiting flowers such as Common Mallow. Not attracted to currently available pheromone lures.

Life cycle Overwinters usually once or sometimes twice as a larva. Larva August-May. The larva tunnels into the tap roots of larger, often isolated, plants. Those affected may appear unhealthy.
Larval foodplants Curled Dock, Common Sorrel and probably other species of dock.
Habitat Well-drained sites with a warm micro-climate. Shingle at the top of beaches or similarly bare man-made features including railway ballast, rough herb-rich grassy sward, broken chalk under-cliff, cliff-tops and nearby roadside verges.
Status & distribution Resident. Red Data Book species. Found very locally along the coast and a short distance inland in Kent, between Folkestone and Dover, including Folkestone Warren where it was first discovered in 1836. Recently rediscovered on the north Kent coast where it was first reported in 1944. In the 19th century, recorded from Hampshire (Hayling Island, Gosport and Southsea), Sussex (Eastbourne) and Essex (between Leigh and Southend-on-Sea), with an unconfirmed record from Dorset (Portland Bill).

Lasiocampidae – Eggar moths

This family of about 1,000 species occurs throughout the world. Ten species are resident in the British Isles, an eleventh is almost certainly extinct and a twelfth is a suspected immigrant. Eggars are thickset, medium-sized or large moths with deep, rounded, usually warm brown or yellowish wings, generally bearing a small central spot or two cross-lines on the forewings.

Oak Eggar

Drinker

The males have broadly feathered antennae with which they can detect the scent of unmated females from several hundred metres. The males of two of the largest British species (Oak Eggar and Fox Moth) do this by day and are often seen flying rapidly on sunny afternoons. Females of these species and both sexes of others are nocturnal and come to light-traps. None are able to feed. Some species, such as the Oak Eggar, broadcast their eggs in flight, but most attach them to the foodplant. The larvae are covered in dense hairs, which protect them from being eaten by most birds, except cuckoos, and can sometimes cause skin irritation in humans when handled. Some feed openly by day and are often seen basking in the sun. Pupation occurs in a substantial, sometimes tough, cocoon formed above ground, attached to vegetation and generally incorporating some of the larval hairs.

December Moth
page 50

Poecilocampa populi (L.)

Common. T   1631(6728)

Field characters FW 15-22mm. Unlikely to be confused with any other moth which flies at the end of the year. The creamy-white markings on charcoal-coloured forewing can be striking. Very little variation, but female much larger.

Similar species Small Eggar is browner, has a prominent white oval, and flies later (may overlap).

Flight season One generation. Late October-early January in southern Britain, from early October in the north. Nocturnal. Comes to light, sometimes in large numbers, otherwise seldom seen.

Life cycle Overwinters as an egg, attached to the bark of twigs or trunk. Larva April-June. Feeds at night, resting along a twig or on bark by day. Pupates under bark or among plant debris.

Larval foodplants Broadleaved trees, including oaks, birches, elms, hawthorns, Blackthorn, poplars and sallows.

Habitat Most numerous in woodland, but also frequent in scrub, hedgerows and established gardens.

Status & distribution Resident. Common. Distributed over most of England and Wales except the highest ground, and at low altitude throughout mainland Scotland and the Inner Hebrides. One record from Man, in 1970. Widespread in Ireland, but more frequent in the west. Local and rare on Guernsey.

Pale Eggar
page 50

Trichiura crataegi (L.)

Common. T   1632(6731)

Field characters FW 14-17mm. The only pale grey eggar found in the British Isles, and distinguished from other small-sized eggars by the flight season. The wavy, black or dark grey outer edge of central band on forewing is also diagnostic. Markings vary little, but ground-colour is darker in the cooler climate of upland areas.

Similar species See Pine Processionary.

Flight season One generation. August-September. Both sexes are nocturnal and come to light, sometimes in numbers, especially male.

Life cycle Overwinters as an egg on the foodplant. Larva April-June, but in upland parts of Scotland and possibly northern England a second winter is sometimes passed as a nearly fully grown larva. Pupates in a cocoon formed in leaf litter.

Larval foodplants Principally birches, Blackthorn and hawthorns, favouring sunny locations, and also recorded from sallows, Hazel, Crab Apple, oaks, Bilberry, Bell Heather and Heather.

Habitat Open woodland, hedgerows, heathland, moorland, scrub and gardens.

Status & distribution Resident. Common. Well distributed and frequent in most of England north into Yorkshire, but scarce to the west of the Pennines. Scattered through lowland Wales, but more frequent on the limestone of north Wales. Widespread in mainland Scotland, especially in the river valleys, but rare in the south-west. Also found in the Inner Hebrides. Very local in Ireland and only recorded from the Burren, Co. Clare, and old woodlands on light soils in Co. Fermanagh.

Small Eggar
page 50

Eriogaster lanestris (L.)

Nb. S,C   1633(6738)

Field characters FW 15-21mm. Combination of flight time, relatively small size, deep reddish-brown colour, a whitish spot in centre of forewing and a whitish cross-line is diagnostic. Female is larger and has a large tuft of grey hair at the end of abdomen, which is used to cover the egg batches.

Similar species See December Moth.

Flight season One generation. February-March. The nocturnal adults are rarely seen, except occasionally in light-traps.

Life cycle Overwinters as a pupa, in a hard, brown, rounded cocoon, usually near the ground. The pupa often passes two or three winters before the adult emerges, and in captivity sometimes up to seven. Larvae April-July. Larvae live gregariously until part way through the final instar, spinning a compact web, basking on this during warm sunshine, feeding mainly at night. Hedges and bushes lightly trimmed in the autumn are preferred to uncut ones.

Larval foodplants Chiefly Blackthorn or Hawthorn, occasionally elms, Spindle, Apple and Grey Willow.

Habitat Hedgerows and scattered bushes in open country.

Status & distribution Resident. Nationally Scarce B and much decreased. Most frequent in Somerset and Dorset; also in Gloucestershire, Wiltshire and Sussex, and locally in Oxfordshire, Northamptonshire, Huntingdonshire, Norfolk, North Yorkshire (Pickering, Scarborough) and Lancashire (Morecambe Bay). In Wales, found in Monmouthshire (near Abergavenny) and Montgomeryshire. In Northern Ireland not found in recent searches of several former localities in the east, but a male was recorded at light at Monmurray, Co. Fermanagh, in 2000, and there are old records for the Enniskillen area. Populations are subject to large fluctuations in numbers, for reasons which are unclear but are propably related mainly to weather.

Lackey
page 50

Malacosoma neustria (L.)

Common. S,C,(N)   1634(6743)

Field characters & Similar species FW M 13-16mm F 16-21mm. Rather variable in colour, from straw yellow to reddish brown, although usually easily recognisable (but see Ground Lackey). Rests like related species. Diagnostic features are two roughly parallel cross-lines (only rarely weak or absent) on forewing, brown and white chequered fringes with

35

two very distinct reflective white patches (duller in Ground Lackey), and hindwing either the same colour as forewing, or paler. Female larger in both species.

Flight season One generation. July-August. Both sexes are nocturnal and are fairly frequent at light, especially male.

Life cycle Overwinters as an egg, laid in bands around a twig of the foodplant. Larva April-June, living in groups in webs on which they bask, until almost fully grown. Pupates in a tough yellow cocoon among low stems or plant debris.

Larval foodplants Many broadleaved trees and shrubs, particularly of the rose family, including Hawthorn, Blackthorn, cherries, Plum, Apple and cultivated *Potentilla* shrubs, but also oaks and willows.

Habitat Open, sunny situations, especially hedgerows, scrubby places, gardens and open woodland.

Status & distribution Resident. Common. Well distributed and frequent throughout southern England to Yorkshire, but rare to the immediate west of the Pennines. In Wales, mainly in the lowlands and on the coast. Further north there are scattered records near the west coast north to Kirkcudbrightshire in Scotland. Local and rare on Man. Widespread in Ireland, more especially in the south, notably in Co. Clare. There are old records from the Mountains of Mourn, Co. Down, Northern Ireland. Widespread and frequent in the Channel Islands.

Ground Lackey   page 50

Malacosoma castrensis (L.)

Na. SE,SW   1635(6744)

Field characters & Similar species FW M 13-16mm F 17-21mm. Similar in colour and markings to Lackey, but differing in several respects. Two cross-lines (often weak or absent) on forewing form a waist at the centre as a result of an outward-facing kink in first cross-line, more obviously in male, and first cross-line curves strongly towards the base in trailing half of wing. Also, forewing margin is chequered with brown and buff; hindwing is same colour as forewing, or darker, with paler margin (darker than wing in Lackey).

Flight season One generation. July-August. Nocturnal. Occasionally found at rest but normally only seen at light.

Life cycle Overwinters as a single layer of eggs around a standing stem of a saltmarsh plant, usually remaining in place during winter inundations by the sea. Larva April-July, pupating among saltmarsh plants in a light cocoon through which the pupa remains visible.

Larval foodplants Herbaceous saltmarsh plants, including Sea Plantain, Common Sea-lavender, Sea Wormwood, Sea-purslane, Grass-leaved Orache and Golden-samphire. Also Wild Carrot. Can be reared on hawthorns and Blackthorn but must have warmth, and preferably sunshine.

Habitat Saltmarshes and coastal shingle.

Status & distribution Resident. Nationally Scarce A. Largely confined to the saltmarshes of the south-east coast of England, namely the north Kent marshes, including Fowley Island, the estuaries of Essex, in the Suffolk marshes around Orford Ness, and north to Benacre Ness, near Southwold. In 1995, adults and over 100 larvae were reported from the shingle and saltings at Axmouth, Devon, with more larvae in subsequent years. Nineteenth-century records from near Exeter suggest this may be an overlooked population of long standing. Also reported from the coast of Sussex on at least three occasions.

Grass Eggar   page 50

Lasiocampa trifolii ([D. & S.])

Na. S,WC   1636(6749)

Pale Grass Eggar

f. *flava* C.-Hunt

RDB. SE

Field characters FW M 21-24mm F 25-30mm. Grass Eggar is a quite distinctive reddish-brown moth, with a curved outer cross-line on forewing and a clear white spot near centre. Considerable geographical variation, with darker, sometimes blackish-brown forms in more northern and western colonies. Pale Grass Eggar is the straw yellow or brownish yellow form, with similar markings to Grass Eggar. The infrequent f. *obsoleta* Tutt lacks cross-lines and central spot has no dark ring.

Similar species Female Pale Grass Eggar might be confused with female Oak Eggar, which is usually larger, has more rounded forewing tip and a wider outer cross-band.

Flight season One generation. August-September. Both sexes nocturnal and come to light; unlikely to be seen otherwise.

Life cycle Overwinters as an egg, laid loose among short vegetation. Larva late March-July, feeding at night. Pupates in a tough brown cocoon on the ground, usually attached to vegetation.

Larval foodplants Seems to vary from colony to colony: mainly False Oat-grass at Dungeness; Tree Lupin on Hayling Island, Hampshire; Marram at Studland, Dorset; Bramble at Prawle Point, Devon; and Creeping Willow at Formby, Lancashire. Also recorded on Kidney Vetch, Common Bird's-foot-trefoil, Purple Clover, Spiny Restharrow and Thrift.

Habitat Lightly vegetated sand-dunes, sea-cliffs, coastal shingle and acid heathland inland.

Status & distribution Resident. Grass Eggar: Nationally Scarce A. Very local on sand-dunes on the coasts of Scilly, Dorset, Hampshire, Somerset, Glamorgan, Cheshire and Lancashire. Also on sea-cliffs in south Devon and Cornwall, and heathland inland in Dorset and formerly in Hampshire. Pale Grass Eggar: Red Data Book species, is confined to Dungeness, Kent, but until the 1950s also occurred at the Crumbles, near Eastbourne, Sussex. Widespread and frequent in the Channel Islands.

Oak Eggar
page 51

Lasiocampa quercus (L.)

Common. S,C
1637(6752)

Northern Eggar

f. *callunae* Palmer

Common. N,W

Field characters FW M 25-34mm F 33-40mm. Rich deep brown colour of male Oak Eggar, together with white central spot and broad pale band on forewing, is unmistakable. Buff or light brown female, with a similar pattern, is also distinctive. Northern Eggar is larger, and in male the pale basal patch on forewing is often larger; female Northern Eggar is darker and browner than female Oak Eggar. The blackish-brown f. *olivacea* Tutt is found in Oak Eggars on sand-dunes on the Cheshire and Lancashire coasts, and in Northern Eggars on moorland in Yorkshire and the northern half of Scotland.

Similar species See Grass Eggar, which is usually smaller.

Flight season One generation. July-August in the south, late May-July in the north. Male flies fast in a zigzag fashion by day, usually in afternoon sunshine. Female flies from early dusk and comes to light early in the night.

Life cycle In the south, overwinters once, as a third instar larva; larva August-June, often basking in sunshine. In the north, overwinters once as a small larva and once as a pupa; larva July-May. Larval hairs may cause skin irritation. Pupates among leaf litter in a very tough brown cocoon.

Larval foodplants On heaths and moors, mainly heathers, and also Bilberry. Also Bramble, Blackthorn, hawthorns, sallows, Hazel and Sea-buckthorn and other woody plants. In captivity, also Garden Privet and Ivy.

Habitat Heathland, moorland, woodland edges, hedgerows, breckland, downland, fens, sand-dunes and sea-cliffs.

Status & distribution Resident. Common. Widespread and often frequent over most of Britain, including the Outer Hebrides and Orkney, and in Ireland. Scarce in the intensively farmed areas of the central lowlands of England. Formerly on Man, but now apparently extinct. Widespread and frequent in the Channel Islands. Although nominally split into two main forms, the situation is more complex, and key features vary within populations. Moths with a one-year life cycle (Oak Eggars) are found in south-east, south-west, eastern and southern England, East Anglia, the south Midlands, and the Cheshire and Lancashire coasts. However, those from Hampshire, Dorset and south-west England (and females from the north-west coast) appear more like Northern Eggars. Typical Northern Eggars, with a two-year life cycle, occur on moorland in northern England, Wales, Scotland and Ireland. There appears to be an intermediate zone with sometimes one-year and two-year life cycles in the Midlands and the Welsh borders.

Fully grown larva of Fox Moth.

Fox Moth
page 51

Macrothylacia rubi (L.)

Common. T
1638(6755)

Field characters FW M 22-26mm F 26-31mm. Combination of large size and two narrow, roughly parallel (less so in female) pale cross-bands on otherwise plain forewing make this moth unmistakable. Male is predominantly red-brown, female largely grey-brown. Moths from the cooler northern and upland areas are often darker, less red and greyer than those from southern lowlands.

Similar species The absence of a central white spot on forewing distinguishes this from other large eggars.

Flight season One generation. May-June. Male flies rapidly by day, but sometimes comes to light. Female is strictly nocturnal and can be frequent at light.

Life cycle Overwinters as a fully grown larva, on or just beneath the ground under moss or leaf litter. Larva June-April, feeding until September. Emerges briefly, without feeding again, to bask in spring sunshine and pupates in a long, cigar-shaped cocoon near the ground.

Larval foodplants Heathers, Bilberry and Creeping Willow on moors and heaths, Bramble and Meadowsweet in wet flushes and Salad Burnet on downland.

Habitat Heathland, moorland, downland, damp meadows, coastal grassland, sand-dunes and open woodland.

Status & distribution Resident. Common. Widely distributed and locally frequent throughout most of the British Isles, including the Outer Hebrides and Orkney (discovered as a larva on Hoy, in 1999). In Ireland, mainly in the north and west. Frequent on Man. In the Channel Islands widespread and occasional on Jersey; rare on Guernsey.

Pine-tree Lappet
page 51

Dendrolimus pini (L.)

Rare immigrant.
1639(6763)

Field characters FW 31-40mm. Quite distinctive. Male is reddish brown with a white central spot on forewing and a fine, dark, scalloped central cross-line, a jagged outer band and whitish frosting. Female, not yet seen in the British Isles, is larger, more golden brown, with a paler outer band and margin on forewing.

Flight season June-August in mainland Europe. Comes to light.

Status Rare immigrant. A male was recorded on 12 August 1996 at Freshwater, Isle of Wight, during an exceptional period of immigration of moths into the British Isles. Also recorded as single males on Guernsey, on 9 July 1989, and subsequently in 1997 and 2000. In addition, there is a record of a male in Norwich in 1809, and a larva near Richmond Park, Surrey, in 1748. Widespread in mainland Europe and sometimes a pest of pines and Norway Spruce.

Drinker page 52
Euthrix potatoria (L.)
Common. S,C,NW   1640(6767)

Field characters FW M 21-25mm F 28-35mm. Distinguished from other large eggars by outer cross-line on forewing, which runs diagonally to wing tip, and the small additional white spot near middle of leading edge. Male is normally warm reddish brown, with yellowish patches. Female varies from deep yellow to very pale buff, whitish, or reddish brown like male (f. *obscura* Tutt). In the fens of East Anglia entirely yellowish male is not infrequent (f. *pallida* Tutt), but is rare elsewhere.

Similar species None.

Flight season One generation. July-August. Nocturnal. Both sexes come to light, male more frequently.

Life cycle Overwinters as a small larva. Larva August-June. Pupates in a tapering, cream-coloured papery cocoon spun above ground, usually on a grass stem, but sometimes under a log.

Larval foodplants A wide range of coarse grasses and reeds, including Cock's-foot, couches, Common Reed, Reed Canary-grass and Wood Small-reed.

Habitat Most frequent in tall, damp grassland, fens, marshes, boggy areas on heathland and low moorland, and damp open woodland, scrub and ditches, but also occurs in drier places, including urban gardens.

Status & distribution Resident. Common. Well distributed throughout England, becoming more coastal north to Northumberland, on the western side of mainland Scotland and in the Inner Hebrides. Local and rare on Man. Well distributed in Ireland. Widespread and abundant on Jersey, but rare on Guernsey.

Small Lappet page 52
Phyllodesma ilicifolia (L.)
Former resident; presumed extinct.   1641(6771)

Field characters FW 18-20mm. Like a very much smaller Lappet in shape, markings and resting posture, but with a light brown forewing, greyer

towards outer edge.

Similar species None.

Flight season One generation. Late April-May. Comes to light, but rarely found by this method in Britain. Occasionally found at rest by day on the foodplant.

Life cycle Overwinters as a pupa in a cocoon formed near the ground. Larva June-mid August.

Larval foodplants Bilberry.

Habitat Moorland and open woodland.

Status & distribution Former resident, now probably extinct. The first British records were from Yorkshire in 1850 near Ripon, Dallongill Moors in Nidderdale and Blubberhouses Moor, where it was found in small numbers until 1882. It was discovered at Cannock Chase, Staffordshire, in 1851 and found occasionally there as larvae up to about 1900, and from the Long Mynd, Shropshire, in 1889. There are unconfirmed records of a larva in 1864 at Lynton, North Devon, and another in August 1938 from Porlock, Somerset. The last confirmed records are of one to light on 15 May 1965 at Weston-super-Mare, Somerset, and another in 1939 at the Rugeley end of Cannock Chase. A report of larvae in 1985 in south-west England was a hoax. It remains possible that undiscovered populations exist in some remote places, but Cannock Chase has subsequently been searched many times without success.

Lappet page 52
Gastropacha quercifolia (L.)
Common. S,EC   1642(6777)

Field characters FW 28-42mm. The large size, purplish-brown coloration, scalloped outer edge of wing, resting posture and prominent snout are diagnostic. Little variation. Pale buff and blackish forms have been reported, but are very rare.

Similar species None.

Flight season One generation. Late June-mid August. Both sexes are nocturnal and come to light in small numbers.

Life cycle Overwinters as a small larva. Larva August-late May. Feeds at night, and when large rests low on a main stem by day. Pupates in a tough cocoon near the ground, attached to vegetation.

Larval foodplants Chiefly Blackthorn, Hawthorn, Crab Apple and cultivated Apple. Also sallows, and reportedly Buckthorn and Alder Buckthorn. Most often found on small, isolated bushes.

Habitat Hedgerows and thorn scrub on downland, and open woodland; occasionally in rural gardens.

Status & distribution Resident. Common. Well distributed in England south of a line between the Severn and the Wash, except the extreme south-west, but rarely seen in numbers, and has declined since the 1980s, if not for longer. Extends more locally to the Humber, with recent increases in Lincolnshire and Yorkshire. Recorded from a few localities near the coast in south Wales. Occasional in the Channel Islands.

Saturniidae – Emperor moths

This family comprises about 1,300 species. The distribution is world-wide, but more of the species occur in the tropics of Central and South America than elsewhere. Only one species is resident in the British Isles. The adults do not feed.

Emperor Moth

Emperor Moth   page 52
Saturnia pavonia (L.)
Common. T   1643(6794)

Field characters FW M 27-32mm F 35-41mm. Unmistakable. Variation is rare, but both sexes from northern or upland sites are more intensely coloured, with female even bluish. Smoky individuals and a form lacking eye-spots have occurred.
Similar species Great Peacock Moth *Saturnia pyri* ([D. & S.]) has eye-spots on both forewing and hind-wing. It has occasionally been found in Britain, prob-ably as accidental introductions, but is darker than female Emperor and very much larger.
Flight season One generation. April-late May. Males fly rapidly by day in sunshine and could be mistaken for a nymphalid butterfly, such as Small Tortoiseshell. Adults are seldom seen in numbers, unless a virgin female is found. One female may attract many males, especially if it is a captive moth prevented from mating by netting. Female flies at night and comes to light in small numbers, usually early in the night, and can sometimes be found at rest by day.
Life cycle Overwinters as a pupa, within a light brown, tough, papery, droplet-shaped cocoon, with a closed circle of upward-pointing spines around the narrow opening to repel predators. It is attached to a plant stem near the ground. Eggs are laid in batches, attached to the foodplant. Larva late May-August, living in groups at first and often sitting exposed by day.
Larval foodplants Mostly woody plants, including heathers, Meadowsweet, Alder Buckthorn, Bramble, hawthorns, Blackthorn, sallows and birches.
Habitat Heathland, moorland bogs, fens, hedgerows, field margins, woodland rides, mature sand-dunes and other open scrubby places.
Status & distribution Resident. Common. Widely distributed in most parts of mainland Britain, the Channel Islands, Man, Orkney, the Hebrides and Ireland, but at low density in some parts of the south.
1643a see Appendix

Endromidae

This family includes just one species in the British Isles, the Kentish Glory, which has been recorded from almost every country in Europe except Ireland, Albania, Greece and Turkey. It occurs in birch forests from Europe, through Asia to southern Siberia and the Far East.

Kentish Glory

Kentish Glory   page 52
Endromis versicolora (L.)
Na. NE   1644(6784)

Field characters FW M 27-30mm F 34-39mm. Large, rather stout moth with unmistakable brown and white forewing markings. Slightly smaller, darker male has orange-brown hindwing, whereas that of female is largely brownish white.
Similar species None.
Flight season One generation. Late April-mid May. The extinct southern populations emerged from late March. Male flies in sunshine or warm cloudy weather, from mid morning to early afternoon. Both sexes fly from dusk and come to light; they can sometimes be found by day at rest on birch twigs or other vegetation, up to 2-3m from the ground.
Life cycle Overwinters as a pupa, in a coarse webbed cocoon formed on the ground. Larva mid May-mid August, feeding at first gregariously and then singly. Egg batches are laid on the outer twigs of low birch scrub, less than 2m above the ground in

open, sunny, sheltered places.
Larval foodplants Silver Birch, and less often Downy Birch and Alder.
Habitat Open birch woodland and lightly wooded moorland.
Status & distribution Resident. Nationally Scarce A. Restricted to the central and eastern Highlands of Scotland, at Rannoch and the Upper Tay valley in Perthshire, the Spey catchment in Inverness-shire, the Morayshire coast, Deeside in Aberdeenshire and Kincardineshire, and possibly at Glen Strathfarrar,

south-west of Inverness. It has declined at sites such as Aviemore and Rannoch where the birch has become mature, but has increased in central Deeside, where birch re-growth has become extensive. In the 19th century, this moth was local in Kent, Sussex, Berkshire, East Anglia, Herefordshire, Worcestershire and Monmouthshire. It survived in the West Midlands in the 20th century, but was last seen in southern Britain in the Wyre Forest, Worcestershire, in about 1970.

Drepanidae – Hook-tips

Of the 400 or so species worldwide, only eight occur in Europe. They have broad wings and slender bodies, like the

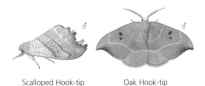

Scalloped Hook-tip   Oak Hook-tip

geometrid moths to which they are closely related. Six are resident in the British Isles and a seventh is an occasional immigrant. On all but one of these, the tips of the forewings are strongly hooked. Some rest with their wings in a rather tent-like position, others hold them flat to the surface. They are sometimes disturbed by day from among the foliage of the larval foodplants, or netted on the wing at dusk. However, they are most frequently encountered in light-traps, to which they come quite regularly, but usually in small numbers. Some adults are able to feed, but have a rather short tongue and do not visit flowers, and are only occasionally attracted to baits, aphid honeydew and oozing sap. The larvae of all the British species feed on the foliage of trees and shrubs. The females attach the eggs to the leaves, either singly or in rows. The hind pair of claspers of the larvae are pointed and the tail end is held in a characteristic raised position. Pupation takes place in a slight cocoon, spun between leaves of the food-plant. The cocoon drops with the leaves to the ground in the overwintering generation. See also the unrelated Beautiful Hook-tip *Laspeyria flexula* (2473).

Scalloped Hook-tip   page 53
Falcaria lacertinaria (L.)
Common. T   1645(7501)

Field characters FW 14-18mm. Unmistakable, with outer edge of forewing irregularly scalloped, two dark parallel cross-lines and a small dark central dot. Rests with wings raised, tent-like. There is little variation in markings but second-generation moths are smaller and paler brown. First-generation moths often have stronger brown lattice-like or flecked markings and are more silvery grey, especially in northern Britain.
Similar species Beautiful Hook-tip has only two projections on outer edge of forewing, has two dark central dots and rests with its wings flat.
Flight season Two generations. Late April-late June

and mid July-August, except in Scotland where there is one generation from late May-June. Nocturnal. Comes to light, sometimes in numbers, and can be disturbed by day from the foodplant.
Life cycle Overwinters as a pupa in a cocoon, in a folded leaf. Larva June-July and August-September, July-August in Scotland. Can be frequent on birch re-growth only 2m tall, and is more numerous in warm sunny situations.
Larval foodplants Downy Birch and Silver Birch.
Habitat Usually in woodland, scrub, heathland and bogs; also hedgerows and gardens.
Status & distribution Resident. Common. Widely distributed in England north to Yorkshire and Cumbria, Wales and mainland Scotland and some of the Hebrides. Widespread in Ireland, with most recent records from the north and south-west. Rare in the Channel Islands, with one on Jersey in 1999.

Oak Hook-tip
page 53

Watsonalla binaria (Hufn.)

Common. S,C   1646(7503)

Field characters FW 13-18mm. Quite a distinctive orange-brown moth, with two well-defined pale cross-lines on forewing, and a lilac tinge when freshly emerged. Two prominent blackish spots in centre of forewing, and two small dots on hindwing. Male is often darker and female differs in being generally larger and having orange hindwing. Varies little, but individuals of first generation are larger and more richly coloured. Rests with wings spread flat.

Similar species Barred Hook-tip has a more distinct, darker central cross-band on forewing, only one brown central spot and no central dots on hindwing. Like Oak Hook-tip, rests with wings flat.

Flight season Two generations. May-June and late July-mid September. Male occasionally flies high around oaks by day and both sexes may be disturbed from lower branches. Flies from dusk and comes to light.

Life cycle Overwinters as a pupa, in a tough brown cocoon spun in a tightly folded oak leaf. Larva June-July and late August-September.

Larval foodplants Both Pedunculate and Sessile Oak, and almost certainly Turkey Oak. Reported occasionally on Silver Birch.

Habitat Most numerous in oak woodland, but occurs in hedgerows, parkland and gardens.

Status & distribution Resident. Common. Well distributed in England, north to Cumbria, and Wales, mainly in the lowlands and near the coast. Recently reported from southern Scotland. Widespread and occasional in the Channel Islands.

Barred Hook-tip
page 53

Watsonalla cultraria (Fabr.)

Local. S,C   1647(7505)

Field characters FW 12-17mm. Broad, darker central cross-band on orange-brown forewing is the main diagnostic feature. Also, there is only one (rarely two) often rather faint, brown central dot, and there are no such dots on hindwing. Little variation in markings, and only slight variation in colour.

Similar species See Oak Hook-tip.

Flight season Two generations. May-June and mid July-early September. Male sometimes flies by day, rather high around the foodplant. Both sexes fly at night and come to light.

Life cycle Overwinters as a pupa, in a white cocoon within a curled Beech leaf or between two leaves spun together. Larva June-July and September.

Larval foodplants Beech.

Habitat Beech woods, especially on calcareous soils, and in places with mature, isolated Beeches. Has colonised many areas where Beech is an introduction.

Status & distribution Resident. Local. Well distributed in England south of a line from the Severn to the Wash. More local northwards to the Humber and through Wales, with occasional records from

Lancashire, Cumbria and southern Scotland. An adult on 4 September 1999 at an actinic trap on sand-dunes at Ballykinler, Co. Down, appears to be the only record from Ireland.

Pebble Hook-tip
page 53

Drepana falcataria falcataria (L.)

Common. S,C   1648(7508)

ssp. *scotica* Byt.-Salz

Local. N

Field characters FW 17-21mm. In ssp. *falcataria* central, rather pebble-like spot on forewing and distinct purplish-brown blotch along outer edge, near wing tip, are the main diagnostic features. Also, hindwing is generally paler, especially in leading half. Rests with wings spread flat. F. *pallida* Stephan is very pale, approaching ssp. *scotica*, but less strongly marked. In ssp. *scotica* ground-colour of wings is straw-white and outer markings are darker than in ssp. *falcataria*.

Similar species Dusky Hook-tip could be confused with ssp. *falcataria*, but central spots on forewing are all quite small and hindwing is not paler in the leading half.

Flight season Ssp. *falcataria* has two generations. Late April-June and mid July-early September, with occasional individuals of a possible third generation in October. Ssp. *scotica* has one generation, from mid May-late July. Occasionally found at rest by day near larval foodplant. Both sexes come to light, usually in small numbers.

Life cycle Overwinters as a pupa, in a cocoon between leaves. Larva late June-late July and September in southern Britain, July-August in the north.

Larval foodplants Downy Birch, Silver Birch and sometimes Alder.

Habitat Woodland, heathland and other habitats with birch scrub, including town gardens. Also Alder carr.

Status & distribution Resident. Common. Ssp. *falcataria* is found in suitable habitat throughout England and Wales and southern Scotland, except on high ground. Rare on Man. Widepread but thinly scattered in Ireland. Local and rare in the Channel Islands. Ssp. *scotica* is widespread in the northern half of Scotland north to Caithness, and the Inner Hebrides, particularly in river valleys.

Dusky Hook-tip
page 53

Drepana curvatula (Borkh.)

Immigrant. S,E   1649(7507)

Field characters & Similar species FW 16-21mm. A brown hook-tip, with a lilac tinge when freshly emerged. Not dissimilar to ssp. *falcataria* of Pebble Hook-tip and, like that species, rests with wings spread flat, but central spots on forewing are small, hindwing is same colour as forewing and hindwing has cross-line (absent in Pebble Hook).

Flight season Two generations in mainland Europe. May-June and late July-August. Both sexes nocturnal

41

and come to light.
Life cycle Overwinters as a pupa. Larva June-July and September in mainland Europe.
Larval foodplants Birch, Alder and oak in mainland Europe.
Status & distribution Immigrant. First recorded on 13 August 1960, a female at Dover, Kent, with over a dozen more since at scattered locations on or near the coast of southern and eastern England, from Hampshire to Lincolnshire. Most have been in August, with some also in May. All but three of the records have been since 1990, which suggests that this species might colonise Britain. Recorded once from the Channel Islands, in Guernsey in 1996.

Scarce Hook-tip   page 53
Sabra harpagula (Esp.)
RDB. SW   1650(7510)

Field characters FW 17-20mm. Distinctive. Forewing is more strongly hooked than in related species. In addition, there is a second distinct projection roughly halfway along outer edge. The brown and gold blotch in centre of forewing and lilac and black outer markings are also diagnostic. Second generation moths from mainland Europe are noticeably smaller.
Similar species Pebble and Dusky Hook-tip do not have the large central blotch, and both have smoothly curved outer edges to forewing.
Flight season One generation. Early June-mid July. Seldom seen, except in light-traps, to which it comes quite readily, more especially male.
Life cycle Overwinters as a pupa, in a tough thin cocoon spun in a curled leaf, which later falls to the ground. Larva late July-late September, sometimes mid October. Apparently lives high in the canopy, since it is rarely beaten from the lower branches.
Larval foodplants Small-leaved Lime.
Habitat Woodland in which Small-leaved Lime is abundant.
Status & distribution Resident and occasional suspected immigrant. Red Data Book species.

Currently appears to be restricted to the Wye Valley, on the border between Monmouthshire and Gloucestershire, where it was discovered in June 1961. Here, the population seems to be stable, since it is regularly seen at light-traps, sometimes several per trap. Formerly found at Leigh Woods, near Bristol, but not seen since 1938 despite recent searches. On 26 August 2000 a suspected immigrant example was recorded at Rye Harbour Nature Reserve, East Sussex.

Chinese Character   page 53
Cilix glaucata (Scop.)
Common. S,C,(N)   1651(7512)

Field characters FW 10-13mm. Unmistakable. When at rest, with wings held steeply over the body, it closely resembles a bird dropping. There is little variation, but first generation tends to be more intensely marked than second.
Similar species None.
Flight season Two generations. Late April-early June and July-early September, apt to overlap in the north. Sometimes found at rest on vegetation by day. Nocturnal and comes regularly to light, usually in small numbers. Often seems to escape predation by birds on the outside of moth traps in the morning.
Life cycle Overwinters as a pupa, in a cocoon attached to leaves, debris or bark. Larva mid June-mid July and late August-September.
Larval foodplants Mainly Blackthorn, Hawthorn and Crab Apple. Bramble, Rowan and Pear are also recorded.
Habitat Hedgerows, scrub and open woodland, on many soil types and in both damp and dry situations, also in gardens.
Status & distribution Resident. Widespread and generally distributed throughout England, Wales and Man, except on the highest ground. Local in Scotland, mainly in the south, but recorded north to Easter Ross. Widespread in Ireland. Widespread and frequent in the Channel Islands.

Thyatiridae

A small family of about 200 species worldwide, with ten in Europe, nine of which are resident in the British Isles (some of the more recent works treat this as a subfamily of Drepanidae). Superficially, members of this family resemble the noctuid moths, although they are slightly slimmer in build and all hold their wings close to the body when fully at rest. The thorax often has prominent tufts. The larvae of Peach Blossom and Buff Arches feed exposed, whereas the remainder of the group conceal themselves between spun leaves. Pupation occurs either on or under the ground, or between leaves of the food-plant which then fall to the ground. Most overwinter in this stage.

Buff Arches

Yellow Horned

Peach Blossom
page 53

Thyatira batis (L.)

Common. T   1652(7481)

Field characters FW 16-19mm. The pink and brown petal-like markings on forewing are diagnostic. There is hardly any variation.
Similar species None.
Flight season One generation. Late May-late July. Occasionally, there is a partial second generation from late August-September in southern England. Hides in ground cover by day, becoming active from dusk, when it is attracted to sugar and wine ropes. Regular at light, usually in small numbers. Often fails to enter the trap, instead fluttering around in short, hopping flights.
Life cycle Overwinters as a pupa in a cocoon on the soil surface or just below it. Larva early July-mid September. Remains on the foodplant when small, but when larger hides in leaf litter by day, feeding mainly at night.
Larval foodplants Bramble.
Habitat Most numerous in light woodland and scrub but also breeds at lower density in many other places where Bramble grows, including urban areas.
Status & distribution Resident. Common. Throughout England and Wales, Man and Ireland. More local in Scotland, found north to Caithness and in the Hebrides. Widespread in the Channel Islands.

Buff Arches
page 53

Habrosyne pyritoides (Hufn.)

Common. S,C   1653(7483)

Field characters FW 17-20mm. Forewing markings have a flint-like quality and are unmistakable, etched with white and orange-brown 'arches', as seen when at rest.
Similar species None.
Flight season One generation. Late June-early August, with occasional individuals in the autumn. Active from dusk and often attracted to sugar and wine ropes. Comes frequently to light, and is sometimes numerous.
Life cycle Overwinters as a pupa in a loose cocoon underground. Larva late July-mid October. Reportedly more frequent on Bramble beneath trees than in the open; feeds mainly at night.
Larval foodplants Bramble and Dewberry. Possibly also Raspberry, which it will accept in captivity.
Habitat Most numerous in open woodland, particularly coppiced areas and young plantations; also scrubby grassland and many other places where Bramble grows, including gardens.
Status & distribution Resident. Common. Throughout England and Wales, north to Cumbria, north Yorkshire and Man. Formerly rare in Northumberland and Co. Durham, and considered extinct by the 1980s. Very rare in Scotland, with a scatter of old records. Widespread in Ireland, mainly round the coasts and in areas with well-drained soils. Abundant in the Channel Islands.

Figure of Eighty
page 53

Tethea ocularis (L.)

ssp. *octogesimea* (Hb.)

Common. S,C   1654(7485)

Field characters FW 16-20mm. White and rather finely etched number '80' in centre of each forewing is diagnostic. Cross-lines generally rather fine, and that beyond '80' mark curves more or less around it before reaching leading edge. Forewing varies in colour from light to dark brown, often with a purplish sheen. The dark f. *fusca* Cock. was first recorded in south and south-east England in the 1940s, and has since spread; it is suspected to have arrived by immigration.
Similar species Poplar Lutestring has only vaguely numerical markings on forewing and has dark wavy cross-lines, usually three or four, between these and thorax. See also Figure of Eight.
Flight season One generation, late May-July. Nocturnal. Comes to light, wine ropes and sugar.
Life cycle Overwinters as a pupa, in a frail cocoon formed between leaves of the foodplant, which fall to the ground in autumn. Larva mid July-September. Rests by day between two leaves spun flatly together; feeds at night.
Larval foodplants Aspen and other poplars.
Habitat A wide variety, including broadleaved woodland, carr, river valleys, plantations, parkland, hedgerows and gardens.
Status & distribution Resident and possibly immigrant. Common. Throughout most of England and Wales north to Cumbria and Yorkshire, with old records from Northumberland. Thinly distributed in western Wales and Cornwall. First recorded on Man in 1998. Widespread but only occasional in the Channel Islands.

Poplar Lutestring
page 53

Tethea or or ([D. & S.])   1655(7486)

Local. S

ssp. *scotica* (Tutt)

Local. N

ssp. *hibernica* (Turn.)

Ireland

Field characters & Similar species FW 16-19mm. Ssp. *or* is not unlike Figure of Eighty. One diagnostic feature is the series of dark cross-lines and bands or 'lute-strings' on forewing, which are wavier, generally thicker and more numerous. Central whitish mark does not clearly form figure '80', and cross-line beyond it turns toward wing tip before reaching leading edge. Variable in colour and intensity of markings. Central markings may be faint or occasionally replaced by a dark mark. See also Yellow Horned Oak Lutestring and Figure of Eight.
Ssp. *scotica* usually has the dark markings more sharply defined and ground-colour paler grey, sometimes with a purplish tinge when freshly emerged, although indistinctly marked brownish forms also occur.

43

Larva of Poplar Lutestring.

Ssp. *hibernica* is midway between ssp. *or* and ssp. *scotica* in terms of colour, but with weaker markings.
Flight season One generation. Late May-early August in England and Wales, June-early July in Scotland and Ireland. Nocturnal. Comes to light, sugar and wine ropes.
Life cycle Overwinters as a pupa, in a cocoon formed between leaves of the foodplant, which fall to the ground in autumn. Larva mid July-September. Lives by day between two leaves spun flat together; feeds openly at night.
Larval foodplants Aspen, and sometimes other poplars.
Habitat Broadleaved woodland and other habitats with well-established Aspen, including low regrowth.
Status & distribution Resident. Local. Ssp. *or* is widespread in most of the southern half of England (except the south-west, where it is rare) and in Wales. Very local in northern England, including sites near Scarborough. Ssp. *scotica* is widespread but local in Scotland, including the Hebrides, mainly in the west, near the coast and in river valleys. Ssp. *hibernica* has been recorded from scattered locations in Ireland, mainly in the west, but there are old records from the north-east.

Satin Lutestring   page 53
Tetheella fluctuosa (Hb.)
Local. SE,W   1656(7488)

Field characters & Similar species FW 17-21mm. Similar to Common Lutestring, but generally larger. Diagnostic features are the small dark crescent or dash in centre of forewing and small dark dash arising on leading edge just inside pale outermost cross-line. Most examples in the south have the outer part of forewing broadly pale. F. *albilinea* Lempke, which is darker with narrow whitish bands, predominates in Scotland and has occurred elsewhere. The populations in the west of Ireland have a paler ground-colour. F. *unicolor* Lempke has more uniformly dark greyish-brown forewings. This form has occurred regularly at Hamstreet, Kent, since 1955, and also in Surrey, Sussex and Staffordshire.
Flight season One generation. June-early August. Sometimes disturbed by day from tree foliage. Nocturnal. Comes to light, often in quite large

numbers, especially in the west of its range, and occasionally to sugar or wine ropes.
Life cycle Overwinters as a pupa, in a cocoon formed between leaves of the foodplant, which fall to the ground in autumn. Larva late July-mid September. Rests in spun leaves by day and feeds at night.
Larval foodplants Birches. Also recorded on Alder.
Habitat Mainly long-established, mature broadleaved woodland; wooded heathland in south-east England.
Status & distribution Resident. Local. Locally widespread and frequent in south-east England, mainly the Weald of Kent, Sussex and Surrey. Also in the Wye Valley and Severn Estuary, north and west Wales, the Lake District, Cumbria and the Great Glen, Inverness-shire. There are also scattered records from Hampshire to Devon, the Midlands, Pennines, Carmarthenshire, Arran, Mull, Perthshire and Wester Ross. Occasional, probably vagrant, in the east Midlands and East Anglia. In the Irish Republic, occurs locally in the west and south-east. Local and rare in the Channel Islands.

Common Lutestring   page 53
Ochropacha duplaris (L.)
Common. T   1657(7490)

Field characters & Similar species FW 14-18mm. Rather like Satin Lutestring, but usually smaller. One diagnostic feature is the pair of small dark dots in centre of forewing (although they occasionally almost merge) and diagonal black dash arising from forewing tip (Satin Lutestring also has a dash, but this arises before the pale outermost cross-line). Considerable variation in strength of cross-lines and bands. The more or less uniform grey-brown f. *obscura* Tutt predominates in many parts of England, and blackish-brown melanic forms are found in the London area, the Midlands and Scotland. Strongly banded forms are more frequent in the north and west, including Ireland, where outer area of forewing is often white. The paired spots and dash remain visible in all forms.
Flight season One generation. Mid June-mid August. Nocturnal. Comes to light and sugar, sometimes in fair numbers, but at many sites only occasionally.
Life cycle Overwinters as a pupa, in a cocoon formed between leaves of the foodplant, which fall to the ground in autumn. Larva late July-early October. Rests in spun leaves by day and feeds at night.
Larval foodplants Birches. Also reported from Alder, Hazel and oaks.
Habitat Light woodland and scrub where birches are frequent, often river valleys in northern Britain and woodland and heathland further south. Not unusual in suburban gardens in south-east England.
Status & distribution Resident. Common. Very widely distributed throughout England, but scarcer on calcareous soils, for instance in the Chilterns and Cotswolds. Widespread in Wales and mainland

Scotland, and found in the Hebrides and Orkney (especially Hoy). Very local and rare on Man. Widespread in northern and western Ireland but rather thinly recorded. Local and occasional in the Channel Islands.

Oak Lutestring   page 53
Cymatophorima diluta ([D. & S.])

ssp. *hartwiegi* (Reisser)

Local. S,C   1658(7492)

Field characters FW 15-17mm. Usually easily recognised by the two strong, black-edged, brown cross-bands on pale grey forewing. There are several darker forms. In f. *nubilata* Robson, forewing is largely brown, but darker cross-lines remain. This form is frequent and widely distributed. There are rare forms in which forewing is grey-brown, with a broad, dark grey-brown or black central cross-band.
Similar species Poplar Lutestring can perhaps be superficially similar, but has grey cross-bands and flies earlier in the year.
Flight season One generation. Late August-September, sometimes early October. Flies from early dusk, coming to sugar and wine ropes, and later to light, sometimes in fair numbers.
Life cycle Overwinters as an egg, attached to a twig of the foodplant. Larva April or early May-early July. Hatches after bud-burst; emerges from spun leaves to feed at night. Pupates in a cocoon, formed among foliage on the tree.
Larval foodplants Pedunculate Oak and Sessile Oak.
Habitat Long-established broadleaved woodland containing mature oak trees. Occasionally gardens.
Status & distribution Resident. Local. Well distributed in southern England, from Dorset to Kent and northwards to the clay vale between Oxford and Peterborough, the Midlands, Wye Valley, north and west Wales and Cumbria. More thinly scattered and local in the rest of England and Wales south of the Humber. Also recorded from southern Scotland.

Yellow Horned   page 53
Achlya flavicornis (L.)

ssp. *galbanus* (Tutt)

Common. S,C   1659(7498)

ssp. *scotica* (Tutt)

Common. N

Field characters FW 17-20mm.
Ssp. *galbanus* is quite distinctive, with orange antennae which give the moth both its English and scientific names. Forewing grey with greenish-white or white frosting, especially on central portion of leading edge, but varying in extent. Pale central markings vary somewhat in size and shape, as do cross-lines.
Ssp. *scotica* is larger, with darker, mauvish-grey forewing, and more heavily marked than ssp. *galbanus*. Central markings are greenish white, but

frosting on leading edge is usually whitish. Intermediate examples occur in northern England.
Similar species Poplar Lutestring does not have orange antennae and flies much later in the year.
Flight season One generation. Late February-mid April. Comes to light. Also visits sugar, sap runs and sallow catkins. Sometimes found at rest on posts, particularly in open habitats, or with wings pressed close around twigs of small birches; occasionally flies on sunny afternoons.
Life cycle Overwinters as a pupa, in a thin cocoon among leaf litter on the ground. Larva mid May-mid July. Hides by day between two leaves tightly spun together and feeds at night.
Larval foodplants Both Silver and Downy Birch.
Habitat Woodland, and on heathland and moorland with birch scrub.
Status & distribution Resident. Common. Ssp. *galbanus* is well distributed and fairly frequent in most parts of England, more so on clays than on lighter, calcareous soils, from Cornwall to Northumberland, also large parts of lowland Wales. Widespread in Ireland. Ssp. *scotica* is widely distributed in mainland Scotland, particularly along the major river valleys, and in the Inner Hebrides and Orkney.

Frosted Green   page 53
Polyploca ridens (Fabr.)

Local. S   1660(7494)

Field characters FW 15-17mm. Rather distinctive, predominantly dark green, with prominent tufts on thorax and a variable mixture of black and greenish-white marbling on forewing. The most frequent form in much of south-east England and the Midlands is blackish green. An extreme version of this is f. *unicolor* Cock., which is without markings and is found in Surrey and Hertfordshire. The brightest forms are more frequent further north and west.
Similar species Sometimes confused with worn Clouded Drab.
Flight season One generation. Mid April-mid May. Comes to light, often in numbers, but seldom to sugar or other baits.
Life cycle Overwinters as a pupa, in a compact cocoon formed under moss at the base of a tree, in leaf litter or in soil. Larva late May-mid July. Eggs are laid singly on the twigs of the foodplant. Larva feeds at night and rests by day on the underside of a leaf curled downwards by silk threads.
Larval foodplants Pedunculate and Sessile Oak; possibly Turkey Oak.
Habitat Mainly long-established broadleaved woodland, with mature trees. Will breed on oaks in hedgerows in well wooded areas.
Status & distribution Resident. Local. Widespread in the southern half of England, north to Lincolnshire (the ancient lime woods near Bardney), Nottinghamshire (Sherwood Forest), and throughout Wales. Recorded near Scarborough, Yorkshire, in the 19th century; there are old records from Cumbria.

Hepialidae Swift moths pages 20-21

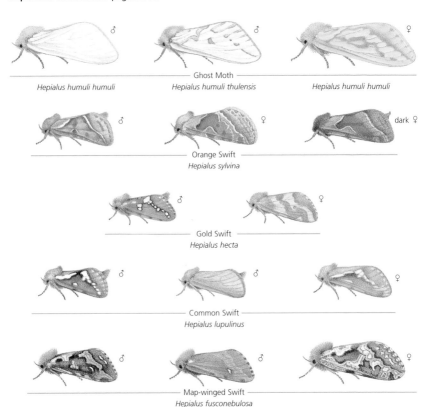

———————————— Ghost Moth ————————————

Hepialus humuli humuli   *Hepialus humuli thulensis*   *Hepialus humuli humuli*

———————————— Orange Swift ————————————
Hepialus sylvina

———————————— Gold Swift ————————————
Hepialus hecta

———————————— Common Swift ————————————
Hepialus lupulinus

———————————— Map-winged Swift ————————————
Hepialus fusconebulosa
f. *gallicus*

Cossidae Leopard and goat moths pages 22-23

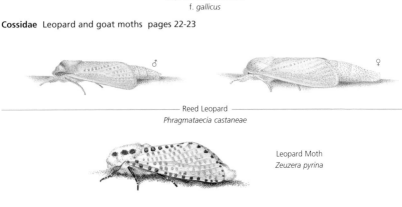

———————————— Reed Leopard ————————————
Phragmataecia castaneae

Leopard Moth
Zeuzera pyrina

Goat Moth
Cossus cossus

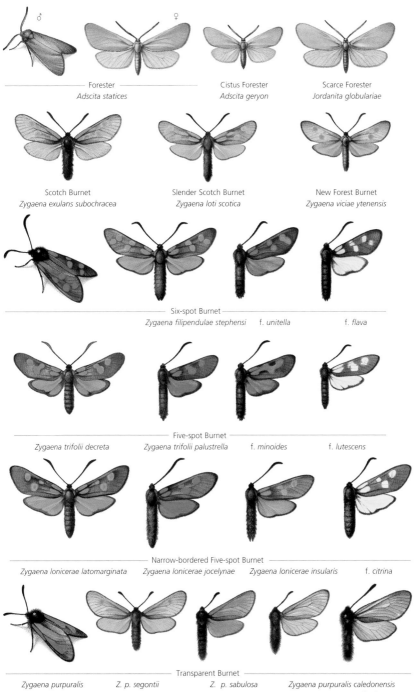

♂ ♀

Forester
Adscita statices

Cistus Forester
Adscita geryon

Scarce Forester
Jordanita globulariae

47

Scotch Burnet
Zygaena exulans subochracea

Slender Scotch Burnet
Zygaena loti scotica

New Forest Burnet
Zygaena viciae ytenensis

Six-spot Burnet
Zygaena filipendulae stephensi   f. *unitella*   f. *flava*

Five-spot Burnet
Zygaena trifolii decreta   *Zygaena trifolii palustrella*   f. *minoides*   f. *lutescens*

Narrow-bordered Five-spot Burnet
Zygaena lonicerae latomarginata   *Zygaena lonicerae jocelynae*   *Zygaena lonicerae insularis*   f. *citrina*

Transparent Burnet
Zygaena purpuralis   *Z. p. segontii*   *Z. p. sabulosa*   *Zygaena purpuralis caledonensis*
f. *obscura*

Limacodidae pages 27-28

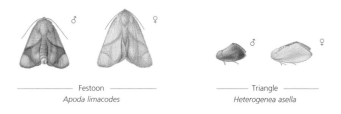

Festoon
Apoda limacodes

Triangle
Heterogenea asella

Sesiidae Clearwing moths pages 28-30

all shown ×1.25

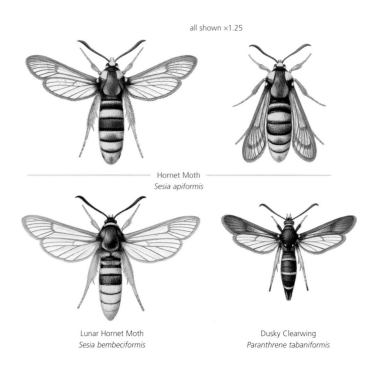

Hornet Moth
Sesia apiformis

Lunar Hornet Moth
Sesia bembeciformis

Dusky Clearwing
Paranthrene tabaniformis

all shown ×1.25

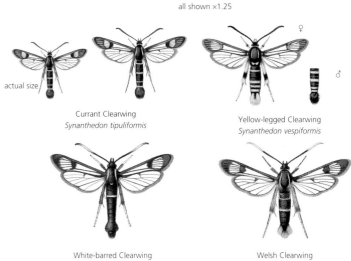

actual size

Currant Clearwing
Synanthedon tipuliformis

Yellow-legged Clearwing
Synanthedon vespiformis

49

White-barred Clearwing
Synanthedon spheciformis

Welsh Clearwing
Synanthedon scoliaeformis

Sallow Clearwing
Synanthedon flaviventris

Orange-tailed Clearwing
Synanthedon andrenaeformis

Red-belted Clearwing
Synanthedon myopaeformis

Red-tipped Clearwing
Synanthedon formicaeformis

Large Red-belted Clearwing
Synanthedon culiciformis

Six-belted Clearwing
Bembecia ichneumoniformis

Thrift Clearwing
Synansphecia muscaeformis

Fiery Clearwing
Pyropteron chrysidiformis

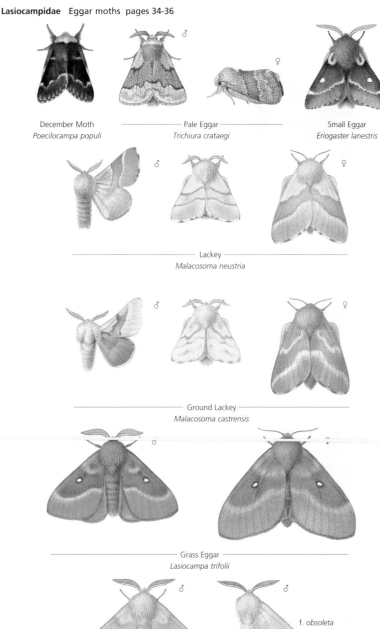

December Moth
Poecilocampa populi

Pale Eggar
Trichiura crataegi

Small Eggar
Eriogaster lanestris

Lackey
Malacosoma neustria

Ground Lackey
Malacosoma castrensis

Grass Eggar
Lasiocampa trifolii

f. obsoleta

Pale Grass Eggar
Lasiocampa trifolii f. flava

50

— Oak Eggar —
Lasiocampa quercus

f. *olivacea*

— Northern Eggar —
Lasiocampa quercus f. *callunae*

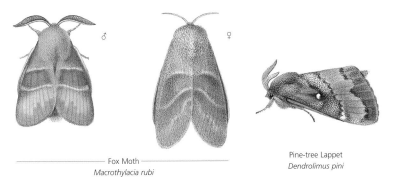

— Fox Moth —
Macrothylacia rubi

Pine-tree Lappet
Dendrolimus pini

Lasiocampidae Eggar moths page 38

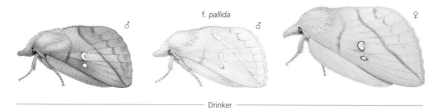

f. pallida

— Drinker —
Euthrix potatoria

Small Lappet
Phyllodesma ilicifolia

Lappet
Gastropacha quercifolia

Saturniidae Emperor moths page 39

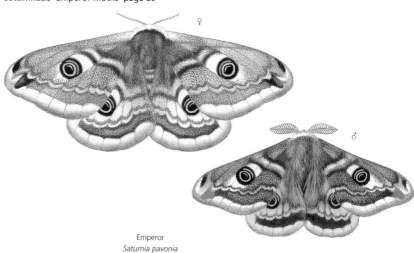

Emperor
Saturnia pavonia

Endromidae page 39

— Kentish Glory —
Endromis versicolora

Drepanidae Hook-tips pages 40-42

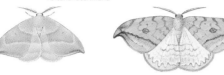

Scalloped Hook-tip
Falcaria lacertinaria

Oak Hook-tip
Watsonalla binaria

53

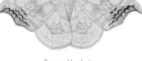

Barred Hook-tip
Watsonalla cultraria

Pebble Hook-tip

Drepana falcataria falcataria

Drepana falcataria scotica

Dusky Hook-tip
Drepana curvatula

Scarce Hook-tip
Sabra harpagula

Chinese Character
Cilix glaucata

Thyatiridae pages 43-45

Peach Blossom
Thyatira batis

Buff Arches
Habrosyne pyritoides

Figure of Eighty
Tethea ocularis octogesimea   f. *fusca*

Poplar Lutestring
Tethea or or   *Tethea or scotica*

Satin Lutestring
Tetheella fluctuosa   f. *albilinea*

Common Lutestring
Ochropacha duplaris   f. *obscura*

Oak Lutestring
Cymatophorima diluta hartwiegi   f. *nubilata*

Yellow Horned
Achlya flavicornis galbanus   *Achlya flavicornis scotica*

Frosted Green
Polyploca ridens

Geometridae

There are two families of macro-
moths in the British Isles which are
much larger than the others: the
Geometridae, with over 300
species, and the Noctuidae, with
over 400 species. The Geometridae
comprises at least 20,000 described
species in total, and is distributed
worldwide. The British members are
divided very unevenly into six subfamilies: the Archiearinae – orange
underwings (two species); the
Alsophilinae – March Moth (one
species); the Geometrinae – emeralds (ten resident species); the
Sterrhinae – mochas and waves
(about 40 species); the Larentiinae –
carpets, pugs and allies (nearly 170

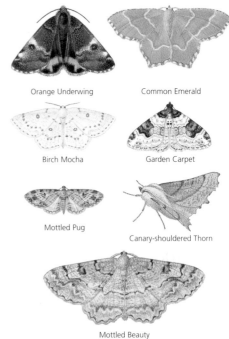

Orange Underwing

Common Emerald

Birch Mocha

Garden Carpet

Mottled Pug

Canary-shouldered Thorn

Mottled Beauty

species, some possibly invalid); and the Ennominae – thorns, beauties, umbers and
allies (about 95 species). The European list is arranged with the Archiearinae at the
start, followed by the Ennominae before the Alsophilinae (Oenochrominae),
Geometrinae, Sterrhinae and Larentiinae.

The Geometridae are a varied group, but most have broad, rather triangular
forewings and rather light, slender bodies, enabling low-energy flight rather than
power and speed. Probably as a consequence, only three species regularly arrive in the
British Isles as immigrants in any numbers, and it is likely that these are carried on jet-
streams for much of their journey.

They are readily distinguished from butterflies by their antennae, which are feathery
in the males and slender in the females, and never clubbed.

Many species fly at dusk, before light-traps are fully effective, and are best searched
for with a net, tapping vegetation to disturb them. Others come readily to light, but
sometimes only late at night, and some have dawn or daytime flights. The females of a
number of species have reduced or vestigial wings, and walk to disperse eggs rather
than flying. This uses less energy than flight and enables them to remain active on
winter nights at temperatures at or below freezing. These females are seen at light-traps
only on the rare occasions they crawl in, and instead are best searched for on woody
vegetation. Many geometrids have functional tongues and can drink moisture, but relatively few can be found reliably by searching flowers or by trying to attract them to
sugary baits, probably because low-energy flight requires less frequent re-fuelling.

Another feature of the family which distinguishes it is that the caterpillars have only two pairs of hind legs, or prolegs. These consist of a pair of claspers at the back end and another pair a short distance in front of them. A few species, notably the two orange underwings and the Light Emerald, have traces of a much smaller third pair of prolegs, indicating that they have evolved from forms with more than two. The central region of the body has no legs and is looped up when the caterpillar moves, drawing the hind end up to the three pairs of legs at the head end. Some can cover distances quickly, which is likely to be an advantage when moving about in trees, and a large proportion eat the foliage of woody plants. The geometrids are often referred to as 'loopers' or 'inch-worms' after this mode of progression, while 'geometrid' means 'ground-measurer' in Greek. If dislodged, the caterpillars are likely to fall on a silken thread; they then clamber back up this or up the plant stem, or may be wind-blown on these threads. Some pupate in cocoons attached to the plant and need never leave the tree canopy, but the majority pupate in the earth below.

Archiearinae
Orange underwings

Orange Underwing   page 131
Archiearis parthenias (L.)

Local. T   1661(7517)

Field characters & Similar species FW 16-19mm. A day-flying moth that appears orange-brown in flight, and which should be netted for examination to distinguish it from the very similar Light Orange Underwing, particularly if mature Aspen is present. Those netted are usually males. Antennae of male Orange Underwing are finely serrated, whereas those of Light Orange Underwing are slightly feathered. On underside of hindwing of Orange Underwing, orange band projects centrally into dark outer band, often reaching outer margin. In Light Orange Underwing, dark outer band is unbroken, and central projection of orange band is absent (or at most slight). Forewing of Orange Underwing is generally longer, usually with a stronger white central cross-band (especially male). Their flight periods vary slightly with each season, but Orange Underwing starts flying two weeks earlier. Male Vapourer is another small orange-brown moth which flies in sunshine around birch trees, but not until they are well into leaf.

Flight season One generation. March-April. Usually seen flying in sunshine high around the tops of birch trees before they come into leaf. They fly lower as the afternoon progresses, and drink and bask at puddles. Copulating pairs can be knocked out of trees in late afternoon.

Life cycle Overwinters as a pupa. Larva April-June. The eggs are laid on twigs and hatch in time for the larvae to begin feeding on the catkins in April, before completing development on the young leaves by night, making a spinning between them by day.

Pupates in the surface of soft bark.

Larval foodplants Downy Birch and Silver Birch. Also reportedly on Rowan.

Habitat Open woodland and birch scrub on heathland, embankments and other rough, open ground.

Status & distribution Resident. Local. Widespread and locally frequent over much of England, Wales and the major river valleys of mainland Scotland, including some large populations in north-east Scotland.

Light Orange Underwing   page 131
Archiearis notha (Hb.)

Nb. S   1662(7518)

Field characters & Similar species FW 15-17mm. Very similar in appearance and habits to Orange Underwing. See under that species for differences.

Flight season One generation. Late March-April, occasionally early May. Seen flying around Aspen in sunshine, or up from puddles on paths in open woodland in the spring.

Life cycle Overwinters as a pupa spun into soft bark, sometimes for two or three years. Larva April-June. The larvae feed on the foliage, spinning a shelter among the leaves by day. It is not clear if they start feeding on young catkins, but the moths are associated with mature or over-mature catkin-bearing trees, rather than low and shaded Aspen growth.

Larval foodplants Aspen. Probably not other poplars, which often produce catkins at slightly different times.

Habitat Open woodland in which mature catkin-bearing Aspen are frequent; usually ancient woods.

Status & distribution Resident. Nationally Scarce B. Largely restricted to England south of the Wash and east of the Severn, where it is widespread but local and seldom as numerous as the Orange Underwing. There are some strong populations at its northern-most limits in Lincolnshire, but it is poorly represented in East Anglia. Reported from the Wye Valley, Monmouthshire, but not for 100 years.

Alsophilinae

 ♂ ♀

Geometrinae
Emeralds

Small Emerald

March Moth
page 131

Alsophila aescularia ([D. & S.])

Common. T   1663(7953)

Field characters & Similar species FW 16-19mm. The rather triangular, grey-brown forewing of the male, overlapped when at rest and with two jagged, dark-edged whitish cross-bands, distinguishes this slightly-built moth from all others flying in early spring. Usually shows only slight variation, but rarely there is a dark grey central cross-band. Female is completely wingless, barrel-shaped, with a conspicuous tuft of brown hair on tail end. This distinguishes it from female Winter Moth, Spring Usher and Pale Brindled Beauty. The flightless females of all other winter species either have very obvious vestigial wings or much fatter, furrier bodies. Male Spring Usher has dark, wavy cross-lines and (usually) a distinct paler central cross-band. Forewings do not overlap.

Flight season One generation. Late February-April. Male flies after dark and can be frequent in light-traps. Female can be seen climbing tree trunks at night and found at rest in the bark early in the morning.

Life cycle Overwinters as a pupa. Larva late April-June. Pupates underground below the larval food-plant, in a fragile cocoon.

Larval foodplants Oaks, Hawthorn, Blackthorn, Crab Apple, willows, Field Maple, birches and many other broadleaved trees and shrubs.

Habitat Most numerous in open woodland but occurs in most places where the foodplants grow, including urban parks and gardens.

Status & distribution Resident. Common. Widespread, well distributed and often abundant throughout Great Britain, except on high ground. Local on Man. Locally widespread in Northern Ireland and the Republic. Widespread and frequent on Jersey, rarely recorded on Guernsey.

Rest Harrow
page 131

Aplasta ononaria (Fuessl.)

RDB. SE   1664(7961)

Field characters FW 13-14mm. At rest, this delta-shaped moth hangs from stems in an open grassy sward, rather than spreading out flat like the mochas. Reddish banding and freckling, heaviest on male, and lack of central spots or other sharp markings is a distinctive combination.

Similar species None.

Flight season One generation. Late June-July. Partial second generation in late August-September. As an immigrant, from mid July-early October. Nocturnal and comes to light, but flies up from the sward if disturbed by day.

Life cycle Overwinters as a small larva on the food-plant, near the ground. Larva August-late May or early June. Pupates in a light cocoon under the food-plant.

Larval foodplants Common Restharrow. Will eat Spiny Restharrow.

Habitat At both main sites the larvae occur on Restharrow growing in a calcareous, short-grass sward, in open but sheltered sun-trap locations.

Status & distribution Resident, also suspected immigrant. Red Data Book species. Only two long-term breeding colonies are known, both in Kent, at Folkestone Warren and on the coastal sand-dunes between Sandwich and Deal. A small colony was reported to exist between Dungeness and New Romney in 1948-49. Single examples have occurred on several occasions elsewhere in Kent, and in Essex, Sussex and Hampshire, and on Jersey in 1994 and Guernsey in 1998, and these are presumed immigrants.

Grass Emerald
page 131

Pseudoterpna pruinata (Hufn.)

ssp. *atropunctaria* (Walk.)

Common. T   1665(7965)

Field characters & Similar species FW 14-19mm. Bluish-green colour (often fading to greyish-white) and rather jagged, dark green or blackish central cross-lines on forewing distinguish this from most other emeralds, which have white cross-lines, except

56

the newly-discovered Jersey Emerald (see under that species for differences).

Flight season Mainly one generation. Mid June-August. Occasional second generation individuals have been reported as far north as southern Scotland in September and October. Often disturbed by day from among or near its foodplant. Active after dark and comes to light, usually in small numbers.

Life cycle Overwinters as a tiny larva among the food-plant. Larva July-early June. Pupates in plant debris.

Larval foodplants Gorse, Broom and Petty Whin.

Habitat Heathland, moorland, open woodland and scrub, shingle beaches, also gravel pits and roadside embankments where Gorse and Broom are some-times introduced to stabilise the banks. Seldom on Broom in gardens unless the larval foodplants are abundant nearby.

Status & distribution Resident. Common. Widely and well distributed, and often frequent, where Gorse or Broom grows in England, Wales and mainly western Scotland. Fairly well distributed and frequent on Man and throughout Ireland. Apparently absent from the Channel Islands (records from Jersey prior to 2001 refer to Jersey Emerald).

Jersey Emerald
Pseudoterpna coronillaria (Hb.)
Jersey   1665a(7966)

page 131

Field characters & Similar species FW 16-20mm. In shape and markings, quite like Grass Emerald, but grey, dusted with darker scales, and central cross-lines dark brown. Cross-line beyond middle of forewing usually more jagged but this is quite vari-able in Grass Emerald.

Flight season June-July.

Life cycle Not known on Jersey. Large larvae found in April-May in mainland Europe.

Larval foodplants Not known on Jersey. Recorded from Broom and Gorse in mainland Europe.

Habitat Open areas with Broom and Gorse, including Grouville golf course.

Status & distribution Resident on Jersey only. Overlooked until 2001, and previously misidentified as Grass Emerald. Old specimens labelled as that species indicate that it has been present for many years. Mainly found in southern and south-west Europe, the Jersey population being very isolated.

Large Emerald
Geometra papilionaria (L.)
Common. T   1666(7969)

page 131

Field characters FW 24-29mm. This large, distinctive green moth is further distinguished by its butterfly-like resting posture, with wings spread and raised at an angle from the horizontal, as if it had just settled briefly and was about to fly off again. Edges of wings are wavy. The green colour is more stable than for most other emeralds. Shows little variation, but one or more of the whitish cross-lines may be absent.

Similar species None.

Flight season One generation. Late June-late August. Comes readily to light, sometimes several per trap, usually after midnight, often landing a metre or more from the light and failing to enter the trap. Occasionally flies high in the canopy on warm, sunny days.

Life cycle Overwinters as a small larva, on a silk pad on a twig or stem of the foodplant. Larva July-June. Pupates in leaf litter.

Larval foodplants Downy Birch, Silver Birch, Hazel, Alder and reported from Beech.

Habitat Woodland, scrubby heathland and grass-land, substantial hedgerows and some well estab-lished gardens and parks.

Status & distribution Resident. Common. Widely and well distributed, and often frequent, throughout Great Britain but mainly in the valleys and coastal plains in the Highlands of Scotland. Local on Man. Widespread and fairly well distributed throughout Ireland. Local and occasional on Jersey, one on Guernsey in about 1889.

Blotched Emerald
Comibaena bajularia ([D. & S.])
Local. S,C   1667(7971)

page 131

Field characters FW 14-17mm. The peculiar cream and fawn blotch in trailing corner of forewing is diagnostic. Ground-colour often fades from green to buffish or pinkish white. Outer edges of wings are chequered red and white, and are rounded rather than pointed.

Similar species None.

Flight season One generation. Late June-July. Male comes readily to light, sometimes in numbers, female much less so, but is sometimes disturbed by day from oak foliage.

Life cycle Overwinters as a small larva. Larva late July-early June. Pupates in a flimsy cocoon among oak leaves.

Larval foodplants Pedunculate Oak and probably Sessile Oak.

Habitat Established woodland with mature oaks. Also breeds on hedgerow oaks in well wooded areas.

Status & distribution Resident. Local. Most densely distributed in woodlands of central southern England, where often abundant. More thinly distributed throughout England north to Yorkshire and in eastern Wales, with occasional records from west Wales.

Essex Emerald
Thetidia smaragdaria (Fabr.)
ssp. *maritima* (Prout)
Was RDB; presumed extinct. SE   1668(7975)

page 131

Field characters & Similar species FW 14-17mm. The only emerald likely to be seen on open salt-marsh, although Small Emerald might be seen on the shrubby edges or access routes. The combination of gold leading edge to forewing, normally prominent white central forewing spot, plain fringes and, when fresh, rich velvety green colour show little variation,

57

Larva of Essex Emerald.

58

but the two lines across forewing are sometimes very weak. Never roosts flat on leaves, but hangs below them. See Small Emerald.

Flight season One generation. Mid June-mid July. Nocturnal and comes to light. May fly up if disturbed by day but usually reluctant to move from rest among vegetation. The female sometimes begins moving and egg laying in late afternoon.

Life cycle Overwinters as a larva low down on foodplant. Larva August-May. Pupates head upwards in a very flimsy cocoon attached to a vertical stem, usually of the foodplant.

Larval foodplants Sea Wormwood.

Habitat Upper saltmarsh zones, including the belt of foodplant sometimes found at the base of old sea walls, provided this is not scoured by the tide.

Status & distribution Very localised resident, now presumed extinct. A British sub-species. Only ever recorded from the coastlines of Essex and Kent, where larvae were formerly collected in hundreds in some sites. Recorded from at least ten 10km squares in the late 19th and early 20th centuries. The last Essex colony died out in 1985. Major surveys of Essex and Kent in 1987 and 1988 found larvae in only one saltmarsh system, in Kent. This was monitored pre- and post-hibernation annually up to 1993, with another search in September 1999. Wild larvae have not been seen in Britain since April 1991. Reported once from the Channel Islands, one on Guernsey in 1965, but probably a misidentification.

Common Emerald — page 131

Hemithea aestivaria (Hb.)

Common. S,C   1669(7980)

Field characters FW 14-17mm. Combination of pointed forewing, wavy cross-lines, single projection on hindwing and chequered fringes, is diagnostic.

Similar species Sussex Emerald looks similar, but has two points on each hindwing.

Flight season One generation. Late June-late July. Flies from dusk and comes to light, though not usually in numbers. Visits flowers after dark, such as Wild Privet and Creeping Thistle.

Life cycle Overwinters as a small larva. Larva July-early June. Pupates among leaves of the foodplant.

Larval foodplants Hawthorn, Midland Hawthorn, Blackthorn, Hazel, oaks, willows, birches, wild and cultivated barberries and many other native and exotic woody plants. Also reportedly some herba-

ceous plants before hibernation, such as Mugwort.

Habitat Woodland, hedgerows, scrub on heathland and downland. In gardens, parks and urban amenity plantings such as roadside Thunberg's Barberry.

Status & distribution Resident. Common. The larvae are much more numerous than the adults appear to be. Widely and well distributed, and often frequent, over most of England and Wales, except high ground. Very rarely in the extreme south of Scotland. Rather local on Man. Thinly recorded in Ireland, but more widespread than pre-1980 records suggest. Widespread and frequent in the Channel Islands.

Small Grass Emerald — page 131

Chlorissa viridata (L.)

Na. S,WC   1670(7982)

Field characters FW 11-13mm. Combination of size, dull green colour (when newly emerged), gold leading edge and fairly straight cross-lines is diagnostic.

Similar species See Little Emerald, but Small Grass Emerald does not fade to whitish when alive.

Flight season One generation. June-early July. Easily disturbed by day among the foodplant but flies from dusk, sometimes coming to light.

Life cycle Overwinters as a pupa, suspended by flimsy threads among the foodplant or in leaf litter. Larva late July-August.

Larval foodplants Woody plants, including Heather, Cross-leaved Heath, birches, Creeping Willow and Gorse.

Habitat Damp heaths and mosses.

Status & distribution Resident. Nationally Scarce A and probably declining. Still fairly frequent on some heaths in the New Forest, Hampshire. Very local and usually in small numbers in Cornwall, Devon, Somerset, the heaths of south-east Dorset, Surrey and Sussex. Still present in one site in Cumbria. No longer found on the mosses of Lancashire and Westmorland. A scattering of old records from central and southern counties, including Wiltshire, Gloucestershire and Worcestershire, and occasional presumed vagrants or immigrants have been reported in the south (Isle of Wight) and east (Kent, Lincolnshire and Norfolk). The literature is plagued with misidentifications and unconfirmed records. Widespread and occasional in the Channel Islands.

1671 see Appendix

Sussex Emerald — page 131

Thalera fimbrialis (Scop.)

RDB (Protected species). SE   1672(7998)

Field characters FW 15-16mm. The two projections on margin of hindwing distinguish this from all other emeralds.

Similar species See Common Emerald.

Flight season One generation. July-early August. Mainly active at dusk and dawn, coming to actinic and mercury vapour lights. Roosts low down among plants.

Life cycle Overwinters as a part-grown larva, probably at rest on a plant stem. Larva August-early June. Pupa not yet found in the wild but among plant debris in captivity.

Larval foodplants Mainly Wild Carrot, very occasionally Common and Hoary Ragwort. Reports from Yarrow may be erroneous. Usually found on foodplants in the shelter of slightly taller herbs or grasses.

Habitat Coastal shingle at Dungeness, but the foodplant and larvae are almost exclusively confined to disturbed areas where finer-grained material has been added, usually imported.

Status & distribution Resident and immigrant. Red Data Book species. One breeding colony only known in the British Isles, at Dungeness, Kent, discovered in 1950 and still extant. Adults fairly frequent in traps operated on site (c100 records per year at the Bird Observatory). Possibly resident on the Crumbles, Eastbourne, Sussex, 1950-56, when a number of adults were reported. Single examples recorded very occasionally from 1902 onwards along the south coast from Dorset to Kent, with one at Bradwell-on-Sea, Essex, in 1946. One was recorded on the Isle of Wight (at Binstead), on 24 June 2001.

Small Emerald
page 131
Hemistola chrysoprasaria (Esp.)
Local. S,(C)   1673(8000)

Field characters & Similar species FW 17-20mm. The rather rounded wings, rich blue-green colour (when newly emerged), and sweeping curves of white cross-lines distinguish this from other emeralds, including Light Emerald. Absence of both a central spot and a gold leading edge on forewing, and presence of a curved white line on hindwing further distinguish it from Essex Emerald. May fade to white while still alive, but cross-lines remain visible.

Flight season One generation. Late June-early August. Very occasional second generation individuals in late September in southern England after hot summers. Comes to light in small numbers. Less often seen at dusk, and occasionally disturbed from the larval foodplant.

Life cycle Overwinters as a small larva on the foodplant. Larva July or August-June. Pupates among the foodplant.

Larval foodplants Traveller's-joy and cultivated species of Clematis.

Habitat Most situations where the native foodplant grows, which tend to be on chalk or limestone, including hedgerows and scrub on downland, open woodland and some gardens.

Status & distribution Resident. Local. Widely and well distributed, and fairly frequent, in England and Wales north to the Wash, except on high ground, acid soils and heavy clays. Local in Lincolnshire, the Midlands and up the west coast of England north to the limestone of southern Cumbria. Occasional individuals have been recorded in southern Scotland and the north-east of Ireland, possibly the result of accidental transport on garden varieties of Clematis. Local and frequent on Jersey, rare on Guernsey.

Little Emerald
page 131
Jodis lactearia (L.)
Common. S,C,NW   1674(8002)

Field characters FW 11-13mm. A delicate greenish-white colour when newly emerged, but this rapidly fades to white in the wild, although cross-lines catch the light and remain visible. Male has finely feathered antennae, and there are usually two white cross-lines on hindwing, inner one often faint.

Similar species Small Grass Emerald, even when faded, is duller, with only one cross-line on hindwing, and antennae of male not feathered. Small, whitish wave moths have darker cross-lines.

Flight season One generation. May-June. In the Channel Islands there is a large second generation in August. Mostly seen on the wing as dusk falls, particularly around low birch scrub or along hedgerows, sometimes in numbers. Comes to light in much smaller numbers.

Life cycle Overwinters as a slender green pupa among leaves. Larva late June-early October.

Larval foodplants Downy Birch, Silver Birch, Hazel, Hawthorn, Blackthorn; also reported from oaks, Sweet Chestnut, Hornbeam, Bilberry, Dogwood, sallows and Broom.

Habitat Open woodland, mature hedgerows and scrubby heathland, moorland and grassland, including ride-side birch in conifer plantations. Infrequent in gardens away from its major habitats.

Status & distribution Resident. Common. Widely and quite well distributed, and locally numerous, throughout England and Wales, becoming scarcer north of the Humber, and mainly on the west coast in Scotland. One record from Man (in 1891). Mainly western in Ireland, with most records from Co. Kerry, Co. Cork and the Burren, Co. Clare. Local and occasional on Jersey. Not seen on Guernsey since about 1889.

Sterrhinae
Mochas and waves

Maiden's Blush   Mullein Wave

Dingy Mocha
page 132
Cyclophora pendularia (Cl.)
RDB. S   1675(8012)

Field characters & Similar species FW 12-14mm. The heavy, rather coarse freckling on this pinkish-grey moth separates freshly-emerged individuals from related species. The combination of location, presence of foodplant and absence of birch is likely

59

Larva of Birch Mocha.

to help in identification. Only likely to be confused with dark forms of Birch Mocha, from which it is further distinguished by forewing shape. In Dingy Mocha forewing is slightly more hooked, the trailing corner is more curved and inset and hindwing has a more distinctive point, but these features can be obscured if individual is worn.

Flight season Two generations. May-early June and July-early August. Flies at dusk. Both sexes occasionally come to light.

Life cycle Overwinters as an exposed pupa, attached to a leaf by a silk girdle. Larva June-July and August-September, the timing depending on weather.

Larval foodplants Small-leaved sallow species such as Eared Willow and Grey Willow, growing as single small bushes or in larger clumps.

Habitat Sallow scrub on open heathland and damp grassland, not shaded by other trees.

Status & distribution Resident. Red Data Book species. Confined to south-east Dorset and west Hampshire, occurring on the Purbeck heaths between Studland and Wareham, and on at least two non-heathland, grassland sites about 25km away, also in Dorset; and on heathland in the Ringwood area of the New Forest. The expansion of Bournemouth has made much intervening land unsuitable, although a colony survives in the Luscombe Valley nature reserve. Formerly larvae found in south Wiltshire and records also from Sussex, Surrey and Kent. Many old records of 'pendularia' refer to Birch Mocha, which was formerly known by this name; this is sometimes evident when mention is made of the foodplant or woodland habits.

Mocha
page 132
Cyclophora annularia (Fabr.)
Nb. S 1676(8014)

Field characters & Similar species FW 11-14mm. The most distinctive of the mochas, with unique and exquisite wavy black markings, including an outer cross-band, on all four yellowish-cream wings. The markings vary somewhat in extent and intensity and the central rings are occasionally missing, and these ring-less specimens could be confused with Maiden's Blush.

Flight season Two generations. Mid May-mid June

and late July-August. Flies from dusk. Both sexes come to light in small numbers, occasionally disturbed by day from larval foodplant or nearby vegetation.

Life cycle Overwinters as a naked, silk-girdled pupa attached to a leaf or among moss. Larva June-July and late August-September.

Larval foodplants Field Maple, both large trees and smaller bushes. Will eat Sycamore and other *Acer* species in captivity.

Habitat Scrub, woodland and hedgerows, preferring maples growing in long-established hedges and woods.

Status & distribution Resident. Nationally Scarce B. A species of southern Britain, like its larval foodplant, but the moth is much more restricted. Two main areas of distribution, one extending north-eastwards from south Devon, through Somerset and along the Severn Valley through Gloucestershire to Worcestershire, roughly following Triassic mudstones and Lower Lias clay beds, with scattered records from south Wales. The other area is centred on the Isle of Wight and southern Hampshire, extending into Dorset, south Wiltshire and West Sussex, and then north-eastwards roughly following Cretaceous greensands towards the Wash and Lincolnshire, with records scattered more widely eastwards to Essex and Kent. In the Channel Islands, not recorded from Jersey and rare on Guernsey.

Birch Mocha
page 132
Cyclophora albipunctata (Hufn.)
Local. T 1677(8016)

Field characters FW 12-14mm. The plain greyish or whitish ground-colour of wings distinguishes most examples. Some have a diffuse, pinkish-red or greyish central cross-band, and the extent of the blackish markings varies. Second generation sometimes darker, more greyish; Scottish moths are palest, and larger. F. *subroseata* Woodforde is rather dark grey, often with an extensive rosy flush. It occurs in most populations as a variable percentage.

Similar species See Dingy Mocha.

Flight season Two generations in the south, early May-late June and late July-end August; one generation in the north, May-early July. Occasionally disturbed from birch by day. Active from dusk. Comes to light, sometimes in numbers. Occasionally visits flowers such as Creeping Thistle and Ragwort, and sugary baits.

Life cycle Overwinters as a pupa attached to a birch leaf. Larva late June-July and, in the south, late August-mid October.

Larval foodplants Downy and Silver Birch. Will eat Alder in captivity.

Habitat Mainly woodland and heathland, seldom in gardens or among scattered, recently established trees.

Status & distribution Resident. Local. The most widespread and frequent of the mochas. Most densely distributed in south-east England, more thinly scattered through the rest of England and Wales north to Cumbria and Yorkshire. Local on Man, where first recorded in 1986. Thinly scattered and local in Ireland. Widely distributed throughout the Scottish mainland. In the Channel Islands one record only, from Guernsey in 1979.

Blair's Mocha
page 132
Cyclophora puppillaria (Hb.)
Immigrant. S
1678(8017)

Field characters FW 12-15mm. The rather plain, or softly-speckled light or darker pinkish-brown forewing helps to distinguish this from related species. Both fore- and hindwing have a small, central black-edged dot. The colour and markings of those reared in captivity can be much more intense, ranging from pinkish-buff to orange-brown or deep red.

Similar species Second-generation Clay Triple-lines are often pinkish, sometimes with rather faint cross-lines, and may have central dark-edged white spots, larger on hindwing. However, forewing more tapering and more strongly hooked, usually without the tiny oblique black fleck at forewing tip of Blair's Mocha, although occasionally dark outer margin dashes go right to tip. False Mocha is more coarsely freckled, usually has dark blotches near outer edge of forewing (unlike Blair's Mocha) and forewing tip is usually blunter. Genitalia should be examined to verify doubtful, atypical specimens.

Flight season Immigrants usually arrive August-October, particularly the latter month. Unlikely to be seen except in light-traps.

Larval foodplants In mainland Europe, Evergreen Oak, possibly also Strawberry-tree, rock-roses and myrtles. Has been reared on young leaves of Pedunculate Oak and privets.

Habitat As immigrants, mostly recorded in coastal and open situations, but occasionally woodland.

Status & distribution Scarce and irregular immigrant, but over 100 have been recorded since the first in 1946. The largest annual total is 25, in 1969. Most have been recorded on or near the south coast of England, occasionally further inland, north to Warwickshire. First recorded in Ireland in 1982, when two were reported from Co. Cork. In the Channel Islands a rare suspected immigrant, but possibly also breeding. Resident in southern and eastern Europe.

False Mocha
page 132
Cyclophora porata (L.)
Nb. S,C
1679(8019)

Field characters & Similar species FW 12-14mm. Fore- and hindwing buff or light pinkish brown, sometimes with a pink blush, and with a central white dot. Maiden's Blush lacks central spots. Second-generation Clay Triple-lines sometimes has circular spots but lacks freckling. See also Blair's Mocha.

Flight season Two generations. Mid May-early July and late July-late August. Second generation usually

more numerous, reaching peak numbers in mid August. Flies from dusk. Comes to light, including actinic traps, but usually in small numbers compared with Maiden's Blush. Occasional at sugar and wine ropes.

Life cycle Overwinters as a pupa, attached by a silk girdle to the underside of an oak leaf, falling with it to the ground. Larva mid June-late July and late August-early October.

Larval foodplants Pedunculate Oak and probably Sessile Oak.

Habitat Oaks in woodland, heathland and carr. May prefer scrubby oak and oak coppice regrowth, in warm sheltered locations, to canopy of dense oak woodland. Appears to be associated mainly with large, long-established areas of habitat, and possibly with coppicing or other active felling and regrowth.

Status & distribution Resident. Nationally Scarce B, formerly Local. In decline. Recorded from a wide but sparse scatter of sites throughout southern England, from Cornwall to Gloucestershire and Shropshire and eastwards to Essex, through parts of the Midlands, such as the Clay Vale of Oxfordshire and Buckinghamshire. Reported also from Nottinghamshire and Yorkshire, possibly as strays. Scarce and local in Wales. Declines in numbers of sites since 1960 reported for Surrey and Sussex, and considered probably extinct in the London area. Now rare in Dorset and Hampshire. Possible causes of decline include the cessation of small-scale rotational woodland management. The moth has survived large-scale conifer-planting on some sites but may be largely dependent on the unplanted portions.

Maiden's Blush
page 132
Cyclophora punctaria (L.)
Local. S,C
1680(8022)

Field characters & Similar species FW 13-16mm. Absence of dark-edged circular spots in centre of fore- and hindwing distinguishes Maiden's Blush from all mochas except Clay Triple-lines, which lacks freckling. Some individuals, particularly summer generation, have a large area of reddish blush in centre of fawn forewing. Others have only a single reddish cross-line. Either one or two reddish or grey squares are sometimes present near outer edge of wing. Occasionally, bands are dark grey or there is extensive dark grey speckling.

Flight season Two generations. Early May-early July and mid July-late September. Sometimes seen by day at rest on leaves of the foodplant, or on Bracken and other vegetation below, and can be found by tapping the lower branches of oaks. Visits flowers after dark, such as Alder Buckthorn, and can be seen flying in numbers around the oak canopy. Often frequent at light, including actinic traps.

Life cycle Overwinters as a pupa, attached to a fallen oak leaf. Larva late June-July and mid August-September.

Larval foodplants Oaks, certainly Pedunculate Oak, probably Sessile Oak and possibly Turkey Oak, larvae

feeding both in the canopy and in lower foliage.
Habitat Oak woodland, from open scrubby growth
to densely standing mature oaks.
Status & distribution Resident. Local. Widely distributed in England and Wales north to Yorkshire,
including the south-west, but most densely represented in the ancient woodlands of central southern
England and the Wye and Severn Valleys, where
often locally abundant. Very local in Scotland north to
Moray. Very local in Ireland, mainly in the west. Local
and occasional in the Channel Islands.

Clay Triple-lines
page 132

Cyclophora linearia (Hb.)

Local. S,C   1681(8024)

Field characters & Similar species FW 14-16mm.
First generation is distinctive in having one, two or
three strong grey lines across plain pale or richer pale
orange-brown forewing. Second-generation adults
generally smaller and more pinkish brown, cross-lines
generally weaker and sometimes with a distinct dark-
edged central spot on hindwing. See Blair's Mocha
for differences. False Mocha has dark freckling of
grey or red scales and forewing tip is usually only
slightly hooked. See also Maiden's Blush.
Flight season Mainly one generation. Late May-
early July, but individuals of a partial second generation, mid August-mid October, becoming more
frequent and widespread, perhaps in response to
warming of the climate. Nocturnal. Both sexes come
to light. Occasionally seen at rest by day on the
upper surface of Bracken or other foliage.
Life cycle Overwinters as a pupa, attached to a leaf
or stem. Larva late June-late August, second generation, if present, September-October.
Larval foodplants Beech.
Habitat Can be numerous in mature Beech woods
but also found on hedgerow trees, in parks and in
garden Beech hedges. May be introduced to new
areas on nursery plants.
Status & distribution Resident. Local. Widespread,
quite well distributed and often frequent in England
north to Lancashire and Yorkshire and in Wales, but
more thinly distributed in the northern part of its
range. Extends right through south-west England and
locally in southern Ireland. Rare in the Channel Islands.

Blood-vein
page 132

Timandra comae (Schmidt)

Common. S,C,(N)   1682(8028)

Field characters FW 15-18mm. Larger than related
species and easily recognisable, with light, creamy
brown wings and a variable degree of very fine, dark
speckling. The virtually straight, diagonal pink or
brownish-red line running from forewing tip to
trailing edge and across hindwing, and the bright
pink fringes, are diagnostic. Pink colour may fade to
brown with age, but pattern varies little. Entirely
dark, smoky brown or purplish-black forms (f. *nigra*
Rebel) are rare.

Similar species None.
Flight season Usually two generations, occasionally
a partial third in the south. May-early July, early July-
mid September, and mid September-November.
Often seen on or disturbed from low vegetation by
day. Comes to light.
Life cycle Overwinters as a larva. Larva July and
September-April. Pupates near the ground among
plant debris.
Larval foodplants Docks, Common Orache,
Common Sorrel, Knotgrass and probably other
related plants.
Habitat A wide range, but particularly damp places
with rank, herb-rich vegetation, including hedgerow
ditches, woodland rides, wet meadows and gardens.
Status & distribution Resident. Common. Well
distributed and fairly frequent in England and Wales
to north Yorkshire. Has recently become fairly widespread in Northumberland and Co. Durham, but rare
in eastern Scotland. On the west side of Britain rare
north of Lancashire, but a few records from the west
coast of Scotland and from Man. Local in Ireland,
mainly in the south-west but also reported, as a
rarity, from Northern Ireland. Widespread and
frequent in the Channel Islands. Two recorded in
Orkney on 8 August 1969 coincided with immigrant
moths of suspected Scandinavian origin.

Lewes Wave
page 132

Scopula immorata (L.)

Former resident; presumed extinct.   1683(8036)

Field characters FW 11-14mm. The mixture of
whitish, brown and blackish scales give this moth a
soft, grey-brown appearance. Several wavy bands are
usually visible across forewing, the outermost of
which is whitish and often broken. The fringes are
chequered and male has slightly feathered antennae,
barely visible to the naked eye. Initially settles with
wings spread and slightly raised, exactly like a
Grizzled Skipper butterfly.
Similar species Common Heath can be somewhat
similar, but is more coarsely marbled and male has
strongly feathered antennae.
Flight season One generation. Early June-mid July,
rarely from late May. Partial second generation
August-September after hot summers. Flies from
dusk and comes to light. Easily disturbed from low
vegetation by day.
Life cycle Overwinters as a larva. Larva August-May.
Larval foodplants Never confirmed in Britain.
Possibly Heather. Wild Thyme and Marjoram quoted in
mainland Europe but not present on the British site.
Habitat An open, heathy area with much Heather, on
Weald Clay and Tunbridge Wells Sand, surrounded by
conifer plantations. In mainland Europe, fallow fields
and other warm, dry, open situations.
Status & distribution Extinct former resident. Only
unquestionably recorded from one locality in Britain,
the north-western section of the Vert Wood
complex, near Laughton, East Sussex, where it was
first collected about 1850 and last seen on 22 June

1961. Often numerous at this site, but breeding grounds lost to agriculture and forestry, and the remnants probably became too overgrown for this moth (waist-high Heather was reported).

Sub-angled Wave

page 132

Scopula nigropunctata (Hufn.)

RDB. SE   1684(8042)

Field characters FW 14-16mm. Wings brownish white, with very fine brown speckling. Both fore- and hindwing have a small black central dot, and several grey-brown wavy cross-lines, the central of which is broader with diffuse edges, fairly straight and angled at leading edge of forewing. Hindwing has a small but distinct point mid-way along outer edge.
Similar species Cream Wave and Lesser Cream Wave have less angled and more or less wavy cross-lines, and hindwing has no distinct point on outer edge. On Cream Wave, if there is a small black central dot on forewings it is weaker than that on hindwing. Lesser Cream Wave may have a small black spot on forewing, but it is smaller and cross-lines are generally curved. See also Rosy Wave.
Flight season One generation. July-early August. Can be disturbed from foodplant by day. Both sexes come to light from dusk onwards.
Life cycle Overwinters as a part-grown larva, probably on the foodplant or other plant stems above ground rather than in litter, based on observations in captivity. Larva August-May. Pupation reported both between leaves and in earth in captivity.
Larval foodplants Unknown in the wild. Adults have been beaten from Traveller's-joy, on which larvae have been reared in captivity. Also accepts many small herbs, including Smooth Tare, other legumes and Tormentil, which are consistently present where the moth occurs.
Habitat Open, bushy coastal grassland, broad flowery woodland rides and clearings.
Status & distribution Resident and occasional immigrant. Red Data Book species. Breeds only in the extreme south-east of England, Folkestone Warren, Kent, being the only long-term breeding site (present at intervals since 1858). Intermittent breeding in the Hamstreet/Orlestone woodland complex in Kent (where it was first noted in 1951 but is not currently resident), in Friston Forest, Sussex (discovered in 1984 but not seen for some years), and possibly in a wood near Charing, Kent (two individuals in 2002). Appears to be occurring increasingly frequently as a presumed immigrant, on or near the south coast from Dorset and the Isle of Wight to Kent, and further colonisation may be just a matter of time.

1685, 1686 see Appendix

Lace Border

page 132

Scopula ornata (Scop.)

Na. S   1687(8045)

Field characters FW 12-13mm. Aptly-named; the chalky white wings, with grey-brown banded outer edges, brown blotches and a very fine, irregular, blackish outer cross-line make this moth unmistakable. There is very little variation.
Similar species None.
Flight season Two generations. May-June and mid July-early September. Easily flushed from grass by day. Flies from dusk, comes to light in small numbers and recorded at sugar.
Life cycle Overwinters as a part-grown larva in the sward. Larva June-July and August-April. Pupates in a slight cocoon on the ground.
Larval foodplants Thyme, Wild Marjoram and probably other herbs. Has been reared on Garden Mint.
Habitat Calcareous grassland, both on chalk and limestone. Some sites are lightly grazed downland and one is the bank of a disused railway line.
Status & distribution Resident. Nationally Scarce A and much declined. Local but still sometimes frequent on a number of sites on the North Downs of Surrey and north Kent, regular at one site in Norfolk, several in Gloucestershire, with only scattered records elsewhere, including recent records from Devon (Yarner Wood, 20 August 1984, one in unsuitable habitat) and Somerset (Millwater Mead, 1980s). Formerly recorded in other localities in the Cotswolds and in other parts of southern England, from the Isle of Wight and Hampshire to Essex and Suffolk, and from south Wales. Overlooked colonies may await discovery but some undoubtedly lost or much reduced due to changes in agriculture. Recorded once on Jersey in the 1930s.

Tawny Wave

page 132

Scopula rubiginata (Hufn.)

RDB. SE   1688(8054)

Field characters FW 9-11mm. A rich, deep pinkish-brown moth when fresh. The intensity of the pink varies and some examples are dull brown. Early season immigrants are often paler than those produced in the wild and in captivity in Britain. Three dark cross-lines are usually apparent across forewing.
Similar species Bright Wave is sandy brown and forewing is more pointed. There is a series of tiny dark dots in fringes, and cross-lines are generally less distinct, especially that closest to base. Ochraceous Wave has four cross-lines or bands, and a more orange colour. The dark form of Purple-bordered Gold is a more vivid pink, has only a single, purple, outer cross-line and usually retains a small yellow spot near centre of wings.
Flight season Two generations. Mid June-mid July and mid August-early September. Readily flushed by day, flies a short distance and then rests on a stem. Flies from dusk onwards and comes to light. Most of the suspected immigrants have been taken at light in

late July-early August, slightly in advance of the residents.

Life cycle Overwinters as a part-grown larva in the sward. Larva July-August and September-May. Pupates in a light cocoon among plant debris on the ground.

Larval foodplants As yet undiscovered in the wild. Reared in captivity on Dandelion and Knotgrass (both unlikely to be the wild foodplants), Field Bindweed, and various legumes including clovers, trefoils and Black Medick.

Habitat, Status & distribution Resident. Red Data Book species. Breeding probably confined to a few of the surviving Breckland areas around the Norfolk/Suffolk border, including the rides in Thetford Forest, and to coastal sand-dunes in the Aldeburgh-Thorpeness area of Suffolk. Reported as suspected immigrants, usually as singletons, at various points along the coast of south-east England as far north as the Wash, also south Cornwall and the Channel Islands, and occasionally inland, including the Norfolk Broads.

Mullein Wave   page 132

Scopula marginepunctata (Goeze)

Local. S,C,(N)   1689(8059)

Field characters FW 12-15mm. Quite distinctive, usually with a creamy ground-colour on both wings, fine blackish markings and a variable scattering of blackish scales. F. *mundata* Prout is white and without dusting, with fine blackish cross-lines, and occurs in Sussex, Dorset and the Isle of Wight. Heavily-dusted examples can have a coarse grey or grey-brown appearance, and a blackish form, usually with whitish fringes (f. *aniculosata* Ramb.) has been found in south-west England and Scotland.

Similar species Weaver's Wave is somewhat similarly marked, but significantly smaller, with usually larger dark blocks on a narrower forewing.

Flight season Mainly two generations. June-July and August-September. One generation in Scotland, June-July. Often seen at rest on rocks. Comes to light, sometimes in fair numbers.

Life cycle Overwinters as a larva. Larva July and September-May. Pupates in loose earth.

Larval foodplants Herbaceous plants, including Wild Marjoram, Wood Sage, Horseshoe Vetch, Yarrow, Mugwort and stonecrops.

Habitat Mainly on or near the coast, especially rocky places and coastal grassland, but also saltmarshes. Also found inland, chiefly along the Thames Valley.

Status & distribution Resident. Local. Well distributed and locally fairly frequent around the coast of England and Wales from Cumbria to Suffolk, including Anglesey and the Isle of Wight. Locally abundant in urban parts of the London area. In northern Britain there are a few records scattered around the coast of Scotland, Northumberland and Yorkshire. Rather local on Man and in Ireland. Widespread and frequent in the Channel Islands.

Small Blood-vein   page 132

Scopula imitaria (Hb.)

Common. S,C   1690(8062)

Field characters FW 13-15mm. A distinctive sandy brown moth, with three fine darker wavy cross-lines on forewing, the central of these usually having dark shading on its outer edge, is slightly curved and is continuous with a similar line on hindwing when moth is at rest. All four wings have a small but distinct point mid-way along outer edge, less pronounced on forewing, and a small black central dot.

Similar species None.

Flight season Usually one generation. July-August. Occasionally a small partial second generation September-October in southern Britain. Sometimes seen at rest or disturbed by day. Comes to light in small numbers.

Life cycle Overwinters as a larva, probably on foodplant. Larva August-May. Probably pupates in debris on the ground.

Larval foodplants Apparently rarely recorded in the wild, but has been found on Garden Privet and Honeysuckle, and may also feed on herbaceous plants, which it eats in captivity.

Habitat A wide range, including gardens, hedgerows, broadleaved woodland and open coastal sites.

Status & distribution Resident. Common. Well distributed and fairly frequent in England north to Lincolnshire. More local in Cheshire, Yorkshire and southern Ireland. Widespread and frequent in the Channel Islands.

Rosy Wave   page 132

Scopula emutaria (Hb.)

Nb. S,E,W   1691(8072)

Field characters FW 11-13mm. The milky-white wings often have a delicate pastel pink tinge and a thin scattering of dark scales. Central cross-line is the broadest and is straight, extending towards forewing tip, but usually fading before reaching it. Beyond it is a row of small dark dots. Hindwing has a small but distinct point mid-way along outer edge. Varies slightly, mainly in strength of markings.

Similar species Sub-angled Wave is similar in shape, but substantially larger. Lesser Cream Wave has rounded wings and curved cross-lines. Both are without a line of small dark dots toward outer edge of forewing, and are never pinkish.

Flight season One generation. Late June-July. Often disturbed by day, seldom flying more than a few metres. Flies from just before dusk. Can be found in numbers by torchlight, resting on grass stems after dark in coastal sites. Less frequent to light.

Life cycle Overwinters as a part-grown larva, several of which have been found on stems of Sea Beet at one coastal site, in north Kent. Larva August-May. Pupates in a cocoon in debris or on the ground.

Larval foodplants As yet undiscovered in Britain. Although found on Sea Beet, they have not been successfully reared from the egg on it, and this plant is absent from many occupied sites. Larvae reared on Knotgrass and chickweeds, and on Hop Trefoil, Common Bird's-foot-trefoil and Sea Campions. Sea-lavender is a suspected foodplant.

Habitat, Status & distribution Resident. Nationally Scarce B. Locally fairly frequent in the Oxwich/Gower area of the Glamorgan coast, the wetter heaths of south-east Dorset, a number of the bogs in the New Forest, Hampshire, and at various places eastwards along the coast, including Titchfield Haven, Hayling Island and the Isle of Wight. Also a few places on the Sussex and Kent coasts, more extensively on the salt-ings and estuaries of the Essex coast, and then locally northwards to Gibraltar Point, Lincolnshire, and Spurn Head, Yorkshire, where it has been recorded annually since the 1960s. Also present on Whixall Moss, Shropshire, and recorded from the west coast of Wales. Two recorded on Jersey in 1999.

Lesser Cream Wave
page 132

Scopula immutata (L.)
Local. S,C   1692(8064)

Field characters FW 12-13mm. Wings rather rounded, white or creamy white, with a fine scatter of black scales and several slightly wavy or curved pale brown cross-lines. Hindwing has a small blackish central dot and is not pointed. There is frequently a similar dot on forewing, but it is sometimes faint or absent.

Similar species Cream Wave is larger, forewing is more pointed, with leading edge more arched near tip, and cross-lines generally more irregular and generally less well-defined. See also Smoky Wave, Rosy Wave and Sub-angled Wave.

Flight season One generation. Late June-early August. Flies from dusk, when sometimes seen in fair numbers, and comes to light in smaller numbers.

Life cycle Overwinters as a larva in plant debris, in which it later pupates. Larva late August-May.

Larval foodplants Meadowsweet and Common Valerian. In captivity, eats a wider range of plants, including hawthorns, Purple-loosestrife and Groundsel.

Habitat Damp grassland and marshes with rank vegetation, in river valleys and other low-lying areas, and on dry breckland heaths.

Status & distribution Resident. Local. Widespread, thinly distributed but sometimes locally frequent throughout England and Wales, and recorded from south-west Scotland. More densely distributed in west Wales, southern and eastern England than else-where. Local on Man and in Ireland.

Cream Wave
page 133

Scopula floslactata (Haw.)
Local. S,C   1693(8069)

f. *scotica* Cock.
Local. NW

Field characters FW 13-16mm. Has creamy-white wings, with a thin scattering of dark scales and three or four distinct light or dark brown wavy cross-lines. Forewing rather pointed, with leading edge notice-ably arched toward tip and outer edge fairly straight. Hindwing more or less rounded. There is a very small but discernible black central dot on hindwing, and only occasionally an even fainter one on forewing. F. *scotica* is similar in shape, but smaller and darker, with thicker (occasionally very thick) dark speckling.

Similar species Smoky Wave is somewhat similar, especially to f. *scotica*, but has no dark central dots and cross-lines are straighter and often less distinct, especially in male. See also Lesser Cream Wave and Sub-angled Wave.

Flight season One generation. May-June, into July in Scotland. Often disturbed from hedgerows, under-growth and low branches by day. Comes to light in small numbers.

Life cycle Overwinters as a fully grown larva. Larva July-April. Pupates in loose earth.

Larval foodplants Bedstraws, Woodruff and Bush Vetch reported. Will eat other herbaceous plants in captivity.

Habitat Broadleaved woodland, hedgerows, damp scrubby grassland and some gardens.

Status & distribution Resident and possibly an occasional immigrant. Local. Fairly well distributed and sometimes frequent in most parts of England and Wales. Widespread but more local in Scotland, mainly in the west. Local on Man and in Ireland, where recorded from Northern Ireland and the Republic, but particularly the south-west. Rare in the Channel Islands. Two possible immigrant (or second generation) examples came to a light-trap in very open habitat at Worth Matravers, Dorset, on the unusually late dates of 19 and 20 August 1996.

Smoky Wave
page 133

Scopula ternata (Schr.)
Local. N,W   1694(8067)

Field characters FW 12-15mm. Wings dull greyish white with fine grey-brown speckling, generally heavier in the larger male, and no black dots. The slightly wavy, brownish cross-lines are often blurred, especially in male.

Similar species Lesser Cream Wave has a small black central dot on hindwing and sometimes also on forewing, and cross-lines generally more curved. See also Cream Wave.

Flight season One generation. June-July. Easily disturbed from low vegetation by day, sometimes in fair numbers. Comes to light in small numbers.

Life cycle Overwinters as a larva. Larva August-late May. Pupates close to the ground in plant debris, or just below it.

Larval foodplants Heather and Bilberry. On calcareous soils the foodplant is apparently unknown.

Habitat Heathland, moorland and very locally on rocky limestone grassland with a short sward.

Status & distribution Resident. Local. Quite well distributed and fairly frequent in north Wales, north

65

Cumbria, south-west Scotland, the central belt, the west coast and along the Spey and Dee. More local elsewhere in Scotland, northern and south-western England and in Wales. Recorded only twice from Man and once from Northern Ireland.

1695 see Appendix

Bright Wave
page 133

Idaea ochrata (Scop.)

ssp. *cantiata* (Prout)

RDB. SE
1696(8099)

Field characters FW 10-12mm. A small, sandy-brown moth with rather pointed forewing, which often fades to a lighter shade of brown. There are small blackish-brown dots, not dashes, in fringes of wings, which may be visible only with a hand-lens. Two central cross-lines are usually distinct, the inner stronger, and a third innermost line is usually weak.
Similar species See Ochraceous Wave and Tawny Wave.
Flight season One generation. Mid June-early August, but usually ending by third week of July. Easily disturbed by day from grass swards, where it rests on stems. Flies from late afternoon, at dusk and after dark. Comes to light, sometimes in large numbers.
Life cycle Overwinters as a part-grown larva, low down on stems near the ground. Larva August-May. Pupates in a light cocoon among debris on the ground.
Larval foodplants Probably a progression of herbs. Has been found after winter on Smooth Tare, of which it eats the flowers, seedpods, foliage and stems. Also found in association with Hare's-foot Clover flowers, on which plant they can complete their whole development. Also flowers of other species, including vetches, Lesser Stitchwort and daisies.
Habitat On the nature reserve, breeds on vegetated shingle, outside the grazed areas only. The golf-course breeding sites are in the 'roughs', open areas with fine grasses and herbs growing on stabilised sand. On shingle with sand-dunes at Kingsdown, Kent, and formerly in Suffolk. On sandy undercliff on the north shore of Pegwell Bay.
Status & distribution Resident and suspected immigrant. Red Data Book species. Now confined to three

Larva of Bright Wave.

golf courses and a nature reserve in a continuous population from just north of Sandwich to Deal, in Kent, where it is quite numerous, with outlying populations on the north shore of Pegwell Bay and on the upper beach of vegetated shingle at Kingsdown. Formerly reported nearby as singletons from Kingsdown Golf Course, but no current evidence of breeding. Formerly resident on the Suffolk coast between Thorpeness and Aldeburgh, but not seen since 1990. Previously at Colne Point near St Osyth, Essex, where it was last seen in 1985. One trapped at Rye Harbour Nature Reserve, East Sussex, on 25 July 1996. Other presumed immigrants were singletons at Portland, Dorset, on 15 July 1994, Axminster, Devon, on 21 July 1987, Bradwell-on-Sea, Essex, on 16 July 1985, Harpenden, Hertfordshire, on 19 July 1983; Bournemouth, Dorset, on 19 July 1900 and Setley, Hampshire, in 1915/16. Very local and occasional on Jersey, rare on Guernsey.

Ochraceous Wave
page 133

Idaea serpentata (Hufn.)

Rare immigrant; Jersey resident
1697(8100)

Field characters & Similar species Forewing narrower and not as pointed as Bright Wave, and brighter orange-brown. Cross-bands stronger; generally four visible across forewing, three on hindwing. Blackish markings on outer edge stronger than in Bright Wave, and may be extended.
Flight season One generation in the northern half of mainland Europe, July. Readily disturbed by day, and comes to light.
Life cycle Overwinters as a larva. Larva August-May. Probably pupates in debris on the ground.
Larval foodplants Unknown. Docks and bedstraws in captivity.
Habitat In central Europe, dry meadows, woodland glades and forest clearings.
Status & distribution Resident on Jersey. Rare immigrant elsewhere. Very local and rare on Jersey, where a breeding population was discovered in 1941. Recorded once on Guernsey, in 1984. Several poorly-labelled specimens from 19th-century collections possibly from England. Two in Surrey, at Leigh and at Reigate Heath or Redstone Wood, both near Redhill, in 1865 and 1869, and a third, near Dartford, Kent, in 1909, may be genuine. Not seen in Britain since. Widely distributed and fairly frequent in mainland Europe.

Purple-bordered Gold
page 133

Idaea muricata (Hufn.)

Nb. S,C
1698(8104)

Field characters FW 8-10mm. The vivid pink and yellow markings distinguish this from all other small geometrids. Extent of the pink varies considerably. F. *auroraria* Borkh., with large yellow patches and margins, is the most frequent. F. *totarubra* Lambillion is almost entirely pink, apart from small central yellow spots, a fine purple outer cross-line and yellow fringes.

Similar species There are several purple and yellow day-flying pyralid moths, such as *Pyrausta* spp. (see pages 12-13) and Gold Fringe *Hypsopygia costalis* (Fabr.), but some have proportionately longer, narrower forewings and their markings are somewhat different. See also Tawny Wave.

Flight season One generation. Late June-July. Easily disturbed from low vegetation by day, flying from dusk onwards and at sunrise, and comes to light.

Life cycle Overwinters as a larva. Larva July-late May. Pupates in a cocoon among plant debris on the ground.

Larval foodplants Marsh Cinquefoil is recorded in the wild. Dandelion and Knotgrass accepted in captivity.

Habitat Damp heaths, bogs, mosses, marshes, fens and wet grassland.

Status & distribution Resident. Nationally Scarce B. Appears to be limited to England and Wales, with no records from Scotland. It occurs in several discrete areas: the heathlands of east Dorset and Hampshire; the New Forest bogs; heathland in Surrey, in particular Chobham Common; some of the fens, heaths, bogs and broads of East Anglia, from Dersingham Bog and Roydon Common near King's Lynn to the Ant and Bure Marshes, to the pingos and other wet places in Breckland; the surviving mosses of Shropshire, Cheshire, Lancashire and Cumbria; and at Thorne Moors, straddling the Lincolnshire/Yorkshire border. Recorded from Borth Bog/Cors Fochno NNR, in west Wales. Scattered pre-1980 records from other counties, but also some confusion with pyralid moths mentioned above. Occurred at Ham Fen, east Kent, in the late 19th century. Resident on Man in the 19th century. In the Republic of Ireland recorded very locally in the south-west and west.

Least Carpet
page 133

Idaea rusticata ([D. & S.])

ssp. *atrosignaria* Lempke

Local. S   1699(8107)

Field characters FW 9-11mm. A small, distinctive, whitish species due to the position of the dark blackish-brown markings on forewing, which form both a central band and extend broadly along leading edge to thorax. Markings vary in intensity.

Similar species None.

Flight season Mostly one generation. Late June-late August, but sometimes reported from late May, with a partial second generation from mid September-late October. Found by day by tapping bushes, but flies at night and comes to lighted windows and other lights.

Life cycle Overwinters as a larva. Larva August-late May or June, sometimes July-August and October-May. Pupates in a cocoon among plant debris on the ground.

Larval foodplants Ivy, Traveller's-joy, the garden crucifer Golden Alyssum and probably many other plants, the larvae eating withered and dead leaves.

Habitat Gardens, verges, hedgerows, scrubby downland and chalk embankments.

Status & distribution Resident and probable immigrant. Local. First recorded in 1831 in the London area but local and rare until the mid 20th century. Now locally numerous. The distribution centres on the banks of the Thames and on the calcareous strata north of the Wealden Clay, in south Essex, the London area, north Kent, Surrey and Sussex. Currently expanding in range, with more frequent records along the south coast to Dorset, including the Isle of Wight. A number of records from Devon and Cornwall, including Scilly, and inland northwards as far as Cheshire (in 1999). Formerly established on Portland, Dorset, in the late 19th century. There is an old unconfirmed record from St Kilda. Widespread and frequent in the Channel Islands.

1700 see Appendix

Dotted Border Wave
page 133

Idaea sylvestraria (Hb.)

Nb. S,C   1701(8123)

Field characters FW 10-11mm. Wings usually brownish white, with a thin scattering of blackish scales and usually rather indistinct, wavy brownish cross-lines that vary in strength. Both wings have a small, distinct central black dot, and a line of blackish dots along outer margins, which are visible to the naked eye. F. *circellata* Guen. is brown, with distinct cross-lines. It is found mainly in Lancashire and Cheshire, but forms approaching it have occurred elsewhere.

Similar species Silky Wave is more tawny brown, usually lacks black central forewing dots, those on hindwing are faint or absent, those on wing edges absent or very inconspicuous. Satin Wave has at most faint central and marginal dots and is nearly always whiter. See also Dwarf Cream Wave.

Flight season One generation. Late June-early August. Sometimes disturbed from heathers by day, flying from dusk onwards and coming to light.

Life cycle Overwinters as a larva. Larva August-end May. Pupates on the ground.

Larval foodplants Unknown in the wild, but unlikely to be dependent on a single genus because Dandelion, Knotgrass, Bramble and others accepted in captivity.

Habitat Open heathy areas, often scattered with bushes.

Status & distribution Resident. Nationally Scarce B. Well established on heathland in Devon, Dorset, Hampshire, Surrey and Berkshire but otherwise appears to have only a few scattered colonies from Sussex to Yorkshire, Lancashire, Cheshire and Cumbria, such as Hartlebury Common, Worcestershire, Lower Hollesley Common, Suffolk, Scotton Common, north Lincolnshire, and Thorne Moors and Strensall Common, Yorkshire. Rare in the Channel Islands, where three were reported on Guernsey in 1997.

68

Small Fan-footed Wave   page 133
Idaea biselata (Hufn.)
Common. T   1702(8132)

Field characters FW 10-11mm. Both whitish-buff wings have a prominent black central dot. Leading edge of forewing is arched toward tip, and second cross-line beyond the black dot usually curves around it. Strength of markings variable, but usually a broad, dark outer cross-band, with an irregular pale cross-line running along its outer edge. In the frequent f. *fimbriolata* Steph. this band is dark grey, and wings are occasionally darker generally.

Similar species Dwarf Cream Wave is smaller. Central dots are smaller, that on forewing is usually after second cross-line, and outer area is not noticeably darker.

Flight season One generation. Late June-late August. A possible second generation occasionally reported in October. Can be disturbed by day from low branches and thickets. Visits flowers from dusk, such as Creeping Thistle. Comes to light, sometimes in large numbers.

Life cycle Overwinters as a larva. Larva August-May. Pupates in leaf litter.

Larval foodplants Apparently little known in the wild. In captivity will eat herbaceous plants such as Dandelion and plantains, preferring withered leaves. This suggests it normally lives close to the ground.

Habitat Broadleaved woodland, where it can be abundant; also conifer plantations, hedgerows and mature gardens in suburban and rural areas.

Status & distribution Resident. Common. Well distributed and fairly frequent throughout the Channel Islands, England, Wales, Man, Ireland, mainland Scotland and the Inner Hebrides, except on higher ground. Recorded once on Orkney, on 13 August 1980, as a suspected immigrant with other moths of more southern distribution.

1703 see Appendix

Silky Wave   page 133
Idaea dilutaria (Hb.)
RDB. W   1704(8136)

Field characters FW 8-10mm. Wings cream, with light brown, slightly wavy, somewhat indistinct cross-lines. The central dark dots of related waves are usually absent or very small, especially on forewing. Outer edges are often, but not always, without dots or dashes and these are never conspicuous.

Similar species Dotted Border Wave and Dwarf Cream Wave have distinct dark central dots on both forewing and hindwing, and conspicuous dark dots or dashes along outer edges. Satin Wave is larger and whiter. See also Isle of Wight Wave.

Flight season One generation. Late June-late July, with peak numbers in early July. Easily flushed by day from ground vegetation. Flies from dusk and comes to light.

Life cycle Overwinters as a part-grown larva, low

down in the sward, on or near the foodplant. Larva August-end May. Pupates in a cocoon on the ground.

Larval foodplants Common Rock-rose and possibly other low-growing plants, the larvae stripping the stems and then feeding on the withering leaves.

Habitat Sparse swards containing well established and not overgrazed Common Rock-rose, on well-drained, mainly south-facing, calcareous slopes.

Status & distribution Resident. Red Data Book species. Breeding colonies have been confirmed from only three localities in Britain in recent years: the Avon Gorge, near Bristol, where it was discovered at Durdham Down in 1851 but has since been found on both sides of the gorge, though mainly the north side, extending in fair numbers over several kilometres; on the Great Orme, Caernarvonshire, where it has been known for many decades, now in small numbers; and on the Gower, Glamorgan, where it was rediscovered in the 1990s and has a strong population. One was recorded from Gloddaeth Hill, south of the Great Orme, in the 1970s. There are a scattering of other records, many of which are unconfirmed, possibly including a single record from Alderney, Channel Islands, in 1980.

Dwarf Cream Wave   page 133
Idaea fuscovenosa (Goeze)
Local. S,C   1705(8137)

Field characters FW 9-11mm. Wings creamy white with fairly distinct, usually light brown cross-lines and a small but noticeable blackish central dot on both wings. Base of leading edge of forewing is brownish. There is a series of very fine blackish dashes along outer edges, best seen with a hand-lens.

Similar species Dotted Border Wave has brownish-white wings, with conspicuous dots rather than dashes along outer edges, and is on average slightly larger. See also Silky Wave and Small Fan-footed Wave.

Flight season One generation. Early June-late July. Sometimes disturbed by day from scrub, hedgerows, tall herbs or rough grass. Flies from dusk and comes to light in small numbers.

Life cycle Overwinters as a larva. Larva August-May.

Larval foodplants Apparently little known in the wild, but in captivity will eat either fresh or withered leaves of Dandelion, Knotgrass and Bramble.

Habitat Hedgerows, scrubby grassland, woodland edges and rides, the edges of marshes, rural and suburban gardens, and other places, usually with tall herbaceous growth. More frequent in sandy or calcareous situations, scarcer on acid heathland and heavy clays.

Status & distribution Resident. Local. Quite well distributed and fairly frequent in central southern and eastern England north to the Humber, including much of suburban London, with a few sites in Yorkshire. Also widespread and fairly well distributed in south-west England. A few, mainly coastal, records from Wales. Local in the West Midlands. Seldom recorded north of the Mersey. Widespread and frequent in the Channel Islands.

Isle of Wight Wave
page 133

Idaea humiliata (Hufn.)

Former resident; presumed extinct. 1706(8140)

Field characters & Similar species FW 9-10mm. Similar to Silky Wave and Dwarf Cream Wave but with a reddish-brown streak along leading edge of forewing, which is narrower and yellower. Sometimes a very fine, brown line along outer edges of both wings. Both these markings are best seen with a hand-lens.

Flight season One generation. July. Flies at sunset and at sunrise.

Life cycle Overwinters as a small larva. In mainland Europe, larva August-May. Pupates in a cocoon on the ground.

Larval foodplants Restharrows, speedwells and a range of other herbaceous plants recorded in mainland Europe. Reared on Dandelion and docks.

Habitat Steep, grassy, chalk sea-cliffs.

Status & distribution Former resident, presumed extinct, and suspected immigrant. As resident, known only from the sheer chalk cliffs to the west of Freshwater, Isle of Wight, where it was discovered in the early 1890s. It was captured intermittently in fair numbers for the next 20 years, and again in July 1931, when last seen. The main grassy ledge from which it was known subsequently collapsed into the sea. Other ledges remain, but are virtually inaccessible. One individual captured in Portsmouth, Hampshire, in 1954, raised hopes that it may have been a wanderer from a resident population, but none has been found.

Small Dusty Wave
page 133

Idaea seriata (Schr.)

Common. S,C,NE 1707(8155)

Field characters FW 9-11mm. Both wings are light to dark grey, usually dusted with dark grey, with a distinct central dot and a line of very fine dark dashes or sometimes dots along outer edges. Usually a narrow, rather diffuse, fairly straight central crossband, but other cross-lines often very faint. The uncommon melanic f. *bischoffaria* La Harpe is blackish, with pale outer edges.

Similar species Unlike any related species, but sometimes mistaken for one of the pugs. Of these, it is most similar in size, colour and markings to Slender Pug and Maple Pug. However, neither is dusted in appearance, cross-lines are distinctly angled near leading edge and hindwing often lacks a distinct central dot.

Flight season Two generations in the south, June-July and August-September. One generation in the north, July-August. Sometimes seen on walls, or disturbed from hedges or other thick vegetation by day. Often sits on lighted windows, or enters houses and is found on interior walls. Comes to light regularly, in small numbers.

Life cycle Overwinters as a larva. Larva September-May and July. Pupates in a cocoon on the ground.

Larval foodplants Shows a general preference for withered leaves and other plant debris. Has been beaten from Ivy clumps, and in captivity will eat herbaceous plants such as Dandelion and docks.

Habitat Gardens, hedgerows and rough ground, often near human habitation; also window-boxes and potted plants.

Status & distribution Resident. Common. Widely and fairly well distributed throughout England, including Scilly, and the lowlands of Wales and Scotland, and recorded north to the Moray Firth. Only a few records from Man. Widespread and frequent in the Channel Islands.

Single-dotted Wave
page 133

Idaea dimidiata (Hufn.)

Common. S,C,NW 1708(8161)

Field characters FW 9-11mm. Diagnostic feature is a darkening of outer area towards trailing corner of the rounded, straw-white forewing. On well-marked examples, this is clearly evident as a dark brown band, but even those that are lightly marked have at least two small dark blotches.

Similar species Small Fan-footed Wave and Treble Brown Spot have much less rounded forewing, with outer area not noticeably darker towards trailing corner.

Flight season One generation. June-August. Visits flowers from dusk, such as Creeping Thistle. Comes regularly to light, usually in small numbers.

Life cycle Overwinters as a larva. Larva August-May. Pupates in a slight cocoon in plant debris.

Larval foodplants In the wild, recorded on the flowers of Cow Parsley, Burnet-saxifrage and Hedge Bedstraw, but in captivity will eat herbaceous plants such as Dandelion, preferring withered leaves.

Habitat Woodland, hedgerows and gardens, marshes and fens. Often, but not always, in damp situations.

Status & distribution Resident. Common. Well distributed and fairly frequent throughout England, Wales, Man, Ireland and the Channel Islands. Local in southern Scotland.

Satin Wave
page 133

Idaea subsericeata (Haw.)

Common. S,(C) 1709(8167)

Field characters FW 10-12mm. Wings greyish white and rather silky. Cross-lines fairly distinct and quite angled. Central and marginal dots very small and faint, or absent.

Similar species See Dotted Border Wave and Silky Wave, both of which are much rarer and more localised.

Flight season Usually one generation. June-July. Occasionally a partial second generation in the south, mid August-late September. Comes to light, usually in small numbers.

Life cycle Overwinters as a larva. Larva August-May. Pupates in loose earth.

Larval foodplants Apparently little known in the wild, but in captivity will eat Dandelion, Knotgrass and other herbaceous plants.

Habitat Woodland, scrub, hedgerows, rough grassland, and some gardens, especially on chalk and limestone, but also on heathland.

Status & distribution Resident. Common. Well distributed and fairly frequent in central southern and south-eastern England. Widespread but more thinly distributed in south-west England, Wales, the Midlands and East Anglia, where it is most frequent in Breckland. Very local in Lincolnshire and Yorkshire, and local along the west coast of northern England to Cumbria and in south-west Scotland. Very local on Man and in Ireland, where most of the records are coastal. Widespread and frequent in the Channel Islands.

Weaver's Wave
Idaea contiguaria (Hb.)

ssp. *britanniae* (Müll.)

Na. WC   1710(8170)

Field characters FW 9-11mm. The elongate shape of forewing, fine blackish cross-lines and blackish-brown patches along leading edge, coupled with the geographical distribution, single out this species.

Similar species See Mullein Wave.

Flight season One generation. Late June-July. By day the moth sits with spread wings in sheltered spots, in crevices and under ledges of rocks, sometimes quite openly. Not very flighty or alert, so easy to box. Flies from dusk and comes to light.

Life cycle Overwinters as a part-grown larva among the foodplant. Larva early August-May. Pupates in a slight cocoon.

Larval foodplants Mostly on Heather, shoots of which the larvae may defoliate in the spring. Also found away from Heather, eating other plants such as Crowberry and Navelwort.

Habitat Heather-clad hillsides, either preferring or most easily found in areas with exposed lichen-covered rocks.

Status & distribution Resident. Nationally Scarce A. Almost certainly restricted to north-west Wales, where it occurs on the mountains and hillsides of Merionethshire and Caernarvonshire. Records from Skokholm and Skomer Islands during the 1970s are probably misidentifications of Mullein Wave.

Treble Brown Spot   page 133
Idaea trigeminata (Haw.)

Local. S   1711(8174)

Field characters FW 10-11mm. Usually unmistakable. The constant, diagnostic feature is dark brown outer cross-band on otherwise rather plain straw-white forewing, which is pinched in two places, more or less forming three dark brown blotches extending neatly outwards from the cross-line. The blotch near leading edge is only linked by a thin cross-line, but hind pair are often merged. Hindwing

only faintly marked. Conspicuous central dot in all four wings.

Similar species In f. *fimbriolata* Steph. of Small Fan-footed Wave, the dark outer band on forewing is less pinched. There is an additional dark band along outer edge and this pattern continues on hindwing. See also Single-dotted Wave.

Flight season Two generations. Late May-July, with a smaller second generation late July-late September, annual in the London area but less frequent further north and west. Sometimes found by day at rest on wooden fences. Flies from dusk and comes to light.

Life cycle Overwinters as a larva. Larva August-May. Pupates in loose earth.

Larval foodplants Apparently little known in the wild, but recorded on withered and dead leaves of Ivy and possibly from birch and Field Maple. In captivity will eat herbaceous plants.

Habitat Most frequent in woodland rides and edges, but occurs regularly in some suburban garden light-traps and in hedgerows and chalk downland.

Status & distribution Resident. Local. Well distributed and fairly frequent in the London area and south-westwards through Surrey to Hampshire and the Isle of Wight. Widely but more thinly distributed in Sussex, Kent, East Anglia and the Midlands. Widespread and fairly frequent in Gloucestershire, Herefordshire and Worcestershire, more so than formerly, and in Somerset, but rare in Devon, Cornwall and Scilly. Local in east Monmouthshire and scarce in south Wales. Locally frequent on Jersey; also reported from Guernsey and Alderney.

Small Scallop   page 133
Idaea emarginata (L.)

Local. S,C   1712(8183)

Field characters FW 11-13mm. The scalloped outer edges of the wings, fine curved cross-lines and central dots on both wings make this rather plain, sandy brown moth easily recognisable. Female tends to be smaller and darker. Some examples have a diffuse dark central cross-band, but otherwise there is little variation.

Similar species None.

Flight season One generation. Mid June-late August. Flies from dusk and comes to light in small numbers.

Life cycle Overwinters as a very small larva. Larva August-May. Pupates in a cocoon among debris on the ground.

Larval foodplants Bedstraws, and recorded on Field Bindweed. In captivity will eat other herbaceous plants, including Groundsel, docks and withered Dandelion.

Habitat Generally rather damp places, including woodland, fens, rough grassland and hedgerow ditches; also mature gardens.

Status & distribution Resident. Local. Well distributed, usually at low density, in south-eastern and eastern England, to the east Midlands and Lincolnshire. Occurs north to Yorkshire, where largely restricted to Strensall and Allerthorpe Commons, with occasional records from Spurn. Still widespread but in decline in Hampshire. Widely but thinly scattered in western England and Wales north to Lancashire. Recorded once on Jersey, in 1931.

Riband Wave page 133
Idaea aversata (L.)

Common. T   1713(8184)

Field characters FW 14-16mm. Forewing rather long and tapering, sometimes slightly hooked, with leading edge strongly arched to tip. Ground-colour is fawn to sandy brown and wings are peppered, sometimes heavily, with blackish scales, giving them a slightly rough appearance. A helpful feature is the third cross-line, which usually has a distinct kink near leading edge. The ribboned form has a dark grey cross-band, and may be more frequent in dense woodland than in open habitats. This form is more frequent in southern Britain than in the north, and is apparently absent from parts of north-east Scotland. The plain f. *remutata* L. is as frequent in the south and predominates in the north.

Similar species See Plain Wave and Portland Ribbon Wave.

Flight season Usually one generation, but occasionally a partial second in the south. Mid June-mid August and September-October. Sometimes disturbed by day, both from low swards and from tree trunks. Visits flowers from dusk, such as Creeping Thistle. Comes to light, sometimes in quite large numbers.

Life cycle Overwinters as a small larva. Larva July-May. Pupates in a slight cocoon near the ground, in plant debris.

Larval foodplants A range of low-growing herbaceous plants, including bedstraws, Wood Avens, Primrose, Dandelion and docks.

Habitat Most habitats, including gardens, hedgerows, woodland, heathland, calcareous grassland, fens, river valleys and coastal situations.

Status & distribution Resident. Common. Well distributed and generally frequent to abundant throughout England, Wales, Man, lowland mainland Scotland, the Hebrides, Ireland and the Channel Islands.

Portland Ribbon Wave page 133
Idaea degeneraria (Hb.)

RDB. S   1714(8186)

Field characters & Similar species FW 13-15mm. Similar to Plain Wave in size, shape and ground-colour. Diagnostic feature is dark brown shading between first and second cross-lines of forewing. This varies in strength but is always darkest near inner edge of second line. Basal area is usually somewhat darkened, and hindwing usually darker near base. The dark band on some Riband Waves is between second and third lines.

Flight season One generation, mid June-mid July. Occasional individuals in late August-September,

probably immigrants. Occasionally disturbed by day, but usually seen at light.

Life cycle Overwinters as a larva. Larva late July-late May. Pupates in loose earth.

Larval foodplants Unknown in Britain, but in captivity accepts various unrelated plants, including Bramble, Lady's Bedstraw, Traveller's-joy, Honeysuckle and Dandelion.

Habitat Open grassy and bushy areas of coastal limestone, including under-cliff and hollows, which experience hot microclimates.

Status & distribution Resident and immigrant. Red Data Book species. Since 1980, the species has been recorded regularly only from the east coast of the Isle of Portland, Dorset, where it was first noted in 1831 and where it is certainly resident. Other records since 1980 are of very occasional singletons, presumed immigrants or wanderers, usually second-generation individuals, in late August and September. These have occured in Cornwall, Devon, Dorset, Hampshire and Scilly. Up to about 1927, there may have been a colony near Torbay, Devon. Locally frequent on Jersey, rare on Guernsey.

Plain Wave page 133
Idaea straminata (Borkh.)

Local. T   1715(8187)

Field characters & Similar species FW 13-15mm. Very similar to some examples of the un-banded form of Riband Wave, but slightly smaller and distinguished by its smooth and rather silky, muddy brown wings and generally fainter cross-lines. Third cross-line on forewing is not kinked at leading edge, as it usually is in Riband Wave. See also Portland Ribbon Wave.

Flight season One generation. Late June-early August. Flies from dusk. Comes to light, usually in small numbers.

Life cycle Overwinters as a larva. Larva August-May. Pupates among plant debris.

Larval foodplants Apparently little known in the wild, but in captivity will eat herbaceous plants such as Dandelion and Knotgrass, and also sallows.

Habitat Mainly open woodland and scrubby heathland but sometimes hedgerows, country lanes, permanent rough grassland and some gardens.

Status & distribution Resident. Local. Locally and thinly distributed and seldom numerous throughout England, Wales and mainland Scotland. Fairly widespread but scarce on Man. Somewhat local in Ireland. Rare on Jersey and Guernsey.

Vestal page 133
Rhodometra sacraria (L.)

Immigrant.   1716(8211)

Field characters FW 12-14mm. Quite variable in colour, but forewing pattern and upright resting posture with forewings held close to body at a steep angle, covering the white hindwings, make it easily recognisable. The colour of the adults depends on the temperatures experienced by the pupae. High temperatures produce a lemon yellow ground-colour and a vivid pink cross-band (sometimes with extensive pink clouding). At lower temperatures, ground-colour can be a duller, straw yellow or leaden brown to deep crimson, and cross-band is brown or even black. Thus, immigrants from southern Europe are generally brighter than those that have developed further north.

Similar species Some male examples of Straw Belle are somewhat similar but larger, with fine speckling on forewing and a dark band on underside of hindwing, visible from upperside. They also have a different resting posture, as do certain pyralid moths, which are similar in colour. See also Yellow Belle.

Flight season Immigrants arrive from April-November, but the majority are found from August-September, when any homebred moths also emerge. Easily disturbed by day, but does not usually fly far, often resting on a grass stem. Comes to light.

Life cycle Unable to overwinter. Breeds continuously in southern Europe and North Africa, but unlikely to produce more than one generation in Britain and Ireland.

Larval foodplants Has been found on Knotgrass in the wild. In captivity will eat other herbaceous plants, such as docks.

Habitat Warm, open sunny places. Has been found breeding on weeds in wheat fields in years of great abundance.

Status & distribution Immigrant. Annual and fairly frequent visitor to Britain, Man, Ireland and the Channel Islands since the 1980s. Particularly numerous in 1947 and 1983, when over a thousand were reported on each occasion. Has reached northern Scotland but the majority occur near the south coast of England. Widespread and often abundant in southern Europe and north Africa.

Larentiinae Carpets, pugs and allies

Silver-ground Carpet

July Highflyer

Brindled Pug

Treble-bar

1717 see Appendix

Oblique Striped   page 134
Phibalapteryx virgata (Hufn.)
Nb. S,WC   1718(8227)

Field characters FW 10-12mm. Forewing grey or grey-brown and rather pointed, quite sharply in female, which is generally smaller. Dark cross-bands before and after central dot are of more or less even thickness, and are edged with greyish white. There is usually a short, dark, narrow diagonal dash at wing tip, not reaching the dark cross-bands.

Similar species Oblique Carpet has a longer, thicker dark streak running from forewing tip. Like Many-lined, it is browner, with unevenly thickened cross-bands.

Flight season Two generations. May-June and August. Readily disturbed from grassy swards by day, often abundantly. Flies from sunset and comes to light, sometimes in large numbers.

Life cycle Overwinters as a pupa, in a cocoon on the surface of the ground among plant debris. Larva June-July and September.

Larval foodplants Lady's Bedstraw. Will eat other bedstraws in captivity.

Habitat, Status & distribution Resident. Nationally Scarce B. This localised species is found in the Breckland of Suffolk and Norfolk, where it is widespread and fairly common, on limestone in Somerset, on chalk downland in Wiltshire, Hampshire, Berkshire, the Isle of Wight and Sussex, on coastal sand-dunes at Hayling Island, Hampshire, Camber Sands, East Sussex, Sandwich to Deal in Kent, the Isle of Wight, Dorset, Somerset, Glamorgan, Lancashire and Cumbria, and possibly at or near Saltfleetby, Lincolnshire, and Spurn, Yorkshire. Also resident in Essex in the Colne Estuary. There are records from various places on the coast of north Wales (most recently near Bangor), from Devon (most recently at Hopes Nose in 1989) and Cornwall (not since 1904). Singletons occasionally occur some distance from known habitat, either as windblown residents or as immigrants (e.g. at Clumber Park, Nottinghamshire, and Helpston, Northamptonshire) and elsewhere. Not reliably recorded from Ireland. Widespread and frequent on Jersey, rare on Guernsey.

Oblique Carpet
page 134

Orthonama vittata (Borkh.)

Local. T 1719(8245)

Field characters FW 11-14mm. Key features are straw-coloured forewing, with a dark streak running from wing tip to join the fine, dark outer cross-lines. Outermost area is pale, and there is a darker central cross-band, which is paler around the small black central dot, its outer edge angled around it. Intensity of markings varies.

Similar species See Many-lined and Oblique Striped.

Flight season Two generations in the south, late May-June and August-September. One generation in the north, July. Flies from dusk. Comes to light in small numbers.

Life cycle Overwinters as a larva. Larva September-April and July in the south. August-early June in the north.

Larval foodplants Marsh Bedstraw, Heath Bedstraw and possibly other bedstraws.

Habitat Fens, marshes, bogs, water meadows, damp woodland and ditch banks.

Status & distribution Resident. Local. Thinly distributed, in small numbers, in many parts of England, Wales and Scotland, including the Hebrides and Orkney, and in Ireland. Local and scarce on Man. Local and occasional on Jersey, rare on Guernsey.

Gem
page 134

Orthonama obstipata (Fabr.)

Immigrant. 1720(8246)

Field characters FW 12-14mm. Forewing of male is orange-brown with a narrow, irregular, sometimes broken, dark central cross-band and a rather ill-defined dark streak at wing tip. That of female has a similar pattern, but is deep rosewood-brown with a small, black, white-ringed central dot and sometimes very fine, wavy whitish cross-lines. There is only minor variation.

Similar species None.

Flight season Immigrants arrive from April-November. Any homebred moths usually emerge in August or September. Seldom seen except at light, usually as singletons.

Life cycle Unable to overwinter. Breeds continuously in southern Europe and North Africa, but unlikely to produce more than one generation in Britain and Ireland.

Larval foodplants Apparently little known in the wild in Britain and Ireland, but in captivity will eat a wide range of herbaceous plants, including

Groundsel, Ragwort, Field Bindweed, docks and Chrysanthemum.

Habitat Warm, sunny places of all kinds, including gardens.

Status & distribution Immigrant. Has arrived annually in recent years, mostly in southern England and southern Ireland, but with a scatter of records from coastal and inland sites in northern England and the west coast of Scotland. Has reached Orkney. Occasional immigrant in Man and the Channel Islands. Numbers vary considerably from year to year, with breeding in some years.

Balsam Carpet
page 134

Xanthorhoe biriviata (Borkh.)

Uncommon. S,SE 1721(8248)

Field characters FW 12-14mm. Distinguished from most carpets by outer edge of dull black and dark grey central cross-band on forewing, which has a pronounced, quite pointed, tooth-like projection, and is generally less irregular. Spring generation is quite pale, with a whitish cross-band beyond central one; it is tinged with brown, and with noticeably brown banding near base of forewing. Summer generation is generally darker, without the white band.

Similar species First-generation Common Carpets are greyer, basal area is not noticeably browner than remainder of forewing, and hindwing more strongly banded. Sharp-angled Carpet and Wood Carpet are somewhat similar to the spring generation, but fly later in the year. Central band of Dark-barred Twin-spot Carpet does not have different shades within it, and has much more wavy edges.

Flight season Two generations. Late April-June and July-early September. Flies in late afternoon and evening sunshine, as well as from dusk. Comes to light.

Life cycle Overwinters as a pupa. Larva June and August-September.

Larval foodplants Found mainly on Orange Balsam, an introduced plant, but adults have been trapped in woods away from Orange Balsam. Has also been found on Small Balsam, another introduction, long naturalised in woods and shady waste places as well as being a common garden plant.

Habitat In lightly wooded water meadows and other damp pasture, and tow-paths bordering rivers and canals alongside which Orange Balsam often grows. Recently in several damp woods away from rivers.

Status & distribution Resident. Uncommon; status equivalent to Nationally Scarce but this category normally reserved for species which feed in the wild on at least one native foodplant. First captured in Britain in 1951, and reported in 1955, then rapidly found over a wide area of England, suggesting it had been in Britain for some time, but overlooked. Recorded very locally but sometimes in numbers in Middlesex, Surrey, north Hampshire and also from Buckinghamshire, Oxfordshire, Cambridgeshire, Sussex, Norfolk and most recently Nottinghamshire. Single records for Derbyshire (about 20km west of the Nottinghamshire records) at Repton, on 26 May 1978, and at Yarner Wood, Devon, on 2 August 1982, and recorded from Pembrokeshire. One was recorded on 31 July 1999 at Westonbirt, Gloucestershire, with singles at Landguard, Suffolk, in 1996, 1998 and 1999.

Flame Carpet
Xanthorhoe designata (Hufn.)
Common. T

page 134

1722(8249)

Field characters FW 11-14mm. Grey forewing with rather narrow, rosewood-red-brown and black striped central cross-band is diagnostic. This band has a double projection on its outer edge in leading half of wing, and narrows toward trailing edge. Rather variable, especially in extent of the black and pinkish red.

Similar species See Red Carpet.

Flight season Two generations in the south, May-June and late July-August. Usually one generation in Scotland, June-July, but sometimes two in warm summers. Occasionally disturbed from bushes and low vegetation by day. Comes regularly to light.

Life cycle Overwinters as a pupa. Larva early June-mid July and late August-September in the south. July-August in Scotland.

Larval foodplants Apparently little known in the wild, but will eat Wallflower and other plants of the cabbage family in captivity.

Habitat A wide range, including upland grassland and moorland, and lowland woodland, hedgerows and downland.

Status & distribution Resident. Common. More numerous in northern and western Britain. Well distributed in south-east and south-west England, Wales, northern England and lowland Scotland, including the Hebrides, and on Man and throughout Ireland. Local and occasional in the rest of England and in the Channel Islands.

Red Carpet
Xanthorhoe decoloraria decoloraria (Esp.)
Common. N,W

page 134

1723(8251)

ssp. *hethlandica* (Prout)
Shetland

Field characters FW 12-15mm.
Ssp. *decoloraria* Forewing is rather pointed and outer area is plain, with a short, dark diagonal mark at tip, which is sometimes rather obscure. Forewing colour varies from light grey to tawny brown. Central band is pinched or narrowed in trailing half. It is usually reddish and often edged with blackish brown, but in one recurrent form it is as pale as ground-colour. Ssp. *hethlandica* Forewing rather dull tawny brown, with a dull red band. Examples resembling this subspecies occur elsewhere, especially in Scotland, but they are generally brighter.

Similar species Flame Carpet has two distinct projections on outer edge of central band. Red Twin-spot Carpet usually has two blackish spots near outer

edge of forewing. Both have more rounded forewings, with no diagonal mark at tip.

Flight season One generation. Late June-mid August. Easily disturbed by day from shaded rocks, stone walls and tree trunks, and flies at dusk. Comes to light.

Life cycle Overwinters as a small larva. Larva August-late May. Pupates in a cocoon formed among plant debris.

Larval foodplants Lady's-mantle, and in captivity on groundsels, bedstraws and chickweeds.

Habitat High moorland and grassy hillsides with exposed rock. Less restricted in the Orkney and Shetland Isles, occurring in a variety of situations, including roadside verges and coastal sand-dunes.

Status & distribution Resident. Common. Local in Shropshire, the northern half of Wales, Staffordshire, the Peak District of Derbyshire and in north-west Yorkshire. Well distributed in Cumbria and most parts of Scotland, including the Hebrides and Orkney. Recorded at Dhoor Ramsey, on Man, on 6 August 1999. Local in the northern half of Ireland. Ssp. *hethlandica* in Shetland.

Red Twin-spot Carpet
Xanthorhoe spadicearia ([D. & S.])
Common. T

page 134

1724(8252)

Field characters & Similar species FW 12-13mm. Very similar to reddish-banded form of Dark-barred Twin-spot Carpet but that species has a distinct notch on inner edge of broad, dark central forewing cross-band near leading edge, absent in Red Twin-spot Carpet. Other reasonably consistent features are that Red Twin-spot Carpet generally has brighter markings, central band is more distinctly edged with white, and pale, narrow band immediately beyond is slightly thicker and contrasts more sharply with ground-colour (especially outer area). It therefore has a more bluish appearance than Dark-barred, which has more understated markings. Both species are variable and some examples may be indistinguish-able.

Flight season Two generations in the southern half of England, mid April-June and late July-August. One generation elsewhere, May-July. Often found at rest on leaves by day. Easily disturbed from bushes and low vegetation. Flies from dusk and comes to light.

Life cycle Overwinters as a pupa, in a cocoon formed among plant debris. Larva July and September in the south, late June-late August else-where.

Larval foodplants A range of herbaceous plants, especially bedstraws; also Ground-ivy and Wild Carrot. In moorland favours Heath Bedstraw with some cover from Bracken or bushes.

Habitat A wide range, including gardens, woodland, hedgerows, downland, fenland, moorland and coastal sand-dunes.

Status & distribution Resident. Common. Well distributed and frequent throughout most of England, Wales, and lowland Scotland, becoming more local northwards to the Inner Hebrides and Orkney. Local and less frequent on Man and in Ireland. Widespread and abundant in the Channel Islands.

Dark-barred Twin-spot Carpet page 134
Xanthorhoe ferrugata (Cl.)

Common. T	1725(8256)

Field characters & Similar species FW 12-13mm. In the most frequent form, central cross-band on forewing is blackish-grey (f. *unidentaria* Haw.). This form is usually unmistakable when upperside is visible in good light. Red Twin-spot Carpets with a very dark band can look similar at first glance, especially when worn, but retain at least a hint of reddish or purplish in the band. The reddish-brown banded form is very similar to Red Twin-spot Carpet. This form is usually considered uncommon, but appears to be frequent in some places. See under that species for differences.
Flight season Two generations in the southern half of England, May-June and late July-August. One generation elsewhere, May-July. Easily disturbed by day from bushes and low vegetation. Flies from dusk and comes to light.
Life cycle Overwinters as a pupa, in a cocoon formed among plant debris. Larva July and September in the south, late June-late August elsewhere.
Larval foodplants The leaves of herbaceous plants, including bedstraws, docks and Ground-ivy.
Habitat A wide range, including gardens, woodland, hedgerows, downland, fens, moorland and coastal sand-dunes.
Status & distribution Resident. Common. Well distributed and frequent in England and Wales to south Cumbria, more local in north-eastern England, mainland Scotland and the Inner Hebrides. Fairly widespread and frequent on Man and in Ireland, more so than the Red Twin-spot Carpet. Widespread and frequent in the Channel Islands.

Large Twin-spot Carpet page 134
Xanthorhoe quadrifasiata (Cl.)

Local. S,C	1726(8254)

Field characters FW 14-16mm. A fairly distinctive, light brown or greyish-brown moth, generally larger than related species. The prominent, broad central cross-band on forewing is usually grey, with darker cross-lines running through it, and usually a slightly elongated, dark central dot. In the less frequent f. *thedenii* Lampa, it is entirely black. The dark 'twin-spots' near outer edge are often faint.
Similar species Dark-barred Twin-spot Carpet and Balsam Carpet are smaller, generally with broader, darker, less irregular central cross-band, with less conspicuous central dot and lacking the rather broad dark outer edge to forewing.
Flight season One generation. Mid June-early August. Sometimes flushed from bushes and tree trunks by day. Flies from dusk and comes to light, sometimes in fair numbers.

Life cycle Overwinters as a small larva. Larva August-May. Pupates in loose earth.
Larval foodplants Herbaceous plants, including bedstraws, Primrose and violets.
Habitat Damp broadleaved woodland, especially ancient woodland, fenland carr and scrubby heathland.
Status & distribution Resident. Local. Well distributed and locally sometimes frequent in the Thames Valley, the Midlands and in the eastern half of England, north to Yorkshire where it appears to be extending its range northwards. Local in Hampshire and rare westwards, with some of the reports possibly mis-identifications. Local and infrequent in the West Midlands north to Staffordshire. Old records from south Wales. Singletons recorded in Jersey in 1983 and Guernsey in 1976.

Silver-ground Carpet page 134
Xanthorhoe montanata montanata ([D. & S.])

Common. T	1727(8255)

ssp. *shetlandica* (Weir)
Shetland

Field characters FW 14-17mm. Ssp. *montanata* is quite a variable moth, but nonetheless distinctive. Diagnostic features are white or brownish-white wings, an irregular brown cross-band on forewing, and relatively plain hindwing. Central band varies considerably in width, and is occasionally split into two blotches (f. *degenerata* Prout) or reduced to a small blotch near leading edge (f. *costimaculata* Rebel). It also varies in colour from light greyish brown to intense blackish brown, usually with a whitish component, especially near leading edge. Ssp. *shetlandica* is smaller than ssp. *montanata*, and more brownish, with central band often no darker than ground-colour.
Similar species See Garden Carpet.
Flight season One generation. Mid May-late July. Easily disturbed from vegetation by day. Often numerous on the wing at dusk and comes to light.
Life cycle Overwinters as a larva. Larva July-May. Pupates in a cocoon in loose earth.
Larval foodplants Herbaceous plants, including Cleavers, Hedge Bedstraw and Primrose.
Habitat Rather damp places with tall herbaceous vegetation, including hedgerows, scrub, woodland rides, fens, chalk downland, gardens and heathland.
Status & distribution Resident. Common. Well distributed and abundant throughout England, Wales, Man, Ireland and Scotland, including the Hebrides and Orkney. Local and occasional in the Channel Islands. Ssp. *shetlandica* in Shetland only, where widespread and frequent.

Garden Carpet page 134
Xanthorhoe fluctuata fluctuata (L.)

Common. T	1728(8256)

Field characters FW 13-16mm. A grey or greyish-white moth, occasionally pale buff-tinted, with three distinct black or dark grey patches on forewing, and a blackish or grey thorax contrasting with whitish abdomen. Blackish central cross-band on forewing usually fades away, or becomes paler, before reaching trailing edge, a diagnostic feature. This band varies in thickness, and is occasionally reduced to a small spot at leading edge (f. *costovata* Haw.). F. *thules* (Prout) is darker, sometimes entirely blackish, so that central band often contrasts less sharply with ground-colour. This form predominates in the Northern Isles and in northern and north-east Scotland, and occurs elsewhere, including urban parts of London where frequencies up to 40% are recorded.

Similar species Occasional examples with cross-band more or less entire somewhat resemble Galium Carpet, which has less rounded, more pointed, elongated forewing with a slightly concave leading edge, and the whitish areas form distinct narrow bands either side of dark central band. See also the larger Silver-ground Carpet and Striped Twin-spot Carpet.

Flight season Two or three overlapping generations in the south, April-October. One or two generations in the north, May-September. Sometimes found at rest on walls by day. Flies from dusk and comes to light.

Life cycle Overwinters as a pupa, underground. Larva June-late October or early November.

Larval foodplants Herbaceous plants of the cabbage family, including Garlic Mustard, Shepherd's-purse, wild Horse-radish, Hairy Bitter-cress, Yellow Alyssum, White Alyssum and cultivated Brassicas; also garden Nasturtium.

Habitat Particularly numerous in gardens, allotments and rough ground in urban areas, but found in most habitats, including woodland and open coastal situations.

Status & distribution Resident. Common. Well distributed and frequent to abundant throughout England, Wales, Man, Ireland, the Channel Islands and lowland Scotland, including the Hebrides, Orkney and Shetland.

Fortified Carpet   not illustrated
Scotopteryx moeniata (Scop.)
Suspected rare immigrant.   1729(8229)

Field characters & Similar species FW 17-19mm. A striking moth, in size and general pattern not unlike Shaded Broad-bar, but outer edge of dark grey central cross-band on forewing has a large, pointed central outer projection and inner edge is almost straight. Ground-colour is cold grey. Spanish Carpet may have dark cross-bands merged in trailing half of wing forming a central band, but outer projection is rounded and its inner edge is bent; it is also a smaller moth.

Status & distribution Suspected rare immigrant to the Channel Islands and perhaps Britain. One on Guernsey in 1973. There are two records reported as British, supported by specimens, one individual captured 'near Baron Wood, Carlisle, some years prior to 1855' and another, from Holgate, near York,

on 19 August 1866. Resident mainly in central and south-eastern Europe where it flies from June-August, and recorded from Denmark.

Spanish Carpet   page 134
Scotopteryx peribolata (Hb.)
Immigrant; resident Channel Islands. S
                                       1730(8235)

Field characters FW 13-15mm. A distinctive light grey moth, with several narrow brown and blackish cross-bands on forewing. Easily distinguished by shape of third blackish cross-band, the middle part of which bulges out strongly toward outer edge.

Similar species Superficially similar to Lead Belle and July Belle, which both have a much straighter third cross-line and generally simpler markings.

Flight season One generation. Late August-September. Easily disturbed by day from the food-plant. Comes to light.

Life cycle Overwinters as a larva. Larva September-May. Probably pupates on the ground.

Larval foodplants Broom and Gorse.

Habitat Among prostrate Broom on cliffs in the Channel Islands. Hot, scrubby situations in mainland Europe.

Status & distribution Resident in the Channel Islands, where it is locally frequent. Immigrant to the British Isles, possibly establishing a breeding population in Dorset in the hot dry summers of the early 1990s, although this was never proven and does not seem to have persisted. The first British record was one in 1890 or 1899 at Westward Ho, north Devon, the second not until 26 August 1951 when one was taken at Fernhurst, Sussex, followed by a third on 6 September 1962, in Devon again, at Bishopsteignton. Subsequently one at Studland, Dorset, on 12 September 1990, two there on 29 August 1991 and three on 3 September 1991, one on 6 September 1994 at Greatstone, Kent, and one on 9 September 1996 at Lizard Point, Cornwall, the last of the 20th century.

Chalk Carpet   page 134
Scotopteryx bipunctaria ([D. & S.])
ssp. *cretata* (Prout)
Nb. S,C   1731(8236)

Field characters FW 15-18mm. Quite a distinctive, delicately-marked moth. The only species with quite pointed, cold grey forewing, numerous finely scal-loped grey and brownish cross-lines and bands, and two small black central dots on forewing. Little variation in markings, but some examples have slightly darker ground-colour or darker central cross-bands, which are sometimes merged.

Similar species None.

Flight season One generation. July-August. Easily disturbed from the ground or rocks by day and sometimes flies of its own accord. Comes to light, sometimes in numbers.

Life cycle Overwinters as a part-grown larva. Larva August-June. Feeds at night, and pupates in a

cocoon on the ground.
Larval foodplants Common Bird's-foot-trefoil and other trefoils, clovers and vetches.
Habitat Limestone and chalk grassland, cliffs and quarries, both on the coast and far inland. Areas of bare ground or rock are favoured for roosting and basking and may be essential.
Status & distribution Resident and possible immigrant. Nationally Scarce B. In calcareous localities in southern England and along the south coast of Wales. Local in the Midlands and north Wales, and on carboniferous limestone in the Buxton-Matlock area in north Derbyshire. Extends north to include coastal chalk in Yorkshire, particularly around Flamborough Head, and chalk and Magnesian limestone sites in Co. Durham, including inland quarries. Also on limestone around Arnside Knott, Cumbria, and the Northumberland coast opposite Lindisfarne. Occasionally reported away from chalk and limestone, e.g. two on the Kent coast at Lydd-on-Sea, on 17 September 1986 and at Greatstone on 2 August 1990, suggesting possible immigration. Not reliably recorded from Ireland.

Shaded Broad-bar page 134

Scotopteryx chenopodiata (L.)
Common. T   1732(8239)

Field characters FW 16-19mm. Quite variable in colour, but easily recognisable. Forewing smooth, light tawny or dull brown, with a distinct darker central cross-band, itself composed of several narrower bands, the central one of which is paler and often greyish. Usually a dark diagonal streak at wing tip. Examples from the north tend to be darker.
Similar species Some examples look superficially like Mallow, which usually flies later in the year, and has inner edge of central cross-band either jagged or with two notches. It is also usually larger and finely dusted and marked with whitish on edges of cross-lines, and there is a pale zigzag line along outer edge. Snout is superficially similar, but with very long palps.
Flight season One generation. Late June-August, sometimes September in the north. Frequently disturbed from grass swards and other low herbage by day. Can be found feeding at flowers after dark, but only comes to light in small numbers.
Life cycle Overwinters as a larva. Larva August-June. Probably pupates in plant debris.
Larval foodplants Clovers and vetches.
Habitat A wide range of open grassy places, including hedgerows, calcareous grassland, neutral meadows, acid heathland, woodland rides, rough roadside verges, coastal sand-dunes and some suburban gardens near these habitats.
Status & distribution Resident. Common. Well distributed and frequent in England, Wales, Man, Ireland and lowland Scotland, including the Inner Hebrides and Orkney. Local and occasional on Jersey. Rarely recorded on Guernsey. A pronounced decline reported in Hampshire.

Lead Belle page 134

Scotopteryx mucronata (Scop.)
ssp. *umbrifera* (Heydemann)
Local. SW   1733(8240)
ssp. *scotica* (Cock.)
Local. WC,N

Field characters & Similar species FW 15-19mm. Ssp. *umbrifera* is very similar to July Belle. Typically, forewing rather light grey (although sometimes darker) and the zigzag outermost cross-line is well defined. Small black central spot is usually tear-shaped, and placed roughly midway between the second and third cross-lines, or sometimes closer to third. However, these characters are somewhat variable. The later flight period of July Belle is helpful, but they may overlap, making it sometimes necessary to examine genitalia for confirmation. Ssp. *scotica* is darker but quite variable. The darkest forms are found in Scotland, including f. *luridaria* Borkh., which is blackish grey with bright-edged cross-lines. See also Spanish Carpet.
Flight season One generation. Mid May-mid June. Easily disturbed from the foodplant by day. Comes to light.
Life cycle Overwinters as a larva on the foodplant, feeding during mild weather. Larva August-March. May pupate on foodplant or in debris below.
Larval foodplants The leaves of Gorse, Broom, Petty Whin and Dyer's Greenweed.
Habitat Usually acid heathland and moorland, but sometimes other scrubby places and rough pasture.
Status & distribution Resident. Both subspecies Local. Ssp. *umbrifera* is found locally, sometimes in fair numbers, in south-west England and near the south coast of Wales. Ssp. *scotica* occurs locally in the more northern part of Wales, northern England, Man, Scotland and Ireland.

July Belle page 134

Scotopteryx luridata (Hufn.)
ssp. *plumbaria* (Fabr.)
Common. T   1734(8241)

Field characters & Similar species FW 15-19mm. Very similar to and sometimes indistinguishable from Lead Belle. On the whole, a slightly darker, more leaden grey than Lead Belle. Usually black central spot on forewing is smaller, round and dot-like, and tends to be nearer to second cross-line than third. Also, zigzag outermost cross-line is usually rather faint. However, these characters are variable and some examples closely resemble Lead Belle, when the more limited known distribution and earlier flight season of Lead Belle may be helpful. See also Spanish Carpet.
Flight season One generation. Mid June-early August. Frequently disturbed from the foodplant and other low vegetation by day. Flies at dusk.
Life cycle Overwinters as a larva. Larva September-May. Pupates in a cocoon in plant debris.

Larval foodplants Dyer's Greenweed, Gorse and Petty Whin.

Habitat A range of open, scrubby places, including heathland and moorland. Also on downland, very open woodland and shingle beaches, unlike Lead Belle.

Status & distribution Resident. Common. Locally distributed throughout Britain and Ireland, including those parts without heathland and moorland. Very locally frequent on Man. One on Jersey, in 1975. More widespread and better distributed than Lead Belle but problems with identification bedevil the records of both species.

Ruddy Carpet   page 135
Catarhoe rubidata ([D. & S.])
Nb. S   1735(8268)

Field characters FW 13-15mm. Unmistakable when fresh. Ground-colour of forewing dull pink or pinkish brown. Grey central cross-band is thickly edged with black, except in trailing half of its outer edge. Here, it consists of a very fine, deeply-scalloped black line. No other species has this combination. There is only slight variation.

Similar species Worn examples could be confused with worn Barberry Carpet.

Flight season One generation. June-July. Can be beaten from hedgerows by day. Flies from just before dusk, and occasionally comes to light, usually as singletons.

Life cycle Overwinters as a pupa, in an earthen cocoon. Larva July-August, more easily found than the adults.

Larval foodplants Lady's Bedstraw and quite frequently Hedge Bedstraw.

Habitat Downland, hedgerows, banks, field margins, other scrubby places and sea-cliffs, generally on calcareous strata.

Status & distribution Resident. Nationally Scarce B. Apparently declined in numbers and range since the 1940s. Recorded in small numbers from a wide scattering of sites in southern England, from Cornwall and Devon, where fairly frequent in the south, to Kent, including the Isle of Wight, northwards to Leicestershire, with old records from Derbyshire and, in 1999, the first record from Yorkshire in over 100 years. Also present in the eastern half of Wales. Local and occasional in the Channel Islands.

Royal Mantle   page 135
Catarhoe cuculata (Hufn.)
Local. S,(N)   1736(8269)

Field characters FW 12-14mm. Unmistakable. Ground-colour is whitish, and basal area of forewing is broadly black and brown. Outer black cross-band only extends across leading third of wing. In the remainder, its outer edge consists of a very fine, deeply-scalloped line. Beyond it, there is a reddish-brown blotch near leading edge. This combination is

diagnostic.

Similar species None.

Flight season One generation. Late June-July. Flies from dusk and comes to light, usually in small numbers.

Life cycle Overwinters as a pupa, in the soil surface below plant debris. Larva late July-early September.

Larval foodplants Lady's Bedstraw and Hedge Bedstraw, mainly on the flowers.

Habitat Grassland on calcareous soils, including chalk downland, limestone quarries, hedge banks, open breckland, wide rides in plantations and coastal cliffs.

Status & distribution Resident. Local. Locally, usually in small numbers, on calcareous sites in southern England, East Anglia, eastern Central Scotland and in Ireland in the Burren, Cos. Clare and Galway. Local and rare in the Channel Islands.

Small Argent & Sable   page 135
Epirrhoe tristata (L.)
Common. N,W   1737(8274)

Field characters & Similar species FW 11-13mm. Not unlike a small, dark example of Common Carpet, but with brown or dark greyish-brown markings and brightly chequered fringes. Outer borders are as dark as central and basal cross-bands, and white outer cross-bands of both forewing and hindwing have a series of small dark dots running through them. See also Argent & Sable.

Flight season One generation in many places. Late May-early July. A partial second generation in south-west England and Ireland, in August. Flies by day in sunshine and at dusk.

Life cycle Overwinters as a pupa, in a cocoon on the ground. Larva late June-August, and again in the autumn in south-west England and Ireland.

Larval foodplants Heath Bedstraw.

Habitat High moorland, including those recently planted with conifers, high limestone grassland; also upland woodland and hedgerows and a few lowland localities on heaths and mosses.

Status & distribution Resident. Common. Well distributed in the uplands of Wales and the Black Mountains, extending into Herefordshire, in Co. Durham, Northumberland, mainland Scotland and the Inner Hebrides. Sometimes seen in hundreds at some of the larger sites in Scotland and Northumberland. Widespread but more local in Yorkshire and Cumbria. Very local in other parts of northern England and the Midlands, with a few sites per county south to Nottinghamshire. Rare in Cornwall but quite a number of sites in Devon and Somerset. Occasional records in the west, either as wanderers or misidentifications. Recorded once from Orkney, where status unclear. Local in Ireland, mainly in the Burren, Co. Clare, but occurs elsewhere, including Northern Ireland.

Common Carpet page 135

Epirrhoe alternata alternata (Müll.)

Common. T 1738(8275)

ssp. *obscurata* (South)

Outer Hebrides

Field characters FW 13-14mm. Although rather variable, this is not a difficult species to recognise. Dark central cross-band on forewing is rather irregular but has only one, rather blunt, outer projection, and sometimes has a distinct grey component. Rarely, central band on forewing is reduced to a spot or patch. Basal area of hindwing is well marked, and white bands running across outer half of forewing and hindwing have a distinct grey line running through them, although this is sometimes rather faint. Ssp. *obscurata* is quite different in appearance. Generally paler, particularly the central cross-band, and brownish.

Similar species See Wood Carpet, Galium Carpet and Sharp-angled Carpet.

Flight season Two generations at least as far north as Northumberland. The first, in May-June, is the most numerous. The second, in July-early September occurs annually in smaller numbers. Sometimes three generations in the south, with the moth seen continuously from May-October. Where one generation, in the far north, June-July. Frequently disturbed from low vegetation by day. Visits flowers from dusk, such as Ragwort. Comes to light, sometimes in fair numbers.

Life cycle Overwinters as a pupa, in a cocoon on the ground. Larva June-July and September-October in the south, July-August in the north.

Larval foodplants Cleavers, Hedge Bedstraw, Lady's Bedstraw and other bedstraws.

Habitat A very wide range, including hedgerows, woodland, calcareous grassland, acid heathland and moorland, fens, marshes, sand-dunes, gardens and other urban situations.

Status & distribution Resident. Ssp. *alternata* Common. Well distributed and frequent to abundant throughout England, Wales, Man, Ireland, Scotland, including the Inner Hebrides and Orkney and the Channel Islands. Ssp. *obscurata* is restricted to the Outer Hebrides, where it is frequent.

Wood Carpet page 135

Epirrhoe rivata (Hb.)

Local. S,(C) 1739(8277)

Field characters & Similar species FW 14-16mm. Easily confused with Common Carpet, but slightly larger. The white cross-band beyond central band on forewing is broader and the thin grey line running through it is very faint or largely absent, although sometimes stronger near leading edge. Central white band on hindwing is also broader and has no thin grey line. See also Sharp-angled Carpet.

Flight season One generation. Mid June-early August. Occasionally netted at dusk. Comes to light.

Life cycle Overwinters as a pupa, in a cocoon on or just below ground. Larva late July-late September.

Larval foodplants Hedge Bedstraw and Lady's Bedstraw. Accepts Cleavers in captivity.

Habitat Woodland rides and edges, small copses, old hedgerows and boundary banks, chalk lanes, scrubby downland and small grassy fields. Also reported from sea-cliffs and mature sand-dunes.

Status & distribution Resident. Local. Probably under-recorded due to confusion with the Common Carpet. Widely and quite well distributed throughout England and Wales north to the Humber, particularly on lighter soils. Local and mainly western in northern England and southern Scotland, with a few coastal records further north. Recorded once from Man, on 6 July 1974, at Knock-e-Dooney, Andreas. Not reliably recorded from Ireland. Rare in the Channel Islands.

Galium Carpet page 135

Epirrhoe galiata ([D. & S.])

Local. S,C,(N) 1740(8279)

Field characters FW 13-15mm. Main diagnostic feature is leading edge of forewing, which is slightly concave in middle. Also, forewing rather narrower and more tapering than in similar species, and dark central cross-band is relatively broad. Ground-colour usually either white or greyish white, contrasting sharply with dark central cross-band. This varies from blackish to paler with grey and brown components, and has a very irregular outer edge, with either a single or double outer projection. Dark, brownish-grey forms with black forewing bands occur in western Ireland.

Similar species In Common Carpet, apart from forewing shape, central cross-band is narrower and its outer edge less irregular. Also, hindwing is more heavily marked. See also Garden Carpet.

Flight season Two generations in southern Britain and in Ireland, late May-mid July and August. One generation further north, June-early August. Sometimes disturbed by day. Flies from dusk and comes to light.

Life cycle Overwinters as a pupa. Larva late June-July and September in the south and in Ireland; August in the north.

Larval foodplants Lady's Bedstraw, Heath Bedstraw and Hedge Bedstraw.

Habitat Open grassy places on the coast, including coastal cliffs, sand-dunes and shingle. Also on calcareous grassland inland and locally on moorland.

Status & distribution Resident. Local. Well distributed and sometimes fairly frequent in western Wales and along the coasts of England north to the Severn and Thames. More local inland but recorded locally throughout England and Ireland, and very locally in Scotland north to the Moray Firth. Local and infrequent on Man. Widespread and abundant in the Channel Islands.

Many-lined page 135

Costaconvexa polygrammata (Borkh.)
Extinct; recent rare immigrant. 1741(8287)

Field characters FW 11-12mm. Forewing dull straw-coloured, hindwing paler, all wings crossed with many fine lines. Male has two conspicuous dark brown or blackish streaks across forewing, the inner one running from trailing edge and ending just short of a small central spot, the outer one arising on leading edge but fading near central spot. In female these are weak and light brown. In both sexes a pale streak runs from wing tip and outermost area is dark. Markings vary in intensity.
Similar species See Traveller, Oblique Carpet and Oblique Striped.
Flight season Probably two generations. Adults recorded in April, June, August and possibly September. Flies in the late afternoon and from dusk.
Life cycle Overwinters as a pupa. Larva probably May-June and August-September, as in mainland Europe, but possibly never found in Britain.
Larval foodplants Bedstraws.
Habitat Fens and wet meadows.
Status & distribution Extinct former resident and recent rare immigrant. Recorded at Burwell Fen and Wicken Fen, Cambridgeshire, in the mid 19th century but not since 1879, and reported from some damp meadows near Bristol prior to 1870. Two, presumed immigrants, were reported in June 2000, one on Portland, Dorset, on 18 June, the other at Closworth, Somerset, on 29 June, with a third in east Devon on 23 September. It is possible the latter was a British descendent of a wider June influx. Singletons recorded on Jersey in 1984, 1999 and 2000. Recorded from most countries in Europe, including Denmark and Sweden.

Traveller page 135

Costaconvexa centrostrigaria (Woll.)
Probable import. 1741a(-)

Field characters & Similar species FW 11-12mm. Similar to Many-lined, but the numerous cross-lines of female and heavy black or dark brown streaks of male are much more wavy. Central black spot on forewing is larger and further from inner cross-lines, and pair of dots near wing tip are much stronger and more conspicuous.
Status & distribution Probable accidental import. The only British record is of a male captured at light in a garden at Hampton, Middlesex, on 12 June 1973 and not reported until 1988, when it was misidentified as the Many-lined. Correctly identified and reported in 1999. A New World species, established on Madeira and other Atlantic Islands but not in Africa or mainland Europe, it is most likely to have arrived as a stowaway on a plane to Heathrow Airport.

Yellow Shell page 135

Camptogramma bilineata bilineata (L.)
Common. T 1742(8289)

ssp. *atlantica* (Stdgr.)
Shetland, Outer Hebrides

ssp. *hibernica* Tutt
W. Ireland

ssp. *isolata* Kane
Blasket Islands, W. Ireland

Field characters FW 13-16mm.
Ssp. *bilineata* Unmistakable. No other species has the combination of yellow or orange-yellow ground-colour on both forewing and hindwing, and numerous fine wavy brownish cross-lines. Bright yellow forms are more frequent in the south, sometimes with two distinct brown cross-bands, especially in female. Examples with brownish forewing are more frequent further north, but bright yellow forms occur as far north as Skye, Inner Hebrides and Sutherland.
Ssp. *atlantica* Smaller than ssp. *bilineata*, and yellowish brown, often with strong bands and cross-lines, sometimes with yellowish hindwing.
Ssp. *hibernica* Similar in size to ssp. *bilineata*, but with brown forewing.
Ssp. *isolata* Very distinctive. Dull, blackish brown.
Similar species None.
Flight season One generation. June-August, occasionally from late May. Often disturbed by day. Comes only sparingly to light, compared with numbers seen at dusk on the wing or visiting flowers such as Creeping Thistle and Betony.
Life cycle Overwinters as a larva on the foodplant. Larva July-late May. Pupates in loose earth.
Larval foodplants Cleavers and other bedstraws, wormwoods, including Sea Wormwood, docks, sorrels, Dandelion and other low-growing broad-leaved plants.
Habitat Many lowland situations, particularly the bases of hedgerows and fences, gardens, fields and meadows, especially at the margins, but larvae found throughout, in urban areas; also woodland rides, downland, heathland, moorland, riversides, fens and coastal habitats.
Status & distribution Resident. Common. Well distributed throughout the British Isles, but less so in the uplands and high moorland. Ssp. *atlantica* is found in Shetland and the Outer Hebrides. Ssp. *hibernica* is found only on sea-cliffs in Cos. Cork and Kerry, south-west Ireland, although forms quite like it occur in northern Scotland. Ssp. *isolata* is found only on the islands of Inishvickilean and Tearaght, the remotest of the Blasket Islands, off the coast of Co. Kerry. Widespread and abundant in the Channel Islands.

Yellow-ringed Carpet
page 135

Entephria flavicinctata flavicinctata (Hb.)
Nb. NW   1743(8299)

ssp. *ruficinctata* (Guen.)
Local. NW

Field characters FW 17-18mm. On ssp. *flavicinctata*, the dusting of bright golden-orange scales through central bands of forewing is diagnostic. However, some individuals have only a few such scales and others have a very dark ground-colour (ssp. *ruficinctata*), so examine closely.
Similar species Grey Mountain Carpet has no hint of orange or golden scales, and often present alongside Yellow-ringed Carpet and seen at the same time.
Flight season On the west coast of mainland Scotland and the Inner Hebrides, two generations, in May and August, of predominantly the pale ssp. *flavicinctata*. In central and north-west Scotland, one generation in July-early August, of the dark ssp. *ruficinctata*, which can produce two generations in captivity. Fond of resting on bare vertical rock surfaces and is flighty if disturbed by day. Flies after dark and comes to light in small numbers.
Life cycle Overwinters as a larva. Larva September-April and June-July where two generations, September-early June when only one generation. Pupates in a cocoon in earth or a rock crevice.
Larval foodplants Ssp. *flavicinctata* has been found on English Stonecrop in several parts of mainland Scotland and the Inner Hebrides and on Mossy Saxifrage in Yorkshire. Ssp. *ruficinctata* has been found on Yellow, Mossy and Purple Saxifrage, and sometimes Roseroot. Prefers the flowers, but will eat the leaves.
Habitat Rocky places, ravines and gorges. Associated with limestone or other strata containing lime fraction.
Status & distribution Resident. Nationally Scarce B. Ssp. *flavicinctata* occurs on the west coast of mainland Scotland and on the Inner Hebridean islands of Canna, Rum, Muck, Coll, Mull, Iona, Islay and Jura. Ssp. *ruficinctata* with one generation is in central and north-west Scotland, but a population with two generations and with the adult appearance of ssp. *ruficinctata* has been reported from Lang Craigs, Dumbarton, and dark forms are occasional elsewhere, e.g. on Rum. The species occurs in the Yorkshire Dales, near Grassington, where the moths are pale (ssp. *flavicinctata*) but have one generation, like other inland colonies. Old records from Cumbria, and reported again in 1995, at Knock Fell. Also occurs in the Black Mountains of Breconshire and Herefordshire. Two specimens were captured at Dovedale, Derbyshire, in 1882 and 1886 respectively, but the species is now considered extinct in the county. Recently rediscovered in Snowdonia, north Wales. Present in Ireland, where long-established colonies exist on the north coast at Fair Head/Murlough Bay, Co. Antrim, by Lough Erne, Co. Fermanagh, and it probably awaits discovery elsewhere.

Grey Mountain Carpet
page 135

Entephria caesiata ([D. & S.])
Common. WC,N   1744(8302)

Field characters FW 16-19mm. Size, habitat, flight season and habit of resting on vertical rock surfaces by day help in distinguishing this upland moth from other geometrids. Central band across forewing is usually conspicuous and edged with white. Otherwise forewing is mottled in appearance. Hindwing plain and pale brownish white, with chequered border. Some forms are very dark, some almost blackish, but with a darker central band.
Similar species Yellow-ringed Carpet has a dusting of golden-orange scales through central bands of forewing. Striped Twin-spot Carpet is much smaller and less boldly marked.
Flight season One generation. Late June-early August, later in the north, and in northern Scotland late July-early October. Easily disturbed by day from rocks and vegetation. Flies from dusk and comes to light, sometimes in numbers.
Life cycle Overwinters as a small larva. Larva July or August-late May or June. Pupates in a cocoon among the stems or debris of the foodplant.
Larval foodplants Heathers and Bilberry.
Habitat Mountains and moorland, usually where there are exposed rocks.
Status & distribution Resident. Common. Well distributed and frequent in the uplands in mid and north Wales, northern England and Scotland, and in the Hebrides, Orkney and Shetland. Frequent but more localised in the uplands of south Wales and the English border counties. Local and infrequent on Man. Widespread in Ireland, but with scattered records and no doubt under-recorded.

81

Mallow
page 135

Larentia clavaria (Haw.)
Common. S,C,(N)   1745(8304)

Field characters FW 19-22mm. Comparatively large. The deep, distinctly pointed reddish-brown forewing is diagnostic. Cross-bands finely edged with white, inner edge of central one jagged or with notches, and a light whitish dusting. There is also a pale zigzag line along outer edge. Little variation.
Similar species See Shaded Broad-bar.
Flight season One generation. September-early November. Comes to light in small numbers, seldom seen otherwise.
Life cycle Overwinters as an egg. Larva April-June. Pupates underground.
Larval foodplants Common Mallow, Marsh-mallow, Tree-mallow and Hollyhock.
Habitat Roadside verges, rough, weedy or marshy places, riversides and gardens.
Status & distribution Resident. Common. Fairly well distributed in southern, south-eastern and eastern England north to the Humber. Local further north and west but recorded into southern Scotland, Northumberland, Cumbria, all parts of Wales, and

locally in central and western England to Devon, Cornwall and Scilly. Mainly southern on Man, where local and infrequent. Local in southern Ireland. Widespread and frequent in the Channel Islands.

Shoulder Stripe   page 135

Anticlea badiata ([D. & S.])
Common. S,C,(N)   1746(8309)

Field characters FW 14-18mm. The brown or charcoal-brown forewing is quite broad and often somewhat pointed. There is a distinct straw yellow, brownish-yellow or brown central cross-band, which is almost always paler than the reddish-brown or blackish-brown outer area of wing. Cross-lines are variably edged with black, more so the inner ones, hence the English name.
Similar species None.
Flight season One generation. March-April, sometimes from late February in the south. Often seen flying from dusk onwards and comes to light. Recorded drinking fluid on rose-hips.
Life cycle Overwinters as a pupa, in a cocoon in loose earth. Larva April-July.
Larval foodplants Dog-rose and other wild rose species.
Habitat Woodland, hedgerows and other scrubby places, including gardens.
Status & distribution Resident. Common. Well distributed and frequent throughout England, Wales and parts of mainland Scotland north to Caithness, except the upland areas. Also the Inner Hebrides. Local and infrequent on Man. Widespread and fairly frequent in Ireland. Rare in the Channel Islands.

Streamer   page 135

Anticlea derivata ([D. & S.])
Common. T   1747(8310)

Field characters FW 14-16mm. Quite distinctive. Some examples have a violet tint when freshly emerged. The quite rounded forewing has a pale central band, thickly edged with black on basal side, and with a deeply elbowed outer margin, which is only darkened in leading half. The name 'streamer' refers to this black marking streaming from leading edge. The pattern varies very little, but central band may be whitish, grey or brown.
Similar species Could be confused with worn Barberry Carpet.
Flight season One generation. April-May, sometimes from late March in the south. Occasionally found on fences by day. Flies from dusk and comes to light.
Life cycle Overwinters as a pupa, in a cocoon in loose earth. Larva May-July.
Larval foodplants Dog-rose and probably other species of wild rose. Also more rarely Hawthorn and Blackthorn.
Habitat Open woodland, rides and edges, hedgerows, gardens and other scrubby places.
Status & distribution Resident. Common. Fairly

well distributed and locally frequent throughout England, Wales, Ireland and lowland Scotland, including the Inner Hebrides and very locally on Orkney. Local and infrequent on Man. Rare in the Channel Islands.

Beautiful Carpet   page 136

Mesoleuca albicillata (L.)
Common. S,C,(N)   1748(8312)

Field characters FW 15-18mm. Unmistakable, with very broad, rounded white or creamy-white forewing and broad, white central cross-band. Dark basal area and blotch near tip consist of black, brown and purplish-blue lines. A key feature is that there is no central dark band, which separates it from other black and white carpet moths. There is very little variation.
Similar species None.
Flight season One generation. Late May-early August. Sometimes disturbed by day and comes to light in small numbers.
Life cycle Overwinters as a pupa in loose earth. Larva July-September.
Larval foodplants Bramble, Dewberry, Raspberry and Hazel.
Habitat Mainly open broadleaved woodland and in conifer plantations on ancient woodland sites. Sometimes in long-established scrub and hedgerows, especially on chalk. Occurs on heavy clays but more numerous on well-drained soils.
Status & distribution Resident. Common. Fairly well distributed throughout England, Wales and the southern half of mainland Scotland, and on Mull, but everywhere usually in small numbers. Local and infrequent on Man and in Ireland. Rare on Jersey.

Dark Spinach   page 136

Pelurga comitata (L.)
Common. S,C,(N)   1749(8314)

Field characters FW 16-18mm. Forewing broad and quite rounded, straw-coloured or light brown. Central cross-band wavy, always darker, with a strong, single, often curved central projection, and with increasingly paler bands towards its centre, marked by wavy contours. Has a small dark dot in palest band. The pattern varies only in minor detail.
Similar species Northern Spinach has a double projection on central band. Spinach has a distinctive resting posture. Both lack a central dark dot.
Flight season One generation. July-August. Flies from dusk and comes to light.
Life cycle Overwinters as a pupa underground. Larva late August-October.
Larval foodplants The flowers and seeds of goosefoots and oraches.
Habitat A range of rough open places, including derelict urban plots and some gardens and allotments. Records suggest that it is more numerous in gardens than in the wider countryside, but this is possibly a result of more intensive light-trapping. The

foodplants are very much associated with disturbed ground and coastal situations.

Status & distribution Resident. Common. Well distributed and locally frequent in the London conurbation, more so than elsewhere in Britain. Also well distributed in East Anglia, Essex, the east Midlands, and in the Liverpool-Manchester area. Local or very local in the rest of England and Wales, and more frequently on or near the coast. In Scotland, largely coastal north to Caithness and reported from Skye and the Outer Hebrides. Local and scarce on Man. Widespread but local in Ireland. Local and occasional in the Channel Islands.

Water Carpet   page 136
Lampropteryx suffumata ([D. & S.])
Common. T   1750(8316)

Field characters FW 14-17mm. This moth has a somewhat shiny, rather tapering forewing with leading edge curved. Broad, dark brown central cross-band has a strong, double outer projection. Usually ground-colour is brownish white or light brown. The colours are usually rich and bright, highlighted by white edging. F. *piceata* Steph. is almost uniformly dark brown, but with the usual markings still evident. The infrequent f. *porritii* Robson has an intensely blackish-brown central band contasting sharply with pale ground-colour, and mainly occurs in northern England.

Similar species Devon Carpet is smaller, forewing less tapered (see also under that species). Small Phoenix does not have a shiny texture, cross-band lacks an outer projection and there is a series of well-defined tooth-like marks near outer edge. See also Phoenix, which flies in July-August.

Flight season One generation. April-May. Sometimes disturbed by day, especially in open habitats. Flies from dusk and comes to light, especially to actinic traps near dense vegetation. Usually recorded in small numbers but sometimes locally numerous.

Life cycle Overwinters as a pupa among plant debris. Larva May-June.

Larval foodplants Lady's Bedstraw, Hedge Bedstraw, Cleavers and Heath Bedstraw.

Habitat Damp woodland, scrub, hedgerows, ditches, high moorland, fens and some mature gardens.

Status & distribution Resident. Common. Somewhat thinly distributed but found throughout England, Wales, Man, Scotland, including the Inner Hebrides, and Ireland. Local and occasional in the Channel Islands. Probably under-recorded due to early flight season and often rural habits.

Devon Carpet   page 136
Lampropteryx otregiata (Metc.)
Nb. S,SW   1751(8317)

Field characters & Similar species FW 12-14mm. Not unlike a diminutive Water Carpet, but forewing is less tapering, and in addition to straighter first third of outer edge of central band, its inner edge is

irregular, but with less sharp indentations than in Water Carpet. Small Phoenix lacks a strong central projection on outer edge of central cross-band. Some individuals have rather dark forewing with weak markings.

Flight season Two generations. Mid May-June and early August-mid September. Occasionally disturbed by day among shrubs near larval foodplant. Flies at early dusk and later, and comes to light.

Life cycle Overwinters as a pupa, probably on the ground below moss or plant debris. Larva June-July and September-October. The eggs are laid on the foodplant, near the flowers.

Larval foodplants Marsh Bedstraw and probably Fen Bedstraw.

Habitat Damp woodland, on heavy soils.

Status & distribution Resident. Nationally Scarce B. Occurs locally in south-western and southern England, from Devon and Cornwall to Hampshire, the Isle of Wight, Sussex, Berkshire and Gloucestershire, and in southern and western Wales, from Monmouthshire westwards to Pembrokeshire and northwards to Caernarvonshire and Anglesey. Recorded from one site in Herefordshire, but status unclear. Reliable post-1980 records from a wood near Ashbourne, Derbyshire, and in Sherwood Forest, Nottinghamshire. Some older records suggest it may have a scattering of local colonies in other parts of central and southern England. Recorded once in Jersey, in 1974.

Purple Bar   page 136
Cosmorhoe ocellata (L.)
Common. T   1752(8319)

Field characters FW 13-15mm. When freshly emerged, this moth has a smooth, silky texture. Ground-colour is creamy white, and the broad, dark central cross-band is composed of purplish grey, black and brown. These features are diagnostic. There is little variation.

Similar species None.

Flight season Two generations in the south, May-early July and a partial second early August-mid September. One generation in the north, June-July. Sometimes disturbed by day. Flies from dusk, and comes to light.

Life cycle Overwinters as a cocooned fully-grown larva. Larva June-July and September-April in the south, July-August in the north.

Larval foodplants Bedstraws, such as Hedge Bedstraw and Heath Bedstraw.

Habitat A wide range, including hedgerows, scrub, woodland, calcareous grassland, heathland, breckland, sand-dunes and gardens. In smaller numbers on heavy clay soils.

Status & distribution Resident. Common. Well distributed and fairly frequent throughout England, Wales, Man, Ireland and Scotland, including the Hebrides, Orkney and the Channel Islands.

83

Larva of Chevron.

Striped Twin-spot Carpet page 136

Nebula salicata (Hb.)

ssp. *latentaria* (Curt.)

Common. N,W,(SW)   1753(8321)

Field characters FW 12-15mm. A rather weakly marked, light to dark grey moth. There are numerous faint cross-lines and a slightly darker central cross-band, often with a paler band within it, always with a small blackish, somewhat elongated central spot.
Similar species Garden Carpet f. *thules* has leading half of central cross-band darker, often obscuring the small blackish central spot. See also Twin-spot Carpet and Grey Mountain Carpet.
Flight season Mainly one generation. May-July. In some places at low altitude there is a second generation. August-early September. Often disturbed by day. Comes to light.
Life cycle Overwinters as a cocooned fully-grown larva. Larva July-early August, in some places again in autumn, then remaining dormant in the cocoon until April or May.
Larval foodplants Bedstraws.
Habitat Mainly moorland, particularly where rocks are exposed, but also open woodland, sand-dunes and other grassy places in upland and northern areas.
Status & distribution Resident. Common. Fairly well distributed and frequent in northern England from Lancashire, where somewhat local, northwards, in Scotland, including the Hebrides and Orkney, where local, and in Ireland. Not reliably recorded from Shetland. Well distributed in north and west Wales, local and infrequent in other parts of Wales and on Man. Local and scarce in south-west England. Singletons have been recorded from Dorset, Surrey and Sussex on several occasions, presumably as windblown wanderers.

Phoenix page 136

Eulithis prunata (L.)

Common. T   1754(8330)

Field characters FW 17-19mm. Quite distinctive. Larger than similarly marked moths, with broader forewing and very wavy outer edge to broad brown central band. Varies only slightly in colour and in fine detail of markings. Male rests with end of abdomen curled upwards.
Similar species Water Carpet is smaller and flies in April-May.
Flight season One generation. July-August. Flies from dusk. Comes to light but in small numbers.
Life cycle Overwinters as an egg on the foodplant. Larva April-June. Pupates between spun leaves on foodplant.
Larval foodplants Black Currant, Red Currant and Gooseberry. More frequent on shaded plants.
Habitat Gardens, allotments and woodland, especially along streamsides.
Status & distribution Resident. Common. Widely distributed and regularly seen, in small numbers, throughout England and Wales, more densely in the west and in the London area than elsewhere. Also in lowland Scotland, north to Caithness and Orkney. Fairly widespread and frequent on Man. Local throughout Ireland. Widespread and frequent in the Channel Islands.

Chevron page 136

Eulithis testata (L.)

Common. T   1755(8331)

Field characters FW 13-19mm. Quite a distinctive moth. Diagnostic features are the chevron-shaped central cross-band of forewing, and short, diagonal whitish line at wing tip, which usually forms part of the outline of an orange or brown, roughly triangular blotch on outer edge. Ground-colour varies considerably, from bright brownish orange to light or dark reddish brown, with a variable degree of whitish frosting, another characteristic feature. Female much smaller than male, with narrower forewing. Darkest forms usually found in the north.
Similar species Northern Spinach lacks whitish frosting, has a dark line at forewing tip and central cross-band is not or is less V-shaped, with a distinct double outer projection.
Flight season One generation. July-mid September. Male flies at dusk. Comes to light and rests at night on low vegetation.
Life cycle Overwinters as an egg on the foodplant. Larva May-June. Pupates between spun leaves on foodplant.
Larval foodplants Sallows, Creeping Willow, Aspen and probably other poplars. Also reported from birches, Hazel, Heather and, in the Hebrides, Rowan.
Habitat Most numerous in moorland and scrubby upland grassland, but also in lowland heathland and open woodland, fens, marshes and dune-slacks.
Status & distribution Resident. Common. Throughout Great Britain, including the Outer Hebrides, Orkney and Shetland. Well distributed and frequent in regions with moorland or heathland; more thinly distributed, local and less frequent elsewhere. Fairly widespread and frequent on Man and in Ireland. Local and occasional in the Channel Islands.

Northern Spinach
Eulithis populata (L.)
Common. SW,W,C,N   1756(8332)

page 136

Field characters FW 13-18mm. Forewing varies in colour from straw yellow to orange-brown or dark brown. There is a distinct double tooth-like outer projection on darker central cross-band, which often has a chain of round or oval blotches running through its centre, pale in trailing half. There is a short, dark diagonal line at wing tip, forming one side of the dark, roughly triangular blotch along outer edge. These features are often faint in dark brown examples, which are most frequent in the north, the darkest of all in Orkney and Shetland. Female much smaller.

Similar species See Chevron, Spinach and Dark Spinach.

Flight season One generation. July-August. Easily disturbed by day from low vegetation, rocky outcrops and isolated bushes. Flies from dusk and can be found at rest on heathers and Bilberry after dark. Comes to light, sometimes in numbers.

Life cycle Overwinters as an egg on the foodplant. Larva April-June. Pupates in a light cocoon on food-plant or in debris below.

Larval foodplants Bilberry.

Habitat Moorland, heathland and open, upland woodland.

Status & distribution Resident. Common. A northern and western species, well distributed and frequent to abundant in the uplands of south-west England, throughout Wales, Man, the West Midlands, northern England, and throughout Scotland, including the Hebrides, Orkney and Shetland. There are scattered records from other parts of England, some presumed wanderers but others indicating small past and extant populations on relict heathlands and mosses. Fairly well distrib-uted and frequent throughout Ireland. In the Channel Islands, one reported from Alderney in 1980 and a very old record from Guernsey, both accepted by the Channel Islands Recorder.

Spinach
Eulithis mellinata (Fabr.)
Common. S,C,(N)   1757(8334)

page 136

Field characters & Similar species FW 16-18mm. This moth shares a unique resting posture with Barred Straw: the wings are held out horizontally, away from body and well clear of the surface, with trailing edge of hindwing and tip of abdomen curled upwards. Both species have straw-yellow forewing, but on Spinach outer edge of central cross-band has a large central tooth-like projection and fringes are chequered. Northern Spinach can be somewhat similar, but central band is darker and it rests with wings flat against the surface and closer to the body. See also Barred Straw and Chevron.

Flight season One generation. Mid June-late August. Flies from dusk. Comes regularly to light,

sometimes in fair numbers.

Life cycle Overwinters as an egg on the foodplant. Larva April-May. Pupates among spun leaves on foodplant or on the ground.

Larval foodplants Black Currant and Red Currant.

Habitat Gardens and allotments, including in major urban areas, and woodland. A lowland moth, unlike Northern Spinach.

Status & distribution Resident. Common. Well distributed and fairly frequent throughout England and Wales, except upland areas. Has probably declined in numbers because fewer households grow the foodplants now. Particularly well distributed in and around the London conurbation and in Essex, and the conurbations centred on Birmingham and Liverpool-Manchester. Local in lowland Scotland to the Moray Firth. Local and infrequent on Man, but recorded in most years during the 1990s. Very rare in Ireland, recorded only from the Dublin area, and possibly introduced with cultivated foodplants. Widespread and occasional in the Channel Islands.

Barred Straw
Eulithis pyraliata ([D. & S.])
Common. T   1758(8335)

page 136

Field characters & Similar species FW 15-18mm. Similar in colour and unusual resting posture to the Spinach, also with central cross-band not usually darker than ground-colour. However, this band is narrower in Barred Straw and looks more like two parallel V-shapes and its outer edge does not have a strong projection. Other markings few and simple. Fringes plain brown. Usually a row of brown spots or smears in outer part of forewing, faint or absent in Spinach, which has chequered fringes.

Flight season One generation. Late May-late August, occasionally to early September. Sometimes disturbed from dense vegetation by day. Flies from dusk, and comes to light.

Life cycle Overwinters as an egg. Larva mid April-mid June. Pupates among plant debris.

Larval foodplants Cleavers and other bedstraws.

Habitat Gardens, hedgerows, ditches and roadside verges; also woodland rides and edges, and rough, scrubby grassland.

Status & distribution Resident. Common. Well distributed and frequent throughout England, Wales, Man, Ireland and lowland Scotland north to Caithness, and recorded from Skye. One record from Orkney, on 18 July 1976, a suspected immigrant. Widespread and frequent in the Channel Islands.

Small Phoenix
Ecliptopera silaceata ([D. & S.])
Common. T   1759(8338)

page 136

Field characters FW 13-17mm. Male rests with tip of abdomen curled upwards. There are two main forms in most populations, one in which the broad dark central band across forewing is broken by two broad white lines on wing-veins (f. *insulata* Haw.), and the typical form in which band is unbroken. Both have a distinctive series of dark wedge-shaped markings beyond central band.

Similar species See the spring-flying Water Carpet, the abundant Broken-barred Carpet, the less frequent Phoenix and the rare Netted Carpet.

Flight season Two generations, with individuals from the end of April in the south, May-June elsewhere, with second generation in late July-August, which becomes occasional from Man northwards. Readily disturbed from among the larval foodplant by day. Flies from dusk, and comes to light and sugar.

Life cycle Overwinters as a pupa among plant debris. Larva late June-late July and late August-September.

Larval foodplants Various species of willowherbs, including Rosebay Willowherb and the related Enchanter's-nightshade. May feed on the unrelated Touch-me-not Balsam in Wales, where larvae of this or a closely-related moth may have been mistaken for those of Netted Carpet in recent years.

Habitat Most numerous in woodland rides and glades, but found wherever the foodplants occur, in gardens, overgrown allotments, hedgerows, roadside verges, canal banks, calcareous grassland, heathland, fens and derelict urban sites.

Status & distribution Resident. Common. Well distributed throughout mainland Britain, the Inner Hebrides and Ireland, but not recorded from Man. Usually fairly frequent except on high ground. Rare, presumed immigrant on Orkney. Local and occasional in the Channel Islands.

Red-green Carpet   page 136

Chloroclysta siterata (Hufn.)

Common. T   1760(8341)

Field characters FW 14-17mm. Quite variable. Central cross-band and basal blotch may be weak or strong. In one striking form they are largely greenish black. Most examples can be distinguished from other green geometrid moths by reddish-brown marbling on forewing, often in the form of streaks radiating from base. However, this may be reduced to a small blotch or absent altogether. Also usually a distinct white or pale blotch on leading edge, just beyond central band, which in male has a solid black bar on or near trailing edge. Female generally a slightly darker, richer green, and slightly larger on average. Hindwing grey.

Similar species See Autumn Green Carpet and Beech-green Carpet.

Flight season One generation. September-November, and March-May after hibernation. Comes to light, Ivy flowers and sallow catkins.

Life cycle Overwinters as adult female. Larva June-August. Pupates in plant debris.

Larval foodplants The leaves of various broadleaved trees, perhaps mainly oak, but recorded from Blackthorn, Apple, Cherry, Dog-rose and Rowan (all rose family), and also birches, lime and possibly Ash.

Habitat Broadleaved woodland, hedgerows and gardens with trees in well-wooded areas, particularly in moorland regions.

Status & distribution Resident. Common. Recorded from most parts of Great Britain and Ireland, including a single record for Orkney, on 6 September 1980, possibly an immigrant. Fairly well distributed and fairly frequent in the north and west of Britain. Distinctly local and infrequent over most of England but has increased in range and numbers since the 1980s, for example in Hampshire, Surrey and, to a lesser extent, in the east Midlands. Local and infrequent on Man and in the Channel Islands.

Autumn Green Carpet   page 136

Chloroclysta miata (L.)

Local. T   1761(8342)

Field characters & Similar species FW 15-17mm. Similar to Red-green Carpet, but generally paler and with broader forewing. There are no reddish-brown streaks, and cross-lines and bands are usually more evenly and extensively whitish, with no solid black bar near trailing edge in male. Pale outer cross-band is uniform in colour, but in Red-green Carpet is interrupted by a dark middle patch. Some examples are as dark as some Red-green Carpets, but hindwing whitish, although sometimes with extensive dark grey dusting. An uncommon form is reddish brown either side of central cross-band.

Flight season One generation. September-November, and March-May after hibernation. Often found at rest on leaves by day. Comes to light, Ivy flowers and sallow catkins.

Life cycle Overwinters as adult female. Larva June-August. Pupates in plant debris.

Larval foodplants Sallows, birches, Alder, lime, wild rose, Rowan and probably other broadleaved trees.

Habitat Broadleaved woodland, scrub, hedgerows and gardens in well-wooded areas, particularly in upland and moorland regions.

Status & distribution Resident. Local. Recorded from most parts of Britain and Ireland, including Hoy, Orkney, where larvae found annually. Quite well distributed and fairly frequent in the north and west of Britain where sometimes seen in large numbers, especially in the autumn, along with Red-green Carpet. More local and declining in the south and east, but sometimes frequent where it occurs and may wander. In Yorkshire appears recently to have extended its distribution in lowland areas. Local and infrequent on Man.

Dark Marbled Carpet   page 137

Chloroclysta citrata citrata (L.)

Common. T   1762(8343)

ssp. *pythonissata* Mill.

Shetland and Orkney

Field characters & Similar species FW 14-19mm. Ssp. *citrata* is variable, and very similar to equally variable Common Marbled Carpet, and Arran

Carpet. However, the most reliable character is the central projection of outer edge of central band on forewing which is longer and more pointed. On hindwing, central cross-line usually has a sharp central point and is acutely angled (more rounded and at an obtuse angle in Common Marbled Carpet). These characters are most obvious on underside. Dark-banded examples often have a distinct white flash in leading half outside central band, usually much less distinct in dark forms of Common Marbled Carpet. Most populations are equally variable, but darker forms are more frequent in industrial areas in the Midlands and northern Britain. Ssp. *pythonissata* is darker and less variable than ssp. *citrata*, often with narrow white cross-lines.

Flight season One generation. July-August in the south, late July-September with stragglers into October in northern Scotland. Emerges later than first generation of Common Marbled Carpet, but usually earlier than any second generation. Easily disturbed by day, and comes frequently to light.
Life cycle Overwinters as an egg. Larva April-June. Pupates among plant debris.
Larval foodplants The leaves of many plants, mainly woody species, including birches, heathers, Bilberry and sallow. Also recorded from Wild Strawberry.
Habitat Most frequent in woodland, heathland and moorland, but also in scrub, hedgerows and gardens.
Status & distribution Resident. Ssp. *citrata* Common. Fairly well distributed and moderately frequent in most parts of Britain and Ireland. Possibly under-recorded due to confusion with Common Marbled Carpet. More frequent and often abundant on moorland in the north; local and more restricted to woodland and heathland in some southern parts of England. Fairly widespread but infrequent on Man. Rare in the Channel Islands. Ssp. *pythonissata* throughout Shetland and Orkney.

Arran Carpet   page 137
Chloroclysta concinnata (Steph.)

Na. NW   1763(8344)

Field characters & Similar species FW 14-19mm. Very similar to some darker forms of Common Marbled Carpet, but pattern of white on central band is more irregular and often rather blotchy, and outer edge of band is more irregular and sometimes more pointed. However, some examples are indistinguishable from the Common Marbled Carpet occurring in the same areas and elsewhere in Scotland. See also Dark Marbled Carpet.
Flight season One generation. July-August, as with Common Marbled Carpet in northern and upland locations. Easily found resting on heather after dark, sometimes in numbers. Comes to light.
Life cycle Overwinters as a small larva. Larva September-mid June. Pupates among leaves or plant debris.
Larval foodplants Heather and Bilberry.
Habitat Open moorland.

Status & distribution Resident. Nationally Scarce A. Endemic. The taxonomic status of this moth is uncertain. Now considered by many authorities to be a local form or race of the Common Marbled Carpet, possibly in the process of evolving into a distinct species. Reliably recorded only from extreme western locations in Scotland, including Arran, the Inner Hebrides (Islay, Colonsay, Oronsay, Eigg, Rum, Canna, Skye) and Outer Hebrides (Harris and Lewis, South Uist).

Common Marbled Carpet   page 137
Chloroclysta truncata (Hufn.)

Common. T   1764(8348)

Field characters & Similar species FW 14-19mm. One form of this highly variable moth has a large central light brown patch on forewing, and is unmistakable. Many other forms are very similar to Dark Marbled Carpet (for differences see under that species). Dark grey or blackish forms predominate in some places, especially in southern areas. See also Arran Carpet in north-west Scotland.
Flight season Two generations in most places, May-June and late August-early October. One generation from early July-August at high altitude in Scotland and parts of Ireland, also at low altitude in north-east Scotland and some parts of western Scotland. Easily disturbed by day. Comes readily to light and occasionally visits sugar, over-ripe blackberries and Ivy flowers.
Life cycle Overwinters as a larva. Larva September-May and June-August, or late August-June where there is one generation. Pupates among foliage on the foodplant.
Larval foodplants Many plants, mainly woody species, including sallow, birches, Bilberry, Bramble, heathers, privets and Hawthorn, but also recorded from docks.
Habitat A wide range, including suburban gardens and urban parks, broadleaved woodland and scrub, hedgerows and bushes on calcareous grassland, in fens, heathland, moorland and many coastal situations.
Status & distribution Resident. Common. Well distributed and frequent throughout most of Britain and Ireland. Doubtfully recorded from Shetland. Widespread and frequent on Man and in the Channel Islands.

Barred Yellow   page 137
Cidaria fulvata (Forst.)

Common. T   1765(8350)

Field characters FW 12-14mm. The bright orange-yellow forewing with an irregular reddish-brown and purplish-brown central cross-band makes this moth unmistakable. There is very little variation.
Similar species None.
Flight season One generation. June-early August. Often seen flying around the foodplant from dusk. Comes to light.
Life cycle Overwinters as an egg on the foodplant.

Larva May-June. Pupates in flimsy cocoon in plant debris on the ground.
Larval foodplants Dog-rose, Burnet Rose and probably other wild and cultivated roses.
Habitat Open broadleaved woodland, scrub on calcareous grassland, hedgerows and gardens.
Status & distribution Resident. Common. Well distributed and fairly frequent in most parts of England, Wales and lowland Scotland, including Orkney. Rather local on Man and in Ireland. Widespread and occasional on Jersey, rare on Guernsey.

Blue-bordered Carpet   page 137
Plemyria rubiginata rubiginata ([D. & S.])
Common. S,C   1766(8352)

ssp. *plumbata* (Curt.)
Local. N

Field characters FW 12-15mm. In ssp. *rubiginata* somewhat narrow, rounded forewing with chalky white ground-colour and cold grey or blue-grey outer border is distinctive. Brown central cross-band is reduced to a large blotch on leading edge, and sometimes a small spot on trailing edge. Ssp. *plumbata* differs in that central cross-band is usually either complete or almost so, and outer border is darker. In f. *semifumosa* Cock. forewing is dark grey, with central band still discernible, and in extreme examples hindwing is also grey. This form is frequent in ssp. *plumbata*, but rare in ssp. *rubiginata*.
Similar species None.
Flight season One generation. Late June-early August. Flies at early dusk and again later, when it comes to light in small numbers.
Life cycle Overwinters as an egg, in the fork of a twig on the foodplant. Larva late April-early June. Pupates in a slight cocoon on the foodplant.
Larval foodplants Alder and Blackthorn mainly, but also birches, Hawthorn, Plum and Apple.
Habitat Alder stands by streams and flood meadows, damp woodland (especially around ponds), hedgerows, scrub, orchards and sometimes gardens.
Status & distribution Resident. Ssp. *rubiginata* Common. Fairly well distributed in the lowlands in England, Wales and Ireland, but adults seldom seen in numbers. Local and infrequent on Man. Widespread and occasional in the Channel Islands. Ssp. *plumbata* thinly distributed but locally frequent throughout northern England, lowland mainland Scotland and the Inner Hebrides.

Pine Carpet   page 137
Thera firmata (Hb.)
Common. T   1767(8354*)

Field characters & Similar species FW 13-16mm. Forewing sandy, greyish brown or dark reddish brown. Diagnostic feature is inner edge of central cross-band, which is sharply indented, greatly narrowing the band; in Grey Pine Carpet this edge is

rather irregular or obtusely angled and does not pinch a section out of band. Varies only slightly in detail. Female generally larger.
Flight season One generation. July-November. Easily disturbed from branches of the foodplant by day. Comes to light, sometimes in large numbers.
Life cycle Overwinters as an egg or a very small larva, on the foodplant. Larva usually autumn-July, sometimes later, individual rates of growth being highly variable. Pupates among pine needles on the tree or in fallen debris.
Larval foodplants Scots Pine and Corsican Pine.
Habitat Coniferous woodland, plantations and shelterbelts, especially in sandy areas.
Status & distribution Resident. Common. Well distributed and often abundant in the areas of native and planted pine forest throughout mainland Scotland and in the large plantations of Wales, northern and southern England, East Anglia and on a smaller scale elsewhere, especially on sands and light soils. Recorded once from Orkney, in the company of immigrant moths. Local and infrequent on Man. Widespread but somewhat local in Ireland. Occasional in the Channel Islands.

Grey Pine Carpet   page 137
Thera obeliscata (Hb.)
Common. T   1768(8356)

Field characters FW 13-17mm. This moth is highly variable in ground-colour, ranging from light sandy brown, light or dark greyish brown or blackish. Central cross-band can be reddish brown, dark brown or dark greyish brown. This varies slightly in shape, but is always narrowed (but not pinched out) toward trailing edge. Edges of band are usually fairly smooth or slightly fluted. Female generally larger.
Similar species See Spruce Carpet and Pine Carpet.
Flight season Two generations. May-July and September-November. Often disturbed from trunks and branches of the foodplant by day. Comes to light, sometimes in large numbers.
Life cycle Overwinters as a larva. Larva September-June and July-August. Pupates underground.
Larval foodplants Many coniferous trees, including Scots Pine, Norway Spruce, Douglas Fir, Western Hemlock-spruce, Red-cedar, Lawson's Cypress and Monterey Cypress.
Habitat Coniferous woodland, plantations, parkland and gardens, on many soil types.
Status & distribution Resident. Common. Well distributed and frequent to abundant throughout most parts of Britain and Ireland, including the Inner Hebrides. Recorded from Orkney but possibly immigrant from Caithness where well established. The distribution and number of sites in the British Isles has been greatly increased by large-scale planting of conifers during 19th and 20th centuries. On many more sites than Pine Carpet. Locally frequent, mainly in conifer plantations, on Man. Widespread and frequent in the Channel Islands.

Spruce Carpet

page 137

Thera britannica (Turn.)

Common. T   1769(8358)

Field characters & Similar species FW 13-17mm.
Similar to some forms of Grey Pine Carpet and some
examples, especially very dark ones, are quite difficult
to distinguish. Ground-colour varies from light grey
to blackish grey, often heavily marked and dusted
with white, especially either side of central cross-
band, which is sometimes tinged with brown and is
often more fluted. Edges of central band of Grey
Pine Carpet are smoother. Other cross-lines are often
quite strong. See also Juniper Carpet and Cypress
Carpet.
Flight season Two generations. May-July and
September-November. Frequently disturbed by day
from rest on trunks or among branches of the foodplant. Comes to light, sometimes in large numbers.
Life cycle Overwinters as a small larva. Larva
autumn-May and late June-July. Pupates on or below
ground.
Larval foodplants Many coniferous trees, mainly
Norway Spruce, Sitka Spruce and Western Hemlock-
spruce; also Scots Pine, Douglas Fir, Red-cedar and
occasionally Lawson's Cypress.
Habitat Most abundant in coniferous woodland and
plantations, but also found in parkland and many
gardens.
Status & distribution Resident. Common. Well
distributed, frequent to abundant and increasing in
distribution throughout England, Wales, Man and
Ireland. More local than Grey Pine Carpet in
Scotland, but on the increase. Rare in the Channel
Islands.

Chestnut-coloured Carpet

page 138

Thera cognata (Thunb.)

Nb. C,N   1770(8361)

Field characters FW 11-14mm. The chestnut
ground-colour, rather broad rounded forewing and
small size distinguish this moth from related species.
Central bar across forewing broad throughout, with
no waist or major indentation. Moths from the
Hebrides, Orkney and Shetland are larger and darker
than mainland forms and those from western Ireland
are large and pale, sometimes with violet tints.
Unlikely to be seen far from Juniper.
Similar species Juniper Carpet and Cypress Carpet
have black streaks near tip of forewing.
Flight season One generation. July-August. Comes
to light, sometimes in numbers.
Life cycle Overwinters as a small larva. Larva
September-early June. Pupates in a light spinning
among the leaves of the foodplant or among fallen
needles.
Larval foodplants Common Juniper.
Habitat Moorland, lightly wooded hillsides and
rocky outcrops, including coastal situations.
Status & distribution Resident. Nationally Scarce B.
Widely and well distributed in Scotland, wherever the

Larva of Juniper Carpet.

foodplant grows, including the Hebrides, Orkney and
Shetland. Also present locally in Cumbria, Yorkshire,
north Wales, Glamorgan and Pembrokeshire. Not
recorded from Man. Widespread in western Ireland,
including the Aran Islands.

Juniper Carpet

page 138

Thera juniperata juniperata (L.)

Common. S,C   1771(8362)

ssp. *scotica* (White)

Local. N

ssp. *orcadensis* Cock.

Possibly extinct; resident Orkney

Field characters FW 11-14mm.
Ssp. *juniperata* is a finely-marked, light brownish-
grey moth. Central cross-band is variable and often
consists of a series of rounded, rather pebble-like
blotches, finely etched in black, often with a sharp
indentation on basal side and sometimes broken or
missing in trailing half. One to three more or less
diagonal black dashes near wing tip, sometimes
reaching central band. Female is smaller, with
narrower forewing.
Ssp. *scotica* is smaller and somewhat darker than
ssp. *juniperata*.
Ssp. *orcadensis* is also small, but generally with a
paler, creamier ground-colour, and more boldly
banded than ssp. *scotica*. Moths from south-west
Ireland are also reported to be very pale, but less
strongly marked and larger than ssp. *orcadensis*.
Similar species Cypress Carpet has a black bar on
trailing edge of forewing, central band is indistinct or
not apparent at all, and date of capture may help.
Spruce Carpet is larger, more clouded, and the only
dark dash is a short, diagonal one at forewing tip.
Flight season One generation. Ssp. *juniperata* late
September-early November, ssp. *scotica* September-
October. Sometimes found at rest on foodplant by
day. Much more obvious after dark on outside of
foodplant, sometimes in large numbers, with mating
pairs. Comes to light.
Life cycle Overwinters as an egg on the foodplant.
Larva mid July-early September. Pupates either spun
up among living needles of the foodplant or among
fallen needles accumulating in the plant or below it.
Larval foodplants Junipers, including garden
varieties.

Habitat Ssp. *juniperata* found in native stands of the foodplant, mainly on chalk downland and limestone grassland, but now many additional sites in gardens and parks, on a much wider range of soil types. Ssp. *scotica* and *orcadensis* found in moorland, upland grassland and coastal situations, often on prostrate forms of the foodplant.

Status & distribution Resident. Ssp. *juniperata* was originally local and confined mainly to the chalk downs of south-east, south and central England, the Cotswolds, and the limestone of north Wales, Cumbria and Co. Durham. Since the1960s, it has massively increased its distribution to cover much of England and Wales by exploiting junipers now popularly cultivated in gardens. Single bushes can support populations for many generations and the eggs, larvae and pupae are transported on plants by the nursery trade. All moths examined from gardens conform to ssp. *juniperata,* which is now probably everywhere junipers are grown, including lowland Scotland. First recorded in the Channel Islands in 1999, on Jersey. Ssp. *scotica* is widespread but local in mainland Scotland, particularly the north-east, and on the Inner Hebrides. Ssp. *orcadensis* restricted to Orkney, where found on Hoy in the 19th century but not recently.

Cypress Carpet

Thera cupressata (Geyer)

Uncommon. SE   1771a(8364)

page 138

Field characters & Similar species FW 12-15mm. Distinguished from related species by its more streaky appearance. Has several dark brown streaks or dashes near forewing tip, another in central band and a dark bar placed centrally on or close to trailing edge. Brown central cross-band on forewing is often indistinct, whereas this is well-defined and finely-etched in Juniper Carpet, which may have several dark streaks towards forewing tip. Spruce Carpet, although superficially similar, is without dark streaks.

Flight season Two generations. Late June-July and October-November. Can be found at rest on the foodplant at night. Comes to light.

Life cycle Overwinters as a larva. Larva November-May and late July-September.

Larval foodplants Monterey Cypress and in captivity, Leyland Cypress.

Habitat Parkland and gardens.

Status & distribution Resident (recent colonist) and suspected immigrant. Uncommon. Frequent in the Channel Islands, where it was first recorded in 1985. First recorded in mainland Britain in 1984 in West Sussex, where it is now well established. Also breeding on the Isle of Wight, in Hampshire, Dorset and Devon, and recorded from Cornwall and Surrey. A male at Dungeness, Kent, on 25 October 1999 was the first record for Kent. Widespread and frequent in the Channel Islands.

Netted Carpet

Eustroma reticulatum ([D. & S.])

RDB. WC   1772(8366)

page 138

Field characters FW 13-14mm. Forewing has a distinctive, complex network of white stripes, most of which follow smooth curves. Dark central bar is so broken up with white stripes, especially on veins, that it hardly reaches trailing edges where forewings meet. Some variation in size and shape of dark areas on forewing. Hindwing grey, with a scalloped darker outer band.

Similar species Male Small Phoenix curls its abdomen tip upwards at rest, and in both sexes dark central bar remains pronounced at trailing edge. Central bar and patterns on Broken-barred Carpet have jagged edges.

Flight season One generation. Early July-mid August. Sometimes disturbed by day among foodplant or seen at rest nearby. Flies at dusk, and comes to light.

Life cycle Overwinters as a pupa, in an earthen cocoon on surface of moist ground by the foodplant. Larva late July-early September, occasionally later. Rests under a leaf on the foodplant by day, usually along the mid-vein. Feeds at night, initially making holes in the leaves, then eating into the seed pods.

Larval foodplants Touch-me-not Balsam. Accepts other balsams such as Orange Balsam in captivity but not, apparently, Indian Balsam, which is widely naturalised in the Lake District habitats of the moth and often out-competes Touch-me-not Balsam.

Habitat Wet woodland, by streams or seepages, often on lake shores, below 150m, in very wet, shaded flushes, in areas of high rainfall. Minor ground disturbance required for foodplant establishment; the plant will grow and flower in open situations, but larvae are more frequent where there is dappled shade.

Status & distribution Resident. Red Data Book species. Recorded from the Lake District, Cumbria, since 1856 and from north Wales at intervals since 1886. As a native species the foodplant is virtually confined to these two areas of Britain. The main localities for the moth in the Lake District are Lake Windermere, Coniston and, until recently, Derwent Water. The Welsh sites are all within 20km of each other, near Bala (1930) and Dolgellau (1973), but despite annual searches throughout the 1990s, the only recent records are of two larvae in 1991 and two in 1994, which were small, on late dates, were not reared and are now suspected to have been the Small Phoenix.

Broken-barred Carpet

Electrophaes corylata (Thunb.)

Common. T   1773(8368)

page 138

Field characters FW 14-16mm. Diagnostic feature is narrow, very irregular dark cross-band on forewing, the trailing half of which is usually pinched or broken in two. The whitish edgings to the dark patches are extensive, generally with buff within main white cross-lines, and forewing has an intricately patterned or frosted appearance. F. *albocrenata* Curt., without the central band, is an infrequent form found in Scotland.

Similar species Large female might be confused with Water Carpet, which has a smooth, rather shiny texture, and outer edge of dark central band is less irregular. See also Small Phoenix and Netted Carpet.

Flight season One generation. May-early July. Can sometimes be disturbed from bushes by day. Flies from dusk. Comes to light, sometimes in numbers.

Life cycle Overwinters as a pupa, probably in plant debris. Larva July-September, sometimes early October, growing very slowly.

Larval foodplants Various broadleaved trees, including Common and Midland Hawthorn, Blackthorn, Downy Birch and Pedunculate Oak.

Habitat Mainly broadleaved woodland, hedgerows and other scrubby places; also some parks and gardens.

Status & distribution Resident. Common. Well distributed and locally frequent throughout most of England, Wales, lowland mainland Scotland north to Caithness, the Inner Hebrides and Ireland. The only record from Man was on 5 July 2000, on the Calf of Man. Local and occasional in the Channel Islands.

Beech-green Carpet page 138

Colostygia olivata ([D. & S.])

Local. N,WC,(S) 1774(8371)

Field characters FW 13-15mm. The rounded, dull green (or sometimes lighter) forewing, with numerous fine wavy black cross-lines, and distinct, continuous, fine white edging of darker central band, make this moth distinctive when in fresh condition. However, colour fades with age to yellowish or brownish. Hindwing brownish grey, with chequered fringes. Markings vary only slightly, but examples from northern Britain are darker.

Similar species Red-green Carpet and Autumn Green Carpet lack continuous fine white edging on outside of central band on forewing. Autumn Green Carpet has whitish hindwing. Both these species fly in the autumn and spring.

Flight season One generation. July-August. Easily disturbed by day from trees, rocks, fences and hedgerows. Flies from dusk. Comes to light in small numbers.

Life cycle Overwinters as a small larva. Larva September-May. Pupates among plant debris.

Larval foodplants Hedge Bedstraw, Lady's Bedstraw and Heath Bedstraw.

Habitat Woodland and moorland. In southern Britain usually restricted to calcareous soils.

Status & distribution Resident. Local. Well distributed and sometimes frequent in north Wales, northern England and mainland Scotland. Recorded from Mull and Rum in the Inner Hebrides. Very local in southern Britain, being most frequently found along the coasts of Devon, Dorset and the south side

Larva of Broken-barred Carpet.

of the Isle of Wight, in the Chilterns and in the Cotswolds. Other scattered populations inland, for example at Selborne, Hampshire. Very local in western Ireland and the east coast of Northern Ireland. Reported twice from Guernsey, in 1970 and 1973.

Mottled Grey page 138

Colostygia multistrigaria (Haw.)

Common. T 1775(8376)

Field characters FW 13-17mm. The delicate markings, rather shiny texture (when fresh) and chequered veins on forewing distinguish this moth from all others that fly in the early spring. Forewing somewhat tapered, especially in male, and narrower in female, which is smaller. Ground-colour is usually straw white, sometimes yellowish-tinged. Dark brownish-grey f. *nubilata* Tutt is found in the Midlands, northern England and Scotland.

Similar species None.

Flight season One generation. March-April. Flies from dusk. Often found at rest on short vegetation at night. Comes to light in small numbers.

Life cycle Overwinters as a pupa. Larva May-June.

Larval foodplants Lady's Bedstraw, Heath Bedstraw, Cleavers and probably other bedstraws.

Habitat Heathland, moorland, downland, and woodland rides and clearings.

Status & distribution Resident. Common. Fairly well distributed and almost certainly under-recorded, due to early flight season, in England, Wales, mainland Scotland and the Inner Hebrides. Usually seen in small numbers but can be numerous. Local and infrequent on Man. Widespread but local in the northern half of Ireland.

Green Carpet page 138

Colostygia pectinataria (Knoch)

Common. T 1776(8385)

Field characters FW 12-15mm. When freshly emerged, green ground-colour of forewing separates this often abundant moth from most others, but this quickly fades to white or pinkish white. The arrangement of black blotches and cross-lines on forewing is distinctive, and once the pattern is learned, the moth can be recognised in any condition.

Similar species None.
Flight season Two generations in southern England, May-mid July and August-early September. The second generation was formerly considered occasional and partial but is now annual, and sometimes numerous. One generation in northern Britain, June-August. Easily disturbed by day. Frequently seen at dusk, and comes to light, usually in small numbers.
Life cycle Overwinters as a larva. Larva June-July and September-May where there are two generations, August-May where there is one. Pupates in a cocoon in loose earth.
Larval foodplants Hedge Bedstraw, Heath Bedstraw and other bedstraws, probably including Cleavers. Suspected to feed on Sheep's Sorrel in damp moorland on Orkney, and Marjoram and White Deadnettle also reported.
Habitat Most habitats, including suburban gardens, hedgerows, roadside verges, calcareous grassland, heathland, open woodland, fens and high moorland.
Status & distribution Resident. Common. Well distributed and frequent throughout England, Wales, Man, Ireland and Scotland, including the Hebrides and Orkney. Widespread but occasional in the Channel Islands.

July Highflyer
page 138
Hydriomena furcata (Thunb.)
Common. T   1777(8391)

Field characters FW 14-18mm. Forewings of all three 'highflyer' moths are distinctly shouldered at base, best seen when at rest. July Highflyer flies later in the year than Ruddy and May Highflyers, and lacks pointed black streaks near forewing tip, but has diagonal dash at tip. Also, hindwing usually dull grey, with at most a faint dark central cross-line. It is extremely variable. In shaded southern woodland, it is usually green or blackish brown. In more open habitats, especially in the north and west, paler, greyish or reddish forms are frequent, often incorporating a whitish central cross-band. Of these, the populations associated with moorland, especially those fed on Bilberry, tend to be smaller.
Similar species See May Highflyer and Ruddy Highflyer.
Flight season One generation. July-August in southern Britain. Late July-early October in northern Scotland. Adults are often disturbed by day in shady carr and woodland. Comes to light, sometimes in large numbers.
Life cycle Overwinters as an egg on the foodplant. Larva April-early June, probably slightly later in the north. Feeds at night and hides between spun leaves by day. Pupates near or below ground.
Larval foodplants Hazel, sallows, Creeping Willow, Bilberry and Heather. Also reported on Lodgepole Pine and Sitka Spruce.
Habitat Quite varied. In the south, most numerous in woodland, especially mature Hazel coppice. Also fens, carr, heathland and other scrubby places, including mature parks and gardens, and on moor-

land, particularly in the north.
Status & distribution Resident. Common. Well distributed and frequent to locally abundant throughout England, Wales, Ireland and Scotland, including Orkney and Shetland. Local on Man but abundant in curragh (hedged meadow) areas. Widespread and frequent in the Channel Islands.

May Highflyer
page 138
Hydriomena impluviata ([D. & S.])
Common. T   1778(8392)

Field characters & Similar species FW 13-16mm. As in Ruddy Highflyer, there are two to three short, parallel blackish streaks near forewing tip, and sometimes a diagonal dash at tip. A frequent form is either grey or greenish grey, usually with a fairly broad, whitish-grey central cross-band. F. *obsoletaria* Schille is blackish grey, with only faint markings, and accounts for up to half of the London population. In northern Britain, there is more variation but it is never reddish, like some forms of the Ruddy Highflyer, and has shorter, deeper forewing. See also Ruddy Highflyer.
Flight season One generation. May-early July. Occasionally found by day resting on trunks. Comes to light.
Life cycle Overwinters as a pupa, often under loose bark on the foodplant. Larva July-September or October, even early November, growing slowly. Feeds at night and hides by day between leaves spun together.
Larval foodplants Alder.
Habitat Damp woodland, carr and the banks of watercourses.
Status & distribution Resident. Common. Fairly well distributed throughout most parts of England, Wales, Ireland and Scotland, including the Inner Hebrides and in Orkney, where it is breeding on Alders introduced in the 1850s. Usually seen in small numbers but may be locally numerous. Distinctly local in parts of central England. Rarely recorded on Man.

Ruddy Highflyer
page 138
Hydriomena ruberata (Freyer)
Local. N,W,(S,E)   1779(8393)

Field characters & Similar species FW 14-17mm. In many places, the least frequent highflyer and very rare in southern England. The reddish-brown forms are distinctive, since May Highflyer is never this colour. Greyish forms can be distinguished by the generally slightly longer, relatively narrow forewing. There is sometimes a paler, whitish-grey central cross-band, but seldom contrasts so sharply with ground-colour as in May Highflyer.
Flight season One generation. May-June. Readily disturbed among foodplants by day, sometimes resting on sallow trunks. Often seen flying at dusk. Comes to light.
Life cycle Overwinters as a pupa. Larva July-

September. Feeds at night and hides by day between leaves spun together.
Larval foodplants Broadleaved willows. In some habitats particularly Eared Willow, often on low, often sickly, growth less than about 30cm in height. Abundant on Grey Willow on Orkney.
Habitat Moorland, heathland, bogs, marshes, sallow carr and open woodland.
Status & distribution Resident. Local. Mainly a northern, western and upland species, like one of its preferred foodplants, Eared Willow. Fairly well distributed in north and west Wales, northern England and Scotland north to Caithness and Orkney, including the Inner Hebrides. Somewhat local but sometimes frequent on Man, in Ireland and in south-west England. There are a number of records from southern and eastern England, with confirmed breeding, but the moth is certainly very local in these areas.

Slender-striped Rufous page 139
Coenocalpe lapidata (Hb.)
Na. N   1780(8397)

Field characters FW 13-16mm. Both sexes are distinctive and rest on vertical stems with the paler hindwing partially exposed. Male has sandy brown forewing, quite deeply coloured when in fresh condition but fading on wing. There are numerous deeper red-brown wavy cross-lines but two or three are particularly conspicuous. Forewing has slightly bulbous shoulders and a swept back pointed tip, much more prominent in female, which tends to be a paler, whitish brown, and smaller.
Similar species None.
Flight season One generation. September-early October. Flies during the afternoon in sunny, dry weather and can be numerous, but hides in vegetation if dull or cloudy. From dusk adults can be found at rest on plant stems, probably having crawled up from daytime hiding places. Seldom on the wing at dusk but both sexes, especially male, fly after dark. Male comes to light fairly readily if these are on the breeding site, and occasionally wanders.
Life cycle Overwinters as an egg, on the ground or often attached to plant stems. Larva April-early August. Pupates in an earthen cocoon in the soil surface.
Larval foodplants Uncertain. Probably Meadow Buttercup (frequent at the Lairg site); has been reared on this and on the related Traveller's-joy in captivity, but the latter is absent on the breeding sites.
Habitat Rough, upland pasture and open moorland; often associated with wet flushes dominated by rushes.
Status & distribution Resident. Nationally Scarce A. Almost certainly under-recorded due to remote locations and late flight season. Merited Red Data Book status on the basis of records from 1980-99 (about a dozen sites), but recorded from additional widely scattered sites in recent years. Records are

Larva of Slender-striped Rufous.

scattered through Scotland, mainly in the west, but including Killiecrankie, Perthshire and extending north to Watten, Caithness. Also Farr, near Inverness, and in south Aberdeenshire. Substantial populations at Trinafour, Perthshire and Lairg, East Sutherland. Also recorded from the islands of Canna and Rum, and in the 19th century from Shap Fell, Westmorland. There is an unconfirmed record from Widdybank Fell, Co. Durham, between 1980 and 1982. In Ireland recorded from Cos. Antrim, Donegal, Fermanagh, Sligo, Mayo and Galway. Last recorded in Northern Ireland on 20 September 1914, between Cuilcagh mountain and Florencecourt, Co. Fermanagh.

Small Waved Umber page 139
Horisme vitalbata ([D. & S.])
Common. S,C   1781(8400)

Field characters FW 14-17mm. The broad, blackish band from leading half of outer edge to middle of trailing edge, which merges with band on hindwing when this moth is at rest, make it distinctive. There is slight variation in width of band, intensity of markings and in ground-colour.
Similar species None.
Flight season Two generations. May-June and August. Comes to light.
Life cycle Overwinters as a pupa, in plant debris. Larva June-July and September-October.
Larval foodplants Traveller's-joy.
Habitat Open woodland, scrub and hedgerows on calcareous soils.
Status & distribution Resident. Common. Well distributed and frequent in central southern and south-eastern England and East Anglia. Much more thinly distributed in the south-west and northwards to Lincolnshire, the West Midlands and westwards into south Wales where very local. Recorded in Yorkshire for the first time, in 1996, at Potteric Carr. Rare on Jersey.

Fern page 139
Horisme tersata ([D. & S.])
Common. S,(C)   1782(8402)

Field characters FW 14-18mm. The fine black line across front end of abdomen coincides with second cross-line on forewings when moth is at rest, making a single black streak which is diagnostic. Rather a plain moth, with a slightly rough texture, emphasised by the faint, broken cross-lines and brown flecks on veins. In shape, not unlike an un-banded version of Small Waved Umber, but browner, and quite distinctive. Varies only slightly in shade and in intensity of markings.

Similar species None.

Flight season One generation. Mid June-mid August. Occasionally disturbed from the foodplant by day and seen flying at dusk. Comes to light, usually in small numbers.

Life cycle Overwinters as a pupa, on or below ground. Larva late July-September.

Larval foodplants Traveller's-joy, and probably cultivated Clematis.

Habitat Open woodland, hedgerows and scrub on chalk and limestone, including downland. Increasingly, found in suburban gardens on a greater range of soil types, more so than Small Waved Umber, suggesting breeding on cultivated species of Clematis.

Status & distribution Resident. Common. Quite well distributed and fairly frequent on calcareous soils in England and Wales south of a line from Glamorgan to Lincolnshire. Widespread but occasional in the Channel Islands.

1783 see Appendix

Pretty Chalk Carpet   page 139
Melanthia procellata ([D. & S.])
Common. S,(C)   1784(8411)

Field characters FW 16-18mm. A moth that lives up to its name, with chalky-white wings. Forewing pattern is diagnostic, with dark brown central cross-band stopping abruptly before the middle and a white blotch in the dark brown outer border. There is little variation, chiefly being in the strength of the very fine dark scalloped lines that extend from the central band to the trailing edge.

Similar species None.

Flight season One generation. Early June-late August. Sometimes disturbed by day and comes to light.

Life cycle Overwinters as a pupa, in plant debris or underground. Larva August-September.

Larval foodplants Traveller's-joy.

Habitat Woodland, scrub, hedgerows and some rural gardens on calcareous soils.

Status & distribution Resident. Common. Well distributed and fairly frequent on calcareous soils in south-east England and the southern half of East Anglia. More local westwards to Cornwall and north to Lincolnshire, the West Midlands, Monmouthshire and along the south coast of Wales to Pembrokeshire.

Barberry Carpet   page 139
Pareulype berberata ([D. & S.])
RDB (Protected species). S   1785(8414)

Field characters FW 13-15mm. The dark edging to the twin projections of outer central cross-band, in leading half, often forming a crescent mark, is diagnostic, and remains visible when moth is in worn condition. There is a bold, dark brown belt across central area of forewing and sometimes a smaller one nearer wing base, but extent of dark brown shading near thorax and pale central band are variable. Individuals from Hampshire and Wiltshire tend to be darker than those from Suffolk. Hindwing pale brownish white, with darker border.

Similar species See the more widespread and frequent Streamer, which usually has a greyish tint, and Ruddy Carpet, which is reddish pink.

Flight season Two generations. Early May-mid June, occasionally to late June, and late July-August. Flies from dusk, comes to light and sometimes disturbed from the foodplant by day.

Life cycle Overwinters as a pupa in a light cocoon, sometimes in leaf litter but usually just below ground. Larva early June-mid July, occasionally to late July; and late August-September, often pupating by mid September. Larvae bask in sunshine.

Larval foodplants Barberry. On one site, breeds on an introduced *Berberis turcomanica*. Will accept some widely-grown soft-leaved cultivated species, including Thunberg's Barberry and *B. ottawensis*, but no colonies known on these in the wild.

Habitat Mainly open hedgerows, both on pastoral and arable farms. Occasionally edges of woods. Highest densities of larvae on hedges not trimmed until late autumn, after pupation; lowest on untrimmed, overgrown hedges.

Status & distribution Resident and suspected immigrant. Red Data Book species. Ten wild breeding populations were recorded during the 1990s: Suffolk (known since the 1860s, monitored annually but now probably lost owing to a fire); Hampshire (last seen in 1992); Dorset (found in 1997, probably a rediscovery of a colony known in the 1920s); Gloucestershire (recorded at intervals since 1960); and six in Wiltshire (all discovered between 1997-99, two of which are extensive). Occasionally reported in light-traps elsewhere, suggesting undiscovered colonies, e.g. Devon (1959), West Sussex (1969), Oxfordshire (1979 and 1981), Hampshire (1984 and 1990). Formerly widespread in southern Britain, extending northwards at least to Yorkshire and from Somerset to Sussex, but many colonies lost through removal of Barberry. There is one record for Scotland (Kinlochewe, 1937), which needs researching. In 1996, two males were recorded as suspected immigrants, on the south coast of Kent in areas without the wild foodplant, one on 17 August, at Dungeness, the other nearby on 21 August, at Greatstone, during a period of much immigrant activity.

White-banded Carpet
page 139

Spargania luctuata ([D. & S.])

Na. SE   1786(8417)

Field characters FW 14-15mm. The single broad and angled white band across centre of otherwise largely dark forewing is diagnostic; band is continued, but wider, on hindwing, which has a broadly blackish border. A blunt dark tooth, with two rounded lobes, projects into band.

Similar species Cloaked Carpet has green scales, like algae, on forewing bases near thorax. Outer edge of dark central band of Sharp-angled Carpet has a single sharp tooth. Both have paler outer areas.

Flight season Two generations. Mid May-mid June and mid July-late August, but the second generation may be only partial. Easily disturbed from low vegetation, and sometimes flies in afternoon sunshine and in the early evening. Comes readily to light. Sometimes, in Orlestone Forest, 100 or more have been recorded at a single Robinson trap in a night.

Life cycle Overwinters as a pupa on the ground, among plant debris. Larva mid June-late July and late August-September.

Larval foodplants Rosebay Willowherb. Has been reared on Broad-leaved Willowherb and Square-stalked Willowherb, so may not be totally dependent on Rosebay.

Habitat Broad rides, clearings and bonfire sites in woodland or recent plantations, rather than on open ground such as railway embankments, where the foodplant also grows.

Status & distribution Resident. Nationally Scarce A. A fairly recent colonist. The first British specimen was recorded on 2 June 1924 in north-west Kent, and widespread colonisation took place in the 1950s. Now well established in the large woodland complexes of the Orlestone Forest area of south-east Kent, the Beckley Wood area of East Sussex and throughout the Thetford Forest area in Norfolk and west Suffolk. Wanders and has sometimes established breeding colonies elsewhere, which have persisted for some years. Occasional individuals recorded as far afield as Brentwood, Essex (15 June 1974), Usk, Monmouthshire (17 May 1975), and Harpenden, Hertfordshire (1 June 1992). Currently does not appear to be breeding west of the Isle of Wight.

Argent & Sable
page 139

Rheumaptera hastata hastata (L.)

Nb. S,C   1787(8419)

f. *nigrescens* (Prout)

Nb. N

Field characters Easily recognised by distinctive black and white pattern on wings. Ssp. *hastata* is generally larger, FW 16-19mm, and black markings are intensely black. In f. *laxata* Krul., the main white band across forewing is expanded at the expense of the central black markings, making the moth look much whiter. Sometimes this form is almost as small

as f. *nigrescens*. Occasionally the dark markings are extremely reduced (f. *demolita* Prout).

F. *nigrescens* is smaller, FW 13-15mm, markings are more intricate and often tend to brownish black or greyish black.

Similar species Small Argent & Sable is superficially similar to f. *nigrescens* but smaller, with a straighter leading edge to forewing and central dark band across forewing rarely broken.

Flight season One generation. May-June. Active by day, especially in sunny or warm weather. Males seen searching for scent of females. Female seen egg laying by day.

Life cycle Overwinters as a pupa, in plant debris. Larva late June-mid August in southern Britain, early July-early September further north, living between spun leaves.

Larval foodplants Ssp. *hastata* on seedlings and low regrowth of Downy Birch and Silver Birch, usually on plants less than 40cm tall, in full sunshine, and on Bog-myrtle. F. *nigrescens* on Bog-myrtle and possibly birches.

Habitat Open and partially cleared or coppiced broadleaved woodland, newly established conifer plantations, moorland and bogs.

Status & distribution Resident. Nationally Scarce B. Ssp. *hastata* formerly throughout most of England to the southern uplands of Scotland, except East Anglia, but now only thinly scattered, mainly in the West Midlands and south. In Ireland, widespread but mainly in the west, where a fair proportion conform to f. *laxata*. The moths in the southern borders of the Scottish Highlands are diminutive but recognisable as ssp. *hastata* f. *laxata*. Such small-sized, whitish forms have also been recorded in north Wales and parts of Yorkshire. F. *nigrescens* occurs in the Hebrides and far north-west of Scotland, especially near the coast and at higher altitudes inland. There is some doubt as to whether f. *nigrescens* occurs in Ireland due to possible confusion with f. *laxata*. Considered vagrant on Man, where the only records are singletons in 1893 and 1954. Two reported from Guernsey about 1889.

Scarce Tissue
page 139

Rheumaptera cervinalis (Scop.)

Local. S,C   1788(8421)

Field characters & Similar species FW 19-22mm. Similar to Tissue, but with forewing slightly narrower and more pointed, with a rather rough texture, not shiny, and not marked with pink. Central cross-lines are closer together, often merged, and usually blackish brown. Hindwing outer margins are irregularly saw-toothed rather than scalloped. On underside, small dark central spots are bold and intense, and there are two small dark spots on leading edge, near base. In Tissue, this area is either plain or has a dark, roughly elliptical mark, with a pale inner spot. See also Irish Annulet.

Flight season One generation. April-June. Can be seen flying over foodplant at dusk, and female can

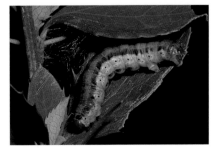

Larva of Scarce Tissue.

be found laying eggs after dark. Comes to light in small numbers.
Life cycle Overwinters as a pupa underground. Larva June-July.
Larval foodplants Barberry, and cultivated *Berberis*, including Thunberg's Barberry, Mrs Wilson's Barberry, *B. ottawensis*, and *Mahonia*, in sunny situations.
Habitat Hedgerows, gardens, parks and amenity plantings such as on roadside verges in suburbs.
Status & distribution Resident. Local. Evidently overlooked. Searches for larvae in recent years have revealed the moth in many rural places not previously recorded. Quite well distributed in southern and eastern England and found throughout most parts of England and Wales wherever Barberry grows or has been planted, north to Northumberland, and west to Pembrokeshire and Cornwall. Apparently not yet recorded from Man, Ireland or the Channel Islands but likely to be present on cultivated plants. Likewise, probably present quite widely in southern Scotland.

Scallop Shell   page 139
Rheumaptera undulata (L.)
Local. S,C,(N)   1789(8423)

Field characters FW 16-19mm. The numerous, tightly-packed, contoured, dark brown wavy cross-lines on whitish-buff wings are diagnostic. There is little variation, but sometimes cross-lines are more broadly spaced across centre of forewing, or somewhat thicker and forming a dark band.
Similar species None.
Flight season One generation. June-July. Occasionally seen feeding by day at flowers such as Common Valerian. Comes to light, usually in small numbers.
Life cycle Overwinters as a pupa, in a fragile cocoon in loose earth. Larva August-September.
Larval foodplants Sallows, Aspen and Bilberry.
Habitat Damp woodland, sallow scrub and carr.
Status & distribution Resident. Local. Widespread but rather thinly distributed throughout England, southern Scotland and Ireland. Better distributed in south-west and southern England and western Wales than elsewhere, but sometimes locally frequent even

on sites in eastern England. Local and infrequent on Man, in the north of the island, and on Jersey.

Tissue   page 139
Triphosa dubitata (L.)
Local. S,C   1790(8428)

Field characters FW 19-22mm. Forewing very broad and quite rounded, brown or greyish brown, and smooth and rather shiny. Some examples are delicately marbled with pink. Intensity of markings varies, but usually two narrow, darker brown central cross-bands are discernible, with conspicuous dark patches, well separated by a paler area. Both wings have scalloped outer edges, the hindwing more so, emphasised by a very fine black line. On underside, dark central spots on both wings are quite small and that on forewing is narrow.
Similar species See Scarce Tissue and Irish Annulet.
Flight season One generation. August-October, and after hibernation April-May. Comes to light in small numbers, and to flowers such as sallow, Ivy and buddleias. More frequent in hibernation sites and as larva.
Life cycle Overwinters as an adult, in caves, disused buildings, outhouses and bunkers, sometimes in large aggregations of 40 or more. Larva May-early July.
Larval foodplants Buckthorn and Alder Buckthorn.
Habitat Woodland, scrub and hedgerows, both on calcareous grassland, neutral clays and acid heathland.
Status & distribution Resident. Local. Somewhat thinly distributed, usually at low density, throughout England, Wales, Ireland and southern-most Scotland. Local and rare on Man and in the Channel Islands.

Brown Scallop   page 139
Philereme vetulata ([D. & S.])
Local. S,(not SW),C   1791(8432)

Field characters FW 13-16mm. A muddy, rather light grey-brown moth, with numerous very faint cross-lines and a very small round dark dot near centre of each forewing. Fringes are chequered grey and buff and outer margins of hindwing are scalloped. Female is slightly larger.
Similar species See Dark Umber, which often breeds on the same bushes, is larger and darker, with a more conspicuous dark central band on forewing.
Flight season One generation. Late June-July. Occasionally disturbed from the foodplant by day, and seen on the wing at dusk. Comes to light in small numbers.
Life cycle Overwinters as an egg on the foodplant. Larva May-June. Feeds at night and hides between spun leaves by day.
Larval foodplants Buckthorn. Apparently not recorded on Alder Buckthorn, and national distribution coincides with the more restricted distribution of Buckthorn.
Habitat Woodland, scrub and hedgerows, particu-

larly on calcareous soils, including fens, but also on neutral clays and on a number of more acid sites, especially in Yorkshire.

Status & distribution Resident. Local. Widely and well distributed in the southern half of England, north to the Wash, from the Welsh border to East Anglia. Very scarce or absent in Devon and Cornwall (one record, Bodmin, pre-1906) and on the Wealden Clay of south-east England, as is Buckthorn but not Alder Buckthorn, which is very well distributed in these areas. Occurs more locally north to Yorkshire, and at Roudsea Woods, Cumbria, where Buckthorn is near its northern limit. Very local in south Wales. Present in Ireland but under-recorded. Discovered in 1996 near Crom Castle, Co. Fermanagh, where it has since proved locally frequent, and at Lough Cutra, Co. Galway. The only previous Irish records were of larvae at Kenmare, Co. Kerry, in 1939.

Dark Umber   page 139
Philereme transversata (Hufn.)

ssp. *britannica* Lempke

Local. S,(not SW),C   1792(8433)

Field characters FW 17-20mm. A rich brown to very dark brown moth, with broad and rather tapering forewing. The darker central cross-band is strongly angled at leading edge, and has a strong, double-pointed (usually), tooth-like projection on its outer edge, at the angle. Outer margins of both wings are scalloped, especially hindwing. This combination of features is diagnostic. The strength of the cross-lines varies considerably.

Similar species See Brown Scallop, which is smaller and paler.

Flight season One generation. July-August. Occasionally disturbed from the foodplant by day and seen on the wing at dusk. Comes to light.

Life cycle Overwinters as an egg. Larva late April-early June. Feeds at night and hides between spun leaves by day.

Larval foodplants Buckthorn and also Alder Buckthorn.

Habitat Woodland, scrub and hedgerows, particularly on calcareous soils, including fens, but also on neutral clays and more acidic sites.

Status & distribution Resident. Local. Widely and well distributed in the southern half of England, from the Welsh border to East Anglia, but much scarcer in Devon and Cornwall and on the Wealden Clay of south-east England, as is Buckthorn but not Alder Buckthorn, which is very well distributed in these areas. More local from the Wash northwards to Yorkshire and south Cumbria. Very local in south Wales. In Ireland known from the Burren, Co. Clare, since 1952, and in July 2000 discovered in numbers on the Crom Estate, Co. Fermanagh. Reported once from Guernsey about 1889.

Cloaked Carpet   page 139
Euphyia biangulata (Haw.)

Nb. W,S,SE   1793(8435)

Field characters & Similar species FW 14-17mm. The most conspicuous feature is dark central band across forewing, with its double-toothed outer edge projecting into a whitish band, but see also Sharp-angled Carpet and White-banded Carpet. However, the greenish scales on base of forewing, like a growth of algae, distinguish this moth. Hindwing pale brownish white, with darker border.

Flight season One generation. Late June-mid August. Occasionally disturbed by day. Comes to light, usually from about midnight.

Life cycle Overwinters as a pupa, in a cocoon in loose earth. Larva late July-mid September, feeding at night.

Larval foodplants Stitchworts. Accepts Common Chickweed in captivity.

Habitat Damp, mossy woodland and wooded rocky ravines with streams. Also in old banked hedgerows along sunken lanes.

Status & distribution Resident. Nationally Scarce B. Quite well distributed, but usually found in small numbers, in south-west England and Wales north to Man, where it is local. Reported in Kirkudbrightshire in 1998. Local but increasing in range in east Dorset, Hampshire, the Isle of Wight and west Surrey. Also present locally in woodlands in the West Midlands and near the coasts of Essex and north Kent. Occurs locally in central and southern Ireland. Recorded from Jersey, as singletons in 1970, 2000 and 2002.

Sharp-angled Carpet   page 139
Euphyia unangulata (Haw.)

Local. S   1794(8436)

Field characters FW 13-15mm. Outer edge of central cross-band sweeps cleanly from trailing edge, to form a sharp point. This contrasts starkly with whitish band beyond, which usually has only the faintest of grey lines running through it. Usually, cross-band is fairly uniformly dark. Also, hindwing largely whitish, with grey borders and only faint grey lines near base.

Similar species Common Carpet and Wood Carpet both have a more irregular central cross-band, with a blunt outer projection and sometimes a noticeable grey component. Also, markings near base of hindwing are stronger. See also White-banded Carpet and Cloaked Carpet.

Flight season One generation. Late June-early August. May be disturbed from bushes and other vegetation by day. Flies from dusk and comes to light in small numbers.

Life cycle Overwinters as a pupa underground. Larva July-September.

Larval foodplants Unknown in the wild. Common Chickweed and stitchworts in captivity.

Habitat Woodland and wooded hedgerows.

Status & distribution Resident. Local. Quite well

97

distributed, usually in small numbers, from Scilly to Kent, northwards to the Wash, especially in central southern England, western Wales and East Anglia. Distinctly local in the Midlands. Local and rare on Man. A very few records from northern England and mainland Scotland, some of which may be misidentifications, but a single confirmed specimen was captured at Kielder Castle, Northumberland, in 1971, where it was presumed a stray. Widespread and fairly well distributed in Ireland.

Epirrita male genitalia

November Moth
E. dilutata

Pale November Moth
E. christyi

Autumnal Moth
E. autumnata

Epirrita November moths

The four species of *Epirrita* found in Britain are at first sight confusingly similar. The Small Autumnal Moth can be distinguished on the basis of its earlier flight season, generally smaller size and restriction to moorland habitat. The other three species have forewings which vary from almost uniform unbanded dark grey-brown to light grey-brown with distinct banding. Strongly-patterned individuals can usually be identified by subtle differences in wing markings, these forms seem to be more frequent in the north and uplands, while the drab forms are more frequent in lowlands.

The live males of all four species can easily be identified by examination of the underside of the abdomen tip under a hand-lens or low-power microscope. This is facilitated by the removal of some of the scales from the abdomen tip with a damp brush. The scales are much easier to remove, and the details much easier to see, in live or freshly-dead moths than in dried specimens, in which the abdomens are shrunken. Rather than man-handle live moths, another possibility is to anaesthetise them by placing them in ethyl acetate vapour until they are still. The females differ from the males in having narrower wings, with more of a 'shouldered' appearance when at rest, due to more bulbous wing bases. Their leading edges are more curved and the hindwings protrude more beyond them at rest. They are generally more heavily banded. To confirm identity of females requires examination of the genitalia.

A few adults of each species can sometimes be seen flying just before dusk, but the main flight is after dark. They often come to light in large numbers. While some individuals may be particularly difficult to identify, examination of large samples should soon reveal which of the species are present on any site. Usually the November Moth is the most numerous of the three species found in woodland and gardens, where many individuals are particularly dark and drab. Accepting that the differences in wing pattern given in 'Field characters' are tendencies rather than absolute differences, sometimes even differing between the two forewings of the same individual, these and the abdominal differences of the males can be used to select from large samples a few likely individuals of each species for

abdomen or genitalia examination, confirmation of identity and retention as voucher specimens, thereby avoiding killing larger numbers. It is also the case that one gets to know how the various species look at a particular site, improving reliability of diagnosis at that site, although in another locality the moths may look quite different.

November Moth   page 140
Epirrita dilutata ([D. & S.])
Common. T   1795(8442)

Field characters & Similar species FW 15-20mm. Clasper (valve) of male, viewed from underside of abdomen tip, has a curved spur, which distinguishes it from Autumnal Moth. Trailing edge of last plate on underside of abdomen (8th sclerite or octaval) has two tooth-like projections which are widely spaced (0.43mm apart on average), compared with about 0.23mm in Pale November Moth. On forewing, in well marked individuals inner margin of outer band across centre usually extends inwards to run through central spot where this is present; in Pale November Moth and Autumnal Moth, central spot is usually clearly separate from the band running outside it, and in Autumnal Moth the band angles more sharply around it. Uniformly dark *Epirrita* moths are usually November Moth, unless they have a conspicuous dark, often smeared, V-mark where the vein forks in centre of forewing. The latter are usually Autumnal Moths, but examination of genitalia is needed for confirmation.
Flight season One generation. Early October-November, but from mid-September in northern Britain.
Life cycle Overwinters as an egg on a twig or bark. Larva late April-June. Pupates underground.
Larval foodplants Most broadleaved trees and shrubs, including oaks, birches, elms, sallows, Aspen, Ash, Hazel, hawthorns, Blackthorn, Plum, Crab Apple and Bilberry.
Habitat The least choosy *Epirrita* species, most abundant in broadleaved woodland but frequent in scrub, hedges and gardens.
Status & distribution Resident. Common. Well distributed and abundant throughout most of the British Isles, including Man and Ireland, but not confirmed from Orkney or Shetland. Widespread and abundant on Jersey and probably elsewhere in the Channel Islands.

Pale November Moth
page 140
Epirrita christyi (Allen)
Common. S,C,(N)   1796(8443)

Field characters & Similar species FW 15-20mm. Teeth on outer edge of underside of eighth abdominal segment are closely spaced (0.23mm apart on average), unlike both November and Autumnal Moths, and clasper (valve) has a ventral spur unlike Small Autumnal Moth. Once learned, these characters can lead to quick identification of males. This is otherwise a difficult species to distinguish with certainty from November Moth. Central spot, when present, usually stands separate from the inner margin of outer central forewing band, as in Autumnal Moth, but not so widely separate. Central V-mark where vein forks tends to be more sharply defined and narrow, where present. Banded pale grey *Epirrita* moths tend to be Pale November Moth. Brown forms often have central forewing bands amalgamated, forming a broader brown area.
Flight season One generation. Late September-November. Peak numbers usually mid-late October, a little later than the November Moth.
Life cycle Overwinters as an egg on a twig or bark. Larva late April-June. Pupates underground.
Larval foodplants Beech, elms, birches, Alder, Hazel, hawthorns, sallows. Beech and Wych Elm appear to be favoured foodplants and the species is sometimes the most numerous of the November moths where these are abundant. Accepts Hornbeam in captivity.
Habitat Most often reported from mature woodland, from which large samples of *Epirrita* moths can be obtained to search out this species. In Lancashire, more frequent in upland woodland than in the lowlands. Foodplants, habitat preferences and distribution incompletely known due to difficulties of identification of the moth and its larvae.
Status & distribution Resident. Common. Likely to be misidentified as a November Moth and therefore overlooked, but almost certainly more localised. Confirmed records are widespread but thinly scattered throughout England, Wales, southern Scotland, Northern Ireland and the Irish Republic. Sometimes abundant, as in one sample from Yorkshire and another from Essex, but apparently unrecorded in some northern counties of Scotland. Not confirmed from Man and the Channel Islands.

Autumnal Moth
page 140
Epirrita autumnata (Borkh.)
Common. T   1797(8444)

Field characters FW 16-20mm. Clasper (valve) of male, viewed from underside of abdomen tip, has no spur. Both sexes are usually slightly larger than other *Epirrita* species on same site but size is very variable. Forewing usually banded, frequently strongly, with a prominent heavy dark V-mark in centre where vein forks. Upper vein radiating from this point bears several alternate bands of dark brown and white

scales, and above point of the V there is a small spot, usually distinctly and widely separated from outer of the two central bands which angles sharply around it. Occasionally spot is completely absent or very close to the angle of the outer central cross-band. The sharp angle is almost diagnostic even if the spot is not visible. Ground-colour often silvery. Some examples may have almost uniformly dark forewing, but V-mark is usually darker, heavy and conspicuous.
Similar species Both November Moth and Pale November Moth have a spur on lower edge of clasper, not present in Autumnal Moth, but the scales must be removed to see it. Forewing spot in November Moth is usually incorporated into outer of the two central bands where present, and less well separated in Pale November Moth.
Flight season One generation. October-November, usually starting two or three weeks later than the November Moth in the same area.
Life cycle Overwinters as an egg on a twig or bark. Larva late April-June. Pupates underground.
Larval foodplants Birch (both Silver and Downy) and Alder, and also Heather, with occasional records from other broadleaved species. Has also been reported from Larch and Scots Pine. Accepts Hawthorn in captivity.
Habitat Possibly prefers the foodplants in more open situations such as in rides and paths in woodland, where the larvae are sometimes frequent on young re-growth. Abundant in Scottish birch woods. Also mixed broadleaved woodland, some gardens and scrub in uplands and lowlands, including on heathland and moorland.
Status & distribution Resident. Common. Confirmed records are thinly scattered but widespread throughout mainland Britain, where it is often abundant in both north and south, likewise on Man and in Ireland. Not confirmed from Orkney and Shetland. Confirmed from Jersey but apparently rare.

Small Autumnal Moth
page 140
Epirrita filigrammaria (H.-S.)
Common. N,C,W   1798(8445)

Field characters FW 14-18mm. An *Epirrita* moth in August, in northern moorland, is almost certain to be this species. Like Autumnal Moth, clasper (valve) of male has no spur, but moth is normally noticeably smaller and generally darker. However, the largest examples may be as large as Autumnal Moth, and indistinguishable on wing markings. Banding on forewing varies from weak to very strong and dark. Central spot distinct and widely separated from banding when present, but often obscure or absent.
Similar species See the other three *Epirrita* species and the two Winter moths *Operophtera* species, all of which are unlikely to be seen before late September.
Flight season One generation. August-September. Often seen in large numbers, hanging from stems of Heather just after dark.
Life cycle Overwinters as an egg attached to the

99

foodplant. Larva mid April-late May. Larvae are quite distinct from the other *Epirrita* species, having a pronounced yellow sub-dorsal stripe from head to tail, a dark green dorsal line and a more olive body colour. Pupates underground.

Larval foodplants Heather, Bilberry and sallows. Has been reported from European Larch.

Habitat Moorland. Tall heathers preferred.

Status & distribution Resident. Common. Apparently endemic to Britain. Locally widespread and sometimes abundant in northern upland areas, including mainland Scotland, Inner Hebrides, Isle of Arran, Orkney, also South Barrule on Man, north and central Wales, northern England and south to Leicestershire and Shropshire, and well represented in Northern Ireland and the Republic.

Operophtera Winter moths

The males of both the Winter Moth and the Northern Winter Moth are noticeably smaller than the November moths, especially obvious at rest, and have more rounded tips to the forewing. The female is wingless, unlike female *Epirrita* moths.

Winter Moth   page 140
Operophtera brumata (L.)
Common. T   1799(8447)

Field characters FW 13-16mm. The males of this species are the brownish moths most often seen in numbers flying weakly in car headlights in the late autumn and early winter, especially by woods and hedgerows. They are a drab light to dark brown, with a darker central forewing band which is often indistinct. Hindwing brown. Male varies quite markedly in size, even on the same site. Female cannot fly and has only rudimentary black-banded wings, and is sometimes carried in flight during copulation by the male. It is much smaller than the other wingless female geometrid moths found in the autumn.

Similar species See Northern Winter Moth. The November moths are usually greyer and larger, with

Larva of Winter Moth.

more pointed forewing tip. See also March Moth (female).

Flight season One generation. October-January. Comes well to light, including lighted windows. Both sexes can be found at rest or walking up tree trunks after dark.

Life cycle Overwinters as an egg on a twig or in a bark crevice near a leaf bud. Larva April-early June, falling to the ground to pupate in a tough cocoon on or below ground.

Larval foodplants Almost any broadleaved tree or shrub, including oaks, birches, sallows, hawthorns, Blackthorn, Hazel, Sycamore, Wild Service-tree and Apple. Also heathers and Bog-myrtle. Recently reported in northern plantations, as a major pest on Lodgepole Pine, and on Sitka Spruce, especially where planted under broadleaved trees, but also on previously open sites.

Habitat Wherever there are trees and shrubs, including hedgerows and gardens, except at high altitude.

Status & distribution Resident. Common. Well distributed and abundant throughout the British Isles, including Orkney and Shetland, Man and Ireland and in the Channel Islands. Occasionally a pest, sometimes blamed for defoliating plantations and orchards, stressing the plants and reducing productivity, but this is likely to be the cumulative effect of several species of moth.

Northern Winter Moth   page 140
Operophtera fagata (Scharf.)
Common. T   1800(8448)

Field characters & Similar species FW 14-18mm. Male is quite similar to Winter Moth, but paler and somewhat silky in appearance. Forewing is more tapering and hindwing whitish. In the distinctive female, wings reach half length of abdomen and forewing is noticeably black-banded. See also November moths.

Flight season One generation. October-December, but mainly November. Male frequently seen in light-traps. Both sexes sometimes found by searching foodplants after dark.

Life cycle Overwinters as an egg on foodplant. Larva April-June. Pupates underground.

Larval foodplants Mainly birches and Alder in woodland, but also reportedly on Beech and fruit trees such as Apple, Plum and Cherry.

Habitat Woodland, heathland, scrub, gardens and orchards.

Status & distribution Resident. Common. Records almost certainly confused with the Winter Moth. Fairly well distributed and sometimes locally frequent throughout much of England, except the south-west, but seems to have become less numerous and more local in recent years. Widely but thinly scattered in Wales, mainland Scotland and the Inner Hebrides. Local and rare on Man. Unconfirmed from Ireland.

Barred Carpet   page 140
Perizoma taeniata (Steph.)
Na. C,N   1801(8454)

Field characters FW 11-12mm. Forewing brown, sometimes heavily marked with dark grey, with a grey basal blotch and a gently curved, grey central cross-band, darkest on veins, thinly edged with white on either side. Outer edge of band is finely scalloped, and has a kink at leading edge. A dark outer band starts at leading edge, but stops abruptly before middle, where there is sometimes a white patch. Hindwing only faintly banded.

Similar species Barred Rivulet, normally found in more open lowland habitat, is smaller, and outer edge of warmer central band on forewing is more irregular. Tip of forewing is less rounded, with two small dark spots close by, and no distinct white patch near outer edge. Foxglove Pug and Toadflax Pug can have similar forewing markings, but have intricately banded hindwing and a distinctive resting posture. See also Yellow-barred Brindle.

Flight season One generation. Late June-mid August or even early September. Sometimes flies in late afternoon. Has been seen at rest on moss-covered rocks and found by beating the branches of trees and shrubs such as Holly and Yew. Flies soon after dark and has been reported at the flowers of rushes and grasses. Comes to light in very small numbers.

Life cycle Overwinters as a larva, probably among moss or plant debris. Larva August-May.

Larval foodplants The only report of a wild larva dates from the 19th century, when one was found and reared on the seed capsules of a moss growing in a damp situation. Apparently, the only flowering plants present were Wild Strawberry, Dog's Mercury, Germander Speedwell and Ivy. It has been reared on moss capsules subsequently and accepts a range of stand-bys, including Chickweed, Knotgrass, Dandelion, Ivy-leaved Toadflax (avidly), Wild Strawberry and, recently, Selfheal.

Habitat Damp woodland and other sheltered, damp places on base-rich rocks.

Status & distribution Resident. Nationally Scarce A. Somewhat under-recorded. A thin scatter of records in mainland Scotland north to Inverness-shire, in northern England and north Wales. Discovered in Cardiganshire in the 1980s. Known from the Tintern area of Monmouthshire since 1859. Occasional records from south-west England, including Watersmeet, near Lynton, north Devon, where it has been recorded for over 100 years. Occasionally seen in numbers (e.g. over 100 at Loch Arkaig, on 2 August 1978). Other well-known localities include Dovedale, Derbyshire (known since 1866), Arnside Knott, Cumbria, and below Dib Scar near Grassington, Yorkshire. Widely distributed in Ireland, mainly in the north and west. Some reports of the species in southern Britain are mis-identifications of the Yellow-barred Brindle, a much more widespread and frequent species.

Rivulet   page 140
Perizoma affinitata (Steph.)
Common. T   1802(8455)

Field characters FW 12-15mm. Forewing dark grey-brown. There is a single narrow white cross-band just beyond middle, with a fine dark line running through it. This band usually has a single rounded indentation near centre of inner edge, with sometimes an extra, smaller indentation present. There is at most a faint suggestion of a pale cross-band before the middle. Hindwing usually has a distinct whitish central cross-band.

Similar species See Small Rivulet, which starts flying about two weeks later.

Flight season Two generations recorded from Cornwall to Monmouthshire and Essex, late May-mid July and August-September. One generation, late May-July further north. Sometimes disturbed from near the foodplant by day. Flies from dusk, usually near the foodplant, and comes to light in very small numbers.

Life cycle Overwinters as a pupa underground. Larva July-early September.

Larval foodplants The flowers and seeds of Red Campion.

Habitat Open woodland, hedgerows, roadside verges and light scrub, especially on chalk downland but on many other soils.

Status & distribution Resident. Common. Well distributed and fairly frequent in south-west and south-east England, Wales, the West Midlands, East Anglia, and in many places in northern England and southern Scotland. Recorded more locally in the rest of mainland Scotland, the Inner Hebrides, central southern England and the northern half of Ireland. Fairly widespread but occasional on Man and Jersey. One recorded on Guernsey, in 1993.

Small Rivulet   page 140
Perizoma alchemillata (L.)
Common. T   1803(8456)

Field characters & Similar species FW 9-11mm. Very similar to Rivulet, but noticeably smaller. There are two more or less equal-sized indentations on inner edge of white cross-band (second, if present, is smaller in Rivulet), and often a second, usually fainter white, cross-band nearer to base. Hindwing usually only faintly banded.

Flight season One generation. Early June-August. Sometimes disturbed by day from near the foodplant. Flies from dusk, and comes regularly to light.

Life cycle Overwinters as a pupa underground. Larva July-early September.

Larval foodplants The flowers and seeds of Common Hemp-nettle, and possibly Hedge Woundwort.

Habitat Quite a wide variety, including open woodland and rides, hedgerows, country lanes, scrubby chalk downland, marshes, derelict open sites and some suburban and rural gardens, sometimes regularly in the absence of Hemp-nettle, suggesting use

101

of alternative foodplants.
Status & distribution Resident. Common. Well
distributed and fairly frequent throughout England,
Wales, lowland mainland Scotland, the Inner
Hebrides, Man and Ireland. Breeding in gardens on
Orkney. Local and occasional on Jersey, rare on
Guernsey.

Barred Rivulet page 140
Perizoma bifaciata (Haw.)
Local. S,C,(N)   1804(8459)

Field characters FW 9-11mm. Dull grey-brown
forewing and fine chalky-white edging of rather
narrow, dark grey central cross-band are diagnostic.
There is slight variation in strength of white markings.
Similar species See Barred Carpet. Heath Rivulet
bears a superficial resemblance but is generally
smaller and grey, with coarse whitish markings.
Flight season One generation. July-August.
Occasionally disturbed by day near the foodplant.
Flies from dusk, feeds at flowers and comes to light
in small numbers.
Life cycle Overwinters as a pupa underground,
sometimes for up to five years. Larva August-
October, living inside the seed capsules until growing
too large, when it remains on the foodplant.
Larval foodplants The ripening seeds of Red
Bartsia, and occasionally Eyebright.
Habitat Most numerous on chalk downland and
other calcareous places with short turf, including the
edges of well-trodden paths in woodland rides,
particularly where limestone chippings are laid. Also
on derelict, open ground and sometimes on clay
soils.
Status & distribution Resident. Local. Fairly well
distributed and locally fairly frequent in the southern
half of England, Wales and north-west England.
Local in north-east England, southern Scotland and
Ireland, where most frequently recorded in the
Burren, Co. Clare, but also reported recently from
several sites in eastern Northern Ireland. Local and
southern on Man. Local and occasional in the
Channel Islands.

Heath Rivulet page 140
Perizoma minorata (Treit.)
ssp. *ericetata* (Steph.)
Nb. N,C   1805(8461)

Field characters FW 8-10mm. The grey, coarse-
textured forewing markings, with strong, well-
defined, irregular whitish cross-lines and bands make
this very small geometrid fairly distinctive. There is
slight variation in strength of pale and dark bands.
Similar species See Barred Rivulet.
Flight season One generation. July-August. Flies in
the afternoon, especially in hot sunshine. Also comes
to light.
Life cycle Overwinters as a pupa, in an underground
cocoon. Larva mid August-September.
Larval foodplants The flowers and seed capsules of

Eyebright.
Habitat Moorland, upland pasture and limestone
grassland.
Status & distribution Resident. Nationally Scarce B.
A northern species, widely distributed but poorly
recorded in Scotland, occurring particularly in the
Cairngorms, the Spey Valley and around Aviemore,
and also on both the east and west coasts north to
Caithness. Present on Rum, Coll and Orkney but not
Shetland. Apparently very local in England, mainly
from Cumbria and the Pennines. The only modern
record for the Northumberland and Durham area is
from Beacon Meadows, Durham, in 1977. The few
recent records from Yorkshire include Thruscross,
Washburndale, in 1981, Dib Scar, Grassington, in
1983 and a confirmed singleton from Harrogate in
1973. There are a number of old records from Britain
south of the Humber, but these require confirmation
or are doubted. Reported from Carmel Woods SSSI,
near Ammanford, Carmarthenshire, in July 1992.
Recorded from the Mourne Mountains in the north-
east of Ireland and the Burren, Co. Clare.

Pretty Pinion page 140
Perizoma blandiata blandiata ([D. & S.])
Local. N,W   1806(8462)
ssp. *perfasciata* (Prout)
Hebrides/Rum

Field characters FW 9-11mm. Ssp. *blandiata* White
ground-colour, grey markings and black discal spot
make this quite a distinctive moth. Diagnostic feature
is central cross-band, which is dark grey near leading
and trailing edges and faint in the middle, but there
is some variation, with the dark grey more extensive
on some examples. Sometimes band is pinched or
even broken in the middle. Ssp. *perfasciata* is more
strongly marked, and central band is more or less
entirely dark grey.
Similar species Lime-speck Pug, but distinguished
by wing shape.
Flight season One generation. Late May-July or
even early August. Flies in the late afternoon,
possibly most active around dusk, but also comes to
light.
Life cycle Overwinters as a pupa, in an earthen
cocoon. Larva early August-mid September.
Larval foodplants Flowers and seeds of Eyebright.
Habitat A wide range of open habitats, including
moorland and rough upland pasture, and reported
from limestone hills. Seems to prefer places where
Eyebright grows among slightly taller vegetation, as
on roadside verges, to those which are carpeted with
it.
Status & distribution Resident. Local. Ssp.
blandiata is widespread and well distributed in
Scotland north of the central belt, and including
Orkney, Shetland and some of the Hebrides. Also
found very locally in Cumbria. Occasional singletons,
assumed to be wanderers, have been recorded elsewhere, including Bedlington, Northumberland, on 12
July 1977 and Midhurst, West Sussex, on 2 August

1989. There are several records from the Wye and Severn Valleys, Gloucestershire, most recently in 1990, and larvae and adults were reported from the Forest of Dean in 1909. In Ireland, well distributed in the Burren, Co. Clare, and recorded from a few additional widely scattered sites, from the extreme south-west to Northern Ireland. Recorded once from Man, on 19 June 1974, at Knock-e-Dhooney, where considered vagrant. Also once from Guernsey, in 1889. Ssp. *perfasciata* occurs in the Hebrides and is frequent on Rum.

Grass Rivulet page 140

Perizoma albulata albulata ([D. & S.])
Local. T 1807(8463)

ssp. *subfasciaria* (Boh.)
Shetland

Field characters FW 10-12mm. Ssp. *albulata* Extensive, soft grey-brown cross-bands on chalky-white forewing make this a fairly easy moth to recognise. Intensity of markings varies. Some examples from chalky areas in the south are predominantly white, and the moth is generally darker in the north. Ssp. *subfasciaria* is smaller and darker. Many examples are entirely soft grey-brown, with only faint, slightly paler markings, although others have strong white cross-bands.
Similar species None.
Flight season One generation. May-early July. Flies by day, especially towards dusk, sometimes in large numbers, and comes to light.
Life cycle Overwinters as a pupa underground. Larva mid June-August. Lives inside the seed capsules.
Larval foodplants The ripening seeds of Yellow-rattle.
Habitat Grassland, usually on calcareous soils, dune-slacks and coastal shingle, from dry to damp situations.
Status & distribution Resident. Local. Ssp. *albulata* is widely distributed throughout England, Wales and Scotland, including the Hebrides and Orkney. Fairly well distributed and locally frequent in the above habitats, mainly in lowland areas and around the coast, but by no means reported from everywhere the foodplant is known. Local and rare on Man, at the north end. Widespread in Ireland but records thinly scattered, mainly from the east in Northern Ireland. Ssp. *subfasciaria* occurs on Shetland; those on Orkney are like those on the mainland.

Sandy Carpet page 140

Perizoma flavofasciata (Thun.)
Common. T 1808(8464)

Field characters FW 11-14mm. The irregular, sandy brown cross-bands and lines on white forewing make this moth quite distinctive. Central cross-band has a double projection on its outer edge. There is only slight variation.
Similar species None.
Flight season One generation. June-July. Sometimes disturbed by day. Flies mainly at dusk, and best found by searching around the foodplant. Comes to light in small numbers but its flight is largely over once it is dark.
Life cycle Overwinters as a pupa. Larva mid July-early September. Lives inside the seed capsules.
Larval foodplants The flowers and ripening seeds of Red Campion, and less often White Campion and Bladder Campion.
Habitat Open woodland, on rides and edges, mature hedgerows, country lanes, calcareous grass-land and sand-dunes. Less frequently in suburban gardens and roadsides, and rare in urban areas.
Status & distribution Resident. Common. Fairly well distributed and locally frequent in England and Wales. Well distributed but rather infrequently recorded on Man. Widely distributed in lowland mainland Scotland, to the extreme north, and in the Inner Hebrides. Apparently very local in Ireland, including the eastern half of Northern Ireland, but probably under-recorded. Widespread and frequent in the Channel Islands.

Twin-spot Carpet page 140

Perizoma didymata didymata (L.)
Common. T 1809(8465)

ssp. *hethlandica* (Rebel)
Shetland

Field characters FW 11-15mm. Ssp. *didymata* The 'twin-spots' refer to the two blackish spots just inside the pale, scalloped outermost cross-line in leading half of wing. These are often joined at base to form a thick U-shape which, along with the rather coarse texture, is diagnostic. Ground-colour in male is grey, and in generally smaller female brownish white or sometimes greyish white. In ssp. *hethlandica*, many examples, of both sexes, are browner and duller than ssp. *didymata*, although some are very similar to it in colour, suggesting a more varied population rather than a separate race. On Orkney, male is mostly very dark grey to blackish and female pale, but in sandy coastal areas of Deerness male is reddish brown.
Similar species Striped Twin-spot Carpet and Garden Carpet f. *thules* are superficially similar to some males, but both lack the twin spots and have less pointed forewing.
Flight season One generation. June-August. Male is mainly active by day and at dusk, and is often seen in numbers, flying freely in warm, dry weather, especially mid-afternoon. Female is less inclined to fly and is most often found at rest on vegetation at night. Both sexes fly from dusk and feed at flowers, including Heather, ragworts and grasses. Comes to light, sometimes in fair numbers in upland habitats, usually in small numbers elsewhere, and more easily found by dusking.
Life cycle Overwinters as an egg. Larva April-June.
Larval foodplants A wide range of plants, including Bilberry, Heather, sallows, also Greater Stitchwort, Red Campion, willow-herbs and Cow Parsley. Has also been reported rarely from the flowers of coarse

103

Larva of Marsh Carpet.

Woodwalton, Holme, Wicken and Chippenham Fens. Subsequently found in certain fens and marshes in Norfolk and Suffolk, on Misterton Carr in the flood-plain of the River Idle, north Nottinghamshire, in 1960 and later at nearby Misson Carr, and at Askham Bog, Yorkshire, in 1978. Discovered in several sites in Lincolnshire from 1880 onwards, and still present near Haxey. Greatly at risk from inappropriate cutting and grazing, and subject to extreme fluctuations in population size – during the 1940s it was considered to be extinct.

grasses and wood-rushes, Sitka Spruce and Lodgepole Pine (one larva in 1969).
Habitat Most abundant in moorland and light upland woodland. Also in woodland and hedgerows in lowlands, and on derelict open ground, sand-dunes and sea-cliffs.
Status & distribution Resident. Common. Ssp. *didymata* is well distributed and often numerous in northern and western Britain, on Man and in Ireland. Widely but more thinly distributed and less frequent in East Anglia and south and south-east England, where it appears to have become rather more local and infrequent in recent years, particularly in Hampshire. Local and rare in the Channel Islands. Ssp. *hethlandica* occurs on Shetland.

Marsh Carpet   page 140
Perizoma sagittata (Fabr.)
Na. EC   1810(8468)

Field characters FW 13-17mm. Unmistakable. The dark grey or blackish, white-edged central cross-band, with strong outer projection, on sandy brown forewing is diagnostic. Little variation, but occasionally central band is broken in middle.
Similar species None.
Flight season One generation. Late June-July, occasionally even mid-August in cool, wet summers. Flies from dusk. Comes to light. Female often disperses from breeding areas.
Life cycle Overwinters as a pupa, at the base of the foodplant, in a cocoon among plant debris or underground. Larva late July-mid September, sometimes from early July.
Larval foodplants Common Meadow-rue, on the ripening seeds. Also reported from Lesser Meadow-rue, a much scarcer plant, which occurs within the range of the moth in western Suffolk and into Cambridgeshire. Most larvae are on the largest and most visible flowerheads, even when newly hatched. Plants swamped by taller species, such as Common Reed, have fewer or no larvae.
Habitat Fens, marshes, wet meadows and the banks of ditches, dykes and rivers.
Status & distribution Resident. Nationally Scarce A. First discovered in Britain in the fens of Huntingdonshire and Cambridgeshire in 1847, and still present in the remnants of these, notably at

Eupithecia
Pug moths

This group of moths, most of which belong to a single genus, *Eupithecia*, causes macro-lepidopterists the most identification problems. As a group, they are not too difficult to distinguish from other moths (except perhaps the Small Dusty Wave) because most have a quite distinct resting posture and outline. The forewings are stretched out so that their leading edges are in line, or form a shallow arc, and often the abdomen is curled upwards. There are 52 species on the British list, of which two are suspected rare immigrants. Four more were regarded as species until recently, but many authorities now consider them subspecies of the above total, and this is how they are treated in the current list.

The majority are brown or grey, and require detailed examination of wing and body markings to distinguish them. Often it is not possible to be certain of the identity based on wing pattern alone, particularly if the individual is worn, and these are delicate moths that wear rapidly. It is often necessary to examine the underside of the abdomen (males only) or the genitalia (see Riley & Prior 2003). This will be especially helpful to those learning the group.

The following scheme sorts the pugs into smaller groups by their most obvious features. Within each group, close examination of wing shape, ground-colour and wing markings will enable you to distinguish most species. The very dark, or melanic, forms of some species can be the most difficult to determine, but there are helpful differences in wing shape. The taxonomic order is indicated by the checklist numbers, which are also handy for quick location of the accounts in the text. In some cases, the larvae are more distinctive than the adults and are confined to particular foodplants, leading to more reliable identification in this stage. Most of the species are undoubtedly under-recorded and will be found more widely as, hopefully, more people learn to identify this group.

The colour plates are arranged in taxonomic order, as in the rest of the book, but the following identification scheme may prove helpful. Work through these groups sequentially to narrow the range of possibilities, then study the field characters in individual accounts, checking also flight season, habitat and known distribution. Some species are listed in more than one group, to cover variation.

Pug with notched hindwing margins:
Dentated Pug (1863).

Pugs with large white areas on forewing:
Marbled Pug (1818); Pinion-spotted Pug (1820); Lime-speck Pug (1825); Bordered Pug (1839); Shaded Pug (1840); Scarce Pug (1847).

Pugs with obvious greenish tints on forewing (these may fade):
Green Pug (1860); V-Pug (1858); some fresh Bilberry Pug (1861); very fresh Sloe Pug (1859) (has pink band on abdomen, unlike the other three).

Pug with large plain orange patch on forewing:
Tawny Speckled Pug (1838).

Pugs with prominent banding or other strong patterns across wings:
Foxglove Pug (1817); Toadflax Pug (1816); Pinion-spotted Pug (1820); Netted Pug (1823); Scarce Pug (1847); Narrow-winged Pug (1846); Juniper Pug (1854); Cypress Pug (1855); Double-striped Pug (1862); Goosefoot Pug (1842a) (rare immigrant).

Pugs with very narrow, pointed wings:
Narrow-winged Pug (1846); Angle-barred Pug (1848)/Ash Pug (1849)/Tamarisk Pug (1850).

The remaining pugs are mainly brownish or greyish and can be usefully subdivided as follows:

Noticeably smaller pugs (forewing only 8-10mm):
Slender Pug (1811) (distinct black central spot; broader, more rounded wings than Maple Pug); Maple Pug (1812) (yellower brown than Slender Pug, with a rougher, blotched appearance due to three dark brown patches on forewing; central spot generally less conspicuous, sometimes minute; black broken line around outer edges of all four wings conspicuous, even when worn); Haworth's Pug (1813) (distinguished from Lead-coloured Pug and Valerian Pug by reddish band on base of abdomen, and latter also has distinct central spot); Lead-coloured Pug (1814) (central spot grey or absent, no spot in trailing corner of forewing); Valerian Pug (1821) (spot in trailing corner of forewing distin-guishes it from Lead-coloured Pug); Marsh Pug (1822) (straight leading edge to forewing, warm dark brown ground-colour and chequered fringes); Thyme Pug (1843) (recognised by black dashes on leading edge of forewing and slit-like central spot); Channel Islands Pug (1855a) (central spot elongate, smaller than Thyme Pug); Juniper Pug (1854) (variable, but a small whitish halo on outer edge of the dark central spot is usually visible, even in melanic individuals); Double-striped Pug (1862) (many individuals boldly

marked, often with red but later generations often small and markings weaker; cross-line beyond central spot black nearest leading edge).

Large pale grey pug, with fine markings and small central spot in middle of forewing:
Fletcher's Pug (1824); Grey Pug (1837) (has larger, less discrete black central spot and heavier markings); Larch Pug (1856) (has small central dot, stronger markings and a white spot or crest on thorax).

Conspicuous dark spot in middle of forewing and distinct whitish spot in trailing corner:
Wormwood Pug (1830) (a most frequent pug, ground-colour plain brown with reddish tint); Ling Pug (1831) (can be as large as Wormwood Pug, of which it is generally considered a greyer subspecies); Currant Pug (1832) (smaller than Wormood Pug, with more rounded brown forewing, usually with some small, creamy-whitish spots on outer edge of forewing, the trailing one being especially large and obvious); White-spotted Pug (1835) (greyer than Currant Pug, with fine cross-lines, generally three conspicuous whitish spots near outer edge of forewing, one whitish spot on trailing edge of hind-wing, which is not covered by forewing at rest, one on thorax and one on either side of abdomen); Common Pug (1834) (the most frequently encoun-tered pug; central spot and tiny corner spot always small; grainy brown appearance); Jasione Pug (1836) (greyish, quite small, corner spot often minute); check also Pimpinel Pug (1845) (on which corner spot is an enlarged trailing end to a weak, pale, outer cross-line).

Conspicuous dark spot in middle of forewing but no distinct whitish spot in trailing corner:
Cloaked Pug (1815) (a large fawn-grey pug with distinctive dark bar from near central spot to leading edge of forewing); Mottled Pug (1819) (has several stacked, dark, wedge-shaped dashes by central spot); Freyer's/Edinburgh/Mere's Pug (1827), (Freyer's Pug frequent in gardens; strong, fine, angled cross-lines); Triple-spotted Pug (1826) (not pale, two bold rather straight-edged spots on leading edge and long central spot); Bleached Pug (1833) (large, pale with two conspicuous brown spots on leading edge); Satyr Pug ssp. *curzoni* (1828) (chequered veins, n.b. compare with Golden-rod Pug 1851); Campanula Pug (1836); Grey Pug (1837); Larch Pug (1856) (a white crest on thorax); Tawny Speckled Pug (1838) (three forms); Yarrow Pug (1841) (sometimes a small, central orange patch near central dot); Plain Pug (1842) (generally has a fairly straight pale band beyond central spot); Pimpinel Pug (1845) (light greyish borders, double-check not Wormwood Pug (1830), or Common Pug (1834), and see also Yarrow Pug (1841)); Golden-rod Pug (1851) (compare with Grey Pug (1837), and Satyr Pug (1828)); Brindled Pug (1852) (flies early in the year, before most other pugs; distinctly curved leading edge on fairly elon-gate, pointed forewing; this works for melanics, too;

central spot usually elongated); Oak-tree Pug (1853) (has small black dashes in outer area of forewing, as does Brindled Pug (1852) but central spot usually round); see also Dwarf Pug (1857), and Juniper Pug (1854)); Ochreous Pug (1844) (pale, yellowish brown, rather plain pointed forewing); Dwarf Pug (1857) (pale with conspicuous dark spots on leading edge, giving rise to strong, dark cross-lines); Bilberry Pug (1861) (like a faded Green Pug but cross-line beyond central spot is in the form of a series of small dark dots); Goosefoot Pug (1842a) (rare immigrant).

Pugs not falling easily into the above groupings:
Satyr Pug (1828) – two chequered or black-flecked veins.
Common Pug (1834) – the dark central spot may be completely absent.
Shaded Pug (1840) – white markings indistinct in some examples.
Sloe Pug (1859) – pink and black transverse bands on abdomen; has the appearance of a small, faded Green Pug – with rarely a trace of green.
Green Pug (1860) which has faded.
Cloaked Pug (1815) – the dark central spot may be so amalgamated with the dark bar from leading edge of forewing that it is not distinct.
Doubleday's Pug (1829) – one British record; resembles Satyr Pug (1828) but larger and yellower.

Melanics – wings almost uniformly blackish brown or dark grey:
Some very dark forms, or melanics, can be identified using forewing shape. Most melanics in gardens turn out to be Grey Pug (1837), which has a distinctive, almost triangular, forewing, or Green Pug (1860), which usually has some paler outer markings and hindwing as dark as forewing.

Slender Pug
page 141
Eupithecia tenuiata (Hb)
Common. T
1811(8475)

Field characters FW 8-10mm. Combination of size, rounded forewing with distinct, round, black central spot and predominantly greyish-brown ground-colour is usually diagnostic. Dark, often brown, blocks along leading edge often noticeable on well-marked examples. F. *johnsoni* Harr. is a darker grey-brown form occurring in north-east England and the Midlands.
Similar species See Maple Pug and Small Dusty Wave.
Flight season One generation. June-July. Sometimes found by day at rest on trunks of large sallows. Comes to light, usually in small numbers.
Life cycle Overwinters as an egg attached to food-plant. Larva March-April, within catkins, pupating among them or in plant debris below.
Larval foodplants The catkins of Goat Willow, Grey Willow, Eared Willow and probably other *Salix* species.
Habitat Damp woodland, scrub, sallow carr, fens,

marshes, dune-slacks, banks of ditches, ponds, lake edges, flooded gravel pits and gardens.
Status & distribution Resident. Common. Records somewhat thinly scattered throughout Great Britain and Ireland, to northern Scotland but not Orkney and Shetland. Undoubtedly under-recorded. Easy to find when searched for as a larva, and often fairly frequent. Considered local and rare on Man and the Channel Islands.

Maple Pug
page 141
Eupithecia inturbata (Hb.)
Local. S,C
1812(8476)

Field characters & Similar species FW 8-10mm. Very similar to Slender Pug. Their flight seasons overlap, and both are somewhat variable. Maple Pug is often yellowish brown, generally has rougher, more blotchy appearance and forewing is, on the whole, slightly narrower and less rounded. Slender Pug is grey-brown, with more rounded forewing margins. Central dark spot sometimes inconspicuous on well-marked Maple Pug. Black broken line around outer edges of all wings usually conspicuous, even when worn. Darker and almost black forms occur in some areas. Common Pug is usually larger, richer brown and bands beyond central spot (if present) more sharply kinked near leading edge. With the exception of Valerian Pug, the other small pugs lack distinct central spot. See also Small Dusty Wave.
Flight season One generation. July-August. Sometimes present in very large numbers, and can be readily disturbed from rest on maple trunks and the vegetation below, and by tapping the branches. Comes readily to light, sometimes in large numbers, particularly if light-trapping under a closed canopy of Field Maple.
Life cycle Overwinters as an egg attached to food-plant. Larva early May-early June, pupating in a cocoon among the flowers.
Larval foodplants Field Maple, feeding on the flowers. The maples must be large enough to produce plenty of flowers. Ability to exploit introduced maples and other *Acer* species requires investigation. Accepts Sycamore in captivity.
Habitat Woodland, scrub on chalk and limestone, and hedgerows.
Status & distribution Resident. Local. Predominantly south-eastern Britain. The bulk of records are south of a line from the Severn and Wye Valleys to the Humber. Well distributed and locally numerous in this area, except in the extreme south-west, but breeding at Looe, Cornwall. Recently recorded from many sites in Yorkshire, particularly southern Yorkshire. Scattered records north to the Borders and Dumfries & Galloway, and including central and north Wales. Also recorded from a Rothamsted light-trap at Elgin, Moray. In Ireland there have been unconfirmed reports from the south. The only record from the Channel Islands is one on Guernsey in 1981.

Haworth's Pug
page 141
Eupithecia haworthiata Doubl.
Local. S,C   1813(8477)

Field characters FW 8-9mm. Reddish band at base of abdomen helps distinguish this small, grey-brown, rather weakly-marked pug. Central forewing spot is faint or absent and outer bands are only slightly kinked near leading edge, and leading edge is rather curved.

Similar species See Lead-coloured Pug. Slender Pug has a distinct central spot.

Flight season One generation. June-July. Easily flushed from larval foodplant by day. Comes readily to light.

Life cycle Overwinters as a pupa, in a cocoon in the surface of the earth. Larva July-August, feeding within flower buds.

Larval foodplants Flower buds of Traveller's-joy and cultivated species of Clematis.

Habitat Most places where the native foodplant occurs, which tends to be on chalk or limestone, including open woodland, scrub, hedgerows and some gardens.

Status & distribution Resident. Local. Quite well recorded and distributed, often in abundance, in the main areas where the foodplant grows in England, north to the Humber, Yorkshire, and Arnside Knott, south Cumbria; also in north Wales and Anglesey. Recorded from the Harrogate district north of the Humber, where the foodplant and its relatives are introductions. In Ireland records are thinly distributed from Co. Kerry to Northern Ireland, but the moth is undoubtedly under-recorded. Local and occasional in the Channel Islands.

Lead-coloured Pug
page 141
Eupithecia plumbeolata (Haw.)
Nb. S,C,NW   1814(8479)

Field characters & Similar species FW 9-10mm. Very similar to Haworth's Pug, but without reddish band on abdomen and with straighter leading edge to the more pointed forewing. Cross-lines very wavy. Ground-colour usually a washed-out, yellowish-grey. Central spot inconspicuous or absent. Slender Pug has a distinct central spot. Valerian Pug has a distinct, wavy, whitish outermost cross-line on forewing, often forming a spot in trailing corner. See also Marsh Pug.

Flight season One generation. Late May-late June. Not easily flushed by day. Occasionally flies briefly in the afternoon, with a more pronounced flight just before dusk. Comes to light throughout the night, sometimes in numbers.

Life cycle Overwinters as a pupa, in plant debris or loose earth. Larva late June-mid August.

Larval foodplants Flowers of Common Cow-wheat. Also reported from Yellow-rattle.

Habitat Open woodland, the foodplant benefiting from coppicing. Also in meadows, dune-slacks and sand-dunes.

Status & distribution Resident. Nationally Scarce B. Widespread but local in England and Wales north to the Humber. Very local northwards but recorded in North Yorkshire, Cumbria, the central belt of Scotland and in Easter Ross. A few mainly scattered records from Northern Ireland to the extreme south-west of the Republic.

Cloaked Pug
page 141
Eupithecia abietaria (Goeze)
Uncommon; suspected immigrant. T   1815(8481)

Field characters FW 11-15mm. One of the largest pugs in Britain, although quite variable in size, and quite distinctive. Forewing broad, with large, bold, black central spot. Central cross-bands edged with black, especially on leading edge where they form two black blocks, the inner of which often merges with central spot to form a bar. Tawny cross-bands near base and outer edge, and across abdomen near base. Strength of black margins and detail of cross-lines somewhat variable.

Similar species Dwarf Pug is smaller and lacks tawny bands.

Flight season One generation. June-July. Sometimes disturbed by day from foodplant. Comes to light in small numbers.

Life cycle Overwinters as a pupa, in a flimsy cocoon among fallen conifer needles or other plant debris on the ground. Larva late June-mid September. Feeds on the ripe seeds between the cone-scales, generally high on the tree, often more than one larva per cone, producing clumps of reddish-brown frass which can be seen hanging from the cones.

Larval foodplants Mainly Norway Spruce. Also recorded from Sitka Spruce, Noble Fir, Silver Fir and unspecified larch. Trees must be sufficiently mature as to produce good numbers of large cones.

Habitat Plantations and shelterbelts of introduced conifers.

Status & distribution Resident and suspected immigrant. Uncommon on recent alien hosts. Recent evidence of breeding colonies in Northamptonshire, Warwickshire, mid Wales, Co. Durham, Northumberland, Inverness-shire and in Co. Down, Northern Ireland. In the late 19th century, best known from the New Forest, Hampshire. Recorded from an additional thin scatter of sites throughout England, Scotland and Wales. Most of these records are of singletons and are correlated with influxes of known immigrant moths, but additional breeding populations are likely. Records from Co. Down in 1999 were the first from Ireland for many years. Previously, the moth had been recorded from a few sites in the Republic.

Toadflax Pug
page 141
Eupithecia linariata ([D. & S.])
Common. T   1816(8483)

Field characters & Similar species FW 9-10mm. Similar to Foxglove Pug, but slightly smaller, with neater markings and emerges later in the summer.

107

Larva of Mottled Pug.

Outer edge of grey central cross-band is curved near leading edge (kinked in Foxglove Pug). The rare Barred Carpet has a charcoal-coloured thorax and forewing base.

Flight season One generation. July-August. Seldom seen by day. Comes to light.

Life cycle Overwinters as a pupa, on the ground or in loose earth. Larva August-September, feeding in the flowers and later on the seed capsules.

Larval foodplants Common Toadflax. Use of Purple Toadflax needs investigation, as it is often frequent where Common Toadflax grows in south-east England. Accepts Snapdragon in captivity.

Habitat Rough chalk and limestone grassland, including roadside verges. Also broken ground and derelict land, including many urban sites. Breeds in some gardens on Snapdragon.

Status & distribution Resident. Common. Quite well distributed throughout England and Wales, with scattered records to northern Scotland, although most Scottish records are from the central belt. One record from Man, in 1893. Local and rare in the Channel Islands.

Foxglove Pug   page 141

Eupithecia pulchellata pulchellata Steph.
Common. T   1817(8484)

ssp. *hebudium* Sheld.
Hebrides/Wales

Field characters FW 10-12mm. The broad grey central cross-band, with its outer edge kinked near leading edge, is the diagnostic feature. The western ssp. *hebudium* has a greyish-white ground-colour and brown bands are dull.

Similar species See Toadflax Pug and Barred Carpet which has a charcoal thorax and deeper, more rounded forewing.

Flight season One generation. May-June, into late July in the north. Elsewhere, sometimes a partial second generation in August. Often seen at rest or disturbed from vegetation near larval foodplants. Frequent at light.

Life cycle Overwinters as a pupa, in loose earth. Larva late June-mid August.

Larval foodplants Foxglove, feeding inside the flower, especially on the stamens.

Habitat A wide range of situations in which the foodplant grows, from sheltered woodland to open hillsides, moorland, calcareous grassland and sea-cliffs. Also urban sites such as railway cuttings and derelict land.

Status & distribution Resident. Common. Widespread, well distributed and sometimes frequent throughout England, Wales, Scotland and on Man. Resident on Orkney but apparently reported in error from Shetland. Widely recorded in northern and western Ireland. Widespread and occasional in the Channel Islands. Ssp. *hebudium* found in Hebrides and Wales.

Marbled Pug   page 141

Eupithecia irriguata (Hb.)
Nb. S   1818(8490)

Field characters FW 9-11mm. The rather pointed, narrow, whitish forewing, with discrete dark blotches on leading and outer edges and large, black, usually quite elongated central spot, are diagnostic. Conspicuous central spot on hindwing.

Similar species Lime-speck Pug has only a single forewing blotch. Bordered Pug is much larger, with continuous dark forewing borders, and flies later in the year.

Flight season One generation. Late April-May. Occasionally found at rest by day on trunks and branches of mature oaks. Comes to light, sometimes in numbers.

Life cycle Overwinters as a pupa, in loose earth. Larva late May-early July, feeding on the leaves.

Larval foodplants Pedunculate Oak. Confirmation required for Sessile Oak.

Habitat Oak woodland and large oaks in hedgerows in well wooded areas. Strongly associated with concentrations of mature oaks.

Status & distribution Resident. Nationally Scarce B. Best known from the New Forest, Hampshire, where it remains frequent. Increasingly being discovered elsewhere, mainly in central-southern England and the south-west, as more mature oak woodlands are investigated. There are strong populations in Oxfordshire and Northamptonshire but most records are from further south, extending to south Devon, east Cornwall and Sussex. Also recorded in recent years from Gloucestershire, Herefordshire, Monmouthshire, from Aberystwyth between 1965-1970 and from Newtown, Powys, in 1988-1989. Now virtually absent from the eastern counties of England, but one was recorded in a light-trap in a garden at Hockwold, Thetford, Norfolk, in May 1995. A record from Danbury Ridge, Essex, on 31 May 1985 was the first in Essex since the 19th century, when it was reported from Epping Forest.

Mottled Pug   page 141

Eupithecia exiguata exiguata (Hb.)
Common. S,C,(N)   1819(8491)

ssp. *muricolor* Prout
Aberdeenshire

Field characters FW 11-12mm. Forewing warm grey,

leading edge curved. Central spot conspicuous, rather elongated, with a series of small black wedges beyond it. A narrow, pale outer cross-band, angled near leading edge, with two straw-coloured smears extending towards outer edge. This combination of features is diagnostic. Species is darker and more heavily marked in the north, reaching the mousey-grey form ssp. *muricolor* from specimens collected in east Aberdeenshire.
Similar species Brindled Pug is similar in shape, size and general pattern, but forewing is brownish and mottled, with a smaller central spot and black wedges, and it flies earlier in the year, mainly in March and April.
Flight season One generation. May-June. Comes to light, sometimes in numbers.
Life cycle Overwinters as a pupa, in loose earth. Larva late June-early October.
Larval foodplants Hawthorn, Midland Hawthorn, Blackthorn and Dogwood. Regularly found on Barberry in rural hedgerows. Also reported from Sycamore. In upland areas on Rowan.
Habitat Woodland, scrub and hedgerows. Often in rural and suburban gardens.
Status & distribution Resident. Common. Widespread, well distributed and often abundant throughout England and Wales. Few records from Man. A scatter of records from mainland Scotland, mainly in the south, suggesting it is very local. The records from Ireland are somewhat localised, but it is present quite widely in Northern Ireland and the Republic. Rarely recorded in the Channel Islands, but noted from Alderney and Guernsey.

Larva of Valerian Pug.

and less so on the edges of woods and in more shaded locations. Occasionally found as an adult in gardens and orchards with large, well-established but not necessarily very old Apple trees, but hawthorns seldom absent and difficult to rule out.
Status & distribution Resident. Nationally Scarce B. A moth of central and southern England but extending up the east coast to Scarborough, Yorkshire, and into East Anglia, particularly the Thetford area. It is absent from much of south-east England but occurs in north Kent and the Romney Marsh area. Reaches its western limits in Dorset and Gloucestershire. Seldom seen in numbers anywhere. Apparently no recent records from Wales.

Valerian Pug page 141
Eupithecia valerianata (Hb.)
Nb. T   1821(8494)

Field characters FW 8-10mm. The zigzagged whitish outer cross-line, sometimes reduced to a row of spots, and distinct white spot at trailing corner distinguish this from other small, grey-brown, weakly-marked pugs. Central forewing spot is elongated, but often faint or absent. Hindwing also has whitish spot in trailing corner.
Similar species Common Pug has rougher texture, usually browner and larger, with a round central spot. See also Lead-coloured Pug.
Flight season One generation. June-early July, sometimes later in Scotland. Flies at dusk and rests on the flowers of the foodplant and on adjacent plants.
Life cycle Overwinters as a pupa, on the ground among plant debris. Larva July-mid August.
Larval foodplants Common Valerian, feeding on the flowers and ripening seeds.
Habitat Most often found in fens, broads and in other wet open ground, but also occurs in damp woodlands and in much drier habitats, such as the limestone quarries at Portland, Dorset.
Status & distribution Resident. Nationally Scarce B. The records are thinly scattered but rather evenly distributed throughout England, Wales and Scotland, north to Sutherland. Appears to have declined, but easily overlooked and less frequently sought as larvae than in the past. There is a concentration of records in the Thetford area of Norfolk, where the Norfolk

Pinion-spotted Pug page 141
Eupithecia insigniata (Hb.)
Nb. S,C,not SW   1820(8493)

Field characters FW 10-12mm. The delicate, narrow, mauvish-grey forewing and sinuous black markings along leading edge are diagnostic and constant features of this pug. Some variation in the shade of grey ground-colour and extent of black markings. Sinuous streaks often faint on worn examples but blotches on leading edge remain.
Similar species See Netted Pug.
Flight season One generation. Late April-May, occasionally early June. In most areas appears to fly for about a fortnight only, usually just after the main Apple blossom is over. Seldom seen, except at light, usually after 1.30am.
Life cycle Overwinters as a pupa, in a light cocoon in cracks and crevices of bark, among plant debris or in loose earth. Larva mid June-early August.
Larval foodplants Mainly Hawthorn. Midland Hawthorn has been beaten extensively in occupied areas, without success. Will accept Crab Apple and cultivated Apple, and sometimes beaten from these. Unusually for moths associated with hawthorns, it does not thrive if supplied with Blackthorn and does not appear to exploit it in the wild.
Habitat Larvae found in various situations but most frequent in hedgerows along open, ancient lanes,

Moth Group makes targeted searches for larvae. However, the habitats are also vulnerable to loss and damage. Local and rare on Man. Reported from western Ireland, where there are records from Co. Cork northwards through Cos. Clare to Donegal, and also from Armagh.

Marsh Pug
page 141

Euphithecia pygmaeata (Hb.)

Nb. S,C,N   1822(8495)

Field characters FW 8-9mm. A small, rich dark brown pug, distinguished by very straight leading edge of forewing and rather pointed wing tip. Broken, white outermost cross-line and trailing corner spot usually present. Fringes usually chequered brown and white, and central spot faint or absent.

Similar species When worn, might be mistaken for Lead-coloured Pug, which has more rounded forewing and is usually larger, without white outermost cross-line and trailing corner spot.

Flight season One generation. May-June. Can be seen flying in sunshine around flowers of the foodplant, sometimes in numbers. Occasional at light.

Life cycle Overwinters as a pupa, probably among plant debris. Larva June-July.

Larval foodplants Flowers and seed capsules of Field Mouse-ear and probably other mouse-ears.

Habitat Marshy ground, wet meadows, fens, but also breckland, vegetated coastal sand-dunes, duneslacks and derelict open ground.

Status & distribution Resident. Nationally Scarce B. Recorded very locally from a very thin scatter of widely distributed sites throughout England, Wales and Scotland, north to Sutherland and Caithness. Discovered in numbers on a single site on Orkney, in 1977. Rarely reported in southern and south-west England, with typically only one or two records per county, but not seen recently in some. In Wales associated mainly with the calcareous strata in the north and south. Local and rare on Man. Few records from Ireland, where it is most frequently reported from the Burren, Co. Clare, but also recorded in Northern Ireland, although not for many years.

Netted Pug
page 141

Euphithecia venosata venosata (Fabr.)

Local. S,C,NE   1823(8502)

ssp. *hebridensis* W. P. Curt.
Hebrides

ssp. *fumosae* Gregs.
Shetland/Orkney

ssp. *ochracae* Gregs.
Orkney

ssp. *plumbea* Huggins
Ireland

Field characters FW 10-14mm. Ground-colour of the full, rounded forewing varies from milky-brown to dark grey in different parts of Britain, but the diagnostic dark brown, net-like markings and narrow, dark-edged whitish cross-bands are fairly consistent in pattern, although varying in intensity. In ssp. *fumosae* the ground-colour is a darker sandy brown than typical, in ssp. *ochracae* it is light sandy brown and dark markings are weak, and in ssp. *plumbea* it is dark grey. Ssp. *hebridensis* is usually darker than typical but sometimes sandy.

Similar species Pinion-spotted Pug has smaller, narrower, pointed forewing, with heavy markings concentrated along leading edge.

Flight season One generation. May-June. Flies from dusk, near foodplant. Occasional at light.

Life cycle Overwinters as a pupa in loose earth, sometimes over a second winter. Larva mid June-late July, sometimes later in northern Britain.

Larval foodplants Ripening seed capsules of Bladder Campion and Sea Campion.

Habitat Mainly on chalk and limestone, including sites where tracks of limestone chippings have been laid. Hedgerows, field margins, verges of woodland rides, calcareous sea-cliffs and rocky coastlines and occasionally gardens.

Status & distribution Resident. Local. Ssp. *venosata* is fairly well distributed on calcareous strata throughout England, Wales and the Channel Islands, sometimes locally frequent, but usually seen in small numbers in light-traps. Also recorded throughout the central belt of Scotland. It may have become scarcer in recent decades, but this may only reflect over-reliance on light-trapping and failure to search for larvae. Local and rare on Man. Ssp. *hebridensis* is found in the Hebrides. Ssp. *ochracae* is found on the coasts of Orkney. Ssp. *fumosae* occurs on Shetland and has also been reported from Orkney. Ssp. *plumbea* occurs around the coast of western Ireland, with pre-1980 records also from the east coast of Northern Ireland. A specimen resembling this subspecies has been reported from the Lizard, Cornwall.

Fletcher's Pug (Pauper Pug)
page 141

Euphithecia egenaria H.-S.

RDB. SW,E   1824(8507)

Field characters FW 11-13mm. A fairly easily recognised, rather large, usually pale grey pug with faint cross-lines and a small, black, obliquely elongate central spot. Delicate blackish dots and cross-lines are visible on fresh individuals.

Similar species Grey Pug and the grey form of Tawny Speckled Pug are more heavily marked, and Larch Pug has much more angular cross-lines and a small white crest on back of thorax.

Flight season One generation. May-June. Occasionally disturbed by day from the trunks and branches of lime trees. Lives in the canopy but at night comes readily to light-traps placed on the ground nearby, the male often in large numbers.

Life cycle Overwinters as a pupa, in a cocoon among fallen leaves or in loose earth. Larva late

June-July, often fully grown by mid July.

Larval foodplants The flowers of limes, feeding mainly on the stamens and styles. Small-leaved Lime is the most abundant and probably the main food-plant at the known sites, except in the Thetford area of Norfolk, where Large-leaved Lime and the hybrid *T. x europea* are also present. Here, larvae have been found on all three, but most plentifully on the Large-leaved Lime, which is also present but not frequent in the Wye Valley.

Habitat Ancient lime woodland. At Thetford, also on limes that were planted as avenue and park trees at the end of the 19th century, preferring the more sheltered sites and avoiding trees in the open. The limes must be mature enough to flower.

Status & distribution Resident. Red Data Book species. Known from the Wye Valley in Monmouthshire and Gloucestershire (first discovered new to Britain in 1962), the Thetford area of south-west Norfolk/north Suffolk and Hockering Wood to the north-east (records from 1984 onwards), several sites in Suffolk where it was first found in King's Forest (adults and larvae in 1993, more subse-quently), three of the limewoods around Bardney, Lincolnshire (discovered in 1995), and a wood in Surrey (one captured in 1994 and others confirmed in 1996). Discovered in Orchard Wood, Taunton, Somerset, in 2001, with more in 2003. The first Norfolk specimen was captured in 1953 but not identified for nearly 20 years. One was captured at a garden light-trap at Walberton, West Sussex, on 1 June 1987. On 7 June 2002 one was captured in Fernham, Oxfordshire, and confirmed by genitalia examination. There are several other scattered records of singletons which await confirmation. This suggests the species may prove to be more wide-spread in avenues and woodlands of lime.

Lime-speck Pug
page 141

Eupithecia centaureata ([D. & S.])

Common. T   1825(8509)

Field characters FW 10-12mm. The only white pug with a single bluish-grey or black blotch on leading edge beyond central spot. Sometimes this is very faint. Rarely, ground-colour is grey rather than white.

Similar species See Marbled Pug and Pretty Pinion.

Flight season Two protracted and overlapping generations in the south, the second being only partial in some areas, late April-October, with a reduction in numbers in July. One extended genera-tion in northern Britain, May-August. Often seen at rest by day on vertical surfaces such as posts, sheds, walls and windows. Usually hides under leaves if disturbed. Frequent at light.

Life cycle Overwinters as a pupa, in loose earth or among plant debris. Larva any time from late May-late October, usually in two overlapping generations.

Larval foodplants The flowers of many low-growing plants, including ragworts, Mugwort, Sea Wormwood, Burnet-saxifrage, Common Knapweed, Field Scabious, Hemp-agrimony, Yarrow, Wild

Angelica, Traveller's-joy, Goldenrod, Canadian Goldenrod and Michaelmas-daisies in gardens.

Habitat Coastal saltmarsh. Many open, inland habi-tats, including urban gardens, roadsides, hedgerows, scrub and open areas in woodland.

Status & distribution Resident. Common. Well distributed and frequent in most of England, Wales, lowland mainland Scotland, and the Hebrides and the Channel Islands. Local and occasional on Man. Fairly widespread and frequent in Ireland, more so around the coast.

Triple-spotted Pug
page 141

Eupithecia trisignaria H.-S.

Local. T   1826(8517)

Field characters & Similar species FW 10-11mm. The name refers to the two strong brown spots on leading edge of forewing, either side of central spot, making a group of three. Forewing nearly always lacks a white trailing corner spot, which helps to distinguish it from Currant and Common Pug. Forewing is rather rounded and almost uniform in colour. F. *angelicata* Prout is a darker brown form, common in many places, usually still with an obvious group of three spot markings. Forewing rather compact, short and broad. Melanic Grey Pug has a longer, fuller forewing.

Flight season One generation. Late June-July. Occasional at light, otherwise rarely seen.

Life cycle Overwinters as a pupa, probably among plant debris. Larva early August-early October.

Larval foodplants Ripening fruits of Wild Angelica and Hogweed.

Habitat Fens, marshy fields, roadside verges and damp woodland rides.

Status & distribution Resident. Local. Widespread. Apparently very local in England and Wales, although probably overlooked and under-recorded. Best found by searching or shaking flowerheads for the green larvae and rearing them to adult. Few records from Scotland, mainly from the east. Local and rare on Man. In Ireland there are old records from Cos. Cork, Dublin and Fermanagh, and recent records from several sites in the east of Northern Ireland.

Freyer's Pug
page 141

Eupithecia intricata (Zett.)

ssp. *arceuthata* (Freyer)

Common. S,C   1827(8519)

Edinburgh Pug
page 141

ssp. *millieraria* Wnuk.

Common. N

Mere's Pug
page 141

ssp. *hibernica* Mere

Ireland

Field characters FW 12-13mm. All three subspecies have numerous sinuous cross-lines, angled near leading edge. Central spot in hindwing is conspicuous. Dark brown or blackish belt near base of abdomen. Short lines of black scales on veins on forewing. Freyer's Pug is quite large, brown, or grey-brown in colour. Edinburgh Pug is smaller, sandy grey-brown, and often darker, with weaker markings. Mere's Pug is strongly marked and has a greyish-white tint, especially in central part of forewing. Worn Edinburgh Pug especially may require examination of genitalia, as northern forms of Common Pug can look quite similar (but with more curved leading edge to forewing).

Flight season One generation. All three subspecies fly May-June, from dusk onwards, and come to light.

Life cycle All three subspecies overwinter as pupae, in cocoons among the foodplant. Larva August-September.

Status & distribution, Habitats and Larval foodplants

Freyer's Pug is a widespread and frequent resident in central and southern England north to Yorkshire and in south Wales, where the larvae feed on various species of exotic Junipers, cypresses (*Cupressus* spp. and *Chaemaecyparis* spp.) and other introduced conifers in gardens, parks and plantations. Long known from Common Juniper, but reported only occasionally.

Edinburgh Pug occurs in north-west England and much of mainland Scotland and the Inner Hebrides, feeding on Common Juniper on moorland, roadside verges and coastal habitats.

Mere's Pug is confined to the Burren, Co. Clare, western Ireland, where it feeds on prostrate Juniper. Not recorded on Man but is likely to be present. Reported on Jersey and Guernsey, but few records.

Satyr Pug
page 142

Eupithecia satyrata satyrata (Hb.)
Local. S
1828(8526)

ssp. *callunaria* Doubl.
Common. Northern moorland form

ssp. *curzoni* Gregs.
Shetland

Field characters FW 9-13mm. Ssp. *satyrata* A pale, weakly-marked, rather non-descript, soft grey-brown pug. Leading edge of forewing is very straight, the tip quite pointed, and veins are chequered black and white, although this may not be clear if worn. Whitish spots near outer edge, the largest in trailing corner. Central spot small or absent. Ssp. *callunaria* is a smaller, often more banded, darker brown upland race. Ssp. *curzoni* has bold dark brown and white cross-lines and bands.

Similar species Most likely to be confused with Common Pug which is more reddish brown, at least in the south (it can be greyer and strongly banded in the north), without chequered veins. Common Pug and Golden-rod Pug have an arched leading edge and central spot of latter is larger. Ssp. *curzoni* could be mistaken for Narrow-winged Pug, which has a more pointed forewing.

Flight season One generation. May-June. In upland habitats sometimes flies in numbers in late afternoon on warm, still days, and can be frequent at light. Elsewhere, comes to light in small numbers.

Life cycle Overwinters as a pupa, probably in loose earth. Larva late June-September.

Larval foodplants Flowers of many plants, including Meadowsweet, ragworts, Devil's-bit Scabious, knapweeds, hawkweeds, Heather and Cross-leaved Heath. Reported feeding on the soft young shoots of newly-planted Sitka Spruce and Lodgepole Pine, but cannot eat the hardened needles.

Habitat Most abundant on moorland and upland grassland but found in most upland habitats. Apparently very local and scarce in the lowlands, occurring mainly on heathland, chalk downland, fens, flowery open woodland and derelict rough ground, where best sought as a larva.

Status & distribution Resident. Local. Ssp. *satyrata* is widespread in southern and eastern England but the records suggest it is very local, with more records from the chalk of Hampshire and Surrey than elsewhere. However, it is easily overlooked in light-trap catches. Two in Guernsey, in 1999, appear to be the only records in the Channel Islands. Ssp. *callunaria* Resident. Common. Fairly well distributed and locally frequent in Northumberland, mainland Scotland, the Inner Hebrides, Orkney and in parts of Ireland, but appears to be rather local and scarce on Man. Also found locally in Wales, the West Midlands and some parts of northern England. Ssp. *curzoni* is widespread and frequent in Shetland, and some individuals from Orkney are similar.

Doubleday's Pug
not illustrated

Eupithecia cauchiata (Dup.)
Uncertain.
1829(8523)

Only a single individual has been recorded in Britain, by Henry Doubleday, in the mid-19th century, in Essex. The moth looks like a larger, more yellow version of the Satyr Pug. Found in most countries in mainland Europe, where it flies in June-July. The larva recorded from Goldenrod.

Wormwood Pug
page 142

Eupithecia absinthiata (Cl.)
Common. T
1830(8527)

Ling Pug
page 142

E. absinthiata f. *goossensiata* Mab.
Local. T
(1831)(8528)

Field characters FW 11-13mm. Wormwood Pug is an often encountered species worth learning at an early stage. The most frequent of the rather plain, reddish-brown pugs, with conspicuous dark spots on leading edge of forewing, and large dark central and whitish trailing corner spots, which all vary in size and extent. Forewing somewhat elongated. Black band on abdomen. Ling Pug is lately considered by some authorities to be a heathland and moorland form of Wormwood Pug. It is usually smaller and greyer but otherwise similar, sometimes with a mauvish tint when fresh.

Similar species Currant Pug is smaller, with much more rounded forewing and a larger, more prominent, often double, white trailing corner spot. Bleached Pug has a black band on abdomen, but is paler, with fuller, more rounded forewing, a weak trailing corner spot and a more elongate dark central spot, and is usually larger. See also Campanula Pug, White-spotted Pug and Pimpinel Pug.

Flight season One generation. June-July. Often seen at dusk. Comes regularly to light in small numbers.

Life cycle Overwinters as a pupa, in loose earth. Larva late July-October.

Larval foodplants The flowers of many plants of the family Asteraceae (composites), including Mugwort, Yarrow, ragworts, Wormwood, Sea Wormwood, Sea Aster, Michaelmas-daisy, Goldenrod and Canadian Goldenrod. Ling Pug feeds on the flowers of Heather.

Habitat A familiar pug in gardens, particularly in urban and suburban areas, but occurs in many habitats, from saltmarshes and other coastal habitats to grasslands and open woodland, in lowlands and uplands.

Status & distribution Wormwood Pug: Resident. Common. Fairly well distributed throughout England and Wales, lowland mainland Scotland, the Inner Hebrides and Ireland. Local on Man. Local and occasional in the Channel Islands.

Ling Pug: Resident. Local. Widespread and often abundant on heathland and moorland throughout the British Isles, including Orkney. Very local and rarely recorded on Man.

Currant Pug
page 142

Eupithecia assimilata Doubl.

Common. T   1832(8531)

Field characters & Similar species FW 9-12mm. Conspicuous, large cream corner spot and other cream markings near outer edge are key features. Has strong black central and leading edge spots on warm, plain brown forewing (when fresh), which is shorter, rounder and more compact than the quite similar Wormwood Pug. Usually, Wormwood Pug is larger, with longer forewing and often with stronger black markings on leading edge. See also Triple-spotted Pug and White-spotted Pug.

Flight season Mainly two generations, May-June and August. One generation in the north of its range, June-July. Sometimes disturbed among foodplants by day. Comes to light.

Life cycle Overwinters as a pupa, in loose earth. Larva early June-late July and late August-September.

Larval foodplants Wild Hop, Black Currant and Red Currant.

Habitat Often seen in gardens and allotments but also frequent on Wild Hop in hedgerows and open woodland.

Status & distribution Resident. Common.

Larva of Wormwood Pug.

Widespread, quite well distributed and fairly frequent in lowland England, Wales and Scotland, including the Inner Hebrides and Orkney, and in Ireland. Local and rarely recorded on Man. Widespread and occasional in the Channel Islands.

Bleached Pug
page 142

Eupithecia expallidata Doubl.

Nb. SE,(W),(N)   1833(8530)

Field characters FW 12-13mm. A large, pale, plain pinkish grey-brown pug, with a bleached look. Forewing broad and rounded. Several black marks on leading edge. Central spot elongated, with black dotted cross-lines either side. Whitish corner spot weak or absent. Has a black band on abdomen.

Similar species Pale Wormwood Pugs are often misidentified as Bleached Pug. Forewing of Wormwood Pug is darker, more reddish, narrower, especially in male, leading edge is less arched with black spots less striking and trailing corner spot generally bolder. Central spot is usually circular or oval and relatively small, but it is sometimes elongated which adds to the confusion.

Flight season One generation. Late June-August. Sometimes disturbed among foodplant by day, flies at dusk and later occasionally comes to light.

Life cycle Overwinters as a pupa, in a cocoon in loose earth. Larva late August-mid October.

Larval foodplants Flowers of Goldenrod. Wild Angelica has been suggested as an alternative but this seems unlikely.

Habitat Woodland rides and clearings, especially recently coppiced areas.

Status & distribution Resident. Nationally Scarce B. Reported very locally throughout England, mainly south of the Humber, and in Wales. Recent records from East Anglia appear to be misidentifications, and this may be the case elsewhere. Limited by the localised distribution of the larval foodplant. A few reports from north-west England, south-west Scotland north to Inverness-shire and from western Ireland, with at least two records from the east coast of Northern Ireland. One record from Man, on the Calf of Man, on 24 August 1998.

Common Pug
page 142

Eupithecia vulgata vulgata (Haw.)

Common. S,C
1834(8534)

ssp. *scotica* Cock.
Common. N

ssp. *clarensis* Huggins
Burren, Ireland

Field characters FW 10-12mm. Ssp. *vulgata* This very common pug is worth learning at an early stage. Forewing somewhat narrow with curved leading edge and a rather rough, grainy texture. Very small central spot, sometimes absent, whitish outermost cross-line and trailing corner spot, and subtle patterns of grey and warm, tawny brown or reddish brown, darker along leading edge. Cross-lines very variable in strength, always angled near leading edge. A series of black dashes along side of abdomen. The dark, melanic f. *atropicta* Dietze and f. *unicolor* Lempke are widespread alongside the typical form. The rather narrow forewing shape helps recognition. Ssp. *scotica* is often greyer, with stronger cross-lines. Ssp. *clarensis* is a whitish-brown race associated with limestone, with chalky, whitish hindwing.

Similar species Smaller and more weakly marked than other common brown garden pugs such as Wormwood and Tawny Speckled Pugs. See also Grey Pug, Edinburgh Pug, Maple Pug, Triple-spotted Pug, Satyr Pug and Valerian Pug.

Flight season Two generations. May-June and August. Normally one generation in Scotland and Ireland, May-July. Often netted at dusk. Comes to light, sometimes in fair numbers.

Life cycle Overwinters as a pupa, on the ground or in loose earth. Larva June-July and late August-early October.

Larval foodplants The leaves of various trees, including Hawthorn and sallows; also Bramble, and the flowers and leaves of various low-growing plants, including ragworts, Yarrow and Hogweed.

Habitat Many situations, including urban and rural gardens, hedgerows, and most open scrubby habitats from fens to heathland, and woodland.

Status & distribution Resident. Ssp. *vulgata* Common. Widespread, well distributed and frequent throughout England, Wales, parts of lowland Scotland and the Channel Islands. Ssp. *scotica* Common. Widespread and frequent in Scotland, including the Hebrides, also Man and Ireland. Less frequent and more localised on Orkney. Reported from Shetland, possibly in error. Ssp. *clarensis* Restricted to the Burren, Co. Clare, where it is locally frequent.

White-spotted Pug
page 142

Eupithecia tripunctaria H.-S.

Local. S,C,(N)
1835(8535)

Field characters & Similar species FW 10-12mm. The white spots on well-marked examples of this brownish-grey pug, at trailing corner of both fore- and hindwing, along outer edge of forewing, on back of thorax (as a crest) and on side of abdomen (near base), are diagnostic. Some spots may be absent, or become worn off, but most remain discernible. Larch Pug has white spot or crest on thorax only, and more sharply-angled cross-lines, and any whitish spot at trailing corner is indistinct, as in Grey Pug and Golden-rod Pug. Forewing never reddish. The widespread melanic f. *angelicata* Barr. is brownish-black all over. It is particularly frequent in the Midlands, but infrequent in the London area, and cannot be distinguished with certainty from melanic Grey Pug or female melanic Golden-rod Pug without examination of genitalia. Currant Pug and Wormwood Pug are redder brown, and black central spot and leading edge markings are larger.

Flight season Two generations. Mainly May-June and August, but also recorded in July and September. Seldom seen except regularly at light, in small numbers.

Life cycle Overwinters as a pupa, in plant debris or loose soil. Larva late June-late September.

Larval foodplants First generation on Elder flowers, the second on the developing fruits of Wild Angelica, and occasionally other umbellifers such as Cow Parsley, Hogweed, Wild Parsnip and Wild Carrot.

Habitat Woodland, hedgerows, roadside verges, the banks of rivers and ditches, damp field corners, fens and unkempt parts of parks and gardens.

Status & distribution Resident. Local. Widespread and fairly well distributed in England and Wales. Local in lowland Scotland north to the Moray Firth. Occasional on Man. Somewhat local in Northern Ireland and probably in the Republic, where it has been reported mainly near the west coast. Widespread and occasional in the Channel Islands.

Campanula Pug
page 142

Eupithecia denotata denotata (Hb.)

Na. S,E
1836(8536)

Jasione Pug
page 142

ssp. *jasioneata* Crewe
Na. SW,WC

Field characters & Similar species FW 11-13mm. Campanula Pug is a rather plain, brownish pug. Leading edge of quite broad forewing is slightly curved, central spot is oval, quite large and conspicuous. Markings on leading edge, cross-lines and trailing corner spot all weak. No black band on abdomen. Sometimes a weak chequering effect on veins. This combination distinguishes it from Wormwood Pug. Pimpinel Pug has greyer, more tapering forewing and is more strongly marked. Jasione Pug is smaller, grey, with narrower forewing and stronger markings than Campanula Pug. Golden-rod Pug is very similar, but leading edge of forewing is more curved, chequered veins usually noticeable and cross-lines weaker. In cases of doubt, examination of abdominal plates is advisable. Could

114

also be mistaken for Larch Pug, which has a white spot on thorax.

Flight season One generation. July. Occasional at light, otherwise both subspecies seldom seen as adults.

Life cycle Overwinters as a pupa in loose earth. Larva August-September.

Larval foodplants Campanula Pug feeds on the ripening seed capsules of Nettle-leaved Bellflower and Giant Bellflower. Also found on garden Campanulas. Recent searches of Clustered Bellflower on the chalk in Surrey have been unproductive. Jasione Pug feeds on the seedheads of Sheep's-bit (*Jasione montana*), usually as the heads are maturing and drying out.

Habitat Campanula Pug is found in woodland rides and edges, hedgerows and scrubby grassland, usually in calcareous, often slightly damp situations; sometimes in gardens. Jasione Pug, like its foodplant, is mainly western, favours dry grassy places, heaths and cliffs, usually near the sea, and avoids calcareous situations. Hedgebanks and overgrown stone walls have proved productive for its larvae.

Status & distribution Campanula Pug: Nationally Scarce A; probably under-recorded. Apparently very local and southern, mainly on the chalk in Hampshire and the North Downs of Surrey and Kent, but reported from several sites as far north and east as Lincolnshire, and from Gloucestershire and the Silurian Limestone of Herefordshire in the west. There are old records from south Wales. Jasione Pug: Nationally Scarce A. Reported locally, usually near the sea, in south-west England, including Scilly, from scattered sites in west Wales, as local and occasional in the south of Man, and from a number of sites near the coast in south-west Ireland, from Cos. Kerry to Mayo. Two reported as accidental introductions to Orkney on 2 August 1970, with plants from Co. Clare. In the Channel Islands Jasione Pug is recorded only from Guernsey, in 1913 and 1932, with no reports of Campanula Pug.

Grey Pug   page 142
Eupithecia subfuscata (Haw.)
Common. T   1837(8537)

Field characters FW 10-12mm. A common, brownish-grey pug, which needs to be memorised. Forewing has a conspicuous black central spot. Ground-colour darkest at wing base, leading edge and outer border, with various wavy cross-lines. Melanic f. *obscurissima* Prout is widespread and frequent. Hindwing paler than forewing in both forms.

Similar species Golden-rod Pug has chequered veins on forewing, and tends to have fainter cross-lines. Larch Pug has a white thoracic spot or crest, more pointed forewing, straighter leading edge and more oblique cross-lines. Difficult to distinguish from female Golden-rod Pug without examination of genitalia. In males, plate on eighth abdominal segment is quite different: in Grey Pug this is dark, with two long pincers, while in Golden-rod Pug it is pale,

broader and with an indentation at the end. Melanic Grey Pugs are distinguished from those of Green Pug by wing shape, complete lack of lighter markings and absence of black belt on abdomen. See also Fletcher's Pug, White-spotted Pug, Triple-spotted Pug and Yarrow Pug.

Flight season Mainly one generation. May-June. In some years a partial second generation in August in some places. Fairly frequent at light.

Life cycle Overwinters as a pupa in loose earth, plant debris, or occasionally behind loose bark. Larva late June-October.

Larval foodplants The flowers and leaves of many herbaceous and woody broadleaved plants. Frequent on Blackthorn, Hawthorn, regular on Barberry in many counties, sallows and Aspen. Also ragworts, Mugwort, knapweeds, Yarrow, Burnet-saxifrage and Betony.

Habitat Gardens, hedgerows, scrub, heathland, downland, woodland and wetland in many situations, from coastal to uplands.

Status & distribution Resident. Common. Well distributed throughout most of England, Wales and lowland Scotland, north to Caithness. Unconfirmed reports from Shetland. Fairly widespread but occasional on Man and in Ireland. Widespread and frequent in the Channel Islands.

Tawny Speckled Pug   page 142
Eupithecia icterata (Vill.)
ssp. *subfulvata* (Haw.)
Common. T   1838(8538)

Field characters FW 11-13mm. A large pug, variable in colour, with two distinct forms. The typical form has a large, orange-brown central patch on forewing, which contrasts sharply with dark grey-brown leading and outer edges. F. *cognata* Steph. often has the tawny orange coloration reduced, and has distinct, whitish cross-lines. This form predominates in northern Britain, especially in Scotland. Both forms have well-defined black central spots and dull grey or brownish-grey hindwing.

Similar species Some examples of f. *cognata* are superficially similar to Grey Pug, which is smaller, flies earlier in the year and lacks any hint of tawny colour.

Flight season One generation. July-August. Flies from dusk, visits flowers such as ragworts and buddleias. Regular at light in small numbers.

Life cycle Overwinters as a pupa in loose earth. Larva September-October.

Larval foodplants Flowers and leaves of Yarrow and Sneezewort. Recorded from Southernwood in gardens.

Habitat Many situations, from suburban and rural gardens, hedgerows and roadside verges to calcareous, neutral and acid grassland, fens, open woodland and coastal habitats.

Status & distribution Resident. Common. Well distributed throughout mainland Britain and on some of the Hebrides. Fairly widespread but occasional on Man. Found in widely separated sites throughout

Ireland, but under-recorded. Local and occasional in the Channel Islands.

Bordered Pug
page 143
Eupithecia succenturiata (L.)
Common. S,C,(N)   1839(8539)

Field characters FW 12-13mm. A large, easily recognisable pug, with brown forewing borders, white central patch and white thorax. In f. *disparata* Hb., much of the white is replaced by grey, but central black spot remains large and conspicuous.
Similar species Shaded Pug is also marked with white, but is smaller, with paler wing borders, weaker markings and a tiny central spot.
Flight season One generation. July-August. Rarely seen except regularly at light, in small numbers.
Life cycle Overwinters as a pupa in loose earth. Larva mid August-mid October, feeding by night and hiding near the base of the plant by day when large.
Larval foodplants Mugwort.
Habitat Disturbed open ground, roadside verges, and other rough places, including gardens.
Status & distribution Resident. Common. Well distributed and fairly frequent in most parts of England, but much more local in the south-west, in Wales, northern England, Scotland and Ireland. Local and rare on Man. Local and occasional on Jersey. Rare on Guernsey and Alderney.

Shaded Pug
page 143
Eupithecia subumbrata ([D. & S.])
Local. SE,(T)   1840(8546)

Field characters FW 10-12mm. The chalky-white component of markings, rather narrow forewing with almost straight leading edge and small central spot, are diagnostic. Usually, forewing whitish apart from a band around edge, but some examples are merely banded with white, or have it even further reduced. Central spot tiny. Sometimes there are bold, fine cross-lines and even wedge-like markings on forewing. Thorax grey-brown.
Similar species Dark, atypical examples could be mistaken for Grey Pug, but wing shape is diagnostic. See also Bordered Pug.
Flight season One generation. June-early July. Readily disturbed by day from sward, flies from dusk. Comes to light, sometimes in large numbers.
Life cycle Overwinters as a pupa in loose earth. Larva July-September.
Larval foodplants Flowers of many herbaceous plants, including hawk's-beards, ragworts, Field Scabious, St John's-worts, Wild Marjoram, Spanish Catchfly and Flixweed.
Habitat Chalk downland, breckland, flowery field margins and roadside verges, wide rides in plantations and woodland, saltmarshes, soft-rock cliffs and other coastal habitats.
Status & distribution Resident. Local. Mainly south-eastern England, where it is quite well distributed and frequent on calcareous soils from Portland,

Dorset, to East Anglia and the downs of Kent. Also found in a scatter of other locations, mainly coastal or inland limestone exposures, such as the Gower, Glamorgan, north Wales, south Cumbria, and in Yorkshire. Local and somewhat rare on Man. Widespread but local in Ireland, though sometimes frequent where it occurs, such as in the Burren, Co. Clare. In the Channel Islands, recorded from Guernsey, but not since 1889.

Yarrow Pug
page 143
Eupithecia millefoliata Rössler
Nb. SE   1841(8551)

Field characters FW 12-13mm. Quite a large greyish pug. Forewing rather pointed and tinged with brown, lightly patterned with numerous slightly wavy cross-lines and bands, that beyond central spot is kinked near leading edge. Leading edge rather straight until near tip. Pale broken line usually runs near outer edge, widening in trailing corner.
Similar species Fletcher's Pug lacks any brownish tint and has more arched leading edge. Plain Pug is sometimes greyish, but the fuller, more rounded forewing, with arched leading edge and gently-curved, white outer band, is diagnostic. Grey Pug has forewing less pointed, more rounded, and is usually smaller. Tawny Speckled Pug f. *cognata* is browner, with more curved leading edge to forewing, and is usually found in the north and west. Abdominal plates or genitalia should be checked, especially if the moth is worn.
Flight season One generation. June-July. Comes to light.
Life cycle Overwinters as a pupa among plant debris. Larva late August-late October.
Larval foodplants Flowers, ripening and later on ripe seedheads of Yarrow, preferring ripe seedheads when large.
Habitat Open, derelict coastal ground, especially sand-dunes and shingle beaches; also roadside verges and rough or scrubby grassland.
Status & distribution Resident and suspected immigrant. Nationally Scarce B. First captured in the British Isles from Hamstreet Woods, east Kent, in 1933. Now breeding in coastal sites as far west as Dorset, particularly around Weymouth and Christchurch, north to Essex and including the north coast of the Isle of Wight. Well distributed along both sides of the Thames, where first recorded in 1961, from the estuary westwards into Middlesex, Berkshire and Surrey, mostly within 10km of the river. Also recorded inland in Essex, Norfolk, Suffolk and Cambridgeshire. Singletons at light at Gibraltar Point, Lincolnshire, in 1992 and 1993. In the Channel Islands recorded only from Guernsey, one in 1989.

Plain Pug
page 143
Eupithecia simpliciata (Haw.)
Local. S,C   1842(8553)

Field characters FW 11-13mm. A fairly large, full-

116

winged, light sandy brown pug. Sometimes tinged with grey, and with a distinct, gently-curved, narrow white cross-band beyond dark central dot, which is small, usually conspicuous but sometimes weak.
Similar species See Yarrow Pug.
Flight season One generation. Mid June-early August. Flies from dusk. Visits flowers such as ragworts and Marram. Sometimes seen at rest on or near foodplant after dark. Comes to light.
Life cycle Overwinters as a pupa in loose earth. Larva August-September.
Larval foodplants Ripening seedheads of goosefoots and oraches, preferring the prostrate kinds.
Habitat Edges of saltmarshes, banks of estuaries and tidal rivers, coastal cliffs, derelict and disturbed open ground, often in urban situations, regularly inland away from rivers. Favours lighter soils, especially calcareous formations.
Status & distribution Resident. Local. Chiefly coastal and in the Thames Valley. Occurs at scattered sites along the coasts of southern England and Wales north to Lancashire in the west, including Scilly. In the east, recorded north to the Tees marshes, near Saltholme, near Hartlepool, Co. Durham, where long known. Well distributed along the Thames. Also recorded in the Severn Valley. There are thinly scattered records inland, in southern England, the Midlands, East Anglia and Yorkshire. Local and rare on Man. Very local in southern Ireland and eastern Northern Ireland. Local and occasional in the Channel Islands.

Goosefoot Pug
page 143
Eupithecia sinuosaria (Eversm.)
Suspected rare immigrant. S   1842a(8557)

Field characters FW 10-12mm. A greyish-brown pug. Diagnostic feature is irregular, narrow, brown, dark-edged central cross-band on forewing, the inner edge of which is strongly angled in leading half, and outer edge usually runs through elongated central spot. Usually dark blotches or dashes near forewing tip. Varies relatively little.
Similar species None.
Flight season One generation. June-August in mainland Europe.
Life cycle Overwinters as a pupa in loose earth. Larva July-September in mainland Europe.
Larval foodplants Goosefoots and oraches.
Habitat Open, disturbed ground.
Status & distribution Suspected rare immigrant. Recorded twice in the British Isles, both males at light at Berrow, Somerset, on 13 June 1992 and at Harpenden, Hertfordshire, between 18-21 June 1992. Apparently extending its distribution westwards from eastern Europe and Scandinavia in recent decades, and now established in the Netherlands.

Thyme Pug
page 143
Eupithecia distinctaria H.-S.
ssp. *constrictata* Guen.
Nb. T,not SE   1843(8556)

Field characters FW 8-10mm. Bold, black, linear central and leading edge spots on forewing, grey colour and small size are a diagnostic combination. Two fine, black central cross-lines are normally present. Hindwing usually well marked.
Similar species Ochreous Pug can be quite grey, but has narrower, more pointed, usually plainer forewing, and weakly-marked hindwing. See also Channel Islands Pug.
Flight season One generation. June-July. Sometimes disturbed from foodplant by day in hot weather. Flies from dusk. Comes to light fairly regularly.
Life cycle Overwinters as a pupa in loose earth. Larva August-September.
Larval foodplants Flowers of Wild Thyme.
Habitat The steep, hot faces of rocky coastal cliffs, limestone quarries and broken chalk; also partly vegetated sand-dunes.
Status & distribution Resident. Nationally Scarce B. Largely western and coastal, occurring very locally from the Lizard, Cornwall, and Lundy, Devon, along the west coast of England and coasts of Wales to the mainly south-facing parts of the Hebrides and the west coasts of Scotland and Ireland. Also recorded on the south coast of England, particularly at Portland, Dorset, and on the south coast of the Isle of Wight. Recorded from a scatter of inland sites in southern England, mainly on chalk and limestone, including recent records from Bentley Wood, Wiltshire, various sites in Hampshire, the dales of Derbyshire and Staffordshire, Yorkshire (frequent at Austwick), Cumbria and in central Scotland. Local and rare on Man.

Ochreous Pug
page 143
Eupithecia indigata (Hb.)
Common. T   1844(8565)

Field characters FW 8-10mm. A rather small and fairly distinctive pug. Narrow, pointed, pale sandy (sometimes greyish) forewing is rather plain, except for a conspicuous slightly elongated black central spot, and dark spots (often weak) along leading edge.
Similar species See Thyme Pug.
Flight season One generation. April-May. Sometimes beaten from foodplant by day. Flies from dusk. Comes to light, sometimes in large numbers.
Life cycle Overwinters as a pupa, in a flimsy cocoon among needles on or below the foodplant. Larva mid June-mid September.
Larval foodplants Mainly Scots Pine, preferring the buds and young needles. Also reported from Lodgepole Pine and larch. Accepts cypresses and Common Juniper in captivity. Also observed feeding on aphids.
Habitat Long established in Caledonian pine forest.

117

Larva of Scarce Pug.

Also in pine plantations and in gardens in areas where pine is abundant.

Status & distribution Resident. Common. Recorded locally throughout mainland Britain, from Cornwall and Kent to Sutherland, and from the Isle of Wight and the Inner Hebrides. Recorded from scattered sites in Ireland, mostly in the south-west. In the Channel Islands, recorded from Guernsey in 1980.

Pimpinel Pug   page 143
Eupithecia pimpinellata (Hb.)
Local. S,C   1845(8567)

Field characters & Similar species FW 11-12mm. Easily confused with Wormwood Pug, but with a characteristic soft, light grey tinge to forewing, especially along leading edge, which has smaller dark markings. See also Campanula Pug.

Flight season One generation. June-July. Occasional at light, otherwise rarely seen.

Life cycle Overwinters as a pupa, in a cocoon in loose earth. Larva late July-mid October.

Larval foodplants Ripening seed capsules of Burnet-saxifrage.

Habitat Mainly calcareous grassland on light soils, including downland, derelict limestone quarries, roadside verges and woodland rides, occasionally on heavier soils.

Status & distribution Resident. Local. Greatly under-recorded, in part owing to resemblance of adult to more widespread and frequent species. Targeted searches for the larvae in Essex found them in most 10km squares with the foodplant, often previously overlooked. Elsewhere, records thinly scattered throughout much of England north to Yorkshire and south Cumbria, with a few pre-1980 reports scattered through Wales and into southern Scotland. Occasionally recorded from Somerset and Devon, but appears to be genuinely scarce in south-west England. A few scattered records from southern Ireland and Londonderry, Northern Ireland.

Narrow-winged Pug   page 143
Eupithecia nanata (Hb.)
Common. T   1846(8570)

Field characters FW 9-12mm. The very narrow, elongated forewing, with complex marbling of light

and dark, tightly-packed, grey-brown, strongly-angled cross-lines with white edges, is a diagnostic feature of this small to medium-sized pug. Ground-colour varies from whitish to the brown f. *oliveri* Prout, often on the same site. A pale cross-band with a conspicuous angle beyond central spot on forewing is generally apparent, as is a small pale spot in trailing corner. This blackish central spot is always present, but not very conspicuous, often with a distinctive white patch just before it. Hindwing lighter and plainer than forewing. The illustration shows one in resting position, but this species also rests with wings more fully spread, like the other pugs.

Similar species Smaller than Scarce Pug, which is confined to coastal saltmarshes and has broader forewing with straight leading edge. See also the Shetland f. *curzoni* of Satyr Pug, which has shorter forewing, with a more rounded outer edge.

Flight season Mainly one generation. Late April-June. Partial second generation in southern Britain, late July-August. Sometimes seen on, or disturbed among, foodplant by day. Flies from dusk. Comes to light, sometimes in large numbers.

Life cycle Overwinters as a pupa, in a cocoon in loose earth. Larva mid June-late September.

Larval foodplants Flowers of Heather.

Habitat Heathland and moorland. Occasionally elsewhere, including gardens, probably as a vagrant.

Status & distribution Resident. Common. Well distributed in heaths and moors throughout the British Isles, from Scilly to Orkney and Shetland, and including the Hebrides, Man and western Ireland. Local and occasional on Jersey, rare on Guernsey.

Scarce Pug   page 143
Eupithecia extensaria occidua Prout
RDB. EC   1847(8571)

Field characters FW 11-13mm. An unmistakable, fairly large brownish pug, with forewing leading edge straight. Forewing crossed by three light brown oblique bands on a silvery white ground-colour. Hindwing light grey with a narrow central whitish cross-band. Looks very elongated as it rests, wings spread to maximum extent along the length of the plant stems.

Similar species See Narrow-winged Pug.

Flight season One generation. June-July. Sometimes disturbed among foodplant by day. Comes to light fairly readily.

Life cycle Overwinters as a pupa in a cocoon among plant debris or soft earth. Larva August-September.

Larval foodplants Flowers and leaves of Sea Wormwood.

Habitat The fringes and higher ground of salt-marshes.

Status & distribution Resident. Red Data Book species. Limited to the east coast of England, mainly in the vicinity of the Wash, where it occurs in a few restricted sites in north Norfolk and Lincolnshire. Also present around the mouth of the Humber in

Yorkshire and in a single saltmarsh system in Essex. The larval foodplant was examined much more widely in Essex and Kent during searches for Essex Emerald in the 1980s and 1990s, and no further colonies of Scarce Pug were found.

Explanatory note to moths 1848-1850:
Angle-barred Pug/Ash Pug/Tamarisk Pug
The Angle-barred Pug *Eupithecia innotata* (1848) has been recorded from most of Europe. In the European checklist it is listed separately from the Ash Pug *E. fraxinata*, with a note that further research is needed to determine whether the Ash Pug really is a distinct species or a form of the Angle-barred Pug. Opinion is divided. The latest version (2000) of the British list follows the view that there is one species, *E. innotata*, the Angle-barred Pug, which exploits a number of plants which are not closely related and happen to be toxic to most moth larvae. One of these is Ash. It is possible that the moths on Ash, until recently known as the Ash Pug, never meet and breed with those on other foodplants, and constitute a distinct lineage separated by foodplant and habitat (an ecotype), but this is not proven and these moths do not appear to have developed distinct physical differences from those on other foodplants. Currently indistinguishable moths are also found regularly, and in numbers, as larvae on Sea-buckthorn and Tamarisk. In the past, these have been considered variously as Angle-barred Pug and Tamarisk Pug, the latter described as *E. tamarisciata*, or alternatively as forms of the Ash Pug. In addition, other apparently identical moths have been reared occasionally from hawthorns, Blackthorn and Elder, and supposedly from Mugwort and Sea Wormwood, and reported either as Angle-barred Pug or Ash Pug. It seems sensible to keep the vernacular name Angle-barred Pug linked to the scientific name *E. innotata*, especially because it is so descriptive and fits all the various populations. This also keeps the names Ash Pug and *E. fraxinata* available should the Ash populations be found to be a distinct species in the future. So in the British list, the Ash Pug is now listed as f. *fraxinata* Crewe of the Angle-barred Pug *E. innotata*. Its number in the list, 1849, is no longer a valid species number, so is shown in parentheses. This is still a useful code number for current databases. Likewise, those moths reared from Tamarisk are considered f. *tamarisciata* Freyer of the Angle-barred Pug *E. innotata*. Those found occasionally on other foodplants are simply referable as Angle-barred Pug. It must be stated that some leading authorities disagree and take the view that only large continental-type moths fit Angle-barred Pug, and these have never been recorded in Britain. In this view, all the British moths are considered Ash Pug on different foodplants.

Angle-barred Pug   page 143
Eupithecia innotata (Hufn.)
Common. T   1848(8573)

Ash Pug
Eupithecia innotata f. *fraxinata* Crewe
Common. T   (1849)(8575)

Tamarisk Pug
Eupithecia innotata f. *tamarisciata*
(Freyer)
Uncommon on alien foodplant.   (1850)(8573)

119

Field characters FW 10-12mm. A large, rather plain brown or grey-brown pug, with narrow, elongated forewing, a small black elongated central spot and usually a partial outer cross-line sharply angled near leading edge. Adjacent lines, when present, also sharply angled. Usually a light outer line, widened in trailing corner to form a hint of a corner spot. The often smaller, all brown melanic f. *unicolor* Prout is easily distinguished from melanic forms of other species by wing shape. It is frequent in northern England and occasional to rare elsewhere.
Similar species None.
Flight season Two generations. Late May-mid June, and August. Regular at light, usually in small numbers.
Life cycle Overwinters as a pupa, under moss or bark on or at the base of the foodplant, or in loose earth. Larva mid June-late July and late August-September.
Larval foodplants Ash, Sea-buckthorn, Tamarisk, hawthorns, Blackthorn and Elder. Reportedly Mugwort and Sea Wormwood, but these have not been confirmed in the British Isles.
Habitat Ash Pug: woodland, hedgerows, parks and gardens, including free-standing trees. Tamarisk Pug: a range of coastal habitats, including gardens. Other populations of the Angle-barred Pug: coastal sand-dunes on Sea-buckthorn. Various other open habitats, including woodland rides. It has yet to be shown that the Ash Pug is a distinct species and it may be that moths in the above habitats sometimes move from Ash to complete development or breed on other plants.
Status & distribution Resident. Angle-barred Pug: Has been reared from Sea-buckthorn locally in Kent, Essex, Lincolnshire, Yorkshire, and possibly else-where, sometimes reported as Angle-barred Pug, sometimes as Ash Pug due to confused nomenclature. Ash Pug: Records of the Ash Pug are widely scattered over Britain, from the south coast of England to southern Scotland and Wales. It appears to occur at low density in most places where Ash is frequent. Recorded from Orkney, where considered introduced with Ash. Local and occasional on Man and throughout Ireland. Rare in the Channel Islands. Tamarisk Pug: Reared from Tamarisk in Kent, Hayling Island, Hampshire, and from the Isle of Wight. Following the 2000 list, all above are Angle-barred

Pug, for which the National Status is therefore 'Common', and the Distribution 'Throughout'.

Golden-rod Pug
page 143

Eupithecia virgaureata Doubl.

Local. W,(E)   1851(8577)

Field characters & Similar species FW 10-11mm. Examples in good condition have a conspicuous white tuft of scales at the hind end of thorax. Features of male antennae have not been found useful in distinguishing this species from very similar Grey Pug. In male Golden-rod Pug the plate on the underside of the eighth abdominal segment is pale, broad, and has an indentation at the end, while in Grey Pug it is dark, with two long pincers. Central spot is generally larger and rounder in Golden-rod Pug and some of the veins are chequered with black on this otherwise greyish-brown, medium-sized pug, but female cannot be reliably distinguished from Grey Pug on wing markings. A melanic f. *nigra* Lempke, almost uniformly dark grey, is frequently predominant in the Midlands and Lincolnshire, and occurs elsewhere. See also Jasione Pug, Satyr Pug, Larch Pug and (melanic) White-spotted Pug.

Flight season Mainly two generations. May-June, and August. One generation in parts of Scotland, May-June. Rarely seen, except regularly at light.

Life cycle Overwinters as a pupa, in loose earth. Larva June-July and September-October.

Larval foodplants Second generation larvae readily found on ragworts and Goldenrod. Foodplants of first generation unresolved. One such larva has been found on Grey Willow. Fresh young leaves of Hawthorn accepted in captivity.

Habitat A wide range, from roadside verges and derelict open ground, to farmland, and rides and cleared areas in woodland.

Status & distribution Resident. Local. Predominantly western in England and Wales. Recorded locally from Scilly, and a scatter of sites in south-west England and the West Midlands to Cumbria, but reaches eastwards to Lincolnshire and Yorkshire. Apparently very local and rare in southern and south-east England, with few genuine records, others proving to be misidentified Grey Pug. Formerly frequent in coppiced woodland in Kent. Reported from widely scattered sites throughout lowland, mainland Scotland, the Inner Hebrides and Ireland. Local and rarely recorded on Man. Rare on Guernsey.

Brindled Pug
page 143

Eupithecia abbreviata Steph.

Common. T   1852(8578)

Field characters & Similar species FW 10-12mm. An abundant spring pug with mottled, usually brown forewing, generally with a small but usually distinct, and normally elongated black central spot. The pale outer central cross-band has a series of very fine, black streaks or wedges projecting inwards, and often a whitish patch beyond the central dot. The

almost blackish f. *hirschkei* Bast. is widespread and frequent alongside the normal form. It can be distinguished from other similar melanic pugs by forewing shape. See also Mottled Pug and Oak-tree Pug.

Flight season One generation. March-early May. Sometimes found, or disturbed from rest, on trunks and branches of foodplant. Flies from dusk. Comes to light, sometimes abundantly.

Life cycle Overwinters as a pupa, behind loose bark on foodplant or in loose earth. Larva June-July.

Larval foodplants Pedunculate Oak and Sessile Oak and hawthorns. Possibly also Turkey Oak.

Habitat Woodland dominated by or containing large amounts of oak. Also hedgerows and gardens in well-wooded districts.

Status & distribution Resident. Common. Fairly well distributed and in many places locally abundant in England, Wales and lowland mainland Scotland. Locally frequent on Man. Proving to be quite well distributed and frequent in Northern Ireland and recorded from a wide scatter of sites in the Republic.

Oak-tree Pug
page 143

Eupithecia dodoneata Guen.

Common. S,C   1853(8579)

Field characters & Similar species FW 8-11mm. Very similarly marked to Brindled Pug, but smaller, more variegated, with a comparatively large, round central dot and less pointed forewing. Black wedges beyond central spot often more prominent. Several black dashes often visible on veins just beyond central spot. Often with orange-brown scales along leading and trailing edges of forewing. Most like Dwarf Pug, which flies at the same time and may also occur in the same habitat, where exotic conifers have been introduced. Dwarf Pug has a larger black central spot, stronger cross-lines and borders, a whiter hindwing, and lacks wedges or a white patch beyond central spot. See also Juniper Pug.

Flight season One generation. April-early June. Flies from dusk. Comes to light, sometimes in large numbers.

Life cycle Overwinters as a pupa, bark on foodplant or in loose earth. Larva late June-early August.

Larval foodplants Mainly the calyx of berries, but also the leaves, of mature Hawthorn; also the leaves of Pedunculate Oak.

Habitat Long-established woodland, shelterbelts, hedgerows and scrub.

Status & distribution Resident. Common. Has proved to be much more widespread and frequent as recording effort has increased. Fairly well distributed and locally frequent throughout England north to south Cumbria and north Yorkshire, where recorded in 1976 for the first time in many years and now widespread. Also recorded from widely scattered sites in Wales. A few very scattered reports from mainland Scotland which may refer to Dwarf Pug, and require confirmation. Occurs locally in Northern Ireland and in the Irish Republic. Local and occasional in the Channel Islands.

Juniper Pug
page 143

Eupithecia pusillata pusillata ([D. & S.])
Common. T   1854(8583)

ssp. *anglicata* H.-S.
Former resident; extinct.

Field characters FW 9-11mm. Very variable. Best identifying features are a small whitish or fawn unmarked patch just beyond small black central spot, and two black dashes usually present on veins halfway between central spot and forewing tip. Cross-lines vary in intensity, but when present sharply angled near central spot, with a blackish cross-line passing through it. Ground-colour varies from whitish, particularly in rural Scotland, to dark brown or grey. Some populations contain many variants. The lighter individuals look finely striped with grey. Melanics usually retain a hint of the pale patch. Hindwing weakly marked, with darker border and tiny central spot. A whitish race ssp. *anglicata* was discovered on the chalk sea-cliffs near Dover, Kent, in 1849, but has not been seen since 1915 and is believed to be extinct.

Similar species Oak-tree Pug can also have pale patch beyond central spot and black dashes, but is slightly smaller and flies earlier in the year.

Flight season One generation. July-September. Occasionally seen flying near foodplant in hot sunshine. Main flight at dusk, but later comes readily to light.

Life cycle Overwinters as an egg on the foodplant. Larva April-early June. Pupates in a slight cocoon among needles on the foodplant.

Larval foodplants Common Juniper and cultivated Junipers, both erect and prostrate. Also reported from cypresses and Red-cedars.

Habitat Moorland, calcareous grassland; frequent in gardens, parks and plantations on cultivars.

Status & distribution Resident. Common. Well distributed, and locally frequent where Common Juniper is well established, particularly southern and south-eastern England, northern England, north Wales, mainland Scotland, and the Inner Hebrides. Recorded widely in other areas throughout Britain where Junipers and cypresses have been planted. Occurs locally on Orkney and Shetland. Very local and rare on Man. Recorded locally in the eastern part of Northern Ireland and from scattered sites in the Republic – Common Juniper is native mainly in the west, but records of the moth include urban areas elsewhere.

Cypress Pug
page 144

Eupithecia phoeniceata (Ramb.)
Uncommon. S   1855(8584)

Field characters FW 10-11mm. Easily recognised by the unique black streaks in central part of pale brown forewing and the black belt on abdomen just behind thorax. Forewing distinctly narrow and ground-colour is paler brown than most pugs.

Similar species None.

Flight season One generation. Mainly August-September, but occasional individuals reported May-October. Easily beaten from mature foodplant in early evening. Flies from dusk and comes readily to light.

Life cycle Overwinters as a larva, feeding from October, including mild periods throughout the winter, until April or May, pupating in a slight cocoon among needles on the foodplant.

Larval foodplants Monterey Cypress. Accepts Lawson's Cypress and Leyland Cypress in captivity and probably uses them in the wild.

Habitat Gardens, parks and plantations where the foodplant is well established.

Status & distribution Resident. Uncommon, on alien host. A recent colonist first recorded in Britain at Lamorna, Cornwall, on 11 September 1959, found in gardens in the same area in 1960 and now well established and locally frequent in Scilly and along the south coast of England from Cornwall to Kent, inland to Basingstoke, north Hampshire, Surrey, the London area and Essex. Also resident in Somerset and Glamorgan. Individuals have been recorded north to Warwickshire. In Ireland, well established in Co. Cork. Widespread and frequent in the Channel Islands.

Channel Islands Pug
page 144

Eupithecia ultimaria Boisd.
Uncommon.   1855a(8593)

Field characters & Similar species FW 7-10mm. A small grey-brown pug, with conspicuous dark elongated central spot and numerous weak cross-lines. Smaller than Thyme Pug, with less bold cross-lines and more rounded forewing. Most likely to be found and recognised as larvae on distinctive foodplant. Reared individuals often darker than adults in the wild.

Flight season One generation. Late June-late August. Comes to light occasionally.

Life cycle Overwinters as a pupa, among plant debris. Larva July-August.

Larval foodplants Tamarisk, an introduced plant.

Habitat Coastal situations where Tamarisk has been planted or is naturalised.

Status & distribution Resident, recent colonist and immigrant. Uncommon, on alien host. Southern England, mainly on the coast, and Channel Islands. Localised and occasional on Guernsey, where first recorded at light at St Martin's on 20 August 1984, then found to be well established as larvae in 1986. On 20 June 1989, one taken at light at Bishop's Stortford, Hertfordshire. Two individuals were recorded at light at Southsea, Hampshire, on 29 June and 30 July 1995. In 1995 and 1996 searches in late July and August produced larvae in some abundance on Hayling Island, Hampshire, and at various points eastwards along the Sussex coast, including West Wittering, Selsey, Atherington and Climping, and in various places on the south-east and north-east coasts of the Isle of Wight. Subsequently, specimens

Larva of Sloe Pug.

122

at light at Walberton, West Sussex, on 3 August 1990 and 28 July 1995 and at Littlehampton, West Sussex, on 27 June 1992 were confirmed.

Larch Pug   page 144
Eupithecia lariciata (Freyer)
Common. T   1856(8595)

Field characters & Similar species FW 10-12mm. White spot or crest on back of thorax and cross-lines sharply angled around central spot separate this grey-brown pug from Fletcher's Pug, which also has a much more rounded outer edge to forewing, and Grey Pug. In some areas, such as London, the melanic f. *nigra* Prout comprises up to half the population. It is blackish, with slightly paler hindwing and a conspicuous central spot on forewing, and is very difficult to distinguish with certainty from Grey Pug, Golden-rod Pug and White-spotted Pug melanics on wing markings. See also Jasione Pug.
Flight season One generation. May-July. Sometimes disturbed from branches of foodplant. Comes readily to light.
Life cycle Overwinters as a pupa, in loose earth. Larva mid June-early August.
Larval foodplants Mature European Larch. Accepts other larch species.
Habitat Plantations, shelterbelts, gardens and parks.
Status & distribution Resident. Common. Fairly well distributed and frequent in mainland Britain wherever there are mature stands of the foodplant. Recorded from Cornwall to Caithness, and on the Hebrides and Shetland. Local and occasional on Man, and throughout Ireland.

Dwarf Pug   page 144
Eupithecia tantillaria Boisd.
Common. T   1857(8596)

Field characters FW 9-11mm. A medium-sized, mottled, brownish-grey pug, with rather rounded forewing and a large, obvious, rather elongated central spot.
Similar species See Oak-tree Pug and Cloaked Pug.
Flight season One generation. May-June. Readily found by day by tapping branches of foodplants. Flies from dusk. Comes to light, sometimes in large

numbers.
Life cycle Overwinters as a pupa, in loose earth. Larva late June-late August.
Larval foodplants Particularly Norway Spruce, Sitka Spruce and Douglas Fir, but also recorded from Lawson Cypress, Western Red-cedar, Western Hemlock-spruce, Giant Fir and other introduced conifers.
Habitat Mainly plantations of introduced conifers. Also shelterbelts, parks and gardens.
Status & distribution Resident. Common. Increasing in distribution. Found throughout England, Wales, mainland Scotland and Ireland. Well distributed and often abundant where large-scale conifer plantations have been established. More local elsewhere. Resident on Man, but few records.

V-Pug   page 144
Chloroclystis v-ata (Haw.)
Common. T   1858(8601)

Field characters FW 8-11mm. The bold black V-shaped marking near leading edge of otherwise rather faintly-marked, rounded forewing distinguishes this from all other pugs. Green when fresh, but may fade to yellowish-fawn. Hindwing greyish white. Abdomen green, with two parallel rows of black spots and a black belt. Rests with forewings drawn further back than other pugs.
Similar species None.
Flight season Mainly two generations, May-June and mid July-late August. One generation, June-July in northern Britain. Occasionally seen by day on fences and sheds. Flies from dusk. Regular in small numbers at light.
Life cycle Overwinters as a pupa underground. Larva mid June-mid July and late August-early October. Late June-August in northern Britain.
Larval foodplants Flowers of various plants, including Dog-rose, Hawthorn, Traveller's-joy, Hemp-agrimony, Bramble, Elder, Wild Angelica, Mugwort and Goldenrod.
Habitat Parks and gardens, even in urban areas; also farm hedgerows, scrub and lowland woodland on many soils, but especially calcareous areas.
Status & distribution Resident. Common. Well distributed and frequent over much of lowland England and Wales, north to Yorkshire, Cumbria and south-west Scotland and the central belt. Fairly widespread but occasional on Man. Proving to be quite well distributed in Northern Ireland and recorded from a wide scatter of sites in the Republic, especially in the south-west and in the Burren, Co. Clare. Widespread and frequent in the Channel Islands.

Sloe Pug   page 144
Pasiphila chloerata (Mab.)
Common. S,C   1859(8604)

Field characters & Similar species FW 9-10mm. Very similar to some forms of Green Pug, but only faintly green when fresh, fading to brownish grey.

Two diagnostic features, one (best seen with hand-lens) is a salmon pink belt near base of abdomen (blackish in Green Pug), striking in fresh examples but fading to pinkish brown. On forewing, pale cross-band beyond central spot is only slightly wavy in leading half of wing. In Green Pug, this band is less obvious and inner edge is wavy and strongly edged with black in leading half (some variation in degree of waviness in Sloe Pug, however). Central spot elongated and often connected to leading edge of forewing by dark line. See also Bilberry Pug.
Flight season One generation. May-early July. Occasional at light, otherwise seldom seen.
Life cycle Overwinters as an egg on the foodplant. Larva late March-April. Pupates among plant debris on the ground.
Larval foodplants Flowers of Blackthorn.
Habitat Long-established hedges, thorn scrub and the edges of lowland woodland, especially on heavy soils.
Status & distribution Resident. Common. Not discovered in the British Isles until 1971, but since found to be widespread and fairly frequent, at least as larvae, from the Isle of Wight to Yorkshire and south Cumbria, and as far south-west as east Devon and Glamorgan. The majority of records are from the Thames Valley, Essex and the Midlands, where it is quite well distributed, especially on clay and on sites of ancient woodland, suggesting it was a long-over-looked resident.

Green Pug   page 144
Pasiphila rectangulata (L.)
Common. T   1860(8603)

Field characters & Similar species FW 8-11mm. Bright green colour of freshly-emerged individuals precludes confusion with any pugs other than V-Pug, which is easily distinguished by the heavy black V-shape near centre of forewing. Faded Green Pug can begin to resemble Sloe Pug, but this is smaller and readily distinguished by salmon-pink belt around abdomen, just behind thorax. Green Pug has a thick black band in this position. The frequent, almost uniformly dark brown f. *anthrax* Dietze has the same broad, rounded forewing of the genus *Pasiphila*, and the central spot remains conspicuous. There are other darker and lighter melanic forms, often with a light greenish line near outer edge of forewing, and in urban areas such as London and in northern Britain the bright green form can be rare.
Flight season One generation. June-early August. Adults sometimes beaten from foodplants by day. Comes readily to light.
Life cycle Overwinters as an egg on the foodplant. Larva April-May. Pupates on the ground or in loose earth.
Larval foodplants Flowers of Crab Apple, cultivated Apple, Pear, Hawthorn, Blackthorn and Cherry.
Habitat A wide range, from urban parks and gardens, hedgerows, scrub and woodland. On many soils, both in damp and dry situations, mainly in the lowlands.
Status & distribution Resident. Common. Well distributed and frequent, sometimes locally abundant, throughout lowland England, Wales and southern and eastern mainland Scotland. Local and infrequently reported in the far north-west. Local and occasional on Man. Proving to be fairly well distributed in the eastern half of Northern Ireland, with a wide scatter of records elsewhere in Ireland. Widespread and frequent in the Channel Islands.

Bilberry Pug   page 144
Pasiphila debiliata (Hb.)
Nb. S,W   1861(8605)

Field characters FW 9-11mm. Has the full, deep, rather rounded wings and arched leading forewing edge of a *Pasiphila* pug, but much lighter in colour and more sparsely marked than most examples of related species. Fresh individuals are a delicate pale lime green, with constant black central spot on forewing, flanked by inner and outer cross-lines of black dots. The green fades to light brown. Hindwing whitish grey.
Similar species Green Pug is usually darker green and cross-lines are almost always continuous, not dotted. Both species have a black belt on front of abdomen and a single row of black dots along top of abdomen. See also Sloe Pug, which has a pink band on abdomen, and is darker.
Flight season One generation. June-July. Often found from dusk onwards, flying among the food-plant. Comes to light, sometimes in large numbers.
Life cycle Overwinters as an egg on the foodplant. Larva April-May, in spun leaves, conspicuous when dark frass accumulates within. Easily swept at night. Pupates underground or among the foodplant.
Larval foodplants Bilberry.
Habitat Heathland, moorland and woodland, usually sheltered by trees with abundant foodplant below.
Status & distribution Resident. Nationally Scarce B. Very local in the southernmost parts of England, the Midlands, Monmouthshire, Pembrokeshire and north Wales. The main areas in England are south Devon, the New Forest, Hampshire, and the heaths of Surrey and Berkshire, and also in the Wyre Forest, Worcestershire and woods in Staffordshire. Recent records are needed for more of the north coast of Devon and Somerset, where the species has been recorded widely in the past. Few records, mainly old ones, north of the Humber, even though the food-plant is increasingly common and widespread further north, but still present at Strensall Common, Yorkshire. The foodplant is rare or absent from much of central and eastern England. Recorded in Aberdeenshire in the 19th century, Kincraig, Inverness-shire, in July 1959 and Kirkconnell Flow NNR, near Dumfries, from 1995 onwards. In Ireland recorded locally, mainly from the west but also from Cos. Waterford and Wicklow in the south-east.

Double-striped Pug
page 144

Gymnoscelis rufifasciata (Haw.)

Common. T
1862(8599)

Field characters FW 8-10mm. Very variable in size, with later generations generally smaller. Some individuals have strikingly reddish-brown markings near edges of the brownish or whitish forewing or are more uniformly reddish, hence the specific name. The two black-edged cross-lines in forewing, which give this pug its English name, are usually conspicuous. Characteristically, black on outer cross-line tends to peter out halfway across forewing. More strongly-marked individuals have other conspicuous black markings near tip of forewing. Scottish and Irish examples tend to be more brightly marked and may puzzle moth recorders.

Similar species None.

Flight season Mainly two generations, late March-May and July-August. Occasional and partial third generation in southern England, September-October. One generation in parts of northern Britain, June-July. Easily disturbed from bushes by day and sometimes flies in hot sunshine. Main flight is just before dusk. Visits flowers. Regular at light in small numbers. Mating pairs sometimes numerous on Heather on moorland at night.

Life cycle Overwinters as a pupa in plant debris. Larva early May-late October.

Larval foodplants Flowers of many plants, including Holly, Ivy, Gorse, Broom, Heather (and cultivars), Rowan, Traveller's-joy, cultivated buddleias and roses; also ragworts, Sea Aster and Wild Marjoram.

Habitat A wide range, from urban parks and gardens to hedgerows, roadside verges, heathland, moorland and woodland.

Status & distribution Resident. Common. Well distributed and frequent over much of England, Wales, Ireland and Scotland, including the Hebrides, Orkney and Shetland, and in the Channel Islands. Local and occasional on Man.

Dentated Pug
page 144

Anticollix sparsata (Treit.)

Na. S,C
1863(8607)

Field characters FW 11-13mm. Larger than most pugs (and not really a pug at all), with a diagnostic notch in outer edge of hindwing, producing the 'teeth' which give rise to the English name and enabling easy identification even of individuals in worn condition. Ground-colour fawnish brown. All the black markings are small and rather delicate. Central spot in forewing is conspicuous, but not large. The many fine black lines become obscured with wear, but dark patches on leading edge of forewing usually remain evident.

Similar species Brown Scallop is superficially similar but larger, with evenly-scalloped hingwing margin.

Flight season One generation. June-July. Sometimes disturbed by day by tapping bushes near the foodplant, in which it seems to roost. Flies at dusk.

Comes to light occasionally.

Life cycle Overwinters as a pupa, in a cocoon spun among the foodplant. Larva August-September.

Larval foodplants Leaves and sometimes flowers of Yellow Loosestrife, usually on plants in shaded and sheltered situations.

Habitat Carr woodland, edges of scrub and verges of droves in fens, marshes and along banks of rivers and canals; also turf moors where peat is dug.

Status & distribution Resident. Nationally Scarce A. A scattered distribution in England, north to Yorkshire. Recent records from a few sites in Yorkshire, Lincolnshire, Norfolk, Suffolk, Huntingdonshire, Cambridgeshire, Hampshire (New Forest and the north-east), Surrey and the Isle of Wight. There are more isolated colonies in Staffordshire and Somerset. Discovered in Nottinghamshire at Misson Carr in 1996. Rediscovered in one of the Oxfordshire fens in 1990. Found in Wales in 1995, possibly for the first time, at Crymlyn Bog NNR, Glamorgan. The larval foodplant is widely distributed in Wales and Scotland but there seem to be no records of the moth from the latter.

Streak
page 144

Chesias legatella ([D. & S.])

Common. T
1864(8609)

Field characters FW 17-19mm. Long, pale streak in leading half of rounded, tapering forewing, roughly triangular or elliptical central mark, and tented resting posture, are diagnostic. Ground-colour of forewing varies from dark brownish grey to lighter grey.

Similar species See Broom-tip, which is similar in shape, colour and resting posture, but lacks the diagnostic pale streak and flies earlier in the year.

Flight season One generation. September-early November. Flies at dusk and later comes to light, often a considerable distance from the nearest foodplant.

Life cycle Overwinters as an egg on the foodplant. Larva May-June. Pupates underground.

Larval foodplants Broom. Also found recently on Tree Lupin. Use of other related plants may explain some records of the adult.

Habitat Most frequent on heathland, moorland and in open woodland. Also hedgerows, scrubby embankments, suburban gardens and some dune systems.

Status & distribution Resident. Common. Widely but patchily distributed throughout mainland Britain north to Caithness. Well distributed and locally frequent on sandy or heathy ground from south-east Dorset, eastwards to south-east England and in East Anglia. Fairly well distributed in Wales, parts of the Midlands, northern England and eastern lowland Scotland. Thinly distributed in south-west England. Rare or absent from large areas of chalk and clay in southern England, although sometimes occurring locally in gardens and roadsides in these areas. Occasionally recorded on Orkney but possibly not resident. Local on Man. Recorded from a number of sites in the eastern part of Northern Ireland. Local and rare in the Channel Islands.

Broom-tip   page 144

Chesias rufata rufata (Fabr.)

Nb. SE,W   1865(8610)

ssp. *scotica* Rich.

Nb. N

Field characters FW 14-16mm.
Ssp. *rufata* Diagnostic features are a large black comma-mark, which forms leading half of a narrow dark central cross-band, and a pale reddish-brown band beyond it. Forewing rather rounded and tapering, grey, diffusely banded with pale brown. Markings vary little, and ground-colour varies slightly. Ssp. *scotica* Ground-colour of forewing is bluish grey and markings are somewhat stronger.
Similar species See Streak.
Flight season One generation, often protracted. April-July. Sometimes found at rest by day on posts and after dark on the foodplant. Comes to light.
Life cycle Overwinters as a pupa underground, often for two winters in captivity. Larva July-September.
Larval foodplants Broom.
Habitat Heathland, breckland, heathy commons, open woodland, scrub, moorland and rocky stream-sides. Occasionally where Broom is planted to stabilise embankments, such as on roadsides and railway-lines. Usually associated with large and long-established stands, and by no means found wherever the plant grows within the range of the moth. No evidence yet of colonisation of gardens and suburban habitats, unlike the closely-related Streak.
Status & distribution Resident. Nationally Scarce B but under-recorded, especially in Scotland. Ssp. *rufata* occurs very locally in southern and south-east England, from the New Forest, Hampshire, a few sites in Surrey, very local and rare in Sussex and north-east Kent to the coastal belt of Essex and Suffolk. Also in the Thetford area of Norfolk, a few sites in Bedfordshire, such as Sandy, and in Gloucestershire near the Severn, with scattered localities from Devon and Cornwall to Cheshire, west Wales, Cumbria and Beltingham Gravels, Northumberland. There is an apparently isolated colony in Nottinghamshire. Occasional on Jersey. Rare on Guernsey. Ssp. *scotica* occurs in central and northern mainland Scotland.

Manchester Treble-bar   page 145

Carsia sororiata (Hb.)

ssp. *anglica* Prout

Nb. N,C   1866(8617)

Field characters FW 11-15mm. Distinctive. The cold grey ground-colour of forewing, jagged leading half of outer dark cross-band, and reddish flush on its outer edge, are diagnostic. Undersides are pinkish brown, and fringes are chequered. Cross-bands are

Larva of Broom-tip.

quite variable in shape, and are often joined in trailing half.
Similar species Treble-bar and Lesser Treble-bar are much larger, with less extensive reddish flush.
Flight season One generation. July-September. Flies readily if disturbed on warm days, even in overcast weather. Active from dusk and visits flowers. Comes regularly to light.
Life cycle Overwinters as an egg. Larva late April-June. Pupates in a cocoon among plant debris.
Larval foodplants Bilberry, Cowberry and Cranberry, feeding on the flowers and leaves.
Habitat The open, wetter parts of damp moorland, heathland and raised mosses.
Status & distribution Resident. Nationally Scarce B. A northern species. Widespread, quite well distributed, locally frequent and probably under-recorded in northern and central Scotland, including the Hebrides, Orkney and Shetland. Local in southern Scotland, mainly in the Borders. Widespread in Northumberland and present in Co. Durham, where it probably occurs on virtually all suitable bogs and mosses. Still found on some of the remnant raised bogs and mosses in western England, from Cumbria south to Shropshire, where it is well established and often numerous on Whixall and Fenn's Mosses, but is not known elsewhere in the county. In Staffordshire, survives at Chartley Moss but lost from Chorlton Moss. Reported from Gyffin, near Conway, north Wales, in 2002. Considered vagrant on Man, with one record, in 1939. Recorded locally in central Ireland, with old records from a single locality in Co. Tyrone, Northern Ireland.

Treble-bar   page 145

Aplocera plagiata plagiata (L.)

Common. T   1867(8620)

ssp. *scotica* (Rich.)

Common. N

Field characters FW 19-22mm. Ssp. *plagiata* On this grey, boldly-banded moth, the narrow basal cross-band on forewing is angled slightly obtusely or at 90° near leading edge, and this angle is usually rounded. Also, tip of abdomen is pointed in male, and if viewed from below claspers are long, narrow and pointed. However, forewing markings show some variation. In ssp. *scotica* ground-colour of

Treble-bar   Lesser Treble-bar

Detail of Aplocera abdomens.

forewing is bluish grey.
Similar species See Lesser Treble-bar (very similar) and Purple Treble-bar.
Flight season Two generations in southern Britain, May-June and August-September. One generation in northern England and Scotland, July-August. Easily disturbed by day. Flies from dusk and comes to light in small numbers.
Life cycle Overwinters as a larva. Larva September-May and late June-early August in the south, August-June in the north. Pupates underground.
Larval foodplants St John's-worts.
Habitat A wide range, including gardens, field margins, calcareous grassland, heathland, moorland, woodland rides, sand-dunes and soft-rock sea-cliffs. Especially frequent in hot, dry, well-drained open habitats.
Status & distribution Resident. Common. Fairly well distributed and fairly frequent throughout Britain and Ireland, including the Hebrides and Orkney. Local and infrequent on Man. Rare in the Channel Islands.

Lesser Treble-bar   page 145
Aplocera efformata (Guen.)
Common. S,C   1868(8622)

Field characters & Similar species FW 16-19mm. Very similar to Treble-bar, but slightly smaller and generally with less intense dark cross-bands, and tip of abdomen is blunt in both sexes. Claspers of male, viewed from below, are short and bent inwards. Usually, angle of narrow basal cross-band is slightly acute and angle is quite sharp. However, on some the angle is very close to 90°, so other features must be taken into consideration. Sometimes, two central cross-bands are broadly merged, or less often faint. Single examples of the rare f. *fimbriata* Cock., lacking bold cross-bands, have been found in Hampshire, Hertfordshire and Buckinghamshire, and most recently in Northamptonshire (1991) and in Oxfordshire (1993 and 1999).
Flight season Two generations. May-June and August-September. Easily disturbed by day. Flies from dusk and comes to light in small numbers.
Life cycle Overwinters as a larva. Larva September-May and late June-early August. Pupates underground.
Larval foodplants St John's-worts.
Habitat A wide range, including gardens, field margins, woodland rides, calcareous grassland, sand-dunes and sea-cliffs.

Status & distribution Resident. Common. Largely restricted to southern Britain, unlike the Treble-bar. Well distributed in central southern and south-eastern England, except on the Wealden clays. Local in Wales and northern England. In Yorkshire more numerous than Treble-bar in higher areas. Occurs very locally north to Cumbria and Co. Durham. Rare on Jersey.

Purple Treble-bar   page 145
Aplocera praeformata (Hb.)
Suspected rare immigrant.   1869(8624)

Field characters & Similar species FW 20-25mm. Larger than Treble-bar, and somewhat darker, with a short brown bar before first dark central cross-band, and angle of basal cross-band is pointed and acute.
Status & distribution Suspected rare immigrant. There are only two recognised British records, one from Chinnor on the Oxfordshire/Buckinghamshire border, in 1919, the other from Lawrenny Park, Pembrokeshire, in 1946. In mainland Europe recorded from June to August, in similar habitats to the Treble-bar and dependent on St John's-wort.

Chimney Sweeper   page 145
Odezia atrata (L.)
Common. N,C,(S)   1870(8631)

Field characters FW 12-15mm. Unmistakable. Almost entirely plain sooty black, fading to brownish black. Only distinct features are fringes of forewing, which are chalky white around wing tip. Shows very little variation.
Similar species None.
Flight season One generation. June-July, sometimes into August in Scotland. Flies by day, usually in sunshine, but male may fly in dull weather.
Life cycle Overwinters as an egg. Larva April-early June. Pupates just below ground.
Larval foodplants The flowers and seeds of Pignut.
Habitat In southern Britain, chalk downland, limestone grassland, old hay meadows and other open, agriculturally-unimproved permanent grassy places, including hedgerows and woodland edges. In northern and upland Britain on a wider range of soil types, especially along streamsides and other damp places.
Status & distribution Resident. Common. Well distributed and fairly frequent in northern England from the north Midlands northwards, and in mainland Scotland and on Mull. Much more local in the southern half of England, with recent records from a thin scatter of sites, more frequently in the west. Very local in East Anglia. Resident on Man in 1892, but not seen since. Local in both Northern Ireland and the Republic but recently recorded from a fair number of sites. Recorded once in the Channel Islands, one on Guernsey, in 1889.

Grey Carpet
page 145

Lithostege griseata ([D. & S.])

RDB. E
1871(8638)

Field characters FW 14-16mm. Unmistakable. The almost plain pale grey, rather pointed forewing has a very fine blackish line on outer edge, white fringes and sometimes a faint, narrow outer cross-band. Shows little variation.
Similar species None.
Flight season One generation. Late May-early July. Occasionally disturbed by day. Comes to light from dusk onwards, sometimes in numbers, and can be seen on the wing around the foodplant as darkness falls. Often disperses from suitable habitat.
Life cycle Overwinters as a pupa, in a cocoon usually in sandy soil, sometimes for two winters. Larva late June-August, usually fully grown by early August. Easily swept by day.
Larval foodplants The seedpods of Flixweed. A report from Treacle-mustard probably the result of plant misidentification; larvae found on Flixweed are not inclined to feed on Treacle-mustard if offered.
Habitat Field margins, agricultural set-aside and fallow fields, roadside verges, disturbed ground on breckland heaths and in newly-established breckland conifer plantations. The foodplant requires frequent soil disturbance to persist.
Status & distribution Resident and possible immigrant. Red Data Book species. Occurs very locally in the Breckland of East Anglia; currently breeding in good numbers in at least four localities. Recorded only four times outside Breckland, as suspected immigrants or internal migrants, as singletons at light-traps at Bradwell-on-Sea, Essex, on 15 June 1995; Howdales near Skidbrooke, Lincolnshire, on 31 May 2002, Spurn, Yorkshire, only 18km to the north, on 7 June 2002, and at Holme-next-the-Sea, Norfolk, on 8 June 2002.

Blomer's Rivulet
page 145

Discoloxia blomeri (Curt.)

Nb. S,C,W
1872(8650)

Field characters FW 10-13mm. The large, rusty brown blotch, with its inner side distinctly edged with black near tip of pale grey forewing, and very fine, scalloped blackish cross-lines, make this moth unmistakable. Basal and central cross-lines are usually faint. Shows very little variation.
Similar species None.
Flight season One generation. Late May-early July. Sometimes seen at rest on tree trunks and low foliage by day. Flies from dusk onwards and comes readily to light.
Life cycle Overwinters as a pupa, in a cocoon on or just below ground. Larva late July-mid September.
Larval foodplants Wych Elm. Apparently unrecorded from other elms.
Habitat Woodland, and hedgerows in well-wooded districts, where Wych Elm occurs in a moist climate.
Status & distribution Resident. Nationally Scarce B.

Locally frequent. Closely associated with various calcareous strata, usually in areas with more than 70cm annual rainfall, including exposed carboniferous limestone sites from Devon north to the Severn, Worcestershire and the Buxton area of Derbyshire. Also the Magnesian limestone running north from Nottinghamshire through Yorkshire to the coast of Co. Durham. In Wales, the carboniferous limestone of Glamorgan and Breconshire, Denbighshire and Anglesey. In Cumbria, at Arnside, and there are pre-1980 records from Northumberland. Recorded on chalk in Wiltshire, the Chilterns and in north Lincolnshire, on oolitic limestone (including Cornbrash) in Yorkshire, and in base-enriched flushes, such as in the Aberystwyth area. Has occasionally occurred elsewhere, including two at light-traps in 1974 in Hampshire: at Minstead, on 14 June and at Crawley, on 1 July. Also noted at a number of sites in Cornwall, most recently at Sheviock, on 14 August 1990, the only Cornish record in the last 20 years.

Welsh Wave
page 145

Venusia cambrica Curt.

Local. W,N
1873(8652)

Field characters FW 13-15mm. Diagnostic feature is the pair of blackish spikes projecting outwards from centre of fine blackish cross-line near middle of forewing. Usually shows slight variation, and there are sometimes further smaller spikes along this line in leading and trailing half of wing. In f. *bradyi* Prout, found frequently in northern England, ground-colour is dark grey, so most of markings are obscured.
Similar species Waved Carpet is superficially similar, but lacks black cross-lines or spikes, and is smaller.
Flight season One generation. June-August. Rests by day on rocks and tree trunks, and comes to light, sometimes in numbers.
Life cycle Overwinters as a pupa, among plant debris. Larva July-September.
Larval foodplants Rowan and sometimes birches, which it will also eat in captivity.
Habitat Moorland, at both low and quite high altitudes, and open woodland.
Status & distribution Resident. Local. Quite well distributed and locally frequent on the fringes of the Quantocks and the Blackdown Hills in Devon, throughout upland Wales and in upland areas from the north Midlands northwards. Found throughout the low to middle altitudes of mainland Scotland and the Inner Hebrides. Local on Man and in Ireland, including Northern Ireland, where there is a wide scatter of recent records.

Dingy Shell
page 145

Euchoeca nebulata (Scop.)

Local. S,C
1874(8654)

Field characters FW 9-12mm. This moth always rests with wings closed. Sandy brown undersides have several faint, darker cross-lines, cream and brown chequered fringes and a small central projection on margin of hindwing. On upperside, forewing is sandy brown near base and along leading edge, dusted with muddy-brown scales, and outer area is entirely brown. Shows slight variation, mainly in extent of brown dusting on upperside.

Similar species See Small Yellow Wave, from which Dingy Shell is distinguished by resting posture; otherwise by fewer, fainter cross-lines, the chequered fringes and lack of dark central spot in forewing.

Flight season One generation. Late May-early August. Easily disturbed by day from near the foodplant. Flies from dusk and later comes to light in small numbers.

Life cycle Overwinters as a pupa. Larva late June-August. Pupates in plant debris on the ground, or under moss on the lower parts of the trunk.

Larval foodplants Alder.

Habitat Damp woodland, carr and other marshy areas, including river valleys and along other watercourses. Seldom strays far from breeding habitat and undoubtedly under-recorded as a consequence.

Status & distribution Resident. Local. Locally distributed, but often fairly frequent, where the foodplant grows, throughout much of England and Wales, from Cornwall and Kent to Northumberland, and from Anglesey to East Anglia. Very local in Scotland north to Aberdeenshire. Not recorded from Man nor reliably from Ireland. Recorded from Jersey in 1941 and 1964.

Small White Wave   page 145
Asthena albulata (Hufn.)
Common. T   1875(8656)

Field characters FW 9-11mm. The small size, pure white ground-colour and brown, very wavy cross-lines distinguish this moth from all superficially similar species. Slight variation in detail of markings, and occasionally outer lines are faint or absent.

Similar species None.

Flight season Usually one generation. May-early July. Sometimes a partial second generation in southern England, August-mid September. Easily disturbed by day. Flies mainly from sunset until dark. Comes to light in very small numbers.

Life cycle Overwinters as a pupa, among plant debris. Larva late June-August, and sometimes again in September in the south.

Larval foodplants Hazel, Hornbeam, birches and wild roses.

Habitat Broadleaved woodland, particularly ancient woodland. Larvae often found on mature Hazel, such as overgrown coppice, occasionally in younger re-growth, in dense Hornbeam, and less frequently on birches.

Status & distribution Resident. Common. Fairly well distributed throughout England and Wales north to Cumbria and Northumberland. Usually seen in small numbers, formerly more numerous. Widespread in mainland Scotland north to Caithness, but records are few and mainly from the west. Resident on Man but seldom seen. There are a few,

widely scattered records for Northern Ireland and the west of the Irish Republic. Rare in the Channel Islands.

Small Yellow Wave   page 145
Hydrelia flammeolaria (Hufn.)
Common. T   1876(8660)

Field characters FW 9-11mm. Unmistakable. Straw-yellow ground-colour, very irregular sandy brown cross-lines on both wings, and small but distinct black discal spot make this moth easily recognised. Outer cross-lines are often linked centrally by a brown bar, usually on forewings, which extends into fringes.

Similar species See Dingy Shell.

Flight season One generation. Late May or June-July. Can be disturbed from low branches of the foodplant by day. Comes to light.

Life cycle Overwinters as a pupa, among plant debris. Larva late July-September.

Larval foodplants Field Maple, Sycamore and Alder.

Habitat Broadleaved woodland, riverine scrub, hedgerows and sometimes isolated trees in the south. Alder carr in the north. Field Maple reaches its natural northern limit in Northumberland.

Status & distribution Resident. Common. Fairly well distributed and locally fairly frequent in England and Wales north to the Humber. Much more local further north and in western mainland Scotland, where there are a few scattered records north to Inverness-shire. Resident on Man but seldom seen. A single specimen from Killarney, Co. Kerry, in 1953, appears to be the only record from Ireland. Local and occasional in the Channel Islands.

Waved Carpet   page 145
Hydrelia sylvata ([D. & S.])
Nb. W,SE,SW   1877(8661)

Field characters FW 11-13mm. Diagnostic features are two narrow, wavy, brown central cross-bands, darker brown wavy cross-lines (often rather indistinct), general peppering of brown scales, and greyish-white ground-colour. Variation in amount of dark scales. Darker forms and intermediates frequent in Sussex and Kent.

Similar species Welsh Wave typically rests with wings less widely spread (useful for identifying dark forms), and otherwise has bolder cross-lines with a pair of black spikes on outer edge of central band.

Flight season One generation. June-early August. Rests on tree trunks and branches by day. Comes to light, usually in small numbers, but over 100 recorded at one m.v. light in one night in Sweet Chestnut coppice in Kent.

Life cycle Overwinters as a pupa. Larva July-September.

Larval foodplants Alder, birches, sallows and Sweet Chestnut. Reported to prefer the youngest leaves. Hazel may be worth investigating as it is often abundant where the moth occurs and is accepted by many other geometrids associated with birches and sallows. An old report from Blackthorn.

Habitat Woodland and scrub, often by watercourses, but also known from scrub on heathland, chalk, hilly sites on sandstone, coastal cliffs and vegetated shingle.

Status & distribution Resident. Nationally Scarce B. Currently restricted mainly to south-west England, the extreme south and west of Wales and the extreme south-east of England, particularly Sussex, where there are more populations known than ever before. Formerly recorded more widely in Wales, northern England to Cumbria and in the West Midlands. Still present in a few sites in Herefordshire. Local in central Surrey and the extreme south-west of the county. Very rare in Hampshire.

Drab Looper   page 145
Minoa murinata (Scop.)
Nb. W,S,(SW)   1878(8663)

Field characters FW 9-11mm. Unmistakable, with entirely plain, light to dark muddy-brown wings.

Similar species None.

Flight season One main generation. May-June, occasionally late April, with a partial second generation in August. Male flies during the middle of the day, in sunshine, sometimes in numbers, and has occasionally been recorded at light. Seen feeding by day at thistle flowers near larval foodplant.

Life cycle Overwinters as a pupa, in a cocoon of silk and earth on the ground. Larva late June-early September.

Larval foodplants Wood Spurge, preferring the flowers and floral leaves.

Habitat Sunny, but sheltered, open, mainly ancient woodland. The foodplant follows clearance, coppicing and other disturbance. Also at lower density along ride edges.

Status & distribution Resident. Nationally Scarce B. Restricted to southern Britain, as is the larval foodplant, and unrecorded north of the Wash. Now two main centres of distribution: central southern England – Dorset, Hampshire, Wiltshire, Berkshire and West Sussex – and the border of England and Wales, from Gloucestershire and Monmouthshire northwards through Herefordshire and Worcestershire. There are also a few scattered colonies surviving elsewhere, particularly in Somerset and Kent. Lost from woods in Oxfordshire, Buckinghamshire, Bedfordshire and Essex since the 1940s and probably from south Wales.

Seraphim   page 145
Lobophora halterata (Hufn.)
Local. T   1879(8665)

Field characters FW 12-15mm. Diagnostic feature is dark grey cross-band near base of broad, rounded forewing, present on even most obscurely marked examples. Shows considerable variation, and plain examples are sometimes tinged with creamy buff. A

peculiarity of this species and also Small Seraphim is that in the male, the rather small hindwing has on upperside a doubly-folded lobe along trailing edge, which is only attached to wing near base, almost like an extra, rudimentary wing, somewhat like the haltere of the Diptera to the naked eye. Their function is unclear, but closely-related species such as Early and Barred Tooth-striped have similar structures, although in these they are fully attached to hindwing.

Similar species Early Tooth-striped is usually larger, with less rounded, more tapering forewing (in male) and any dark basal cross-bands are either very narrow or inconspicuous.

Flight season One generation. May-June. Rests by day on tree trunks, from where it can sometimes be disturbed. Flies from dusk. Comes to light, sometimes in fair numbers.

Life cycle Overwinters as a pupa, in a cocoon formed just beneath the ground. Larva late June-July.

Larval foodplants Aspen, Black-poplar and occasionally cultivated poplars.

Habitat Mainly broadleaved woodland; sometimes poplar plantations.

Status & distribution Resident. Local. Fairly well distributed in southern England north to the Wash and the Mersey, in the eastern half of Wales and in central mainland Scotland. Very local in northern England, southern Scotland and Ireland, but recorded from many more sites in Yorkshire in recent years. An infrequent resident on Man. One record from Guernsey, in 1989.

Barred Tooth-striped   page 145
Trichopteryx polycommata ([D. & S.])
Na. T   1880(8667)

Field characters FW 14-17mm. Diagnostic feature is brown and blackish central cross-band, elbowed and divided in two in leading half of rounded, tapering forewing. This pattern shows little variation, but occasionally cross-band is entire, with a pale blotch within it. Forewing varies in colour from light to dark grey-brown, and central band varies in intensity and width.

Similar species None.

Flight season One generation. Mid March-mid or late April, depending on season, sometimes later in northern Britain. Can be found at rest on foodplants and flitting about after dark. Comes to light in small numbers.

Life cycle Overwinters as a pupa, in an underground cocoon. Larva mid April-early June.

Larval foodplants Wild Privet, Ash. Accepts Garden Privet, Lilac and Honeysuckle in captivity.

Habitat Open scrub, especially on chalk downs. Also hedgerows, open woodland, rides and edges of woods.

Status & distribution Resident. Nationally Scarce A. The main strongholds are on the chalk of Dorset, northern Hampshire, Wiltshire and the southern half of Sussex, in Breckland on the Norfolk/Suffolk border, and on limestone in the south of Cumbria. There are scattered records through the east Midlands and West Midlands, at Grass Wood, Malham, Yorkshire, and north to the Ardnamurchan peninsula of Argyll, and in Perthshire and the Great Glen, but apparently none in recent years from Wales. Recorded once on the Isle of Wight, one at Chale Green, on 3 April 1993.

Early Tooth-striped   page 145
Trichopteryx carpinata (Borkh.)
Common. T   1881(8668)

Field characters FW 13-18mm. Quite variable, but usually distinctive among moths flying in spring. Broad, somewhat rounded forewing (more tapering in male) is most often pale grey, but can be darker, or brownish grey, or greenish grey, sometimes with a delicate pink flush along leading edge when freshly emerged. Central cross-bands are usually faint and pale, but in f. *fasciata* Prout they are bold and dark, and sometimes broadly merged. This form is frequent in Wales and Scotland.
Similar species See Seraphim.
Flight season One generation. April-May. Can be found at rest on tree trunks and posts by day. Flies from dusk. Visits sallow catkins. Comes to light, sometimes plentifully.
Life cycle Overwinters as a pupa. Larva May-July.
Larval foodplants Sallows, birches, Honeysuckle and Alder.
Habitat Broadleaved woodland, scrubby heathland and fens.
Status & distribution Resident. Common. Quite well distributed and fairly frequent in south-west, central southern and south-east England, Wales, the West Midlands, northern England, much of lowland mainland Scotland, the Inner Hebrides and Ireland. More local in central and eastern England. Local on Man, where first recorded in 1995.

Small Seraphim   page 145
Pterapherapteryx sexalata (Retz.)
Local. T   1882(8675)

Field characters FW 9-12mm. Diagnostic feature of this delicately banded grey and white moth is the broad, grey central cross-band on broad forewing, paler in trailing half, with small but conspicuous black central spot situated close to its inner edge. Like related species, hindwing is small in male, with a lobe along trailing edge (see also comments under

Seraphim). Shows little variation.
Similar species None.
Flight season Two generations in the southern half of England, May-June and July-early August. One generation north of the Midlands, June-July. Flies over the foodplant at dusk and later comes to light. Usually seen in small numbers, but sometimes quite plentiful.
Life cycle Overwinters as a pupa, in plant debris or moss. Larva mid June-mid July and mid August-mid September. Early July-mid August in the north.
Larval foodplants Sallows. Also recorded on White Willow.
Habitat Damp broadleaved woodland, scrub, fens and other marshy places.
Status & distribution Resident. Local. Quite well distributed in southern England and East Anglia. Local and rather sporadic in the Midlands, Wales, central Scotland and the western half of Ireland. Rare in the Channel Islands.

Yellow-barred Brindle   page 145
Acasis viretata (Hb.)
Local. S,C,NW   1883(8681)

Field characters FW 10-14mm. Quite distinctive. Although green when freshly emerged, this moth rapidly fades to yellowish green. Most examples have a distinct broad, blackish-grey central cross-band, usually with a green component. On some, this is reduced to a number of fine, wavy cross-lines, with short dashes on veins.
Similar species See the much rarer Barred Carpet, which has dark forewing base and thorax.
Flight season Two generations in southern Britain, May-June and late July-early September. One generation elsewhere, May-June. Rests on tree trunks by day. Flies from dusk and comes to light quite regularly, but in small numbers.
Life cycle Overwinters as a pupa. Larva June-July, and again in September-October in the south.
Larval foodplants The leaves, flowers and buds of Holly, Ivy, Wild Privet, Dogwood, Guelder-rose and Hawthorn.
Habitat Broadleaved woodland, hedgerows, parkland and gardens.
Status & distribution Resident. Local. Quite well distributed in the southern half of England and in Wales and Ireland. Very local in north-west England and western Scotland. Local on Man but more frequently recorded since 1988. Widespread and frequent in the Channel Islands.

 ♂   ♀  ♂   ♀

――――――― Orange Underwing ―――――――
Archiearis parthenias

――――― Light Orange Underwing ―――――
Archiearis notha

131

♂ ♀ × 1.25   ♂ ♀

―――――――――― Rest Harrow ――――――――――
Aplasta ononaria

――――――― March Moth ―――――――
Alsophila aescularia

Grass Emerald
Pseudoterpna pruinata atropunctaria

Jersey Emerald
Pseudoterpna coronillaria

Large Emerald
Geometra papilionaria

Blotched Emerald
Comibaena bajularia

Essex Emerald
Thetidia smaragdaria maritima

Common Emerald
Hemithea aestivaria

Small Grass Emerald
Chlorissa viridata

Sussex Emerald
Thalera fimbrialis

Small Emerald
Hemistola chrysoprasaria

Little Emerald
Jodis lactearia

Geometridae (Sterrhinae) Mochas and waves pages 59-65

Dingy Mocha
Cyclophora pendularia

Mocha
Cyclophora annularia

Birch Mocha
Cyclophora albipunctata

Birch Mocha

Cyclophora albipunctata f. *subroseata*   Scottish form

Blair's Mocha
Cyclophora puppillaria

Blair's Mocha
Cyclophora puppillaria

False Mocha
Cyclophora porata

Maiden's Blush
Cyclophora punctaria

Clay Triple-lines
Cyclophora linearia

Clay Triple-lines
Cyclophora linearia
2nd generation

Blood-vein
Timandra comae

Lewes Wave
Scopula immorata

Sub-angled Wave
Scopula nigropunctata

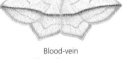

Lace Border
Scopula ornata

Tawny Wave
Scopula rubiginata

Mullein Wave
Scopula marginepunctata

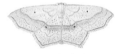

Small Blood-vein
Scopula imitaria

Rosy Wave
Scopula emutaria

Lesser Cream Wave
Scopula immutata

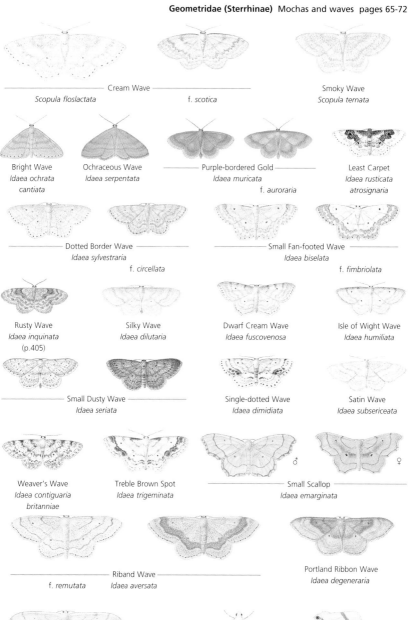

Cream Wave
Scopula floslactata

f. *scotica*

Smoky Wave
Scopula ternata

Bright Wave
Idaea ochrata
cantiata

Ochraceous Wave
Idaea serpentata

Purple-bordered Gold
Idaea muricata
f. *auroraria*

Least Carpet
Idaea rusticata
atrosignaria

133

Dotted Border Wave
Idaea sylvestraria
f. *circellata*

Small Fan-footed Wave
Idaea biselata
f. *fimbriolata*

Rusty Wave
Idaea inquinata
(p.405)

Silky Wave
Idaea dilutaria

Dwarf Cream Wave
Idaea fuscovenosa

Isle of Wight Wave
Idaea humiliata

Small Dusty Wave
Idaea seriata

Single-dotted Wave
Idaea dimidiata

Satin Wave
Idaea subsericeata

Weaver's Wave
Idaea contiguaria
britanniae

Treble Brown Spot
Idaea trigeminata

♂   ♀

Small Scallop
Idaea emarginata

f. *remutata*

Riband Wave
Idaea aversata

Portland Ribbon Wave
Idaea degeneraria

Plain Wave
Idaea straminata

Vestal
Rhodometra sacraria

Geometridae (Larentiinae) Carpets, pugs and allies pages 72-78

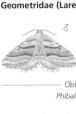

———————————— Oblique Striped ————————————
Phibalapteryx virgata

Oblique Carpet
Orthonama vittata

Gem
Orthonama obstipata

134

Gem
Orthonama obstipata

———————————— Balsam Carpet ————————————
Xanthorhoe biriviata
spring generation   summer generation

Flame Carpet
Xanthorhoe designata

——————————— Red Carpet ———————————
Xanthorhoe decoloraria   *Xanthorhoe decoloraria*
decoloraria   *hethlandica*

Red Twin-spot Carpet
Xanthorhoe spadicearia

Dark-barred Twin-spot Carpet
Xanthorhoe ferrugata

Dark-barred Twin-spot Carpet
Xanthorhoe ferrugata

Large Twin-spot Carpet
Xanthorhoe quadrifasiata

Silver-ground Carpet
Xanthorhoe montanata
montanata

————————— Silver-ground Carpet —————————
Xanthorhoe montanata
montanata

————————— Garden Carpet —————————
Xanthorhoe fluctuata   *Xanthorhoe fluctuata*
                                      f. *thules*

Spanish Carpet
Scotopteryx peribolata

Chalk Carpet
Scotopteryx bipunctaria
cretata

————————— Shaded Broad-bar —————————
Scotopteryx chenopodiata

———————————— Lead Belle ————————————
Scotopteryx mucronata   *Scotopteryx mucronata*
umbrifera   *scotica*

July Belle
Scotopteryx luridata
plumbaria

Ruddy Carpet
Catarhoe rubidata

Royal Mantle
Catarhoe cuculata

♂ ♀

Small Argent & Sable
Epirrhoe tristata

135

Common Carpet

Epirrhoe alternata alternata

Epirrhoe alternata obscurata

Wood Carpet
Epirrhoe rivata

Galium Carpet
Epirrhoe galiata

dark form, Co. Clare

Many-lined
Costaconvexa polygrammata

Traveller
Costaconvexa centrostrigaria

Yellow Shell

Camptogramma bilineata bilineata

Camptogramma bilineata atlantica

Yellow Shell

C. b. hibernica

C. b. isolata

Yellow-ringed Carpet

*Entephria flavicinctata
flavicinctata*

*Entephria flavicinctata
ruficinctata*

Grey Mountain Carpet
Entephria caesiata

Mallow
Larentia clavaria

Shoulder Stripe
Anticlea badiata

Streamer
Anticlea derivata

Beautiful Carpet
Mesoleuca albicillata

Dark Spinach
Pelurga comitata

————— Water Carpet —————
Lampropteryx suffumata   f. *piceata*

Devon Carpet
Lampropteryx otregiata

Purple Bar
Cosmorhoe ocellata

Striped Twin-spot Carpet
Nebula salicata latentaria

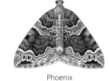

Phoenix
Eulithis prunata

♂   ♀

————— Chevron —————
Eulithis testata

————————————— Northern Spinach —————————————
Eulithis populata   dark form, Scotland

Spinach
Eulithis mellinata

Barred Straw
Eulithis pyraliata

————— Small Phoenix —————
Ecliptopera silaceata   f. *insulata*

————— Red-green Carpet —————
Chloroclysta siterata

Autumn Green Carpet
Chloroclysta miata

————————————————— Dark Marbled Carpet —————————————————
Chloroclysta citrata citrata ———— C. c. pythonissata ————

Arran Carpet ————————————————— Common Marbled Carpet —————————————————
Chloroclysta concinnata *Chloroclysta truncata*

views of
undersides

Dark Marbled Carpet Arran Carpet Common Marbled Carpet
Chloroclysta citrata citrata *Chloroclysta concinnata* *Chloroclysta truncata*

Barred Yellow ————— Blue-bordered Carpet —————
Cidaria fulvata *Plemyria rubiginata* *Plemyria rubiginata*
rubiginata plumbata f. semifumosa

————— Pine Carpet ————— ————— Grey Pine Carpet —————
Thera firmata *Thera obeliscata*

————— Spruce Carpet —————
Thera britannica

———— Chestnut-coloured Carpet ————
Thera cognata
Orkney specimen

———————— Juniper Carpet ————————
Thera juniperata juniperata　　*T. j. scotica*

Cypress Carpet
Thera cupressata

Netted Carpet
Eustroma reticulatum

———————— Broken-barred Carpet ————————
Electrophaes corylata　　f. *albocrenata*

Argyll
specimen

———————— Beech-green Carpet ————————
Colostygia olivata

———— Mottled Grey ————
Colostygia multistrigaria　　f. *nubilata*

———— Green Carpet ————
Colostygia pectinataria
faded specimen

———————————— July Highflyer ————————————
Hydriomena furcata

———— July Highflyer ————
Hydriomena furcata

———— May Highflyer ————
Hydriomena impluviata

———— Ruddy Highflyer ————
Hydriomena ruberata

♂ ♀

Slender-striped Rufous
Coenocalpe lapidata

139

Small Waved Umber
Horisme vitalbata

Fern
Horisme tersata

Pretty Chalk Carpet
Melanthia procellata

Barberry Carpet
Pareulype berberata

White-banded Carpet
Spargania luctuata

Argent & Sable
Rheumaptera hastata hastata *Rheumaptera hastata f. nigrescens*

Scarce Tissue
Rheumaptera cervinalis

Scallop Shell
Rheumaptera undulata

Tissue
Triphosa dubitata

Brown Scallop
Philereme vetulata

♂

Dark Umber
Philereme transversata britannica

♀

Cloaked Carpet
Euphyia biangulata

Sharp-angled Carpet
Euphyia unangulata

Geometridae (Larentiinae) Carpets, pugs and allies pages 98-104

 ♂ ♂ ♂ ♀

November Moth
Epirrita dilutata

 ♂ ♂

Pale November Moth
Epirrita christyi

 ♂ ♀

Autumnal Moth
Epirrita autumnata

Small Autumnal Moth
Epirrita filigrammaria

 ♂ ♀ × 1.5 ♂ ♀ × 1.5

Winter Moth
Operophtera brumata

Northern Winter Moth
Operophtera fagata

Barred Carpet
Perizoma taeniata

Rivulet
Perizoma affinitata

Small Rivulet
Perizoma alchemillata

Barred Rivulet
Perizoma bifaciata

Heath Rivulet
*Perizoma minorata
ericetata*

Pretty Pinion
*Perizoma blandiata
blandiata*

Grass Rivulet
*Perizoma albulata
albulata*

*Perizoma albulata
subfasciaria*

Sandy Carpet
Perizoma flavofasciata

Twin-spot Carpet
Perizoma didymata didymata

Wigtownshire specimen   Ross-shire specimen   Berkshire specimen

Marsh Carpet
Perizoma sagittata

All pugs shown × 1.25

f. johnsoni

Slender Pug
Eupithecia tenuiata

Maple Pug
Eupithecia inturbata

Haworth's Pug
Eupithecia haworthiata

Lead-coloured Pug
Eupithecia plumbeolata

Cloaked Pug
Eupithecia abietaria

141

Toadflax Pug
Eupithecia linariata

Foxglove Pug

Eupithecia pulchellata
pulchellata

Eupithecia pulchellata
hebudium

Marbled Pug
Eupithecia irriguata

Mottled Pug

Eupithecia exiguata exiguata

Eupithecia exiguata muricolor

Pinion-spotted Pug
Eupithecia insigniata

Valerian Pug
Eupithecia valerianata

Marsh Pug
Eupithecia pygmaeata

Netted Pug

Eupithecia venosata
venosata

Eupithecia venosata
fumosae

Eupithecia venosata
plumbea

Eupithecia venosata
ochracae

Fletcher's Pug
Eupithecia egenaria

Lime-speck Pug
Eupithecia centaureata

Triple-spotted Pug

Eupithecia trisignaria
f. angelicata

Freyer's Pug
Eupithecia intricata
arceuthata

Edinburgh Pug
Eupithecia intricata
millieraria

Mere's Pug
Eupithecia intricata
hibernica

Geometridae (Larentiinae) Carpets, pugs and allies pages 112-116

All pugs shown × 1.25

——————————— Satyr Pug ———————————

Eupithecia satyrata satyrata   *Eupithecia satyrata callunaria*   *Eupithecia satyrata curzoni*

——————— Wormwood Pug ———————   Ling Pug
Eupithecia absinthiata   *Eupithecia absinthiata* f. *goossensiata*

Currant Pug   Bleached Pug
Eupithecia assimilata   *Eupithecia expallidata*

——————————— Common Pug ———————————

Eupithecia vulgata vulgata   *Eupithecia vulgata*   *Eupithecia vulgata*
    f. *unicolor*   scotica   clarensis

——————————— White-spotted Pug ———————————
Eupithecia tripunctaria   f. *angelicata*

Campanula Pug   Jasione Pug
Eupithecia denotata denotata   *Eupithecia denotata jasioneata*

——————————— Grey Pug ———————————
Eupithecia subfuscata   f. *obscurissima*

——————————— Tawny Speckled Pug ———————————
Eupithecia icterata subfulvata
f. *subfulvata*   f. *cognata*

All pugs shown × 1.25

Bordered Pug
Eupithecia succenturiata f. *disparata*

Shaded Pug
Eupithecia subumbrata

Yarrow Pug
Eupithecia millefoliata

Plain Pug
Eupithecia simpliciata

Goosefoot Pug
Eupithecia sinuosaria

Thyme Pug
Eupithecia distinctaria constrictata

Ochreous Pug
Eupithecia indigata

Pimpinel Pug
Eupithecia pimpinellata

f. *oliveri*

Narrow-winged Pug
Eupithecia nanata

Scarce Pug
Eupithecia extensaria occidua

Angle-barred Pug
Eupithecia innotata

f. *fraxinata* (Ash Pug)

f. *unicolor*

Golden-rod Pug
Eupithecia virgaureata

f. *nigra*

f. *hirschkei*

Brindled Pug
Eupithecia abbreviata

Oak-tree Pug
Eupithecia dodoneata

Scottish specimen

melanic form

Juniper Pug
Eupithecia pusillata pusillata

All pugs shown × 1.25

Cypress Pug
Eupithecia phoeniceata

Channel Islands Pug
Eupithecia ultimaria

144

———————————— Larch Pug ————————————
Eupithecia lariciata   f. *nigra*

Dwarf Pug
Eupithecia tantillaria

V-Pug
Chloroclystis v-ata

Sloe Pug
Pasiphila chloerata

——————————— Green Pug ———————————
Pasiphila rectangulata   f. *anthrax*

Bilberry Pug
Pasiphila debiliata

————————— Double-striped Pug —————————
Gymnoscelis rufifasciata

Dentated Pug
Anticollix sparsata

——————————— Streak ———————————
Chesias legatella

Broom-tip
Chesias rufata rufata

Manchester Treble-bar
Carsia sororiata anglica

——————————— Treble-bar ———————————
Aplocera plagiata plagiata   *Aplocera plagiata scotica*

————————— Lesser Treble-bar —————————
Aplocera efformata   f. *fimbriata*

Purple Treble-bar
Aplocera praeformata

Chimney Sweeper
Odezia atrata

Grey Carpet
Lithostege griseata

Blomer's Rivulet
Discoloxia blomeri

————— Welsh Wave —————
Venusia cambrica   f. *bradyi*

————— Dingy Shell —————
Euchoeca nebulata

Small White Wave
Asthena albulata

Small Yellow Wave
Hydrelia flammeolaria

———————— Waved Carpet ————————
Hydrelia sylvata

Drab Looper
Minoa murinata

————— Seraphim —————
Lobophora halterata

Barred Tooth-striped
Trichopteryx polycommata

Early Tooth-striped
Trichopteryx carpinata

——— Early Tooth-striped ———
Trichopteryx carpinata
f. *fasciata*

Small Seraphim
Pterapherapteryx sexalata

——— Yellow-barred Brindle ———
Acasis viretata

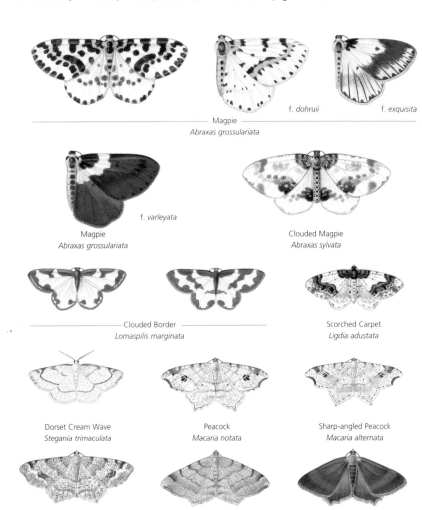

f. dohruii   f. exquisita

Magpie
Abraxas grossulariata

f. varleyata

Magpie
Abraxas grossulariata

Clouded Magpie
Abraxas sylvata

Clouded Border
Lomaspilis marginata

Scorched Carpet
Ligdia adustata

Dorset Cream Wave
Stegania trimaculata

Peacock
Macaria notata

Sharp-angled Peacock
Macaria alternata

Dusky Peacock
Macaria signaria

Tawny-barred Angle

Macaria liturata   f. nigrofulvata

Netted Mountain Moth
Macaria carbonaria

V-Moth
Macaria wauaria

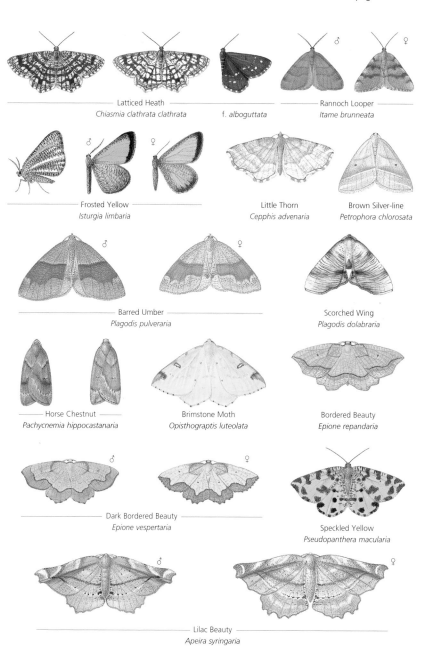

Latticed Heath
Chiasmia clathrata clathrata

f. *alboguttata*

♂ ♀
Rannoch Looper
Itame brunneata

♂ ♀
Frosted Yellow
Isturgia limbaria

Little Thorn
Cepphis advenaria

Brown Silver-line
Petrophora chlorosata

♂
♀
Barred Umber
Plagodis pulveraria

Scorched Wing
Plagodis dolabraria

Horse Chestnut
Pachycnemia hippocastanaria

Brimstone Moth
Opisthograptis luteolata

Bordered Beauty
Epione repandaria

♂
♀
Dark Bordered Beauty
Epione vespertaria

Speckled Yellow
Pseudopanthera macularia

♂
♀
Lilac Beauty
Apeira syringaria

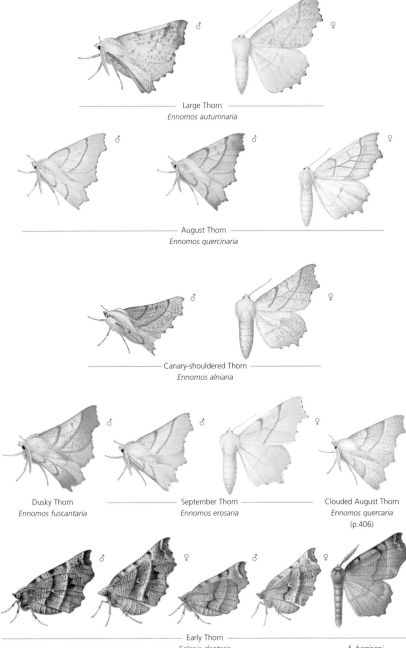

Large Thorn
Ennomos autumnaria

August Thorn
Ennomos quercinaria

Canary-shouldered Thorn
Ennomos alniaria

Dusky Thorn
Ennomos fuscantaria

September Thorn
Ennomos erosaria

Clouded August Thorn
Ennomos quercaria
(p.406)

Early Thorn
Selenia dentaria

1st generation

2nd generation

f. *harrisoni*

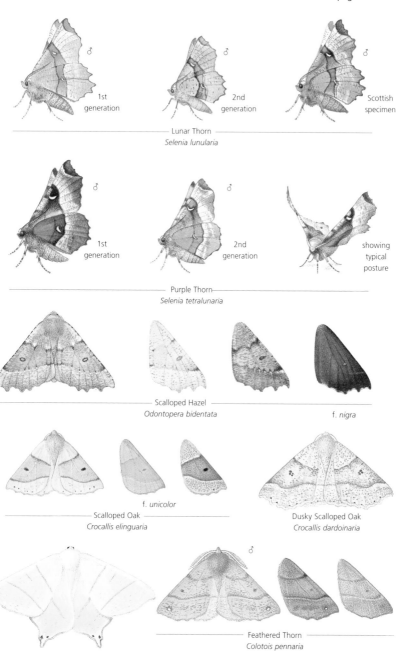

♂ 1st generation

♂ 2nd generation

♂ Scottish specimen

Lunar Thorn
Selenia lunularia

149

♂ 1st generation

♂ 2nd generation

showing typical posture

Purple Thorn
Selenia tetralunaria

Scalloped Hazel
Odontopera bidentata

f. *nigra*

f. *unicolor*

Scalloped Oak
Crocallis elinguaria

Dusky Scalloped Oak
Crocallis dardoinaria

♂

Feathered Thorn
Colotois pennaria

Swallow-tailed Moth
Ourapteryx sambucaria

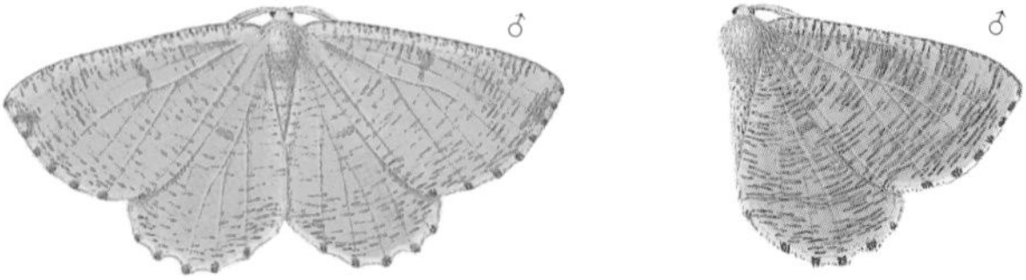

♂

♂

Orange Moth
Angerona prunaria

♀

♀

♂

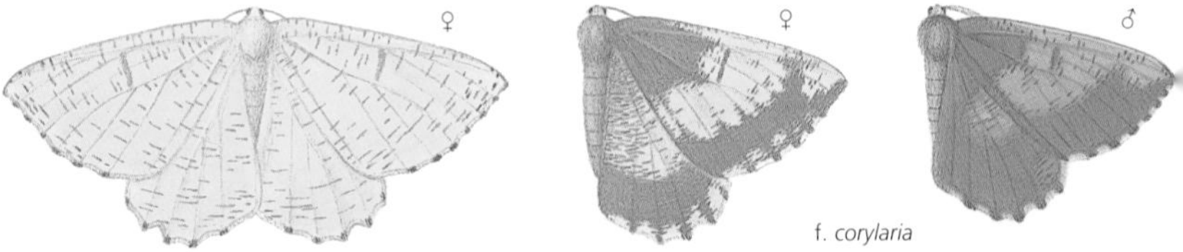

f. *corylaria*

Orange Moth
Angerona prunaria

♂

♂

♀

dark form

Small Brindled Beauty
Apocheima hispidaria

♂

♂

♀

f. *monacharia*

Pale Brindled Beauty
Phigalia pilosaria

♂

♀

♀

Brindled Beauty
Lycia hirtaria

f. *nigra*

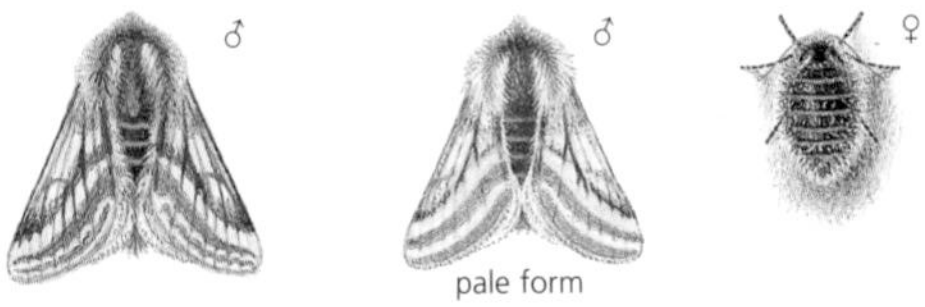

♂

♂

♀

pale form

♂

♀

Belted Beauty
Lycia zonaria

Rannoch Brindled Beauty
Lycia lapponaria scotica

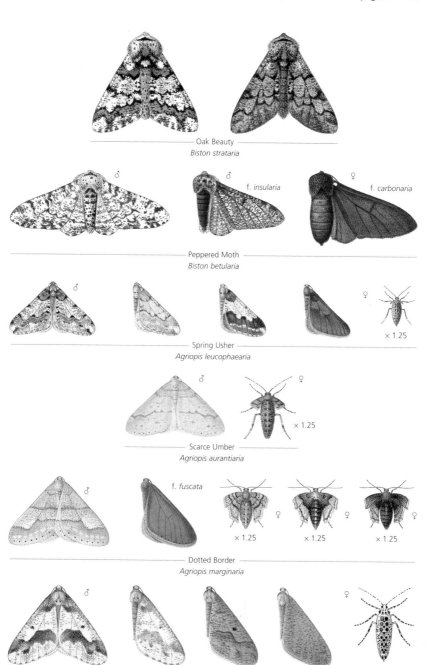

Oak Beauty
Biston strataria

♂   ♂ f. *insularia*   ♀ f. *carbonaria*

Peppered Moth
Biston betularia

♂   ♀ × 1.25

Spring Usher
Agriopis leucophaearia

♂   ♀ × 1.25

Scarce Umber
Agriopis aurantiaria

♂   f. *fuscata*   ♀ × 1.25   ♀ × 1.25   ♀ × 1.25

Dotted Border
Agriopis marginaria

♂   ♀ × 1.25

Mottled Umber
Erannis defoliaria

Waved Umber
Menophra abruptaria

f. *fuscata*

Willow Beauty
Peribatodes rhomboidaria

f. *perfumaria*

f. *rebeli*

Feathered Beauty
Peribatodes secundaria

f. *nigrata*

Lydd Beauty
Peribatodes ilicaria

Bordered Grey
Selidosema brunnearia scandinaviaria

Ringed Carpet
Cleora cinctaria cinctaria

Cleora cinctaria bowesi

152

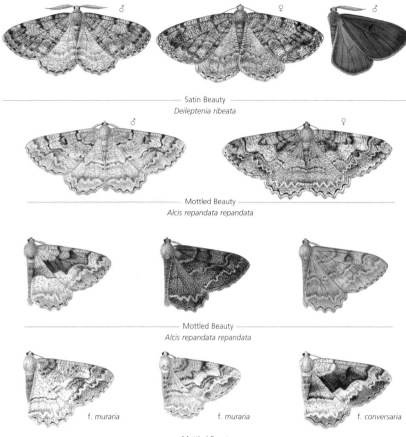

153

Satin Beauty
Deileptenia ribeata

Mottled Beauty
Alcis repandata repandata

Mottled Beauty
Alcis repandata repandata

f. *muraria*   f. *muraria*   f. *conversaria*

Mottled Beauty
Alcis repandata repandata

Dotted Carpet
Alcis jubata

154

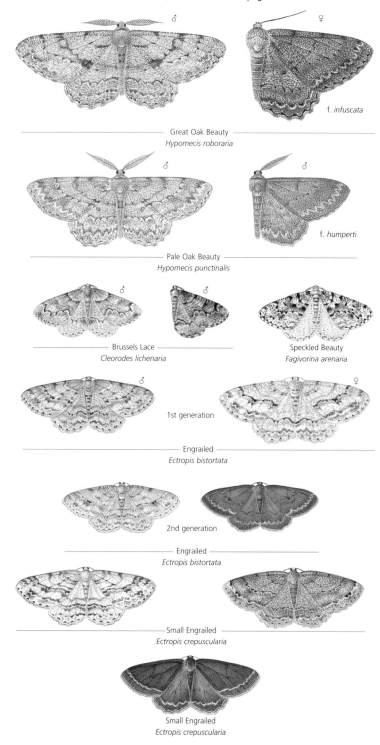

♂ ♀

f. *infuscata*

Great Oak Beauty
Hypomecis roboraria

♂ ♂

f. *humperti*

Pale Oak Beauty
Hypomecis punctinalis

♂ ♂

Brussels Lace
Cleorodes lichenaria

Speckled Beauty
Fagivorina arenaria

♂ ♀

1st generation

Engrailed
Ectropis bistortata

2nd generation

Engrailed
Ectropis bistortata

Small Engrailed
Ectropis crepuscularia

Small Engrailed
Ectropis crepuscularia

155

Square Spot
Paradarisa consonaria

Square Spot
Paradarisa consonaria

Brindled White-spot
Parectropis similaria   f. *variegata*

Grey Birch
Aethalura punctulata

Common Heath
Ematurga atomaria atomaria

Common Heath
Ematurga atomaria atomaria   f. *unicoloraria*

northern specimens   southern specimens

Bordered White
Bupalus piniaria

Common White Wave
Cabera pusaria

Common Wave
Cabera exanthemata

White-pinion Spotted
Lomographa bimaculata

Clouded Silver
Lomographa temerata

Sloe Carpet
Aleucis distinctata

♂ ♀

Early Moth
Theria primaria

Light Emerald
Campaea margaritata

♂ ♀ ♂ ♂

Barred Red
Hylaea fasciaria
f. *prasinaria*

♂ ♀

Irish Annulet
Odontognophos dumetata hibernica

Scotch Annulet
Gnophos obfuscatus

♂ ♀ ♂ ♀

Annulet
Charissa obscurata

specimen from Lulworth, Dorset
Swanage, Dorset
Wareham, Dorset   Portland, Dorset

156

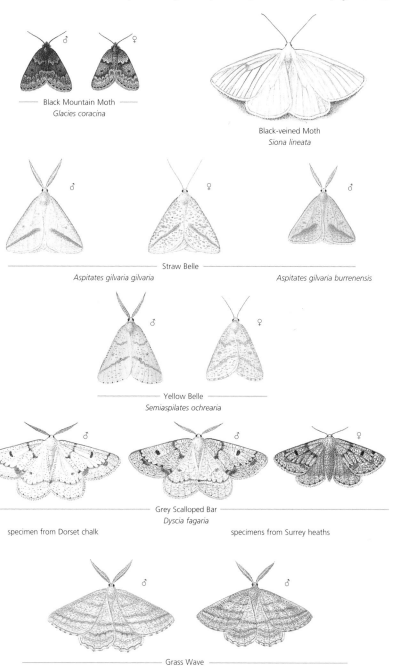

Black Mountain Moth
Glacies coracina

Black-veined Moth
Siona lineata

Straw Belle

Aspitates gilvaria gilvaria

Aspitates gilvaria burrenensis

Yellow Belle
Semiaspilates ochrearia

Grey Scalloped Bar
Dyscia fagaria

specimen from Dorset chalk

specimens from Surrey heaths

Grass Wave
Perconia strigillaria

Ennominae Thorns, beauties, umbers and allies

the lowlands, river valleys and coasts but occurs north to John O'Groats. Very well distributed throughout the west coast of Scotland and the Hebrides, where it occurs at greater densities than elsewhere. Recorded only rarely from Orkney and Shetland and possibly not resident. Widespread and frequent in Ireland and the Channel Islands.

Early Thorn

Brindled Beauty

Engrailed

Magpie   page 146

Abraxas grossulariata (L.)

Common. T   1884(7522)

Field characters & Similar species FW 18-25mm. The large size separates it from all other black and white carpet moths except the closely-related Clouded Magpie, which lacks heavy black spots around borders of wings and central black band across forewing. Extent of black and yellow markings can vary from almost all black to almost all white wings, but such extreme forms are rare in the wild. See also Small Magpie (pages 12-13).

Flight season One generation. Late June-August. Comes to light, usually in small numbers in southern Britain. Sometimes found at rest flat on Bramble and other low foliage. In the Hebrides, large numbers fly up from roosting in heathers. Plays 'dead' if captured and handled.

Life cycle Overwinters as a small larva on the foodplant. Larva late August-mid June. Pupates in a flimsy cocoon on the plant, with the yellow and black pupa easily visible.

Larval foodplants Blackthorn, Hawthorn, Midland Hawthorn, Hazel, Garden Privet, Black Currant, Red Currant, Gooseberry, Spindle, Evergreen Spindle and related trees and shrubs. Also Heather in northern Scotland.

Habitat Most abundant in northern heather moorland. Fairly frequent and familiar in gardens and allotments. Also woodland and hedgerows.

Status & distribution Resident. Common. Well distributed throughout England and Wales but often at rather low density and probably less frequent than 30 years ago. Also undergoes short-term cycles of local abundance and rarity. Fairly widespread and frequent on Man. In Scotland, largely restricted to

Clouded Magpie   page 146

Abraxas sylvata (Scop.)

Local. S,C   1885(7524*)

Field characters FW 18-22mm. Rests with wings partly spread, exposing blurred black and yellow blotches on hindwing as well as those on forewing near thorax and at trailing corner. Grey markings along leading edge are limited, and forewing tip is white.

Similar species See Magpie.

Flight season One generation. Late May-July. Sometimes seen by day resting flat on the upper side of low foliage. Comes well to light, sometimes in numbers, usually settling around light-traps rather than inside them.

Life cycle Overwinters as a pupa underground. Larva mid July-early October.

Larval foodplants Confirmed from Wych Elm, English Elm and the cultivated Japanese Golden Elm.

Habitat Mainly woodland. Sometimes parkland and scrub.

Status & distribution Resident. Local. Widespread but rather thinly distributed in England and Wales. Especially local in Cornwall, Devon, the Weald of Kent and parts of the east Midlands and East Anglia (but well established in the Thetford Forest area). Recorded annually at various sites in Dumfries & Galloway but seldom reported further north in Scotland. Locally numerous on Man. Widespread but local in Ireland, with populations scattered through Northern Ireland and south to Co. Kerry. Rare in the Channel Islands, one on Guernsey in 1983.

1886 see Appendix

Clouded Border   page 146

Lomaspilis marginata (L.)

Common. T   1887(7527)

Field characters FW 11-14mm. Distinguished by combination of its small size and the irregular brownish-black borders on both hindwing and forewing. Extent of these markings varies, sometimes extending with extra spots or a band into centre of wings. Rests with wings fully spread.

Similar species None.

Flight season One generation. From mid May in the south, but mainly June-July. Occasional second generation individuals, from August onwards, have been reported as far north as southern Scotland. Often disturbed from foodplant by day. Flies from dusk. Comes to light, sometimes in large numbers.

Life cycle Overwinters as a pupa underground. Larva

mid July-mid September.

Larval foodplants Aspen, poplars, sallows and willows. Also reported from Hazel.

Habitat Woodland, carr, wetlands, heathland and poplar plantations. Larvae obtained from mature trees, low sucker growth and coppice regrowth.

Status & distribution Resident. Common. Very well distributed and often abundant throughout England, Wales and much of Scotland, Man and Ireland, but not recorded from Orkney and Shetland. Widespread and frequent in the Channel Islands.

Scorched Carpet page 146
Ligdia adustata ([D. & S.])

Local. S,(C)   1888(7530)

Field characters FW 12-14mm. The blackish basal patch and broad black outer cross-band, both with blue-grey scales when freshly emerged, on creamy white wings, make this moth unmistakable. Shows very little variation.

Similar species None.

Flight season Two generations in the southern half of England, late April or May-June and late July-early September. One generation in northern England and parts of Wales, June-early July. May be disturbed from bushes by day. Flies from dusk and comes to light in small numbers.

Life cycle Overwinters as a pupa. Larva June-July and again late August-September in the south, early July-August in the north. Often seen at night, hanging from foodplant on a short silk thread.

Larval foodplants Spindle.

Habitat Broadleaved woodland, scrub and hedgerows on chalk, limestone, clays and occasionally more heathy places; also in gardens.

Status & distribution Resident. Local. Quite well distributed and fairly frequent in the southern half of England and Wales, north to the Wash and including East Anglia. Local from the Midlands northwards to south Cumbria and Yorkshire, where recorded from many more sites in recent years. Local in Ireland, where most frequent in the east of Northern Ireland and in the Burren, Co. Clare. Rare in the Channel Islands.

Dorset Cream Wave page 146
Stegania trimaculata (Vill.)

Rare immigrant.   1888a(7533)

Field characters FW 10-13mm. A fairly unmistakable creamy-white moth, with two fine, dark cross-lines on forewing, both angled near leading edge, where they are thickened to form spots, with a further dark spot closer to wing tip, and sometimes blotches along outer edge of outer line. Hindwing has a single, curved outer cross-line.

Similar species None.

Larval foodplants Poplars, in June and September in mainland Europe.

Status & distribution Rare, presumed immigrant. Only British record is one at light at Stowborough,

Dorset, on 13/14 June 1978. Mainly southern European but recorded from Belgium and the Netherlands.

Ringed Border not illustrated
Stegania cararia (Hb.)

Rare immigrant.   1888b(7532)

Field characters FW 10-12mm. Wings straw yellow, extensively speckled with brown, and with brown markings. Fore- and hindwing have an undulating outer cross-line, with the points or extensions reaching, or almost reaching, outer edge. Area beyond this line is often less heavily speckled.

Status & distribution Rare immigrant, Channel Islands only. One reported in a Rothamsted light-trap on Jersey in early August 1981.

Peacock Moth page 146
Macaria notata (L.)

Local. S,WC,NW   1889(7539)

Field characters & Similar species FW 14-16mm. The black, paw-print mark beyond centre, and the dark-edged concavity in leading half of outer edge of whitish, grey-brown speckled forewing, and strongly pointed hindwing readily distinguish this moth from all but the similar Sharp-angled Peacock (for differences see under that species).

Flight season Two generations in southern England, late May-early July and, often in smaller numbers, late July-August. One generation elsewhere, late May-June. May be disturbed from bushes by day. Flies from dusk and comes to light in small numbers.

Life cycle Overwinters as a pupa among plant debris. Larva late June-early August and again in September in southern England.

Larval foodplants Birch. Also reported from sallow.

Habitat Open broadleaved woodland with birch scrub, often on chalk, and wooded heathland.

Status & distribution Resident. Local. Very well distributed from the heathy parts of southern and south-east England, from Dorset to Essex, and especially in Kent. More thinly distributed in south-west England and south-west Wales. Very local in Monmouthshire and the West Midlands, but still locally frequent at one site in Staffordshire. In eastern England very local north of the Thames, but occasional individuals recorded north to Yorkshire, more frequently since the 1970s, and resident in Roudsea Wood, Cumbria. Also recorded from a wide scatter of sites in central and western Scotland, including the Inner Hebrides, and in south-west Ireland. Local and occasional in the Channel Islands.

Sharp-angled Peacock page 146
Macaria alternata ([D. & S.])

Local. S,(C)   1890(7540)

Field characters & Similar species FW 13-15mm. Very similar to Peacock Moth, and often confused with it. Forewing usually has a distinct grey cross-

159

band running through paw-print mark, continuing across hindwing (although some individuals are extensively grey, obscuring this band). Concavity, including fringes, on outer edge of forewing is very dark, blackish (lighter, brownish in Peacock). Paw-print mark is often smaller and less well-formed, and brown blotch on leading edge is often narrower and more tapered (roughly rectangular on Peacock). On hindwing, fine dark line around edges is usually well broken or consists of dots (usually continuous in Peacock). For worn or atypical examples, it may be necessary to examine genitalia to be certain.

Flight season Two generations. Late May-mid July and in smaller numbers in August. Flies from dusk and comes to light, sometimes in fair numbers.

Life cycle Overwinters as a pupa, in a cocoon formed just beneath the ground. Larva July and September.

Larval foodplants Sallows, willows, Blackthorn, Sea-buckthorn and Alder.

Habitat Open broadleaved woodland, scrubby heathland and well vegetated coastal sand-dunes.

Status & distribution Resident. Local. Well distributed and fairly frequent in south-west and southern England, from Cornwall to Hampshire and the north-west part of the Isle of Wight, and in south-west Wales. Much more local and less frequent in south-east England. Scattered records further north, mainly up the east coast north to Spurn, Yorkshire, where recorded several times, suggesting local movement or immigration. Resident very locally in south Cumbria at Roudsea Wood, Witherslack and Lyth Valley. In Ireland found in Co. Wexford in July 1969. Locally frequent in the Channel Islands.

Dusky Peacock   page 146
Macaria signaria (Hb.)
Immigrant.   1891(7541)

Field characters FW 13-14mm. Rather an indistinctly marked moth, with thickly-speckled dirty white wings, a roughly square dark grey blotch beyond centre of forewing, three diffuse dark spots on leading edge and slightly pointed hindwing.

Similar species Might possibly be mistaken for a worn Tawny-barred Angle, which has an orange-brown outer cross-band on broader forewing.

Flight season One generation. Has been recorded in Britain from late May-end July. In mainland Europe can be disturbed from branches of the foodplant by day. Flies from dusk and comes to light.

Life cycle Overwinters as a pupa. Larva August-September. No evidence of breeding in Britain at time of writing.

Larval foodplants The needles of various coniferous trees, including Norway Spruce and Scots Pine.

Habitat Coniferous woodland and plantations in mainland Europe.

Status & distribution Immigrant. Thirteen examples have been recorded up to 2000, all at light, from southern and south-eastern England and East Anglia (Sussex to Kent, Hertfordshire and Norfolk), since the

first in Essex, in 1970. A possible future colonist.

1892 see Appendix

Tawny-barred Angle   page 146
Macaria liturata (Cl.)
Common. T   1893(7542)

Field characters FW 14-17mm. A fairly distinctive, usually greyish-brown moth. Diagnostic features are orange-brown outer cross-band on both fore- and hindwing, slight concavity in leading half of outer edge of forewing, and slightly pointed hindwing. F. *nigrofulvata* Collins is dark brownish-grey, apart from the orange-brown cross-bands.

Similar species See Dusky Peacock.

Flight season Two generations in some parts of southern Britain, mid May-mid June and August-September, elsewhere one protracted generation. In Scotland, late April-mid September, with a peak in early July. Sometimes seen at rest on leaves of Hazel and other understorey plants. Readily disturbed by tapping conifer branches. Comes to light, sometimes in very large numbers.

Life cycle Overwinters as a pupa, among fallen conifer needles or below ground. Larva late June-early August and September-early October in southern Britain, mainly July-August in the north.

Larval foodplants Mainly Scots Pine and Norway Spruce, but also reported from Corsican Pine, Sitka Spruce, Japanese Red-cedar and Western Hemlock-spruce.

Habitat Most abundant in conifer plantations but occurs in most places where suitable conifers are native or planted, including urban situations.

Status & distribution Resident. Common. Well distributed and often abundant throughout England, Wales, mainland Scotland, and some of the Hebrides. Local and not frequent on Man. Widespread and locally frequent throughout Ireland. Rare on Jersey and Guernsey.

1894 see below 1897

Netted Mountain Moth   page 146
Macaria carbonaria (Cl.)
RDB. NE   1895(7545)

Field characters FW 10-11mm. Wings patterned with wavy, parallel blackish-brown cross-bands, running from leading to trailing edge. Varies from forms with substantial whitish frosting to smoky, almost completely black, individuals.

Similar species Small upland forms of the highly variable Common Heath (especially female), on which central bands on forewing converge or unite in trailing half, and male (usually larger) has more strongly feathered antennae. See also dark f. *unicolraria* of Common Heath, and Latticed Heath.

Flight season One generation. April-early June, varying with altitude and season. Both sexes active by day. Male often seen flying in numbers on calm sunny afternoons. In windy weather they walk or make short hopping flights just above the vegetation. Visits flowers, including those of the larval foodplant.

Life cycle Overwinters as a pupa, in a cocoon among mosses, lichens or plant debris on the ground. Larva late May-early July.

Larval foodplants Bearberry. The small larvae eat only the young shoots and are unable to manage the mature leaves. Appears not to accept the alternative foodplants stated in some previous works (Grey Willow and birches).

Habitat Mountains and moorlands.

Status & distribution Resident. Red Data Book species. Could prove to merit Nationally Scarce A if systematically surveyed. Scattered distribution in central Scottish Highlands, within which it is probably under-recorded; the Newtonmore area is a favourite with visiting entomologists but searches elsewhere have been limited. Occurs on several national nature reserves, including Morrone Birkwood and the Muir of Dinnet, Aberdeenshire.

1896 see below 1897

V-Moth
page 146

Macaria wauaria (L.)

Local. T   1897(7543)

Field characters FW 14-17mm. Bold black V on pale grey forewing is diagnostic. Three additional black markings are also conspicuous on leading edge of forewing. Intensity of ground-colour and markings varies, sometimes with a violet tinge. Rarely the wings are smoky grey (f. *vau-nigraria* Hatchett) or blackish brown (f. *fuscaria* Thunb.).

Similar species None.

Flight season One generation. July-August. Occasionally disturbed from the foodplant or seen on the wing at dusk. Comes to light, almost always in small numbers.

Life cycle Overwinters as an egg on the foodplant. Larva mid April-mid June, pupating in a cocoon among the leaves of the foodplant.

Larval foodplants Black Currant, Red Currant and Gooseberry, preferring the young shoots.

Habitat Mainly gardens and allotments where the foodplants are grown. The extent to which 'pick-your-own' farms and other commercial crops are exploited needs investigation, but insecticidal sprays are sometimes used.

Status & distribution Resident. Local. Recorded in small numbers from many localities throughout England, Wales and Scotland north to Banffshire, where it is occasional. More densely distributed in south-east England and the Home Counties than elsewhere, but everywhere probably less numerous than formerly, probably because the foodplants are less frequently grown in gardens, and the use of insecticides by non-commercial growers has increased. Local and scarce on Man. Appears rare in the Irish Republic, with a few widely scattered

records. In Northern Ireland not seen between 1960 and 2000, but several older records. In the Channel Islands, recorded from Jersey, but very rare.

Latticed Heath
page 147

Chiasmia clathrata clathrata (L.)

Common. S,C,N   1894(7547)

ssp. *hugginsi* (Baynes)
Ireland

Field characters FW 11-15mm. Often lands and perches with wings partly raised, like a butterfly. Ssp. *clathrata* Crisp network effect created by dark cross-lines and veins on upper- and undersides of wings is characteristic of the normal form, and the two joined outer bands on forewing are somewhat like a distorted swastika. Width of bands varies greatly. In the infrequent f. *alboguttata* Fettig most of wing area is dark brown but borders remain chequered. Other extreme variation is unusual but includes the rare f. *obsoletissima* Cock., which is creamy yellow without dark cross-bands. Ssp. *hugginsi* has a striking, pure white ground-colour.

Similar species On Common Heath (and Netted Mountain Moth if in a northern upland habitat), markings are less crisp, and without dark veins. Also, male has strongly feathered antennae and the wings tend to be held flat.

Flight season Usually two generations. May-June and July-September. One generation in north-west Britain, May-July. Active by day and often disturbed from low vegetation. Comes to light, occasionally in huge numbers near Lucerne fields.

Life cycle Overwinters as a pupa underground. Larva June-July and mid August-September, or July-August where one generation.

Larval foodplants Clovers, trefoils and Lucerne.

Habitat Most abundant around Lucerne crops. Generally occurs in smaller numbers in open ground, including gardens, and ranging from calcareous grassland and fens to acid heathland and moorland. Sometimes open woodland and derelict or unkempt urban sites.

Status & distribution Resident and suspected immigrant. Common. Well distributed in central and southern England, East Anglia, western Wales, northern England and southern Scotland, including Skye, Mull and the smaller Inner Hebridean islands of Canna, Rum, Islay and Colonsay. Local and not frequent on Man. Locally frequent in the Channel Islands. Ssp. *hugginsi* quite well distributed in Ireland, with many records from Northern Ireland in recent years.

Rannoch Looper
page 147

Itame brunneata (Thunb.)

Na. NE   1896(7567)

Field characters FW 11-13mm. A distinctive small orange-brown moth, with deep wings and rather

161

rounded forewing tips. Female is more strongly marked than male, with slightly narrower, more pointed wings. Both sexes have four darker red-brown lines across forewing and male often has a central dot. Intensity of colour varies and worn male can be pale, with weak markings.

Similar species None.

Flight season One generation. Late June-July. Male flies over the foodplant by day from just before noon until late afternoon. Easily disturbed from vegetation, even on dull days. Comes to light, sometimes in numbers.

Life cycle Overwinters normally as an egg, not as a larva as stated in some previous works. Possibly pupae sometimes also overwinter, based on observations in captivity, where pupae have remained dormant for up to four years. Larva late April-late May, pupating just beneath the ground.

Larval foodplants Bilberry. Possibly also Cowberry.

Habitat Long-established native pine and birch woodland, with Bilberry ground cover. Also among birch regeneration and in more open areas. Prefers substantial growth of Bilberry and vulnerable to over-grazing.

Status & distribution Resident and suspected immigrant. Nationally Scarce A. With systematic survey, this species might be found in sufficient squares to merit Nationally Scarce B. Quite widely and well distributed, and locally numerous, in central Scotland, where it occurs from Perthshire east to Aberdeenshire, with colonies to the north-west in Easter Ross. About 50 have been recorded elsewhere in Britain. Most of these are singletons at light, mainly in eastern England and south-eastern Scotland but occasionally south to the Isle of Wight, and are presumed immigrants.

1898 see Appendix

Frosted Yellow   page 147
Isturgia limbaria (Fabr.)
Former resident; presumed extinct.   1899(7561)

Field characters FW 13-15mm. Unmistakable. Both sexes have orange-yellow, rather rounded wings with chocolate-brown borders, less pronounced in female. Extent of brown frosting varies, f. *fumata* Mathew being mostly smoky brown with an orange tinge. At rest wings are brought together over back, like a butterfly, with hindwing showing a mostly greenish-brown underside, with strong speckling and white streaks. Male has feathered antennae.

Similar species None.

Flight season Two generations in southern Britain, May-early June and late July-August. Probably one generation in Scotland, from where the few surviving set specimens appear all to have been captured in June. Flies in sunshine. Readily disturbed from foodplant.

Life cycle Overwinters as a pupa underground, sometimes for more than one year. Larva June and September.

Larval foodplants Broom.

Habitat Well-drained, sunny situations in bushy places. Formerly quite numerous along a railway embankment near Colchester, Essex. Reported from Kent as 'not uncommon among high broom', suggesting mature stands favoured.

Status & distribution Former resident, presumed extinct. Always very local, in East Anglia and north and central Scotland. Last seen at Kelvedon, near Chelmsford, Essex, in 1914. Most records are from Suffolk during the 19th century, when it was seen in numbers at Stowmarket and reported around Needham, Barham and Ipswich. Also occurred very locally in north Kent but lost during the 1860s. A few were collected in Perthshire and Ross-shire, but these were little known and not mentioned in most of the standard works of the 19th and early 20th centuries.

1900 see Appendix

Little Thorn   page 147
Cepphis advenaria (Hb.)
Nb. W,S,not SW   1901(7594)

Field characters FW 14-17mm. Rests with wings held partly open up over back, somewhat like Purple Thorn. The small size, distinctive golden patterning, double-pointed hindwing and greyish clouding are also diagnostic. Occasionally individuals are more reddish. A uniformly dark brown form with white fringes has been recorded (f. *fulva* Gillmer).

Similar species None.

Flight season One generation. Late May-June. Sometimes disturbed from foodplants by day. Female occasionally seen flying among Bramble in late afternoon. Comes to light in small numbers, often settling outside the trap.

Life cycle Overwinters as a pupa underground. Larva late June-early August.

Larval foodplants Recorded on Bilberry, but must have alternative foodplants because it occurs on sites without this plant. Bramble is accepted in captivity and wild roses, Dogwood, Ash and sallows have also been proposed.

Habitat Sunny, open woodland and low vegetation along the verges of rides. Sometimes in long-established scrub. Often on heavy, damp clay, sometimes lighter, heathy soils.

Status & distribution Resident. Nationally Scarce B. Two main centres of distribution, with some notable apparently isolated colonies elsewhere. One is centred on Hampshire, extending into east Dorset, Isle of Wight, south Wiltshire, Berkshire, West Sussex and extensively into Surrey. It is known to have occurred more widely in Sussex and northwards into Kent in the past but disappeared from East Sussex early last century, the last record being from Hastings in 1939. The other main centre is the area bordering the Bristol Channel, Severn and Wye, from north Somerset up through Gloucestershire and Monmouthshire into Herefordshire. There is an outlying colony at Flitwick Moor, Bedfordshire. Not seen in Shropshire since 1969, in Derbyshire since 1922, in Yorkshire since 1958 and in Essex since the 19th century. In Ireland recorded only from the southern counties of Cork, Waterford, Limerick, Clare and Tipperary. Local and occasional in the Channel Islands.

Brown Silver-line page 147
Petrophora chlorosata (Scop.)
Common. T   1902(7596)

Field characters FW 15-18mm. Fairly unmistakable. Holds forewings back to cover hindwings when at rest, like a noctuid. The two fairly central silvery cross-lines on forewing, edged with brown, and the dark central spot are constant features. Hindwing paler, with a single, similar cross-line. Varies slightly in size and colour (often browner than illustration) and in prominence of cross-lines.
Similar species None.
Flight season One generation. May-June, individuals from mid-April in the south. Frequently disturbed by day among Bracken, often in numbers. Comes to light, sometimes in abundance.
Life cycle Overwinters as a pupa underground. Larva mid June-early September.
Larval foodplants Bracken.
Habitat Most places where the foodplant occurs, particularly woodland, heathland and moorland.
Status & distribution Resident. Common. Widely and well distributed, and abundant in many places throughout England, Wales, Man, Ireland and lowland Scotland north to Caithness. Widespread and frequent in the Channel Islands.

Barred Umber page 147
Plagodis pulveraria (L.)
Local. T   1903(7606)

Field characters FW 17-19mm. Jagged outer edge of dark brown central cross-band on soft brown, dark-speckled forewing is most striking and diagnostic feature. Less obvious is unique red and gold freckled underside. Central cross-band contrasts more distinctly with ground-colour in some individuals, varies slightly in shape and sometimes outer edge blurs with rest of forewing. Some individuals have a pinkish or purplish tinge, others are more greyish brown. Female has a more curved leading edge to forewing.
Similar species None.
Flight season One generation. May-June. Comes to light, mainly male but occasionally female.
Life cycle Overwinters as a pupa underground. Larva mid June-mid August.
Larval foodplants Particularly Hazel, also Downy and Silver Birch, some sallows and Hawthorn.
Habitat Mainly ancient broadleaved woodland, including low Hazel growth in cracks in limestone pavement.
Status & distribution Resident. Local. Well distrib-

Larva of Scorched Wing.

uted, but not numerous, in south-west, south-east and southern England and in Wales. More thinly distributed through the Midlands, East Anglia and northwards, and recorded locally throughout northern England and mainland Scotland. Widespread but local throughout Ireland.

Scorched Wing page 147
Plagodis dolabraria (L.)
Local. T   1904(7607)

Field characters FW 16-19mm. Unmistakable. Tip of male's abdomen is curled up at rest. Trailing corners of both fore- and hindwing are darkened, as if scorched, and these marks are brought together at rest. The many fine, brown, curved lines on forewing almost make wings look like they are in motion. The forewing shape, with slight cut-aways at trailing corner and crumpled appearance, is distinctive. There is little variation.
Similar species None.
Flight season One generation. Mid May-late June. Male frequent at light. Female hardly seen, but reported at sugar. Seldom seen by day, so possibly roosts in the tree canopy.
Life cycle Overwinters as a pupa, in a cocoon on the ground. Larva late June-mid September.
Larval foodplants Mainly oaks, Downy and Silver Birch. Also sallows. Sometimes Beech, Sweet Chestnut and probably Turkey Oak.
Habitat Broadleaved woodland and scrub. Sometimes in parks and gardens if stands of large trees present.
Status & distribution Resident. Local. Well distributed and sometimes frequent in England and Wales north to Yorkshire and Cumbria. Also occurs more locally in parts of south-west Scotland north to Argyll. Widespread but local in Ireland, including Northern Ireland. Local and occasional in the Channel Islands.

Horse Chestnut page 147
Pachycnemia hippocastanaria (Hb.)
Nb. S,EC   1905(7609)

Field characters FW 14-16mm. The narrow, rounded forewing is distinctive, but hardly that expected of a geometrid moth. Wings overlap at rest. Two cross-lines are usually conspicuous, the inner sharply angled, the outer curved. The area between them is sometimes darker, particularly in female. Ground-colour varies from light to dark brown or greyish brown, and sometimes has a purplish tinge. Hindwing paler, off-white.

Similar species None among the macro-moths. Could be mistaken for a large micro-moth, but no British species really resembles it.

Flight season Two generations. April-May and August, the second generation annual but only partial. Odd records from January and November. Occasionally disturbed from foodplant by day. Flies from dusk and comes to light, often abundantly.

Life cycle Overwinters as a pupa underground. Larva late May-early July, with a partial second generation in September. Larva may also overwinter.

Larval foodplants Heather, Cross-leaved Heath.

Habitat Closely associated with lowland heathland. Regularly recorded up to 1950 in the Itchen Valley, Hampshire, an area of watermeadows and chalk woodland through which the moth was presumably prone to travel.

Status & distribution Resident. Nationally Scarce B. Abundant throughout the surviving lowland heaths of Dorset, Hampshire, Isle of Wight and Surrey, with colonies in Berkshire and Sussex, the south and east of Devon and north coast of Somerset, but not on the high moorland. Occurs very locally in Lincolnshire. Formerly in other English counties south of the Humber, where occasionally examples are still reported, sometimes in unlikely habitat. Also previously reported from Cumbria and Glamorgan. Locally frequent on Jersey. Recorded once from Guernsey, in 1972.

Brimstone Moth   page 147

Opisthograptis luteolata (L.)

Common. T   1906(7613)

Field characters FW 14-21mm. An unmistakable yellow moth, with chestnut brown marking on forewing tip. Small white crescent or dash, with a dark reddish-brown outline, near centre of leading edge of forewing. Varies only slightly. Female is generally larger and later-generation moths are usually smaller.

Similar species None.

Flight season Usually two or three generations. April-October, with the emergence time of the spring individuals and their progeny dependent on the stage at which they overwintered. Some authors consider there is a consistent pattern of three generations over two years. One generation in northern Scotland and Orkney, June-July. Sometimes disturbed on or near foodplant by day. Frequently seen on the wing from just before dusk and comes regularly to light, sometimes in fair numbers.

Life cycle Some overwinter as part-grown larvae on the foodplant, others as pupae in cocoons on the plant, in debris below it, or in a crack in a wall.

Larval foodplants Blackthorn, Hawthorn, Midland

Hawthorn, sometimes Plum, Bullace and related species. Rowan is the main foodplant on Orkney and Wayfaring-tree has been reported elsewhere.

Habitat Hedgerows and gardens, woodland, scrub on calcareous grassland and acid heathland.

Status & distribution Resident. Common. Very well distributed and usually frequent throughout Great Britain, Man, Ireland and the Channel Islands, north to Orkney, but not Shetland.

Bordered Beauty   page 147

Epione repandaria (Hufn.)

Common. T   1907(7615)

Field characters FW 13-16mm. The broad pinkish or fawnish-brown border of the orange forewing tapers to a point at forewing tip. Intensity of orange and colour of border varies.

Similar species In male Dark Bordered Beauty, dark border does not taper towards forewing tip.

Flight season One generation. July-September. Readily disturbed from foodplant from dusk. More often seen on the wing just after dark, but also comes to light, usually in small numbers. Female sometimes found after dark, flying gently among willow foliage, laying eggs.

Life cycle Overwinters as an egg on the foodplant. Larva early May-mid July. Pupates among leaves, not necessarily of the foodplant when in mixed stands.

Larval foodplants Sallows, certainly Grey Willow. Also Black-poplar, Alder and Hazel.

Habitat Mainly carr woodland and rides and clearings in damp woods, but also occasionally in scrub, hedgerows and gardens away from woodland.

Status & distribution Resident. Common. Widespread and quite well distributed, but seldom seen in numbers and somewhat local, in England and Wales north to the Humber, and in Yorkshire. Much more local and infrequent in Cumbria and northwards. Occurs in the lowlands and river valleys throughout much of mainland Scotland. Widespread but somewhat local and infrequent on Man and in Ireland. Local and occasional in the Channel Islands.

Dark Bordered Beauty   page 147

Epione vespertaria (L.)

RDB. NE   1908(7616)

Field characters FW 12-14mm. Forewing border of male runs roughly parallel with wing edge and is broad throughout. Female is virtually un-freckled, lemon yellow, with a deep indentation in middle of reddish-brown wing border on forewing.

Similar species See Bordered Beauty.

Flight season One generation. Mid July-late August (from late June in 2003). Male active by day and both sexes often disturbed from foodplant, especially in the afternoon. Comes to light, mainly the male, and usually well after midnight or just before dawn. Also flies at dawn and just after, sometimes in numbers.

Life cycle Overwinters as an egg on the foodplant. Larva May-early July. Pupates on the foodplant or in debris below it.

Larval foodplants Aspen less than 50cm tall at the three Scottish sites. Creeping Willow at the Yorkshire site and probably at the site in Northumberland, although possibly other willows may be used.

Habitat Open and damp scrubby grassland and heathy grassland, usually near taller trees.

Status & distribution Resident. Red Data Book species. Currently three small populations are known in Scotland (Aberdeenshire and Moray) and two in England (Strensall Common, Yorkshire, and Newham Bog, Northumberland). Individuals recorded at Aviemore, Moray, on 10 August 1975 and at Middleton-in-Teesdale, Co. Durham, on 13 August 1976, indicate there may be more populations awaiting discovery. Reported from Adderstonlee Moss, Roxburghshire, but not for many years, despite searches.

Speckled Yellow
page 147

Pseudopanthera macularia (L.)

Common. T
1909(7620)

Field characters FW 13-15mm. Bold brownish blotches on yellow fore- and hindwing are diagnostic. Slight variation in intensity of yellow and dark patterning.

Similar species None.

Flight season One generation. Mid May-late June. On the wing by day, particularly in sunshine, and often seen in numbers.

Life cycle Overwinters as a pupa underground or in plant debris. Larva mid June-early August.

Larval foodplants Wood Sage. Also reported from White Dead-nettle, Woundwort and Yellow Archangel.

Habitat Mainly open woodland. Also open scrub and bushy grassland.

Status & distribution Resident. Common. Well distributed and locally frequent throughout south-west and south-east England, south-east and north-west Wales. More local in central southern England, East Anglia, the West Midlands, Cumbria and central and western Scotland, with scattered records throughout the eastern half of Britain north to the Moray Firth. Local in southern Ireland, with most records from the Burren. Not recorded from Northern Ireland. In the Channel Islands locally frequent on Jersey, with single records from Guernsey and Sark.

Lilac Beauty
page 147

Apeira syringaria (L.)

Local. S,C
1910(7630)

Field characters FW 19-22mm. Resting posture, with forewings slightly raised and with leading edge broadly creased, is diagnostic, as are the invariable lilac markings and bold brown line running obliquely across forewing. Male is smaller and more brightly coloured than female, with more orange. Female is greyer. Second-generation individuals of both sexes

smaller.

Similar species None.

Flight season Mainly one generation. Late June-July. Individuals of an occasional partial second generation recorded from late August-mid September in southern England northwards to Cheshire. Sometimes seen on the wing at dusk. Comes to light in small numbers.

Life cycle Overwinters as a small larva on the food-plant. Larva normally August-end May. Larvae producing individuals in late August must hatch in early July.

Larval foodplants Honeysuckle, Ash and Wild Privet. Recorded on cultivated varieties of honey-suckles and Garden Privet.

Habitat Broadleaved woodland, scrub and some gardens, occurring both in more open areas and in narrow woodland rides or under the tree canopy.

Status & distribution Resident. Local. Fairly well distributed and fairly frequent throughout England and Wales and locally north to southern Scotland. Local and infrequent on Man and throughout Ireland. Local and occasional on Jersey, rare on Guernsey.

Large Thorn
page 148

Ennomos autumnaria (Werneb.)

Nb. SE
1911(7632)

Field characters & Similar species FW 21-28mm. Rests with wings half raised, like most other *Ennomos* thorns, but quite distinct. August Thorn holds its wings much flatter. Female is much larger than other female thorns (all with un-feathered antennae). Male (feathered antennae) can be the same size as females of other species. Amount of dark speckling is highly variable, but rarely absent.

Flight season One generation. September-early October. Comes to light, otherwise seldom seen.

Life cycle Overwinters as an egg on the foodplant. Larva late April-early August. Pupates under a leaf or on the ground.

Larval foodplants A wide range of broadleaved trees and shrubs, including birches, Alder, Hazel, hawthorns, Blackthorn, Plum, Cherry, Apple, oaks, Sycamore and poplars.

Habitat Broadleaved woodland and scrub. Has been recorded in suburban gardens.

Status & distribution Resident and suspected immigrant. Nationally Scarce B. Largely restricted to south-eastern England but has extended its range since the 19th century. Regularly recorded and assumed to be breeding locally from Bedfordshire and Cambridgeshire east and south into Norfolk, Suffolk, Essex and Hertfordshire. Also in east Kent, Sussex and along the coast of south-east Hampshire to Southampton Water, including Hayling Island. Often recorded from a site for several years and then disappears, suggesting establishment of temporary colonies, with Peterborough about the northern limit of this pattern. Numbers may be reinforced by immigration and presumed wanderers or suspected immi-

165

grants have been recorded as far north as Spurn, Yorkshire, and from a few scattered localities west of the main distribution. In Ireland one individual only reported, from Co. Wexford in 1931. Widespread and frequent on Jersey. Recorded once in Guernsey, in 1989.

August Thorn
page 148

Ennomos quercinaria (Hufn.)

Local. S,C   1912(7633)

Field characters & Similar species FW 18-22mm. August Thorn and September Thorn cannot be distinguished on the basis of flight season, the latter appearing first, in July! Slimmer than related thorns, with generally broader forewing, especially in male (except the much larger Large Thorn). Also holds wings at a lower angle when at rest than similar species. These are probably the best diagnostic features. On forewing, outer cross-line is usually kinked near leading edge, turning towards then usually away from base as it meets edge. Inner one usually has longer, more pronounced angle at leading edge. Male is quite orange, female is much paler, straw-coloured. Forewing in both sexes usually speckled, but not infrequently plain, and may have extensive brown outer shading. Usually at least a trace of central spot or crescent on forewing. See also Canary-shouldered Thorn, September Thorn and Dusky Thorn.
Flight season One generation. Mid August-late September. Comes to light, sometimes in fair numbers. Occasionally found at rest on vegetation by day.
Life cycle Overwinters as an egg on the foodplant. Larva early May-mid July. Pupates among leaves of foodplant.
Larval foodplants Pedunculate Oak and probably Sessile Oak. Also limes, Small-leaved Elm and probably other elms. Also reported from Beech, birches, Hawthorn and Blackthorn.
Habitat Woodland, parkland, hedgerows (in west), scrubby downland and sometimes gardens.
Status & distribution Resident. Local. Widespread but fairly local in England and Wales, north to Yorkshire and Cumbria. More numerous in the west of its range. Few records from Scotland but recorded north to Ross-shire. Fairly widespread but not frequent on Man. Widespread and fairly frequent in Ireland and in the Channel Islands.

Canary-shouldered Thorn
page 148

Ennomos alniaria (L.)

Common. T   1913(7634)

Field characters & Similar species FW 16-20mm. In most cases, the bright canary-yellow thorax distinguishes this thorn. Also, outer cross-line on forewing is quite steeply angled and sweeps in a gentle arc to leading edge (usually kinked in August Thorn, straighter and less angled in Dusky and September Thorns), meeting it between three-quarters to four-fifths to the wing tip (about two-thirds on

September Thorn). Central crescent or dash normally present (absent or faint in September Thorn). Ground-colour orange-yellow (sometimes darker), with variable dark speckling. A form with a buff thorax has been reported from Kent, mainly towards the end of the flight period. A very rare form has dark grey wings, but the thorax remains yellow.
Flight season One generation. Late July-mid October. Comes to light, sometimes in numbers. Otherwise seldom seen.
Life cycle Overwinters as an egg on the foodplant. Larva early May-July. Pupates among plant debris or occasionally spun to small plants.
Larval foodplants Downy and Silver Birch, Alder, limes, elms. Also reported from Goat Willow.
Habitat Woodland, scrub, parks and gardens, but less frequent in densely urban areas.
Status & distribution Resident. Common. Widespread, generally well distributed and frequent throughout England, Wales, mainland Scotland, Ireland and the Channel Islands. Fairly widespread but not frequent on Man.

Dusky Thorn
page 148

Ennomos fuscantaria (Haw.)

Common. S,C   1914(7635)

Field characters & Similar species FW 17-21mm. Generally distinguished by the dark mauvish-grey or grey-brown shading between outer cross-line and outer edge of wing. Shape of cross-lines on forewing slightly variable. Closest to Canary-shouldered Thorn, but usually less curved. A rarer but widespread darker f. *perfuscata* Rebel has uniform dark shading over all four wings. See also August Thorn, September Thorn, Large Thorn and buff form of Canary-shouldered Thorn.
Flight season One generation. Late July-early October. Comes to light, often in numbers. Otherwise seldom seen.
Life cycle Overwinters as an egg on the foodplant. Larva early May-mid July. Pupates among spun leaves of foodplant.
Larval foodplants Ash. Probably also privets, which are accepted in captivity.
Habitat Most places where Ash occurs within the range of this moth, including woods, hedgerows, rural and suburban gardens and urban centres.
Status & distribution Resident. Common. Fairly generally distributed and often frequent in England and Wales north to Yorkshire, where numbers and colonies are prone to fluctuate. Occasionally recorded in Northumberland and Co. Durham, mainly as suspected wanderers from further south. Not reliably recorded on Man. Widespread and occasional in the Channel Islands.

September Thorn
page 148

Ennomos erosaria ([D. & S.])

Common. S,C,(N)   1915(7636)

Field characters FW 17-21mm. Distinguished by

plain or very slightly speckled, orange-brown or fawn wings, and almost always absence of central crescent. Cross-lines slightly variable, but generally converging closely to trailing edge. Moths emerging early in the flight period are distinctly paler.

Similar species Stouter than plain form of August Thorn, without a kink in the outer cross-line, which usually points to forewing tip at leading edge or widens to point to both tip and base. Also holds wings at a steeper angle. See also Canary-shouldered Thorn and Dusky Thorn.

Flight season One generation. July-early October. Comes to light, sometimes in numbers. Otherwise seldom seen.

Life cycle Overwinters as an egg on the foodplant. Larva late April-early July. Pupates between spun leaves.

Larval foodplants Oaks, birches, limes and Beech.

Habitat Woodland, parkland and gardens.

Status & distribution Resident. Common. Fairly well distributed and frequent in most parts of England and Wales. More local in northern England and mainland Scotland north to Inverness-shire. Apparently, the only confirmed records from Ireland are three individuals captured in Killarney, Co. Kerry, in 1966, 1970 and 1988. Previous records from Co. Kildare in 1931 and 1938 are considered mistaken. Local and occasional on Jersey; old records only from Guernsey and Alderney.

1916, 1916a see Appendix

Early Thorn   page 148
Selenia dentaria (Fabr.)
Common. T   1917(7641)

Field characters & Similar species FW 14-23mm. Resting position distinguishes Early Thorn from all other thorns, with wings held up over back and pressed together, like a butterfly. Summer generation moths are smaller and paler, usually with larger tawny orange patches on undersides. Scarce f. *harrisoni* Wagner is rather uniform dark brown, with pale cross-lines. Less extreme brownish and greyish forms are more frequent.

Flight season Generally two generations. Mid February-May and July-September. In parts of northern Britain, including Orkney, one generation, May-June. Sometimes seen on the wing from dusk onwards. Often comes to lighted windows and frequent at light-traps.

Life cycle Overwinters as a pupa, spun between leaves or among plant debris. Larva mid May-late June and August-early October, except where one generation, June-August.

Larval foodplants Blackthorn, Hawthorn, Hazel, Downy and Silver Birch, Alder, sallows, Honeysuckle, Bog-myrtle and other woody broadleaved plants.

Habitat Woodland, scrub, hedgerows, parks and gardens, including urban areas.

Status & distribution Resident. Common. Well distributed and frequent throughout England, Wales,

mainland Scotland, Man, Ireland and the Channel Islands. Resident on Orkney.

Lunar Thorn   page 149
Selenia lunularia (Hb.)
Local. T   1918(7642)

Field characters & Similar species FW 16-22mm. Resting posture is like that of similar Purple Thorn. On upperside of forewing, cross-line beyond small central silver crescent is either virtually straight or slightly wavy (sometimes slightly kinked in leading half) and there is no dark central spot near outer edge of hindwing upperside, which is distinctly scalloped, with a much bigger, deeper central indentation. Very variable in colour, from pale straw to reddish or purplish brown, especially in Scotland. Second-generation moths are much smaller, often more richly coloured and more strongly marked, sometimes pinkish. Often extensively speckled, sometimes very darkly, but not infrequently plain. See also Purple Thorn for differences.

Flight season Mainly one generation. May-June. A second and probably partial generation sometimes occurs in southern England, in July-August, and is annual in the Channel Islands. Seldom seen except at light, arriving late at night.

Life cycle Overwinters as a pupa, just below ground. Larva late June-late August.

Larval foodplants Ash, Blackthorn, Dog-rose, birches, elms, oaks and probably other broadleaved trees and shrubs.

Habitat Open woodland and scrub.

Status & distribution Resident and suspected immigrant. Local. Recorded usually very locally, sometimes in fair numbers but often as singletons, throughout mainland Britain, Ireland and some of the Hebrides, north to Caithness. First recorded on Man in 2000. Local and occasional on Jersey. Seen on Guernsey in 1982 and 1999. Second generation individuals occasionally recorded at Dungeness, Kent, where the moth is not known to be resident and first generation individuals are very rarely seen. These invariably coincide with southerly winds and migrant species, and are probably immigrants.

Purple Thorn   page 149
Selenia tetralunaria (Hufn.)
Common. S,C,(N)   1919(7643)

Field characters & Similar species FW 17-23mm. Rests with wings open and half-raised, with forewings slightly curled. Distinguished from Lunar Thorn by dark central spot towards outer edge of hindwing upperside. Central silver crescent on forewing is larger than in Lunar Thorn, and cross-line beyond it is distinctly bowed in leading half, and often in trailing half. Hindwing usually less deeply scalloped. Second-generation moths much smaller and paler, often tawny rather than purple.

Flight season In southern Britain two generations, April-May and July-August, with occasional individuals

of a partial third generation, late September-October. In northern Britain one generation, May-June. Fairly frequent at light, otherwise seldom seen.
Life cycle Overwinters as a pupa, just below ground. Larva late May-early July and August-September in southern Britain, June-July in northern localities.
Larval foodplants Hazel, birches, Alder, hawthorns, oaks and many other broadleaves.
Habitat Woodland and scrub, from calcareous substrates to acid heathland and wet clay. Often in rural and suburban gardens.
Status & distribution Resident. Common. Fairly well distributed and sometimes frequent in England and Wales north to the Humber. Has become widespread and frequent in Yorkshire since the 1980s. Very much more local further north, but reported north to Ross-shire. Local on Man, only one old record until the 1990s. Rare on Jersey and Guernsey where there are several recent records and the oldest is 1963.

Scalloped Hazel   page 149
Odontopera bidentata (Cl.)
Common. T   1920(7647)

Field characters FW 20-24mm. Rests with wings flat. Very triangular in appearance, with strongly and irregularly-scalloped forewing edges. Area between two cross-lines on forewing may be darker, producing a central band, but may also be the same colour as rest of wing, or even slightly paler. Overall ground-colour varies from whitish brown to deep chocolate brown (f. *nigra* Prout), but the usual forms are tawny with white edging on cross-lines. Dark forms, including f. *nigra*, are widely recorded in small numbers, such as in London and the Midlands, but are more frequent in north-west England and western Scotland. Those from Orkney are smaller and rather greyish brown. All forms have central spot in shape of a ring on fore- and hindwing.
Similar species See Scalloped Oak, which does not have jagged wing edges.
Flight season One generation. May-June. Sometimes found at rest on walls, fences and in the bases of hedges. Often seen flying along hedgerows after dark. Comes to light, sometimes in fair numbers.
Life cycle Overwinters as a pupa. Larva early June-September, feeding slowly. Pupates on the ground among plant debris or mosses.
Larval foodplants A wide range of woody plants, including Hazel, Downy and Silver Birch, Hawthorn, Midland Hawthorn, Blackthorn, oaks, willows, limes, privets, Barberry and conifers, including pines, spruces, Monterey Cypress, Lawson Cypress, Juniper and Larch.
Habitat Woodland, scrub and hedgerows, on both calcareous and acid soils. Conifer plantations, parks and gardens, including in urban centres.
Status & distribution Resident. Common. Well distributed and fairly frequent throughout mainland Britain and some of the Hebrides, Man and Ireland. Local on Orkney. Widespread and frequent in the Channel Islands.

Scalloped Oak   page 149
Crocallis elinguaria (L.)
Common. T   1921(7654)

Field characters & Similar species FW 18-22mm. Like Scalloped Hazel, wings also held flat at rest, but smaller, with more rounded, only slightly scalloped outer edge to forewing, and flies later in the year. Most familiar form is a yellowish moth with a brown central band and conspicuous blackish central spot on forewing, and slightly paler, more uniform hind-wing. Some forms are uniformly orange-brown (f. *unicolor* Prout), deep brown, even blackish (f. *fusca* Reutti), although cross-lines tend to remain paler and visible. Darker forms are more frequent in north-west England, Scotland and Ireland. See also Dusky Scalloped Oak.
Flight season One generation. July-August, occasionally from late June and as late as early September. Comes to light, sometimes in fair numbers.
Life cycle Overwinters as an egg on the foodplant. Larva late March-June.
Larval foodplants Hawthorn, Blackthorn, Downy and Silver Birch, oaks, Honeysuckle, Bilberry and Heather. Also reported from many other broadleaved woody plants, including cultivars, but not from conifers, unlike somewhat similar Scalloped Hazel.
Habitat Woodland, scrub, hedgerows, parks and gardens, including urban centres.
Status & distribution Resident. Common. Well distributed and generally frequent throughout main-land Britain, some of the Hebrides, Man and Ireland. Widespread and frequent in the Channel Islands.

Dusky Scalloped Oak   page 149
Crocallis dardoinaria Donzel
Guernsey   1921a(7655)

Field characters & Similar species FW 18-24mm. Distinguished from Scalloped Oak by forewing, which is usually straw-coloured, sometimes dull reddish-brown, rather than yellowish or orange-brown, with central mark composed of four small black spots (usually one solid spot in Scalloped Oak). Some examples are quite plain, but others, especially female, have heavy, rough freckling.
Flight season Possibly two generations, in June and September, based on occurrence of adults in Guernsey.
Life cycle, Larval foodplants & Habitat Not known on Guernsey. Larva reported from Gorse and Broom in mainland Europe.
Status & distribution Probable Resident. Guernsey only. Likely to be breeding locally on Guernsey but rare. First recorded at Icart, Guernsey, on 4 September 1990 and Petit Bot on 11 September 1990. At the time presumed to be an immigrant. Subsequently, three at Icart, in 1999, one in early June and singles on 8 and 12 September, and appears to be resident. In the rest of Europe, recorded only from France, Spain, Portugal, Corsica, Sardinia and Sicily.

Swallow-tailed Moth

page 149

Ourapteryx sambucaria (L.)

Common. T   1922(7659)

Field characters FW 22-30mm. Unmistakable, with a diagnostic pointed tail on hindwing, with two dark brown spots at base of tail. Pale lemon yellow when fresh, becoming whiter with age. Two darker cross-lines and a central dash on forewing, one cross-line on hindwing. Little variation, but female generally larger.

Similar species None.

Flight season One generation. Late June-mid August. Occasional individuals of a partial second generation in early October. Sometimes disturbed by day. Frequently comes to lighted windows soon after dark, and to light-traps, sometimes in fair numbers.

Life cycle Overwinters as a larva in a bark crevice. Larva late August-early June. Forms a loose cocoon on the foodplant.

Larval foodplants Woody broadleaves such as Blackthorn, Hawthorn, Goat Willow and Black Currant. Also plants often avoided by generalist feeders, such as Elder, Horse-chestnut, Garden Privet and Ivy. Several larvae have been found on cultivated Canadian Goldenrod.

Habitat Woodland, scrub, hedgerows, parks and gardens. Frequent in urban centres, including Ivy-shrouded cemeteries.

Status & distribution Resident. Common. Well distributed and fairly frequent throughout most of England and Wales, the lowlands of southern Scotland, Man, Ireland and the Channel Islands. Has colonised Deeside in recent years.

Feathered Thorn

page 149

Colotois pennaria (L.)

Common. T   1923(7663)

Field characters FW 19-23mm. Flies later in the year than other thorns, and unlike any other moth flying late in the year. Rests with wings flat. Male has wide feathery antennae, more so than other thorns. Both sexes have a slightly hooked tip to otherwise rather smooth outer edge of forewing, and often a unique and diagnostic whitish spot near tip. Two cross-lines are usually conspicuous on forewing but can be blurred or incomplete. Overall colour of male is usually orange, sometimes fawnish brown or brick-red, but many females are greyish brown. Female has un-feathered antennae, somewhat narrowed fore- and hindwing and cross-lines generally well defined.

Similar species Orange Moth is larger and flies during the summer. See also Scalloped Oak f. *unicolor*.

Flight season One generation. Mid September-early December. Occasionally found at rest below trees and bushes or low on trunks. Male often seen on the wing after dark, comes readily to light, often in numbers, usually several hours after dusk. Female much less frequent at light.

Life cycle Overwinters as an egg on the foodplant.

Larva of Feathered Thorn.

Larva April-June. Pupates just below ground.

Larval foodplants A wide range of broadleaved trees, including Pedunculate Oak, Hawthorn, Midland Hawthorn, Blackthorn, Crab Apple, Dog-rose, Downy and Silver Birch, Hazel, Goat Willow, Black-poplar, elms and Wild Service-tree. Also reported from Larch.

Habitat Most numerous in broadleaved woodland. Frequent in most situations with trees, including parks and gardens, but less so in urban areas.

Status & distribution Resident. Common. Quite well distributed, and usually fairly frequent throughout England, Wales, Ireland and locally throughout mainland Scotland and the Inner Hebrides. Local and infrequent on Man. Widespread but occasional in the Channel Islands.

Orange Moth

page 150

Angerona prunaria (L.)

Local. S   1924(7665)

Field characters FW 20-30mm. Unmistakable, but with two main forms. In one, male is truly orange, with variable brown flecking, sometimes forming curved streaks and normally, a brown central dash or crescent on both fore- and hindwing; antennae feathered. Female similar, but pale yellow and with un-feathered antennae. In f. *corylaria* Thunb. ground-colour is largely restricted to central bands, or panels of variable size, being otherwise uniformly dark brown. This form occurs in all populations, but is usually the less frequent form. Fringes chequered, except in extreme panelled forms.

Similar species None.

Flight season One generation. Late June-July. Male often seen flying along woodland rides, particularly just before dusk. Female sometimes found or disturbed among vegetation. Both sexes come to light but males greatly predominate. Female flies late in the night.

Life cycle Overwinters as a small larva on the food-plant. Larva August-late May. Pupates between spun leaves.

Larval foodplants Many woody broadleaved plants, including Blackthorn, Hawthorn, birches, Heather, Broom, Traveller's-joy and apparently herbaceous garden plants such as Mint.

Habitat Broadleaved woodland, generally long-

Larva of Pale Brindled Beauty.

established and particularly on clay. Also wooded heathland, scrub and large ancient hedgerows.

Status & distribution Resident. Local. Quite well distributed and sometimes frequent in woodlands in southern and south-east England, from Hampshire to Suffolk. Also locally in south-west England from Cornwall to Gloucestershire, and in the eastern half of Monmouthshire, particularly the Wye Valley woodlands. Present very locally in central England north to the Wyre Forest in Shropshire and the ancient Bardney limewoods in Lincolnshire. One record from Man, 15 July 1937, presumed vagrant. Very locally in southern Ireland. Rare in the Channel Islands.

Small Brindled Beauty   page 150

Apocheima hispidaria ([D. & S.])

Local. S,(C)   1925(7671)

Field characters FW 15-17mm. Male is much smaller than related species found in woodland, with rather narrow, tapering forewing, rounded at tip, and a massively hairy thorax. Generally two dark brown wavy cross-lines are conspicuous, the outer one somewhat jagged, but in some forms these are lost, with dark brown scales covering most of wing. Most forms have a notably paler region at outer edge of forewing but some are entirely dark. Hindwing paler than forewing. Wingless female is generally dark or blackish brown, and rather more squat and stocky at front end than other wingless females in woodland and lowland habitats.

Similar species Female Pale Brindled Beauty is noticeably thinner at head and thorax, less furry and generally paler. Brindled Beauty flies later in the spring, is larger, with much broader wings and has a winged female.

Flight season One generation. Mid February-March. Female regularly found by searching near base of tree trunks, after dawn. Male comes to light, sometimes in large numbers in woodland.

Life cycle Overwinters as a pupa underground. Larva late April-mid June.

Larval foodplants Pedunculate Oak. Probably Sessile Oak. Also reported from Hawthorn, Silver Birch, Hazel, English Elm, Hornbeam and Sweet Chestnut.

Habitat Mature oak woodland and hedgerows

containing large oaks in well wooded areas. Seldom wanders from oaks.

Status & distribution Resident. Local. Fairly well distributed and often locally abundant in south-east England, from Dorset to Essex and Kent. Much more local elsewhere but with records scattered through England, Wales and south-east Scotland.

Pale Brindled Beauty   page 150

Phigalia pilosaria ([D. & S.])

Common. T   1926(7672)

Field characters & Similar species FW 19-24mm. Superficially somewhat similar to Brindled Beauty, but slighter in build, generally paler, without the heavy black cross-lines and dusting, and flies earlier in the year. The dark brindle markings in male vary in extent. Some have almost plain pale greyish or greenish-grey forewing, others grade through to the practically all-dark brown f. *monacharia* Stdgr. The dark form comprises some 60% of catches in central London, but is much less frequent towards the outskirts. It also predominates in parts of north-west Britain, and occurs at lower frequency elsewhere. Fresh examples have pinkish abdomen. The wingless female is brownish and not particularly hairy. See also female March Moth.

Flight season One generation. January-March. Occasionally found in late December. Female regularly found near base of tree trunks, just after dawn, sometimes later. Male comes readily to light, often in large numbers in woodland.

Life cycle Overwinters as a pupa, in an underground cocoon. Larva mid April-mid June.

Larval foodplants Many broadleaved trees and shrubs, including oaks, Hawthorn, Midland Hawthorn, Blackthorn, Apple, Downy and Silver Birch, Alder, Hazel, Goat Willow, poplars, limes, elms, Ash, Purging Buckthorn and Alder Buckthorn. Also reported from Larch.

Habitat Broadleaved woodland and many other situations with trees or scrub, on many soil types, including urban gardens.

Status & distribution Resident. Common. Quite well distributed and frequent throughout most of England, Wales and lowland Scotland north to Caithness and including the Inner Hebrides. Rather local and infrequently recorded on Man. Proving to be fairly widespread and quite well distributed in Ireland. Only record for the Channel Islands on Jersey, in 1903.

Brindled Beauty   page 150

Lycia hirtaria (Cl.)

Common. S,C,(N)   1927(7674)

Field characters & Similar species FW 19-23mm. A fairly distinctive, furry moth. Distinguished from male Pale Brindled Beauty by the much thicker thorax and abdomen and broader wings. Wings are thickly scaled. Wing pattern variable but all forms have some heavy blackish cross-lines and/or banding, especially conspicuous at leading edge of forewing. Many examples have a golden-yellow component, but others are predominantly grey. Female is rather thinly scaled, with forewing leading edge more arched. A rare, almost uniformly blackish f. *nigra* Cock. is recorded from London and elsewhere in southern England. Scottish examples are larger and brightly marked.

Flight season One generation. Early March-late May. Sometimes found on tree trunks and fences by day. Male comes readily to light late at night and is sometimes trapped in large numbers if lights are operated all night. Female seldom seen at light.

Life cycle Overwinters as a pupa underground. Larva early May-early July.

Larval foodplants Many broadleaved trees and shrubs, including Downy and Silver Birch, Hawthorn, Midland Hawthorn, limes, elms, Alder, sallows, Pedunculate and Evergreen Oak.

Habitat Broadleaved woodland, scrub, hedgerows, parks and gardens, including those in urban centres.

Status & distribution Resident. Common. Well distributed and often frequent to abundant in southern and eastern England north to the Humber. More local in the West Midlands, south-west England and south Wales. Previously very rare in Yorkshire, where it has greatly increased its range and numbers since 1974. Found locally in central and northern Scotland, mainly in the major river valleys. Local and mainly western in Ireland, including the extreme west of Northern Ireland. In the Channel Islands recorded only from Guernsey, where rare.

Belted Beauty
page 150

Lycia zonaria ([D. & S.])

ssp. *britannica* (Harr.)
RDB. WC
1928(7680)

ssp. *atlantica* (Harr.)
Na. NW

Field characters FW 13-16mm. Male is easily recognised by the silvery-grey and brown stripes on forewing. Amount of brown varies greatly, even within same population. Female wingless. In both sexes abdomen has orange rings. Ssp. *atlantica*, of questionable validity, was described from the Isle of Baleshare on the basis that male is slightly smaller than mainland specimens. This is not a general feature of Belted Beauty on the other Hebridean islands, and some are larger than mainland individuals.

Similar species Female Belted Beauty somewhat similar to female Rannoch Brindled Beauty but both sexes are distinguished by orange markings on abdomen, which form a mid-line of spots along the back of Rannoch Brindled Beauty.

Flight season One generation. March-April. Male sometimes flies on sunny afternoons. Can be found at rest low down on vertical plant stems after dark, also flying late at night and coming to light. Female often encountered in sunshine on posts and dry

Larva of Brindled Beauty.

plant stems, as if basking. After dark they can be found climbing plant stems to lay eggs.

Life cycle Overwinters as a pupa, just below ground. Larva May-July.

Larval foodplants Mainly Common Bird's-foot-trefoil and Kidney Vetch, but clovers, Yarrow, Creeping Willow, Burnet Rose and plantains have been reported, and also, surprisingly, Yellow Iris.

Habitat Machair habitat (shell-sand vegetated with herbs) on the Hebrides. Elsewhere in sand-dunes only semi-stabilised by vegetation, and on golf courses and coastal paths. Occurs below the strand-line at Morecambe Bay, on sandy saltings that are annually inundated by saltwater.

Status & distribution Resident. As a species, Nationally Scarce A, but ssp. *britannica* merits Red Data Book species. Larvae often abundant where they occur. Restricted to the west coast of Scotland and the coasts of north Wales and north-west England, and Ireland. Occurs in the Hebrides, Sanna Point on the Ardnamurchan peninsula of western Argyll, Mull, Iona, Colonsay and Islay, with additional colonies at Morfa Conwy, Caernarvonshire, Sunderland Point/Morecambe Bay and Ainsdale, Lancashire, and Meols, the Wirral, Cheshire. No post-1980 records from the coastal sand-dunes of Flintshire (where it was formerly known at Talacre Warren), or from Deganwy Dunes, Caernarvonshire, or most of the sites of earlier records on the Wirral, where it now appears to be confined to one damaged site. In Ireland recorded from Cos. Galway and Mayo in the west of the Republic and from Co. Antrim in Northern Ireland. There are no post-1960 records for the latter, despite searches.

Larva of Belted Beauty.

Larva of Rannoch Brindled Beauty.

172

Rannoch Brindled Beauty   page 150
Lycia lapponaria (Boisd.)
ssp. *scotica* (Harr.)
Na. N   1929(7678)

Field characters FW 14-16mm. Both male and the black, furry wingless female have a row of orange spots, starting at thorax and forming a broken dorsal stripe along abdomen, which makes them easier both to find and identify. Male has several narrow, dark cross-bands on wings which are grey and semi-transparent, rather than silvery white. These markings vary greatly in extent but a central crescent and a dark curved outer cross-line are usually conspic-uous. A brown form of the male has been taken regularly at Dalwhinnie quarry, Morayshire.
Similar species See Belted Beauty, but note differ-ence in range and habitat.
Flight season One generation. Late March-early May, depending on altitude and season. Both sexes can be found by day resting on plant stems, rocks and fence posts. Male presumably flies at night and would come to light, but traps are seldom operated in the breeding areas at this time. Female has been seen laying eggs at night.
Life cycle Overwinters as a pupa underground, sometimes remaining dormant for up to four years in captivity. Larva mid May-early August.
Larval foodplants Most frequently Bog-myrtle, but reported in abundance on Bilberry and also on Eared Willow, Heather, Bell Heather and Cross-leaved Heath.
Habitat From boggy acid moorland, especially by streams, to mixed, dry, rather basic heathland which does not include Bog-myrtle but in which Bilberry and various heathers are common. Tolerates a wide range of climatic conditions.
Status & distribution Resident. Nationally Scarce A. Restricted to the central Highlands of Scotland, where it has been regularly recorded in the Rannoch and upper Speyside areas since its discovery there in 1871. However, recent work has found it to be much more widespread, extending east from the Spey into the Dee river system, with much suitable moorland habitat between yet to be searched. There are outlying colonies such as at Flanders Moss to the

south and sites in Wester Ross to the north. To the west it occurs on the moors around Fort William and extends to the Ardnamurchan peninsula.

Oak Beauty   page 151
Biston strataria (Hufn.)
Common. S,C,(N)   1930(7685)

Field characters FW 17-27mm. Both sexes similar but female often whiter. Male has feathered antennae. The two broad brown bands across forewing are diagnostic. These vary in width and are edged with black. Ground-colour varies from white to greenish grey. The banding is present, but less conspicuous, in the darker forms.
Similar species Peppered Moth never has light brown banding, no matter how dark the form.
Flight season One generation. Late February-April. Freshly-emerged adults sometimes found by day at base of tree trunks. Male comes readily to light, sometimes in numbers, female only very occasionally.
Life cycle Overwinters as a pupa underground. Larva May-July.
Larval foodplants Oaks, Hazel, Aspen, Alder, elms, sallows and other broadleaved trees and shrubs.
Habitat Most numerous in mature oak woodland, but also occurs in other types of woodland and scrub. Fairly frequent in some suburban areas with mature trees but only occasional in urban centres.
Status & distribution Resident. Common. Well distributed and often frequent in south-east England and quite well distributed elsewhere in England and Wales, northwards to the Humber. Occurs locally further north to central Scotland. First recorded from Man in 2000. Widespread but very local in Ireland, including Northern Ireland. Widespread but occa-sional in the Channel Islands.

Peppered Moth   page 151
Biston betularia (L.)
Common. T   1931(7686)

Field characters FW 22-28mm. The usual form in most rural areas is white, peppered with black on wings and body. The classic pattern of variation includes f. *carbonaria* Jord., sooty black except for white spots at base of forewing, and a genetic inter-mediate f. *insularia* Thierry-Mieg. The frequency of the black form was 60-80% in the London area in the 1980s and has been higher in this and other industrial areas in the past, correlating with levels of atmospheric pollution. However, its frequency has been steadily declining in many areas in the last few decades. A different intermediate form is very common and is not the result of mixed mating between black and white parents but an unrelated form which also tends to be more frequent in polluted areas. A rare aberration with black forewing and white hindwing has been recorded.
Similar species Dark forms of Oak Beauty, but this species has an earlier flight season.
Flight season One protracted generation. Early

May-late August. Unusual to find adults at rest. Comes to light, sometimes in numbers.

Life cycle Overwinters as a pupa just below ground. Larva early July-late September.

Larval foodplants A wide range of trees, shrubs and smaller plants, including Blackthorn, Hawthorn, Midland Hawthorn, Downy and Silver Birch, limes, sallows, poplars, oaks, Sweet Chestnut, Beech, rose, Bramble, Broom, Black Currant, Hop, Mugwort, Michaelmas-daisy and Goldenrod.

Habitat Woodland, scrub, hedgerows, parks and gardens, including urban centres.

Status & distribution Resident. Common. Very well distributed and fairly frequent throughout most of England, Wales and lowland Scotland, north to Caithness and including the Inner Hebrides. Well distributed and frequent on Man, Ireland and the Channel Islands.

Larva of Peppered Moth.

flight season. Recorded twice from Man, in 1940 and 1959, and apparently only twice from Ireland, in Cos. Wicklow and Fermanagh. Local and occasional on Jersey. Recorded as 'not uncommon' on Guernsey in the 19th century, but not seen recently.

Spring Usher   page 151

Agriopis leucophaearia ([D. & S.])

Common. T   1932(7693)

Field characters & Similar species FW 14-17mm. Male distinguished from those of closely-related species by its smaller size. Forewing is very triangular, but with rounded tip and a slightly kinked leading edge. Wing patterning is variable, but has a wavy outer cross-line and a curved inner one, both of which are sometimes dark and distinct against a pale whitish or brownish background, sometimes forming the edges of dark regions at base of wing and at outer edge. In some individuals the whole forewing is uniformly dark brown. Male March Moth has a similar wing shape, but rests with forewings folded. Flightless female Spring Usher is dark grey or blackish, has only tiny wing stumps, generally smaller than those of Winter Moth, which is a similar size and colour and may also be found in January or early February. Other flightless female geometrids are larger or have larger wing stumps.

Flight season One generation. From early January but usually early February-mid March, depending on the pattern of mild nights. Male sometimes rests by day on tree trunks, but usually hides behind bark and in crevices. Female regularly found near base of tree trunks in early morning. Male flies soon after dark and comes to light, sometimes in large numbers.

Life cycle Overwinters as a pupa underground. Larva early April-mid June.

Larval foodplants Pedunculate and Sessile Oak. Reported at least once from Apple.

Habitat Most abundant in mature and usually long-established oak woodland. Also mature oaks in hedgerows in well-wooded areas, parks, arboreta, orchards, cemeteries and gardens.

Status & distribution Resident. Common. Widespread, quite well distributed and locally abundant throughout England and Wales, with a scatter of records throughout mainland Scotland north to Ross-shire. Likely to be under-recorded due to early

Scarce Umber   page 151

Agriopis aurantiaria (Hb.)

Common. T   1933(7695)

Field characters FW 17-21mm. Male has warm, golden orange-yellow forewing with two usually distinct darker cross-lines, often with a spot between them and surrounded by variable greyish-brown edging, blotches and freckling, but much less variable than Dotted Border (which flies in early spring) and Mottled Umber. Flightless female is dark brown. Wing stumps are obvious, also dark brown, usually with two black bands on each wing.

Similar species Worn or unusually dark male could be mistaken for Mottled Umber, which never has golden ground-colour. Female Mottled Umber is usually paler, and wing stumps are hardly visible to the naked eye. See also Dotted Border, which generally flies in spring.

Flight season One generation. October-December. Female found by trunk-hunting in the morning. Male comes to light, sometimes in large numbers.

Life cycle Overwinters as an egg on the foodplant. Larva April-mid June.

Larval foodplants Broadleaved trees and shrubs, including Downy and Silver Birch, Hazel, Blackthorn, Hawthorn, Midland Hawthorn, Pedunculate Oak, Dog-rose, English Elm, limes, sallows and Hornbeam.

Habitat Most abundant in open broadleaved woodland with mature trees. Also long-established scrub and gardens in well wooded districts.

Status & distribution Resident. Common. Very well distributed and locally abundant in south-east England from Dorset to Essex, and quite well distributed throughout the rest of England, Wales and lowland Scotland north to Caithness, including the Inner Hebrides. Resident on Orkney, where it may have been imported with foodplants during the 1960s or earlier. Local on Man. Proving to be widespread but local in Northern Ireland and has been recorded south to Co. Kerry. Rare in the Channel Islands.

Dotted Border
Agriopis marginaria (Fabr.)
Common. T   1934(7696)

Field characters & Similar species FW 16-20mm.
Male has brownish forewing and is quite variable,
but distinguished by a conspicuous row of black dots
along edges of both fore- and hindwing, not present
in Mottled Umber (in which the fringes may be
spotted) and usually much less conspicuous in the
golden Scarce Umber. These dots are less obvious in
worn individuals and may be absent in dark forms
such as uniformly-dark brown f. *fuscata* Mosley,
which is not rare and occurs in most populations. On
Orkney, Dotted Border is small and rather dark
greyish brown, while mainland forms are generally
orange-brown. Outer cross-line elbowed, inner one
almost straight. Forewing clouded to a greater or
lesser extent by darker brown. Flightless female has
substantial wing stumps, usually with dark cross-lines
or bands, and varies from fawnish white to very dark
brown. Flightless female of the micro-moth *Diurnea
fagella* ([D. & S.]) is similar in size, also occurs in
spring and also has relatively large wings, but these
are very pointed, and greyish. See also Scarce Umber.
Flight season One generation. February-April.
Occasional individuals from late December onwards.
Male comes to light, sometimes in large numbers,
particularly to actinic traps operated all night in
woodland. Female regularly found by trunk-hunting
in the morning.
Life cycle Overwinters as a pupa underground. Larva
April-mid June.
Larval foodplants Many broadleaved trees and
shrubs, including Pedunculate and Sessile Oak,
Hawthorn, Midland Hawthorn, Blackthorn, Downy
and Silver Birch, Hazel, Goat and Grey Willow, elms,
Field Maple, Sycamore, Apple and Plum. Locally
abundant on Heather in Orkney.
Habitat Most abundant in woodland. Also in scrub,
hedgerows, gardens, scrubby calcareous grassland,
heathland and moorland.
Status & distribution Resident. Common. Well
distributed and often abundant throughout most of
England, Wales and lowland Scotland north to
Orkney. Local and infrequently recorded on Man.
Proving to be quite well distributed in Northern
Ireland and widespread in the Republic. Local and
occasional in the Channel Islands.

Larva of Mottled Umber.

Mottled Umber
Erannis defoliaria (Cl.)
Common. T   1935(7699)

Field characters FW 18-25mm. Forewing patterning
of male is very variable, but has several easily recognisable elements. Both inner and outer cross-bands,
when present, are brown or blackish, and rather
irregular. These forms usually have a dark central
spot. Ground-colour varies from off-white to orange-
brown. Hindwing generally off-white, with a dark
brown central spot. In the dark brown f. *nigra* Band,
all markings are obscured and speckled, but otherwise unmarked brown forms are frequent. All forms
often numerous on same site. Flightless female is
usually yellowish white with black dots, but there is
also a black form, which has minute wings barely visible
to the naked eye.
Similar species See Scarce Umber and Dotted
Border.
Flight season One generation. October-January.
Male sometimes seen on the wing in numbers just as
darkness is falling, flying about 2m above ground
among standing trees. Comes to light, sometimes in
large numbers, from early in the evening until well
after midnight. Female found by trunk-hunting after
dark.
Life cycle Overwinters as an egg on the foodplant.
Larva early April-late June.
Larval foodplants Many broadleaved trees and
shrubs, including Pedunculate and Sessile Oak,
Downy and Silver Birch, Hazel, Hawthorn, Midland
Hawthorn, Blackthorn, Apple, Dog-rose, Goat
Willow, Field Maple, Sycamore, Hornbeam, Sweet
Chestnut and elms. Also reported from Sitka Spruce.
Habitat Most abundant in woodland. Also in scrub,
hedgerows, scrubby calcareous grassland, heathland,
moorland and scrubby upland pasture. Occurs in
some gardens.
Status & distribution Resident. Common. Well
distributed and usually abundant throughout
England, Wales and lowland Scotland north to
Caithness, and including the Inner Hebrides and
Orkney. Local and infrequently recorded on Man.
Proving to be quite well distributed in Ireland.
Widespread but occasional in the Channel Islands.

Waved Umber
Menophra abruptaria (Thunb.)
Common. S,(C)   1936(7724)

Field characters FW 18-21mm. Rests with wings
flat, so that dark brown, rather straight-edged markings on fore- and hindwing line up like parallel
fissures on a wood surface. Diagonal, straight-edged
banding across hindwing is unique among British
moths. Hindwing edges are quite deeply scalloped.
Ground-colour of normal form varies from whitish
brown, especially in female, to deep tawny brown.
F. *fuscata* Tutt is almost entirely dark brown, with
markings faintly represented. It is quite frequent in
London and occurs throughout southern England.

Similar species None.

Flight season One generation. Mid April-June. Very occasionally a partial second generation in July and August in particularly hot summers. Sometimes found by day, at rest on trunks and fences. Comes to light in small numbers.

Life cycle Overwinters as a pupa, in a cocoon on the foodplant. Larva early June-mid September.

Larval foodplants Garden Privet, Lilac and Winter Jasmine in gardens. Occurs in many rural sites where even Wild Privet is not found, but no reports of other foodplants. Ash is likely to be used and is accepted in captivity, as is birch.

Habitat Broadleaved woodland, scrub, hedgerows, parks and gardens. Frequently in many urban and suburban areas.

Status & distribution Resident. Common. Particularly well distributed and fairly frequent in south-east England, including the London area. Also well distributed in East Anglia, the east Midlands and northwards to Yorkshire. More thinly distributed in the western half of England and Wales, becoming very local in Cornwall. Occurs north to Cumbria. One record from Man, in 1893. In Ireland unconfirmed records from Cos. Wicklow and Fermanagh. Widespread and frequent on Jersey. Rare on Guernsey and Alderney.

Willow Beauty   page 152
Peribatodes rhomboidaria ([D. & S.])
Common. S,C,(N)   1937(7754)

Field characters FW 17-24mm. A key feature is the cross-line on forewing beyond middle, which is fine, strongly-kinked near leading edge, more or less straight in trailing half, and forms a dot on each vein. On underside of hindwing, outer cross-line (when present) is angled centrally. Male antennae feathered, with feathering tapered and ending 2mm from tip. A preliminary identification feature is the way the two central cross-lines on forewing begin broadly apart at leading edge but converge at trailing edge, the outer line sweeping inwards, whereas on similar species they usually do not converge, or usually do so less strongly. Ground-colour varies from light brown, through grey (f. *perfumaria* Newm.) to blackish grey, and dark markings vary in intensity and extent. The almost uniformly black or dark brown f. *rebeli* Aigner is widespread and sometimes numerous in industrial areas. Second-generation individuals often smaller.

Similar species See Feathered Beauty, Mottled Beauty, Great Oak Beauty and Satin Beauty.

Flight season Mainly one generation. Mid June-August. From early June in southern Britain, where a second generation in late August-early October has become regular and substantial. Both sexes sometimes found at rest by day on tree trunks, more so in light woodland in the Highlands of Scotland than elsewhere. Comes readily to light in numbers, especially if light-trap placed by the shady cover of stands of conifers or dense broadleaved woodland. Visits flowers after dark, such as Creeping Thistle and Ragwort.

Life cycle Overwinters as a small larva on the foodplant. Larva July-June. In southern Britain some individuals develop more rapidly and produce adults from late August onwards. Cocoon is attached to the foodplant or plant debris.

Larval foodplants A wide range of broadleaved trees, shrubs and climbers, including Hawthorn, Plum, Garden Privet, birches, Alder Buckthorn, Honeysuckle, Traveller's-joy and Ivy. Also conifers including Yew, Scots Pine, Norway Spruce and Monterey Cypress.

Habitat Woodland, scrub, hedgerows, parks, gardens and other places where the foodplants grow, including central London and other urban centres.

Status & distribution Resident. Common. Well distributed and often abundant in most of England, Wales and much of lowland Scotland north to Caithness. Not reliably recorded from Orkney and Shetland. Local and infrequent on Man. Quite well distributed in the eastern half of Northern Ireland and widely distributed elsewhere in Ireland. Widespread and abundant in the Channel Islands.

Feathered Beauty   page 152
Peribatodes secundaria (Esp.)
Uncommon on alien foodplant. SE   1937a(7762)

Field characters & Similar species FW 17-20mm. Similar to Willow Beauty and Lydd Beauty, but cross-line beyond middle of forewing is strongly curved in trailing half, and usually less kinked near leading edge. In male, antennae more broadly feathered, with feathering ending abruptly 1mm from tip. Outer line on underside of hindwing not angled centrally. Slightly smaller than Willow Beauty on average, and in most cases more heavily speckled with dark scales, including underside. The almost uniformly blackish f. *nigrata* Sterneck occurs occasionally.

Flight season One generation. July-early August. Occasionally disturbed by day among conifers. Comes to light.

Life cycle Overwinters as a small larva on the foodplant. Larva late August-early June. Pupates in a cocoon on the foodplant.

Larval foodplants Norway Spruce.

Habitat Plantations of exotic conifers, largely growing on ancient woodland sites.

Status & distribution Resident and suspected immigrant. First recorded in the British Isles in July 1981, when good numbers were seen in Orlestone Forest, Hamstreet, Kent, where it is still locally frequent. First recorded outside Kent in July 1982, near Plaistow, in the Chiddingfold woodland complex, West Sussex, and in Tugley Wood, Surrey, in the same woodland complex, in July 1985. Also found in Bransland Wood in Surrey and a wood in East Sussex. A few singletons have been recorded elsewhere in south-east England, including Bradwell-on-Sea, Essex, in 1987, Greatstone, Kent, in 1994, and Kirby-le-Soken, Essex, in 1997. These coastal locations suggest immigration, which probably led to the recent colonisation. Recorded throughout most of Europe, including Scandinavia.

175

Lydd Beauty page 152

Peribatodes ilicaria (Geyer)

Rare immigrant. SE 1937b(7765)

Field characters & Similar species FW 16-20mm. Similar to Feathered Beauty and Willow Beauty, but more heavily and coarsely speckled, especially female. A key feature is the strongly-curved outer cross-line on hindwing, partly visible when moth is at rest. In Willow and Feathered Beauty, this line is only slightly curved. Male antennae feathered, but less strongly than in related species.

Flight season One generation. July-September in France.

Life cycle Overwinters as a small larva. Larva September-late June or July. Probably pupates in plant debris or loose earth.

Larval foodplants A wide range of broadleaved trees and shrubs in mainland Europe, including Pedunculate Oak, Evergreen Oak, Blackthorn, birches, Wild Privet and pines.

Habitat Woodland, parks and gardens in mainland Europe.

Status & distribution Rare immigrant. First recorded in the British Isles on 27 August 1990, a male at light at Lydd, Kent. Recorded subsequently on 4 August 1994 at New Romney, Kent, a fertile female from which larvae were reared. Two were trapped at Ninham, Isle of Wight, on 14 and 18 August 1996. On 21 July 2002 another was reported, at Dymchurch, Kent. Rather sparsely recorded from mainland Europe, but reported from Spain to Greece, and north to Denmark.

Bordered Grey page 152

Selidosema brunnearia (Vill.)

ssp. *scandinaviaria* Stdgr.

Na. S,WC,NW,NE 1938(7767)

ssp. *tyronensis* Cock.

Ireland

Field characters FW 16-22mm. A brownish-grey moth, purplish tinged when freshly emerged, with thick, darker brown borders on all four wings. Three very dark brown markings on leading edge of forewing, with a narrow, rather blurred dark brown central cross-line. Male has feathered antennae, female smaller and browner, with simple antennae. A dull brown form (f. *atlantica* West), sometimes with a purplish tinge but with no trace of grey and reduced markings, has been reported from the limestone of Co. Clare. Ssp. *tyronensis* was described from individuals found on a bog near Lough Neagh, Co. Tyrone, on the basis that they were smaller and central and marginal shading on forewing was narrower and lighter. The original site has been destroyed and no specimens conforming to this race have been reported recently.

Similar species None.

Flight season One generation. July-August. Easily disturbed by day from among heathers or patches of bare ground, even in overcast weather. Flies from dusk onwards and comes to light, usually in small numbers.

Life cycle Overwinters as a small larva on the foodplant. Larva September-June. Cocoon formed on or just below ground.

Larval foodplants Heather on heathland and moorland. Common Bird's-foot-trefoil and possibly other legumes in calcareous and sand-dune habitats.

Habitat, Status & distribution Resident and suspected immigrant. Nationally Scarce A. The major centres are the heathlands of the New Forest, Hampshire, south-east Dorset, north-east Hampshire (Aldershot area) and north-west Surrey. Recorded, but not for many years, on heathland/moorland in Berkshire, Devon, west Wight, Sussex and Cheshire. Occurs on the mosses of south Cumbria, such as Meythop Moss, at Whixall Moss (a large population), and Buckland, Shropshire, on the Hebridean islands of Canna and Rum, and on the Ardnamurchan peninsula of Argyll. There are colonies on chalk downland at Swanage and Lulworth, Dorset, and on the sand-dunes of Hayling Island, Hampshire. There are pre-1980 records from south Wiltshire and Caernarvonshire. It also occurs in an apparently isolated colony at St Cyrus NNR, Kincardineshire on the east coast of Scotland. Singletons, presumed immigrants, were recorded near Harrogate, Yorkshire, in 1992, at Gunwalloe, Cornwall, in the 1980s and at Blackheath, London, in 1986. Reported from Man in 1946 and 1959, possibly vagrant. Occurs very locally in the centre of Northern Ireland. Recorded from scattered localities in the Republic, usually on acid bogland, but there are strong colonies on the carboniferous limestone of Co. Clare. Locally frequent on Jersey, rare on Guernsey.

Ringed Carpet page 152

Cleora cinctaria cinctaria ([D. & S.])

Na. S 1939(7773)

ssp. *bowesi* Rich.

Na. NW,WC

Field characters & Similar species FW 16-20mm. Combination of triangular wings, with almost straight leading edge, small, whitish central crescent or dash on both fore- and hindwing (sometimes obscured) and (usually) strong dark basal cross-band, is diagnostic. Dark, elongated 'ring' in centre of forewing is distinctive. Pale Oak Beauty has a hollow central ring but is much larger and flies later in the year. Square Spot and Engrailed both have curved leading edge to forewing, and lack small, pale central crescent. Worn or more obscurely-marked Ringed Carpets might be confused with these, especially female, but see their accounts for distinctive features. Ssp. *cinctaria* is rather brownish, especially male. In Scotland, ssp. *bowesi* has a silvery-white ground-colour and better-defined, blacker wing markings.

Flight season One generation. Late April-May. Rests

by day on trunks of young birches and small pines, on the latter of which they are conspicuous, on fence posts and in heather. Comes to light in small numbers.

Life cycle Overwinters as a pupa, in plant debris or just below ground. Larva late May-early August.

Larval foodplants Birches, Bilberry, Bell Heather and Cross-leaved Heath on the southern lowland heaths, Bog-myrtle in Scotland.

Habitat Damp heathland with stands of scrubby birch, often with small self-set pines. Moorland with Bog-myrtle.

Status & distribution Resident. Nationally Scarce A. Occurs in three widely separated regions. Ssp. *cinctaria* occurs on heathlands in the New Forest, Hampshire, and in Dorset, which are its traditional strongholds, and on one heathland in Berkshire, with occasional records elsewhere. Formerly recorded from south Wiltshire, Sussex and Surrey, but not in recent decades. There is also a series of records, which need verification, from Holme Fen, Huntingdonshire, the last report being 1981. Ssp. *bowesi* has been recorded recently from the Rannoch area of Perthshire and at Ariundle Oakwood NNR in West Inverness-shire, to the west. There are older records from several sites between these two localities. A single male was recorded in Dumfries-shire in 1986 and there are post-1960 records from Kirkcudbrightshire and Wigtownshire. A number of adults and larvae were found from 1978 and during the late 1980s at a site near Porthmadog, Caernarvonshire, from which county there are earlier records. The adults from this site are more like ssp. *bowesi* than ssp. *cinctaria*. Reported from Man in 1862, but not since. Reported in Northern Ireland from a single locality on the east coast of Co. Down, but not for decades. Recorded from scattered sites throughout the Republic, from Cos. Donegal to Kerry.

Satin Beauty   page 153
Deileptenia ribeata (Cl.)
Common. T   1940(7775)

Field characters & Similar species FW 18-26mm. Distinguished from all similar species, notably Mottled Beauty, by the broad, rounded forewing and smooth or faintly-scalloped margins of both fore- and hindwing. Cross-lines, when evident, closest to those of Willow Beauty, but less jagged. The very broad, feathery antennae of the male help distinguish it from some similar species but in Willow Beauty they are as thickly feathered. The predominant form in most places is the rather dark, obscurely-marked f. *sericearia* Curt. (rather variable). The completely dark brown f. *nigra* Cock. is best known from Boxhill, Surrey.

Flight season One generation. Late June-mid August. Comes to light, more so if the trap is placed in the darker areas among trees. Sometimes found by beating the branches of conifers by day.

Life cycle Overwinters as a small larva on the food-

plant. Larva August-late May. Pupates in loose earth.

Larval foodplants Most frequently conifers, including native Scots Pine and Yew, also exotic forestry species, including Norway Spruce, European Larch and Douglas Fir. Reportedly able to feed also on birches, oaks and other broadleaved trees.

Habitat Woodlands, most frequent in conifer plantations. Found on ancient Yew trees, usually on woodland edges and other sheltered situations, sometimes on downland. Other sites are often remnants of ancient broadleaved woodland.

Status & distribution Resident. Common. Widespread, somewhat local, but often fairly frequent, in the southern half of England and in Wales, and more locally northwards through Yorkshire, Co. Durham, Cumbria, and southern Scotland to Perthshire, with populations found from 1999 onwards in Aberdeenshire and Kincardineshire. The large-scale planting of conifers in both lowlands and uplands has enabled this moth to expand its range and distribution. Local and infrequent on Man. Local and infrequent in Ireland, where it is known from the south-east and in 1999 was discovered for the first time in Northern Ireland, at Rostrevor Forest. Two records from the Channel Islands, on Guernsey in 1969 and 2002.

Mottled Beauty   page 153
Alcis repandata repandata (L.)
Common. T   1941(7777)

ssp. *sodorensium* (Weir)
Outer Hebrides

Field characters FW 19-26mm. One consistent and diagnostic feature, visible in all but the very darkest or palest individuals, is the dark cross-line beyond centre of forewing, which is solid, smooth and wavy, with a distinctive large crescent-like curve in leading half. Very variable in both ground-colour and markings. Ground-colour varies from whitish brown (mainly in north-west Britain, f. *muraria* Curt., also present in populations elsewhere) to pale brown, through various shades of grey or brown to almost uniformly black (mainly in industrial areas). Pale forms sometimes have a very dark central band across both fore- and hindwing (f. *conversaria* Hb.). Outer edges of hindwing wavy. Ssp. *sodorensium* is small and dark grey, described from Lewis in the Outer Hebrides.

Similar species Willow Beauty is often abundant in the same habitats, although the main flight period of Mottled Beauty is slightly earlier. The two cross-lines on forewing of Willow Beauty, jagged and converging at trailing edge, are usually the most obvious differences. Hindwing of Willow Beauty has a less deeply-scalloped outer edge, and in male antennae are more strongly feathered. See also Satin Beauty.

Flight season One generation. Early June-mid August. Sometimes found at rest by day on tree trunks from which it is easily disturbed. Visits flowers after dark, such as Wild Privet. Comes to light, especially if trap placed in the shady cover of conifers or in dense broadleaved woodland.

Life cycle Overwinters as a small larva on the foodplant, often pressed along a stem. Larva late August-May.

Larval foodplants Many woody plants, including Blackthorn, Hawthorn, Midland Hawthorn, oaks, Downy and Silver Birch, Ash, Barberry, Broom, Bilberry, Heather, Bramble, Honeysuckle, Traveller's-joy, Juniper, Norway Spruce, Lawson Cypress, Japanese Red-cedar and Western Hemlock-spruce. Also reported from St John's-wort, Yarrow, Angelica and docks.

Habitat Most abundant in woodland, moorland and carr. Also in scrub, hedgerows, heathland and scrubby calcareous grassland, parks and gardens, including urban centres.

Status & distribution Resident. Common. Well distributed and often abundant throughout most of England, Wales, lowland Scotland, the Hebrides, Orkney, Man and Ireland. Questionably recorded from Shetland. Widespread and frequent on Jersey, rare on Guernsey.

Dotted Carpet   page 153
Alcis jubata (Thunb.)
Local. W,N   1942(7779)

Field characters FW 13-16mm. The small size and generally white colour, quite large, conspicuous central black dots on fore- and hindwing and fine outer cross-line, angled near leading and trailing edges, distinguish this species. The black markings are boldest at leading edge of forewing, but vary in intensity. Brownish individuals are occasionally recorded, usually with markings recognisable (f. *obscura* Fuchs).

Similar species See Grey Birch.

Flight season One generation. Late June-mid September, peaking in late July. Can be disturbed from foodplant on tree branches. Comes readily to light, sometimes in large numbers.

Life cycle Overwinters as a larva among the foodplant. Larva late August-June. Pupates among the foodplant.

Larval foodplants Beard Lichen, eating the newest growth. Probably also other lichens.

Habitat Mature woodland and scrub, both broadleaved and coniferous, with abundant lichen growth. Has colonised older conifer plantations with ample lichens. In southern Britain mainly in large ancient woodlands, presumably requiring humidity and clean air for lichen growth.

Status & distribution Resident. Local. Predominantly western and northern in distribution. Well distributed and locally abundant in Cornwall, Devon and western Somerset, western Wales and the west coast of Scotland, but has recently also spread eastwards into Aberdeenshire, with a scatter of records also in the Highlands and Southern Uplands. Extends south into Northumberland, where

it occurs in large numbers at Kielder Forest and is occasionally recorded elsewhere. Formerly resident in the New Forest and Woolmer Forest, Hampshire, but now believed extinct in the county. Also recorded from Dorset and the Forest of Dean, Gloucestershire, but not recently. Not reliably recorded on Man. Apparently only one record from Ireland, from Co. Kerry in 1941.

Great Oak Beauty   page 154
Hypomecis roboraria ([D. & S.])
Nb. S,C   1943(7783)

Field characters & Similar species FW 21-32mm. Usually distinguished by size. Also, central dark cross-lines on forewing are thickened where they converge near trailing edge, often forming a blotch, apparent even on dark individuals. Pale Oak Beauty lacks this, and small dark spot in centre of hindwing is pale-centred. It is generally less strongly marked, and male has less thickly-feathered antennae. Willow Beauty is smaller, and more brownish. The dark grey f. *infuscata* Stdgr. is frequent in some areas.

Flight season One generation. Mid June-mid July. Roosts by day on trunks and branches of foodplant. Comes to light, sometimes in numbers, and occasionally to sugar.

Life cycle Overwinters as a larva on twigs in the canopy of the foodplant. Larva early August-end May. Pupates just below ground.

Larval foodplants Pedunculate Oak.

Habitat Large, long-established oak woodlands with mature trees.

Status & distribution Resident. Nationally Scarce B. A southern species. Fairly well distributed in Hampshire, Sussex, Surrey and Berkshire, which are the main strongholds. Scattered colonies elsewhere in central and southern England, such as Yardley Chase, Buckinghamshire, and the Wyre Forest, Shropshire, with an out-lying population in the Sherwood Forest area of Nottinghamshire. A few scattered records from south-west England. Well established in the Wye Valley. Recorded from two 10km squares in Glamorgan since 1980, suggesting it may be present more widely in south Wales. Not found recently in woods formerly occupied on the Oxfordshire/Buckinghamshire border, despite much light-trapping.

Pale Oak Beauty   page 154
Hypomecis punctinalis (Scop.)
Common. S   1944(7784)

Field characters FW 22-26mm. Rather elongate, somewhat narrower forewing than superficially similar species of about the same size, and much more weakly marked, so the usual impression is of a pale grey-brown moth with a large wingspan. Forewing base slightly darker, except in melanic form. Forewing tip rather rounded. Usually, a small dark pale-centred spot or ring in centre of each hindwing. Female usually whiter. The dark f. *humperti*

Humpert is quite frequent.
Similar species See Great Oak Beauty and Willow Beauty.
Flight season One generation. Late May-mid July. Rarely, individuals as early as late April. Probably a partial second generation in southern England, September-October. Sometimes found by day at rest on tree trunks. Comes readily to light, often in large numbers.
Life cycle Overwinters as a pupa underground. Larva early July-late August.
Larval foodplants Pedunculate Oak, Downy and Silver Birch, Hazel, Hawthorn, Midland Hawthorn, Crab Apple and sallows. Also reported from Sycamore and Larch.
Habitat Mainly broadleaved woodland and long-established scrub. Occurs in smaller numbers in parks and gardens in well-wooded areas.
Status & distribution Resident. Common. Well distributed and locally abundant in south-east England, from Dorset to East Anglia and Kent. Very local, with few records, in south-west England, Wales and central England, but found north to Castle Eden Dene and the Derwent Valley, Co. Durham. Also reported from Kirkcudbrightshire and Fife. Apparently reported from only one locality in Ireland, two in 1914 at Glengariff, Co. Cork. Locally frequent on Jersey, unrecorded elsewhere in the Channel Islands.

Brussels Lace   page 154
Cleorodes lichenaria (Hufn.)
Local. W,WC,(S,N)   1945(7790)

Field characters FW 14-18mm. Fairly small, with a freckled, variable amount of green and black speckling such that ground-colour ranges from off-white to black. Wings often tinted olive-green. Distinguished by the fine, jagged and irregular outer cross-line on fore- and hindwing.
Similar species See Grey Birch and Brindled White-spot.
Flight season One generation. June-mid August. Occasionally a partial second generation, September-October. Comes to light, sometimes in fair numbers in the west. Otherwise seldom seen.
Life cycle Overwinters as a larva. Larva late August-end May. Pupates in a cocoon among lichens.
Larval foodplants Lichens growing on branches and stems of woody plants and sometimes on rocks and walls.
Habitat Dense scrub such as mature Blackthorn and hawthorn thickets, sometimes in otherwise open ground, as well as in the tree canopy in woodland, plantations and shelterbelts. Also on rocky coastlines.
Status & distribution Resident. Local. Well distributed and locally frequent in south-west England, west Wales and the west coast of Scotland. Records are thinly scattered elsewhere throughout Scotland. Also recorded from central and southern England, where colonies may survive very locally. Formerly well established in Surrey, Sussex and Kent but declined

almost to extinction by the 1950s, although occasional individuals continue to be reported. Local and infrequent on Man but recorded almost annually since 1990. Proving to be quite well distributed locally in Northern Ireland, and widely recorded in the Republic. Widespread and frequent on Jersey, rare on Guernsey.

Speckled Beauty   page 154
Fagivorina arenaria (Hufn.)
Former resident; extinct.   1946(7792)

Field characters FW 15-17mm. A white moth with two distinct black lines across forewing, various other black markings, and coarse, irregular brown and black speckling. Diagnostically, the white hindwing is almost unmarked save for faint speckling and two or three black spots along inner edge by abdomen, and has no cross-lines.
Similar species None.
Flight season One generation. July-early August. Females were found resting on tree trunks. The moth was also collected by sweeping the upper branches of oak trees with a long pole.
Life cycle Overwinters as a pupa in a cocoon among lichens. Larva August-September.
Larval foodplants Lichens growing on Pedunculate Oak and Beech.
Habitat Mature oak woodland.
Status & distribution Extinct former resident. Last seen in Britain in July 1898, between Brockenhurst and Lyndhurst in the New Forest, Hampshire, where it was first discovered about 1822. Also found in Sussex at Tilgate Forest, Worth Forest, Henfield and near Brighton in the 19th century, but lost from the county by the 1880s.

Note on the Engrailed and Small Engrailed
In the latest European checklist (1996), the Engrailed is listed as synonymous with Small Engrailed, since it has recently been found that they cannot be distinguished on wing markings or genitalia. However, they have long been considered two species in the British Isles, and the current British checklist (which this book follows) reflects this. There do seem to be, mostly in the south, localised populations that appear slightly different to Engrailed, and fly slightly later in the spring, and have been shown to produce only one generation per year, even in captivity, whereas Engrailed can produce up to three, even in the wild. The situation seems unclear, and further research into the ecology and taxonomy of British and Irish populations of these moths is required to ascertain their true status.

Engrailed   page 154
Ectropis bistortata (Goeze)
Common. T   1947(7796)

Field characters & Similar species FW 15-22mm. Ground-colour is brownish white, brown or grey-brown, and darker markings are usually dark brown,

Larva of Engrailed.

but sometimes greyish. There is a dark brown marking on central cross-line, and two darts near outer edge of forewing which are conspicuous, but also shared with Small Engrailed. Female has more elongate wings. Sometimes a dark band outside the central cross-line, especially in Scotland. Almost uniformly dark brown individuals are fairly frequent. Second generation individuals much smaller than spring generation of Engrailed and Small Engrailed. Small Engrailed flies between the first two generations of Engrailed. See also Brindled White-spot, Ringed Carpet and Square Spot.

Flight season In southern Britain two generations, with occasional individuals of a partial third, March-mid May, mid June-August and September-October. In northern Britain one generation, April-early June. Sometimes found at rest by day on tree trunks. Comes readily to light, sometimes in large numbers.

Life cycle Overwinters as a pupa underground. Larva late April-June and, where a second generation occurs, in late July-early September.

Larval foodplants A wide range of woody plants, including oaks, Downy and Silver Birch, Hazel, Hawthorn, Midland Hawthorn, sallows, Broom, Purging Buckthorn, Spindle, Wild Privet and Hornbeam. Also reported from Yew, Larch and Sitka Spruce.

Habitat Most abundant in broadleaved woodland. Also in scrub, hedgerows, parks and gardens. Less frequent in urban areas.

Status & distribution Resident. Common. Quite well distributed and locally abundant throughout most of England, Wales and lowland Scotland north to Caithness and the Inner Hebrides. Local and not frequent on Man. Widespread but apparently rather local in Ireland, including Northern Ireland. Widespread and frequent on Jersey, rare on Guernsey.

Small Engrailed — page 154

Ectropis crepuscularia ([D. & S.])
Local. S,C,(N)   1948(7796)

Field characters & Similar species FW 16-19mm. Very similar to Engrailed, and difficult or even impossible to distinguish. Ground-colour is sometimes predominantly white, with black scales forming fine cross-lines and other markings, and sometimes coarsely freckling the whole of the wings to such an extent as to make them appear blackish. Outer and

trailing edge of forewing generally form closer to a right-angle than those of Engrailed, which has a more triangular and tapered forewing, particularly in the summer generation. See also Square Spot and Brindled White-spot.

Flight season One generation. Mostly early May-mid June, but some have been recorded late April-late June. Sometimes found at rest by day on tree trunks. Comes to light, often in numbers.

Life cycle Overwinters as a pupa underground. Larva mid June-early August.

Larval foodplants Downy and Silver Birch, sallows, Beech, and probably other broadleaved trees. Also reported from Larch.

Habitat Broadleaved woodland. Also in scrub, hedgerows and gardens in well-wooded districts. Less frequent in urban areas.

Status & distribution Resident. Local. More thinly distributed than Engrailed and less numerous, but occurs widely throughout England and Wales, with a thin scatter of records from southern Scotland. Status uncertain further north, with records from scattered localities to Wester Ross requiring confirmation. First reported from Man in 1972, and recorded at various sites from the 1990s. Proving to be quite well distributed in Northern Ireland and recorded widely in the Republic, but particularly in the Burren, Co. Clare, and the south-west. Recorded in the Channel Islands as 'not common' in the 19th century, but not seen recently.

Square Spot — page 155

Paradarisa consonaria (Hb.)
Local. S,W   1949(7798)

Field characters FW 18-20mm. The name refers to the roughly square-shaped dark brown forewing blotch placed centrally on outside of middle cross-line, which is without outer projections. This is discernible in most forms and is diagnostic. Often a greyish-white, or at least paler, broad central band, contrasting with the darker margins. This assists recognition even when the dark square is faint or obscured by broad dark borders, but not in the rarer almost all-black forms, which retain white wing bases.

Similar species Engrailed and Small Engrailed lack square-shaped dark spot, even if they have some dark markings in this part of the wing. See also Ringed Carpet.

Flight season One generation. Late April-mid June. Occasionally found by day on tree trunks or disturbed from scrub. Comes to light, sometimes in fair numbers.

Life cycle Overwinters as a pupa underground. Larva mid June-mid August.

Larval foodplants Oaks, birches, Beech, Hornbeam, pines, Yew and probably other woody plants. Recently found to be able to reach final instar feeding on algae and lichens, which may help it survive en route from egg in bark crevice to foliage of foodplant.

Habitat Broadleaved and mixed woodland, dense scrub, also some parkland situations and large gardens, particularly in the west.

Status & distribution Resident. Local. Fairly well distributed and sometimes locally frequent in south-east England, from south-east Dorset, Hampshire and the Isle of Wight to the outskirts of London and into Kent. Much more local in south-west and central England. Poorly represented in the east, but occurs locally in the east Midlands. Quite well distributed in Monmouthshire and Gloucestershire, centred on the Wye Valley woodlands, and more thinly spread elsewhere through Wales. Well established in south Cumbria, particularly Roudsea Wood, Witherslack Wood and Meythop Moss. In Ireland, apparently restricted to the extreme south-west.

Brindled White-spot   page 155
Parectropis similaria (Hufn.)

Local. S   1950(7800)

Field characters & Similar species FW 17-20mm. Smaller than similar species. Extensive dark brown markings on straw-yellow wing sometimes suggests a slightly greenish tint. The large, rather square pale patch near outer edge of forewing is diagnostic. Many individuals have a conspicuous dark brown patch or narrow central band across middle of forewing, most obvious at leading edge, which also distinguishes them from small forms of Engrailed and Small Engrailed. See also Brussels Lace, which is smaller, with less conspicuous pale spot nearer trailing corner of forewing.

Flight season One generation. Late May-June. Occasionally disturbed by day from tree trunks, understorey shrubs or conifer branches. Comes readily to light, sometimes in numbers.

Life cycle Overwinters as a pupa underground. Larva late June-early September.

Larval foodplants Pedunculate Oak, Hazel, Hawthorn, Midland Hawthorn, Downy and Silver Birch, and probably Sessile Oak. Also reported from unspecified lime.

Habitat Broadleaved woodland, favouring ancient woodland in rural areas. Occasionally recorded in gardens several kilometres from woodland.

Status & distribution Resident. Local. Quite well distributed and locally frequent in south and south-east England and in the vicinity of the Wye and Severn Valleys of Monmouthshire and Gloucestershire. More local in the West Midlands, central England, the Thetford Forest area of East Anglia, south Devon and the Great Torrington woodlands of north Devon. Widely scattered records from Wales and resident at Kinver Edge, Staffordshire. Recorded once from Man, in 1977.

Grey Birch   page 155
Aethalura punctulata ([D. & S.])

Common. S,C,N   1951(7802)

Field characters FW 13-16mm. A small grey moth with rounded wings and four conspicuous blackish blotches on leading edge of forewing, sometimes the

inner and outermost giving rise to weak, dark cross-lines, the second line sometimes connected to a small central dot. Ground-colour varies from light to dark grey, never white and very rarely black.

Similar species Dotted Carpet is similar in size but whiter, with a larger and more conspicuous black central dot in forewing. It flies later in the summer, from late June. Brussels Lace has a very jagged outer cross-line, and is usually greenish.

Flight season One generation. May-June. Sometimes disturbed by day from trunks in birch woodland. Comes well to light, sometimes in numbers.

Life cycle Overwinters as a pupa, just below ground. Larva June-late August.

Larval foodplants Downy and Silver Birch. Sometimes Alder. Has been obtained from Hazel under birches but uncertain if able to complete growth from egg on Hazel.

Habitat Birch woodland and birch scrub, mainly on long-established sites. Presumably also Alder groves.

Status & distribution Resident. Common. Well distributed and fairly frequent in south-east England, from Dorset to the rural outskirts of London and much of Kent. More local but often frequent in East Anglia, the Midlands, Lincolnshire, Yorkshire, Wales and south-west England. Very local in Cumbria. Recorded widely in Scotland but mainly in the western half. Not seen recently in Northern Ireland and only very locally in the Republic, mainly in the south-west.

Common Heath   page 155
Ematurga atomaria atomaria (L.)

Common. T   1952(7804)

Field characters FW 12-15mm. Very variable, although the forms in southern England are less likely to be confused with any other species. Ground-colour varies from white (especially female) to warm light brown, yellowish brown or dark grey. Both fore- and hindwing often have several dark brown bands which vary in width. Two bands may merge, particularly near trailing edge of forewing. Sometimes there are no bands, only dark freckles, or bands are very blurred. Male has very feathery antennae which readily distinguish it from Dingy and Grizzled Skipper butterflies, which often fly at the same time and in the same habitat. The small form found on northern moorlands has been named f. *minuta* Heydemann.

Similar species Latticed Heath usually has crisper markings on a more uniform background, and two outermost dark bands normally merge in centre to form a swastika or cross. It frequently settles with its wings up over its back, like a butterfly, while Common Heath holds them flat. In northern Britain, see also Netted Mountain Moth.

Flight season One generation. May-June, with a partial second generation, more pronounced in southern Britain, in August. Active by day, especially in warm weather, and frequently disturbed from

181

Larva of Common White Wave.

grass sward or heather.
Life cycle Overwinters as a pupa, in a flimsy cocoon on or just below ground. Larva mid June-mid September.
Larval foodplants Heather, Bell Heather and Cross-leaved Heath on heathland and moorland; trefoils, clovers and vetches elsewhere.
Habitat Most abundant on acid heathland and moorland. Also meadows and other grassland on chalk, limestone and neutral soils, including wood-land rides and roadside verges.
Status & distribution Resident. Common. Most densely distributed in south-east England but found locally and sometimes in abundance throughout most of mainland Britain, the Hebrides, Orkney, Man and Ireland. In the Channel Islands, locally frequent on Jersey.

Dusky Carpet

not illustrated

Tephronia sepiaria (Hufn.)
Suspected rare immigrant.   1953(7812)

Field characters & Similar species FW 9-12mm. A small, slender and fairly unmistakable geometrid. Forewing rather narrow and rounded, with two fine, wavy blackish cross-lines and no other distinct mark-ings. Hindwing paler, with a single curved cross-line. Antennae slightly feathered in male.
Status & distribution Suspected rare immigrant, not recorded in the last 200 years. There is a spec-imen in the Natural History Museum, said to have occurred at Tenby, south Wales, in the early 19th century. A species of central and southern Europe.

Bordered White

page 155

Bupalus piniaria (L.)
Common. T   1954(7822)

Field characters FW 17-19mm. Sexes differ in colour but both rest with wings above the body and pressed flat together, like a butterfly, showing a conspicuous whitish streak and dark cross-lines on underside of hindwing. Male has feathery antennae, with upper wing surfaces dark blackish brown in outer parts, with pale yellow patches near centres in southern Britain, while in northern Britain these light patches are frequently white. Female has thin antennae, generally medium brown on outer parts of

wings and tawny brown nearer the centre, and in northern Britain is slightly darker.
Similar species None.
Flight season One generation. May-June, but flying as late as July and early August in parts of northern Britain. On warm days male flies around conifers, particularly pines which have reached full height. Both sexes sometimes beaten from rest among conifer branches. Both sexes come to light, male sometimes in large numbers.
Life cycle Overwinters as a pupa, among conifer needles on the ground, or just below ground. Larva late June-October or later.
Larval foodplants Mainly mature Scots Pine, often as a pest, but recorded from many other conifers, including Corsican Pine (several pest outbreaks), Lodgepole Pine, Norway Spruce and Larch.
Habitat Native pine woodland and plantations, and shelterbelts of conifers (often planted on heathland). Prefers mature trees.
Status & distribution Resident. Common. Quite well distributed throughout most of mainland Britain and the Inner Hebrides, sometimes in abundance, from the Isle of Wight to Caithness. Not recorded from Orkney and probably only as a vagrant from Shetland. Local and infrequent on Man. Widespread and locally numerous in Ireland, including Northern Ireland. In the Channel Islands, local and occasional on Jersey.

Common White Wave

page 156

Cabera pusaria (L.)
Common. T   1955(7824)

Field characters FW 15-17mm. A white moth vari-ably peppered with grey scales, with three distinct and rather straight silver-grey lines across forewing, and two less distinct lines across hindwing. Occasionally one or more lines may be missing. In the very rare f. *heveraria* H.-S. ground-colour is grey, in less extreme forms it may be pinkish.
Similar species See Common Wave. Larger than other waves, and with a characteristic, rather rounded forewing shape (see also Grass Wave).
Flight season Two generations in southern Britain, May-June and late July-August, but the two genera-tions sometimes merge, making the distinction diffi-cult. In Scotland, recorded continuously from May-September, with a single peak in numbers in late June-July. Often found at rest or disturbed from foliage by day. Flies mainly at dusk, near foodplant, when often seen in numbers. Regular at light but relatively few are captured in light-traps compared with the numbers present in the habitat.
Life cycle Overwinters as a pupa, among plant debris or in the surface of the soil. Larva late June-October, often found in a wide range of sizes.
Larval foodplants Downy and Silver Birch, Alder and sallows.
Habitat Woodland and scrub on calcareous, neutral and acidic ground.
Status & distribution Resident. Common. Well

distributed and often abundant throughout most of mainland Britain, except at higher altitudes. Recorded from the Hebrides. Locally frequent on Man. Proving to be quite well distributed in Ireland. Widespread and frequent in the Channel Islands.

Common Wave
Cabera exanthemata (Scop.)
Common. T   1956(7826)

Field characters & Similar species FW 14-16mm. Similar to Common White Wave, but cross-lines are brown and curved, notably the outer two, and often indistinct. Brownish-grey freckling on wings varies in intensity, usually heavier in female.
Flight season Two generations in southern England. May-early July and early July-early September. In Scotland recorded continuously from May-mid October, with a single peak in numbers in mid June-early July, but some of the later individuals could represent a partial second generation. Frequently disturbed in or near the foodplants by day. Flies mainly at dusk. Visits flowers such as Wild Privet. Comes to light, sometimes in fair numbers, but seen more numerously at dusk.
Life cycle Overwinters as a pupa, among plant debris or in the surface of the soil. Larva late June-October, often in a range of sizes.
Larval foodplants Goat Willow, Grey Willow and other sallows, Aspen and other poplars.
Habitat Woodland and carr, often on very wet sites.
Status & distribution Resident. Common. Quite well distributed and often numerous in England, Wales and lowland Scotland, including the Inner Hebrides. Locally frequent on Man. Proving to be quite well distributed in Ireland. Widespread and frequent in the Channel Islands.

White-pinion Spotted
Lomographa bimaculata (Fabr.)
Common. S,WC   1957(7828)

Field characters & Similar species FW 13-14mm. White, slightly smaller than Clouded Silver, with two blackish spots on leading edge of forewing, each extended into a broken cross-line of dark dots. Hindwing largely white with a weak cross-line. Little variation.
Flight season One generation. May-early July. Some individuals from the end of April in southern England. Sometimes disturbed by day from food-plant. Flies from dusk and comes to light, sometimes in fair numbers.
Life cycle Overwinters as a pupa, just below ground or among plant debris. Larva late June-late August.
Larval foodplants Blackthorn, Hawthorn, Midland Hawthorn. Probably also on other members of the rose family.
Habitat Woodland, scrub, hedgerows and gardens in rural and suburban situations.
Status & distribution Resident. Common. Well distributed and fairly frequent in south-east England

and East Anglia, north to Lincolnshire. Widely and quite well distributed in the rest of southern and south-western England and south Wales. Less frequent though well established in the Midlands. Occasionally recorded in Yorkshire, Derbyshire and Nottinghamshire, particularly since the mid 1980s, and probably expanding its range. Long established locally in south Cumbria. One record from Man, in 1953. Apparently restricted to the extreme south-west of Ireland and Co. Wicklow. In the Channel Islands, recorded only from Jersey.

Clouded Silver
Lomographa temerata ([D. & S.])
Common. S,C,(N)   1958(7829)

Field characters FW 13-15mm. White, with blackish clouding at outer edges of forewing. Extent and intensity of clouding varies; female generally more weakly marked. Clouding is cut in two by at least one wavy white line. There is usually a dark central forewing spot and a mark on trailing edge.
Similar species In White-pinion Spotted the dark spots are confined to leading edge of forewing.
Flight season One generation. May-early July. Sometimes disturbed from rest by day. Often seen on the wing at dusk, particularly along hedgerows. Comes to light, sometimes in fair numbers.
Life cycle Overwinters as a pupa on the ground among plant debris. Larva late June-late August.
Larval foodplants Hawthorn, Midland Hawthorn, Blackthorn, Plum, Cherry, Crab Apple and cultivated relatives. Also reported from Aspen and Wych Elm.
Habitat Woodland, scrub, hedgerows, parks and gardens, including those in urban areas.
Status & distribution Resident and suspected immigrant. Common. Well distributed and frequent throughout most of England and Wales north to Yorkshire, where it has increased dramatically in numbers and range since the 1970s. Also established colonies in Co. Durham and Northumberland from the 1970s onwards. In the west it extends locally north to Argyll. Local and not frequent on Man. Proving to be quite well distributed in Ireland, including Northern Ireland. Widespread and frequent in the Channel Islands.

Sloe Carpet
Aleucis distinctata (H.-S.)
Nb. SE,S   1959(7831)

Field characters & Similar species FW 13-14mm. The jagged edges to darker central band across forewing, pointed forewing tip, faint or absent dark central dot on hindwing and conspicuous white spots on abdomen distinguish this moth from male Early Moth, which flies earlier in the year. Male Early Moth has slightly feathery antennae, and female Early Moth is effectively wingless.
Flight season One generation. March-April. Occurs when Blackthorn is in blossom. Can be found at rest on the outer leafless twigs after dark, is sometimes

Larva of Early Moth.

seen on the wing at dusk and comes to light.
Life cycle Overwinters as a pupa underground. Larva mid May-early July. Feeds mostly at night but remains among the foliage by day, when sometimes beaten in good numbers.
Larval foodplants Blackthorn.
Habitat In Essex and Suffolk, in scrubby hedgerows on farmland. In Surrey, on isolated bushes rather than large thickets, on clay. In Hampshire, associated mainly with small Blackthorn bushes, only 30-60cm high, on damp heaths. Being in a warmer, more sheltered micro-climate near the ground, further west, may be important to a species with such a marked eastern distribution.
Status & distribution Resident. Nationally Scarce B. Probably under-recorded due to early flight season. Found annually at some sites but may be present at others at such low density that it is only recorded every few years. Essex and Suffolk are the strongholds, in the eastern parts of which it is fairly frequent. Surrey, south Hampshire and Sussex continue to support a few colonies. Present but infrequently recorded in south Wiltshire, Berkshire, Buckinghamshire, Oxfordshire, Hertfordshire and Kent.

Early Moth
page 156
Theria primaria (Haw.)
Common. S,C,(N)
1960(7834)

Field characters FW 14-17mm. Flightless female has stumpy, brown, square-ended wings, crossed by a darker brown band. Male is sometimes pinkish brown, with rounded forewing tip and a curved, slightly wavy cross-line either side of a central spot. Hindwing pale brownish white, with a distinctive dark central spot.
Similar species See Sloe Carpet. Female Spring Usher and March Moth are completely wingless, female Scarce Umber has uniformly-coloured wing stumps, female Winter Moth has rounded wing stumps and female Dotted Border has much larger wing stumps. The flightless females of other winter geometrids are generally larger, furrier and almost or completely wingless.
Flight season One generation. January-February, sometimes March. Male flies from dusk, and after dark is easily seen at rest on bare twigs of foodplant,

sometimes mating with female.
Life cycle Overwinters as a pupa just below ground. Larva early April-late May.
Larval foodplants Blackthorn, Hawthorn, Midland Hawthorn.
Habitat Open woodland, woodland margins, long-established scrub and hedgerows.
Status & distribution Resident. Common. Widespread and quite well distributed throughout much of England, Wales and the southern half of Scotland. Probably under-recorded as an adult due to winter flight season. Larvae are often present in large numbers. Apparently local and rather infrequently recorded on Man and in Ireland, including Northern Ireland. Widespread and abundant in the Channel Islands.

Light Emerald
page 156
Campaea margaritata (L.)
Common. T
1961(7836)

Field characters FW 18-26mm. Unmistakably greenish white when fresh, but fades to whitish a few days after emergence. Hooked, reddish forewing tip and a largely straight, white, dark-edged cross-lines readily distinguish this from other green geometrid moths. Individuals of the second generation are smaller and darker.
Similar species Swallow-tailed Moth is yellow, fading to white, with extended tail on hindwing and generally larger. See also Small Emerald.
Flight season Mainly one generation. Late May-early August in southern Britain, continuing to early September in Scotland. Partial second generation, late July-September in southern Britain most years, and also recorded in Scotland, where individuals reported to late October. Often disturbed from rest on the undersides of leaves of trees and shrubs. Comes readily to light, sometimes in fair numbers.
Life cycle Overwinters as a small larva lying flat along stems of the foodplant. Larva mid August-late May or June.
Larval foodplants A wide range of broadleaved trees and shrubs, including Pedunculate Oak, Hawthorn, Midland Hawthorn, Blackthorn, Hazel, Downy and Silver Birch, elms, sallows, Horse-chestnut, Sweet Chestnut and Beech.
Habitat Most abundant in broadleaved woodland. Also found in most other situations with trees and shrubs, including scrub, hedgerows, parks and gardens, even in urban centres.
Status & distribution Resident. Common. Well distributed and generally frequent throughout most of England, Wales, lowland Scotland, and recorded from the Hebrides. Locally frequent on Orkney. Widespread and frequent on Man and in the Channel Islands. Proving to be quite well distributed in Northern Ireland and widely recorded in the Republic.

Barred Red
page 156

Hylaea fasciaria (L.)

Common. T
1962(7839)

Field characters FW 17-21mm. The red forms are unmistakable. Other frequent and widespread forms range from reddish brown to dull grey. The dull green f. *prasinaria* [D. & S.], frequent in mainland Europe, has been recorded in Kent and Suffolk but is rare. All forms have two slightly darker, gently curving lines across forewing, sometimes edged with white or creamy yellow. Inner cross-line in particular may be weak or absent, especially in dark forms. Hindwing slightly lighter in colour, with a single cross-line. Outer edges of all wings smoothly curved.
Similar species None really. Barred Umber has a very jagged outer edge to central band across forewing. Light Emerald has pointed hindwing and cross-lines are much straighter.
Flight season One generation. Mid June-early August. Sometimes seen by day at rest on foliage of plants under conifers, and can be beaten from conifer branches. Comes to light, sometimes in large numbers.
Life cycle Overwinters as a small larva on the food-plant. Larva early September-late May. Pupates among conifer needles and other plant debris on the ground.
Larval foodplants Mainly Scots Pine and Norway Spruce, but recorded from other conifers, including Larch and Western Hemlock-spruce.
Habitat Native pine forest, conifer plantations, shelterbelts, parks, gardens and cemeteries with conifers.
Status & distribution Resident. Common. Quite well distributed throughout mainland Britain and the Inner Hebrides. Very well distributed and often abundant in all the major areas of large-scale conifer planting. Local and not frequently recorded on Man. Widely recorded but somewhat local in Ireland, including Northern Ireland. Widespread and frequent in the Channel Islands.

Irish Annulet
page 156

Odontognophos dumetata (Treit.)

ssp. *hibernica* Forder

Ireland
1962a(7852)

Field characters FW 18-20mm. A fairly large, grey-brown geometrid with scalloped outer edges to both wings, but with a freckled rather than plain appearance. Dark cross-lines on forewing a constant feature. Ssp. *hibernica* is distinct from ssp. *dumetata*, from mainland Europe, which is much browner.
Similar species Scotch Annulet is smaller and has a smooth rather than jagged outer edge to forewing. Tissue has rounded forewing tip, and hindwing much paler than forewing. Scarce Tissue has numerous additional markings on forewing and darker central band. Both Tissue and Scarce Tissue are brownish.
Flight season One generation. August. Reported visiting flowers of scabiouses and Greater Knapweed and flying around the larval foodplant after dark.

Comes to light.
Life cycle Overwinters as an egg on the foodplant. Larva April-early July.
Larval foodplants Purging Buckthorn. Will not eat Alder Buckthorn.
Habitat Scrubby limestone pavement.
Status & distribution Ssp. *hibernica* Resident western Ireland only, where it is apparently endemic. Discovered in August 1991 when two adults were captured at light in the Burren, Co. Clare. Many adults have since been captured and it appears well established on the Burren. However, initial searches have failed to find it outside Co. Clare. Ssp. *dumetata* has a localised central and southern distribution in Europe, including parts of Spain, France and Germany.

Scotch Annulet
page 156

Gnophos obfuscatus ([D. & S.])

Nb. N
1963(7848)

Field characters & Similar species FW 17-21mm. A rather obscurely-marked geometrid. Normally freckled rather than uniformly coloured. Distinguished from the more widespread and highly variable Annulet on size and slightly concave leading edge of forewing. Annulet is smaller with less pointed forewing, usually with more distinct markings. Scotch Annulet has cross-lines and a central spot on each wing but these are frequently not obvious. Central spot is rarely large and hollow. Ground-colour varies from light grey to dark brown or black.
Flight season One generation. July-August. Sometimes found by day at rest in fissures on rocks and stone walls or disturbed from rest. Flies from dusk and comes to light, generally in small numbers.
Life cycle Overwinters as a larva. Larva September-June. Pupates in a cocoon in plant debris or loose earth.
Larval foodplants Yellow Saxifrage, other saxifrages and stonecrops, Heather, Bell Heather, Cross-leaved Heath and Petty Whin. Probably also other small plants. Has been reared on Dyer's Greenweed, but the moth only occurs north of the natural distribution of this plant.
Habitat Mountains and moorlands, especially where there is exposed rock such as in gullies, streamsides and quarries.
Status & distribution Resident. Nationally Scarce B. Widespread but patchy distribution in northern and central Scotland, the west coast and the Inner Hebrides, but not Orkney and Shetland. Not recorded in the southern uplands south of the Clyde, although present on the Isle of Arran. In the Republic of Ireland it has a north-western distribution and has been reported from Cos. Clare, Galway, Mayo and Donegal.

186

Larva of Annulet.

Annulet
page 156

Charissa obscurata ([D. & S.])

Local. T 1964(7857)

Field characters FW 15-18mm. Very variable in colour, but markings rather constant. Ground-colour matches to some degree colour of soil or rocks in habitat. Those from chalk and limestone are lightest, sometimes almost white, those from heaths, bogs and dark rocky coastlines range from various shades of brown to black. Forewing has two jagged cross-lines with a hollow circle between them, but these markings may be obscured, especially in dark forms. Likewise the jagged cross-line and hollow circle on hindwing.

Similar species See Scotch Annulet.

Flight season One generation. July-August. Easily flushed by day from rest on bare chalk, baked earth or hidden among rocks, in small recesses and behind overhanging vegetation on cliffs. Flies at dusk. Visits flowers such as thistles. Comes to light.

Life cycle Overwinters as a small larva near the base of the foodplant. Larva September-late May. Pupates on the ground among plant debris or in earth.

Larval foodplants Sea Campion, Thrift, Common Rock-rose. Also Common Bird's-foot-trefoil, Kidney Vetch, Creeping Cinquefoil, Wild Strawberry, Wild Thyme, Salad Burnet, Shining Crane's-bill and Heather.

Habitat Many coastal situations, from rocky coastlines to limestone cliffs, grassy banks and sandy places by the sea. Heathland, moorland and chalk and limestone grassland and quarries inland.

Status & distribution Resident. Local. Well distributed on the coasts of south-west England and Wales, from Cornwall and Scilly north to Anglesey and east to the Isle of Wight. Breeds widely inland in north Wales. Recorded from scattered localities along the north coast of Wales, in south Cumbria and on the west coast of Scotland to Sutherland. Also very locally on the east coast, from Yorkshire to Aberdeenshire. Few coastal records east of the Isle of Wight. It occurs inland in the major areas of heathland and chalk downland, from Hampshire and the Isle of Wight, through Surrey to the London area, but these populations have declined and some have been lost in recent decades. Other inland populations are scattered throughout England north to

Northumberland, usually on chalk or limestone, and in Scotland, and at some the moth is fairly frequent. Singletons are sometimes reported in other habitats as suspected wanderers. Mainly coastal and infrequently recorded on Man. Occurs locally around the coast of Ireland, from the extreme south-west to Northern Ireland. Local and occasional in the Channel Islands.

Black Mountain Moth
page 157

Glacies coracina (Esp.)

Na. N 1965(7910)

Field characters FW 10-13mm. This moth is unusual in shape, in that forewing and hindwing are roughly the same size. Both sexes frequently crawl because it is often too cold or windy to fly in their high-altitude habitats. Both sexes are dark brownish black, absorbing heat from the sun more effectively than pale moths. Wing shape, dark central band and central spot are the main features, although the latter are often obscured by other dark scales, particularly in male.

Similar species None.

Flight season One generation. June-July, depending on altitude and season. Male flies in sunshine. Female found crawling over rocks and lichens.

Life cycle Incompletely known. Almost certainly has a two-year life cycle, because on some sites the adults appear to be more numerous every other year, generally in odd-numbered years. The first winter is spent as a larva and probably the second also, although the pupal stage has been stated by some authorities. Larvae, pupating larvae and pupae have been found during late May under reindeer-moss.

Larval foodplants Crowberry. Has been reared on Heather and partially reared on Cross-leaved Heath, but mainly fed on the flowers, suggesting these are not the normal foodplants.

Habitat High-altitude moorland and mountainsides, generally above 600m (2000ft).

Status & distribution Resident. Nationally Scarce A. Widespread and quite well distributed in the central Highlands of Scotland, occurring throughout the Cairngorms and in the Monadhliaths. Also recorded from Ross-shire, Sutherland and recently from two sites in Perthshire.

Black-veined Moth
page 157

Siona lineata (Scop.)

RDB (Protected species). SE 1966(7916)

Field characters FW 19-22mm. Quite distinctive. There is no other white or cream geometrid moth in the British Isles with black veins and banding on undersides of wings. Both sexes change from slightly cream, especially near thorax, to white, and the dark veins become more visible on the upperside with age, as scales are lost. When fully at rest, wings are held flat, but often alights, rests and feeds at flowers with them closed or partly closed up over back, like a butterfly. Male has long, slender abdomen which turns up at tip. Female has stiff abdomen, broad at front and tapering to tip, and slightly smaller, more angular wings.

Similar species The quite large micro-moth *Sitochroa palealis* ([D. & S.]) (Pyralidae), with FW 14-16mm, can appear whitish when faded (very pale green or yellowish when fresh) and has a rather similar underside pattern. It is also active by day in rough grassy places (usually in the south), sometimes sitting on flowers. However, it has much narrower forewing and never rests with wings held up. Black-veined White butterfly *Aporia crataegi* (L.) is much larger, with clubbed antennae, and not likely to be seen in Britain.

Flight season One generation. Late May-early July, depending on site and season. Both sexes readily flushed from rough grass by day, and nectar in sunshine. Female often seen egg-laying by day, particularly on blades of Tor-grass. Male patrols breeding grounds at dusk, searching for females. Both sexes come to light.

Life cycle Overwinters as a part-grown larva. Larva late July-May. The cocoon is attached to blades or stems of grass within the main sward or on the edges of tussocks.

Larval foodplants Recorded on Marjoram, Black-knapweed and Common Bird's-foot-trefoil, but probably not restricted to these. Accepts the usual stand-bys such as Knotgrass in captivity, but difficult to rear. It does not feed on grasses, as sometimes reported.

Habitat Current sites are unshaded, rough but fairly herb-rich chalk grassland slopes of various aspects. Formerly also occurred in open woodland and on clay, including sea-cliffs.

Status & distribution Resident. Red Data Book species. Now thought to be restricted to four British sites, all in Kent. Numbers fluctuate depending on grazing and other management. Occurred in various other sites in Kent prior to 1980. Formerly recorded from Essex, Sussex, Somerset, Dorset, Gloucestershire and Hertfordshire. Spuriously reported from one locality in southern Ireland.

Straw Belle page 157
Aspitates gilvaria gilvaria ([D. & S.])
RDB. SE   1967(7922)

ssp. *burrenensis* Cock.
Ireland

Field characters & Similar species FW 15-18mm. Distinguished from all other moths, except the much more widely found Vestal, by its pale yellow forewing, with an oblique red or reddish-brown stripe running across wing from tip. Vestal when reported as Straw Belle, but is a smaller, more fragile moth and rests with its wings held closer to the body, at a steep angle. Straw Belle has a greyish line and central spot on underside of hindwing, while hindwing of Vestal is unmarked. Straw Belle is heavier in build, and has proportionately longer wings. Female is more freckled than male, with thin

antennae. Ssp. *burrenensis* is darker, forewing markings more brownish and heavier and grey stripe on hindwing nearly reaches trailing edge. See also Yellow Belle.

Flight season One generation. From mid June in Kent but July-early September in Surrey. Easily disturbed from among grass by day. Flies from dusk and comes to light.

Life cycle Overwinters as a small larva. Larva September-end May or June. Pupates in a flimsy spinning in the sward.

Larval foodplants Recently found on Common Bird's-foot-trefoil and Fairy Flax. Also reported from Black Medick, Thyme, Creeping Cinquefoil, Wild Parsnip and Yarrow.

Habitat Rough chalk grassland and quarries, with the larvae feeding on herbs, but using dead grass stems for cover throughout the long larval period.

Status & distribution Resident. Red Data Book species. Restricted to the North Downs of Surrey and Kent. Now possibly confined to two sites in Surrey, of which Box Hill is the best known, and several in Kent, most famously around Folkestone and Dover. Formerly recorded from Devon, Somerset, Gloucestershire, Hampshire, Isle of Wight, Sussex, Middlesex, Essex, Suffolk and apparently Cheshire, mainly in the 19th century. In Ireland ssp. *burrenensis* is found fairly extensively and in moderate to fair numbers in the Burren, Co. Clare. Also reported from Cos. Derry, Galway, Dublin and Wicklow. Two were reported on Guernsey in 1989 and have been accepted by the Channel Islands recorder.

Yellow Belle page 157
Semiaspilates ochrearia (Rossi)
Local. S   1968(7926)

Field characters & Similar species FW 12-16mm. The two brownish, often wavy cross-lines on rather rounded, yellowish forewing and curved, rather wavy line on hindwing distinguish Yellow Belle from Straw Belle and Vestal, both of which have more pointed forewing and a single fairly straight brown or reddish-brown cross-line. The grey line on whitish hindwing is wavy. Female is less yellow than male, sometimes almost fawnish white, and has thin antennae. Outer edge of forewing is sometimes chequered, especially in female. Varies greatly in size.

Flight season Two generations. May-June and August-September. Often flushed from ground vegetation by day, or seen on the wing in hot weather. Found at rest on stems after dark. Comes to light, usually in small numbers.

Life cycle Overwinters as a larva on the foodplant or on other vegetation in the sward. Larva September-May and late June-August.

Larval foodplants A wide range of small plants, including Sea Wormwood, Hare's-foot Clover, Smooth Tare, Bird's-foot Trefoil, Common Restharrow, Wild Carrot, Beaked Hawk's-beard, Buck's-horn Plantain and Spanish Catchfly.

Habitat Almost invariably on or near the coast,

187

Larva of Yellow Belle.

except for the few inland grassy heaths mentioned below. Sand-dunes, shingle, the upper parts of beaches and saltmarshes and the grassy or heathy areas further inland, including golf courses and grazing levels.

Status & distribution Resident. Local. Quite well distributed and sometimes frequent along the south coast of England, including the Isle of Wight, the north coast of Cornwall, Devon, Somerset and Gloucestershire into the Severn Estuary, and along the south coast of Wales to Pembrokeshire. On the east coast, from Kent to the Lincolnshire side of the Wash. Seldom found far inland, but notably along the banks of the Thames into rough and derelict sites in East London, in the Brecklands and at Greenham Common, Berkshire. Widespread and frequent in the Channel Islands.

Grey Scalloped Bar page 157

Dyscia fagaria (Thunb.)

Local. T 1969(7931)

Field characters FW 15-21mm. Quite distinctive. Consistent features are the two curved dark cross-lines on forewing and the bold, dark central dot between them, with outer cross-line continued on hindwing, which may also have a central dot. Male is larger than female, has a slightly concave leading edge to forewing and more rounded wing-tip. Ground-colour very variable. Upland forms often white, lowland and heathland forms tend to be grey and some forms are very dark grey or brownish. Female much smaller, generally darker, with a straighter leading edge and more pointed tip to forewing. Her wings are relatively small for her body size, suggesting she flies much less than male.

Similar species None.

Flight season One generation. Late May-early August. Male basks on stones and broken or bare ground, and is easily disturbed by day. Both sexes found at rest on Heather after dark. Comes to light in small numbers.

Life cycle Overwinters as a small larva. Larva July-May. Cocoon is formed on the foodplant or in fallen debris.

Larval foodplants Heather, Bell Heather and Cross-leaved Heath.

Habitat Heathland, moorland, bogs and raised

mosses, probably favouring the shorter swards. Often seen at rest in burned areas.

Status & distribution Resident. Local. Well distributed and fairly frequent on heathlands of south-east Dorset and the New Forest, Hampshire. Local and scarce on heathland elsewhere in Hampshire and west Surrey. One recorded on the Isle of Wight in 2001. Recorded from a thin scatter of sites elsewhere in southern Britain, including a population in Monmouthshire, found in 1995. Fairly well distributed in suitable habitat in northern Wales, the West Midlands, northern England and Scotland, including the Inner Hebrides and Orkney, and in Ireland. Recorded from Man in 1893, 1968 and on Calf of Man in 1989. One recorded in the Channel Islands, on Jersey in 1977.

Grass Wave page 157

Perconia strigillaria (Hb.)

Local. T 1970(7939)

Field characters FW 15-20mm. Silvery grey, heavily marked with diffuse brown stripes and fine speckling, and with rather pointed forewing. Male has wide, feathery antennae. Normally four stripes across forewing and three across hindwing, but one or more on either wing may be reduced or absent. Strength of markings is quite variable, even among individuals on the same site, and there is also considerable variation in size.

Similar species Somewhat larger and with more stripes than dark forms of Common Wave and Common White Wave, which have more rounded forewings.

Flight season One generation. May-July. Readily disturbed and sometimes active by day. Also flies from dusk and comes to light in small to moderate numbers.

Life cycle Overwinters as a small larva. Larva August-late May. Cocoon attached to the foodplant.

Larval foodplants Heather, Bell Heather, Broom and Petty Whin. Reported from the flowers of Gorse and on Blackthorn.

Habitat Most abundant on lowland heathland, the heathy commons of Surrey, and in open woodland where the ride verges and open areas have a heathy character. Also on moorland and bogs.

Status & distribution Resident. Local. Well distributed and locally fairly frequent on the heaths of south-east Dorset, the New Forest and north-east Hampshire, Surrey and Berkshire. More local in Sussex. Very local in the extreme south-west of Cornwall but still present in at least a dozen sites in Devon. Widespread but thinly distributed and very local in the rest of Great Britain. Reported north to Ross-shire. Strong populations or centres of distribution are known in Glamorgan, Worcestershire, Staffordshire, Nottinghamshire, Lincolnshire, Yorkshire and Cumbria, and on a few sites elsewhere. Records thinly scattered in lowland Scotland. Widespread but very local in Ireland, from the extreme south-west to Northern Ireland.

Sphingidae – Hawkmoths

The Sphingidae comprises about 1,050 species and occurs worldwide, with most found in the tropics. There are nine species resident in the British Isles. Eight others occur as immigrants, some regularly breeding, but the early stages are unable to survive the winter, although one species, the Hummingbird Hawkmoth, hibernates as an adult in south-west England. About ten further species of dubious origin have been reported in Britain, in some cases probably imported with cargoes of fruit or vegetables. Hawkmoths are impressive medium to large moths, often strikingly coloured, and include the biggest moths in Britain in terms of wingspan and body size. They are known as hawk-moths because of their fast and manoeuvrable flight and the large size of many species.

Pine Hawkmoth

The Sphinginae include the largest hawkmoths. They tend to hold their wings close to the body at rest. Some have very long tongues and hover in front of the flower to feed, like the Macroglossinae, while others, such as the Death's Head Hawkmoth, have reduced tongues but may still feed.

Within the Smerinthinae, the proboscis is reduced in length and the moths typically do not feed. The hindwings often have circular patches or eye-spots, and the leading edge of the hindwing sometimes projects beyond the leading edge of the forewing at rest. The females are generally bigger than the males, and the males rest with the tip of the abdomen curled upwards.

The Macroglossinae have long tongues, hence the name, and the group includes many species which hover to take nectar from flowers by day or at dusk. Two species have evolved a resemblance to bees, with largely transparent wings and squat bodies. Many of the Macroglossinae look like jet-fighters. Their caterpillars often have eye-spots on the body segments.

The eggs are attached to the foodplant, usually singly or in pairs. The larvae are not hairy and most species have a horn at the tail end. This tends to be long and well developed in the Sphinginae and Smerinthinae, while in the Macroglossinae the tail horn is often reduced; in the Small Elephant Hawkmoth it has disappeared altogether. The larvae feed on the leaves of both woody and herbaceous plants. The pupae of many species can be found by searching at the base of the larval foodplant, either among moss and leaf litter, or by digging in the soil.

With the exception of the day-fliers, the adults of most hawkmoths come regularly to light, and are occasionally found at rest by day, usually when newly emerged. Those which feed can be found by searching out their nectar plants, to which they will return repeatedly. A number have brightly-coloured hindwings and flash these when disturbed, in order to deter predators.

Sphinginae

1971 see Appendix

Convolvulus Hawkmoth   page 225
Agrius convolvuli (L.)
Immigrant.   1972(6828)

Field characters FW 50-55mm. An extremely large moth, with ash grey, variably marbled and extensively streaked forewing. Male is quite heavily marked with blackish streaks and bands, often with a broad, central cross-band. Larger female lacks extensive blackish markings and antennae are shorter and thinner.

Similar species The roof-like way in which Convolvulus Hawkmoth holds its wings close to the body distinguishes it from other hawkmoths except Privet Hawkmoth, which is normally seen only in June and July. Privet Hawkmoth, like Convolvulus Hawkmoth, has pink and black banding on abdomen, but has a dark thorax, a pronounced wavy chocolate-brown stripe running from the trailing edge of forewing towards tip and pinker hindwing, with three strongly marked black bands. Pine Hawkmoth is superficially similar but is smaller, lacks pink bands on abdomen, and forewing markings are less extensive.

Flight season June-December, with the largest numbers from late August-late November. Nocturnal. Feeds at dusk, and sometimes at dawn, at tubular flowers such as tobacco plants, petunia, lilies and phlox. The proboscis is extremely long and no other moth occurring in the British Isles can feed at some of these flowers; white varieties that open at night and have strong scent are particularly attractive to moths. Comes to light, and is occasionally found at rest by day, usually on tree trunks, posts, rocks and walls. Has occasionally been seen on migration, flying a few metres above the sea.

Life cycle Unable to overwinter. Larvae are occasionally found in the British Isles. Pupates underground.

Larval foodplants Field Bindweed, Hedge Bindweed and other members of the Convolvulaceae, including cultivated varieties.

Habitat It can be found anywhere, including gardens.

Larva of Privet Hawkmoth.

Status & distribution Immigrant. Annually on the south and east coastal counties of England, sometimes in large numbers. Recorded more sparsely over the rest of the British Isles north to Orkney and Shetland. Resident in Africa, from where some of the adults that emerge from June-August fly north to Europe and breed, the offspring of which form the majority of those reaching Britain and Ireland.

Death's Head Hawkmoth   page 225
Acherontia atropos (L.)
Immigrant.   1973(6830)

Field characters FW 52-60mm. Unmistakable. The skull-like marking on thorax of this huge moth and banded yellow abdomen and hindwing are diagnostic among British hawkmoths. When disturbed, it makes an audible squeaking sound by expelling air through the short proboscis, past a structure that vibrates like a saxophone reed.

Similar species None.

Flight season Mainly late August-late October, but sometimes as early as May and into late November. Nocturnal. Seldom seen except in light-traps or in beehives, which it is able to enter in order to feed on the honey without being attacked by the bees. Occasionally found at rest by day.

Life cycle Unable to overwinter. Adults arriving in the summer sometimes produce larvae that pupate from August-October. Pupates underground, in a fragile cocoon.

Larval foodplants Usually potato, Deadly Nightshade and occasionally other members of the Solanaceae. Can be reared on Garden Privet.

Habitat Until the use of insecticides, larvae and pupae were often found in potato fields, sometimes in large numbers. They are still found occasionally, with organic crops, allotments and gardens perhaps offering the best opportunities.

Status & distribution Immigrant. Recorded in small numbers most years, usually in the south and east of England, but has reached most parts of the British Isles, including Orkney, Shetland, Man and the eastern half of Ireland. It has been recorded at the lights of oil-rigs in the North Sea. Rare in the Channel Islands.

Folklore Widely regarded as an omen of death, due to the skull marking on the thorax. *Atropos* was one of the Fates that cut the thread of life. The moth featured in the film 'Silence of the Lambs' was actually the closely related Eastern Death's Head *A. styx*, an Oriental species.

1974, 1975, 1975a see Appendix

Privet Hawkmoth   page 225
Sphinx ligustri (L.)
Common. S   1976(6832)

Field characters FW 41-55mm. The dark chocolate-brown, pale-clouded forewing, pink and black banded hindwing and abdomen, and blackish thorax

190

make this very large moth unmistakable. There is some variation in the intensity of the pink and the darker markings. Very rarely the pink is replaced by white (f. *albescens* Tutt) or the abdominal bars are yellow (f. *lutescens* Tutt).

Similar species See Pine Hawkmoth, which is smaller and lacks pink bars on abdomen, and also Convolvulus Hawkmoth.

Flight season One generation. June-July. Sometimes found freshly emerged at rest on vertical surfaces, such as tree trunks and fence posts. Active after dark and comes to light, but does not feed.

Life cycle Overwinters, occasionally twice, as a pupa underground, sometimes at a depth of 30cm or more. Larva July-September.

Larval foodplants Wild and Garden Privet, Ash (particularly young saplings in woodland, sometimes lower branches of big trees), Lilac and Guelder-rose. Also reported on Holly, Honeysuckle, Snowberry and the cultivated shrubs *Viburnum tinus, Forsythia* and *Spirea*.

Habitat Downland, hedgerows, open woodland, gardens, fens and coastal scrub, preferring calcareous soils.

Status & distribution Resident. Common. Recorded widely from Cornwall and Scilly to Kent, and northwards to a line from the Severn to the Wash. Local in Lincolnshire, Nottinghamshire, the West Midlands and formerly in Derbyshire. Largely coastal in Wales. Scattered records from northern England, Man and southern Scotland. Widespread and frequent in the Channel Islands.

1977 see Appendix

Pine Hawkmoth   page 225
Hyloicus pinastri (L.)
Local. S,SE   1978(6834)

Field characters FW 35-41mm. The characteristic features are the rather plain, white-dusted grey or brownish-grey forewing, with three or four black streaks in centre, chequered margin to trailing edge and somewhat uniformly dark brown hindwing. Abdomen has black bars, without any trace of pink banding.

Similar species See Convolvulus and Privet Hawkmoths.

Flight season One generation. May-early August. Sometimes found by day at rest on tree trunks or fence posts. Flies at night and comes to light, sometimes in numbers. Feeds from flowers after dark, particularly Honeysuckle.

Life cycle Overwinters as a pupa. Larva late June-mid September. Found on both small trees and mature trees, but prefers older needles rather than young shoots. Pupates under leaf litter or just beneath the ground.

Larval foodplants Mainly Scots Pine, but occasionally Maritime Pine, Norway Spruce and Cedar of Lebanon.

Habitat Conifer plantations, shelterbelts and wooded heathland. It is regularly recorded in small numbers in light-traps in other habitats, even urban areas, but there is no evidence that it ever becomes established in these places. It is far more likely that these are dispersing or pioneering individuals.

Status & distribution Resident. Local. The increase in conifer plantations in the 20th century has enabled the moth to spread slowly northwards. Well established and frequent in Dorset, Hampshire and the Isle of Wight (since 1947), Surrey, Sussex, Kent and East Anglia. Also found in the London area, and since the 1940s in Bedfordshire, Oxfordshire and Berkshire, and very locally in Cornwall. In the 1990s it became established in Lincolnshire and Yorkshire and was occasionally recorded in Devon, Worcestershire and Nottinghamshire. Widespread and frequent in the Channel Islands.

Smerinthinae

Lime Hawkmoth   page 226
Mimas tiliae (L.)
Common. S,C   1979(6819)

Field characters FW 23-39mm. Its colour, wing shape and markings distinguish this species from all other resident British hawkmoths. The two dark olive-green central forewing markings may be enlarged to form a cross-band, or reduced to one small spot (f. *centripunctata* Clark). F. *brunnea* Bartel is largely reddish brown and central markings are brick-red.

Similar species Willowherb Hawkmoth is superficially similar, but smaller and more thickset.

Flight season One generation. May-early July. Sometimes found at rest on tree trunks, walls and among lime foliage. Comes to light, often early in the night. Does not feed.

Life cycle Overwinters as a pupa just below ground, usually near the larval foodplant. Occasionally the pupa has been found in leaf litter trapped in crooks of branches high above the ground, and in bird nesting boxes. Larva late June-mid September. Larvae sometimes found crawling down the trunks of urban limes, or squashed on the pavement.

Larval foodplants Limes, elms, Downy and Silver Birch and Alder. In the London area, reported from Plane and cultivars of Wild Cherry.

Habitat Most habitats in which the foodplants grow in lowland situations, particularly broadleaved woodland, parks and gardens, including urban areas.

Status & distribution Resident. Common. Widely distributed and fairly frequent in England north to Yorkshire, where it became well established in the 1950s. Occasionally recorded north to Cumbria. Local in Wales, but found in Monmouthshire, Breconshire, Glamorgan and north Wales. Recorded once from Man, in 1936. Local and rare on Jersey.

Eyed Hawkmoth
page 226

Smerinthus ocellata (L.)

Common. S,C
1980(6822)

Field characters FW 36-44mm. Unmistakable. Eye-spots on pink hindwing are diagnostic. When disturbed, it exposes these and rocks to and fro. This has been proved to deter insectivorous birds. Forewing markings vary little, except in colour and degree of contrast, ranging from pinkish brown to deep chocolate or even blackish.

Similar species Poplar Hawkmoth has a similar resting posture but no eye spots.

Flight season Usually one generation. Early May-mid July. Sometimes a partial second generation in the south, early August-late September. Occasionally found at rest by day. Comes to light, usually in small numbers. Does not feed.

Life cycle Overwinters as a pupa underground, below or near the larval foodplant. Larva late June-September, sometimes later. The pupa is shiny blackish brown and easily distinguished from the rough blackish-brown pupa of Poplar Hawkmoth.

Larval foodplants Wild and cultivated willows and sallows, frequently on small bushes, Apple and both wild and ornamental Crab Apple. Occasionally reported from Aspen and poplars.

Habitat Gardens, orchards and most situations in which willows grow, including parks, riversides, fens, scrub and woodland.

Status & distribution Resident. Common. Widely distributed and fairly frequent over most of lowland England and Wales north to Cumbria. Previously recorded in Northumberland and Durham, but rare or absent since the 1970s. Only reported once from Scotland, in Dumfries-shire. Local on Man. Widespread in Ireland. Widely distributed but occasional in the Channel Islands.

Poplar Hawkmoth
page 226

Laothoe populi (L.)

Common. T
1981(6823)

Field characters FW 30-46mm. Unmistakable. Pattern on wings is very constant. Chestnut-brown patches on hindwing are diagnostic. At rest, hindwing can project well beyond leading edge of forewing. Some individuals have a strong pinkish or violet tinge to wings. There is also an uncommon buff-coloured form, which is more frequent in female.

Similar species See Eyed Hawkmoth.

Flight season One generation in most places. May-July or early August. Sometimes a partial second generation in the south, August-September. Comes frequently to light, male usually after midnight, female earlier and in smaller numbers. Does not feed.

Life cycle Overwinters as a pupa underground, near the larval foodplant. Larva June-September, occasionally later.

Larval foodplants Poplars, including Aspen, White Poplar, Black-poplar and Lombardy-poplar. Also frequent on sallows and willows, particularly Goat Willow and Grey Willow.

Habitat Most situations in which the larval food-plants grow, including parks and gardens, fens, woodland, heathland and moorland (but not at high altitude).

Status & distribution Resident. Common. The most widely distributed and frequent hawkmoth in the British Isles. Recorded from all the counties of mainland Britain, on Man and in the Inner Hebrides. Widespread and frequent in Ireland and in the Channel Islands.

Macroglossinae

Narrow-bordered Bee Hawkmoth p.227

Hemaris tityus (L.)

Nb. SW,WC,NW,(E)
1982(6839)

Field characters & Similar species FW 18-21mm. The two bee-hawkmoth species have largely transparent wings and a compact body, but are more agile than the bumble-bees they mimic. They do not alight to feed and are also much larger than bee-flies (*Bombylius*). In Narrow-bordered Bee Hawkmoth, dark brown bands around outer edges of wings are narrower than in Broad-bordered, especially on hindwing and towards trailing edge of forewing. There are two thin blackish bands on abdomen, obscured by golden hairs which may wear off, making bands appear blacker and more extensive. In Broad-bordered, bands are broader and more reddish brown, but may appear blacker as the hairs wear off. When freshly emerged, wings have a thin covering of grey scales, lost on the first flight. See Broad-bordered for further differences. Hummingbird Hawkmoth can look similar in flight, but is very different on close examination.

Flight season One generation. Mid May-June or early July (exceptionally April, as in 2003). Active in sunshine, particularly in late morning and early afternoon. Feeds at flowers such as Bugle, Ground Ivy, lousewort, Viper's-bugloss, Common Bird's-foot-trefoil, Rhododendron and Red Valerian. Can be lured to cut Lilac flowers.

Life cycle Overwinters as a pupa. Larva mid June-mid August. The flimsy cocoon is found among plant litter or just below ground.

Larval foodplants Devil's-bit Scabious. Less frequently Small Scabious and Field Scabious.

Habitat Unimproved grassland, including wet acidic pasture, lightly grazed calcareous grassland, including chalk downland. Also acid bogs and drier heathland.

Status & distribution Resident. Nationally Scarce B. Much decreased, especially in the south and east, probably due to agricultural intensification, including the change from cutting hay to making silage. Still

Larva of Narrow-bordered Bee Hawkmoth.

Larva of Broad-bordered Bee Hawkmoth.

widespread but local in Cornwall, Devon, Somerset, the heaths of Dorset and some of the chalk grasslands of Wiltshire. At least one colony survives in Yorkshire, and one in East Anglia, near Thetford. Rediscovered in Gloucestershire in 1993. There are scattered records from western Wales, particularly Anglesey. In Scotland, found mainly near the west coast and the inner Moray Firth. Widespread in Northern and western Ireland, and in the Burren, Co. Clare. Recorded once from the Channel Islands, on Jersey in 1917.

Broad-bordered Bee Hawkmoth p. 227

Hemaris fuciformis (L.)

Nb. S,EC   1983(6840)

Field characters & Similar species FW 20-24mm. Very similar to Narrow-bordered Bee-hawk. In addition to the broader wing borders, on forewing of Broad-bordered Bee Hawkmoth the transparent window (or cell) near base in leading half is divided in two by a vein running parallel with leading edge. Also, the short, dark central cross-vein is thicker. Band on abdomen is usually reddish brown, although the hairs may wear off to leave the blackish abdomen exposed. When freshly emerged, the wings are covered with a thin layer of light brown scales, lost on the first flight. See Narrow-bordered Bee Hawkmoth for additional differences.

Flight season Usually one generation. Mid May-early July. Occasionally a partial second generation in southern England, August-September. Active in sunshine, particularly in late morning and early afternoon. Feeds at tubular flowers such as Bugle, Honeysuckle, Ragged-Robin, louseworts, Viper's-bugloss, Yellow-rattle, Rhododendron and Aubretia.

Life cycle Overwinters as a pupa just below ground. Larva late June-August.

Larval foodplants Wild Honeysuckle, occasionally cultivated honeysuckles and Snowberry.

Habitat Rides and clearings in open woodland, and heathland.

Status & distribution Resident. Nationally Scarce B. Much decreased due to the decline in coppicing, maturation of dense stands of conifers and browsing of Honeysuckle by increased deer populations. Found only in the southern half of England and in Wales,

north to south Yorkshire (Doncaster area). It has major strongholds in the Thetford Forest and Breckland areas of East Anglia, on heathlands on the Suffolk coast and in the ancient lime woods of Lincolnshire, as well as in large woodlands further south. Thinly scattered in the West Midlands, Wales and south-west England.

Hummingbird Hawkmoth page 227

Macroglossum stellatarum (L.)

Immigrant; suspected resident.   1984(6843)

Field characters & Similar species FW 20-24mm. Resembles a hummingbird as it flits rapidly between plants, hovering to feed at tubular flowers of such species as Viper's-bugloss, Red Valerian, Phlox, Jasmine, Buddleias, Petunia and Lilac. Orange-brown colour of hindwing and undersides of wings is evident on flight. This, together with warm greyish-brown forewings, distinguishes this moth from the two species of bee hawkmoth, which behave similarly but have largely transparent wings.

Flight season Most immigrants arrive from April-December, especially in August and September. Hibernators may fly on warm days from January onwards. Active by day, mainly in sunshine, but sometimes in overcast weather, rain, and occasionally at dusk or after dark.

Life cycle Larva mainly June-October, most frequently found in August. Recorded hibernating as an adult in south-west England in mild winters over the last 30 years or more, in unheated outbuildings, garages, lofts and porches, and in crevices and holes in walls and trees. Pupates in a flimsy cocoon spun close to the ground, among the foliage of the food-plant or in leaf litter.

Larval foodplants Lady's Bedstraw, Hedge Bedstraw and Wild Madder. Also seen laying eggs on Red Valerian.

Habitat Can occur anywhere, from coastal sites to inland gardens, woodland rides and urban window boxes.

Status & distribution A frequent immigrant from southern Europe and north Africa, most numerous near the south coast, but has reached all parts of the British Isles and the Channel Islands. The number recorded varies considerably annually and in some years exceeds 1,000. Suspected breeding resident in south-west England, where it hibernates in small numbers.

Folklore Apparently long considered a messenger of good tidings in Italy and Malta. A small swarm was reported flying over the water in the English Channel, headed to England from France on D-Day, 1944. One seen by the senior author on the day his daughter was born!

Willowherb Hawkmoth   page 227

Proserpinus proserpina (Pall.)

Rare immigrant/import. S,E   1984a(6849)

Field characters FW 18-21mm. This relatively small, thickset hawkmoth, with jagged-edged, banded, green or brownish-green forewing and orange-yellow, black-bordered hindwing, is fairly unmistakable.

Similar species See Lime Hawkmoth.

Larval foodplants Willowherbs, Common Evening-primrose and Purple-loosestrife. Larvae not found in the British Isles.

Habitat Damp woodland clearings and sandy wasteground, in mainland Europe.

Status & distribution Either rare immigrant or accidental import. Two individuals have been recorded in the British Isles. On 25 May 1985, a male was captured at light at Denton, near Newhaven, East Sussex, and on 18 July 1995 one was found at rest on a stone pillar at St Katharine's Dock, East London. Its distribution includes Spain, North Africa, southern France and Italy.

Oleander Hawkmoth   page 227

Daphnis nerii (L.)

Immigrant.   1985(6845)

Field characters FW 48-51mm. The swirling cream and pinkish-brown markings on the green forewing and thorax of this large hawkmoth make it totally unmistakable. Whitish band across front end of abdomen is also distinctive.

Similar species None.

Flight season Usually occurs August-October. In the British Isles usually seen at light. Will feed on the wing at tubular flowers such as Honeysuckle and tobacco plants after dusk.

Larval foodplants Oleander and Lesser Periwinkle. Feeds on privets in captivity. Larvae are very rarely found in Britain.

Habitat Abroad, it breeds in very warm, open places such as scrubby hillsides.

Status & distribution A rare but fairly regular immigrant. Not seen in some years. The most reported in a year is 13, in 1953. Most frequently recorded in southern England, but has occasionally reached Scotland and Ireland. Rare in the Channel Islands. Its distribution as a resident includes Sicily, Crete, Cyprus and northern Africa. It breeds more extensively in southern Europe in most summers, the offspring probably making up a large proportion of the immigrants that reach Britain.

Spurge Hawkmoth   page 228

Hyles euphorbiae (L.)

Immigrant.   1986(6853)

Field characters & Similar species FW 28-31mm. A dull olive-green hawkmoth, with a broad, pale, sometimes pink-tinged and/or speckled stripe along forewing, which extends close to and sometimes reaches leading edge at various points. Undersides of both wings are pinkish. Bedstraw Hawkmoth is similar, but forewing stripe is distinctly narrower and does not approach leading edge; underside of wing is not pink. Striped Hawkmoth is distinguished by white veins on forewing.

Flight season Recorded in Britain in every month from May-October.

Larval foodplants Perennial herbaceous spurges. Larvae are very rarely found in the British Isles.

Habitat Abroad, it breeds in open sunny situations, including coastal sand-dunes and field margins.

Status & distribution A very scarce immigrant to the British mainland, usually recorded in southern England. In recent years, usually at light, but often as larvae in the more distant past. Since 1990, single examples were recorded at Newton Abbot, Devon, on 17 June 1991; Dungeness, Kent, on 12 August 1993 and again on 12 June 1997; Dymchurch, Kent, on 3 August 2002; and Durlston Country Park, Swanage, Dorset, on the same date. A fully grown larva was found at Hastings, East Sussex, on 22 August 1994. Exceptionally, one individual reached Otterburn, Northumberland, in 1860, where it was captured at Rhododendron flowers. The moth breeds fairly widely and commonly in Spain and much of France and formerly in the Channel Islands. Also resident eastwards through central and southern Europe.

Bedstraw Hawkmoth   page 228

Hyles gallii (Rott.)

Immigrant; transitory resident.   1987(6855)

Field characters & Similar species FW 34-38mm. A fairly unmistakable, dark olive-green hawkmoth, distinguished from Striped Hawkmoth by lack of white stripes highlighting the veins across forewing and along top of thorax. See also Spurge Hawkmoth.

Flight season May-August. Flies from dusk and visits nectar flowers. Comes to light.

Life cycle Overwinters as a pupa, but does not usually survive, probably due to the high rainfall since it seems to favour a continental climate. Larva July-September, in the British Isles. Likes to bask in sunshine.

Larval foodplants Bedstraws, Rosebay Willowherb, madders and fuchsias.

Habitat In the British Isles, usually breeds in open coastal habitats such as sand-dunes, or on wasteground inland.

Status & distribution Immigrant. Currently fairly regular in small numbers in most years. Periodically invades in large numbers after long periods of scarcity or absence. For example, 65 adults and about 1,000 larvae were noted in 1888, with 250 in Kent and large numbers also in Suffolk, Cheshire and Lancashire. Subsequently, the highest annual total between 1889 and 1954 was seven in 1935. In 1955, 50 adults were reported, and it was temporarily resident in north Norfolk from 1956-58. Most recently, 65 adults and about 200 larvae were found in 1973, for which an origin in eastern Europe was suggested. It was again suspected of overwintering. Has been recorded from most parts of mainland Britain, Scilly, Man, the Inner Hebrides, Orkney, Shetland, and the Channel Islands. In the Irish Republic, recorded from the south-east and the south-west, including larvae. Resident in southern France and eastwards throughout most of Europe, north to Denmark, southern Scandinavia and Russia.

1988, 1989 see Appendix

Larva of Elephant Hawkmoth.

195

Elephant Hawkmoth
page 228

Deilephila elpenor (L.)

Common. S,C,(N)   1991(6862)

Field characters FW 28-33mm. Unmistakable, with pink and olive-green forewing and pink and black hindwing. Clearly defined pink pattern on olive-green thorax and abdomen, including stripe along abdomen. The sexes are similar and there is very little variation.

Similar species Small Elephant Hawkmoth is pink and yellow, and very much smaller.

Flight season Mainly one generation. May-early August, but very occasionally fresh adults are reported later in the summer. Sometimes found at rest by day among the foodplant. Flies from dusk, feeding on the wing at Honeysuckle and other tubular nectar flowers. Comes to light, sometimes in numbers.

Life cycle Overwinters as a pupa. Larva late June-September. This larva sometimes arouses people's curiosity, often when it is found searching for a pupation site, due to its size and large eye markings. Feeds at night, but comes up to rest on a stem in the late afternoon on fine days, when it can be very conspicuous. Pupates in a flimsy cocoon formed among plant debris on the ground or just below the surface.

Larval foodplants Most frequently found on Rosebay Willowherb, Great Willowherb, other willowherbs and bedstraws. Also recorded on Enchanter's-nightshade, fuchsias and Himalayan Balsam, and less frequently on many other plants.

Habitat A wide variety, including rough grassland, often with disturbed or burnt ground where Rosebay Willowherb has colonised, hedgerows, ditches, gardens, woodland rides and clearings, heathland and sand-dunes.

Status & distribution Resident. Common. Very widely and well distributed throughout England and Wales. More thinly distributed in Scotland, in the Borders, Dumfries-shire, the Clyde Valley and Argyllshire, and has recently expanded its range into the north-east to include Aberdeenshire , Banffshire and north to Easter Ross. Somewhat local on Man. Recently found to be widely and quite well distributed in Ireland. Very local and rare in the Channel Islands.

Striped Hawkmoth
page 228

Hyles livornica (Esp.)

Immigrant.   1990(6860)

Field characters FW 33-42mm. Distinguished by the white stripes highlighting veins on forewing and along top of thorax.

Similar species See Bedstraw, Silver-striped and Spurge Hawkmoths. Striped Hawkmoth was formerly considered to be a subspecies of the White-lined Hawkmoth *Hyles lineata* (Fabr.), an American moth with three white stripes on each side of the thorax. There is a specimen of this species in the Natural History Museum, London, reputedly found in Bridlington, North Yorkshire, in July 1897, which was very probably an accidental introduction.

Flight season April-October, with the main influxes in May-early June and August. Flies mainly at dusk and just before dawn, when it feeds from flowers such as Red Valerian and Petunia, but when migrating can be active late at night. Comes to light.

Life cycle Unable to overwinter. Larva June-July and September-October, only occasionally found in the British Isles.

Larval foodplants An unusually wide range of unrelated foodplants has been reported, but usually on Rosebay and other willowherbs, or Hedge Bedstraw. Also occasionally found on snapdragons, fuchsias, buckwheats, sorrels and docks.

Habitat Usually breeds in open, warm habitats, particularly on the coast and in gardens, but also on rides in open woodland.

Status & distribution Immigrant. Recorded most years, usually in small numbers. There was a major influx in 1931, and another in 1943 when over 540 were reported. Recently, there were 60 in 1992 and 80 in 1996. Recorded from most parts of the British Isles and the Channel Islands, with the greatest number in south-west and southern England, and southern Ireland. Resident all around the Mediterranean coast, and much more widely in northern Africa.

Small Elephant Hawkmoth · page 228
Deilephila porcellus (L.)
Local. S,C,(N) 1992(6863)

Field characters FW 21-25mm. Unmistakable. The only small, pink and yellowish-brown hawkmoth found in the British Isles.
Similar species Elephant Hawkmoth is very much larger, with green rather than yellow markings.
Flight season One generation. May-July. Freshly emerged adults are occasionally found by day. Flies from dusk and visits flowers such as Viper's-bugloss, campions, Honeysuckle, Red Valerian and Rhododendron. Comes to light, occasionally in large numbers, sometimes quite early in the night.
Life cycle Overwinters as a pupa. Larva late June-early September, feeding at night and hiding in the debris at the base of the plant by day. Pupates in a flimsy cocoon formed on the ground among leaf litter, or just below the surface.
Larval foodplants Usually bedstraws, particularly Lady's Bedstraw, but also Hedge, Marsh and Heath Bedstraws. Also recorded on Rosebay Willowherb and Purple-loosestrife.
Habitat Generally in open habitats with a short grassy sward, including chalk and limestone grassland (where it can be very numerous), commons, golf courses, heathland, sand-dunes, shingle beaches and also damp, neutral grassland.
Status & distribution Resident. Local. Recorded widely but locally in England and Wales. More thinly distributed in northern England and Scotland, and from the Tay northwards largely confined to the east coast, reaching Sutherland. Fairly widespread on Man. Widely distributed in Ireland, but largely coastal. Widespread and abundant in the Channel Islands.

Silver-striped Hawkmoth · page 228
Hippotion celerio (L.)
Immigrant. 1993(6865)

Field characters & Similar species FW 33-35mm. The smooth-edged, tapered, cream and silver stripe running along forewing in a gentle curve from body to wing tip is main diagnostic feature. Pinkish areas on hindwing are crossed by several dark brown veins, which distinguishes it further from Striped, Bedstraw and Spurge Hawkmoths. Female is generally slightly smaller than male, and has slightly shorter antennae.
Flight season Two generations. May-October. Most that reach the British Isles are of the second generation, occurring from August. Flies from dusk and visits nectar flowers, including Ivy. Comes to light, sometimes early in the night.
Life cycle Unable to overwinter. Very few larvae have been found in Britain, those that have being mainly in October.
Larval foodplants Mainly Grape-vine and Virginia-creeper, but Lady's Bedstraw, Great Willowherb, fuschias, bindweeds, Honeysuckle and mulleins are among the reported foodplants abroad.
Habitat Generally in open places, particularly on the coast.
Status & distribution Immigrant. In most years fewer than ten are reported, with none in some years. The largest annual total is 41, in 1885. More recently, there were 14 in 1963. Resident in Africa, where it is widespread and abundant and breeds along the north coast. From here, it colonises southern Europe each summer, producing one or two generations between May and October, a few of which reach the British Isles. Most have been recorded along the south coast of England.

Notodontidae – Prominent and kitten moths

Alder Kitten

Buff-tip

This family comprises over 2,500 species, with representatives throughout the world. Twenty-seven have been recorded in the British Isles. Of these, 21 are certainly resident, one has not been seen since 1938 and one is a transitory resident, currently known from a single site. The remaining four are rare immigrants. One species is considered to be a member of the Noctuidae by some authorities.

The Notodontinae are furry, thick-bodied moths, in many cases with rather long, tapering forewings, which are normally held quite close to the body when at rest. The trailing edge of the forewings of some species have prominent projections which are raised over the back when the moth is resting with its wings closed, hence the common name for the group. The adults are unable to feed, and are seldom seen by day, but the males especially come readily to light-traps. The antennae are relatively long and obvious in both sexes, and in most species are feathered in the male. The wing markings are subtle and cryptic, with a preponderance of brown, grey and white, often in beautifully textured patterns, which help them blend with bark and dead leaves. Variation is not usually great, and is largely confined to the ground-colour or the intensity of the dark markings.

The larvae are often striking, and raise both the head and tail end when they feel threatened. Some have prominent lobe-like projections on their backs, or two extended 'tails'. In the case of the Puss Moth, a red whip-like structure is produced from each tail, as an extra deterrent to would-be predators. The Puss Moth and the kittens are probably so-named because the young larvae have two ear-like projections just behind the head, making them appear rather cat-like from behind (although the adults are particularly furry also). Prominent and kitten larvae feed on the foliage of trees and shrubs, resting on the foodplant when not feeding. The majority leave the foodplant to pupate below it, usually in the earth or among leaf litter, or in a hard cocoon on the trunk. The largest species have one generation a year. Some of the smaller species fit two generations into the year in the south, but in northern Britain they grow more slowly and complete only one.

197

Notodontinae

1994 see below 2019

Puss Moth

page 229

Cerura vinula (L.)

Common. T

1995(8704)

Field characters FW 29-38mm. A large, furry, white or greyish-white moth, with a number of small black spots on thorax and near base of forewing, and grey, steeply-contoured lines on outer part of forewing. Female is generally larger and also differs in having grey hindwing and sometimes forewing. The appearance of the adults of this and the following three species undoubtedly contributed to their English names.

Similar species Leopard Moth is superficially similar, but has only black spots on forewing and lacks the contoured lines of Puss Moth. Leopard Moth has distinctive short antennae, those of the male (which is smaller) being feathered in basal half only. Both species may pretend to be dead when handled.

Flight season One generation. May-July. Comes to light in small numbers, but often lands in vegetation near a light-trap rather than entering it.

Life cycle Overwinters as a pupa. Larva July-September. Eggs are laid singly, or in twos and threes on the uppersides of the leaves. Larvae often strip entire stems of leaves. Pupates in a very hard cocoon spun on a tree-trunk or post, incorporating wood macerated by the larva.

Larval foodplants Poplars and willows, particularly low re-growth or suckers of Aspen and Goat Willow in sunny places.

Habitat Gardens, hedgerows, open woodland, moorland, scrub and carr.

Status & distribution Resident. Common. Fairly frequent throughout most of the British Isles, but not recorded from Shetland. Less frequent in upland areas, where it is often confined to the banks of streams. In Ireland, more frequently recorded near the coast, but now known to be well distributed in Northern Ireland. Local and rare in the Channel Islands.

Larva of Puss Moth.

Larva of Alder Kitten.

198

Alder Kitten   page 229

Furcula bicuspis (Borkh.)

Local. SW,SE,E,WC   1996(8709)

Field characters & Similar species FW 16-19mm. Easily distinguished from Poplar and Sallow Kitten by central cross-band and lines on forewing, which are intense blackish grey. Central band is also generally more irregular, more deeply pinched in leading half, and spreads more widely along trailing edge, often reaching trailing corner.

Flight season One generation. Mid May-early July. Comes regularly to light.

Life cycle Overwinters as a pupa. Larva late June-early September. Pupates in a hard cocoon formed on the bark of the foodplant.

Larval foodplants Alder and birches.

Habitat Woodland, copses and sometimes gardens.

Status & distribution Resident. Local. Found mainly in south-east and south-west England, central and south-east Wales and the West Midlands, where fairly frequent. Also found very locally in East Anglia, Nottinghamshire (since 1990), Derbyshire and Lancashire, and previously recorded from Yorkshire and Co. Durham.

Sallow Kitten   page 229

Furcula furcula (Cl.)

Common. T   1997(8708)

Field characters & Similar species FW 14-18mm. Like Poplar Kitten, the central cross-band is grey, and its inner edge is usually more or less straight. However, its outer edge is usually rather irregular and usually only finely (sometimes faintly) outlined in black in the leading half. Antennae feathered in male. See also Alder Kitten.

Flight season Two generations over much of Britain, May-June and July-August. One generation in Scotland and Ireland, June-early July. Comes regularly to light.

Life cycle Overwinters as a pupa. Larva June-mid July and August-September, or July-September where one generation. Can be found both on large trees or small plants consisting of just a few shoots, usually in quite open, sunny places. Pupates in a hard cocoon formed on the bark of the foodplant or on a post.

Larval foodplants Usually willows, including Grey Willow, Goat Willow and White Willow; also Aspen and poplars, including examples only 30cm tall.

Habitat Most frequent in open parts of woodland, scrub and carr; also hedgerows, parkland, moorland, heathland and sometimes gardens.

Status & distribution Resident. Common. Well distributed and fairly frequent in England, especially in the south, and in Wales. Somewhat more thinly distributed in mainland Scotland, the Inner Hebrides and Orkney. Recently recorded from many places in Northern Ireland, with a wide scatter of records in the Irish Republic. Recorded once from Jersey, in 1924.

Poplar Kitten   page 229

Furcula bifida (Brahm)

Local. S,C   1998(8710)

Field characters & Similar species FW 16-22mm. Very similar to Sallow Kitten, but generally larger (female of both species being generally larger, with un-feathered antennae). Outer edge of central cross-band on forewing is obtusely angled or gently curved, but not irregular, and quite thickly outlined with black in the leading half. See also Alder Kitten.

Flight season One generation. Late May-July. Comes to light, usually in small numbers.

Life cycle Overwinters as a pupa. Larva late June-mid September. Pupates in a hard cocoon on the bark of the foodplant.

Larval foodplants Usually poplars or Aspen, but also reported from willows.

Habitat Most frequent in poplar plantations, but found in woodland and sometimes gardens.

Status & distribution Resident. Local. Widely distributed and fairly frequent in England and eastern Wales, but much less frequent in northern England. Rare in Ireland, where most records are from the eastern part of Northern Ireland and from Co. Galway.

1999 see below 2019

Iron Prominent   page 229

Notodonta dromedarius (L.)

Common. T   2000(8716)

Field characters FW 18-24mm. Quite distinctive. Dark grey-brown forewing has reddish-brown, rusty-brown streaks near base and in outer half, where there is also a narrow, broken, rusty-brown cross-band. Central cross-lines are variably edged with straw yellow, and central area may be lightly dusted with pale grey. In northern England and Scotland ground-colour is darker and sometimes markings are rather faint.

Similar species See Large Dark Prominent.

Flight season Two generations in southern and central Britain, May-June and late July-August. One generation in the north, June-July. Comes to light, usually in small numbers.

Life cycle Overwinters as a pupa in a slight cocoon underground. Larva mid June-late July and September-early October, but in the north and in Ireland mainly in August.

Larval foodplants Mainly birches and Alder, sometimes Hazel; also reported on oaks.

Habitat Broadleaved woodland, heathland, carr, riverbanks, and sometimes gardens.

Status & distribution Resident. Common. Well distributed and frequent throughout mainland Britain, Scilly, Man and the Inner Hebrides, but rather restricted to the lowlands, river valleys and coasts in the north. Quite well distributed in Northern Ireland and the Burren, Co. Clare, and with scattered records throughout the Irish Republic. Widespread but occasional on Jersey, rare on Guernsey.

Larva of Pebble Prominent.

199

Large Dark Prominent

page 229

Notodonta torva (Hb.)

Rare immigrant.   2001(8717)

Field characters & Similar species FW 19-25mm. Similar in size and general pattern to Iron Prominent, but in colour rather like a small, dark, unusually plain Great Prominent. Forewing greenish grey, with a rather pale texture, the whole effect being created by a dusting of yellowish scales. There are two darker, sometimes pale-edged and sometimes faint wavy cross-lines and an elongated pale, dark-centred central spot. There is also a blackish form with pale cross-lines. The male, which is smaller and darker, could possibly be overlooked as a worn Iron Prominent, but lacks the light brown blotch at base of forewing, or any trace of rusty brown.

Flight season Usually two generations in central Europe. May and August. Comes to light.

Life cycle Overwinters as a pupa on or below the ground. Larva July and late August-September.

Larval foodplants Aspen, other poplars and apparently birches.

Habitat Damp woodlands and peat bogs.

Status & distribution Rare immigrant, recorded twice only in Britain. The first was reared from either an egg or a larva found in north Norfolk in 1882, and initially identified as a Great Prominent. The second came to a light-trap at Eastbourne, Sussex, on 29 May 1979. A widespread moth in central and northern Europe.

Three-humped Prominent

page 229

Notodonta tritophus ([D. & S.])

Immigrant.   2002(8718)

Field characters & Similar species FW 22-27mm. Quite distinctive, with broad, rounded and extensively blackish-grey forewing and usually rather ill-defined narrow, tawny brown central and outer cross-bands. Somewhat similar to Iron Prominent in markings and Pebble Prominent in coloration, but larger than both, with broader forewing and leading edge more arched, and distinguished by pale oval ring marking in centre of forewing, which is much bigger and more elongated than the ring on Iron Prominent and is absent from Pebble Prominent. Has dark grey patch at base of forewing and lacks the heavy outline marking at inner edge of 'pebble' patch on Pebble Prominent.

Flight season Two generations in much of mainland Europe, April-June and late July-August, but only one in northern parts. Has occurred in the British Isles, May-August.

Life cycle Overwinters as a pupa underground. Larva June-July and late August-September, or July-August where there is one generation.

Larval foodplants Aspen and other poplars.

Habitat In mainland Europe found in woodland, river valleys, poplar plantations, parks and gardens.

Status & distribution Immigrant. First found in Britain as a larva beaten from Aspen in 1842 and reared to adult. Several records of adults or larvae later in the 19th century, including two in Suffolk: an adult at a gas-lamp in Ipswich in about 1867, and one at a lighted shop window in Southwold in 1884. Between 1900-1999 there were nine further records, all of single adults, and mainly at light-traps near the south and east coasts. These were in Bedfordshire (Bedford, 1907), Hampshire (Havant and Waterlooville, 1920), Isle of Wight (Freshwater, 1956; Cranmore, 1960), Suffolk (Walberswick, 1992), Essex (Jaywick, 1998) and Kent (Folkestone, 1955; Dymchurch, 1998). A male came to light at Lydd, Kent, on 3 August 2002.

Pebble Prominent

page 229

Notodonta ziczac (L.)

Common. T   2003(8719)

Field characters FW 17-24mm. Darker, outer pebble-like blotch of light brown forewing usually contrasts with light brown base and central whitish area in leading half. The demarcation is emphasised by the very large, curved, thick, crescent-shaped black central mark. This pattern is diagnostic, although colour and intensity are somewhat variable. Sometimes, especially in Scotland, cross-lines are stronger, white area is brighter, pebble-mark is paler and less well defined, and occasionally ground-colour is reddish brown.

Similar species See Three-humped Prominent.

Flight season Two generations in southern and

central Britain, May-June and late July-August. One generation in the north, June-July. Comes regularly to light.
Life cycle Overwinters as a pupa underground. Larva June-July and mid August-late September in the south, and July-August in northern Britain. Can be found on small plants in open situations, even on cliff faces, as well as on larger trees.
Larval foodplants Sallows, willows, Aspen and poplars, including cultivated varieties.
Habitat Most places where the foodplants grow, from mature woodland to hedgerows and gardens.
Status & distribution Resident. Common. Frequent throughout most of Great Britain and Ireland, although less frequent at higher altitudes, and not recorded from Shetland. Widespread and frequent in the Channel Islands.

2004 and 2005 below 2019

Lesser Swallow Prominent   page 229

Pheosia gnoma (Fabr.)
Common. T   2006(8728)

Field characters FW 20-26mm. Silvery white forewing is strongly tapered, with bold black and brown markings along edges. Diagnostic feature is the distinct, clean white wedge extending from trailing corner, reaching less than halfway to wing base. Variation is slight. In northern Britain, thorax is either very pale or very dark. Antennae are slightly feathered in male.
Similar species See Swallow Prominent.
Flight season Mainly two generations. Late April-June and July-August. One generation in northern Scotland, late May-early August. Comes to light, sometimes abundantly near birch scrub.
Life cycle Overwinters as a pupa, in a strong cocoon underground. Larva June-July and late August-September, and July-September in northern Scotland.
Larval foodplants Silver Birch and Downy Birch.
Habitat Woodland, heathland, moorland, downland, parks and gardens.
Status & distribution Resident. Common. Widely distributed and fairly frequent throughout most of mainland Britain, Ireland and the Channel Islands, except on high ground.

Swallow Prominent   page 229

Pheosia tremula (Cl.)
Common. T   2007(8727)

Field characters & Similar species FW 22-28mm. Very similar to Lesser Swallow Prominent, but often larger (although variable in size), with a longer, narrower, greyish-white and rather indistinct wedge extending from trailing corner, reaching at least halfway to wing base. In Lesser Swallow Prominent this wedge is shorter and more distinct. On hindwing a fine whitish line runs around margin, through dark blotch at trailing corner. Variation is mainly in extent of brownish tint, which may be very faint, especially

in examples from Scotland.
Flight season Mainly two generations. Late April-June and August. One generation in northern Britain, June-August. Comes to light, sometimes in fair numbers.
Life cycle Overwinters as a pupa underground. Larva June-July and late August-September, and July-September in northern Britain.
Larval foodplants Aspen, other poplars, willows and sallows.
Habitat Woodland, poplar plantations and shelter-belts, scrub, carr, gardens and parks.
Status & distribution Resident. Common. Well distributed and fairly frequent in most parts of Great Britain, Ireland and the Channel Islands, but more local in mainland Scotland and the Inner Hebrides and not recorded from the Outer Hebrides, Orkney and Shetland.

Coxcomb Prominent   page 229

Ptilodon capucina (L.)
Common. T   2008(8738)

Field characters FW 17-22mm. The rather uniform, pale or dark warm brown ground-colour of forewing, distinct dark scale tuft on trailing edge and large forward-pointing, quiff-like cream-centred tuft on thorax, are diagnostic. There is little variation in markings.
Similar species Maple Prominent is generally similar, but has a large white patch at forewing margin, and is smaller.
Flight season Mainly two generations. Late April-June and August-early September, except in the far north, where there is almost certainly one generation, May-July. Comes fairly regularly to light, usually in small numbers. Very occasionally active by day.
Life cycle Overwinters as a pupa, in a cocoon underground. Larva June-July and mid August-September, and June-August where there is one generation. Can be found on low growth and larger trees.
Larval foodplants A wide variety of broadleaved trees, including birches, Hazel, Alder, Aspen, sallows, hawthorns, limes, oaks, Beech, Rowan and rose.
Habitat Woodland and scrub in most situations, including parks and gardens.
Status & distribution Resident. Common. Well distributed and fairly frequent throughout most of the British Isles, but not recorded from the Outer Hebrides, Orkney and Shetland. Widespread but occasional on Jersey.

Maple Prominent   page 229

Ptilodon cucullina ([D. & S.])
Local. S,E   2009(8739)

Field characters FW 15-20mm. Easily recognised by large whitish blotch along outer margin of brown forewing. Leading edge and leading half near base are paler. There is very little variation.
Similar species Coxcomb Prominent lacks white forewing patches, has a more uniform ground-colour over forewings and is slightly larger.

Flight season One generation. Mid May-late July, sometimes later. A male in fresh condition came to a light-trap near Sevenoaks, Kent, on 28 September 2001. Male comes regularly to light, female less often.
Life cycle Overwinters as a pupa. Larva June-late August. Pupates in a strong cocoon in moss on the trunk of the foodplant, in leaf litter or underground.
Larval foodplants Field Maple, occasionally Sycamore and cultivated maples.
Habitat Broadleaved woodland and scrub; also hedgerows and gardens, preferring calcareous soils.
Status & distribution Resident. Local. Formerly Nationally Scarce but seems to be expanding its range northwards and westwards. Found mainly in southern and south-east England, west to the Isle of Wight, in East Anglia, and eastern England, where it is now found regularly in Peterborough, which is near its northern limit. Also found in western Somerset and south Devon, and recorded from south Wales.

Larva of Maple Prominent.

201

Apart from a general resemblance to a fragment of broken wood, the most diagnostic characters are the large, upturned palps at the front and divided tail tufts on the long abdomen of male. Forewing greyish-straw with dark veins and dots, sometimes with a rather blurred dark brownish central crossband, or less often generally darker. Has prominent dark scale tuft on trailing edge, and sometimes fringes are distinctly scalloped. Antennae feathered, quite strongly in male, only slightly in female.
Similar species None.
Flight season Mainly two generations, May-June and July-August. One generation in northern Britain, late May-June. Male comes regularly to light, female very infrequently.
Life cycle Overwinters as a pupa, in a cocoon below the foodplant, on or just below the soil surface. Larva July and late August-September, and July-August in the north.
Larval foodplants Aspen, other poplars, and willows, including low re-growth.
Habitat Most situations where the foodplants grow. Often regular in gardens.
Status & distribution Resident. Common. Fairly frequent throughout southern Britain south of the Humber, and apparently expanding its range in Yorkshire. More local and less frequent in the remainder of northern England and in mainland Scotland, particularly favouring the Great Glen and the south-west. Widespread in Ireland. Widespread but occasional on Jersey, rare on Guernsey, Alderney and Sark.

Scarce Prominent   page 229
Odontosia carmelita (Esp.)
Local. S,N   2010(8741)

Field characters FW 18-21mm. Quite distinctive. The creamy-white comma mark in outer part of leading edge of forewing is constant and diagnostic. Forewing reddish brown or purplish brown, heavily dusted with silvery grey, especially in trailing half. Fringes are chequered creamy white and dark brown. There is little variation, but Scottish examples are darker.
Similar species None.
Flight season One generation. April-May. Male comes regularly to light, female only occasionally.
Life cycle Overwinters as a pupa, in a cocoon on or just below ground. Larva May-July. Tall trees are preferred, and larvae are seldom found on low re-growth or isolated trees, or in areas only recently colonised by birches.
Larval foodplants Silver Birch and Downy Birch.
Habitat Mainly long-established birch woodland.
Status & distribution Resident. Local. Somewhat overlooked until the advent of portable ultra-violet light traps. Widely distributed and fairly frequent in southern and south-east England. Also found locally in south-east Wales (Wye Valley), Gloucestershire (Forest of Dean), Nottinghamshire (Sherwood Forest), the West Midlands and Yorkshire. Widespread in Cumbria and Northumberland and in Scotland, where it is most often recorded along the Spey and Dee river valleys. Very few records from Ireland, but known to be present in the south-west in Co. Kerry and the south-east in Co. Wicklow, and since 1980 discovered in Northern Ireland in Cos. Fermanagh and Tyrone.

Pale Prominent   page 229
Pterostoma palpina (Cl.)
Common. T   2011(8732)

Field characters FW 18-25mm. Very distinctive.

White Prominent   page 229
Leucodonta bicoloria ([D. & S.])
Former resident/suspected immigrant. 2012(8736)

Field characters FW 16-19mm. An utterly distinctive white moth, with unique orange markings edged with black on forewing.
Similar species None.
Flight season One generation. June. Comes to light.
Life cycle Overwinters as a pupa in a slight cocoon among leaf litter or just below ground. Larva June-August. Has been beaten from lower branches.
Larval foodplants Birches.
Habitat Long-established woodland with mature birches.

Status & distribution Former resident, possibly still surviving in Ireland, where it was first found near Killarney, Co. Kerry, in June 1859, and for a year or two subsequently. Also recorded from other sites in Co. Kerry, but no reliable records since 1938, despite many searches. A singleton was reported from Burnt Wood, Staffordshire, in 1861, with six more from the same site in 1865. One was reported from near Exeter, Devon, in 1880, possibly an immigrant, and one from Jersey, in 1905.

Plumed Prominent   page 229
Ptilophora plumigera ([D. & S.])
Na. SE   2013(8734)

Field characters FW 16-19mm. The very broadly feathered antennae of male, rather narrow, thinly-scaled wings with smooth outer margins and late flight season are diagnostic. Forewing in male varies from straw yellow with reddish blotches and a darker central cross-band, to largely reddish brown with yellow cross-lines. Female is duller, even more thinly scaled and has un-feathered antennae.

Similar species None.

Flight season One generation. November-December. Male comes to light from about an hour after dark on mild nights, often in numbers. Female arrives in smaller numbers much later in the night.

Life cycle Starts the winter as a pupa suspended in a brittle cocoon among leaf litter below the foodplant. The eggs are laid on bare twigs in November-December. Larva late April-July.

Larval foodplants Field Maple. Occasionally beaten from Sycamore.

Habitat Woodland, shelterbelts and hedgerows on calcareous soils, with mature Field Maple.

Status & distribution Resident. Nationally Scarce A. Found in scattered colonies in southern and south-west England, from Dorset to Suffolk and Kent, with populations in the Chilterns and Cotswolds and old unconfirmed records from Herefordshire and Devon, at least one of which is supported by a specimen. There is also a record from the Gower Peninsula, Glamorgan, of one in a Rothamsted light-trap in 1973.

Marbled Brown   page 229
Drymonia dodonaea ([D. & S.])
Local. S,C,NW   2014(8721)

Field characters FW 17-20mm. Quite variable, from mainly whitish to grey, with rather blurred cross-lines and bands on forewing. The rare f. *nigrescens* Lempke has almost entirely blackish forewing, and is most often found in East Anglia.

Similar species Lunar Marbled Brown has a distinct central black comma or crescent on forewing, clear black cross-lines, and outer area is always grey.

Flight season One generation. Late May-early July. Male comes regularly to light, female rarely. Sometimes found at rest on oak trunks.

Life cycle Overwinters as a pupa in a cocoon underground below the foodplant. Larva late June-early

September, rarely seen or beaten, suggesting they are mainly high in the tree canopy.

Larval foodplants Oak, probably both Pedunculate and Sessile.

Habitat Long-established woodland in which mature oaks remain plentiful.

Status & distribution Resident. Local. Widely distributed and locally frequent in England, Wales, south-west Scotland and north to west Inverness-shire, mainly in areas where substantial oak woodlands remain. Also recorded in Ireland, in Cos. Kerry and Cork. One on Jersey, in 1997.

Lunar Marbled Brown   page 229
Drymonia ruficornis (Hufn.)
Common. T   2015(8722)

Field characters FW 16-20mm. This rather thickset grey and white moth has a prominent black comma in the pale, usually whitish central cross-band on forewing. Basal and outer areas vary from light to dark grey, but markings are fairly constant. Occasionally central band is entirely grey, and there is a rare, almost entirely blackish form.

Similar species See Marbled Brown, which is not normally on the wing until late May.

Flight season One generation. April-May. Comes regularly to light.

Life cycle Overwinters as a pupa just below ground, often near the surface roots of the foodplant. Larva late May-late July, occasionally beaten from lower branches of mature trees.

Larval foodplants Oaks, both Pedunculate and Sessile; also probably Turkey Oak.

Habitat A wider range of habitats than Marbled Brown, including oaks in hedgerows and parks as well as woodlands, often visiting garden light-traps if there are oaks in the vicinity.

Status & distribution Resident. Common. Well distributed in England south of the Wash, and in Wales. More local in the Midlands, northern England and southern and central parts of mainland Scotland. Widespread in Ireland.

Dusky Marbled Brown   page 229
Gluphisia crenata (Esp.)

ssp. *vertunea* Bray
Rare immigrant; possible former resident.
                                            2016(8747)

Field characters & Similar species FW 14-15mm. Not unlike one of the darkest forms of Marbled Brown or Lunar Marbled Brown, but smaller with a small but distinct pale central comma mark, and a brownish central cross-band.

Flight season Two generations in central and southern Europe. April and June-July. Only one generation further north. Comes to light.

Life cycle Overwinters as a pupa in a cocoon, usually spun between leaves of the foodplant.

Larval foodplants Aspen and other poplars.

Habitat In mainland Europe, a wide range of habitats in which poplars grow.

Status & distribution Rare immigrant and possible former resident. There are three records from the mid 19th century that may be authentic: two females at Ongar Park Wood, Essex, one in June 1839 and one in June 1841, and a larva beaten from poplar at Halton, Buckinghamshire, in August 1853. There is also an unconfirmed report of three 'among aspens' on the Isle of Man, in 1870. There have been no further records from mainland Britain since, but a male came to a light-trap at Gorey, Jersey, on 28th July 1995. Recorded from Scandinavia to the Mediterranean.

Pygaerinae

Small Chocolate-tip   page 230
Clostera pigra (Hufn.)
Nb. T   2017(8699)

Field characters & Similar species FW 11-14mm. Distinguished from Chocolate-tip and Scarce Chocolate-tip by its smaller size and poorly-defined chocolate-brown blotch near tip of forewing. Some individuals have a very dark grey ground-colour, especially in the cooler northern and western parts of its distribution, sometimes with brighter, more contrasting markings.

Flight season Two generations in southern Britain, May and August, with occasional individuals in October. One generation in northern Britain and Ireland, June-July. Comes to light, usually late in the night; has also been reported flying by day.

Life cycle Overwinters as a pupa, in a cocoon among spun leaves of the foodplant. Larva late May-mid July and September-early October in the south, and August-mid September in the north. Hides by day between spun leaves, emerging to feed at night.

Larval foodplants Creeping Willow and other low-growing willows such as Eared Willow, and low re-growth of Aspen.

Habitat Open, damp places, including fens, marshes, broads, damp heathland, dune-slacks and moorland. Formerly in open woodland and coppiced areas, but there are rather few records from this habitat recently.

Status & distribution Resident. Nationally Scarce B. Probably overlooked, but possibly in decline as breeding sites become overgrown, shaded or overgrazed. Most easily recorded as a larva. Rather thinly scattered throughout mainland Britain and Ireland, except some central and upland areas. In the south, most frequently recorded in Dorset, Hampshire, Sussex, Surrey and Kent, but now considered local and scarce here. Also recorded from the Hebrides. One reported from Jersey, in 1925.

Scarce Chocolate-tip   page 230
Clostera anachoreta ([D. & S.])
RDB. SE   2018(8700)

Field characters & Similar species FW 14-19mm.

Similar to Chocolate-tip, but the well-defined chocolate-brown blotch at tip of forewing extends both sides of outermost white cross-line, and there is a prominent black spot and a second smaller one near trailing corner. See also Chocolate-tip and Small Chocolate-tip.

Flight season Two generations. April-May and late July-August, with occasional individuals of a partial third generation in October.

Life cycle Overwinters as a pupa spun between leaves of the foodplant, the autumn generation falling with them to the ground. Larva June-July and August-September. Hides by day between spun leaves, emerging to feed at night.

Larval foodplants Sallow scrub, mainly Grey Willow. Eggs and larvae have also been found in Britain on other sallows, willows, Aspen and poplars.

Habitat The single known breeding population is on coastal shingle colonised by scrub.

Status & distribution Nationally rare resident and suspected immigrant. Red Data Book species. Currently known to breed only at Dungeness, Kent, where it has been recorded almost annually since 1978, both as adults and larvae. Previously recorded in south-east Kent at regular intervals, usually as larvae, from 1858-1912, and as occasional adults in light-traps from 1951 onwards. Elsewhere, single examples have been recorded at light at Bradwell-on-Sea, Essex (1976, 1981, 1997), Waldringfield, Suffolk (1956) and Southwold, Suffolk (1976). The adult was also recorded in Ipswich, Suffolk (1898) and Clacton, Essex (1908). Immature stages have been found at St Leonards, Sussex, in 1893 (eggs), Dovercourt, Essex, in 1907 (larvae) and Canford Cliffs, in 1909 (eggs). Very local and rare on Jersey.

Chocolate-tip   page 230
Clostera curtula (L.)
Local. S, (N)   2019(8698)

Field characters & Similar species FW 13-18mm. Quite distinctive. The well-defined chocolate-brown blotch at tip of forewing stops abruptly at outermost white cross-line, in contrast to that of Scarce Chocolate-tip, which extends beyond it. There is little variation. See also Small Chocolate-tip.

Flight season Two generations. April-May and August-September. In Scotland there is one genera-tion, in June. Comes to light, usually late at night and in small numbers.

Life cycle Overwinters as a pupa, in a cocoon formed between leaves of the foodplant, falling with them to the ground in the autumn. Larva May-June and August-September in England, and July-August in Scotland. Hides by day between spun leaves, emerging to feed at night.

Larval foodplants Aspen, other poplars, sallows and willows.

Habitat Woodland, scrub, carr, poplar plantations, shelterbelts, hedgerows and other situations in which the foodplants grow, including gardens.

Status & distribution Resident. Local. Well distrib-uted in south-east, southern and central England and

Larva of Buff-tip.

204

East Anglia, and extending more locally north and west to the ancient woodlands of central Lincolnshire, Somerset, eastern Glamorgan, Monmouthshire and the south-west Midlands. Also found locally in Scotland, in Inverness-shire and Aberdeenshire. This isolated population is probably the result of a previous colonisation from mainland Europe. Rare in the Channel Islands.

Phalerinae

Buff-tip   page 230
Phalera bucephala (L.)
Common. T   1994(8750)

Field characters FW M 22-26mm F 26-34mm. Unmistakable. When at rest, with wings held almost vertically against the body, this large moth closely resembles a broken birch twig. This is due to the buff blotches on the tip of the forewing and front of thorax, both of which are emphasised by dark edging. There is little variation.
Similar species None.
Flight season One generation. Late May-July. Occasionally found at rest by day, either on a twig or on the ground. Comes to light, usually after midnight, sometimes in numbers.
Life cycle Overwinters as a pupa underground in an earthen cell. Larva July-early October. Larvae hatch from large batches of eggs and feed initially in groups by day and night, and later singly. Often

Larva of Lobster Moth.

wanders across the ground before pupation.
Larval foodplants Most frequently on sallows, birches, oaks and Hazel but recorded from many other broadleaved trees and shrubs such as Alder, limes, elms, Beech, Rowan, Hornbeam and Sycamore. Prefers bushes and small trees in sunny locations.
Habitat Open woodland, scrub, hedgerows and gardens.
Status & distribution Resident. Common. Well distributed and frequent throughout England, Wales, Man and the Channel Islands. More local in mainland Scotland, but more frequent in the west, including the Inner Hebrides. Widespread in Ireland, particularly near the coasts. Now known to be well distributed through Northern Ireland; probably under-recorded inland in the Irish Republic.

Heterocampinae

Lobster Moth   page 230
Stauropus fagi (L.)
Common. S,WC   1999(8758)

Field characters FW 24-33mm. Quite distinctive. Forewing and hindwing grey-brown, dusted with grey (especially near base) and yellowish. There is a russet-brown smear along trailing edge of forewing, also yellowish cross-lines and a series of blackish spots near outer edge. The darker f. *obscura* Rebel is widespread, but most frequent near London. Particularly large, pale forms are found in Ireland. Rests with hindwings protruding from under leading edge of forewings, resembling a bunch of dead leaves. Male has feathery brown antennae.
Similar species Great Prominent has a greenish tint. Pale Tussock and Dark Tussock are grey and lack russet patch, have very furry forelegs which are held far forwards at rest, while hindwings are completely hidden.
Flight season One generation. Mid May-July. Comes to light, male frequently but female rarely.
Life cycle Overwinters as a pupa, in a cocoon spun among leaves or in the soil. Larva late June-September.
Larval foodplants Birches, Hazel, oaks and Beech. Has also been reported on hawthorns, Alder, Blackthorn, Apple, Dog-rose and limes. Gravid females have been seen investigating Aspen, on which larvae will feed, and willows are accepted in captivity. Can be found on both mature trees and low scrub.
Habitat Mainly found in areas of long-established woodland, and absent from many woods and plantations within its range although foodplants are present.
Status & distribution Resident. Common. Well distributed and sometimes frequent in southern, south-west and south-east England, and in Wales. More local in East Anglia and the southern half of the Midlands. In Ireland recorded only from the south-west, in Cos. Cork and Kerry. One record from Guernsey, in 1999.

Tawny Prominent
Harpyia milhauseri (Fabr.)
Rare immigrant.

page 230

2004(8760)

Field characters FW 21-24mm. Quite distinctive. Forewing pale grey, obscurely marked and streaked with dark grey. There are two parallel blackish streaks in trailing half near base, and a thick, dark, outer cross-line is evident in trailing half. There is sometimes a rather faint, light brown central cross-band. Hindwing whitish, with a very noticeable blackish blotch at trailing corner, and shoulders are distinctly pale. Basal three-quarters of antennae are feathered, quite strongly in male.
Similar species None.
Flight season In central Europe, one generation. May-June. Comes to light.
Life cycle Overwinters as a pupa, in a hard cocoon behind bark or in leaf litter. Larva June-August.
Larval foodplants Oaks, including Holm or Evergreen Oak, and sometimes Beech, Hornbeam and birches.
Habitat Woodland and also lightly wooded places.
Status & distribution Rare immigrant. Recorded twice in Britain. Both examples were in light-traps, one at Aldwick Bay, West Sussex, on 11 June 1966, and one at Dungeness, Kent, on 24 May 1993. Favours the warmer parts of central and southern Europe, but its distribution includes Belgium and southern Denmark.

Great Prominent
Peridea anceps (Goeze)
Local. S,WC,(NW)

page 230

2005(8754)

Field characters FW 23-32mm. The complex grey, dull yellow and brown marbling and streaking on forewing results in a rather greenish tint, and makes this moth distinctive. Hindwing yellowish white, and when at rest protrude from under leading edge of forewings. The uncommon f. *fusca* Cock. is much darker, almost black in some cases, and is found in the Lake District, occasionally in Surrey and elsewhere.
Similar species Lobster Moth has no trace of green. See also Large Dark Prominent.
Flight season One generation. Late April-June. Male comes regularly to light, female less frequently.
Life cycle Overwinters as a pupa well underground. Larva late May-early August. Seldom beaten and usually associated with the canopy of mature trees, but sometimes found wandering over the ground prior to pupation.
Larval foodplants Mature Pedunculate Oak and Sessile Oak.
Habitat Broadleaved woodland. Also on mature oaks in hedgerows and gardens, in well-wooded districts.
Status & distribution Resident. Local. Widely distributed in the well-wooded parts of southern south-east and south-west England, the south Midlands and Wales. More local in central and

Larva of Great Prominent.

eastern England but extending up the west coast to Cumbria, south-west Scotland and west Perthshire.

Dilobinae

In most recent British publications this moth has been relocated to the end of the Notodontidae, as in mid 19th-century textbooks, although in the current European checklist it is placed back in the Noctuidae.

Figure of Eight
Diloba caeruleocephala (L.)
Common. S,C,(N)

page 230

2020(9331)

Field characters FW 15-19mm. Forewing grey, tinged with lilac and brown. The two yellowish-white, darker-centred central marks on forewing are diagnostic, in that the innermost one resembles the number eight, and is often joined to its outer neighbour, which is more variable. Antennae of male are feathered.
Similar species Figure of Eighty and Poplar Lutestring have somewhat similar central marks, but it is the outer one that resembles the figure eight. Also, they do not normally fly in the late autumn, their forewings are broader and their antennae are not feathered.
Flight season One generation. Late September-mid November. Comes to light and can be numerous in scrubby habitat.
Life cycle Overwinters as an egg, laid in small groups on twigs of the larval foodplant. Larva late April-mid July. Most often found in open, sunny places, but also in shady situations. Pupates in a cocoon formed in soil or leaf litter.
Larval foodplants Blackthorn, hawthorns, Crab Apple, wild roses and fruit trees, including Bullace, Cherry Plum, cultivated Plum and Pear.
Habitat Most habitats in which the foodplants grow, including gardens, hedgerows and woodland.
Status & distribution Resident. Common. Well distributed throughout most of England, Wales and southern Scotland, but apparently absent from Cornwall and rare in south Wales. Very thinly scattered in central and northern mainland Scotland, mainly near the coast north of the Firth of Forth, reaching the Moray Firth, and in Ireland. Local and rare in the Channel Islands.

Thaumetopoeidae – Processionary moths

Pine Processionary

A small family of about 100 species worldwide, with five species in Europe, two of which have been recorded in the British Isles, one as an immigrant, the other as a possible immigrant or accidental import. The adults are stout and furry and somewhat resemble the Lasiocampidae in shape and build. At rest, they hold the coarse-scaled wings close to the body. They have feathered antennae. The hairy larvae live in groups in silken webs and contact with them can cause severe skin irritation. At night, they leave their web in procession to feed, following silk trails produced by the foremost larvae, and pupate in cocoons formed within the larval web. Both species are forest pests in mainland Europe.

Pine Processionary   page 230
Thaumetopoea pityocampa ([D. & S.])
Possible rare immigrant.   2021(8691)

Field characters FW M 16-17mm F 18-22mm. Diagnostic feature is bold dark comma mark in centre of grey forewing. The two wavy cross-lines vary in intensity.
Similar species See Oak Processionary. Pale Eggar lacks a central crescent mark on forewing and cross-lines are much wavier.
Flight season One generation. Late May-early July. Comes to light, especially male.
Life cycle Overwinters as an egg, attached to the foodplant. Larva April-June.
Larval foodplants Pines.
Habitat In mainland Europe, in pine forests, usually on light or sandy soils.
Status & distribution Possible rare immigrant. Originally added to the British list after a highly dubious report of larvae near Southborough, Kent, in 1874. A single example came to light in July 1966 at Burghfield Common, Berkshire, and the recorder speculated that it could have been imported accidentally. Resident in central and southern Europe.

Oak Processionary   page 230
Thaumetopoea processionea (L.)
Immigrant; resident in Channel Islands.
                                          2022(8689)

Field characters & Similar species FW M 14-16mm F 16-17mm. Similar to Pine Processionary, but browner, and also distinguished by pale basal area of forewing, and central crescent mark, which is small and usually rather faint. Cross-lines smooth rather than jagged.
Flight season One generation. July-September. Nocturnal. Both sexes come to light, especially the male.
Life cycle Overwinters as an egg, in batches, attached to the foodplant. Larva May-June.
Larval foodplants Oaks, preferring mature trees.
Habitat Broadleaved woodland.
Status & Distribution Immigrant. Resident locally on Jersey, Channel Islands, where it was first reported in 1984. On Guernsey, first recorded on 18 August 1983, with several subsequently, as suspected immigrants. In mainland Britain 19 immigrants, all males, occurred in the 20th century, the first on 19 August 1983, at Mawnan Smith, Cornwall. In 1992, two were reported at Dungeness and one at nearby Greatstone, Kent, on 9 and 10 August respectively. In 1995, 12 were recorded between 3 and 13 August, in Kent, Essex, Cambridgeshire, Suffolk, Norfolk and Northamptonshire. In 1996, one was trapped at Worth Matravers, Dorset, on 19 August. In 1998 the moth was recorded twice, at Freshwater on the Isle of Wight, on 1 and 6 September, the last of the century. Widespread in central and southern Europe, extending north to Scandinavia.

2023 see Appendix

Lymantriidae – Tussock moths

This family of about 2,700 species is distributed throughout the world, but with more species in the Old World tropics than elsewhere. Eleven have been recorded in the British Isles, of which two are extinct residents and one has established itself only

Dark Tussock   Yellow-tail

briefly. These are furry, medium-sized or fairly large moths. They are collectively called tussocks on account of the characteristic tufts of hair on the backs of the larvae, which are incorporated into their silken cocoons, formed above ground. The males have strongly feathered antennae, whereas those of the females are either simple or slightly feathered. The females of some species cover the eggs with hair from substantial furry tufts on the hind end of their abdomen. Those of two species have highly reduced wings and are flightless. The majority are strictly nocturnal. They come regularly to light, but do not feed. The males of three species fly both by day and night. All but two produce only one generation a year.

The larvae are hairy, and readily lose their hairs, especially when fully grown. The hairs cause skin irritation in some people, so the larvae should be handled with great care, or not at all. The severity varies between species, with Brown-tail larvae by far the worst in this respect, this species being accorded pest status as a result. The larvae of all but one species feed on woody plants.

Reed Tussock page 230
Laelia coenosa (Hb.)
Former resident; extinct. 2024(10410)

Field characters FW 16-21mm. The strong blackish feathering of antennae and pale buff forewing of male are a diagnostic combination. There are either no markings, or simply a curved line of small, rather faint blackish spots in outer part, running roughly parallel with outer margin and trailing corner. Female has plain whitish wings, and antennae are not feathered.
Similar species White Satin is larger, with a strong silky sheen and black and white ringed legs.
Flight season One generation. July-August. Nocturnal. Male comes regularly to light, but often settles in vegetation nearby rather than entering trap.
Life cycle Overwinters as a part-grown larva in vegetation near the foodplant. Larva August-June.
Larval foodplants Common Reed, Great Fen-sedge and Branched Bur-reed were the foodplants reported in Britain.
Habitat Fens.
Status & distribution Extinct former resident.

Discovered in Britain in 1819 at Whittlesea Mere, Huntingdonshire, and later found in nearby Yaxley Fen, and at Wicken and Burwell Fens in Cambridgeshire. Larvae and adults were quite frequent and were sold to collectors by reed-cutters. By 1855 all the known sites had been drained and ploughed up, except Wicken Fen, where the larvae had become scarcer by 1865. Numbers of males came to light-traps from 1871 to 1873, but numbers then dwindled rapidly and the last was seen in 1879.

Scarce Vapourer page 230
Orgyia recens (Hb.)
RDB. EC 2025(10396)

Field characters & Similar species FW M 13-17mm. Quite distinctive. The orange-brown and white marks near forewing tip, along with dark chocolate brown colour, easily distinguish male from that of Vapourer. In female, wings are reduced to tiny stumps and abdomen is swollen like Vapourer, but body is dark grey and furrier.
Flight season One main generation, June-July, with a partial second generation from August-October. Male flies by day with a fluttering, swooping flight.

Larva of Vapourer.

Sedentary female remains on her cocoon.
Life cycle Overwinters as a larva among the leaves of the foodplant. Larva August-June. The eggs are laid on the cocoon of the female, which is formed on the foodplant.
Larval foodplants Mainly hawthorns, oaks and sallows, but birches, Blackthorn, Rose, Bramble, Hazel, Heather, Alder Buckthorn, Meadowsweet, Common Sorrel and Rosebay Willowherb have been reported.
Habitat Lowland heath, wet woodland, fens and bogs. Also hedgerows.
Status & distribution Resident. Red Data Book species. Restricted to a small number of sites in south Yorkshire, north and south Lincolnshire, Nottinghamshire and Norfolk. Formerly widespread but local in central and southern England and parts of Wales. In decline in Yorkshire, where only nine of 26 known breeding sites have produced records since 1980.
Conservation Since either the early stages or the adult female are always on the foodplant, this species is threatened by the removal or over-zealous cutting of hedgerows and other vegetation, and by the draining of its habitats.

Vapourer
page 230
Orgyia antiqua (L.)
Common. T
2026(10397)

Field characters FW M 12-17mm. Male has rather plain orange-brown wings, occasionally darker, with indistinct darker cross-lines and a conspicuous white spot near trailing corner. Female has rudimentary wings and is flightless, light grey-brown with a swollen abdomen.
Similar species See Scarce Vapourer.
Flight season Probably one protracted generation, July-October, in the south. Usually September-October in the north. Male flies by day with an irregular, fluttering flight, often quite high, searching for the scent of female, and is sometimes mistaken for Brown Hairstreak butterfly. Male evidently also flies at night, occasionally coming to light. Wingless female is sedentary, remaining on her cocoon.
Life cycle Overwinters as an egg, in a batch of several hundred on the outside of the empty cocoon of the female, attached to some part of the food-

plant, or to a nearby fence, wall or other structure. Larva May-early September, sometimes with staggered hatching from egg batches.
Larval foodplants Most native broadleaved trees and shrubs, including birches, Hazel, sallows, hawthorns, Blackthorn, elms, limes, oaks and Bog-myrtle, and many cultivated bushes such as Cotoneaster and Pyracantha.
Habitat Frequent in gardens and parks, open woodland, fens, hedgerows, heathland, moorland and other scrubby places.
Status & distribution Resident. Common. Well distributed throughout England, Wales, Man and mainland Scotland and Ireland, except on high ground in the north. Also found in Orkney. Occasionally so numerous in towns that it defoliates small trees. Rare on Jersey, one recorded in 1992.

Dark Tussock
page 231
Dicallomera fascelina (L.)
Local. S,WC,NE
2027(10392)

Field characters & Similar species FW 18-28mm. Both Dark and Pale Tussock have a characteristic resting posture, with the very hairy front legs stretched forward, almost as far as they will go. However, they are quite different from one another and their habitat and flight season do not normally overlap. Forewing of Dark Tussock is usually darker, finely peppered with black. Black cross-lines usually edged with small orange blotches, and antennae grey. Darkest forms are normally found in northern England and Scotland and the palest in southern England. On shingle at Dungeness, Kent, the moths are unusually large.
Flight season One generation. July-August. Nocturnal and comes to light. Occasionally found at rest by day in Heather.
Life cycle Overwinters as a small larva, in a silk shelter. Larva late August-May or early June, except in Scotland, where it may hibernate over two winters.
Larval foodplants Heather is the main foodplant on heathland and moorland, Broom at Dungeness, Creeping Willow and other willows, Bramble, hawthorns and low birch re-growth.
Habitat Heathland, moorland, coastal sand-dunes and shingle.
Status & distribution Resident. Local. Well distributed and fairly frequent on the heaths of south-east Dorset, the New Forest, Hampshire, Surrey and Sussex, and on coastal shingle at Dungeness, Kent. There is a scattering of records from other lowland sites south of the Wash. Widespread on coastal sand-dunes in Cheshire and Lancashire, on moorland in Northumberland and on heathland in Co. Durham. Found in south-east Scotland, but most widespread on the moors of central, north-east and northern Scotland, especially the valleys of the Spey and Dee. Also occurs on coastal moorland in Aberdeenshire and on sand-dunes on the Moray Firth coast, but is apparently scarce or absent in western Scotland and

the islands. Very local on low moorland in Northern Ireland and the Irish Republic. Rare on Jersey and Guernsey.

Pale Tussock   page 231
Calliteara pudibunda (L.)
Common. S,C   2028(10387)

Field characters FW M 21-22mm, F 27-31mm. Resting posture similar to Dark Tussock. Male Pale Tussock has strongly feathered orange-brown antennae. Female is larger, usually without the dark central shading of male. The melanic f. *concolor* Cock., with plain blackish-grey forewing and dark grey hindwing, is now frequent in parts of southern England.
Similar species See Dark Tussock.
Flight season One generation. May-June. Male can be numerous at light, female comes in smaller numbers. Sometimes found at rest by day, particularly as mating pairs, on secluded stems of foodplant, blending with stems and looking like silken webbing.
Life cycle Overwinters as a pupa. Larva late June-early October, growing slowly. The thin silken cocoon is formed on the foodplant or among fallen debris below it.
Larval foodplants A wide variety of broadleaved trees and shrubs, including hawthorns, Blackthorn, Crab Apple, cultivated fruit trees, oaks, birches, Hazel, limes, elms, Hop and Barberry. Abundant in Hop fields prior to the use of insecticides, where it was known as the 'Hop-dog'.
Habitat Frequent in gardens, hedgerows and parks in urban and rural locations, also woodland, scrub and other bushy places, mainly in the lowlands but also along stream valleys in some upland places.
Status & distribution Resident. Common. Very widely and well distributed and frequent in England and Wales, north to Cumbria. Apparently absent from Scotland. Local on Man. In Ireland well distributed on the Burren limestone of Cos. Clare and Galway, in the south-west, and recorded sparsely elsewhere, mainly in the south, and in the southern parts of Northern Ireland. Widespread and frequent in the Channel Islands.

Brown-tail   page 231
Euproctis chrysorrhoea (L.)
Local. S, SE, EC   2029(10405)

Field characters FW M 16-20mm, F 18-19mm. Uppersides of wings usually slightly silky and pure white, although sometimes male has a few tiny black dots near trailing corner of forewing. In male, upperside of abdomen is very furry towards tip, and is deep chocolate-brown, or rusty-brown, but white at base, and antennae are strongly feathered. Female has only slightly feathered antennae, upperside of abdomen is dark brownish grey and there is a large, bulbous, dark brown tuft of hair at tip. The moth often raises or curls the abdomen into view if disturbed, as does Yellow-tail.

Similar species See Yellow-tail.
Flight season One generation. July-August, but occasionally a partial second generation in October. Comes to light.
Life cycle Overwinters as a small larva in a tough communal web on a foodplant stem. Larva late August-May. The eggs are laid in batches, covered with hair from the female's abdomen. The larval webs are usually on low growth, in open conditions exposed to full sun. Pupates in a cocoon formed among foliage or leaf litter, sometimes communally.
Larval foodplants Most frequently Bramble, Hawthorn, Blackthorn, Dog-rose and sallows. Also reported from Plum, Apple, Pear, cherries and Sea-buckthorn.
Habitat Coastal scrub, hedgerows, parks and gardens.
Status & distribution Resident. Local. Mainly found on or near the coast, where it is most frequent from Hampshire to Suffolk, and extends westwards to Cornwall and Scilly. Well established in the London area and increasingly found further west along the Thames Valley. Larvae were found recently in north Hampshire, and the moth may be expanding its range more widely inland. Small numbers (either immigrant or dispersing) are regularly captured elsewhere in southern England and East Anglia, and also further north along the east coast to Northumberland. Exceptionally, one was recorded in Scotland, on 7 August 1996, at Lunan Bay, Angus. Widespread and abundant in the Channel Islands.
Pest status The larval hairs cause severe skin irritation, and in urban areas they can reach pest proportions, such that windblown hairs cause skin rashes on people in the vicinity. For this reason it has been subject to local pest control measures for centuries.

Yellow-tail   page 231
Euproctis similis (Fuessl.)
Common. S,C,(N)   2030(10406)

Field characters & Similar species FW M 16-22mm, F 17-23mm. Not dissimilar to the Brown-tail, but slightly slimmer, with more rounded wings. Male has one or more dark grey or blackish spots near trailing corner of forewing, and occasionally near base. Abdomen is white with a golden yellow or orange-brown tip, larger (but not bulbous) in female. Female is larger, with unfeathered antennae, and with, at most, faint dark spots near trailing corner of forewing. See also White Satin Moth.
Flight season Usually one generation. July-August. Recently, a small partial second generation has been recorded north to Cumbria, usually in mid-October. Comes to light, sometimes in numbers, and may be found at rest by day among leaves of the foodplant, or beaten from low branches.
Life cycle Overwinters as a small larva, in a thin cocoon behind loose bark or among dead leaves. Larva August-June. Sits openly by day and is often quite conspicuous on hedges. Pupates in a cocoon formed on or below the foodplant.

209

Larva of Yellow-tail.

Larval foodplants Many broadleaved trees and shrubs. Particularly frequent on hawthorns and Blackthorn, but also often on birches, Hazel, oaks, sallows, elms and Barberry, especially in sunny situations.

Habitat Hedgerows, woodland, other scrubby places and gardens, including suburban and urban areas.

Status & distribution Resident. Common. Frequent throughout most of the southern half of Britain, except the higher ground of south-west England, Wales and the Pennines. Local in the northernmost counties of England and southern Scotland. Widespread on Man. Widespread but local in Ireland. Widespread and abundant in the Channel Islands.

White Satin Moth   page 231

Leucoma salicis (L.)

Local. S,EC,(WC,N)   2031(10414)

Field characters FW 18-27mm. Readily distinguished from other large, plain white moths by the strong silky sheen, black and white ringed legs and entirely white hair on abdomen. Sometimes a very pale buff streak along leading edge, but otherwise variation is rare. Male has strongly feathered antennae, which are black in centre, with white edges. Female is larger, with un-feathered antennae.

Similar species Black V Moth has central black V mark on forewing. See also extinct Reed Tussock (female), included for those working with old specimens, and Yellow-tail.

Flight season One generation. July-August. Comes to light, sometimes in numbers. Occasionally found by day, resting on the underside of leaves.

Life cycle Overwinters as a small larva, communally in a silk web on the foodplant. Larva late August-late June. Pupates in a hairy cocoon, usually in a bark crevice or among foliage on the foodplant.

Larval foodplants Aspen and other poplars, sallows and willows.

Habitat Sometimes abundant in poplar plantations and willow beds. Also found in hedgerows, scrub, woodland parks and gardens, particularly in river valleys and flood-plains.

Status & distribution Resident and immigrant. Local. Occurs in large numbers in some years, probably as a result of immigration. Found in most of the southern half of England, but most frequent in the south-east, including the London area, and increasingly local toward the south-west, where it may only be immigrant. Extends north to south Yorkshire, Lancashire and Cumbria. In Wales, frequent in the east, but rare in the west. Occasionally recorded on the east coast, north to Aberdeenshire, and in Orkney and Shetland, probably as an immigrant. In Ireland, one confirmed breeding site, near Newcastle, Co. Wicklow. Considered a rare suspected immigrant in the Channel Islands.

Black V Moth   page 231

Arctornis l-nigrum (Müll.)

Immigrant; transitory resident.   2032(10416)

Field characters FW 19-27mm. Wings are greenish white when freshly emerged, but quickly fade to white. The diagnostic thin black V-shaped central mark is usually evident, but may be obscure on worn examples. Other diagnostic features are the quite broad forewing, with a noticeably curved leading edge, the slight silky sheen, and the feathery antennae of the male, which are orange-brown.

Similar species See White Satin Moth.

Flight season One generation. Late June-July. Comes to light, particularly male. Moths fly to the tree-tops when released, suggesting that this is the normal roosting site.

Life cycle Overwinters as a small larva. Larva July-late May or June. Pupates in a cocoon formed among the leaves of the foodplant

Larval foodplants Recorded only on elm in the wild in Britain, but reared successfully on lime. Limes, elms, willows and poplars are the main foodplants in mainland Europe.

Habitat The only recorded breeding to date was in a tall elm hedgerow and shelterbelt.

Status & distribution Suspected immigrant and transitory resident. First reported in the early 19th century, with several adults in Kent and Yorkshire. One in 1904 in Chelmsford, Essex, and a male came to a light trap on 7 July 1946 at Arundel, Sussex. Between 27 June and 1 July 1947, six males came to a light-trap at Bradwell-on-Sea, Essex. Subsequently, it was seen annually at this locality until 1960, a period of hot dry summers, with a total of 102 trapped and released. One larva was found, on 22 June 1953, on an elm hedge. Recorded on Jersey in 1982 and 1986, where it is probably immigrant.

Black Arches   page 231

Lymantria monacha (L.)

Local. S,(C)   2033(10375)

Field characters FW M 18-20mm, F 20-28mm. Most examples have a central V-shaped mark and numerous black jagged cross-lines on the white or creamy white forewing, with pink bands on the abdomen. Sometimes these lines are merged into a broad central band, and pink on abdomen may be very faint, especially on dark examples. In parts of the south-east an almost entirely black form exists

Larva of Gypsy Moth.

and can be best recognised by the pinkish abdomen. Female has a distinctly pointed abdomen. In the infrequent f. *eremita* Ochs., forewing is entirely sooty grey, often with cross-lines obscured.

Similar species F. *eremita* could be confused with male Gypsy Moth, which is, however, distinctly brown. Female Gypsy Moth is thickset, has rather indistinct markings and a very blunt abdomen.

Flight season One generation. Late July-August. Nocturnal. Comes to light, the male frequently. Can sometimes be found at rest by day on tree trunks and posts.

Life cycle Overwinters as an egg, usually laid singly or in pairs in crevices in the bark of the larval food-plant. Larva April-June. Pupates in a flimsy cocoon in a bark crevice or among foliage.

Larval foodplants Mainly Pedunculate and Sessile Oak, but also recorded on a wide range of other trees, including Midland Hawthorn, birches, elms, Hornbeam, Aspen, Scots Pine and Norway Spruce.

Habitat Woodland, especially with mature oaks.

Status & distribution Resident. Local. Well distributed in southern, south-west and south-east England, East Anglia and the south Midlands. Local in Lincolnshire, west Wales and Man. There are 19th century records from Yorkshire, and old records from southern Ireland, in Cos. Cork and Sligo. Widespread and frequent on Jersey, rare on Guernsey.

Gypsy Moth
page 231

Lymantria dispar (L.)

Immigrant; former resident.   2034(10376)

Field characters FW M 20-24mm, F 31-35mm. Male has broad, deep brown forewing, sometimes with diffuse paler cross-bands. There are rather faint wavy cross-lines and a dark central, roughly V-shaped mark. Creamy white female is similarly marked, but thickset, much larger and has a very blunt abdomen, which is dark brown towards tip.

Similar species See Black Arches.

Flight season One generation. July-August. Male comes to light, and also flies by day. Female apparently does not usually fly far from the cocoon.

Life cycle Overwinters as an egg, laid in batches on the bark, twigs and leaves of the larval foodplants. Larva April-late June. The young larvae are wind-

dispersed and can be carried for several miles. Pupates in a flimsy cocoon behind bark or among leaf litter or foliage.

Larval foodplants The extinct English populations fed on Bog-myrtle and Creeping Willow. In mainland Europe it feeds on a wide variety of broadleaved trees and bushes.

Habitat The more acidic, open parts of fens. In mainland Europe it is found in a wide variety of places, such as woodland, scrub, plantations, parks and gardens.

Status & distribution Immigrant and former resident. Well established, probably as a distinct subspecies, in the fens of Huntingdonshire, Cambridgeshire and Norfolk in the first half of the 19th century, but declined from the 1850s, when major breeding sites were cleared and drained. The last accepted record is from Wennington Wood, near Huntingdon, in 1907. Large migrations of males of the continental populations occur, and at least 30 have been recorded in light-traps in southern England, mainly near the coast (and once in Cheshire), since the 1950s, many of these in the 1990s. Local and frequent on Jersey, occasional immigrant on Guernsey.

Pest status In mainland Europe the moth is frequently a serious pest, defoliating timber plantations and ornamental trees, as in North America, where it was accidentally introduced in about 1868. It became re-established briefly in the London Borough of Redbridge in 1995, when many larvae escaped from captivity, but was eradicated by pest-control measures.

Arctiidae – Tiger moths, ermines, footman moths and allies

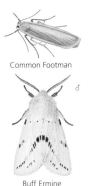

Common Footman

Buff Ermine

Cream-spot Tiger

212

This family comprises about 11,000 species worldwide. Thirty-two species have been recorded from the British Isles, of which 29 are resident, five of these also being immigrants. Another is a scarce immigrant, one a suspected immigrant and the status of the other is uncertain.

The subfamily Arctiinae includes the tiger and ermine moths. Tiger moths are boldly striped and banded, in some cases a reminder to predators that they are poisonous. Despite their size and bright colours, the patterns are often highly cryptic, making the moths hard to see when at rest in vegetation. The ermine moths are so-called because their wings are usually whitish, with black flecks or spots reminiscent of the ermine robes of dignitaries. The Lithosiinae are much slimmer, and often rather plain. Some of the smaller species could initially be mistaken for micro-moths, but they show relatively little variation and once known are easily recognised. They are named footman moths because many have long, narrow forewings and rest with them held over their back or wrapped around the body, bearing a resemblance to the long, stiff coats worn by the eponymous Victorian servants.

Many of the Arctiidae do not feed, but most come to light-traps and some fly by day. The larvae are hairy, especially those of some of the tigers and ermines, but their hairs do not normally cause skin irritation. Larvae of the Arctiinae generally feed on herbaceous plants, whereas those of the Lithosiinae feed mainly on lichens and algae growing on trees, rocks and walls, in dense low vegetation or on the ground. Pupation usually occurs in a cocoon formed above ground, either in a crevice, under bark or among low vegetation.

Lithosiinae

Round-winged Muslin
page 232
Thumatha senex (Hb.)
Local. S,C,(N)
2035(10466)

Field characters FW 10-11mm. A small, delicate and fairly unmistakable cream-coloured moth, with very broad, rounded, slightly translucent wings. Forewing has a small but noticeable dark central dot and usually two cross-rows of dark spots or dashes. Hindwing has a small dark central crescent mark and sometimes a row of dashes beyond it. A smaller, greyer and less distinctly marked form occurs in the Scottish Highlands.

Similar species See Muslin Footman.

Flight season One generation. Late June-late August. Seen flying slowly but with rapid wing-beats among lush swards, sometimes in numbers, from sunset and also at sunrise. Comes to light.

Life cycle Overwinters as a small larva. Larva late August-May, feeding in mild weather during the winter. Pupates in a cocoon among vegetation near the ground.

Larval foodplants Reported from lichens, including *Peltigera* species, and mosses growing on the ground, including *Homalothecium sericeum* and *Dicranoweisia cirrata*. Probably also on algae low down on the dead stems of marsh plants.

Habitat Fens, bogs, wet flushes on moorland, damp grassland, marshes, riverbanks and coastal dune-slacks.
Status & distribution Resident. Local. Well distributed in southern and south-east England, the south Midlands and East Anglia. More thinly scattered in south-west England, Wales and in northern England. Very local in Scotland, mainly recorded from the lowlands between the Clyde and the Forth, but also the Insh Marshes and Nethy River, near Aviemore. Recorded twice on Man, in 1993 and 2000. Recently found to be quite well distributed in Northern Ireland, especially the eastern part, but records from the Irish Republic are thinly scattered. In the Channel Islands, local on Guernsey, first recorded from Jersey in 1999.

Dew Moth   page 232
Setina irrorella (L.)
Na. S,NW   2036(10509)

Field characters FW 11-18mm. Unmistakable. The orange-yellow forewing, with small black spots roughly arranged into three cross-rows, is diagnostic. Leading edge of forewing is quite straight, especially in male, giving it a rather triangular appearance when at rest. Female is smaller, with narrower forewing. Rarely, there is a dark central V-shaped mark and one or more dark lines on forewing (f. *signata* Borkh.).
Similar species None.
Flight season One generation. June-July. Male flies in the afternoon, from dusk and again at dawn. Both sexes come to light in small numbers, and rest on grass stems both by day and night.
Life cycle Overwinters as a larva. Larva August-June. Pupates in a flimsy cocoon between stones or rocks.
Larval foodplants Lichens on rocks, shingle and in grassland.
Habitat Rocky coasts, shingle beaches and calcareous grassland inland.
Status & distribution Resident. Nationally Scarce A. Very scattered along southern and western coasts. On coastal shingle in Kent (Dungeness and Folkestone Warren) and Hampshire (Hurn), and chalky cliff-tops on the Isle of Wight (near Freshwater). Also found on the west coast of Wales, on Man, the west coast of mainland Scotland, the Inner Hebrides and the Burren, Co. Clare, Ireland. Found very locally inland on the scarp slope of the North Downs, Surrey, and also recorded from Gloucestershire (Cotswolds) and from the Black Hills, Breconshire, in south-east Wales.

Rosy Footman   page 232
Miltochrista miniata (Forst.)
Local. S,(C)   2037(10475)

Field characters FW 12-15mm. Unmistakable. Rounded forewing, with a fine, very wavy black cross-line beyond the middle and a line of short dark dashes or dots near outer edge, is diagnostic, with little variation. Forewing normally pinkish red near leading and outer edges and slightly paler centrally. Rarely the pink

is replaced by yellow (f. *flava* Bigneau).
Similar species None.
Flight season One generation. Mid June-early August. Sometimes found at rest on twigs and foliage of woody plants by day. Comes to light, sometimes in numbers.
Life cycle Overwinters as a larva. Larva August-late May, feeding in mild weather during the winter. Pupates in a hairy cocoon.
Larval foodplants Dog Lichen and other lichens on the trunks and twigs of oaks and other trees.
Habitat Broadleaved woodland, wooded heathland and well wooded hedgerows.
Status & distribution Resident. Local. Well distributed in central southern, south-west and south-east England, East Anglia, the western side of Wales and Scilly. Local in old woodland in the south Midlands, including Oxfordshire, Herefordshire and Worcestershire, and in Lincolnshire. In Ireland, recorded only from the south-east, in Co. Waterford. Widespread and frequent in the Channel Islands.

Muslin Footman   page 232
Nudaria mundana (L.)
Local. T   2038(10464)

Field characters & Similar species FW 10-12mm. Somewhat like Round-winged Muslin, but with strongly transparent wings. In addition, forewing narrower and less rounded, with two roughly V-shaped dark cross-lines, and hindwing is entirely plain.
Flight season One generation. Late June-early August. Male comes regularly to light, but female is rarely seen.
Life cycle Overwinters as a larva. Larva August-early June. In the spring, feeds and basks in sunshine or rests under a stone. Pupates in a loose-spun cocoon, formed in a crevice.
Larval foodplants Small lichens on stone walls, rocks, posts and the trunks and branches of isolated bushes.
Habitat Generally open, stony places with dry-stone or other field boundary walls, or hedgerows. Also sometimes in gardens and woodlands.
Status & distribution Resident. Local. Widely and quite well distributed in most of mainland Britain, although more frequent in the west and on calcareous soils, and reaching central and north-east Scotland. It has declined in central southern and south-east England, but is still present in widely scattered sites, often near the coast. Local and infrequent on Man. Widely distributed and fairly frequent in Ireland. Local and occasional in the Channel Islands.

Red-necked Footman   page 232
Atolmis rubricollis (L.)
Local. S,WC,(N)   2039(10483)

Field characters FW 15-18mm. Unmistakable. The only footman moth in Britain and Ireland with constantly plain black wings (velvety when fresh) and a red collar. Very worn or faded examples may

213

appear brownish black. Hind third of abdomen is deep yellow on upperside, and this colour is more extensive on underside.

Similar species None.

Flight season One generation. June-July. Sometimes flies around the tops of oak trees and conifers on hot sunny days, occasionally in large numbers, and is often found at rest on the leaves of bushes. Comes to light, usually in small numbers.

Life cycle Overwinters as a pupa, in a cocoon formed among plant debris. Larva August-October.

Larval foodplants Lichens and green algae growing on oaks, birches, Beech, Larch, spruces and other trees.

Habitat Broadleaved woodland and conifer plantations, including latter established on open moorland.

Status & distribution Resident and suspected immigrant. Local. Quite well distributed and sometimes locally abundant in south-west England, less frequent and more local in southern England and Wales. Also established in south-west Scotland. Recently proving to be numerous in some parts of Northern Ireland, particularly in the west, but only thinly scattered records from the Irish Republic. In the Channel Islands, local and rare on Jersey. Occasional examples in light-traps elsewhere in Britain, particularly in the east, are thought to be immigrants.

Four-dotted Footman   page 232
Cybosia mesomella (L.)
Local. T   2040(10477)

Field characters FW 13-16mm. Fairly unmistakable. Broad forewing either white with leading and outer edges yellow, or dull yellow (f. *flava* de Graaf), constantly with a small black dot placed centrally near both leading and trailing edges. F. *flava* occurs in all populations, but is particularly frequent in south-east England.

Similar species None.

Flight season One generation. Mid June-early August. Often disturbed from low vegetation by day. Flies from early dusk and comes to light, sometimes in numbers.

Life cycle Overwinters as a larva. Larva mid August-late May. Pupates in a cocoon formed among plant debris.

Larval foodplants Algae and lichens on the stems of heathers, sallows and other woody plants.

Habitat Heathland, moorland, damp grassland, fens and open woodland.

Status & distribution Resident. Local. Widely distributed in the southern half of Britain (apart from areas of the Midlands). More local in northern England and Scotland, north to Banffshire. Local and rare on Man and in the Channel Islands. One record only from Ireland, in a Belfast garden on 4 July 1991.

Dotted Footman   page 232
Pelosia muscerda (Hufn.)
RDB. E   2041(10479)

Field characters FW 13-16mm. Forewing rather

slender, soft grey-brown and often paler near leading edge. The pattern of five (occasionally six) small black spots, in two separate rows, is diagnostic.

Similar species See Small Dotted Footman.

Flight season One generation. Mid July-August. Flies at dusk, during the night and again at dawn. Comes to light, sometimes in numbers, but otherwise is seldom seen.

Life cycle In captivity overwinters as a larva. Larva August-June.

Larval foodplants The larva has apparently not been found in the wild, but probably feeds on algae and lichens growing on the stems of bushes and other plants, upon which it has been reared in captivity. Will also eat withered leaves of sallows and Bramble.

Habitat Fens, preferring wetter areas with scattered sallow and alder carr.

Status & distribution Resident and suspected immigrant. Red Data Book species. Currently, known to be resident only in the Norfolk Broads, where it is well established. In the late 19th and early 20th centuries it was resident at Ham Fen, Kent, and was also reported from the New Forest, Hampshire. The occasional examples recorded in other habitats elsewhere in East Anglia, south-east England, Dorset and Yorkshire were probably immigrants. Most have been near the coast, and were caught alongside known immigrant species.

Small Dotted Footman   page 232
Pelosia obtusa (H.-S.)
RDB. E   2042(10480)

Field characters & Similar species FW 12-14mm. Not unlike Dotted Footman, but forewing shorter and browner. Diagnostic features are the very curved leading edge and the arrangement of the small black central spots into a rough V-shape.

Flight season One generation. July. Male comes to light, usually in small numbers. Female has been found at rest on reeds at night.

Life cycle Overwinters as a larva. Larva August-June. Pupates in a thin, grey cocoon.

Larval foodplants The larva has not been found in the wild. In captivity will eat green algae growing on dead wood.

Habitat Old, dense, uncut reedbeds with tall herbs, often with small bushes.

Status & distribution Resident. Red Data Book species. Discovered in 1961, and found in the Norfolk Broads and adjacent fens only, where it is very localised but probably under recorded.

Orange Footman   page 232
Eilema sororcula (Hufn.)
Local. S   2043(10499)

Field characters FW 13-16mm. Shape of plain, orange-yellow forewing is diagnostic, with leading edge very straight in basal half, then strongly curved towards tip. There is little variation, but worn examples are paler.

Similar species None likely to be found in woodland in late spring and early summer. The yellow forms of Dingy and Buff Footman are larger and leading edge of forewing is more evenly curved.

Flight season One generation. Late May-June. Flies from dusk onwards and comes regularly to light, sometimes in large numbers, and is occasionally beaten from branches by day.

Life cycle Overwinters as a pupa, in a flimsy cocoon formed among lichens. Larva late June-September.

Larval foodplants Lichen growing on oaks, Beech, Larch, Blackthorn and other trees.

Habitat Usually larger areas of mature oak or Beech woodland, but also in dense, mature Blackthorn scrub.

Status & distribution Resident and suspected immigrant. Local. Found mainly in south-west, central southern and south-east England, the Isle of Wight and south Wales. Also found very locally in East Anglia and Lincolnshire. Some of the eastern records are suspected to be of immigrants. Widespread and frequent on Jersey, but rare on Guernsey.

Dingy Footman   page 232
Eilema griseola (Hb.)

Common. S,(C)	2044(10488)

Field characters FW 15-18mm. Distinguished from similar species by broad, rounded forewing, which is silky when freshly emerged. Leading edge is strongly curved and in grey form has a pale, narrow and often indistinct stripe. The plain straw yellow f. *stramineola* Doubl. is known from Britain only, and is frequent in some populations.

Similar species See Common, Buff and Orange Footman.

Flight season One generation. July-August. Sometimes seen resting on foliage by day or beaten from hedges. Comes to light, sometimes in numbers, and visits flowers, including Hemp-agrimony and Lesser Burdock.

Life cycle Overwinters as a larva. Larva August-late May. Pupates among plant debris.

Larval foodplants Lichens and algae growing on trees and bushes. In captivity will eat mosses and withered leaves.

Habitat Fens, wet meadows, damp woodland and other marshy places.

Status & distribution Resident. Common. Well distributed in the southern half of England and low-lying parts of Wales. Extends locally north through the Midlands to Yorkshire, and appears to be increasing in the West Midlands. First recorded from Ireland in 1984, one from Co. Cork. A second was captured in woodland in Co. Kildare in 2001. Widespread and frequent in the Channel Islands.

Hoary Footman   page 232
Eilema caniola (Hb.)

Nb. SW	2045(10493)

Field characters FW 15-17mm. Quite distinctive. Forewing narrow, silky, and usually very pale grey,

with a pale orange-yellow stripe along leading edge, and hindwing white. In f. *lacteola* Boisd. forewing is white and stripe is very faint.

Similar species Scarce Footman and Common Footman have darker grey forewing and pale straw-coloured hindwing.

Flight season One generation. Late July-early September. Comes to light from soon after dark, usually in small numbers, and occasionally to sugar.

Life cycle Overwinters as a larva. Larva September-late June, feeding at night. Pupates in a cocoon formed under a stone or in a rock crevice.

Larval foodplants Lichens and algae on rocks and even roof-tiles. Reportedly also Common Bird's-foot-trefoil and related plants.

Habitat Rocky coastlines, shingle beaches and quarries.

Status & distribution Resident and suspected immigrant. Nationally Scarce B. Found along the north and south coasts of Devon and Cornwall, Scilly, Somerset, and the rocky parts of the coast of southern and western Wales, particularly in Pembrokeshire, Cardiganshire, and Skomer and Skokholm Islands. Recently confirmed breeding on Anglesey, at South Stack and Church Bay. Recorded once on Man, at Douglas, in 1868. In Ireland, recorded recently on the south coast in Cos. Cork and Waterford, and in the 19th century from Howth, Dublin. Also recorded breeding in an old quarry 150m above the river in the lower Wye Valley, Monmouthshire, 10km inland from the Severn Estuary, after searches in 1981, 1989 and 1991. Occasional suspected immigrant examples have been recorded on the coasts of Dorset, Sussex and south-east Kent. Widespread and frequent in the Channel Islands.

Pigmy Footman   page 232
Eilema pygmaeola pygmaeola (Doubl.)

RDB. E	2046(10495)

ssp. *pallifrons* (Zell.)

RDB. SE

Field characters FW 10-15mm. Ssp. *pygmaeola* is small, with narrow, silky, greyish-white or light grey forewing, and a distinct and often extensive grey smear in leading half of hindwing. Rests with wings held close to body. Ssp. *pallifrons* has straw-yellow forewing.

Similar species Smaller than all other British footman moths. The abundant micro-moth *Crambus perlella* (Scop.) is superficially similar, but has shiny forewings and rests with them steeply arched, and has long, protruding palps.

Flight season One generation. Mid July-August. Comes to light, sometimes in large numbers, and occasionally to sugar.

Life cycle Overwinters as a small larva. Larva August-June. A tightly-packed 'nest' of some 30 larvae of ssp. *pallifrons* has been found attached to the base of a dead grass stem on shingle in mid-April. Pupates in a flimsy cocoon among lichens and moss.

Larval foodplants Lichens and algae on stones, plant stems and posts, almost certainly including *Cladonia rangiformis*. Will also accept decaying sallow leaves in captivity.

Habitat Coastal sand-dunes and shingle beaches with a mosaic of grasses and lichens.

Status & distribution Resident and suspected immigrant. Ssp. *pygmaeola* Red Data Book species. Locally frequent in Kent between Sandwich and Deal, and in Norfolk between Winterton and Waxham. Also recorded regularly from the Isle of Sheppey, Kent, since 1976, and possibly established there. Suspected vagrants from resident colonies are occasionally recorded in the Norfolk Broads, and suspected immigrants recorded on the coasts of Lincolnshire, Yorkshire, Sussex, Essex, Suffolk and Devon. In the Channel Islands, first recorded on Guernsey in 1997 and 1998, and on Sark in 1998. Ssp. *pallifrons* Red Data Book species. Endemic to Britain and known only from coastal shingle at Dungeness, Kent, where it can be numerous. However, since moths resembling ssp. *pygmaeola* also occur at this locality, the classification of *pallifrons* as a subspecies, rather than a form, seems questionable.

Scarce Footman
page 232

Eilema complana (L.)

Local. S,C
2047(10490)

Northern Footman
page 232

f. *sericea* (Gregs.)

RDB. WC
2048(race of 10490)

Note The taxonomic status of the Northern Footman is uncertain. It is treated here as a form of the Scarce Footman, in line with the most recent British list, although it was originally thought to be a separate species. It is certainly distinct, and apparently restricted by habitat. However, the genitalia are indistinguishable from those of the Scarce Footman and the differences in the wing markings are slight.

Field characters & Similar species
Scarce Footman: FW 15-18mm. Very similar to Common Footman, but rests with wings held tightly around body. Also, orange-yellow stripe along leading edge of forewing reaches wing tip without becoming noticeably narrower. Hindwing pale straw colour, sometimes with a grey smear near leading edge. Another useful character is the collar, which is completely orange-yellow, whereas in Common Footman there is a small central grey area.
Northern Footman: FW 14-17mm. Slightly smaller on average, with narrower forewing. Orange-yellow stripe along edge of forewing often narrows before reaching wing tip, and there is almost invariably a grey smear on hindwing, which is often extensive.

Flight season One generation. July-August. Comes to light, sometimes in numbers, and visits flowers such as knapweeds and thistles after dark.

Life cycle Overwinters as a small larva. Larva August-June. Pupates in a cocoon formed among plant debris or in a crevice.

Larval foodplants Lichens and algae on rocks, walls, posts, plant stems, branches and the ground. Will eat decaying leaves in captivity.

Habitat A wide variety, but perhaps most numerous on heathland, moorland and sand-dunes. Also frequent in woodland, fens, downland, and sometimes found in gardens. Northern Footman is only found on raised peat-bogs and boggy moorland.

Status & distribution Resident. Scarce Footman: Local. Belies its English name by being well distributed and quite frequent in southern and eastern England, north to Spurn Head, Yorkshire, where it is found in large numbers. Somewhat more local in south-west England, Wales and the Midlands, north to Cumbria and Man. Widely distributed in Ireland, but largely coastal. Widespread and fairly frequent in the Channel Islands. Northern Footman: Red Data Book listing. Endemic to Britain, and very local in Lancashire, Cheshire, Shropshire, north Wales (Merionethshire) and Man.

Buff Footman
page 232

Eilema depressa (Esp.)

Local. S,(C)
2049(10487)

Field characters FW 15-17mm. The greyish-white male, with orange-yellow fringes on both wings and a faint yellow stripe along basal third of leading edge, is distinctive. In the slightly larger female, forewing usually brownish grey (occasionally paler, orange-tinged) with a distinct orange stripe along leading edge, and hindwing grey. Another form, frequent in some populations, has orange-yellow forewing (f. *unicolor* Bankes) and hindwing diffusely marked with grey toward trailing edge. There is a very dark f. *plumbia* Cock. In all forms, forewing may be slightly silky.

Similar species Dingy Footman has broader, more rounded, often noticeably silky forewing, and yellow form is paler and lacks grey on hindwing. See also Common Footman and Orange Footman.

Flight season One generation. July-August. Comes to light, usually in small numbers.

Life cycle Overwinters as a small larva. Larva September-late June. Pupates in a cocoon formed in a bark crevice.

Larval foodplants Lichens and algae on the branches of trees and shrubs, including oaks, birches, hawthorns and conifers such as spruces and Yew.

Habitat Mainly in long-established broadleaved or mixed woodland; also among scrub on downland and heathland and in fens.

Status & distribution Resident. Local. Well distributed and fairly frequent in south-west and central southern England. Also found in parts of Sussex and Kent, the London area, and East Anglia, particularly in Breckland. More localised in ancient woodland in the south Midlands and the Wye Valley. Very local further north, extending to north Wales, Lancashire, Lincolnshire and Yorkshire. In Ireland, very local in the south-west. Widespread and frequent on Jersey but rare on Guernsey.

Common Footman
page 232
Eilema lurideola (Zinck.)
Common. S,C,(N)   2050(10489)

Field characters FW 14-17mm. Rests with
forewings gently curled over body. These are leaden
grey, with a well-defined yellow stripe along leading
edge, narrowing distinctly toward wing tip, and
often just failing to reach it. Hindwing pale straw,
sometimes with a grey smear near leading edge.
Similar species See Scarce, Northern and Hoary
Footman. Dingy Footman has much broader
forewing, and streak along leading edge is thin, pale
and indistinct. Dark female form of Buff Footman is
brownish. Both have grey hindwings.
Flight season One generation. July-August. Comes
to sugar, to flowers such as thistles, and frequently
to light, sometimes in quite large numbers.
Life cycle Overwinters as a small larva. Larva
August-late May. Pupates in a cocoon formed in a
crevice. Can sometimes be found basking in spring
sunshine on tree trunks, walls or posts.
Larval foodplants Lichens and algae on trees,
bushes, posts, walls and rocks. Also feeds on leaves,
particularly Hawthorn in hedgerows. Accepts
Blackthorn, Traveller's-joy and Bramble.
Habitat Most lowland habitats, including town
gardens and farmland, wetlands, woodland and
coastal situations.
Status & distribution Resident. Common. The most
widely and well distributed of the footman moths,
occurring throughout England and Wales, but rare on
Man. Thinly distributed but increasing in the north-
east of England. Local in mainland Scotland, and
most frequently found on the east coast, north to
Easter Ross. Widespread but apparently local in Ireland.
Widespread and frequent in the Channel Islands.

Four-spotted Footman
page 232
Lithosia quadra (L.)
Na; immigrant. SW   2051(10485)

Field characters FW M 18-22 F 20-26mm.
Unmistakable. Twice the size of most British footman
moths. Only female has two dark brown spots, on
yellow forewing. In male, the black and yellow
blotches at base of sleek grey forewing are diagnostic. There is little variation.
Similar species None.
Flight season One generation. July-September. Both
sexes come to light, occasionally in large numbers.
Also visits flowers and sugar.
Life cycle Overwinters as a small larva. Larva
September-late June. Pupates in a flimsy cocoon
formed in a crevice.
Larval foodplants Dog lichen (*Peltigera* species),
and other lichens and algae growing on the trunks
and branches of oaks and other trees, and on rocks.
Habitat Mature broadleaved woodland.
Status & distribution Resident and immigrant.
Nationally Scarce A. Resident populations, which can
be locally abundant, exist locally in Scilly, Cornwall and

Devon. These show large annual fluctuations in
numbers of both adults and larvae (suggesting that the
species' tolerance of our climate is limited) and are
probably reinforced by immigration. Also resident in
south-west Ireland, in Cos. Cork, Galway, Kerry and
Clare. Other areas where it occurs regularly and is
probably resident are Hampshire (New Forest), south-
east Dorset and Pembrokeshire. It also occurs rather
infrequently elsewhere as an immigrant, mainly in
southern parts of Britain and Ireland, but exceptionally
north to Easter Ross. Occasional in the Channel Islands.

Arctiinae

Feathered Footman
page 232
Spiris striata (L.)
Uncertain.   2052(10526)

Field characters FW 15-22mm. Unmistakable. In
male, which has feathered antennae, there are
usually numerous black stripes and a black central
crescent on yellow forewing. Female is usually
plainer, with stripes limited to outer edges and
central crescent reduced to two small dots. However,
occasionally male is plainly marked and female
heavily striped. Hindwing usually orange-yellow, with
a central black crescent and a black border which
varies in width and may be broken, or less often
hindwing almost entirely black.
Similar species None.
Flight season One or two generations in mainland
Europe, depending on latitude. May-August. Active
by day.
Life cycle Overwinters as a small larva. Pupates in a
cocoon at ground level.
Larval foodplants A wide range of herbaceous
plants, including grasses.
Habitat Dry, warm slopes with sparse vegetation,
particularly heathland, and woodland clearings.
Status & distribution Uncertain. Four records from
the 19th century are possibly genuine. These are from
Yorkshire (Wharfedale, c.1836), Anglesey (Manachty,
before 1803), Caernarvonshire (Betws-y-Coed, 1859)
and Denbighshire (near Wrexham, 1859). Others from
Berkshire and Essex are considered to be unreliable.
The distribution of these records does not suggest
immigration, and there have been none since. In
mainland Europe it is most frequent in the south, but
extends north to northern France and Denmark.

Speckled Footman
page 232
Coscinia cribraria (L.)
ssp. *bivittata* (South)
RDB. S   2053(10528)
ssp. *arenaria* (Lempke)
Immigrant.

Field characters FW 15-18mm. Rests with
forewings wrapped closely around body and folded

so that tips appear pointed. The rows of blackish spots, arranged into cross-bands and sometimes merged, and blackish streaks on the greyish-white forewing make it fairly unmistakable. Hindwing grey with whitish fringes. Amount of blackish streaking varies, and some examples are extensively clouded. In ssp. *arenaria* the dark markings are highly reduced.

Similar species Thistle Ermine *Myelois cribella* (Hb.) (Pyralidae) and various Yponomeutidae (see pages 12-13) are quite large and frequently seen micro-moths with long, narrow, white forewing spotted with black. They do not have dark streaks.

Flight season One generation. July-August. Sometimes disturbed by day, and comes to light.

Life cycle Overwinters as a small larva. Larva August-June, basking and feeding as early as February. Pupates in a flimsy cocoon among grass or heathers.

Larval foodplants Recently found on the grass Bristle Bent, on which the larger larvae can develop exclusively. Also reported to feed on Bell Heather, Cross-leaved Heath, Heather and Bilberry.

Habitat Open heathland. Has been found breeding in tussocky, free-draining areas that were burned about five years previously, and apparently does not breed in areas of very short growth, or among tall mature heathers.

Status & distribution Resident and immigrant. Red Data Book species. Ssp. *bivittata* was formerly wide-spread and sometimes locally numerous on heaths in south-east Dorset and the New Forest, Hampshire. However, it has greatly declined since the 1970s and is now found only in small numbers in Dorset. A single, presumably vagrant, example was captured at Portland Bill, Dorset, on 1 July 1993. Locally frequent on Jersey, rare on Guernsey. Ssp. *arenaria*, which is resident in mainland Europe, has occurred rarely as an immigrant in Kent, Sussex, Hampshire and Suffolk.

Crimson Speckled   page 232
Utetheisa pulchella (L.)
Immigrant.   2054(10535)

Field characters FW 15-22mm. The pattern of the many red (or pink) and black spots on the creamy white forewing is unmistakable, although the pattern varies in detail. Sometimes the red spots are merged into cross-bands, and occasionally the black spots are reduced to tiny dots. Hindwing white, with an irregular black border and often with small dark central marks.

Similar species None.

Flight season One or more generations, depending on latitude. Immigrants have occurred from March-October, but mainly from July onwards. Easily disturbed by day, flies freely in sunshine and at night, when it comes to light.

Life cycle The early stages have not been found in the British Isles. In southern Europe it overwinters as a larva, and in the sub-tropics breeds continuously.

Larval foodplants A wide range of herbaceous plants.

Habitat In southern Europe and North Africa it is found in dry, open places.

Status & distribution Immigrant. Rare, with about 100 moths recorded since 1900. It was most numerous in 1961 (over 30) and 1990 (25). Most have been in southern England, but a few have reached Scotland, Man and Ireland. These probably originated in the Mediterranean region, where it is resident. A rare immigrant in the Channel Islands.

Beautiful Utetheisa   not illustrated
Utetheisa bella (L.)
Rare immigrant/import.   2055(-)

Field characters & Similar species FW 22mm. Similar to Crimson Speckled but ground-colour of hindwing is pink and there are usually irregular orange or pink bands and blotches on forewing.

Status & distribution Either a rare transatlantic immigrant or accidental import, possibly carried part of the way by a ship. Recorded once, a singleton on Skokholm Island, Pembrokeshire, at the end of July, 1948. Resident in North America, where it is widely distributed.

Wood Tiger   page 233
Parasemia plantaginis plantaginis (L.)
Local. T,(rare SE)   2056(10557)

ssp. *insularum* Seitz
Shetland, Orkney, northern mainland Scotland

Field characters FW 17-20mm. Unmistakable. Ssp. *plantaginis* Variable in colour, extent and detail of markings, but overall pattern is diagnostic. In female, black basal markings on hindwing are more extensive. In northern England and parts of Scotland, males with ground-colour of hindwing white are frequent (f. *hospita* [D. & S.]).
Ssp. *insularum* Similar, but in both sexes ground-colour of hindwing is orange-yellow and black basal markings are extensive.

Similar species None.

Flight season One generation. Late May-July. Both sexes are easily disturbed by day from low vegeta-tion. In sunny weather, male flies rapidly and erratically in search of female. Female is more sluggish but has been reported laying eggs by day, and is active in the late afternoon and after dark.

Life cycle Overwinters as a half-grown larva, low down in the vegetation. Larva July-April or early May. Pupates in a cocoon spun among plant stems.

Larval foodplants A range of herbaceous plants, including Bell Heather, Ribwort Plantain, Greater Plantain, Common Rock-rose, Salad Burnet and Groundsel.

Habitat Moorland, heathland, downland and other scrubby places, including open areas in woodland.

Status & distribution Resident. Local. Ssp. *plan-taginis* is widespread but very local in south-west and southern England, the Midlands, Wales, northern England, Man, and more well distributed in mainland Scotland, the Hebrides and Ireland. Previously found widely in south-east England, but in recent decades it has become very rare, and has also become much more local in central southern England, although strong colonies remain on downland in Wiltshire and the Isle of Wight. Evidence suggests these losses are due to agricultural intensification, overgrazing (especially of downland sites), a decrease in coppicing, an increase in shading of rides by plantation forestry, and possibly in part due to climate change. Ssp. *insularum* is found in northern mainland Scotland, Orkney and Shetland.

Larva of Garden Tiger.

Garden Tiger   page 233
Arctia caja (L.)
Common. T   2057(10598)

Field characters FW 28-37mm. Unmistakable, although dark brown spots and blotches are so highly variable that no two moths are exactly alike. In extreme examples, spots are entirely absent, or merged to almost cover wings. These are rare in the wild, but can sometimes be obtained through selective breeding. F. *lutescens* Cockll., with ground-colour of hindwing and abdomen yellow, and f. *fumosa* Horhammer, which is sooty-brown, are also rare. If disturbed, this moth displays its orange hindwings with blue-black spots, and produces a clear yellow fluid from two ducts just behind the head.
Similar species None.
Flight season One generation. July-August. Flies late at night and comes to light, sometimes in numbers.
Life cycle Overwinters as a small larva. Larva August-late June. The very hairy larva, known as the 'woolly bear', sometimes feeds and basks in sunshine and may be seen moving rapidly across bare ground when fully grown, searching for a pupation site. Pupates in a thin cocoon among vegetation on or near the ground.
Larval foodplants A wide variety of herbaceous plants, including Common Nettle, Broad-leaved Dock, Water Dock, burdocks, Hound's-tongue and many garden plants.
Habitat A wide range of generally rather open habitats, including gardens, damp meadows, fens, riverbanks, sand-dunes (especially mature dunes with scrub, where it can be abundant), and open woodland.
Status & distribution Resident. Common. Well distributed and sometimes numerous throughout most of Britain and Ireland, but absent from Shetland. Widespread and frequent in the Channel Islands. In most areas this moth has decreased significantly since the mid-1980s, and most noticeably in the south-east. This could in part be due to spraying of weedy areas and the general tidying of hedgerows, etc., since it is still frequent in some relatively undisturbed coastal and wetland habitats. However, recent statistical evidence links lower numbers of moths with mild, wet Januarys followed by colder weather in February. Since these are predicted to occur ever more frequently as a result of global climate change, a recovery to previous levels would seem unlikely.

Cream-spot Tiger   page 233
Arctia villica (L.)
ssp. *britannica* Ob.
Local. S   2058(10600)

Field characters FW 25-32mm. The broad, furry black thorax, with creamy-white blotches on shoulders and on black forewing, together with yellow hindwing, are diagnostic. Upperside of abdomen is yellow near base, and bright red towards tip. Considerable variation in detail of markings, although overall pattern usually remains. Extreme examples, with white spots on forewing and black spots on hindwing either highly reduced or greatly enlarged, are rare.
Similar species Very rarely, Scarlet Tiger has yellow hindwing, but forewing iridescent and without a white blotch at base, and it is a more slender moth.
Flight season One generation. Late May-early July. Sometimes found by day, at rest exposed on low herbage or walking across bare ground. Both sexes active after dark and regular at light.
Life cycle Overwinters as a larva. Larva July-late April or early May, feeding in mild weather throughout the winter, and sometimes basking in sunshine before pupating in late April in a flimsy cocoon among plant debris.
Larval foodplants A wide range of herbaceous plants, including White Dead-nettle, chickweeds, hawkweeds, ragworts and Black Horehound.
Habitat Open ground on the coast, including cliff-tops, under-cliff, edges of saltmarshes and mature sand-dunes. Inland, on downland, roadside verges, heathland and open woodland.
Status & distribution Resident. Local. Locally frequent in south-west, southern and south-east England, East Anglia and south Wales, and most frequent on or near the coast, and on heathland. Widespread and frequent in the Channel Islands.

Clouded Buff   page 234
Diacrisia sannio (L.)
Local. T   2059(10583)

Field characters FW M 19-22mm F 17-20mm. The yellow forewing, whitish hindwing and pink fringes of male, and orange forewing with orange-red veins

Larva of Buff Ermine.

September-October, especially in southern England. Comes to light, usually late in the night.

Life cycle Overwinters as a pupa, in a cocoon formed among plant debris. Larva July-September.

Larval foodplants A wide range of herbaceous plants, including Common Nettle and docks.

Habitat Most rural and urban habitats, including gardens, hedgerows, wet and dry grassland, heath-land, moorland, woodland and coastal situations.

Status & distribution Resident. Common. Very well distributed and frequent, and found throughout most of Britain, Man and Ireland, apart from Shetland. Widespread and abundant in the Channel Islands.

of female make this moth unmistakable. Forewing markings hardly vary in both sexes, but amount of blackish shading on hindwing is highly variable, and generally greater in female.

Similar species None.

Flight season One generation. June-July, rarely in late August as a possible second generation. Male is easily disturbed by day and flies in sunshine. Both sexes are active at night, and male comes to light. Female appears to fly little, but can sometimes be found at rest on vegetation.

Life cycle Overwinters as a small larva. Larva July-late April or May.

Larval foodplants Heathers and various herbaceous plants, including Sheep's Sorrel, Devil's-bit Scabious, Common Dog-Violet and plantains.

Habitat Mainly heathland and moorland, and less frequently chalk and limestone grassland and open areas in woodland.

Status & distribution Resident. Local. Widely distributed in mainland Britain, but most frequent in southern, south-west and south-east England, East Anglia, the Midlands, Wales, north-west England and western Scotland, including the Inner Hebrides. Widespread but local in Ireland. Local and occasional on Jersey, rare on Guernsey.

White Ermine   page 234

Spilosoma lubricipeda (L.)

Common. T   2060(10567)

Field characters FW 18-23mm. The pattern of small black spots on forewing and the presence of at least one central black spot on hindwing make most examples of this moth easy to recognise. However, forewing spots vary greatly in number. On some examples they are extensive, often formed into a curved row, or even joined to form streaks along veins, whereas others are almost plain. In the southern half of Britain, forewing is usually whitish with a creamy tint and hindwing is white, but in Scotland and Ireland forewing is often creamy buff, or even brown, and hindwing creamy white. Buff examples are occasionally found further south.

Similar species See Water Ermine, Buff Ermine and Muslin Moth.

Flight season Usually one generation. Mid May-late July. Occasionally a partial second generation in

Buff Ermine   page 234

Spilosoma luteum (Hufn.)

Common. S,C,(N)   2061(10566*)

Field characters FW 17-22mm. Usually quite distinctive, with very broad, yellowish-buff to whitish-buff forewing and slightly paler hindwing. The row of rather elongated spots running from wing tip to trailing edge, present on underside of plain examples, is diagnostic. Number and size of black spots on forewing varies considerably, and they may form streaks. The extreme f. *zatima* Stoll, with mainly black wings, is very rare in the wild but has been obtained through selective breeding.

Similar species White Ermine usually has a general scattering of black dots on forewing. Irish male Muslin Moths are smaller. Both are without a diagonal row of larger spots.

Flight season One generation. Mid May-July. Comes regularly to light, sometimes in numbers.

Life cycle Overwinters as a pupa, in a cocoon formed among plant debris. Larva July-October.

Larval foodplants A wide range of herbaceous plants, especially Common Nettle and also woody species including Honeysuckle, Hop, Wild Plum, Barberry and birches.

Habitat Most habitats, including gardens, hedgerows, parks and woodland; also sand-dunes.

Status & distribution Resident. Common. Very well distributed and frequent throughout England, Wales, Man and Ireland. Local in mainland Scotland and the Inner Hebrides, but more frequent near the west coast, north to Caithness. Widespread and abundant in the Channel Islands.

Water Ermine   page 234

Spilosoma urticae (Esp.)

Nb. SE   2062(10568)

Field characters & Similar species FW 18-21mm. Very like an unusually plain example of the white form of White Ermine, but distinguished by the pure white ground-colour of forewing and absence of a central black spot on hindwing. Forewing usually has one or two central black dots, and sometimes a short row near wing tip, but may be entirely plain. See also Muslin Moth.

Flight season One generation. June-July. Comes to

light.
Life cycle Overwinters as a pupa, in a cocoon formed among plant debris. Larva late June-early September.
Larval foodplants Herbaceous plants, including marshland species such as Water Mint, Water Dock, Yellow Loosestrife, Lousewort and Yellow Iris.
Habitat Fens, wet meadows, marshes, ditches and other waterside places, dune-slacks, vegetated shingle and saltmarshes.
Status & distribution Resident. Nationally Scarce B. Now largely confined to coastal areas in south-east England, from Sussex to Norfolk, with possibly a few inland sites in southern England. Occasionally reported elsewhere in southern England, sometimes in error. Elsewhere, well established at Exminster Marshes, Devon, a single example occurred at Spurn Head, Yorkshire, on 8 June 1992, and one was reared from a larva found in marshy habitat on the Ravensworth Estate, near Darlington, Co. Durham, in September 1968.

Muslin Moth
Diaphora mendica (Cl.)
Common. S,C,(N)   page 234
                                   2063(10572)

Field characters FW M 14-17mm F 17-19mm. Generally smaller than similar species, always with a whitish or grey-brown abdomen. Forewing is broad, with a variable pattern of black spots. In England, Wales and Scotland, male is grey-brown or sooty-grey and unmistakable. In Ireland it is creamy white or creamy brown. Female has white, slightly translucent wings and a whitish abdomen.
Similar species In White, Water and Buff Ermines the abdomen is largely yellow, and these species are generally larger, with opaque wings.
Flight season One generation. May-early June. Male is nocturnal, and comes regularly to light. Female is active by day, flies in sunshine, and may also be found crawling on low vegetation.
Life cycle Overwinters as a pupa, in a cocoon formed among plant debris. Larva mid June-early September.
Larval foodplants Many herbaceous plants, including docks, plantains and Red Dead-nettle. Egg batches have been found and reared on Aspen.
Habitat Many open habitats, including open woodland, downland, sand-dunes, gardens and hedgerows.
Status & distribution Resident. Common. Well distributed throughout England and Wales. Rare on Man. Widespread but very local in mainland Scotland, north to Sutherland. Widespread but somewhat local in Ireland. Widespread and frequent in the Channel Islands.

Ruby Tiger
Phragmatobia fuliginosa fuliginosa (L.)
Common. S,C   page 234
                               2064(10550)
ssp. *borealis* (Stdgr.)
Common. N

Field characters FW 14-19mm. A small, thickset, moth with rather thinly-scaled wings. Forewing pinkish brown, or deep pink, with one or two small dark central spots, sometimes more or less linked to form a crescent. Hindwing bright pink (very rarely yellow), including fringes, with highly variable sooty-grey shading. On some, only trailing third is pink. Moths from northern England and Ireland are generally somewhat darker.
Ssp. *borealis* Forewing is darker, sometimes dull brown, with no trace of pink. Hindwing usually sooty-grey with a pink streak along trailing edge, or entirely sooty-grey, including fringes.
Similar species None.
Flight season Ssp. *fuliginosa* Two generations. Mid April-June and mid July-early September. Ssp. *borealis* One generation. May-July. Sometimes flies by day, more especially the first generation, and pairing has been observed in the mid afternoon. It also flies at night and comes to light, more frequently in the second generation.
Life cycle Overwinters as a fully grown larva. May-July and August-April where there are two generations, July-May where there is one. Often seen crossing bare ground in warm weather in the autumn, and basking in early spring sunshine.
Larval foodplants Many herbaceous plants, including ragworts and plantains; also heathers, Spindle and Broom.
Habitat Most open habitats, including downland, heathland, moorland, sand-dunes, open areas in woodland, set-aside farmland and gardens.
Status & distribution Resident. Common. Ssp. *fuliginosa* is frequent throughout England, Wales, Ireland, Man and the Channel Islands. Ssp. *borealis* is found throughout most of Scotland, although not recorded from Shetland, and moths resembling it sometimes occur further south.

2065, 2066 see Appendix

Jersey Tiger
Euplagia quadripunctaria (Poda)
Nb; suspected immigrant. SW   page 234
                                   2067(10605)

Field characters FW 28-33mm. The black and creamy-white striped markings on forewing, and red, orange or yellow ground-colour of hindwing make this moth unmistakable. Variation is usually slight, but examples with entirely black forewings or more extensively marked with white have been recorded.
Similar species None.
Flight season One generation. Mid July-early September, but usually starting early August. Active on warm days, visiting flowers such as Buddleias and thistles. Also flies at night and comes to light.
Life cycle Overwinters as a small larva among foodplants. Larva September-May.
Larval foodplants Many herbaceous plants, particularly Common Nettle, Hemp-agrimony, White Dead-nettle, plantains and Ground-ivy, and also Bramble.
Habitat Gardens, rough and disturbed ground, hedgerows, coastal cliffs, under-cliff and the higher

Larva of Cinnabar.

parts of beaches.

Status & distribution Resident and suspected immigrant. Nationally Scarce B. Well established and quite numerous along the south coast of Devon, from just west of Dartmouth to just east of Bridport, Dorset. Extends inland around Exeter and to the edge of Dartmoor, and there are also records from the Plymouth area. Single examples have been recorded further east, from Portland, Dorset, to the Isle of Wight and Sussex. Some of these could have been immigrants, but the pattern of records suggests that colonies have been established on the south coast of the Isle of Wight and near Rye, on the Sussex coast. Widespread and abundant in the Channel Islands.

Scarlet Tiger page 235

Callimorpha dominula (L.)
Local. SW 2068(10603)

Field characters FW 23-27mm. Unmistakable, with white and yellow spots and blotches on the iridescent black forewing and largely red hindwing. The markings vary in detail, but extreme forms are rare. These include f. *bimacula* Cock., with outer forewing spots reduced or absent and extensively black hindwing and f. *rossica* Kolenati, with ground-colour of hindwing yellow.

Similar species See Cream-spot Tiger.

Flight season One generation. June-July. Flies by day, and is often seen at rest on leaves. Male patrols wildly in late afternoon and early evening. Also flies at night and comes to light.

Life cycle Overwinters as a larva. Larva August-May. Feeds openly by day, especially in sunshine.

Larval foodplants A wide range, but particularly associated with Common Comfrey, also Hemp-agrimony and Hound's-tongue (on Welsh dunes). When larger, often disperses to feed on other plants, including Common Nettle, Bramble, sallows, Honeysuckle and Meadowsweet.

Habitat Fens and marshes, riverbanks, damp meadows in floodplains, and coastal habitats, including the upper parts of beaches and under-cliff. Disperses widely in years of abundance, appearing in gardens, woodland and along ditches, where colonies may be established, at least temporarily.

Status & distribution Resident. Local. Quite well distributed in southern and south-west England,

from Berkshire, Hampshire, Oxfordshire and Gloucestershire westwards to Cornwall, and in south and west Wales. There are two isolated colonies on the east coast of Kent, and until the early part of the 20th century it was also found elsewhere in south-east England and East Anglia. In the Channel Islands several have been recorded on Jersey, the first in 1986, but it is not known if it is resident.

Cinnabar page 235

Tyria jacobaeae (L.)
Common. S,C,(N) 2069(10607)

Field characters FW 17-23mm. Unmistakable. Little variation, but very rarely the red or pinkish-red markings are replaced by yellow (f. *flavescens* Thiery-Mieg), forewing is red with a black border (f. *coneyi* Watson), or wings are entirely black (f. *negrana* Cabeau). Female is generally smaller.

Similar species Burnet moths, also active by day, have much narrower forewings and are more thickset, with long, thickened antennae.

Flight season One generation. Mid May-early August. Has a long period of emergence, so newly emerged moths may be seen alongside fully grown larvae. Easily disturbed by day, and flies in sunshine. Comes to light, occasionally in large numbers.

Life cycle Overwinters as a pupa, in a flimsy cocoon just under the ground. Larva July-early September. Conspicuous, sitting openly on the foodplant by day.

Larval foodplants Mainly Common Ragwort. Eats the leaves and flowers, and where populations are high reduces the plants to bare stems. Also found on other ragworts, cultivated ragworts, groundsels, and occasionally reported from Colt's-foot.

Habitat Most numerous in well drained, rabbit-grazed grassland, including mature sand-dunes and heathland, but also in many other open habitats, including gardens and woodland rides.

Status & distribution Resident. Common. Well distributed throughout most of England, Wales and Man. More local and mainly coastal in northernmost counties of England and in Scotland, extending north to Angus in the east and Skye in the west. A single example was recorded in Orkney in 1985. Widespread and frequent in the Channel Islands.

2069a see Appendix

Ctenuchidae

This family is closely related to the Arctiidae, of which it is considered to be a subfamily by some taxonomists. Of the 3,000 or so species known, most are tropical and very few are found in the wild in Europe. Of these, two are suspected to have occasionally reached the British Isles unaided. Others, including tropical species, are sometimes accidentally imported with food produce. The adults are day-flying and feed at flowers. They have rather triangular forewings, often with a number of semi-transparent spots and noticeably small hindwings, and superficially resemble burnet moths. The larvae are hairy.

Syntominae

Nine-spotted
page 235

Amata phegea (L.)

Suspected rare immigrant.
2070(10517)

Field characters FW 18-22mm. Unlike any moth resident in the British Isles, with slender, inky blue-black wings scattered with white spots, two yellow bands on abdomen and white-tipped antennae.
Similar species Two species in mainland Europe are quite similar, and these could possibly occur as immigrants, but require examination of genitalia to distinguish.
Flight season One generation. June-July. Flies by day and visits flowers.
Life cycle The early stages have not been found in the British Isles. In mainland Europe it overwinters as a larva. Larva August-May.
Larval foodplants Dead-nettles, dandelions and other herbaceous plants.
Habitat Flowery, well-drained grassland, disturbed ground, farmland, old gravel pits and clearings and rides in woodland.
Status & distribution Suspected rare immigrant, or accidental import, recorded twice. The first was reported as captured in 1872 on the Kent coast between Folkestone and Dover, flying in sunshine, but the recorder suspect. A second example was reported from a photograph, taken at Clacton-on-Sea, Essex, on 24 July 2000. Resident in southern Europe, where it is local.

2071-2074a (including Euchromiinae) see Appendix

Nolidae

A small family found worldwide. Six species have been recorded in the British Isles, of which four are resident, one is an immigrant that sometimes breeds, and one has been recorded once as a prob-able immigrant. All are small, whitish or grey moths with rather rounded forewings with basal and central scale tufts (easily lost), and could well be mistaken for micro-moths. They are not often seen by day, but come to light and sometimes to sugar. The larvae feed on woody plants, and are quite hairy. They pupate above ground in tough, sometimes boat-shaped cocoons, usually formed on a stem of the foodplant, incorporating fragments of bark.

Small Black Arches
page 235

Meganola strigula ([D. & S.])

Na. S
2075(10423)

Field characters & Similar species FW 9-11mm. Similar to Least Black Arches, but slightly larger on average, with broader, greyer forewing, and flies later in the year. Black cross-lines are rather irregular, and there is no distinct central cross-band. Outer area is seldom noticeably darker, and usually has small but distinct blackish streaks, sometimes roughly arranged into a cross-line. Hindwing brown.
Flight season One generation. Late June-early August. Comes to sugar and light, occasionally in numbers.
Life cycle Overwinters as a small larva. Larva August-early June. Pupates in a boat-shaped cocoon formed on a twig of the foodplant.
Larval foodplants Pedunculate Oak.
Habitat Long-established broadleaved woodland and wooded commons with mature oaks.
Status & distribution Resident. Nationally Scarce A. Very local and decreasing in southern England; formerly from Devon to Essex and Kent but now mainly from Dorset, Hampshire, the Isle of Wight, north to Oxfordshire and Buckinghamshire and eastwards to Surrey and Sussex. Dubiously reported from Monmouthshire.

Kent Black Arches
page 235

Meganola albula ([D. & S.])

Nb. SE
2076(10425)

Field characters FW 10-11mm. Ground-colour of forewings is white, and they appear smooth, like polished flint, due to soft, tawny brown or grey-brown markings. These vary considerably in extent, so that some examples have a narrowed central cross-band and reduced chequering on leading edge, whereas others are extensively darkened. A plain white form has also been recorded.
Similar species Scarce Black Arches is smaller, with fine cross-lines, often edged with darker, frequently blackish scales.

Flight season One generation. Late June-early August. Sometimes disturbed from rest under leaves by day. Comes to light.

Life cycle Overwinters as a small larva. Larva September-late May or June. Pupates in a cocoon formed on a vertical stem.

Larval foodplants Dewberry, Bramble, Raspberry and Wild Strawberry.

Habitat Coastal heathland, saltmarshes, shingle and sandy beaches. Inland on chalk downland and open areas in woodland.

Status & distribution Resident. Nationally Scarce B. Well distributed on or near the coast of England from Devon to Norfolk, including the Isle of Wight and Scilly, and inland in Hampshire, Berkshire and Surrey, and also recorded from Wiltshire. Occasionally recorded on the east coast north to Spurn Head and Muston, Yorkshire, and on the coast of Wales. Widespread and frequent in the Channel Islands.

Short-cloaked Moth   page 235

Nola cucullatella (L.)

Common. S,C   2077(10427)

Field characters FW 8-10mm. The sharply demarcated dark base of grey (or less often darker grey-brown) forewing makes this the easiest member of the family to recognise, and gives the appearance of a short cloak when the moth is at rest.

Similar species None.

Flight season One generation. June-July. Both sexes come to light.

Life cycle Overwinters as a small larva. Larva August-June. Pupates in a cocoon on a twig.

Larval foodplants Hawthorn, Midland Hawthorn, Blackthorn, Apple, Pear and Plum.

Habitat Hedgerows, gardens, scrub and woodland.

Status & distribution Resident. Common. Well distributed and fairly frequent in England and Wales, north to Co. Durham and Cumbria. One record from Man in 1893. Widespread and frequent in the Channel Islands.

Least Black Arches   page 235

Nola confusalis (H.-S.)

Local. T   2078(10429)

Field characters FW 9-11mm. Ground-colour of rather narrow forewing is usually whitish, with fine, black cross-lines, the innermost of which is elbowed or V-shaped, and the outermost strongly curved in leading half, and often shaped like a question mark. Usually a narrow but fairly distinct grey-brown band between scalloped, brown (or black) central cross-line and outermost one, and often whole outer area is noticeably darker, sometimes with small blackish dashes. In f. *columbina* Image, found in Epping Forest, Essex, forewing has a grey-brown ground-colour.

Similar species Small Black Arches, Scarce Black Arches, Jersey Black Arches.

Flight season One generation. May-June. Comes

regularly to light, usually in small numbers.

Life cycle Overwinters as a pupa, in a cocoon attached to a twig. Larva June-August.

Larval foodplants A variety of broadleaved trees, including Downy Birch, Blackthorn, Purging Buckthorn and several species of lime. Also reported from Apple, Pedunculate Oak, Beech and Evergreen Oak.

Habitat Woodland and other well-wooded areas, including hedgerows, parkland, orchards and gardens.

Status & distribution Resident. Local. Quite well distributed in the southern half of England and in Wales and Man. Local in northern England, and very local in Scotland, mainly in the west. Local in Ireland. Widespread and frequent in the Channel Islands.

Scarce Black Arches   page 235

Nola aerugula (Hb.)

Immigrant; transitory resident.   2079(10431)

Field characters FW 8-9mm. Ground-colour of forewing is white, variably clouded with brown or grey-brown. Slightly wavy, fine black or brown cross-line beyond middle of forewing is diagnostic, although on some examples it is rather faint.

Similar species Least Black Arches flies earlier in the year, and outer black cross-line is strongly curved. See also Kent Black Arches and Jersey Black Arches.

Flight season One generation. Late June-early August. Mainly seen at light, but has also been found at rest on grass stems from dusk onwards.

Life cycle Overwinters as a larva. Larva August-June. Pupates in a cocoon among stem bases and plant debris.

Larval foodplants Common Bird's-foot-trefoil and clovers.

Habitat Formerly resident on sand-dunes.

Status & distribution Immigrant and transitory resident. Over 50 individuals have been reported since 1900, mostly in light-traps on the coasts of eastern and south-east England, from Sussex to Yorkshire, with records also from Dorset and the Isle of Wight. Resident near Deal, Kent, from 1858-1898, and might establish temporary colonies again. In mainland Europe its distribution includes France, Belgium and Denmark.

Jersey Black Arches   not illustrated

Nola chlamitulalis (Hb.)

Rare immigrant.   2079a(10437)

Field characters & Similar species FW 7-10mm. Easily distinguished by bold dark markings near outer edge of forewing, consisting of blackish-brown blotches and a tawny band along outer edge. Forewing otherwise whitish with faint markings. Most similar in shape to Least Black Arches, but forewing more pointed and angular.

Status & distribution Rare immigrant. Reported from the Channel Islands only, where one was recorded in a light-trap at La Haule, Jersey, on 16 July 1963. Resident in southern Europe.

Convolvulus Hawkmoth
Agrius convolvuli

225

Death's Head Hawkmoth
Acherontia atropos

Pine Hawkmoth
Hyloicus pinastri

Privet Hawkmoth
Sphinx ligustri

f. *brunnea*

f. *centripunctata*

♂

Lime Hawkmoth
Mimas tiliae

♀

Eyed Hawkmoth
Smerinthus ocellata

♂

Poplar Hawkmoth
Laothoe populi

buff form ♀

Narrow-bordered Bee Hawkmoth
Hemaris tityus

Broad-bordered Bee Hawkmoth
Hemaris fuciformis

Hummingbird Hawkmoth
Macroglossum stellatarum

Hummingbird Hawkmoth feeding at a
honeysuckle flower

Willowherb Hawkmoth
Proserpinus proserpina

Oleander Hawkmoth
Daphnis nerii

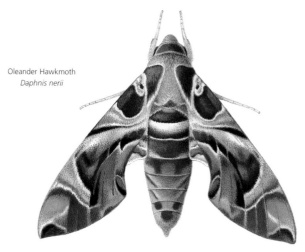

Spurge Hawkmoth
Hyles euphorbiae

Bedstraw Hawkmoth
Hyles gallii

Striped Hawkmoth
Hyles livornica

Elephant Hawkmoth
Deilephila elpenor

Small Elephant Hawkmoth
Deilephila porcellus

Silver-striped Hawkmoth
Hippotion celerio

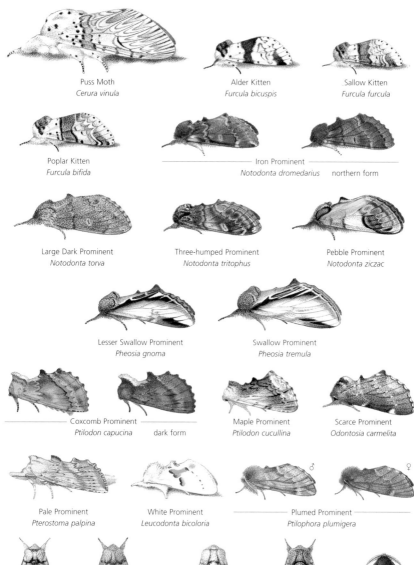

229

Puss Moth
Cerura vinula

Alder Kitten
Furcula bicuspis

Sallow Kitten
Furcula furcula

Poplar Kitten
Furcula bifida

———— Iron Prominent ————
Notodonta dromedarius   northern form

Large Dark Prominent
Notodonta torva

Three-humped Prominent
Notodonta tritophus

Pebble Prominent
Notodonta ziczac

Lesser Swallow Prominent
Pheosia gnoma

Swallow Prominent
Pheosia tremula

——— Coxcomb Prominent ———
Ptilodon capucina   dark form

Maple Prominent
Ptilodon cucullina

Scarce Prominent
Odontosia carmelita

Pale Prominent
Pterostoma palpina

White Prominent
Leucodonta bicoloria

——— Plumed Prominent ———
Ptilophora plumigera

——— Marbled Brown ———
Drymonia dodonaea
f. *nigrescens*

——— Lunar Marbled Brown ———
Drymonia ruficornis

Dusky Marbled
Brown
*Gluphisia crenata
vertunea*

Small Chocolate-tip
Clostera pigra

Scarce Chocolate-tip
Clostera anachoreta

Chocolate-tip
Clostera curtula

230

Buff-tip
Phalera bucephala

———————————————————— Lobster Moth ————————————————————

Stauropus fagi

Stauropus fagi f. *obscura*

Tawny Prominent
Harpyia milhauseri

Great Prominent
Peridea anceps

Figure of Eight
Diloba caeruleocephala

Thaumetopoeidae Processionary moths page 206

——————————— Pine Processionary ———————————
Thaumetopoea pityocampa

——————————— Oak Processionary ———————————
Thaumetopoea processionea

Lymantriidae Tussock moths pages 207-208

Reed Tussock
Laelia coenosa

——————— Scarce Vapourer ———————
Orgyia recens

——————— Vapourer ———————
Orgyia antiqua

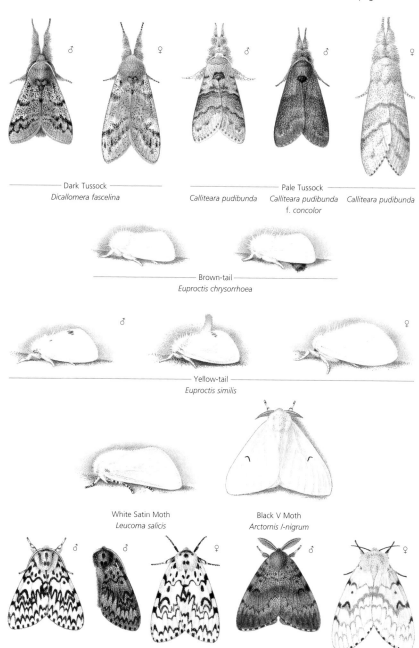

♂ ♀

——— Dark Tussock ———
Dicallomera fascelina

♂ ♂ ♀

——— Pale Tussock ———
Calliteara pudibunda   *Calliteara pudibunda*   *Calliteara pudibunda*
f. *concolor*

——— Brown-tail ———
Euproctis chrysorrhoea

♂ ♀

——— Yellow-tail ———
Euproctis similis

White Satin Moth
Leucoma salicis

Black V Moth
Arctornis l-nigrum

♂ ♂ ♀   ♂ ♀

——— Black Arches ———
Lymantria monacha   *Lymantria monacha*   *Lymantria monacha*
f. *eremita*

——— Gypsy Moth ———
Lymantria dispar

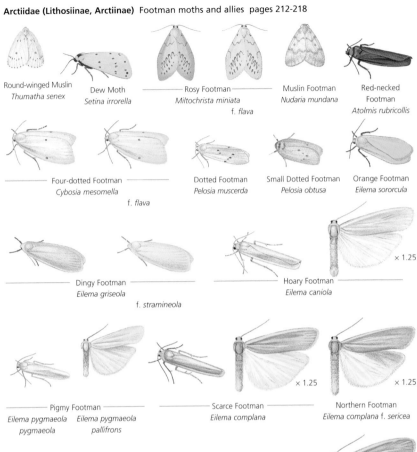

Round-winged Muslin
Thumatha senex

Dew Moth
Setina irrorella

————Rosy Footman————
Miltochrista miniata
f. *flava*

Muslin Footman
Nudaria mundana

Red-necked
Footman
Atolmis rubricollis

————Four-dotted Footman————
Cybosia mesomella
f. *flava*

Dotted Footman
Pelosia muscerda

Small Dotted Footman
Pelosia obtusa

Orange Footman
Eilema sororcula

————Dingy Footman————
Eilema griseola
f. *stramineola*

× 1.25

————Hoary Footman————
Eilema caniola

————Pigmy Footman————
Eilema pygmaeola   *Eilema pygmaeola*
pygmaeola   *pallifrons*

× 1.25

————Scarce Footman————
Eilema complana

× 1.25

Northern Footman
Eilema complana f. *sericea*

————Buff Footman————
Eilema depressa

× 1.25

————Common Footman————
Eilema lurideola

♂   ♀

————Four-spotted Footman————
Lithosia quadra

Feathered Footman
Spiris striata

————Speckled Footman————
Coscinia cribraria bivittata

Crimson Speckled
Utetheisa pulchella

232

— Wood Tiger —

Parasemia plantaginis plantaginis   f. *hospita*

Garden Tiger
Arctia caja

Arctia caja
f. *petriburgensis*

Arctia caja
f. *fumosa*

Arctia caja
f. *lutescens*

Cream-spot Tiger
Arctia villica britannica   ♂

Arctiidae (Arctiinae) Tiger moths, ermines and allies pages 219-222

———————— Clouded Buff ————————
Diacrisia sannio

———— White Ermine ————
Spilosoma lubricipeda

———————— Buff Ermine ————————
Spilosoma luteum

Water Ermine
Spilosoma urticae

———— Muslin Moth ————
Diaphora mendica

———— Ruby Tiger ————
Phragmatobia fuliginosa fuliginosa   *Phragmatobia fuliginosa borealis*

———— Jersey Tiger ————
Euplagia quadripunctaria   f. *lutescens*

♂

Scarlet Tiger
Callimorpha dominula

Scarlet Tiger
f. *bimacula*   *Callimorpha dominula*   f. *rossica*

Cinnabar
Tyria jacobaeae   *Tyria jacobaeae* f. *flavescens*   *Tyria jacobaeae* f. *coneyi*

Ctenuchidae page 223

Nine-spotted *Amata phegea*

Nolidae Black arches pages 223-224

Small Black Arches   Kent Black Arches   Short-cloaked Moth
Meganola strigula   *Meganola albula*   *Nola cucullatella*

Least Black Arches   Scarce Black Arches
Nola confusalis   *Nola aerugula*

Noctuidae – noctuids

The Noctuidae is the largest family of macro-moths in the British Isles, with just over 400 species on the latest British list, although a minority have certainly occurred only as imports or are of dubious origin. Worldwide, there are an estimated 21,000 valid species described, and the family is well represented in every continent.

Heart and Dart

Marbled Coronet

Orange Sallow

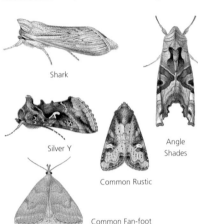

Shark

Silver Y

Common Rustic

Angle Shades

Common Fan-foot

Most British noctuids are medium-sized, stout-bodied, frequently brown moths, with forewings often substantially longer than they are deep. Most are specialised for powerful, manoeuvrable flight and fly mainly at night. The majority of long-distance migrant moths are noctuids. They require regular re-fuelling for flight, and feed at flowers, oozing tree-sap, aphid honeydew or sugary baits. The exceptions in terms of body form are the snouts, fan-foots and allies, which sometimes occur as immigrants and are generally brown, but which have not become specialised for powerful flight and retain deep wings and slight bodies, more like geometrid moths. The Waved Black, for example, rests on vertical surfaces with its wings spread flat and is so like a geometrid moth in build that it is often mistaken for one.

However, most noctuid moths rest with the trailing edges of the forewings brought together or slightly overlapping, over the folded hindwings, and hold their wings tent-like over the body. In the Noctuinae, popularly known as darts, the narrowed forewings are held horizontally over the body in the same plane, and overlap to a much greater extent, making the insect much narrower and more able to slip between vertical stems and grass-blades in the open grassy places in which they predominate.

There is usually a conspicuous kidney-shaped marking and an adjacent oval and other marks in the central area of the forewing of noctuid moths, and as the thyatirid moths are the only other group of macro-moths with these markings, the kidney-mark and oval can be useful recognition features. The size, shape and colour of these markings are also often helpful in distinguishing particular species from close relatives.

The majority of noctuid moths have bald larvae (a notable exception being the daggers). The full complement of five pairs of claspers (prolegs) is usually present, but in the Herminiinae (fan-foots), Catocalinae (red underwings), Hypeninae (snouts) and Plusiinae (Ys and brasses) they are often reduced to three or four pairs, including the anal claspers. Most noctuid larvae feed on the leaves, stems or roots of grasses or broadleaved herbaceous plants, but some feed on the foliage of trees and shrubs, most notably the daggers, quakers, drabs, chestnuts, sallows, red underwings and fan-foots. Those dependent on grasses and herbs tend to overwinter as larvae, feeding in mild periods from autumn to spring. Those on trees and shrubs tend to overwinter as eggs or pupae. The larval period of some coincides with the flowers, fruits or tender spring leaves, but others can cope with the older leaves or seek out new late summer growth. Most noctuids have one generation per year in the British Isles.

While the majority pupate on or below ground, or sometimes in surface leaf litter, some, particularly those feeding in trees and shrubs, pupate in cocoons attached to leaves, tree trunks, fences and other objects, so that the whole life cycle may take place in the tree canopy.

Taxonomy

Although most noctuid moths have a certain jizz which sets them apart from other families of moths, the evolutionary relationships between some species and groups within the family are still not completely understood or agreed upon by taxonomists. Hence, although the British species are divided into 19 subfamilies in both the British and European lists, the arrangement of species into subfamilies and the sequence in which they are presented differs considerably, and further changes are underway.

The familiar arrangement of the British list, broadly used throughout the 20th century, presents the major subfamilies in the following order (with their general characteristics):

Noctuinae – darts, yellow underwings and clays – forewings narrow, square-ended, held flat over body and deeply overlapped, usually sombre in colour.
Hadeninae – brocades, quakers and the wainscots with leaf-feeding larvae – stocky thorax with broad, well-patterned forewings held in shallow tent-like fashion, with ends forming a V-shape.
Cucullinae – sharks, also swordgrasses, shoulder-knots, pinions and allies – elongate pointed forewings, pulled close to body at rest, thorax often

with crest like a shark's dorsal fin, hence common name of group.
Acronictinae – daggers, (sallows and chestnuts) – The daggers have elaborately marked larvae, often hairy. Name refers to dagger-like markings on grey forewings of many species. Sallows and chestnuts are distinctive and easily recognised, but not dagger-like, and are placed in Hadeninae in European list.
Amphipyrinae – arches, brindles, minors, rustics, ears and the wainscots with stem-boring larvae – a large and diverse group in the British list originally grouped together on shared pattern of wing venation, lack of eye-lashes and lack of spines on legs! Easier to recognise by the descriptive common names of the various sub-groups.
Plusiinae – silver and golden Ys and brasses – usually have metallic patches or letters on forewings, which are held close to the body at rest, and conspicuous tufts atop thorax and abdomen.
Catocalinae – underwings – some have brightly coloured and banded hindwings. Forewings broad and sombre in colour. Often prominently spined legs and semi-looper larvae with some reduction in prolegs. Almost half the world's noctuid species may eventually be allocated to this group, but few species in the British Isles.
Ophiderinae – an uneasy rag-bag collection of species which did not seem to fit elsewhere, now being disbanded, with most entering the Catocalinae – very many tropical species but few in Britain, all distinctive, including the Herald, sometimes placed in a subfamily of its own, and the Blackneck, sometimes placed in Catocalinae.
Hypeninae – snouts – head with a 'snout' composed of long palps. Body slender, wings form delta-shape when together.
Herminiinae – fan-foots – slender in body and similar to snouts but forewings usually narrower, often crossed by very wavy central lines.

In contrast to the British list, the current European listing begins with the Acronictinae, and runs through the Herminiinae, Catocalinae, Hypeninae, Plusiinae, Cucullinae, Amphipyrinae (now restricted to the Copper Underwings and close allies), Hadeninae (now a very large grouping) and concludes with the Noctuinae, as can be seen by studying the European serial numbers shown on the species descriptions. Interestingly, Edward Newman's standard British textbook for much of the 19th century also had the Acronictinae at the beginning of the noctuids, but ended with the Plusiinae and Catocalinae, and had the Noctuinae in the middle!

The subfamilies in which the caterpillars have a reduced number of prolegs are grouped together in both the British and European listings, but feature late in the former and early in the latter. The Noctuinae have larvae without such obvious specialisations as leg reduction. Such features suggest placement early in an evolutionary sequence, as in the British listing. However, the adults show a high degree of evolution in wing position, shape and mechanism, which is a reason for placing them at the conclusion of the Noctuidae, as in the European listing.

As in the rest of this guide, the sequence of species adopted here follows the British list exactly, for the reasons explained in the Introduction.

Noctuinae
Darts, yellow under-wings and clays

White-line Dart	Lesser Yellow Underwing	Setaceous Hebrew Character

Square-spot Dart   page 311

Euxoa obelisca ([D. & S.])

ssp. *grisea* (Tutt)

Nb. S,W,NE   2080(10282)

Field characters & Similar species FW 14-18mm. Pale leading edge of forewing near thorax of males and some females is most obvious feature, but this is shared by the much more variable White-line Dart and Coast Dart, and in cases of doubt it may be necessary to examine the genitalia. Square-spot Dart lacks black arrowheads towards outer edge of forewing, a feature of many forms of White-line Dart. Cross-line beyond middle approaches or merges with outer edge of kidney-mark on forewing, and from this line to outer edge of wing the colour is rather uniform and dark. Ground-colour grey-brown to reddish, and rather uniform across forewing. White-line Dart and Coast Dart appear on the wing earlier, flying from July onwards. In both these species, outer third of forewing has generally a more varied pattern of light and dark shades, and outer cross-line usually arcs quite widely around kidney-mark.
Flight season One generation. Early August-early October. Recorded visiting the flowers of ragworts and heathers and attracted to sugar-bait, but most records are to mv light, sometimes in numbers.
Life cycle Probably overwinters as an egg. Larva February-March, pupating underground in July.
Larval foodplants Various low-growing plants. Common Rock-rose and Lady's Bedstraw have been reported specifically but the larval habits in the wild are poorly understood. Has been reared on plantains and bedstraws.
Habitat Rocky and hilly coasts, some of which are

soft rock, earth or chalk. Appears to be absent from most flat, sandy coasts. Also some inland hilly sites.
Status & distribution Resident. Nationally Scarce B. Almost entirely coastal in Britain. Recorded from scattered localities along the south coast of England, including Scilly and the Isle of Wight, as far east as the Crumbles, Eastbourne, Sussex, and as probable wanderers at Dungeness, Kent. Found in many places along the west coast of England, Wales and Scotland north to Arran, Islay, Rum and Canna. Also recorded from the coast of Northumberland (including Lindisfarne) and from the east coast of Scotland (Berwickshire and Midlothian northwards to Kincardineshire and Aberdeenshire). Local on Man. Recorded from several localities on the coast of Northern Ireland and from a thin scatter of places on the south and west coasts of the Irish Republic. Reliably recorded from a number of inland sites recently, including Hillmorton, Warwickshire, the Malvern Hills, Herefordshire, and Matlock, Derbyshire, but some inland records are undoubtedly misidentifications of the White-line Dart. Rare in the Channel Islands.

White-line Dart   page 311

Euxoa tritici (L.)

Common. T   2081(10280)

Field characters FW 13-17mm. Extremely variable in colour and intensity of markings, even in same locality. Also quite variable in size, but distinguished from most related species by up to six short, dark arrowheads towards outer edge. Forewing ranges from blackish grey, dark brown and various shades of grey to pale brown or sandy. Variation often reflects soil type, with moths from coastal sand-dunes and sandy heathland tending to be paler, brighter, and sandy or grey. Those from peaty moor-land tend to be dark and strongly marked. Many individuals have the major vein parallel to leading edge of forewing highlighted with white scales, hence the English name.
Similar species See Square-spot Dart, Coast Dart, Garden Dart and Heath Rustic.
Flight season One generation. Mainly mid July-mid August, occasionally to early September. Comes to light, sometimes in numbers, and feeds at sugar and flowers, notably of Marram-grass, ragworts and heathers, sometimes by day.
Life cycle Overwinters as an egg, laid on the food-plant. Larva late March-July, feeding at night and hiding in the soil by day. Pupates underground.
Larval foodplants A wide range of herbaceous plants, including Hedge and Lady's Bedstraws, Corn Spurrey and mouse-ears.
Habitat Coastal sand-dunes and cliffs, heathland, moorland, downland and open heathy woodland.
Status & distribution Resident. Common. In suit-able habitat in most parts of Great Britain, possibly supplemented by immigration. Local on Man. Mainly coastal in Ireland. Local and occasional in the Channel Islands.

Garden Dart   page 311

Euxoa nigricans (L.)

Common. T   2082(10275)

Field characters & Similar species FW 15-18mm.
Similar in size and shape to White-line Dart, but
plainer and browner or black rather than greyish,
lacking the arrowheads near outer edge and never
with a pale streak along leading edge. Variable in
colour. In southern Britain individuals are often paler.
See also Square-spot Rustic, which has broader
forewing, at least in male.
Flight season One generation. July-mid September,
occasional individuals from mid-June and to early
October. Comes to light and sugar in small numbers,
and to flowers, including ragworts and buddleias.
Life cycle Overwinters as an egg, laid on the foodplant. Larva March-June, feeding at night. Pupates
underground in an earthen cocoon.
Larval foodplants Herbaceous plants, including
clovers, docks and plantains.
Habitat A wide range, but typically gardens, allotments, farmland, downland, rough open ground,
flood-plains and marshes, occasionally in woodland
rides.
Status & distribution Resident. Common.
Throughout most of Great Britain and Ireland. In
lowland Scotland. Not recorded from Orkney or reliably from Shetland. Local and rare on Man.
Widespread as occasional individuals in the Channel
Islands.

Coast Dart   page 311

Euxoa cursoria (Hufn.)

Nb. Nsc. E,WC,N   2083(10284)

Field characters & Similar species FW 14-18mm. A
very variable species, wing colours ranging from
straw and white to dark grey and brown, but generally with a sandy tint. Darker forms predominate in
more northern populations. Some forms resemble
Sand Dart, but differ in that forewings are more
tightly drawn together at rest, leading edge of
forewing is slightly curved and kidney-mark is much
larger. White-line Dart has a similar range of colour
forms. On underside of forewing of Coast Dart,
kidney-mark is large and blurred and there is a
blurred dark band between it and edge of wing.
Kidney-mark of White-line Dart is small and crescent-
like and there is no dark band. Some Coast Dart are
as dark as Garden Dart.
Flight season One generation. Late July-August,
sometimes early September. Hides among vegetation
by day, and from dusk visits flowers such as Marram-
grass and other grasses, ragworts and heathers.
Attracted to sugar-bait and comes to light, sometimes in fair numbers.
Life cycle Probably overwinters as an egg, until
about February or March. Larva early spring-July.
Feeds at night and hides in the sand near the foodplant by day, eventually pupating quite deep in the
sand in an egg-shaped cocoon.

Larval foodplants The leaves of a range of unre-
lated common sand-dune plants, including Sea
Sandwort, violets, Early Hair-grass and Sand Couch,
Hound's-tongue, Sticky Mouse-ear and Sea Spurge.
Has been reared on plantains.
Habitat Coastal sand-dunes. Tends to breed where
the sand-dune vegetation is well established, rather
than in the less stable dunes favoured by the Sand
Dart.
Status & distribution Resident and suspected immigrant. Nationally Scarce B. Largely restricted to the
bigger tracts of sandy beaches on the east, west and
north coasts of northern and central Britain, and
apparently absent from some of these. Present on
Shetland and various of the Hebrides. A special
investigation by B. Skinner in the late 1980s,
including searches for larvae, found no evidence of
breeding from Cheshire southwards on the west
coast of Britain and from Suffolk southwards on the
east coast. Occasional records further south are
either suspected immigrants or are misidentifications
of the Sand Dart, the latter accounting for most of
the reports from the Welsh coast, but confirmed
from Tenby, Pembrokeshire. As suspected immigrants, about a dozen have been found on or near
the coasts of Essex and Kent since 1950, coinciding
with influxes of known immigrants, and generally of
a sandy-coloured form paler than those of populations resident in Britain. Local and scarce on Man. In
Ireland recorded from widely scattered locations on
the north and western coasts. In the Channel Islands
only on Jersey, where local and rare.

Wood's Dart   page 311

Agrotis graslini Ramb.

Jersey   2083a(10357)

Field characters & Similar species FW 15-20mm.
The more pointed forewing and pure white hindwing
distinguish Wood's Dart from similar members of the
group, including sandy-coloured forms of Archer's
Dart, which it resembles in having boldly patterned
forewing with pale-edged kidney-mark, a long,
central, blunt dart-mark and feathered antennae in
male. There are three pale and weak cross-lines,
varying in strength with wing colour. Archer's Dart
has hindwing marked with grey to some extent (may
only be slight). Sand Dart also has less pointed
forewing with daintier markings, and male has un-
feathered antennae. See also Spalding's Dart.
Flight season In mainland Europe, August-October.
Comes to light and sugar.
Larval foodplants In mainland Europe recorded
from Tuberous Hawk's-head, scabious, plantains and
docks.
Habitat Coastal sand-dunes.
Status & distribution Probable resident on Jersey.
Presently known only from Jersey, where it was first
recognised from eight individuals captured at Les
Quennevais, on 22 August 2001. Two singletons
trapped here on 1 and 3 August 1995 have subse-
quently been identified. Most probably there is a

239

240

resident population. The known European range is very limited, being confined to coastal dunes in France, Portugal and Spain. It also occurs on the North African coast.

Light Feathered Rustic page 311
Agrotis cinerea ([D. & S.])
Nb. S,C   2084(10360)

Field characters FW 13-17mm. A dart moth with a relatively broad, rather rounded forewing (narrower in female), with several colour forms, usually with several dark spots on leading edge, from which originate fine, dark, irregular cross-lines. Kidney-mark is reduced sometimes almost to a small circle and oval is tiny or absent. Lacks a bullet-shaped mark in centre of forewing. The light chalky or bluish-grey forms of southern England and south Wales are fairly easy to recognise. Those from Derbyshire, Warwickshire and Forest of Dean, Gloucestershire, are darker, slate-grey, brown or blackish, but usually cross-lines are strongly marked. Female smaller than male.
Similar species Other dart moths of similar size have larger or more prominent kidney-marks and ovals in centre of forewing.
Flight season One generation. May-June, occasional individuals in July. Male comes readily to light, female much less so, but comes to sugar and has been found at rest on short grass stems after dark. Female occasionally active in the sward by day in hot weather.
Life cycle Overwinters as a fully grown larva. Larva late June-September. Feeding is completed by late September, and it pupates underground in spring.
Larval foodplants Wild Thyme and possibly some other low-growing plants. Accepts Dandelion and plantains in captivity.
Habitat Chalk and limestone grassland, from lowland to moderate altitude, quarries, old slag heaps, coastal cliffs and shingle beaches, the main larval foodplant favouring short swards and broken ground.
Status & distribution Resident. Nationally Scarce B. Widespread and quite well distributed in open calcareous habitats, predominantly in southern England and south Wales, but with scattered populations northwards to the dales on the Derbyshire/Staffordshire border, and to Great Orme's Head and Anglesey, north Wales. Individuals have occasionally been trapped away from known populations, which suggests the moth wanders widely. Recorded rarely in Ireland, where there are old records from Co. Kerry in the south and Co. Antrim in the north.

Archer's Dart page 311
Agrotis vestigialis (Hufn.)
Local. T   2085(10356)

Field characters FW 14-18mm. One of the most distinctive members of the 'darts' owing to the bold marks and highly variegated appearance of forewing.

Three marks are particularly prominent: the kidney, the oval and a long bullet-shaped dart-mark by it. There is a row of short, dark arrowheads towards outer edge of wing. Shoulder flaps usually paler than rest of thorax. Shows strong geographical variation, those from heaths of Dorset, Hampshire and Surrey being particularly dark, with silvery grey markings; some coastal sand-dune forms are almost white. Male has feathered antennae.
Similar species Sand Dart has markings much less bold. Coast Dart has more rounded, less angular forewing. Neither has feathered antennae in male, but are found in the same coastal habitat. See also Wood's Dart and Spalding's Dart.
Flight season One generation. July-September. Readily attracted to light and sugar. Regularly seen visiting the flowers of ragworts, as well as heathers, Marram and other plants. Occasionally seen flying by day, and sometimes found resting among ragworts.
Life cycle Larva September-June, feeding throughout the winter except when very cold. Pupates underground in June.
Larval foodplants Herbaceous plants, including bedstraws, stitchworts and Sea Sandwort. Also reported from unspecified grasses.
Habitat Mainly coastal sand-dunes, but also occurs inland on heaths and in the parts of Breckland where sandy soils are present. Occasionally on limestone grassland.
Status & distribution Resident. Local. Has a scattered distribution around the coast of Britain, Man and Ireland, occurring as far north as Orkney. Inland it is found very locally on heathland in Dorset, the New Forest, Hampshire, Surrey, the Breckland of East Anglia, Lincolnshire, Nottinghamshire and Yorkshire. Also in parts of Oxfordshire on sandy soil and on limestone grassland at Sydlings Copse, near Oxford. Sites of other inland populations include the Birmingham plateau and Speyside. Local and occasional in the Channel Islands.

2086 see Appendix

Turnip Moth page 311
Agrotis segetum ([D. & S.])
Common. T   2087(10351)

Field characters FW 16-21mm. Forewing colour ranges from pale sandy through various shades of brown (occasionally greyish) to black. Kidney-mark, oval and central dart-mark may appear hollow-centred or dark, although in darker specimens they may be obscure. Hindwing of male is gleaming white; darker individuals, especially female, have darker veins and marginal shading.
Similar species Pearly Underwing is generally larger, does not have a prominent dart-mark on forewing, oval is larger and hindwing distinctly shines like mother-of-pearl. Male Turnip Moth has much whiter hindwing, with only slight mother-of-pearl effect; female likewise but dark veins.
Flight season Usually two generations. In south and

central Britain, May-June and August-October or November. In northern Britain peak numbers continue into July and the second generation may be absent or only partial. May also appear outside these times, occasionally as early as February, such individuals possibly being immigrants. Strongly attracted to light and sugar.

Life cycle Overwinters as a larva. Larva July-April, sometimes June-August. Second generation October-April. Feeds slowly during the winter and pupates underground in April when fully grown, in an earthen cocoon. Larvae almost entirely subterranean, feeding at night and known as 'cut-worms'.

Larval foodplants The roots and lower shoots of a wide variety of wild and cultivated herbaceous plants, including Turnip, Carrot, Beet, Swede and Cabbage. Regarded as a pest of root crops.

Habitat A wide variety, including gardens, agricultural land, parkland, open woodland and coastal dunes.

Status & distribution Resident and regular immigrant. Common. Found throughout Great Britain, but records more thinly scattered in Scotland. Occurs as an immigrant on Shetland. Local on Man. In Ireland recorded fairly widely from both the north and the south. Widespread and frequent in the Channel Islands.

Heart and Club   page 312

Agrotis clavis (Hufn.)

Common. T   2088(10350)

Field characters FW 14-18mm. Has relatively broad, blunt forewing, and central dart-mark is usually rather blunt and club-like. Lacks dark brown collar of Heart and Dart. Forewing colour ranges from pale straw, greyish brown or pale brown, variably flecked or clouded with dark brown, or entirely dark brown or blackish. Dark individuals have pale streaks along veins. Basal two-thirds of antennae feathered in male.

Similar species See Heart and Dart, Crescent Dart, Great Dart and Turnip Moth.

Flight season One generation. Mid June-early August. Comes frequently to light, sugar and flowers.

Life cycle Overwinters as a fully grown larva in an underground cell, in which it pupates. Larva August-spring, feeding until November, at first on the leaves and when larger on the roots.

Larval foodplants A wide range of herbaceous plants, including Fat-hen, Broad-leaved Dock and Wild Carrot.

Habitat Coastal sand-dunes, where it is most abundant, chalk downland and other open dry habitats, typically on light soils, including gardens. Occasional in woodland rides.

Status & distribution Resident. Common. Throughout southern Britain. Local from the Midlands northwards through mainland Scotland north to Sutherland, on Man and in Ireland. Local and occasional in the Channel Islands.

Heart and Dart   page 312

Agrotis exclamationis (L.)

Common. T   2089(10348)

Field characters & Similar species FW 15-19mm. Variable, but a constant diagnostic feature is the blackish mark on collar, visible even on the darkest individuals. Somewhat similar to Heart and Club, but less blunt and stocky, and usually easy to recognise. Forewing markings similar, but ground-colour usually rather plain, and rarely flecked or streaked, ranging from pale brown or greyish brown to dark brown or blackish. Central dart-mark solid, usually narrow and more dart-like. Male has un-feathered antennae, and is generally paler, with whitish hindwing. Female generally darker, with grey hindwing. Individuals sometimes occur with central marks joined, distorted, blurred or formed into streaks. See also Turnip Moth and Great Dart.

Flight season Two generations. Mid May-late August, usually with a small second generation from September in the south. Comes to light regularly in large numbers. Several hundred per trap is not unusual, sometimes thousands. At the peak of emergence (late June in the south, July in the north) it is often by far the most numerous species in light-traps, especially in gardens. Also feeds commonly at sugar and flowers.

Life cycle Overwinters as a fully grown larva in an underground cell, in which it pupates. Larva July-spring, feeding until October or earlier, hiding in debris or loose soil by day.

Larval foodplants A wide range of wild and cultivated herbaceous plants, including Ribwort Plantain and Fat-hen.

Habitat In all habitats except at high altitude, but most abundant in lowland arable farmland, pasture and gardens.

Status & distribution Resident. Common. One of the most abundant larger moths throughout most of Great Britain, Man and Ireland, except in Scotland where it is widespread but much less plentiful, especially in the north. Very rare immigrant to Orkney and Shetland. Widespread and abundant in the Channel Islands.

Crescent Dart   page 312

Agrotis trux (Hb.)

ssp. *lunigera* Steph.

Local. SW, WC   2090(10347)

Field characters FW 16-19mm. Small, pale oval with a dark outline, a pale area beyond kidney-mark and relatively pointed forewing with very straight leading edge distinguish most individuals from related species. Male has pale or dark grey-brown forewing, flecked, dusted or clouded with dark brown. Oval same as ground-colour in the palest individuals, sometimes with a dark spot in centre. Hindwing whitish. Antennae slightly feathered. Female distinctive, forewing black with a varying degree of grey shading, especially just beyond kidney-mark.

241

Hindwing greyish white, with an ill-defined grey outer band.

Similar species Male can resemble Heart and Club, which has more rounded forewing tip, darker hindwing and more strongly feathered antennae in male. See also Turnip Moth and Great Dart.

Flight season One generation. July-August. Occasional second generation individuals in October. Comes to light and feeds at sugar, especially when it is painted on flowerheads.

Life cycle Overwinters close to or under the ground as a fully grown larva. Larva August-spring. Larvae fully grown by late autumn. Hides near the ground by day and pupates underground in the spring.

Larval foodplants Larvae seldom found in the wild, but recorded on Thrift and reported fully grown among Rock Sea-Spurrey.

Habitat Coastal cliffs and rocky shorelines.

Status & distribution Resident. Local. Scattered along the south and west coasts of Britain, from Sussex and Hampshire, where probably vagrant, and the Isle of Wight to north Wales. Also well established on Scilly, Man and locally on the east and south-west coasts of Ireland. Apparently also reported from Morayshire. Widespread and frequent in the Channel Islands.

Dark Sword-grass   page 312

Agrotis ipsilon (Hufn.)

Immigrant. T   2091(10346)

Field characters FW 15-25mm. Best recognised by its size and presence of a black dart that extends outwards from kidney-mark, almost meeting with two smaller darts extending inwards from outer part of forewing. Variable, some specimens being darker and less contrasting.

Similar species Pearly Underwing lacks black darts on forewing and is plainer in appearance.

Flight season As an immigrant has been recorded during every month of the year, but is most numerous between July and October, and to a lesser extent during the spring. Winter records are infrequent and tend to coincide with mild weather and southerly winds. Strongly attracted to light, sugar and flowering plants.

Life cycle Individuals that arrive in the spring are thought to give rise to summer larvae (most likely in July and August), the resulting adults supplementing the autumn immigrants. However, breeding is unconfirmed.

Larval foodplants Probably many herbaceous plants, feeding near ground level and rarely reported. Accepts Dandelion and plantains in captivity.

Habitat Tends to be most abundant in coastal areas. As an immigrant it has been reported from most habitats, including gardens, open farmland, heathland, moorland, parkland, woodland, marshes and dunes.

Status & distribution Regular immigrant and possible transitory resident. Abundant in some years. Occurs throughout Great Britain as far north as

Shetland, but most abundant in the south. Reported widely and frequently on Man, in Ireland and in the Channel Islands.

Spalding's Dart   page 312

Agrotis herzogi Rebel

Rare immigrant.   2091a(10344)

Field characters & Similar species FW 15-17mm. A distinctive species unlikely to be overlooked in a light-trap. Forewing markings somewhat like a pale male Shuttle-shaped Dart, with flattened, elongated oval. However, forewing much more angular, more so than that of Archer's Dart, which it resembles in having a series of dark wedges near outer edge, but Spalding's Dart is streakier and antennae of male not visibly feathered. Female tends to be darker than male. Wood's Dart is quite similar, but forewing more pointed and male has feathered antennae. Sand Dart has daintier markings.

Status & distribution Rare immigrant. Only one British record. Single male captured in a light-trap in a regularly trapped garden at Praze-an-Beeble, near Camborne, Cornwall, on 22 November 1995. In Europe recorded only from Sardinia, Malta and Greece. More widespread and frequent in northern Africa.

Shuttle-shaped Dart   page 312

Agrotis puta puta (Hb.)

Common. S,C   2092(10343)

ssp. *insula* Rich.

Scilly

Field characters FW 12-16mm. A short, stubby moth with pale oval elongated into a shuttle, pointed at both ends. Male has pale greyish-brown forewing, with a contrasting dark brown kidney-mark and a dark area at base. Female has much darker and more uniformly coloured forewing, but still with pale 'shuttle' mark. Head and face have a rough, twig-like appearance. On Scilly, forewing markings are brighter and more contrasting, and a dark brown form is frequent in male.

Similar species Quite distinctive. Male might be confused with The Flame, which more closely resembles a twig, holds its wings rolled around the body rather than flat, and differs in being more buff with more extensive dark brown markings.

Flight season At least two overlapping generations. April-October, and occasionally in March. There are spring and summer generations but it is not clear whether autumn individuals represent a third brood or slower larval development. Regularly attracted to light and sugar; also visits flowers such as buddleias at night.

Life cycle Overwinters as a larva. Larva May-July when producing a second generation, August-April; June-April where only one generation.

Larval foodplants Reported from docks, Dandelion, Knotgrass, lettuces and other herbaceous plants, but seldom found.

Habitat A wide range of open habitats, including

gardens, farmland, grassland, heathland, wetlands and open woodland.

Status & distribution Resident. Common. Found over much of southern and central England and lowland Wales, north to Yorkshire, where it is becoming more frequent, Cumbria and, in 1998, Kirkcudbrightshire. Rare on Man. Also recorded from Ireland, but few records. Widespread and abundant in the Channel Islands.

Sand Dart
page 312
Agrotis ripae (Hb.)
Nb. S,C,NE   2093(10338)

Field characters FW 14-18mm. All key markings are small and dainty, compared to other darts, including the central oval, kidney-mark, dart-mark and dark wedges. Ground-colour of forewing is usually sandy but in some populations is cream or greyish.

Similar species Coast Dart, but this does not emerge until several weeks after the first Sand Dart, and is more variable, with more rounded, less angular, often narrower forewing, with larger and generally better defined kidney-mark. See also Archer's Dart, Wood's Dart and Spalding's Dart.

Flight season One generation. June-July. Adults fly from dusk, visit flowers such as ragworts, Marram and Lyme-grass, and come to sugar and to light, sometimes in numbers.

Life cycle Overwinters as a larva. Larva August-May. Fully grown by October, when it spins a cocoon deep in the sand, but does not form a pupa until the spring. Feeds by night, hiding in the sand by day.

Larval foodplants Reported from many strandline plants, including members of the Chenopodiaceae such as Prickly Saltwort, Sea-purslane, Annual Seablite, Common Orache and Red Goosefoot, and unrelated plants such as Sea Rocket, Sea-milkwort, Sea-holly, Sea Bindweed and sucker growth of Seabuckthorn. Accepts sliced Carrot in captivity, on which it can be reared to adult to confirm identification.

Habitat The strandline of sandy beaches, which is a feature only of actively accreting beaches, not of those which are eroding. Apparently there are no colonies on inland sands such as the Breckland heaths of East Anglia.

Status & distribution Resident. Nationally Scarce B. Colonies are scattered around the coast of Britain where suitable habitat exists, from the Isle of Wight northwards to Cumbria in the west and Aberdeenshire in the east, and including Scilly. Very occasionally wanders inland. Local on Man. In Ireland recorded from a thin scatter of southern coastal sites. Locally frequent in the Channel Islands.

Great Dart
page 312
Agrotis crassa (Hb.)
Immigrant; former resident; resident Channel Islands   2094(10336)

Field characters FW 16-18mm. Stout thorax and relatively broad forewing with dark kidney-mark and

oval. Two pale cross-lines with dark edges on forewing and a third weaker and more jagged crossline near outer edge. Cross-line nearest thorax projects sharply outwards at trailing edge. A row of dark wedges points inwards from outermost crossline. Male antennae feathered. These features separate Great Dart from most related species. Ground-colour varies considerably, from pale brown to almost black, but markings are visible even on darkest forms. Hindwing pure white in male, rather brownish, especially at borders, in female.

Similar species Heart and Dart and Turnip are smaller and slighter. In both, kidney-mark is smaller than in Great Dart. Antennae of male Turnip Moth are less strongly feathered, those of Heart and Dart are un-feathered.

Flight season One generation. July-September. Most British records are in August. Comes to light, sugar and flowers.

Life cycle In mainland Europe overwinters as a larva. Larva September-May. Pupates underground.

Larval foodplants The roots and stem-bases of various unspecified low-growing plants, including grasses. The larva is an occasional pest in vineyards.

Habitat Generally open ground.

Status & distribution Resident since at least 1874 in the Channel Islands, where it is widespread and frequent. Elsewhere in the British Isles, an immigrant and possible former resident. A number were reported from Essex and Kent during the 1840s but their origins and identification are uncertain and it is not clear whether there was a resident population. In the 20th century, recorded only as a suspected immigrant, some 20 individuals, all after 1986 and almost half from Portland, Dorset. Also recorded from Scilly, Cornwall, Hampshire, Isle of Wight, East Sussex and Co. Cork, with one in Saffron Walden, Essex, on 13 August 1995. Occurs in much of southern and eastern Europe and in northern Africa.

2095, 2096 see Appendix
2097, 2097a see below 2306

Flame
page 312
Axylia putris (L.)
Common. T   2098(10082)

Field characters FW 14-16mm. A distinctive and rather invariable species, which rests with wings tightly folded around body, resembling a broken piece of dry stem. Straw ground-colour of forewing is sometimes strongly tinged with reddish brown.

Similar species A number of other noctuids are straw-coloured with a streaky pattern, but none has the dark streak along the leading edge in combination with the dark kidney-mark.

Flight season One generation. June-July. Occasionally a small second generation in September. Comes to light, sugar and flowers.

Life cycle Overwinters as a pupa. Larva July-October, feeding at night. Pupates underground.

Larval foodplants A wide range of low-growing

plants, including Common Nettle, White Dead-nettle, Hedge Bedstraw and Hound's-tongue.

Habitat A broad range, but typically gardens, farmland, downland, hedgerows, heathland and woodland edges.

Status & distribution Resident. Common. Throughout southern Britain, Man and Ireland, but local in Scotland, occurring mainly in the south and south-west. Widespread and frequent in the Channel Islands.

Portland Moth
page 312

Actebia praecox (L.)

Nb; immigrant. T   2099(10244)

Field characters FW 17-21mm. A distinctive silvery green moth with long, slender forewings which are closely overlapped when fully at rest.

Similar species None.

Flight season One generation. Mid August-September, but late July in Lincolnshire, Northumberland and parts of Scotland. Both sexes nocturnal. Recorded feeding at flowers of ragworts, Heather and Marram. Comes to light, sometimes in numbers.

Life cycle Overwinters as a larva, hatching in about September. Pre-hibernation habits unknown. Post-hibernation larvae hide in the sand by day and pupate there from late June.

Larval foodplants Larvae have been found after hibernation feeding at night on the foliage of Creeping Willow. Also reported from a number of unrelated plants found on sand-dunes such as chickweeds, fine marine grasses, Wormwood, Common Bird's-foot-trefoil, mouse-ears, plantains and, where it is naturalised, Tree Lupin.

Habitat Sandy beaches with well established vegetation, sandy heathland, and sand and shingle banks of rivers.

Status & distribution Resident and occasional immigrant. Nationally Scarce B. Mainly coastal, with colonies scattered around the British coast, most notably at Studland, Dorset, Dawlish Warren, south Devon, and Braunton Burrows, north Devon. Also on the Gower, Glamorgan, various other places in the Welsh coast, including Anglesey, the coasts of Cheshire, Lancashire and Cumbria, the west coast of Scotland, including some of the Inner Hebrides, the sandy coasts of the Moray Firth and probably further east, Tayside and also the coasts of Angus and Northumberland. Larvae found at Dungeness, Kent, in the past. Inland populations exist in the Scunthorpe area of Lincolnshire, Budby Heath and Misson, Nottinghamshire, and there are old records from the sand and shingle banks of the Spey, Inverness-shire. Individuals occasionally recorded in Essex, Sussex and Kent are suspected immigrants, although the moth is seen almost annually at Dungeness, Kent. Local on Man. In Ireland recorded from several locations scattered around the coast, particularly in the south and west, but also in Northern Ireland (Co. Down). Recorded once from the Channel Islands, on Jersey in 1932.

Eversmann's Rustic
page 312

Actebia fennica (Tausch.)

Rare immigrant.   2100(10245)

Field characters FW 16-18mm. Forewing long, narrow and rather rounded at end. In male there is a marked contrast between the orange stripe along trailing edge of forewing and the dark grey-brown of rest of wing. Female's forewing is more uniformly purplish grey or even blackish. Both oval and kidney-mark are conspicuous, with light edges. Two or three small black wedge-shaped marks extend inwards in centre of outer part of forewing. Hindwing dirty white.

Similar species The superficially similar Dark Sword-grass is larger, with a relatively broader, more pointed forewing and a black wedge extending outwards from kidney-mark.

Flight season One generation in mainland Europe. July-August. Comes to light, sugar and flowers.

Life cycle In mainland Europe overwinters as a larva. Larva September-June. Pupates underground.

Larval foodplants Bilberry and various herbaceous plants, including willowherbs. In Sweden, also recorded from Lodgepole Pine.

Habitat Taiga moorland and light woodland.

Status & distribution Rare immigrant. Six British records, the first in August 1850 at Chesterfield, Derbyshire, the rest between 1972 and 1983, all in August, from Warwickshire, Middlesex, Nottinghamshire, Northumberland and Aberdeenshire. Some of these records tie in with arrivals of Great Brocade and Scarce Silver Y. A native of the Scandinavian, Siberian and North American taiga, it migrates into various parts of north-west Europe in some years.

Black Collar
page 312

Ochropleura flammatra ([D. & S.])

Rare immigrant.   2101(10084)

Field characters FW 19-21mm. Broadly black collar behind head and sinuous black line at base of otherwise milky-brown forewing and thorax are diagnostic. In female the black collar is tinged with grey. The black streak is broken in some individuals. Base of forewing is greyer near leading edge, contrasting with brown appearance of moth at rest. Hindwing is lighter brown. Wings held overlapping and quite close to the body at rest, giving a slender appearance.

Similar species Heart and Dart has a narrower blackish mark on collar, is smaller and although very variable has no basal streak on forewing, having instead dark central marks.

Flight season Two overlapping generations in southern Europe, May-September. Comes to light, sugar and flowers from dusk.

Life cycle Overwinters as a larva. Two generations, feeding from autumn to spring and in the summer. Larval stage unrecorded in the British Isles.

Larval foodplants Reported from Wild Strawberry

and Dandelion in southern Europe and probably feeds on other low-growing plants.

Habitat A wide range of mainly open habitats.

Status & distribution Rare immigrant. The most recent record was of an individual on Shetland on 28 June 1997. Prior to that, single examples were recorded in Gloucestershire in June 1968, at Cromer Lighthouse, Norfolk, on 10 August 1875 and on the Isle of Wight in 1859 and 1876. It inhabits southern and central Europe, extending eastwards to central Asia. Also occurs in northern Africa.

Flame Shoulder
Ochropleura plecta (L.)

page 312

Common. T   2102(10086)

Field characters FW 12-15mm. Resembles no other resident species. The English name reflects the most conspicuous and diagnostic feature, a bright, straw-coloured band running along leading edge of forewing. This 'flame' is further emphasised by the black streak behind it, on the rather plain, rich reddish-brown or purplish-brown forewing. Markings show only minor variation but some individuals are very pale. Hindwing glossy yellowish white.

Similar species See Radford's Flame Shoulder.

Flight season In southern Britain, April-September in two generations, peaking in May-June and again in August. In northern Britain, one generation, late May-July. Comes to light, when it flies wildly and has an unfortunate habit of occasionally entering the ears of moth recorders near the light! Also feeds at sugar and flowers.

Life cycle Overwinters as a pupa just below the ground surface. Larva June-July and September-October in the south, August-September in the north, feeding at night.

Larval foodplants A wide range of herbaceous plants, including Groundsel, Ribwort Plantain and bedstraws.

Habitat A broad range, from low to mid-altitude, including gardens, farmland, grasslands, hedgerows, moorland, woodland and wetlands.

Status & distribution Resident. Common. Throughout most of Great Britain, Man and Ireland, but not recorded from Shetland. Widespread and abundant in the Channel Islands.

Radford's Flame Shoulder
Ochropleura leucogaster (Freyer)

page 312

Immigrant.   2102a(10087)

Field characters & Similar species FW 13-16mm. Resembles Flame Shoulder but looks noticeably larger, duller and less reddish. It is distinguished by the relatively longer, narrower wings, usually smaller oval and kidney-mark, cleaner white hindwing with no yellowish gloss and less tendency to a yellowish or reddish edge, and by the greater contrast between the purple thorax and whiter collar and white hairs around front of abdomen (the specific name means 'white stomach'). Black streak on

forewing projects sharply beyond kidney-mark. However, this can sometimes be the case on Flame Shoulder, especially when worn. Tends to be recorded later than the normal flight season of Flame Shoulder.

Flight season All the British records have been between late September and late November, but mainly during October. In mainland Europe it flies from May onwards, so records earlier in the season are possible.

Life cycle In southern Europe overwinters as a larva and has two generations per year. Pupates below ground. The larval stage has not been recorded in the British Isles.

Larval foodplants Reported from Common Bird's-foot-trefoil in mainland Europe, and probably feeds on other low-growing plants.

Habitat A wide range of open habitats.

Status & distribution Immigrant. Less than 15 British records, all from 1983 onwards, mainly from the south coast of England, from Scilly to Kent. Not recorded from the Channel Islands. Mainly Mediterranean in Europe but occurs as far north as Brittany. Also found in northern Africa and parts of Asia.

2103 see below 2117

Northern Rustic
Standfussiana lucernea (L.)

page 313

Local. S,WC,N   2104(10153)

Field characters FW 17-21mm. A rather softly-patterned species. The general indistinctness and blurred nature of the markings, and dark hindwing with pure white fringes help to distinguish it from similar moths. Many individuals have broad, dark grey bands on underside of fore- and hindwing, which is another useful feature, although in others bands are reduced or wings are almost entirely dark grey. Upperside of forewing quite variable in colour, from dark brownish grey, heavily dusted with either pale yellowish brown or greyish brown, to blackish with very faint markings.

Similar species See Dotted Rustic, Stout Dart, Grey.

Flight season One generation. Late June-September. Comes to light, and feeds at sugar and flowers such as Wood Sage, Sea Rocket and ragworts. Also flies wildly on sunny days in the late afternoon.

Life cycle Overwinters as a small larva, low down on the foodplant. Larva October-May, feeding at night.

Larval foodplants Herbaceous plants, including Harebell, Biting Stonecrop and saxifrages, and also reported from grasses such as Sheep's-fescue.

Habitat Coastal cliffs, mountain scree and other rocky, sparsely-vegetated places such as quarries.

Status & distribution Resident. Local. Occurs locally from the Isle of Wight westwards along the coasts of southern and south-western England, Wales, Man, Scotland, including the Hebrides, Orkney and Shetland, and Ireland. Inland in Wales, Derbyshire, Lancashire and Cumbria.

Dotted Rustic
page 313

Rhyacia simulans (Hufn.)

Local. T
2105(10139)

Field characters FW 17-21mm. Typical form has a row of black dots across forewing beyond kidney-mark. The wavy double cross-line between thorax and circular spot is usually conspicuous, and the greyish-buff ground-colour and long forewing is distinctive. The smaller, darker f. *suffusa* Tutt occurs on the Hebrides, Orkney and Shetland and north-west Ireland, in which the above markings are present but harder to see.

Similar species Northern Rustic lacks row of forewing dots and all forewing markings are less well defined. Stout Dart is superficially similar, with similar habits, but is mousy brown, lacks the row of black dots beyond kidney-mark, and usually has a black basal streak.

Flight season One generation. Late June-July in England, reappearing from late August-early October; mainly July-early September in Scotland. The moths emerge and fly briefly, then take up resting positions, often in outbuildings, frequently entering houses and being found behind curtains at this time. Visits flowers such as Red Valerian and buddleias, comes to sugar and both sexes come to light in small numbers.

Life cycle Probably overwinters as a larva. English adults lay eggs in September which hatch after about two weeks. Pupates underground in the spring.

Larval foodplants Unknown. The larva has not been found in the wild. The early instars have been reared on grasses but later instars have required other food, Dandelion and Bramble being accepted, but few captive larvae have survived to produce adults.

Habitat Open countryside, including rural gardens, with hedgerows and light woodland, usually on calcareous soils. On moorland, rough pasture and mountain scree in northern Britain.

Status & distribution Resident. Local. Prone to great fluctuations in numbers and distribution. During the 1960s the West Midlands, particularly the Cotswolds, was considered the main stronghold, with other well-known populations on Portland, Dorset, and in north Wales and south Cumbria, with the darker race present on Orkney and other northern areas as detailed above. In the late 1970s and early 1980s the distribution of the southern form expanded greatly and the moth was reported from over 400 10km squares, covering much of England east of the Severn and the Pennines. It has since declined, but is still reported regularly in small numbers north to Yorkshire, with less frequent records from lowland Scotland. Local and rare on Man and in the northern half of Ireland.

Southern Rustic
not illustrated

Rhyacia lucipeta ([D. & S.])

Suspected rare immigrant.
2106(10141)

Field characters & Similar species FW 24-29mm. Not unlike Dotted Rustic and some forms of Northern Rustic, but much larger, with golden yellow markings on forewing and a greenish tint when fresh.

Status & distribution Suspected rare immigrant. The only individual recorded in the British Isles was a worn female captured in a light-trap at Pulborough, Sussex, after 2am on 15 July 1968. On the night of 30 June 1968, winds from the south brought much red dust to southern England, after which many scarce migrant moths were recorded for about two weeks. The weather system was tracked back to Spain. The Southern Rustic is resident in Spain and parts of France, as well as occurring eastwards through central and south-east Europe.

Large Yellow Underwing
page 313

Noctua pronuba (L.)

Common. T
2107(10096)

Field characters FW 21-26mm. Very variable but distinctive, with long, narrow, rounded forewing, consistently with a small black pip-mark close to leading edge near tip. Hindwing has a narrow black band and no dark crescent or clouding near base, a combination not found in other yellow underwings. Forewing in male rich dark reddish brown or blackish brown, with no or few markings, or paler reddish brown with a pale brown or grey streak along leading edge, and marbled with same colour as streak. Female not marbled, rather uniformly light brown or brownish grey, and slightly or extensively flecked with darker scales, or pale reddish brown. Intermediate colour forms occur in both sexes.

Similar species See Lunar Yellow Underwing, which is smaller.

Flight season One protracted generation. June-October or November. Long-lived, with a peak of activity in late August or early September. Late stragglers regularly occur well into October, or even November. Comes to light, sometimes abundantly – a single Robinson trap occasionally captures several thousand in a night. Also comes avidly to sugar and nectar flowers, often feeding for several hours at a time. May be disturbed from among plant debris or ground vegetation during the day, flying rapidly to cover as do other underwing moths, displaying the brightly coloured hindwings. Early season immigrants arrive carrying matured eggs before resident females have reached this stage.

Life cycle Overwinters underground as a larva. Eggs are laid from July onwards in large batches, which are sometimes conspicuous on grasses or other vegetation. Larva August-early spring, feeding at night and hiding underground during the day. Some are fully grown by December. Pupates underground in the spring.

246

Larval foodplants A wide range of herbaceous plants and grasses, including docks, cultivated Brassicas, Marigolds, Foxglove and Annual Meadow-grass.

Habitat Ubiquitous, from gardens to woodland and high moorland, but most abundant in open grassy lowland habitats.

Status & distribution Resident and immigrant. Common. Widespread and abundant throughout Great Britain, Man, Ireland and the Channel Islands.

Larva of Large Yellow Underwing.

Lunar Yellow Underwing   page 313
Noctua orbona (Hufn.)

Nb. T   2108(10097)

Field characters & Similar species FW 17-20mm. Well-defined black marking on leading edge of forewing, near the tip, distinguishes this moth from much more frequent Lesser Yellow Underwing, which also has a broader forewing. Large Yellow Underwing has the black mark, but lacks a dark central crescent on hindwing, and is larger.

Flight season One generation. Late June-September, apparently hiding away in a dormant state in July, reappearing from late August. Both sexes come readily to light and sugar and have been noted visiting flowers of Heather.

Life cycle Overwinters as a larva. Larva September-late April or May. Feeds mainly at night in mild weather throughout the winter and spring, pupating in a flimsy cocoon in loose earth.

Larval foodplants A range of fine grasses and also small herbaceous plants. Those reported include Sheep's-fescue and Wavy Hair-grass (which appear to be the favourites in Breckland), Cock's-foot, Couch, Reed Canary-grass, Meadow Buttercup, Creeping Cinquefoil, Cowslip and Common Chickweed.

Habitat Fairly dry, sandy, heathy or calcareous sites in open situations and in open woodland, both on the coast and inland. Rare or absent if habitat close-cut or heavily grazed.

Status & distribution Resident. Nationally Scarce B. Formerly widespread in Great Britain. In decline by the 1970s, since when it is most frequently sought and recorded from the Breckland area of Norfolk and Suffolk. Scattered populations survive elsewhere, however, mainly from sandy sites, mudstones and chalk formations including Dorset, south Wiltshire, north Hampshire, Bedfordshire, Somerset and Leicestershire, Pembrokeshire, Lincolnshire and the Menai Straits/Anglesey. Also present on the sandy coasts of Northumberland and around the coast of Scotland, including Fife, Aberdeenshire and Morayshire. Recorded from Ireland, where there are confirmed records for Lough Neagh, Co. Londonderry, in the extreme north, on 1 August 1977, and Killard Point on the east coast of Co. Down on 29 August 1996, although both individuals could have been wanderers from Britain.

Lesser Yellow Underwing   page 313
Noctua comes Hb.

Common. T   2109(10099)

Field characters FW 16-21mm. Most easily recognised by combination of a dark crescent on hindwing, and no well-defined small black markings near tip of forewing, near leading edge. Instead, outermost band may be thickened at this point to form a roughly triangular mark. Forewing very variable in colour, and in the intensity of cross-lines and other markings. Ground-colour pale brown, pale or dark greyish brown (occasionally greenish tinted), bright or dark reddish brown, reddish black or blackish. Blackish and reddish-black forms occur in the northern half of Scotland, and in these the hindwing may also be dusted with black. In Scilly and on Lundy Island individuals with strong, dark cross-lines are frequent.

Similar species Lunar Yellow Underwing has a small black mark near tip of forewing, near leading edge, whereas in Lesser Yellow Underwing there is usually a dark smudge here. See also Least Yellow Underwing.

Flight season One generation. June-September, with smaller numbers well into October. Comes abundantly to light, and feeds at sugar and flowers.

Life cycle Overwinters as a small larva. Larva August-May or June, feeding at night and hiding in leaf litter by day. Pupates underground.

Larval foodplants A wide range of herbaceous plants, such as Common Nettle, Broad-leaved Dock and Foxglove. In spring, climbs into bushes and small trees, including Hawthorn, Bramble, sallows and Broom.

Habitat Ubiquitous, from gardens, downland and heathland to woodland and moorland.

Status & distribution Resident. Common. Throughout Great Britain, Man and Ireland. Widespread and abundant in the Channel Islands.

Broad-bordered Yellow Underwing   page 313
Noctua fimbriata (Schreb.)

Common. T   2110(10100)

Field characters FW 22-27mm. A stout, beautifully-marked species, quite unlike any other. Colour variable but markings very constant. Thorax appears very large, wing-tips pulled together at rest. Male has reddish-brown to olive-green forewing; female pale brown, light green or pale reddish brown. There is also a less common mahogany-coloured form, which occurs in both sexes.

Similar species None.

Flight season One generation. July-September. Emerges in July, hides away for a period and becomes active again in August and September. Comes to light in fairly small numbers, and to sugar.

Life cycle Overwinters close to the ground as a small larva. Larva September-May, feeding at night and hiding by day in leaf litter. Pupates underground.

Larval foodplants A wide range of herbaceous plants, such as Common Nettle, Primrose and Broad-leaved Dock, sometimes climbing to feed on low woody plants such as Bramble, sallows and privets, especially in the spring.

Habitat Most frequent in broadleaved woodland and other well-wooded areas, such as parkland and wooded heathland. Recorded in smaller numbers in gardens.

Status & distribution Resident. Common. Throughout most of mainland Great Britain north to Inverness-shire. Less frequent on Man and in Ireland. Rare presumed immigrant on Orkney and Shetland. Widespread as occasional individuals in the Channel Islands.

Langmaid's Yellow Underwing   p.313

Noctua janthina ([D. & S.])

Suspected rare immigrant.   2110a(10102)

Field characters & Similar species FW 16-18mm. Very similar to Lesser Broad-bordered Yellow Underwing, and retention of a specimen and possibly examination of genitalia would be necessary for confirmation of any further record. Upperside of forewings of the two species are indistinguishable, but Langmaid's is usually darker. However, set specimens of Langmaid's in fresh condition can sometimes be confirmed by careful reference to a combination of characters. Hindwing of Lesser Broad-bordered has a black outer border, which either stops before leading edge or extends diffusely along it, usually with at least a small gap. On Langmaid's, black border is generally broader, and extends along leading edge without a gap, so the overall effect is of a black hindwing with a yellow spot. On underside of forewing of Lesser Broad-bordered, outer edge of black area is usually distinctly toothed and ends well before outer edge of wing, with area beyond it yellowish brown. In Langmaid's, outer edge of black area is usually smooth or diffuse (although toothed effect may be suggested) and it may extend close to outer edge, with area beyond it dull brown.

Status & distribution Only recognised as a distinct species in 1991. Status in the British Isles uncertain; could be immigrant, overlooked resident or both.

First confirmed in the British Isles as a singleton in fresh condition on 9 July 2001 at Southsea, Hampshire. The recorder was alerted by the date, which is two weeks earlier than the Lesser Broad-bordered Yellow Underwing usually appears at this site. If resident, the foodplant and life cycle require investigation, but are likely to be similar to those of Lesser Broad-bordered Yellow Underwing. Widespread in mainland Europe, with a more easterly distribution than Lesser Broad-bordered Yellow, but reaches the west coast of France.

Lesser Broad-bordered Yellow Underwing   page 313

Noctua janthe (Borkh.)

Common. T   2111(10103)

Field characters FW 16-20mm. Several features distinguish this rather invariable species from all except Langmaid's Yellow Underwing. Behind head is a collar of delicate light green when moth is freshly emerged, fading to light brown. This colour also extends about a quarter of the way along leading edge of forewing, which is deep purplish brown or (less commonly) reddish brown, clouded with blue-grey. The oval and kidney-mark are partly outlined with white, but all other markings are usually obscure. Hindwing has no dark crescent, and base is blackish and streaky.

Similar species See Langmaid's Yellow Underwing.

Flight season One generation. Late July-early September. Comes frequently to light, and feeds at sugar and flowers.

Life cycle Overwinters as a half-grown larva, close to the ground. Larva September-May, feeding at night and hiding by day in leaf litter. Pupates underground.

Larval foodplants A wide range of herbaceous plants, including White Dead-nettle, Broad-leaved Dock, Scentless Mayweed and Arum Lily. In spring, climbs to feed in bushes such as sallows, hawthorns and Blackthorn.

Habitat Most habitats, including woodland, hedgerows and gardens, heathland and moorland to medium altitude.

Status & distribution Resident. Common. Throughout most of Great Britain to Shetland; also Man and Ireland. Widespread and abundant in the Channel Islands.

Least Yellow Underwing   page 313

Noctua interjecta Hb.

ssp. *caliginosa* Schaw.

Common. S,C   2112(10105)

Field characters FW 14-17mm. Distinguished by size and rich reddish-brown forewing coloration, together with wavy inner edge of black band on hindwing, which extends along trailing edge to base, from which black streaks project. There may be a small dark crescent on hindwing. Varies relatively little in colour and markings, but forewing is sometimes extensively marked with blackish, and is occasionally pale reddish brown.

Similar species Large individuals could be mistaken for reddish-brown forms of Lesser Yellow Underwing. However, in that species hindwing has a large, conspicuous crescent mark, a straighter black border and is yellow at base.

Flight season One generation. July-August. Comes frequently to light, less often to sugar and also to flowers. Occasionally seen flying wildly around hedgerows on hot sunny afternoons.

Life cycle Overwinters as a half-grown larva, close to the ground. Larva September-May, feeding at night and hiding in leaf litter by day. Pupates underground.

Larval foodplants Herbaceous plants, such as Meadowsweet and Common Mallow, and grasses. In the spring also on bushes such as sallows and hawthorns.

Habitat A range of mainly open places, such as hedgerows, gardens, fens and sand-dunes.

Status & distribution Resident. Common. Widespread in the southern half of England, the north Midlands, Wales and Man. Local in Ireland and northern England, with occasional records from lowland Scotland. Widespread and frequent in the Channel Islands.

Stout Dart
page 314

Spaelotis ravida ([D. & S.])

Local. S,EC   2113(10163)

Field characters FW 18-22mm. Recognised by drab, mousy grey-brown colour of the long narrow rounded forewing, which usually has a reddish tint along leading edge and sometimes more extensively. A diagnostic long black streak at forewing base is normally present, but some reddish forms lack this and are weakly marked. Hindwing dirty white, slightly darker around outer margin.

Similar species Individuals without the black streaks somewhat resemble Northern Rustic, which would normally be found in a very different habitat. It is more softly marked and hindwing is darker, with a pure white fringe. See also Dotted Rustic.

Flight season One generation. June-September. Emerges June-July, then hides away in outbuildings or under loose bark, sometimes gregariously. Becomes active again August-September. Comes to light and feeds at sugar, usually in small numbers, and at flowers such as Common Reed, Red Valerian and buddleias.

Life cycle The larva has not been found in the wild. In captivity, eggs hatch in December, even if kept in a cold outhouse. The larvae feed slowly during the winter until April or May.

Larval foodplants In captivity, at first on the leaves and later the roots of Dandelion, sow-thistles and docks.

Habitat Mainly damp meadows and the edge of marshes, but can also occur on drier ground and in gardens.

Status & distribution Resident. Local. Subject to periodic fluctuations and range expansions, with East Anglia, eastern England and the Midlands being the strongholds. Also recorded in small numbers from Wales, south-west and northern England, and south-east Scotland.

Double Dart
page 314

Graphiphora augur (Fabr.)

Common. T   2114(10171)

Field characters FW 18-21mm. Broad, rather plain forewing with oval, kidney- and dart-marks simply outlined in blackish is diagnostic. Forewing colour ranges from soft light brown to mousy or dark greyish brown, sometimes slightly reddish tinted. Otherwise varies only in the fine detail of the markings.

Similar species None.

Flight season One generation. June-mid August. Comes to light in small numbers, more commonly to sugar, and also to flowers.

Life cycle Overwinters as a small larva, close to the ground. Larva August-May, feeding at night and hiding by day in leaf litter. Pupates just below the ground surface.

Larval foodplants Sallows, birches, Blackthorn and hawthorn scrub, both in the autumn and spring, and herbaceous plants, including Broad-leaved Dock.

Habitat Broadleaved woodland and scrub, hedgerows, parkland, marshes, fens and gardens.

Status & distribution Resident. Common. Throughout most of mainland Britain and Ireland. Resident on Orkney but not recorded from the Outer Hebrides and Shetland. Rare on Man. In the Channel Islands recorded once, from Guernsey in 1889.

Rosy Marsh Moth
page 314

Coenophila subrosea (Steph.)

RDB. WC   2115(10220)

Field characters & Similar species FW 17-22mm. Fairly distinctive, with rather broad forewing and an obvious dark central bar between and before oval and kidney-mark, and feathered antennae in male. In Wales, male has rosy-pink forewing, clouded with light grey, and female has a strong silvery bloom. Moths from Huntingdonshire were greyer. Some forms of Purple Clay and Ingrailed Clay are somewhat similar, but have a small blackish spot below oval. Ingrailed Clay is usually smaller, with more angular forewing, Purple Clay has uniformly grey hindwing, and neither has feathered antennae.

Flight season One generation. Late July-August. Often visits the flowers of Soft-rush and comes to sugar, especially female. Both sexes come to light.

Life cycle Overwinters as a larva, from eggs laid on bog plants. Larva late August or September-mid June, feeding throughout the winter in mild weather, pupating in a loose silken cocoon spun almost vertically among *Sphagnum* moss or other plant material.

Larval foodplants Mainly the catkins, buds and

249

Larva of Rosy Marsh Moth.

then the leaves of Bog-myrtle at Cors Fochno, but other plants are also eaten, particularly Bog-rosemary in the winter when little else is available. Once found on the fleshy pedicel of a flower of a cottongrass. At one site, where Bog-myrtle is absent, or undetected, Crowberry is the main foodplant. In captivity, feeds readily on Crack-willow and other narrow-leaved willows, preferring the ripe female catkins.
Habitat Bogs and mires. At Cors Fochno mainly in the hummock/hollow habitat where Bog-myrtle is 30cm or less in height, but not around the fringes of this domed mire, where the Bog-myrtle is woody and up to 1m tall. This distribution of larvae may be more a reflection of the higher water-table and greater amount of Bog-rosemary in the central portion than the effects of past fires or selection of shorter growth of the foodplant. The larvae are more numerous where there is a fair amount of leaf litter.
Status & distribution Resident. Red Data Book species. Known from five breeding sites in western Wales, the best-known of which is Borth Bog/Cors Fochno, Cardiganshire, where it was discovered in numbers in 1967. Two of the other breeding areas are remnants from this once more extensive site. In the 19th century it was quite numerous in Huntingdonshire, where it was discovered at Yaxley Fen in about 1828, and subsequently at Whittlesey Mere and Holme Fen, disappearing about 1850 when the burning and draining of the fens was completed. There are two specimens (now at Derby Museum) allegedly from Little Eaton, in Derbyshire, one from 1857 and one 'some years prior to 1885', but the species is now considered extinct in the county.

Cousin German page 314
Protolampra sobrina (Dup.)
Na. N   2116(10236)

Field characters & Similar species FW 14-17mm. Forewing varies from a striking mixture of light pink and silvery grey to a dark and rather indistinctly marked reddish grey. The combination of indistinct markings and lack of a black dot on forewing between oval and trailing edge distinguish this species from dark forms of Purple Clay, Barred Chestnut and Ingrailed Clay. Very dark northern forms of Neglected Rustic have cross-lines absent or

very faint and kidney-mark normally more distinctly darker in trailing half. See also Dotted Clay.
Flight season One generation. Late July-August. Flies after dark, comes fairly reliably to light, even on cold nights, sometimes to sugar and has been reported visiting the flowers of Heather.
Life cycle Overwinters as a small larva. Larva late August-June. Feeds mainly in May and June, after dark, and pupates in loose earth, moss or plant debris.
Larval foodplants Initially on Bilberry and Heather, but after hibernation the larvae will climb low birch scrub and Eared Willow to feed on the young leaves.
Habitat Open upland birch woodland and scrub with a ground cover of Heather and Bilberry, at altitudes from c200m upwards. Often but not exclusively associated with the early stages of birch succession, where small birch bushes are growing among Bilberry and Heather.
Status & distribution Resident. Nationally Scarce A. A species of the Scottish Highlands, recorded particularly along the valleys of the Spey and Dee and in the Loch Rannoch area, but also found in the northernmost Caledonian pine forest in Scotland, in Wester Ross.

Autumnal Rustic page 314
Eugnorisma glareosa (Esp.)
Common. T   2117(10156*)

Field characters FW 15-16mm. The black, roughly anvil- or vase-shaped mark between kidney-mark and oval, the other black marks and cross-lines near base, and the narrow, rather angular forewing are diagnostic. Forewing colour ranges from cold whitish grey, darker grey to pale orange-brown, sometimes tinged with pink to a greater or lesser extent, but markings vary little. Scottish individuals tend to be darker grey, pink forms are most frequent in western Britain and the orange-brown form occurs in Kent. In f. *edda* Stdgr., forewing is greyish black, the black anvil and other black marks are still evident, and other markings pale. This form mainly occurs in Shetland and is most frequent where the soil is dark and peaty. Similar forms and intermediates also occur in Orkney and in mainland northern Scotland, occasionally as far south as Aberdeen.
Similar species Superficially similar to the darkest individuals of the Shetland ssp. *thulei* of the Ingrailed Clay, but the latter is usually brownish black rather than greyish black.
Flight season One generation. August-October. Comes to light and flowers, particularly heather, but rarely to sugar.
Life cycle Overwinters as a small larva, close to the ground. Larva October-May, feeding at night and hiding by day in leaf litter. Pupates underground in a fragile cocoon.
Larval foodplants Low-growing plants, including heathers, bedstraws and Bluebell; also birches and sallow scrub. Reportedly also grasses.
Habitat Heathland, moorland, rough grassland,

downland provided it is not heavily grazed, and other open country, on light sandy or chalky soils. Also fens, shingle beaches and open woodland.
Status & distribution Resident. Common. In suitable places throughout most of Great Britain, Man and Ireland, the Hebrides and Orkney. More frequent in the north, and more local south of a line from the Severn to the Humber. Widespread and frequent in the Channel Islands.

Plain Clay   page 314
Eugnorisma depuncta (L.)
Nb. N,WC,SW   2103(10178)

Field characters FW 16-20mm. The form and position of the three main dark chocolate streaks running from leading edge of quite broad, pale brown forewing are diagnostic. Little variation.
Similar species None.
Flight season One generation. July-early September. Both sexes come to light, sometimes in numbers. Also recorded at sugar and visiting ragwort flowers.
Life cycle Overwinters as a very small larva, among low-growing plants. Larva September-June, but feeding mainly in the spring, at night. Pupates in a cocoon underground.
Larval foodplants Probably a wide range of low-growing plants. Reported foodplants include Primrose, Cowslip, Common Sorrel, Sheep's Sorrel, Common Nettle, Dead-nettle and stitchworts.
Habitat Usually in or near broadleaved woodland, but sometimes seen in numbers at light-traps in adjacent rough fields.
Status & distribution Resident. Nationally Scarce B. A species mainly of northern Britain, recorded from many localities in central and eastern Scotland, where records are concentrated principally around the Great Glen, and the Spey, Dee and Tay river valleys. Well established in several sites in Yorkshire and has extended its range south in the county. Rare in Co. Durham and Cumbria. Very local in north Wales. Old records for Glamorgan. Occasionally recorded elsewhere in Wales and in west and south-west England, for example recorded once each in Devon and Cornwall during the 1990s.

True Lover's Knot   page 314
Lycophotia porphyrea ([D. & S.])
Common. T   2118(10113)

Field characters FW 12-15mm. This rather small, usually reddish-brown species is distinguished by the extensive fine black and white markings, the detail of which varies but not the general pattern. The black streaks and dashes are most prominent near outer margin and often run through oval and kidney-mark. Forewing colour may also be deep pinkish brown or purplish brown, or less often greyish brown or blackish grey.
Similar species Heath Rustic occurs in the same habitat but usually later in the year, has a pale streak along leading edge of forewing, a small, pale oval

within a black wedge, and slightly feathered antennae in male. See also Beautiful Yellow Underwing.
Flight season One generation. June-August. Strongly attracted to light and feeds at heather flowers, but rarely at sugar. Active by day in bright sunshine, visiting flowers.
Life cycle Overwinters as a nearly fully grown larva, among plant debris. Larva August-May. Pupates in a cocoon on or just below the ground.
Larval foodplants Heather and Bell Heather. Probably Cross-leaved Heath, but this needs confirmation.
Habitat Acid heathland and high moorland. Also occurs occasionally in light-traps far removed from likely breeding areas and may breed in gardens on cultivated heathers.
Status & distribution Resident. Common. In suitable habitats, often abundantly, throughout Great Britain, Man, Ireland and the Channel Islands.

Pearly Underwing   page 314
Peridroma saucia (Hb.)
Immigrant; possible transitory resident. T
                                    2119(10238)

Field characters FW 19-23mm. This species' name derives from the hindwing, which has a translucent mother-of-pearl quality, with darker veins and outer margin. Large kidney-mark and oval are usually visible on forewing, although not always so on darker individuals. Highly variable, ranging from variegated buff and dark brown to very dark individuals that may show a strong russet coloration. A short 'Mohican-style' crest is visible on head, which in some individuals appears pale grey and contrasting.
Similar species See Turnip Moth and Dark Sword-grass.
Flight season Has been recorded in every month of the year, winter records usually coinciding with milder weather and southerly winds. Most numerous in September and October but also appears regularly during the summer months and to a far lesser extent during the spring. Attracted to light and sugar.
Life cycle Larvae are rarely encountered but are thought to occur July-October, feeding at night. These are the progeny of earlier immigrants and may give rise to autumn adults, which supplement the immigrant population.
Larval foodplants Various low-growing plants, including Dandelion, docks, Red Clover, Cabbage and Rape. Occasionally reported as a pest in glasshouses, where it has been recorded on lettuce.
Habitat May occur almost anywhere. Most abundant in coastal areas.
Status & distribution Regular immigrant and possible transitory resident. Numbers vary greatly from year to year, sometimes frequent. Recorded throughout the British Isles, as far north as Shetland, also on Man and widely in Ireland. Frequent most years in the Channel Islands.

Ingrailed Clay
page 314

Diarsia mendica mendica (Fabr.)

Common. T
2120(10089)

ssp. *thulei* (Stdgr.)
Shetland

ssp. *orkneyensis* (Byt.-Salz)
Orkney

Field characters FW 13-17mm.
Ssp. *mendica* Extremely variable, both within local populations and geographically, but usually aspects of the basic elements of forewing markings can be recognised with practice, particularly outline of kidney-mark and a tiny black spot part way between region of oval and trailing edge of forewing. Forewing usually rather marbled in appearance, in southern Britain ranging from pale straw, yellowish orange, orange-brown, to reddish brown. Some paler individuals are banded or clouded with reddish brown. Even more variable in northern Britain, usually smaller, predominantly darker, often with narrower forewing, and sometimes clouded with pink or grey, often lacking the tiny black spot. Usually a series of tiny but noticeable black arrow-head or crescent-marks along outer edge.
Ssp. *thulei* Darker than the mainland populations, although some are similar to those from the northern mainland. Forewing narrower and more pointed, with the leading edge straight or almost so. Dirty greyish brown, deep pinkish red, dark pinkish brown or reddish brown, blackish brown, or blackish, often dusted with grey. Blackish wedge usually present in the oval and kidney-mark. Cross-lines often conspicuously pale-edged.
Ssp. *orkneyensis* Similar to the Shetland population, but a little brighter and more striking.
Similar species Ssp. *mendica* See Small Square-spot, Purple Clay, Barred Chestnut and Rosy Marsh Moth. Ssp. *thulei* Some individuals are very similar to Autumnal Rustic f. *edda*, which has the third cross-line evenly curved, the oval and kidney-mark pale, outlined only and never brownish.
Flight season One generation. June-July in the south, July-August in the north. Comes to light, often in large numbers, and feeds at sugar and flowers.
Life cycle Overwinters as a small larva, close to the ground. Larva August-May, feeding at night and hiding in leaf litter during the day. Pupates underground.
Larval foodplants Herbaceous plants, including Primrose and violets, and also woody species such as Bramble, heathers, Bilberry, sallows, hawthorns, Blackthorn and Hazel.
Habitat In the south most frequently in woodland, less often in gardens and open habitats without scrub. More widely, frequent on heathland and open moorland with heathers and other woody plants.
Status & distribution Resident. Common. Widespread and frequent throughout Great Britain, Man, Ireland and the Channel Islands.

Barred Chestnut
page 314

Diarsia dahlii (Hb.)

Local. N,WC,SE
2121(10090)

Field characters & Similar species FW 15-18mm. The rather broad forewing and strongly curved leading edge serve to distinguish this species from its closest relatives. Male is orange-brown or reddish brown, clouded and banded with purplish brown, with oval and kidney-mark inconspicuous, and area between them sometimes darker. Similar to some darker forms of Ingrailed Clay. See also Small Square-spot. Female deep pinkish red, dark reddish brown or dark purplish brown. Kidney-mark pale in outline, sometimes largely pale and conspicuous. Superficially similar to Purple Clay, which has area between oval and kidney-mark blackish. See also Square-spotted Clay.
Flight season One generation. August-September.
Life cycle Overwinters as a larva. Larva September-early spring, feeding at night and hiding in leaf litter by day. Pupates in a loose cocoon underground.
Larval foodplants Bilberry, Bramble, sallows and birches; also other woody and herbaceous plants such as docks.
Habitat Broadleaved woodland on acid soils, moorland and wooded heathland.
Status & distribution Resident. Local. Widespread in Scotland, northern England, the north Midlands and Wales. Largely rare south of the Midlands, but locally numerous in woodland on greensand in Surrey. Very local in Ireland, mainly on the west coast.

Purple Clay
page 314

Diarsia brunnea ([D. & S.])

Common. T
2122(10092)

Field characters FW 16-20mm. Forewing quite broad, relatively plain-looking, ranging from pinkish brown to rich, dark, purplish brown. Kidney-mark as ground-colour, with pale outline, or bright straw-coloured and conspicuous. Area between oval and kidney-mark usually blackish.
Similar species Pale individuals could be mistaken for northern Ingrailed Clays, but these are often more extensively orange-tinted and marbled, and slightly smaller. See also female Barred Chestnut, Rosy Marsh Moth and Square-spotted Clay.
Flight season One generation. June-August. Comes to light and feeds at sugar and flowers.
Life cycle Overwinters as a small larva, on or near the ground. Larva August-May, feeding at night and hiding in leaf litter by day. Pupates underground.
Larval foodplants A range of herbaceous plants in the autumn, including Foxglove and figworts, and in the spring also on woody species such as Bilberry, Heather, sallows, Bramble and birches.
Habitat Broadleaved woodland and wooded heathland.
Status & distribution Resident. Common. Throughout most of Great Britain and Ireland. Rare

but probably resident on Shetland. Local on Man. In the Channel Islands widespread but occasional on Jersey, rare on Guernsey.

Small Square-spot   page 314
Diarsia rubi (View.)
Common. T   2123(10093)

Field characters FW 12-16mm. The pale or dark pinkish-brown forewing, to a greater or lesser extent banded and clouded with reddish brown or dark brown, is diagnostic. Has a little black spot between oval and trailing edge, as in Ingrailed Clay. Another useful character is outer edge of third cross-line, which is strongly dark-edged, and either has very fine, short dark streaks extending outwards, or forming a band, fading into a pale wavy line or band. Second generation individuals tend to be smaller and darker and the northern populations that have only one generation tend to be paler.
Similar species See Fen Square-spot. Some dark northern Ingrailed Clays are similar, but are usually more marbled. Male Barred Chestnuts have a much more curved leading edge to forewing and are usually larger and browner.
Flight season Two generations in England, Wales and Ireland, May-early June and August-September. One generation in Scotland, June-July. Comes commonly to light and feeds at sugar and flowers, including ragworts and marsh grasses and rushes.
Life cycle Overwinters as a larva, close to the ground. Where there are two generations, larva September-April and June-late July, feeding at night and hiding low down in leaf litter during the day. Where there is one generation, larva August-May. Pupates underground.
Larval foodplants A range of herbaceous species, including Dandelion, docks and Foxglove. Also Heather, but not known to climb other woody species in the spring.
Habitat Almost everywhere, but most abundant in damp woodland and other marshy places, including damp pasture. Frequent in gardens.
Status & distribution Resident. Common. Well distributed and frequent throughout Great Britain, Man, Ireland and the Channel Islands.

Fen Square-spot   page 315
Diarsia florida (Schmidt)
Local. EC,WC,(N)   2124(10094)

Field characters & Similar species FW 15-17mm. Very similar to Small Square-spot, but larger, paler and brighter buff rather than so pink, where they occur in the same localities, and flight period occurs between the two generations of the latter. In areas where Small Square-spot has only one generation, many moths are as large and pale as the southern Fen Square-spots. No differences have been found in the genitalia of the two species in any population, and they produce fertile hybrids.
Flight season One generation. Late June-July.

Comes to light and feeds at sugar and flowers.
Life cycle & Larval foodplants Early stages have not been found in the wild, but probably have similar habits to single-brooded Small Square-spots.
Habitat Fens and acid bogs.
Status & distribution Resident. Local. Considered to be in the process of evolutionary separation from the Small Square-spot. In the areas where the latter has two generations, distinct local populations with a single generation, considered Fen Square-spot, have been identified in East Anglia, northern England and Wales. It appears that in Scotland there is only one species, at present regarded as the Small Square-spot, but perhaps the form with one genera-tion is the same species, i.e. Fen Square-spot, throughout.

Northern Dart   page 315
Xestia alpicola (Zett.)
ssp. *alpina* (Humph. & Westw.)
Na. N   2125(10194)

Field characters FW 15-17mm. The black or dark brown blazes on both sides of main vein in centre of forewing, near thorax, of this rather thickset species, are distinctive. Forewing rather broad and short. Other markings are very variable between populations. The large kidney-mark and oval are not always obvious. Ground-colour is usually varie-gated, sometimes strikingly so, and may include reds and greys, particularly in Aberdeenshire and Banffshire.
Similar species None.
Flight season One generation. Late June-August. Flies mainly late at night and comes readily to light traps. Occasionally reported flying in hot sunshine.
Life cycle Overwinters twice as a larva. Larva July-August of Year 1, making little growth until the spring of Year 2, reaching the penultimate instar by the end of the year and pupating late May-June of Year 3. Observations suggest that local populations are largely in synchrony, with most adults in most localities emerging in even years. In these years, fully grown larvae and pupae can be found under mosses and lichens.
Larval foodplants Mainly Crowberry. Heather, Bilberry, Cowberry, Bearberry and Mountain Azalea have been reported as additional possible foodplants but require confirmation in the wild.
Habitat Chiefly the upper slopes and tops of moun-tains, usually above 450m but at lower altitudes in the far north and recorded near sea level on Shetland.
Status & distribution Resident. Nationally Scarce A. Recorded rather widely on the high mountains of Scotland, but particularly where road and rail have provided access, such as in the Cairngorms and the mountains around Loch Rannoch, Perthshire. On 2 June 1996 a colony was discovered on a mountain in Banffshire, some 40km north-east of the Cairngorms, when larvae were found at 825m, and there are reports from the west coast and the

Southern Uplands. Also recorded from Harris and Lewis in the Outer Hebrides, Orkney and Shetland. Present in northern England, chiefly in the Pennines (adults mainly in odd years). Regularly recorded at Moor House NNR, Cumbria, at 450m, where it is fairly common, and noted at Skiddaw at 800m and at High Force. A single worn male was found at 850m near the summit of Cheviot, Northumberland, on 17 July 1975. In Ireland reported from Co. Mayo (1972) and Co. Donegal (1973) in the north-west.

Setaceous Hebrew Character page 315

Xestia c-nigrum (L.)

Common. T   2126(10199)

Field characters FW 14-19mm. The bright straw-coloured (or occasionally pinkish-brown) blotch extending centrally to leading edge of forewing is diagnostic. It contrasts sharply against the black, roughly saddle-shaped mark adjoining it which supposedly resembles a letter from the Hebrew alphabet. The straw colouring may extend either way along leading edge, but the triangular blotch is always distinctly paler. Collar is also straw-coloured. Forewing otherwise pale or dark greyish brown (sometimes reddish), or dark grey, occasionally clouded with reddish brown. Hindwing whitish, slightly clouded with grey around outside.
Similar species See Triple-spotted Clay and Double Square-spot.
Flight season Two generations in southern Britain, a relatively small one May-July and a much larger one early August-October. One generation in northern England and Scotland, early July-August. Comes to light, sometimes in large numbers, and feeds on sugar and flowers.
Life cycle Overwinters as a larva. Larva June-July and September-April when two generations, September-May where only one. Feeds at night and hides close to the ground by day. Pupates in a loose cocoon underground.
Larval foodplants A wide range of herbaceous plants, including Common Nettle, White Dead-nettle, willowherbs and burdocks.
Habitat Typically a lowland species, occurring in a wide variety of places, including woodland and marshes, but most abundant in cultivated areas, including gardens.
Status & distribution Resident and suspected immigrant. Common. Well distributed and frequent throughout Great Britain, Man, Ireland and the Channel Islands. The second generation can sometimes be abundant in late summer and autumn. It has been stated that the first generation is too small to have produced such large numbers, so their numbers must be increased by immigrants. However, it is equally possible that winter mortality is high, and populations are able to build up quickly under favourable conditions, whether or not immigration occurs. Widespread and abundant in the Channel Islands.

Triple-spotted Clay page 315

Xestia ditrapezium ([D. & S.])

Local. T   2127(10200)

Field characters & Similar species FW 17-19mm. In shape not dissimilar to Setaceous Hebrew Character, but without a conspicuous pale triangular block. Markings are more similar to Double Square-spot, which tends to have slightly broader forewing, is generally paler and hindwing is grey. Ground-colour varies from reddish brown (sometimes slightly greyish), purplish brown, very dark purplish grey, to purplish black. Hindwing rather dark and brownish, with orange-brown fringes. See also Square-spotted Clay and Double Square-spot.
Flight season One generation. Late June-early August. Comes to light, and feeds at sugar and flowers.
Life cycle Overwinters as a larva. Larva August-May, feeding at night and hiding among leaf litter by day. Pupates on or just below the ground.
Larval foodplants Herbaceous plants, including Primrose, and in the spring also woody species such as sallows, Dogwood and birches.
Habitat Damp and open broadleaved woodland, particularly carr woodland and bushy fens. Sometimes parks and gardens.
Status & distribution Resident. Local. Widespread and quite well distributed in southern and south-west England, the Midlands, East Anglia, Wales, north-west England and the western side of Scotland. Scarce in the east from Lincolnshire northwards. Local and scarce on Man. Few records from Ireland, from Cos. Dublin, Clare and Galway. Recorded once in the Channel Islands, from Guernsey, in 1973.

Double Square-spot page 315

Xestia triangulum (Hufn.)

Common. T   2128(10201)

Field characters FW 17-19mm. Forewing quite broad, generally light greyish brown, occasionally reddish or pinkish tinged, sometimes darker or predominantly grey. Markings vary only slightly. Hindwing uniformly grey, with whitish or grey fringe.
Similar species See Triple-spotted Clay and Square-spotted Clay.
Flight season One generation. June-early August. Comes frequently to light, and feeds at sugar and flowers.
Life cycle Overwinters as a larva. Larva August-May, feeding at night and hiding low down by day. Pupates underground.
Larval foodplants Many herbaceous plants, including buttercups, Primrose, Cow Parsley, Wood Spurge and, particularly in the spring, woody species such as Blackthorn, hawthorns and Raspberry.
Habitat Deciduous woodland, hedgerows, lush riverbanks in open country. Frequently in gardens.
Status & distribution Resident. Common. Throughout most of Great Britain, Man and Ireland,

but not recorded from Shetland. In the Channel Islands, widespread and frequent in Jersey but only once from Guernsey, in 1973.

Ashworth's Rustic
Xestia ashworthii (Doubl.)

Na. WC

page 315

2129(10203)

Field characters FW 16-20mm. Rather slender forewing and ashen colours are distinctive. No major black dashes or bars running along length of wings, only wavy cross-lines. Ground-colour varies from light grey (especially male) to very dark grey.
Similar species None.
Flight season One generation. Mid June-August. Both sexes come readily to light and to sugar.
Life cycle Overwinters as a small larva. Larva August-late May or June, feeding mainly at night, sometimes basking by day in the spring. Pupates in a flimsy cocoon under moss, among rocks or just below ground.
Larval foodplants Many low-growing plants, including Common Rock-rose, Wild Thyme, Sheep's Sorrel, Harebell, Salad Burnet, Bell Heather, Goldenrod, hawkweeds, Lady's Bedstraw, Creeping Willow, Foxglove and Heather.
Habitat On many geological strata including slate and limestone, on hillsides, quarries and mountainsides. There is a belief that the species breeds only on south-facing slopes but larvae have also been found on a steep, shaded east-facing slope. Small, isolated patches of foodplant growing on steep, rocky ground and scree seem to be preferred.
Status & distribution Resident. Nationally Scarce A. The nominate subspecies, distinct from the three forms in mainland Europe. Confined to north-west Wales, where it is locally frequent in Denbighshire (e.g. Llangollen), Caernarvonshire (e.g. Penmaenmawr, Snowdon and Sychnant Pass, and Cader Idris), Merionethshire and Montgomeryshire. The moth extends south well into Cardiganshire, where post-1980 records include Plas Gogerddan, Talybont and the RSPB Ynys-hir reserve. Discovered breeding on Anglesey in 1994.

Dotted Clay
Xestia baja ([D. & S.])

Common. T

page 315

2130(10204)

Field characters FW 17-21mm. The most conspicuous, diagnostic markings are the two small, sharp black dots just below leading edge, close to tip of forewing. Markings such as the cross-lines and kidney-mark (often darker in lower half) are usually weak, but visible. Forewing colour variable, light or dark reddish brown or warm greyish brown, sometimes tinged with pink or grey.
Similar species Six-striped Rustic lacks black wing-tip markings. Neglected Rustic and Cousin German both lack sharp black spots near leading edge of forewing.
Flight season One generation. Late July-late August.

Comes frequently to light, and feeds at sugar and flowers.
Life cycle Overwinters as a small larva. Larva August-May, feeding at night and hiding low down during the day. Pupates just beneath the soil surface.
Larval foodplants Herbaceous plants such as Common Nettle, and in the spring also on woody species such as willows, birches, Blackthorn and Bog-myrtle.
Habitat Woodland, heathland, also scrubby grassland on chalk and limestone, damp neutral grassland, carr woodland, wetlands and lakesides. Occasionally in gardens.
Status & distribution Resident. Common. Throughout Great Britain, Man and Ireland. More numerous in northern Britain.

255

Square-spotted Clay
Xestia rhomboidea (Esp.)

Nb. T

page 315

2131(10206)

Field characters & Similar species FW 17-20mm. Distinguished from related species by the rather broad, sombre, dark grey-brown forewing (usually with a purple tint) with thick, dark, irregular outer band. Shape and central forewing markings most like Double Square-spot (but often with an additional black block) which is paler, with at most a fine dark outer cross-line, and also has a distinct thick black dash on leading edge near tip, as does Triple-spotted Clay. Purple Clay and female Barred Chestnut are distinctly purple or reddish and have narrower, more rounded forewing, often with a bright kidney-mark.
Flight season One generation. Late July-August, sometimes from early July. Adults can be found visiting the flowers of burdocks, teasels, Rosebay Willowherb, Wood Sage and ragworts after dark, and come well to sugar and wine ropes. Both sexes come to light, usually only in small numbers but occasionally into double figures, mainly late at night.
Life cycle Overwinters as a small larva. Larva September-May. Feeds until mid April. Makes a cocoon in the earth, but does not change into a pupa until several weeks later.
Larval foodplants Wild larvae rarely reported but found recently in spring on Common Nettle, Dog's Mercury and Oxlip. In captivity on Primrose, Chickweed, docks, elms, Goat Willow, birches, Bullace and others. Has been reared from egg to adult exclusively on Ribwort Plantain and found in the wild in the absence of woody growth.
Habitat Usually long-established broadleaved woodland on chalk, gravel or clay, mainly at the edges of clearings. Also in more recent shelterbelts and scrub.
Status & distribution Resident. Nationally Scarce B. Rather locally distributed throughout its range. Most recent records are from the eastern half of England but there are also scattered records from the west, Wales and southern Scotland. Most frequently sought and recorded in Norfolk and Suffolk, particularly in Breckland. Locally distributed in the North Downs of Surrey and Kent, the Chiltern Beech

Larva of Square-spotted Clay.

woods of Oxfordshire and Buckinghamshire, the Midlands and in Yorkshire, particularly in the north of the county, with scattered records from other parts of lowland England. Appears to have spread into Hertfordshire from the north-east during the 1990s, but seems to have declined in south-west England. Formerly frequent in the New Forest, Hampshire, but last recorded in the county in 1968. In western Scotland occurs annually at Taynish NNR, Kintyre, suggesting there are thriving populations in this area.

Neglected Rustic   page 315
Xestia castanea (Esp.)
Local. T   2132(10207)

Field characters FW 16-18mm. A fairly unmistakable, finely-marked moth. A constant diagnostic feature is the conspicuous black base of kidney-mark. Extremely variable in colour, from light greyish brown, sometimes tinged with pink or with pink fringes (f. *neglecta* Hb.), to reddish brown. Hindwing uniformly grey with whitish, pinkish or grey-pink fringes. Variation is geographical, with f. *neglecta* dominant in the south. From the north Midlands and Wales northwards, pink and red forms predominate, and the darkest occur in northern Scotland. A yellow form (f. *xanthe* Woodforde) has occurred rarely in Surrey, Hampshire, Staffordshire and Kerry.
Similar species Pale examples of Square-spot Rustic are similar to f. *neglecta*, but kidney-mark paler than ground-colour, or at least pale-outlined and usually squarer. In the Northern Isles, very dark individuals of both species occur with the markings obscured, but Square-spot Rustic is a more rich brownish black, rather than reddish or greyish black, and smaller. See also Cousin German and Dotted Clay.
Flight season One generation. August-September. Comes to light, and feeds at sugar and flowers, particularly of heathers. Often seen on the wing by torchlight, just after dark.
Life cycle Overwinters as a small larva. Larva October-May, feeding at night and hiding low down by day. Spends about six weeks underground before pupating.
Larval foodplants Heather, Bell Heather and Cross-leaved Heath.
Habitat Open and wooded heathland, moorland

and raised bogs.
Status & distribution Resident. Local. In southern England mainly on the heaths of Berkshire, Surrey and the New Forest, Hampshire. In south-west England, Wales, the north Midlands, northern England and Man. Widespread in Scotland, including the Hebrides and Orkney. In the Channel Islands recorded once, from Guernsey, in 1966.

Six-striped Rustic   page 315
Xestia sexstrigata (Haw.)
Common. T   2133(10211)

Field characters FW 15-17mm. The dark veins, fine dark cross-lines and dark-outlined oval and kidney-mark are diagnostic and show little variation. Forewing light brown to warm dark brown.
Similar species See Dotted Clay.
Flight season One generation. July-August. Comes frequently to light, and feeds at sugar and flowers, notably of ragworts.
Life cycle Overwinters as a larva. Larva September-April or May, feeding at night and hiding low down by day. Pupates underground.
Larval foodplants Rarely reported as a larva since it is difficult to distinguish from the abundant Square-spot Rustic larva, but recorded on Hedge Bedstraw, Ribwort Plantain, Bramble, Bluebell and Water Figwort.
Habitat Wet meadows, marshes, fens and damp woodland; also in drier places such as hedgerows, gardens and downland.
Status & distribution Resident. Common. Throughout most of Great Britain, Man and Ireland, but not recorded from Shetland or the Channel Islands.

Square-spot Rustic   page 315
Xestia xanthographa ([D. & S.])
Common. T   2134(10212)

Field characters FW 14-17mm. The pale, or pale-outlined, rather square kidney-mark is a conspicuous diagnostic character, obscured only in some dark examples. Other markings usually weak, but fine dark cross-lines are usually evident, the third sometimes in the form of a series of small dark dots or dashes. Forewing colour varies considerably, from light brown, light or dark reddish or greyish brown, to dark or blackish brown.
Similar species Garden Dart has narrower forewing. White-marked flies in the spring. See also Neglected Rustic.
Flight season One generation. Late July-early October, peaking in late August-early September. Flies over grassland at dusk, sometimes in profusion. Comes to light, sometimes in abundance. Also dependable at sugar, often in large numbers, and flowers such as ragworts, Heather and Marram.
Life cycle Overwinters as a larva. Larva September-April. Feeds at night in mild weather, becoming fully grown in March or April and then spending about six

weeks in an underground cocoon before pupating.
Larval foodplants Mainly grasses, but also herbaceous plants such as plantains and Cleavers.
Habitat All types of grassland, including gardens, pasture and woodland rides, but not at high altitude.
Status & distribution Resident. Common. Well distributed and abundant throughout Great Britain, Man, Ireland and the Channel Islands.

Heath Rustic   page 315

Xestia agathina agathina (Dup.)
Local. T   2135(10216)

ssp. *hebridicola* (Stdgr.)
Hebrides

Field characters FW 14-16mm.
Ssp. *agathina* A constant and diagnostic feature of this rather variegated moth is the small pale straw-coloured or whitish oval, rather elongated and strongly contrasting with the black wedge containing it. Another is the second of the fine dark cross-lines, which is deeply zigzagged. Several black arrowhead marks on inner edge of outermost cross-line and a broad pale streak along leading edge. Forewing colour varies from light greyish brown, to reddish brown, dark grey or blackish, marbled with reddish brown or dusted with grey or white. Antennae in male slightly feathered.
Ssp. *hebridicola* Described from the Hebrides, has a whitish-grey ground-colour.
Similar species Some brightly marked examples of White-line Dart are somewhat similar, but oval is less elongated and does not contrast quite so sharply with black wedge, and antennae not feathered in male. See also True Lover's Knot.
Flight season One generation. Late August-September. Comes to light, and feeds at the flowers of Heather. Often seen flying over Heather at dusk, and again later in the night.
Life cycle Overwinters as a small larva. Larva late September-June, feeding at night and hiding low down by day. Pupates among plant debris or loose earth.
Larval foodplants Heather.
Habitat Acid heathland and moorland. Most numerous where Heather is tall.
Status & distribution Resident. Local. Widespread, chiefly in southern and south-west England, Wales, the north Midlands, northern England, Scotland including the Hebrides and Orkney, and Ireland. Local on Man. In the Channel Islands local and occasional on Jersey, rare on Guernsey.

Gothic   page 315

Naenia typica (L.)
Local. T   2136(10228)

Field characters FW 17-22mm. A greyish-brown moth with very broad forewing with brownish-white veins and cross-lines creating a netted effect, and uniformly dark grey hindwing.
Similar species Bordered Gothic also has a network

pattern, but much narrower forewing and paler hindwing. Feathered Gothic has dark cross-lines, flies later in the year and male has feathered antennae.
Flight season One generation. June-July. Comes to light in small numbers, and more frequently to sugar. Also feeds at flowers.
Life cycle Overwinters as a larva. Larva July-April, feeding at night, gregariously when small, hiding in leaf litter by day. Pupates underground.
Larval foodplants A wide range of wild and cultivated herbaceous and woody plants, including Common Comfrey, willowherbs, Cleavers, sallows, Blackthorn, Apple and buddleias.
Habitat Gardens, riverbanks, marshes, wet meadows, weedy hedgerows and damp woodland.
Status & distribution Resident. Local. In lowland areas throughout most of Great Britain and Ireland, except the Outer Hebrides, Orkney and Shetland. Local on Man. Rare in the Channel Islands.

Great Brocade   page 315

Eurois occulta (L.)
Nb; immigrant. T   2137(10161)

Field characters FW 24-27mm. The relatively long, narrow forewings help to distinguish this moth from other large, dark noctuids. A long, heavy black streak is usually apparent at base of forewing. The resident populations in Britain are darker than those in mainland Europe. They are variable in appearance but usually blackish, with a variable amount of lighter grey markings. Immigrants, which arrive from Scandinavia, the Netherlands and northern Germany, are grey.
Similar species Both resident and immigrant forms could be confused with Grey Arches, which flies at the same time and in similar habitats to the resident populations. Forewing of Grey Arches has a more arched leading edge, and basal streak is absent. Great Brocade holds its wings flatter over the body when walking.
Flight season One generation. July-early August. Immigrants usually arrive later, in August and into September. Seldom found by day, but comes to sugar in numbers and also to light, usually late at night.
Life cycle Overwinters as a small larva. Larva September-June, feeding mainly at night. Pupates in moss or plant debris on the surface of the soil, without a cocoon.
Larval foodplants Mainly Bog-myrtle growing on peaty ground, although the leaves of many herbaceous plants and also birches and sallows are eaten, especially in the later instars after the winter.
Habitat By rivers and boggy areas in scrubby moorland, broadleaved woodland and pine forest.
Status & distribution Resident in the central and western Highlands of Scotland, with a few records as far as the west coast. Nationally Scarce B. Immigrant elsewhere, recorded very widely throughout England, Wales and Scotland, including Orkney and Shetland, but in small numbers in most years. In Ireland and on Man recorded very infrequently, as an immigrant

257

only. Rare in the Channel Islands, where one was reported from Jersey in 1976.

Green Arches

page 315

Anaplectoides prasina ([D. & S.])

Common. T   2138(10232)

Field characters FW 20-25mm. A beautiful rich green moth when freshly emerged, marbled to a varying extent with white, brown and black. Thorax green, with a rusty red tuft. Green pigment fades rapidly on exposure to sunlight, as with many green moths, and worn examples appear yellowish grey. Some variation in fine detail of markings. Central area often darker, sometimes with a dark, narrow, blackish band. Patch beyond kidney-mark usually distinctly paler, often whitish. Hindwing uniformly dark grey, with white fringe.

Similar species None.

Flight season One generation. June-July. Comes to light in small numbers and frequently to sugar.

Life cycle Overwinters as a larva. Larva August-May, feeding at night and hiding in leaf litter by day. Pupates underground.

Larval foodplants A range of herbaceous and woody plants, including Primrose, docks, Honeysuckle, Bramble and Bilberry.

Habitat Broadleaved woodland and carr.

Status & distribution Resident. Common. Throughout most of Great Britain and Ireland but not recorded from the Outer Hebrides, Orkney and Shetland. Local on Man. Rare in the Channel Islands, where one seen on Guernsey in 2002.

Red Chestnut

page 315

Cerastis rubricosa ([D. & S.])

Common. T   2139(10224)

Field characters FW 14-17mm. Forewing rather pointed, with a straight leading edge and outer edge, curved only at trailing corner. Ground-colour is uniform rich pale or dark reddish brown or purplish brown, dusted with light grey to a varying extent, especially along leading edge. Markings rather indistinct. Oval, kidney-mark and cross-lines usually faint, pale, with dark edges. In southern England, reddish forms are usual, but in Scotland and in upland areas further south, the darker, purplish or greyish forms predominate. In some northern populations oval and kidney-mark are distinctly pale and forewing heavily frosted with white.

Similar species See White-marked, the only spring species with similar wing-shape and rich, reddish-brown colour.

Flight season One generation. Late February-April, but April-May in northern Britain. Comes frequently to light, and to sugar and sallow catkins.

Life cycle Overwinters as a pupa in a strong, silk-lined cocoon. Larva late April-June, feeding at night and remaining on the foodplant by day.

Larval foodplants Wild larvae are seldom found, but are recorded as feeding on herbaceous and

woody plants, including bedstraws, sallows and Bilberry.

Habitat Mainly broadleaved woodland and scrub but also in open country, including gardens, and on northern moorland.

Status & distribution Resident. Common. Throughout most of Great Britain, Man and Ireland, except Shetland. In the Channel Islands rare on Jersey, occasional on Guernsey.

White-marked

page 315

Cerastis leucographa ([D. & S.])

Local. S,C   2140(10225)

Field characters & Similar species FW 14-16mm. Similar in size, shape and colour to Red Chestnut, but with oval quite bright and kidney-mark distinct, both largely creamy white, kidney dark in lower third. Third cross-line very fine and blackish, either finely scalloped or represented by a row of white-tipped dashes. A distinct paler band beyond third line, and area along outer edge distinctly darker. Light grey dusting, if present, restricted to leading edge of forewing, which is very slightly curved and is less pointed than that of Red Chestnut. Slightly smaller on average, and darkest individuals deep brown, rather than purplish brown. In Red Chestnut, oval and kidney-mark usually dull but exceptionally may be distinctly pale in outline. The outermost cross-line has a pale component, and cross-band along outer edge of forewing is not distinctly darker. See also Square-spot Rustic.

Flight season One generation. Late March-April. Comes to light and sallow catkins.

Life cycle Overwinters underground as a pupa, with the adult formed inside. Larva May-June.

Larval foodplants It appears wild larvae have never been found. In captivity, various herbaceous and woody plants are accepted, including stitchworts, docks, sallows, Bilberry and oaks.

Habitat Open broadleaved woodland, old hedgerows and scrub.

Status & distribution Resident. Local. Locally widespread in central southern England, parts of the Midlands (Northamptonshire and Nottinghamshire), the southern half of Wales and the Welsh Borders. Local in Dorset, Yorkshire and the Lake District. A male at Lydd, Kent, on 4 April 1999, occurred as a suspected immigrant with an influx of Blossom Underwings, the first Kent record since 1912.

Pale Stigma

not illustrated

Mesogona acetosellae ([D. & S.])

Rare immigrant.   2141(9539)

Field characters & Similar species A reddish-brown moth about the size and shape of Lesser Yellow Underwing, with a conspicuous kidney-mark and oval between two brown cross-lines, which converge to trailing edge of forewing. Hindwing pale brownish or pinkish grey.

Status & distribution Rare immigrant. Recorded

only once in the British Isles. A single female was taken at sugar in a garden at Arlington, about 10km inland from Eastbourne on the coast of East Sussex, on 26 October 1895, during an influx of immigrant moths. A widespread species in central and southern Europe.

Hadeninae
Brocades, quakers and leaf-eating wainscots

Beautiful Brocade   Clouded Drab   Common Wainscot

Beautiful Yellow Underwing page 316

Anarta myrtilli (L.)

Common. T   2142(9907)

Field characters FW 10-12mm. Forewing most often reddish brown (f. *rufescens* Tutt) or less frequently brownish grey, but always marbled with greyish white. A small white blotch in centre of forewing adjacent to oval is usually the most notice-able feature. Hindwing yellow, with a broad black border extending narrowly along both leading and trailing edges.

Similar species Small Dark Yellow Underwing has a large, conspicuous white kidney-mark. True Lover's Knot has somewhat similar forewing and is some-times active during the day on heathland and moor-land, but has dirty brown hindwing and is usually slightly larger. Both species are well camouflaged when sitting on heathers.

Flight season Probably two overlapping generations in southern England, late April-August. In northern Britain one generation, June-July. Flies low over heathers in sunshine, and feeds at flowers.

Life cycle The overwintering stage is not known for certain, but is probably the larva or pupa. Larva April-October or later, or July-September or later in the north. Feeds mostly during the day. Pupates in a tough cocoon or just below the ground surface.

Larval foodplants The terminal shoots of Heather and Bell Heather.

Habitat Heathland and moorland.

Status & distribution Resident. Common. In suit-able habitat throughout most of Britain and Ireland, except Shetland. Local and rare on Man.

Larva of Beautiful Yellow Underwing.

Small Dark Yellow Underwing   p.316

Anarta cordigera (Thunb.)

Na. NE   2143(9908)

Field characters FW 10-12mm. Recognisable by quite large, conspicuous white kidney-mark on otherwise rather uniform dark grey forewing, and yellow, black-bordered hindwing, which is hidden at rest.

Similar species Forewing of Beautiful Yellow Underwing is intricately patterned with white, has smaller, more central white mark and is often reddish brown in ground-colour. Small Yellow Underwing has smaller, more pointed forewing without any prominent white markings, and very different habitat and distribution.

Flight season One generation. Late April-May, sometimes to mid June, depending on altitude and latitude and coinciding with the flowering of Bearberry, which it visits for nectar. Active in sunshine and flies rapidly. In dull weather individuals and mating pairs can be found at rest near Bearberry flowers, or on twigs, rocks and posts, especially in the afternoon.

Life cycle Overwinters as a pupa, in a long silken cocoon on the ground. Larva late May-mid July. Feeds by night on the young shoots and leaves of the foodplant.

Larval foodplants Bearberry is the only foodplant confirmed in the wild. Cowberry, Bilberry and Bog Bilberry accepted in captivity.

Habitat Bearberry-rich moorland, mainly at altitudes of 200-650m, usually on stony glacial moraines and dry gravelly areas, or on roadside banks where Heather growth is poor. Probably benefits from a combination of sparse sward and well-drained bare ground which warms up quickly in sunshine.

Status & distribution Resident. Nationally Scarce A. Confined to Scotland where it occurs mainly in the central Highlands in Perthshire and Inverness-shire, extending eastwards to Aberdeenshire and Angus and northwards to Banffshire and Morayshire. Not recorded north of the Great Glen, although the habitat and foodplant is widespread in that area. There is a doubtful 19th-century report from Shetland.

Broad-bordered White Underwing p.316
Anarta melanopa (Thunb.)
RDB. N   2144(9899*)

Field characters FW 11-13mm. Diagnostic features are grey forewing, marked with black, with no central white spot, and white hindwing bordered with dark brown and with a central dark crescent.
Similar species Small Dark Yellow Underwing and Beautiful Yellow Underwing have yellow hindwing and conspicuous white markings on forewing.
Flight season One generation. Mid May-June. Flies in sunshine or if it is cloudy but warm, and takes advantage of short sunny periods on cloudy days. Feeds at flowers of montane plants such as Bearberry and Cowberry. Can travel at great speed, but often flies only a few centimetres above the vegetation, in a direct, bee-like fashion, especially in windy weather. Can be readily attracted, from distances of 10m or more, to bunches of flowers such as Cherry Laurel.
Life cycle Overwinters as a pupa, in a cocoon among plant debris under the foodplant. Larva July-August. Feeds at night and rests under the leaves of the foodplant by day.
Larval foodplants Crowberry, Cowberry, Bilberry and Bearberry. Sallows, Knotgrass, Common Rock-rose and other unrelated plants have been accepted in captivity, but on these mortality is usually high.
Habitat Usually high moorland, on the slopes, ridges and summits of mountains, at altitudes over 650m. Also near sea level in the far north.
Status & distribution Resident. Red Data Book species. The only record from England is of a single adult near the summit of Cheviot, Northumberland, on 12 June 1974. Otherwise restricted to Scotland, where it is recorded most frequently in the central Highlands. Also recorded in Wester Ross, Caithness, Argyll, Galloway and the Southern Uplands. In 1992 one was recorded in Shetland, from where there are also old records and specimens. The Natural History Museum holds old specimens labelled 'Hebrides'.

Nutmeg   page 316
Discestra trifolii (Hufn.)
Common. T   2145(9895)

Field characters FW 14-18mm. Key characters include kidney-mark, which is quite large with half nearest trailing edge always darker than ground-colour, and shape of forewing which is rather narrow at the base with a straight leading edge. Forewing ground-colour pale to dark brownish grey, or pale sandy brown, usually dusted with grey or sometimes black, to give a finely variegated effect. Outermost cross-line forms a distinct pale-edged W-mark.
Similar species White Colon is usually larger and stockier, outline of kidney-mark is whitish and outer band normally fails to form a W. Dusky Brocade (f. *obscura*) has the W, but again is larger and has a broader forewing. Confused is browner, kidney-mark is edged whitish. In all these species, forewing is

broader near base.
Flight season Two generations in the south, mid April-June and August-September. One generation from the Midlands northwards, June-July. Comes to light, sugar and flowers.
Life cycle Overwinters as a pupa, in a fragile underground cocoon. Larva late June-July and September-October in the south, August-September in the north. Feeds at night.
Larval foodplants Herbaceous plants, particularly goosefoots, Common Orache and other related species, but also recorded on unrelated plants including onions and conifer seedlings.
Habitat A range of rather open places, including gardens, waste-ground, downland, fens and open woodland, favouring light soils. Especially frequent in coastal areas and river valleys.
Status & distribution Resident and suspected immigrant. Common. Widespread and well distributed in southern and south-east England, but more local from the Midlands and Wales northwards to southern Scotland. Has occurred further north to Shetland and (rarely) in Ireland, probably as an immigrant, although temporarily established in Orkney in the 1970s. Local on Man. Widespread and abundant in the Channel Islands.

2146 see Appendix

Shears   page 316
Hada plebeja (L.)
Common. T   2147(9925)

Field characters FW 14-17mm. Diagnostic feature is the bold whitish mark in centre of forewing. This radiates outwards to two sharp points, somewhat like an open pair of scissors or shears, and contrasting sharply with the blackish bar or blotch adjacent to or surrounding it. Shears-mark is somewhat variable in size, and may be restricted to veins, but general pattern is fairly constant. Forewing varies in colour, being whitish grey, sandy, pale to dark brownish grey, or grey.
Similar species See Stranger.
Flight season Mainly one generation, late May-early July, with a small second generation in August in the south. Comes to light and feeds at sugar and flowers, including campions, Wood Sage, Viper's-bugloss and Red Valerian. Can sometimes be found during the day sitting on tree trunks and posts.
Life cycle Overwinters as a pupa, in a cocoon on the ground, under leaf litter or moss. Larva July-August, and again later in the south. Feeds at night.
Larval foodplants Herbaceous plants, including Smooth Hawk's-beard, Mouse-ear-hawkweed and Lucerne.
Habitat Typically, open places on light soils, including heathland, sand-dunes and downland, but also in open woodland.
Status & distribution Resident. Common. Throughout Great Britain, Man and Ireland. Widespread and frequent in the Channel Islands.

Pale Shining Brown
page 316

Polia bombycina (Hufn.)

pRDB. S   2148(9991)

Field characters FW 19-23mm. This pale brown moth has a reflective reddish shine on forewing when fresh, and a heavy, curved, pale, irregularly-edged brownish line (sometimes broken) just inside and parallel to outer edge. Both kidney-mark and oval are large and usually well defined. Occasional silvery grey individuals have been recorded, usually near the coast, in south-east England and are suspected immigrants.

Similar species Unlike Pale Shining Brown, Silvery Arches does not have the dash formed by the brown edging of the outer line in trailing corner, pointing to base of forewing, and Silvery Arches generally looks more marbled and favours acidic and clay soils. Of the superficially similar species, Reddish Light Arches and Large Nutmeg are smaller, and lack the reddish-brown line. Dark Arches is never reddish, with a black basal streak and I-bar on forewing. These latter three also have a W-shaped line near outer edge. See also Scarce Brindle.

Flight season One generation. Early June-mid July. Comes to light and sugar and visits flowers, including Wood Sage, White Campion, Bladder Campion, woundworts, Viper's-bugloss, Martagon Lily and Red Valerian.

Life cycle Unconfirmed in the wild. Almost certainly overwinters as a part-grown larva. Eggs laid by light-trapped females have hatched by early August, and if kept warm and in the dark have produced adults in the winter. Pupates underground.

Larval foodplants Unconfirmed in the wild. Foliage accepted in captivity includes Knotgrass, lettuce, sow-thistles, Dandelion, Common Restharrow, Grey Willow, White Willow and docks. May complete its spring growth on the buds and leaves of deciduous trees and shrubs, like other members of the genus, so scrub may be important.

Habitat Usually on light calcareous soils, both chalk and limestone, the largest numbers from rough, scrubby grassland and downland, but also recorded in open woodland.

Status & distribution Resident and occasional immigrant. Proposed Red Data Book species, formerly Nationally Scarce B. Until the mid 1970s, widely and well distributed in southern and south-east England northwards to a line between the Severn and the Wash. In the 1980s it was considered Nationally Scarce. Since then it has undergone a massive and continuing decline. Still present on the south Wiltshire/north Hampshire border, but has become very hard to find elsewhere and must be at very low population levels if present. Recorded annually in Cambridgeshire until 1980, in Oxfordshire until 1984, in Kent until 1992, with various records from Northamptonshire, Leicestershire, Gloucestershire and Norfolk in the mid 1990s. Singletons at Dungeness and Greatstone, Kent, in 1989 were of the pale grey continental form and are considered immigrants, as

are the few 20th-century records from Sussex and the few more recent ones from Essex and Yorkshire. Reported from Northumberland and southern Scotland in the early 19th century but not since, and occasionally recorded in north Wales up to 1948. Reported but unconfirmed from Man. Recorded from Ireland many years ago, as single records from Cos. Louth, Carlow and Waterford.

Silvery Arches
page 316

Polia trimaculosa (Esp.)

Nb. T   2149(9992)

Field characters & Similar species FW 21-25mm. The richly-marbled, greyish forewing and reddish tufts on grey thorax make this moth fairly easy to recognise. Both the reddish-tinted forms of southern England and the darker silvery grey or even bluish forms in Scotland have a lustre not present in Grey Arches, which has a distinct blackish dash or arrow-mark in trailing corner. Edging of outermost cross-line on forewing of Silvery Arches is black and broken into three distinct sections, with no dash at trailing corner. See also Pale Shining Brown.

Flight season One generation. June-July. Sometimes found at rest on birch trunks by day. Comes to sugar, and in smaller numbers to light.

Life cycle Overwinters as a small larva, probably among ground vegetation. Larva late July or August-May. Pupates underground.

Larval foodplants Pre- and post-hibernation larvae have been beaten from birches and sallows, and post-hibernation larvae also from Bog-myrtle and, less often, Hawthorn and Honeysuckle. Herbaceous plants are also accepted in captivity.

Habitat Scrubby woodland on heathland, moorland and in river valleys, and open woodland on acid soils and clays.

Status & distribution Resident and suspected immigrant. Nationally Scarce B. The main centres of current distribution are the river valleys of the Spey, Dee, Clyde and the Sound of Jura, the Rannoch and Aviemore environs and more widely in Scotland. Also, the acid heaths of Surrey, north-east Hampshire and Berkshire. It has been recorded from other widely scattered locations in south-east England (e.g. Ashdown Forest, Sussex), the Midlands (e.g. Wyre Forest, Shropshire/Herefordshire), central and north Wales, the Morecambe Bay/Grange-over-Sands area of Lancashire and Cumbria (though not recently), and the north-west coast of Scotland, where it is probably under-recorded. Reported from Shetland but almost certainly in error. Suspected immigrants are occasional along the coast of south and south-east England.

Grey Arches
page 316

Polia nebulosa (Hufn.)

Common. T   2150(9993)

Field characters FW 21-26mm. Key features of this normally grey or whitish moth are the leading edge of forewing, which is strongly curved, and oval and kidney-mark, which are large and pale with dark outlines. Also, a blackish dash or arrow-mark in trailing corner. Very variable in colour, ranging from white, light to dark grey, or blackish. The pale form (f. *pallida* Tutt) predominates in western and northern Britain and in Ireland. In the late 19th century, blackish forms with bright white fringes, f. *robsoni* Collins and f. *thompsoni* Arkle, were recorded in northern England, but have now become rare. Hindwing grey, darker towards fringe.

Similar species Immigrant Great Brocades are also grey but are generally larger, leading edge of forewing is straighter, there is a black basal streak, and hindwing uniformly dark brownish grey with a sharply contrasting white fringe. See also Silvery Arches.

Flight season One generation. June-July. Comes to light, and feeds at sugar and flowers. Can sometimes be found by day on tree trunks and posts.

Life cycle Overwinters as a part-grown larva, on the ground in leaf litter. Larva August-May. Feeds at night, and by day rests among the foliage of woody foodplants when small, hiding on or near the ground when larger. Pupates in a cocoon on or in loose earth.

Larval foodplants Woody plants, including Hazel, Downy Birch, Silver Birch, Honeysuckle, sallows and Bramble. Also low-growing plants such as docks.

Habitat Broadleaved woodland and well-wooded country in the south, including rural gardens, but more restricted to woodland in the north.

Status & distribution Resident. Common. Widespread in the whole of southern Britain, but more local in Scotland, mainly in the west. Local on Man. Widespread in Ireland. In the Channel Islands rare on Jersey and Guernsey, but locally frequent on Alderney and Sark.

Feathered Ear
page 316

Pachetra sagittigera (Hufn.)

ssp. *britannica* (Turn.)

Former resident; presumed extinct. S   2151(10068)

Field characters & Similar species FW 17-20mm. Conspicuous chocolate-coloured hoof-shaped mark by oval and whitish square on trailing edge of forewing distinguish Feathered Ear from Bordered Gothic, as do inner cross-lines which are fairly straight on Feathered Ear, rather than widely curved.

Flight season One generation. Mid May-late June. Reported visiting flowers of Wild Privet. Comes to sugar and sometimes to light.

Life cycle Overwinters as a larva and has been found in numbers on grass stems at night in January and February. Larva July-April. Pupates in a flimsy cocoon on the ground.

Larval foodplants Grasses, particularly Annual Meadow-grass and Wood Meadow-grass.

Habitat Calcareous grassland. The moth is reported as hiding among 'grass tufts' by day, suggesting it occupied a rough sward, but the noted Surrey site at Betchworth was heavily grazed by rabbits in 1950 when a number of larvae were found. This was prior to myxomatosis which decimated rabbit populations, after which this and many other swards became much ranker. However, the disappearance of the moth from its stronghold on Wye Downs, Kent, coincided with an intensification of grazing and burning in the 1960s.

Status & distribution Former resident, now considered extinct. Recorded mainly from the North Downs of Surrey (discovered 1855, last seen 1960) and Kent (last seen 1963), particularly the chalk downs between Ashford and Wye, but also in the Folkestone and Tunbridge districts. One was recorded at light on Stockbridge Downs, on the Wiltshire/Hampshire border, about 1950, and in 1921 one was found near High Wycombe, Buckinghamshire.

White Colon
page 316

Sideridis albicolon (Hb.)

Nb. S,C,NE   2152(9969)

Field characters FW 17-20mm. Forewing has a grainy texture. The white comma or sometimes colon-shaped marking, which forms the lower, outer part of the kidney-mark, is quite striking when moth is in good condition and helps to distinguish it from several similar brown noctuid moths.

Similar species In Dusky Brocade, Nutmeg and Cabbage Moth, outermost whitish cross-line of forewing often has a pronounced central W-shaped zigzag. Crescent Striped has a smooth, silky texture.

Flight season Mainly one generation, late May-June, with a small second generation in southern England, late July-August. Visits flowers such as Viper's-bugloss and various grasses, sometimes by day, and comes to sugar and light.

Life cycle Overwinters as a pupa underground, formed in August and lasting until May. Larva late June-July. Second-generation larvae have been found at Sandwich, Kent, in late August and September. Feeds by night and hides in sand near the foodplant by day.

Larval foodplants Sea Rocket, Common Restharrow, Sea Sandwort, Sand Spurrey and Ribwort Plantain, and probably many other plants. Larvae have also been found on the flowers of Sea Bindweed and in Breckland on Flixweed, and reared on straggly plants of oraches, goosefoots and Knotgrass.

Habitat Coastal habitats, particularly vegetated sand-dunes, shingle and marshes. Also breeds inland on heathland.

Status & distribution Resident. Nationally Scarce B. A scattered distribution, on sandy beaches all around the British coast, from the Moray Firth on the east coast to south Cumbria on the west, and including the Isle of Wight. There are older records from the west coast of Scotland. Well established inland in the Breckland of Norfolk/Suffolk, and present but very local on heaths on the Hampshire/Surrey border and in north Lincolnshire. There were a number of records from the lower Thames Valley west of London between 1941 and 1956, but the moth is now considered a scarce vagrant in this area. Local on Man. Apparently very local around the coast of Ireland, but present both in the south-west and the north-east. In the Channel Islands widespread and occasional on Jersey, rare on Guernsey.

Bordered Gothic
page 316

Heliophobus reticulata (Goeze)

ssp. *marginosa* (Haw.)

pRDB. S,EC   2153(9972)

ssp. *hibernica* Cock.

Ireland

Field characters & Similar species FW 17-19mm. Ssp. *marginosa* is the form recorded over most of mainland Britain and is a pale, light brown moth, strikingly different in appearance from the darker, greyer ssp. *hibernica,* which occurs on the extreme south coast of Ireland. However, recent specimens from Portland, Dorset, are dark like those from Ireland. Both subspecies distinguished from Feathered Gothic, which flies later in the year, in having white-edged cross-lines on forewing inside oval and outside kidney-mark. Gothic is larger and has much broader, more obscurely-marked forewing. See also Feathered Ear, which has fewer of the cross-lines and high-lighted veins which give the gothics a latticed appearance, Beautiful Gothic and Mediterranean Brocade.
Flight season One generation. May-July. Has been reported feeding at the flowers of Red Valerian, campions, Viper's-bugloss and Wood Sage, and comes readily to sugar and light.
Life cycle Overwinters as a pupa in loose earth. Larva late June-early September. The larva appears not to have been found in the wild, so the life cycle details are deduced from observations in captivity. Eggs laid by wild-caught females hatch in about two weeks.
Larval foodplants Reared with limited success on Soapwort; Bladder Campion and Knotgrass also accepted. Soapwort has a scattered distribution somewhat similar to the records of the moth.
Habitat Chalk downland, calcareous parts of breck-land heaths, limestone and chalk cliffs, quarries and other exposures such as cuttings and embankments. Also other disturbed ground, including calcareous brownfield sites.
Status & distribution Resident and suspected immigrant. Formerly Nationally Scarce B; in serious decline and now merits RDB status. A series of post-1990 records from Gravesend, Kent, including two in May 2001, suggests at least one population is still present in Britain but searching in 2002 failed to find it. The Breckland of Norfolk, Suffolk and Cambridgeshire was always the best known area, but it has not been seen there since the mid-1990s. Formerly recorded on Portland, Dorset, but not seen since the mid-1990s, despite many searches. Several were recorded

in Yorkshire in the 1980s, but it is unlikely to be established there. Singletons were reported in Glamorgan at Llanishen, Cardiff, in August 1995 and Roath, Cardiff, in July 1996. Reported from Slimbridge, Gloucestershire, in 1989. Previously recorded from a wide scatter of sites in England north to Lancashire and in south Wales. Not recorded in Scotland but there is an old record for Man. Ssp. *hibernica* occurs in the extreme south of Ireland, from Co. Wexford to Co. Kerry. Scattered singletons are reported periodically, as suspected immigrants, such as one resembling the dark conti-nental race at Eccles-on-Sea, Norfolk, on 9 June 1999. Recorded twice from Jersey, in 1983.

Cabbage Moth
page 316

Mamestra brassicae (L.)

Common. T   2154(9987)

Field characters FW 14-22mm. Most noticeable characters on forewing are chalky-white outline of kidney-mark and whitish inner edge of dark outer band, which forms a W-mark in the middle. Ground-colour dark brownish grey, sometimes rather blackish or paler, often with pale brown blotches. Variation is relatively slight.
Similar species In White Colon, most of the kidney-mark is not more distinct than other markings, forewing dusted with grey or brownish grey, giving it a grainy texture, and pale edge of outer band is usually broken and not W-shaped. Dark Brocade has a black bar in centre of forewing joining middle cross-lines.
Flight season Usually two or three generations, May-October, but has been found in every month of the year. In the north, probably only one generation, June-July. Comes to light, usually in rather small numbers, and feeds at sugar and flowers.
Life cycle Overwinters mainly as a pupa, in an underground cocoon, and sometimes as a larva, which can be found at any time of year, but mainly in late summer and autumn. Feeds at night and hides close to or under the ground by day.
Larval foodplants Best known as a pest of culti-vated brassicas, ruining cabbages by burrowing into the heart. However, feeds on the leaves of almost any wild or cultivated herbaceous plant, and is also recorded on woody species, including sallows and oaks.
Habitat A lowland species most frequent in culti-vated areas, but found in many habitats, including open woodland.
Status & distribution Resident. Common. Throughout Great Britain, Man and Ireland, but more thinly distributed in northern Britain. Widespread and abundant in the Channel Islands.

Dot Moth
page 316

Melanchra persicariae (L.)

Common. S,C,(N)   2155(9984)

Field characters FW 16-21mm. The rather broad,

264

Larva of Dot Moth.

glossy black forewing and large, conspicuous white kidney-mark make this moth unmistakable. Little variation and other markings are usually indistinct.
Similar species None.
Flight season One generation. Late June-August. Comes to light and feeds at sugar and flowers.
Life cycle Overwinters as a pupa, in an underground cocoon. Larva August-October. Feeds by day and night and rests on the foodplant.
Larval foodplants A wide range of wild and cultivated herbaceous and woody plants, including Common Nettle, Hop, Field Bindweed, Broad-leaved Dock, Groundsel, Michaelmas-daisy, White Clover, Black Currant, Ivy, Hazel, Elder, willows and larch seedlings. Regularly on Barberry.
Habitat Frequent in gardens and hedgerows. Occurs in a wide range of open and wooded habitats.
Status & distribution Resident. Common. Widespread in the whole of southern Britain, but more local in parts of northern England and the extreme south of Scotland. Local on Man. Widespread in Ireland. Widespread and frequent in the Channel Islands.

Broom Moth   page 316
Melanchra pisi (L.)
Common. T   2163(9985)

Field characters FW 16-20mm. Most conspicuous and diagnostic feature of rather broad forewing is wide, outermost cross-line which is irregular and creamy white, with dark arrowhead marks or blotches along its inner edge. Ground-colour is quite variable, ranging from pale to dark reddish brown or dark purplish brown. Some examples are marbled with grey. Others are variegated with brownish yellow and tinged with pink. The darkest are often dusted with purplish grey and are most frequent on peaty moorland.
Similar species Bright-line Brown-eye, which has a straighter, whiter outermost line on forewing, with a conspicuous tooth or zigzag.
Flight season One generation. Late May-July. Comes to light and feeds at sugar and flowers.
Life cycle Overwinters as a pupa in an underground cocoon. Larva June-September. Most active at night, resting on the foodplant by day.
Larval foodplants A wide variety of herbaceous and

woody plants, including Heather, Bracken, Broom, Bramble, sallows, Sea-buckthorn and larches.
Habitat In all kinds of open country, including gardens. Most numerous on heathland and moorland. Less frequent in woodland and marshland.
Status & distribution Resident. Common. Throughout most of Great Britain, Man and Ireland. Has reached Shetland but unclear if resident or immigrant. Particularly abundant on northern moorland. Widespread and frequent in the Channel Islands.

Beautiful Brocade   page 316
Lacanobia contigua ([D. & S.])
Local. T   2156(9919)

Field characters FW 16-19mm. Distinguishing features are the very marbled appearance and the whitish diagonal band crossing forewing from white oval to trailing corner, broken by second cross-line and often ending at third. The band forms a V when moth is at rest, but may be indistinct on dark individuals. Variable in ground-colour, but predominantly either greyish white, clouded and variegated with grey, pink or orange-brown; or blackish grey, clouded with pale grey.
Similar species This and the following three species are similar in general pattern. In particular, outermost cross-line of forewing forms a distinct white W, there is a pale patch at base of leading edge and a black basal streak. Pale-shouldered Brocade and Dog's Tooth do not have a diagonal white band and are both brownish and less marbled, although sometimes either paler dusted or clouded. Pale-shouldered Brocade has broader forewing than Beautiful Brocade and Dog's Tooth. See also Light Brocade.
Flight season One generation. June-July. Comes to sugar and light.
Life cycle Overwinters as a pupa, in an underground cocoon. Larva late July-September. Feeds by day and night.
Larval foodplants A range of mainly woody plants, including Downy Birch, Silver Birch, oaks, Broom, Bog-myrtle, Heather, Dyer's Greenweed and Bracken.
Habitat On heathland and moorland, and in woodland on neutral and acid soils.
Status & distribution Resident. Local. Well distributed on the heathlands of southern England. Widespread but thinly distributed elsewhere in southern England, the Midlands and Wales. Local in northern England and on Man. Widespread and more frequent in mainland Scotland and the Inner Hebrides. In Ireland mainly near the coast, in the south-west and north-east.

Light Brocade   page 316
Lacanobia w-latinum (Hufn.)
Local. T   2157(9912)

Field characters FW 18-21mm. The easiest of the group to identify, being larger with bold, clear-cut markings and a wide, uniformly light grey cross-band beyond the kidney-mark. Varies very little in colour and markings, although some individuals are tinged with pink.

Similar species Beautiful Brocade is also predominantly greyish, but smaller with a whitish diagonal band and markings less clear. See also Dusky Brocade and Saxon.

Flight season One generation. May-mid July. Comes to light and feeds at sugar and flowers, and is sometimes found by day at rest on fences and tree trunks.

Life cycle Overwinters as a pupa underground. Larva late June-August. Feeds at night.

Larval foodplants A range of woody and herbaceous plants, including Broom, Dyer's Greenweed, Bramble and Redshank.

Habitat Often associated with open ground on calcareous soil, but also frequent on some heaths and heathy commons. Sometimes recorded in open woodland.

Status & distribution Resident. Local. Widespread and well distributed in southern England, including the Isle of Wight and in East Anglia. Local in Wales and the Midlands, and very local in northern England and Scotland north to Perthshire.

Pale-shouldered Brocade   page 317
Lacanobia thalassina (Hufn.)
Common. T   2158(9918)

Field characters FW 16-20mm. Pale patch at base of forewing striking, but shared by other members of the group. Most examples distinguishable by broader forewing with a more curved leading edge, and richer, overall rather dark reddish-brown coloration, variably dusted with light brown and off-white. There is also a light greyish-brown form, f. *humeralis* Haw. In centre of forewing there is a solid black bar or thin line, nearly always joining middle cross-lines. An arm extends inward from near the outer end of this line to form an outlined tooth-like mark. Some females are rather dark, with a less obvious pale patch at base of forewing.

Similar species Dusky Brocade has a duller white W and the eyes are not conspicuously hairy. Dark Brocade has no pale basal patch. See also Dog's Tooth and Beautiful Brocade.

Flight season Mainly one generation. May-late July. A small second generation has been reported in the south in August. Comes to light, sometimes in numbers, and feeds at sugar and flowers.

Life cycle Overwinters as a pupa in an underground cocoon. Larva late June-early September. Feeds at night.

Larval foodplants A wide range of mainly woody plants, including oaks, hawthorns, Apple, sallows, Aspen, Barberry and Honeysuckle.

Habitat Woodland, wooded country, scrub, moorland, fens; sometimes gardens but seldom in urban areas.

Status & distribution Resident. Common. Throughout most of Britain, Man and Ireland, but not recorded from the Outer Hebrides or the Channel Islands.

Dog's Tooth   page 317
Lacanobia suasa ([D. & S.])
Local. S,C   2159(9920)

Field characters & Similar species FW 15-20mm. Diagnostic feature is a distinct, often solid, dark tooth-like mark in centre of forewing. This fails to reach third cross-line, and there is no black bar or line, which eliminates brightly-marked Dusky Brocades and most examples of Pale-shouldered Brocade, which can be a similar colour but also has a broader forewing. There are two distinct colour forms: one is greyish brown, clouded with sandy brown. The other, f. *dissimilis* Knoch, is uniformly dark greyish brown with the only distinct markings the tooth-mark, white W and black basal streak. This form is sometimes less numerous, but seems to occur in all populations. See also Bright-line Brown-eye and Stranger.

Flight season Two generations in southern England, late May-early July and late July-early September. Further north, one generation, June-July. Comes to light, sometimes in numbers, and feeds at sugar and flowers.

Life cycle Overwinters as a pupa underground. Larva late June-July and late August-September in the south, and August-September further north. Feeds at night.

Larval foodplants Herbaceous plants, including Common Sea-lavender, Greater Plantain and goose-foots.

Habitat Most numerous in damp places such as salt-marshes, coastal grasslands, moorland and river valleys, but does occur inland in drier farmland and some urban and suburban areas.

Status & distribution Resident. Local. Widespread in southern mainland Britain, more local in southern and western Scotland and Ireland. Singletons recorded from Man in 1956 and 1974, and from Jersey in 1995 and Guernsey in 1984.

Bright-line Brown-eye   page 317
Lacanobia oleracea (L.)
Common. T   2160(9917)

Field characters FW 14-19mm. Uniformly warm brown forewing slightly dusted with white, orange blotch in kidney-mark (the 'brown eye') and fine pure white outer cross-line forming a W, are all diagnostic features. Variation slight, chiefly in strength of small white oval, extent of dusting and shade of brown.

Similar species Dog's Tooth f. *dissimilis* is duller brown and has a characteristic central tooth-mark on forewing. See also Broom.

Flight season Mainly one generation. May-late July in most places. In southern Britain there is a small second generation, August-September.

Life cycle Overwinters as a pupa underground. Larva June-October. Feeds at night and rests on or under the foodplant during the day.

Larval foodplants A wide range of wild and cultivated herbaceous and woody plants, including Common Nettle, Fat-hen, willowherbs, St John's-worts, Traveller's-joy, Black-bindweed, Tamarisk, English Elm, Hazel, Hop and Reed Sweet-grass. Occasionally a pest of tomatoes, boring into the fruit.

Habitat Occurs in most habitats. Abundant in gardens and other cultivated land, including in glasshouses. Frequent on heathland and on the edges of saltmarshes. Also occurs in woodland rides.

Status & distribution Resident. Common. Throughout most of Great Britain, Man and Ireland, less frequent in the far north but resident north to Shetland. Widespread and abundant in the Channel Islands.

Stranger · · · · · · · · · · · · · · · · · not illustrated

Lacanobia blenna (Hb.)

Rare immigrant; temporary resident. · · · · 2161(9916)

Field characters & Similar species FW 15-17mm. Rather like an unusually pale, whitish-brown Dog's Tooth in shape and markings, but with an oblique, pale straw coloured, roughly elliptical, tapering or crescent-like flash between tooth-mark and kidney-mark, smaller basal streak and markings generally more intricate. Also, hindwing whitish, sometimes with a dark outer band. Tawny Shears is smaller, without central flash and outer W-mark on forewing. Central mark of Shears is branched.

Status & distribution Rare immigrant and possible temporary resident. The only confirmed records are of three captured at Freshwater, the Isle of Wight, in 1857, 1859 and 1879, the first two at sugar; and one captured on the downs near Lewes, Sussex, in 1868. Resident in coastal habitats in Spain, southern and western France, around the Mediterranean and in south-eastern Europe.

Glaucous Shears · · · · · · · · · · · · · page 317

Papestra biren (Goeze)

Local. SW,WC,N · · · · · · · · · · · · · · · 2162(9989)

Field characters & Similar species FW 15-18mm. Narrow, rather pointed, marbled, ash-grey forewing with large, rounded, whitish kidney-mark is diagnostic. Ground-colour varies from pale to dark grey, but the heavy pattern varies only in minor detail. Some examples are marked with yellowish white, especially along outermost cross-line. Despite its name, this species does not possess the characteristic scissor-like marks of Shears, which can also be ash grey. Instead, there is a dark-edged, pale tooth-like mark in centre of forewing.

Flight season One generation. May-June, to mid July or later in the north and at high altitudes. Comes to light and flowers. Can be found at rest on trees and rocks during the day, and sometimes active by day.

Life cycle Overwinters as a pupa underground. Larva June-August. Feeds largely at night.

Larval foodplants Many herbaceous and woody

species, including Bog-myrtle, Meadowsweet, Creeping Willow, Bilberry and Heather.

Habitat Moorland.

Status & distribution Resident and suspected immigrant. Local. South-west England, Wales, the north Midlands, northern England and Scotland, including the Inner Hebrides and Orkney, Man and Ireland. In the Channel Islands recorded only from Alderney, three in 1970, two in 1994. Two fresh, almost black individuals, unlike British forms, were recorded in Orkney in June 1980 with immigrant Silver Y, after the local moths had finished flying, and were presumed immigrants.

2163 see below 2155

Broad-barred White · · · · · · · · · · · page 317

Hecatera bicolorata (Hufn.)

Common. T · · · · · · · · · · · · · · · · · 2164(9928*)

Field characters FW 13-15mm. Broad dark grey or blackish central band on white or greyish-white forewing, which has a straight leading edge, usually makes this an unmistakable species. Occasionally, ground-colour is grey.

Similar species Grey examples superficially resemble Small Ranunculus, which is similar in shape but has greenish-tinged forewing, marked with orange.

Flight season Usually one protracted generation, late May-July. Occasionally a small second generation in southern England, in August. Comes to light, sometimes in numbers, and feeds at flowers, including campions, Red Valerian and Viper's-bugloss, on which it is often found resting by day.

Life cycle Overwinters as a pupa just below the ground. Larva July-late September. Feeds by night and day, often resting exposed on leaves and flowers in dry weather.

Larval foodplants The flowers and flower buds of hawkweeds and hawk's-beards, sow-thistles and other closely-related plants.

Habitat Vegetated coastal dunes, shingle and disturbed rough grassland, particularly on limestone and chalk downland. Sometimes breeds in gardens.

Status & distribution Resident. Common. Widespread and fairly well distributed in southern Britain, becoming less so from the Midlands northwards. Local in mainland Scotland north to Inverness-shire, and on Man. Widespread and frequent in the Channel Islands.

Small Ranunculus · · · · · · · · · · · · page 317

Hecatera dysodea ([D. & S.])

pRDBK; suspected immigrant. SE,S Wales
· 2165(9927*)

Field characters & Similar species FW 14-15mm. Fine mottling of black and orange-gold scales on forewing is distinctive. Feathered Ranunculus and Large Ranunculus share the same type of forewing mottling but are easily distinguished on size. Hindwing of Feathered Ranunculus is largely white;

that of Small Ranunculus has a broad brown border. See also Broad-barred White.

Flight season One generation. June-early August. Comes to light and visits flowers.

Life cycle Overwinters as a pupa underground. Larva July-August, easily found on the foodplant by day.

Larval foodplants Prickly Lettuce; also Great Lettuce. In the 19th century recorded in large numbers on cultivated lettuces. Eats mainly the flowers and seeds.

Habitat Roadside verges, old chalk pits, gardens, allotments, rough open ground; also found on old industrial sites.

Status & distribution Resident, recent colonist and suspected immigrant. Red Data Book – Insufficiently Known/Nationally Scarce. Formerly widespread and locally frequent, mainly in East Anglia and south-east England, but with scattered records along the south coast of England, around the Severn and into south Wales. Had virtually disappeared by 1914, and apart from a half a dozen or so records up to 1939 was not seen again until 1997, when singletons were recorded in a light-trap in a garden in Gravesend, Kent, on 28 June and 6 August, followed by adults and larvae more widely in Kent in 1998. Present distribution imperfectly known and possibly changing rapidly. Larvae have now been found in north-west Kent, at several places in Essex from 1999 onwards, and in 2001 at Newport, Monmouthshire, and in Middlesex and Surrey. An adult was light-trapped at Landguard Bird Observatory, Suffolk, in June 1999 and another in 2000, suggesting possible immigration.

Campion
page 317

Hadena rivularis (Fabr.)

Common. T
2166(9955)

Field characters & Similar species FW 14-16mm. A diagnostic feature of this species when freshly emerged is purplish-pink marbling on forewing, especially strong along cross-line beyond kidney-mark, leading edge and central area. However, this colour fades with age, leaving forewing dark greyish brown, like that of Lychnis, which has similar markings. Campion is slightly slimmer-bodied, with broader forewing, with kidney-mark and oval usually joined, or kidney at least extended from its base towards oval. On Lychnis, these marks are nearly always separate and kidney not usually distorted. On Campion, pale outermost cross-line is zigzagged throughout and turns to finish usually at trailing corner. On Lychnis, it is zigzagged only near leading edge and in the middle, and then curves more smoothly to finish on trailing edge, usually angled towards base of wing.

Flight season Two generations in southern England, late May-June and August-September. Further north, one generation, late May-June. Comes to light, usually in rather small numbers, and feeds at flowers.

Life cycle Overwinters as a pupa, in a fragile cocoon just beneath the soil surface. Larva June-July and

August-September where two generations, July-September where one. Lives inside the seed capsules until too large, then feeds only at night, hiding near the ground by day.

Larval foodplants The ripening seeds of White, Red and Sea Campion and Ragged-Robin.

Habitat A wide range of open, grassy places, including verges, damp meadows, moorland and sea-cliffs; also in woodland rides in calcareous locations.

Status & distribution Resident. Common. Throughout most of Britain, Man and Ireland, including Orkney but not Shetland. Local in the Channel Islands.

Tawny Shears
page 317

Hadena perplexa perplexa ([D. & S.])

Common. S,C
2167(9957)

Pod Lover
page 317

ssp. *capsophila* (Dup.)

Local (Protected on Man). SW,WC,NW

Field characters FW 13-15mm.

Tawny Shears is extremely variable, but characterised by rather broad, pointed forewing with a straight leading edge, quite sharply defined markings and often a variegated appearance. Constant features are several arrowhead marks before outermost cross-line, and a dark-outlined tooth-like or bullet-shaped mark in central area. Ground-colour whitish or pale straw, tawny or dull brown. Pale examples are often rather plain, and some have the markings rather obscure, but most have conspicuous markings, particularly kidney-mark. Hindwing brownish white, sandy, brownish or grey, often with a darker outer band. Whitish forms occur in south-east England. Elsewhere, sandy or tawny brown forms predominate, except in extreme west of mainland Britain, where usual form is dull brown.

Pod Lover is same size and shape, but dull brownish grey or even blackish, extensively marked and dusted with greyish white or straw white. Occasionally somewhat paler tawny brown.

Similar species Pod Lover superficially resembles Lychnis, which is larger with broader, less pointed forewing. Barrett's Marbled Coronet is also larger and broader and more obscurely marked. Pale examples of Tawny Shears are superficially similar to Sand Dart, which is likely to occur in some of the same southern coastal localities. However, Sand Dart has longer, narrower forewing and silky white hindwing, sometimes darkened along veins but without a dark border. See also Stranger.

Flight season One generation, May-July, apart from southern England, where there is a small second generation, in August. Comes to light and to flowers, particularly of Red Valerian, campions and Wood Sage.

Life cycle Overwinters as a pupa, in an underground cocoon. Larva late June-August, and again in the

Larva of Pod Lover.

autumn in the south.

Larval foodplants The ripening seeds of Bladder Campion, White Campion, Nottingham Catchfly, Sea Campion and Rock Sea-spurrey.

Habitat Dry open ground on calcareous soils inland, including field margins and gardens. Many coastal habitats, but Pod Lover is found mainly on rocky coastlines.

Status & distribution Resident. Common. Tawny Shears is well distributed throughout England and Wales, and just reaches southern Scotland. Pod Lover is western and coastal; it has been reported from Cornwall, widely around the Welsh coast, Lancashire, south-west Scotland, Man and northern and southern Ireland. Both subspecies are widespread and frequent in the Channel Islands.

Viper's Bugloss   page 317

Hadena irregularis (Hufn.)

Former resident; presumed extinct. E 2168(9964)

Field characters & Similar species FW 14-15mm. Forewing intricately marked with warm shades of sandy brown. Distinguished from Tawny Shears by absence of a conspicuous central bullet or tooth-mark. Dusky Sallow is superficially similar, but with a distinct, pinched or broken, dark central cross-band.

Flight season One generation. Late May-July. Flies from dusk, comes to light and visits flowers, including those of the larval foodplant.

Life cycle Overwinters as a pupa, in a cocoon just below the ground. Larva July-early August. Feeds on the developing seed capsules of the foodplant, the larger larvae leaving the plant to hide near the ground by day.

Larval foodplants The sole larval foodplant is Spanish Catchfly. The larva does not feed on Viper's-bugloss, as the vernacular name might imply, and the only connection with this plant is that the adult may visit the flowers for nectar.

Habitat Foodplant occurs as a native only in areas of Breckland where the soil is chalky or calcareous sand. Colonies of the moth were found on roadside verges, open grassland, derelict and fallow fields, paths and wood edges. The plant thrives best following small-scale ground disturbance, such as by moles or rabbits.

Status & distribution Former resident, now presumed extinct. In the British Isles only ever recorded reliably from the Breckland, including colonies in Norfolk, Suffolk and Cambridgeshire. Recorded annually as larvae on the foodplant, sometimes in large numbers, until the 1960s. The last substantiated record was of larvae at Icklingham, Norfolk, in 1968, despite extensive subsequent searches of this and other sites.

Barrett's Marbled Coronet   page 317

Hadena luteago ([D. & S.])

ssp. *barrettii* (Doubl.)

Nb. SW   2169(9935)

Field characters FW 15-19mm. There is a pale area on centre of forewing by oval, bordered by a dark line running parallel to trailing edge. Ground-colour of forewing can vary from warm brown with indistinct lines (predominant in south Devon populations) to greyish brown with white lines and clouding (north Cornish coast). Individuals from Ireland, Guernsey and the French coast all differ in appearance and have been named f. *turbata* Don. (greyish), f. *lowei* Tutt (yellowish) and f. *argillacea* Hb. respectively. A recent review showed that while the Guernsey and French forms are *H. luteago*, the British populations are a different species and should be referred to as *H. andalusia* (Stdgr.) ssp. *barrettii* (Doubl.).

Similar species The much more widespread Lychnis has finer, crisper markings. Pod Lover is smaller, with paler hindwing.

Flight season One generation. Early June-July, sometimes August. Recorded visiting campion flowers from dusk. Comes readily to light on the breeding grounds.

Life cycle Overwinters as a pupa. Larva July-September. The larvae bore first into the leaves and leaf-axils, then move into the stems and bore down to the roots, where the cocoon is formed.

Larval foodplants Sea Campion, Rock Sea-spurrey and Sand Spurrey.

Habitat Mainly coastal cliffs and some shingle beaches, but has been found as larva 3km inland and in woodland.

Status & distribution Resident. Nationally Scarce B. In mainland Britain confined to the north and south coasts of Devon and Cornwall and the coast of Carmarthenshire and Pembrokeshire. Two worn specimens were taken in Cardiganshire in 1983, the first county records. One of these was inland at Cors Caron NNR, an apparent wanderer, the other in typical coastal habitat at Aberporth, so it is possible that the moth is locally established on the Cardiganshire coast. There are 19th-century records for Caernarvonshire, Anglesey and Man, and a single fresh individual was recorded at light on the Isle of Wight on 3 June 1952. In Ireland occurs on the south coast. Locally frequent in the Channel Islands.

Varied Coronet
page 317

Hadena compta ([D. & S.])

Common. SE,S,EC
2170(9939)

Field characters & Similar species FW 13-15mm. Bold blackish-grey and white forewing colour is very like that of southern examples of Marbled Coronet, which are slightly larger. However, on Varied Coronet white band is complete and meets trailing edge about halfway along, and is therefore not diagonal as in Marbled Coronet. Little variation, but some more heavily marked and dusted with white, especially along outer edge.

Flight season Usually one generation. June-July. Sometimes also September, as a partial second generation or as immigrants. Comes to light and feeds at flowers. Female often active and laying eggs on the foodplant before dark.

Life cycle Overwinters as a pupa, in an underground cocoon. Larva July-early September. At first lives inside seed capsules of foodplant, then when large feeds only at night, hiding near the ground by day.

Larval foodplants Usually the ripening seed-pods of Sweet-William, but also recorded on Bladder Campion.

Habitat Gardens and calcareous grassland, wandering into other habitats, including woodland.

Status & distribution Resident and suspected immigrant. Recent colonist or introduction. Common. Recorded, possibly as an immigrant, in the late 19th century, but first recorded breeding in Dover in 1948. Since then it has spread rapidly across southern England, East Anglia and the Midlands, northwards to Yorkshire and westwards to Gloucestershire.

Marbled Coronet
page 317

Hadena confusa (Hufn.)

Local. T
2171(9940)

Field characters FW 14-16mm. Examples from southern, central and eastern England have a roughly square greyish-white blotch at tip of forewing and further white blotches in central area and along trailing edge near trailing corner, and are unmistakable. Sometimes central blotches almost merge to form a diagonal band. Further north and west, particularly in south-west England, Wales, Scotland and Ireland, white is often replaced by dull yellow, and blackish ground-colour is strongly tinted dark olive green. In Orkney and Shetland, the pale markings are often reduced or even absent (f. *obliterae* Robson).

Similar species See Varied Coronet.

Flight season In most areas one generation, late May-early July. In south-east England, a small second generation in August. Comes to light and feeds at flowers.

Life cycle Overwinters, sometimes twice, as a pupa in an underground cocoon. Larva July-August. At first lives inside seed capsules of foodplant, then when large feeds only at night, hiding near the ground by day.

Larval foodplants The ripening seed-pods of Sea and Bladder Campion, Rock Sea-spurrey and other related species, including cultivated varieties.

Habitat Open ground on calcareous soils, especially on the coast. Sometimes in gardens.

Status & distribution Resident. Local. Widespread and quite well distributed in England, both inland and on the coast, also in Scilly and on Man. Coastal in Wales. Widespread in Scotland, especially in the far north, including the Hebrides, Orkney and Shetland. Mainly coastal in Ireland. Widespread and frequent in the Channel Islands.

269

White Spot
page 317

Hadena albimacula (Borkh.)

RDB. S
2172(9944)

Field characters FW 15-17mm. Straight-edged, central white blotch on forewing, in combination with large areas of uniform warm brown colour on forewing and thorax, and other small white-edged black forewing markings, are diagnostic.

Similar species Forewing of the more widespread southern form of Marbled Coronet and of Varied Coronet are blackish grey rather than brown, and have a much more variegated appearance, with larger and more numerous white markings and a greater range of dark tones. Marbled Coronet has a prominent white blotch at wing tip.

Flight season Main generation May-mid July (peak in late May), with smaller but regular numbers of a partial second generation or delayed emergence August-mid September. Can be found by day on posts and walls of wooden buildings. Flies from dusk and visits flowers, including those of the larval food-plant and related species, Viper's-bugloss, Wood Sage and Red Valerian. Comes regularly to light.

Life cycle Overwinters as a pupa just below ground. Larva July-August. Rests on seedheads of foodplant by day when young and at the base of the plant among shingle and debris when larger, feeding mainly at night.

Larval foodplants Seed capsules and seeds of Nottingham Catchfly. As these are usually well over by late September-October, the fate of larvae resulting from late adults is uncertain. Has been reared on the flowers and seedheads of other related species, including Sea Campion, Bladder Campion, Red Campion and White Campion, and on cultivated Sweet-William and carnations.

Habitat Apparently confined to the few places on the south coast of England where Nottingham Catchfly grows. At Dungeness, Kent, this is extensive open coastal shingle; elsewhere chalk or limestone coastline with cliffs. The plant favours dry, well-drained situations such as slopes, cliff ledges and shingle beds.

Status & distribution Resident. Red Data Book species. Surveys from 1998-2001 indicate the moth is breeding on at least six sites on the south coast of England: in Dorset (White Noathe, Ballard Down/Studland Cliffs and possibly elsewhere); in Hampshire (Browndown, near Gosport); and in Kent (Dungeness, Hythe Ranges and the recently created Samphire Hoe). Continued breeding at a site near Beer, in Devon, is probable but needs confirmation. Most of these sites have a long history (Kent since 1816; Hampshire since 1865; Devon since1889). A worn female came to a light-trap in Croydon, Surrey, on 3 June 1983 and a few singletons have been noted inland in Devon, Dorset and Sussex. There are a few old records from further north in England which may be erroneous. Not reliably recorded elsewhere in the British Isles. Very local on Jersey.

Lychnis
page 317

Hadena bicruris (Hufn.)

Common. T
2173(9933)

Field characters FW 14-17mm. Forewing quite broad, dark greyish brown with fine, quite crisp, straw-white markings and a dark, solid, square or tooth-like central mark.
Similar species See Campion, Barrett's Marbled Coronet and Pod Lover.
Flight season Two generations in southern England, late May-July and August-September. One generation from the Midlands northwards, June-July. Comes to light regularly and feeds at flowers.
Life cycle Overwinters as a pupa in an underground cocoon. Larva late June-early August and September in the south, July-August in the north. Lives inside the seed capsules of the foodplant, sometimes until quite large, then feeds only at night and hides near the ground by day.
Larval foodplants The ripening seeds of campions, especially White and Red, and Sweet-William.
Habitat A wide range, including gardens, roadside verges, field margins, hedgerows, woodland, and various coastal habitats including sand-dunes.
Status & distribution Resident. Common. Throughout Great Britain, Man and Ireland. Widespread and frequent in the Channel Islands.

Grey
page 317

Hadena caesia ([D. & S.])

ssp. *mananii* (Gregs.)

RDB (Protected on Man). NW
2174(9947)

Field characters FW 15-17mm. Oval and kidney-mark poorly defined and hard to see in comparison with related species. Individuals from Man and most of Ireland are greyish brown and indistinctly marked, those from the Burren, Co. Clare, are bluish.
Similar species Dark forms of the Pod Lover/Tawny Shears are more distinctly marked. Northern Rustic is larger, with white fringe on hindwing.
Flight season One extended generation or partial second generation. Late May-August. Flies rapidly from dusk. Fairly frequent at light.
Life cycle Overwinters as a pupa, in a cocoon

among rocks. Larva June-August, sometimes September. At first feeds in the seed-pods, then on the leaves, hiding under more isolated plants by day.
Larval foodplants Sea Campion.
Habitat Rocky coasts and shingle, breeding mainly on plants within 50m of the strandline.
Status & distribution Resident. Red Data Book species. Recorded from western Ayrshire, western Argyllshire and the west coasts of Arran, Islay, Mull, Rum and Skye. Probably more widespread in this area. Also around the coasts of Man and the south and west of Ireland. Four specimens labelled 'Cumberland 1899' have been reported.

Silurian
page 317

Eriopygodes imbecilla (Fabr.)

RDB. SW
2175(10070)

Field characters FW 10-13mm. A small, rather plain macro-moth with rather rounded forewing (although narrower and more pointed in female). Distinctive features in male are two gently waving lines across forewing, and a distinctive but often faint kidney-mark, but no trace of an oval. Ground-colour of male varies from reddish through sandy brown to fawn. Female smaller and darker reddish brown; the markings can be less distinct than the male's, although sometimes the kidney-mark is highlighted with yellowish.
Similar species None.
Flight season One generation. Late June-July. Male comes to light, sometimes in large numbers, but predominantly between 2am and 4am. Female is rare at light but has occasionally been reported on the wing on sunny afternoons.
Life cycle Not known in the wild. Probably overwinters as a larva because almost fully grown individuals have been found in the spring in Sweden. Eggs laid by wild-caught females hatch within a couple of weeks, showing no signs of dormancy. Larvae kept in captivity, even at close to outdoor temperatures, have consistently produced adults from September to December, depending on temperature.
Larval foodplants Not confirmed. Heath Bedstraw is the most likely of the plants present at the breeding locality. In Sweden, larvae have been found by night on Northern Bedstraw. They accept Cleavers in captivity and can be reared successfully on Dandelion, feeding at night and hiding by day.
Habitat Gullies and hollows in high moorland (400-500m) dominated by Bilberry.
Status & distribution Resident. Red Data Book species. Currently known from a single locality some 4km north to south, in the hills of north-west Monmouthshire, where the species was first discovered when one came to light on 30 July 1972. On 6 July 1999 a single male came to a light-trap in a suburban garden in Abergavenny, about 10km from the known breeding grounds. Another was light-trapped just over the English border in the Black Mountains of Herefordshire, some 20km away, on 12 July 1999, the only record from England.

Antler Moth

page 317

Cerapteryx graminis (L.)

Common. T   2176(10062)

Field characters FW 12-17mm. Elongated, branched, creamy white antler-like mark in centre of forewing is diagnostic. This mark may be reduced or enlarged, but varies relatively little in general shape. However, there is considerable variation in extent and intensity of black streaks, which may be virtually absent. Ground-colour light to dark olive brown or reddish-tinged, with a dull texture. Forewing leading edge straight. Male has slightly feathered antennae; female is larger, with simple antennae.

Similar species None.

Flight season One generation. Mid July-mid September. Comes to light and sugar, sometimes in large numbers, and feeds at flowers. Also flies during the day, especially in the north.

Life cycle Overwinters as an egg, scattered over grassland in flight. Larva March-June. Feeds mainly at night and hides in the sward by day.

Larval foodplants Hard-bladed grasses, including Sheep's-fescue, Mat-grass and Purple Moor-grass; also reported on sedges and rushes.

Habitat Grassland, mainly in open country, particularly acid upland pasture, moorland and downland.

Status & distribution Resident. Common. Throughout Great Britain north to Shetland, also Man and Ireland. Often abundant in northern, upland areas, the larvae occasionally stripping hillsides of grass. Rare in the Channel Islands, where singletons were recorded on Jersey in 1917, and on Guernsey in 2001.

Hedge Rustic

page 317

Tholera cespitis ([D. & S.])

Common. T   2177(10064)

Field characters FW 15-19mm. Forewing of this rather thickset species is quite broad and rather uniformly blackish brown, with straight leading edge. Only conspicuous markings are oval and kidney-mark outlined in golden yellow, and pale cross-lines. Whole wing is finely dusted with golden yellow. Variation is slight. Kidney-mark sometimes extends to a point in direction of oval. Male has slightly feathered antennae. Hindwing usually whitish in male and grey in female, paler toward the base.

Similar species None.

Flight season One generation. August-September. Comes to light, and feeds at sugar and sugared flowerheads.

Life cycle Overwinters as an egg, laid loose in the sward. Larva March-July. Feeds at night, at first on the leaves and when larger at ground level on the stems.

Larval foodplants Hard-bladed grasses, including Mat-grass and Wavy Hair-grass.

Habitat A range of open grasslands and rough grassy places, including suburban gardens.

Status & distribution Resident. Common in England, Wales, Man and Ireland. More local in southern, eastern and western Scotland, including the Hebrides. Locally frequent on Jersey but rare on Guernsey.

Feathered Gothic

page 317

Tholera decimalis (Poda)

Common. T   2178(10065)

Field characters FW 16-22mm. Fine straw-white streaks along veins of forewing and the series of black arrowhead marks on inner edge of outermost cross-line distinguish this from most other species. Male is thickset, with broad forewing and leading edge straight. Forewing very broad in female, with leading edge straight or slightly curved. Male has strongly feathered antennae.

Similar species Bordered Gothic has several pale cross-lines, male lacks feathered antennae and flies much earlier in year, in June and July. See also Gothic.

Flight season One generation. Late August-September. Comes regularly to light.

Life cycle Overwinters as an egg, scattered over grassland in flight. Larva March-July. Feeds at night, at first on the leaves, and when larger at ground level on the stems.

Larval foodplants Hard-bladed grasses, including Mat-grass and Sheep's-fescue.

Habitat Rough grassland, including downland, woodland rides and edges, parkland and some gardens.

Status & distribution Resident. Common. Well distributed throughout southern Britain, more local in Scotland, including the Hebrides, and on Man. Widespread in Ireland. Local and occasional in the Channel Islands.

Pine Beauty

page 317

Panolis flammea ([D. & S.])

Common. T   2179(10052)

Field characters FW 15-16mm. Unmistakable. Large, whitish kidney-mark, drawn out close to leading edge towards wing tip, is the most noticeable diagnostic feature. Forewing rather narrow and pointed, variable in colour. Some examples are orange-brown, reddish brown or brick red, often yellowish along outer edge and sometimes dusted whitish. Others (f. *grisea* Tutt) are variegated with greenish grey, or are intermediate (f. *grisoevariegata* Goeze). Rests with wings folded tightly against body. When sitting head down on the tip of a shoot, the moth closely resembles a pine bud, suggesting that this is the favoured natural roosting place.

Similar species None.

Flight season One generation. March-May. Comes to light, but in very small numbers even when population size is large. Feeds at sallow catkins.

Life cycle Overwinters as a pupa, in a flimsy cocoon in leaf litter or in a crevice in a tree trunk. Larva May-July.

Larval foodplants The needles of pine trees, including Scots Pine, Corsican Pine and Lodgepole

271

Pine, especially on the new shoots. Also recorded from larches.

Habitat Occurs in pine forests and plantations; also in parks and gardens. Became very abundant in northern Scotland in the 1970s when pines were planted extensively; it caused serious damage and is still a major pest in this region.

Status & distribution Resident. Common. Throughout mainland Britain, also Scilly, Man and the Inner Hebrides. Widespread but local in Ireland and the Channel Islands.

2179a, 2180 see Appendix

Silver Cloud   page 318

Egira conspicillaris (L.)

Na. SW   2181(10054)

Field characters & Similar species FW 16-18mm. F. *melaleuca* View. is the most frequent in Britain, the black forewing markings distinguishing it from all other British moths. The brown form has similarities with Pale Pinion but has white hindwing, while that of Pale Pinion is dirty brown and the shoulders are pointed. At rest, forewing tip appears rounded and projecting when viewed from the side.

Flight season One generation. Mid April-late May. Comes to light, usually late at night. Occasional at sugar. Recorded feeding at Blackthorn flowers.

Life cycle Overwinters as a pupa, in a fragile cocoon underground. Larva late May-mid July. Young larvae disperse in the wind on silk threads.

Larval foodplants Unconfirmed in the wild. Egg batches have been found on old dock stems in open ground, and pupae under oaks and elms. In captivity accepts docks, Common Nettle, oaks, elms, Blackthorn and many other plants.

Habitat Rough open ground, grassy fields, hedgerows, scrub, open woodland and orchards.

Status & distribution Resident. Possibly also extensive wanderer and immigrant. Nationally Scarce A. Distribution centred on the lower Severn Valley, extending on both sides of the river. Local in Herefordshire, Worcestershire, Warwickshire, Gloucestershire and Somerset. A fresh female was recorded in Monmouthshire at a garden light-trap at Plas Newydd, Usk, on 18 May 1973, and a second individual at the same site on 28 May 1977, with previous records from Monmouth in 1939. One was reported from the Gower, Glamorgan, in the 19th century, and at least one reliably from south Devon in 1962. The moth was resident at a number of sites in Kent in the 19th century and there are old single records for Essex, Middlesex and doubtfully Suffolk and Surrey.

Small Quaker   page 318

Orthosia cruda ([D. & S.])

Common. T   2182(10039)

Field characters FW 12-15mm. Readily distinguished from all other early spring species by small size, usually light colour and plain appearance of

forewing. This also has a rough texture, created by a fine dusting of black scales, sometimes strong enough to be visible to the naked eye. Often, the only noticeable markings are a narrow kidney-mark and a pale line along outer edge. Some examples have fine dark cross-lines. Ground-colour ranges from pale to dark pastel brown, greyish or reddish-tinged, or delicately frosted with off-white, and occasionally dark brownish grey.

Similar species See Blossom Underwing and Common Quaker.

Flight season One generation. Late February-early May. Comes to light, often in numbers, and feeds at sugar and sallow catkins.

Life cycle Overwinters as a pupa in an underground cocoon, often close to a tree trunk, with the adult fully formed inside. Larva April-early June. Feeds at night and hides between spun leaves of foodplant during the day.

Larval foodplants Mainly oaks, also other trees including Downy Birch, Hazel, sallows and Field Maple.

Habitat Broadleaved woodland, wooded areas and wet heathland. Smaller numbers occur in hedgerows and gardens.

Status & distribution Resident. Common. Throughout southern Britain. Local in Scotland including the Inner Hebrides, north to Easter Ross, and on Man. Local but widespread in Ireland. Widespread and occasional in the Channel Islands.

Blossom Underwing   page 318

Orthosia miniosa ([D. & S.])

Local; suspected immigrant. S,WC   2183(10041)

Field characters FW 15-17mm. Hindwing pinkish white, distinguishing this moth from related species flying in the spring. Warm sandy or pinkish-brown colour, grainy texture and softly defined markings of forewing contrasts with sharper markings and harder colours of the other members of the genus. Forewing fringe pinkish. Kidney-mark rather narrow. Cross-lines always evident, darker brown, pale-edged and finely scalloped. The central area between them is usually a deeper shade, which is occasionally sprinkled with whitish scales. Variation is slight, but an uncommon form is more uniformly dark reddish brown.

Similar species Reddish examples of Small Quaker are usually smaller and have more rounded forewing, central area is not darker, cross-lines (when evident) are fine and blackish and hindwing is grey. See also Common Quaker. The rare Orange Upperwing has a passing resemblance and similar habits in the spring, but forewing pointed, with angular cross-lines, more orange and hindwing lacks any pink tint.

Flight season One generation. Early March-late April. Comes to light, sometimes in numbers; feeds at sallow catkins from dusk and occasionally at sugar.

Life cycle Overwinters as a pupa in an underground cocoon, with the adult fully formed inside. Larva late

April-mid June. Lives gregariously in light webs when small.

Larval foodplants Mainly oak leaves, but also known to eat wasp-galls on oak. Part-grown larvae also recorded from other trees and shrubs such as Blackthorn and Hawthorn, and on herbaceous plants.

Habitat Oak woodland and old hedgerows with mature oak trees. Larvae most numerous on oaks in sunny situations and low oak coppice, often on damp ground.

Status & distribution Resident and occasional immigrant. Local. Widespread in southern and south-west England and in Wales. Local in East Anglia, the Midlands and south Cumbria. Rare in Ireland, recorded only from the south-east. In March and April 1999 a large immigration occurred, with at least 90 moths reported on coasts from Glamorgan to Norfolk. Examination of older coastal records strongly suggests that previous influxes have occurred, but on a smaller scale.

Northern Drab   page 318

Orthosia opima (Hb.)

Local. T   2184(10042)

Field characters FW 15-17mm. Stocky, with a very furry thorax. Forewing pointed, with a very straight leading edge. Quite variable in colour, ranging from cold light grey, yellowish grey, warm dark grey or brown, or greyish black. Dark central band in the brown form f. *brunnea* Tutt may be faint, but usually catches the light and can be seen with care. Dark forms are frequent and appear to have no geographical or habitat association, grading into paler grey forms, but the yellowish-grey form is associated with saltmarshes in south-east England.

Similar species Lead-coloured Drab has forewing rounded at tip, with a curved leading edge and usually black dots on outer cross-line near wing tip. Male has feathered antennae. Clouded Drab has less pointed forewing with leading edge curved, and is usually larger. Any dark shading is usually in small patches or covers whole forewing. Both species lack a broad, darker central band and have a less furry thorax.

Flight season One generation. April-May. Comes to light and sugar, and feeds at sallow catkins and Blackthorn flowers.

Life cycle Overwinters as a pupa in an underground cocoon, with the adult fully formed inside. Larva May-July.

Larval foodplants A range of both woody and herbaceous plants, including sallows and birches, ragworts, Mugwort and Common Sea-lavender.

Habitat A range of open, usually damp places, including saltmarshes, freshwater marshes, heathland, downland, golf-course roughs and sand-dunes. Sometimes associated with river valleys and floodplains, especially in the south.

Status & distribution Resident. Local. Widespread but thinly distributed. Southern, central and northern

Larva of Blossom Underwing.

England, East Anglia and Wales. Also in southern and western Scotland, and in Ireland.

Lead-coloured Drab   page 318

Orthosia populeti (Fabr.)

Local. T   2185(10043)

Field characters FW 15-17mm. A predominantly grey moth, characterised by rather round-tipped forewing with quite large, pale-outlined oval and kidney-mark always evident. Male has visibly feathered antennae. Fine, dark, scalloped cross-lines may be present, and outermost line is pale, often with small brown or black marks on its inner edge, especially centrally. Ground-colour varies from pale leaden grey to blackish grey.

Similar species Easily overlooked among its commoner and very variable relatives. Clouded Drab can be leaden grey, but forewing slightly more pointed and lower half of kidney-mark is noticeably darker, except in the darkest examples. It is also usually larger. Antennae of male Clouded Drab are not visibly feathered, although they appear quite thick, and under a hand-lens can be seen to have short projections. Common Quaker can be similar in pattern, but brownish. See also Northern Drab.

Flight season One generation. March-April. Comes to light and feeds at sallow catkins and occasionally sugar.

Life cycle Overwinters as a pupa in an underground cocoon, with the adult fully formed inside. Larva late April-early June. Feeds at night and hides by day

Larva of Northern Drab.

between two leaves spun flatly together.
Larval foodplants At first inside the catkins, later on the leaves of Aspen, Black-poplar and occasionally other poplars.
Habitat Broadleaved woodland and other areas where poplars are numerous, including some parks and gardens.
Status & distribution Resident. Local. Widespread in southern and south-east England, the Midlands, Wales and central Scotland. Local in northern England and in the central Highlands of Scotland. Very local in Ireland.

Powdered Quaker
Orthosia gracilis ([D. & S.])

page 318

Common. T   2186(10048)

Field characters FW 15-19mm. Rather long, comparatively pointed forewing, more delicate pastel ground-colour and powdered or grainy texture due to fine black speckling separate this from other spring moths. Usually, the only distinct markings are quite large oval and kidney-mark, a curved row of fine blackish dots beyond kidney-mark and a fairly straight, pale, dark-edged outermost cross-line. Extremely variable in ground-colour, from sandy white, through sandy grey, bright orange-brown, reddish brown, warm dark grey-brown tinged with pink or mauve, to blackish. There is huge geographical variation. Pale sandy grey forms predominate in much of lowland Britain. Very dark examples with pale markings have occurred in Hampshire and Yorkshire. Salmon pink, reddish-brown and dark grey-brown forms, which are usually associated with Bog-myrtle, are the most frequent in Scotland, Ireland and parts of Wales. In the New Forest and Somerset the moths are mainly reddish brown, with pale whitish hindwing.
Similar species See Clouded Drab.
Flight season One generation. April-May. Comes to light and sugar and feeds at sallow catkins and Blackthorn flowers.
Life cycle Overwinters as a pupa in an underground cocoon, with the adult fully formed inside. Larva May-July. Lives at first in a spun terminal shoot, later hiding low down by day.
Larval foodplants Herbaceous and woody plants, including willows, Black-poplar, Blackthorn, Bog-myrtle, Meadowsweet, Purple-loosestrife and Common Fleabane.
Habitat Most common in marshes, but also occurs in damp woodland, gardens and open country, more especially in the southern half of Britain. The populations associated with Bog-myrtle are restricted to marshes and bogs.
Status & distribution Resident. Common. Throughout England, Wales, Man and Ireland. The Bog-myrtle-feeding populations are widespread but local in Scotland, including the Inner Hebrides and Orkney, in Ireland, parts of Wales, Somerset and the New Forest, Hampshire. Rare in the Channel Islands.

Common Quaker
Orthosia cerasi (Fabr.)

page 318

Common. T   2187(10044)

Field characters FW 13-17mm. Easily recognised by round-tipped forewing, with large, rounded, pale-outlined oval and kidney-mark, and uniformly grey hindwing. Extremely variable in ground-colour and extent of markings, but always some shade of brown: light sandy, warm sandy or orange-brown, light or dark greyish brown, warm brown, or blackish brown. Outer cross-line generally distinct.
Similar species Small Quaker is usually smaller, with a narrow kidney-mark and usually weak outer cross-line. Blossom Underwing has more pointed forewing, narrower kidney-mark and pinkish-white hindwing. See also Vine's Rustic.
Flight season One generation. March-May, with small numbers sometimes emerging in mild spells during the late autumn and winter. Comes to light, often in abundance, and to sugar, and feeds at sallow catkins and Blackthorn flowers.
Life cycle Overwinters as a pupa in an underground cocoon, with the adult fully formed inside. Larva April-June. Lives at first in developing buds, then in spun shoots or leaves, resting under a leaf in the final instar.
Larval foodplants A wide range of broadleaved trees, including oaks, sallows, birches, elms, hawthorns and Hazel.
Habitat Occurs in most lowland habitats, including gardens, but is most numerous in woodland.
Status & distribution Resident. Common. Frequent throughout the whole of southern Britain, the southern half of Scotland, Man and Ireland. Widespread but less frequent in the rest of mainland Scotland and the Inner Hebrides. Widespread and abundant in the Channel Islands.

Clouded Drab
Orthosia incerta (Hufn.)

page 318

Common. T   2188(10037)

Field characters FW 16-20mm. Extremely variable, although most examples are easily recognised. Forewing somewhat variable in shape, but fairly sharp-tipped and often rather rough-textured. Outermost cross-line paler and slightly irregular, almost always with small dark blotches at leading edge, one third of the way along and at trailing corner. These are less obvious on dark examples and exceptionally are missing on the very palest. In much of southern and eastern England ground-colour is most frequently blackish or dark reddish brown, largely with obscure markings. Further north and west, paler forms become more frequent and can be pale brown, greyish, reddish or light grey, to some extent clouded, dusted, or flecked (sometimes heavily) with dark brown or black. However, fairly plain examples do occur, notably in north-east Scotland.
Similar species Powdered Quaker is a softer pastel

274

shade and more plainly marked, outermost cross-line is straighter, without dark blotches, and forewing not clouded. See also Northern Drab, Lead-coloured Drab and Twin-spotted Quaker.

Flight season One generation. Early March-May, sometimes earlier. Comes to light and sugar, and feeds at sallow catkins and Blackthorn flowers.

Life cycle Overwinters as a pupa in an underground cocoon, with the adult fully formed inside. Larva April-June. Lives at first in developing buds, then in spun shoots or leaves, resting under a leaf in the final instar.

Larval foodplants A wide range of broadleaved trees. Perhaps most numerous on oaks and sallows, but frequent on Downy Birch, Silver Birch, Hawthorn, Hazel, elms and limes.

Habitat Most abundant in woodland, but occurs in many habitats with trees and shrubs, including gardens.

Status & distribution Resident. Common. Throughout most of Great Britain, Man and Ireland, and often numerous. One recorded on Orkney on 16 April 1980, but may not be resident. Not recorded from Shetland. Local and occasional in the Channel Islands.

Twin-spotted Quaker page 318
Orthosia munda ([D. & S.])
Common. S,C,(N) 2189(10050)

Field characters FW 17-20mm. Tawny colouring and two black spots on inner edge of faint pale outermost cross-line, one third of the way in from leading edge of rather broad, curved forewing, are diagnostic. However, spots may be brown and faint, or missing altogether (f. *immaculata* Stdgr.). Ground-colour may also be more reddish or greyish brown, often rather grainy. Male antennae visibly feathered. Female antennae with projections visible under a hand-lens.

Similar species Clouded Drab normally has blotches on outermost cross-line, instead of two distinct spots, and antennae are not feathered.

Flight season One generation. March-April, sometimes earlier. Comes to light and sugar, and feeds at sallow catkins.

Life cycle Overwinters as a pupa in an underground cocoon, with the adult fully formed inside. Larva April-June. Feeds at night and, when small, rests among leaves by day, hiding in bark crevices when larger.

Larval foodplants A wide range of trees and woody plants, including oaks, sallows, Aspen, Field Maple, Ash, Honeysuckle and Hop.

Habitat Broadleaved woodland.

Status & distribution Resident. Common. Well distributed in the southern half of England and in Wales. More local from the Midlands northwards, in southern and western Scotland, including the Inner Hebrides, and on Man. Widespread but somewhat local in Ireland. Local and occasional in the Channel Islands.

Larva of Hebrew Character.

Hebrew Character page 318
Orthosia gothica (L.)
Common. T 2190(10038)

Field characters FW 15-17mm. Named after the black mark in centre of forewing, which is unique among spring-flying moths. This mark is variable, but in most cases is roughly saddle-shaped. It may also be cut in two by the oval, and more rarely a solid rectangle, reduced or bent and distorted. In most examples forewing is greyish or reddish brown, but varies from pale sandy to blackish, and can be tinged with pink or purplish brown. In the reddish f. *gothicina* H.-S., the saddle-mark is a similar colour to the surrounding area and is very indistinct. This form occurs as a small percentage of the population on moorland in parts of the Scottish Highlands and elsewhere in northern Britain. Similar forms with more variable ground-colour can occur as far south as Hampshire, and in Ireland and are known as f. *obsoleta* Tutt.

Similar species None. Even on f. *gothicina* and *obsoleta* forms saddle-mark is discernible, due to pale edging of oval and kidney-mark.

Flight season One generation. March-early May in southern Britain, April-early June in the north and in Ireland. Small numbers sometimes emerge in mild spells during the late autumn or winter. Comes to light and sugar, often flying very late in the night, even in cold conditions, and feeds at sallow catkins.

Life cycle Overwinters as a pupa in an underground cocoon, with the adult fully formed inside. Larva April-July. Feeds mainly at night, at first on buds and then on leaves.

Larval foodplants A wide range of trees, bushes and herbaceous plants, including oaks, birches, hawthorns, sallows, limes, Bilberry, Meadowsweet and Common Nettle.

Habitat Ubiquitous, from moorland to the smallest of urban gardens and yards.

Status & distribution Resident. Common. Throughout Great Britain to Shetland; also Man and Ireland. Widespread and abundant in the Channel Islands.

Double Line page 319
Mythimna turca (L.)
Nb. SW,(SE)   2191(9999)

Field characters FW 18-23mm. A large, rich sandy-coloured moth with two conspicuous dark lines across forewing and a white-tinted slit-like mark between them.
Similar species Clay lacks broad dark cross-lines. The dark f. *bilinea* Haw. of Treble Lines is smaller and lacks central slit-mark on forewing.
Flight season One generation. Mid June-mid July in south-east England but as late as mid August in west Wales. Comes readily to light from dusk onwards, often in numbers. Attracted to sugar.
Life cycle Overwinters as a small larva, low down among grasses. Larva August-May. Feeds by night and pupates in a cocoon just below ground.
Larval foodplants & Habitat In Surrey, Common Bent and Creeping Soft-grass below a lightly-shaded open canopy of Pedunculate Oak in parkland. In south-west England and south Wales, associated with wet, rough, acid grassland along valley bottoms, streamsides, commons and flushed hill-sides, where light cattle- or horse-grazing maintains a herb-rich turf. This habitat is known as Culm grass-land in England and Rhos pasture in Wales, and frequently adjoins thick hedgerows or mature wood-land, with the moth favouring the wood edge or the shelter of gorse, willow scrub or Bracken when avail-able. The larva has been found in this situation, after midnight, feeding on Common Bent among tussocks 10cm tall. Wood Meadow-grass, Cock's-foot, Hairy Wood-rush and Field Wood-rush are also reported foodplants, but the wood-rushes require confirma-tion. In Cardiganshire, breeds on the grassy floor of mature woodland.
Status & distribution Resident and possible immi-grant. Nationally Scarce B. Predominantly south-western, with scattered populations in Somerset, Devon and Cornwall (but not Scilly), and more densely distributed in south Wales westwards to the Gower Peninsula. Also locally numerous in Brecon and Cardiganshire. There is an outlying population in Richmond Park and Wimbledon Common, Surrey, where the moth has been known since the 19th century. Formerly resident in Essex until about 1907, in West Sussex until about the 1950s and in Hampshire where it was last seen in 1978. One was recorded at Eaton Wood, Oxfordshire, on 17 July 1983. Another was reported from Aldringham, near Thorpeness, on the East Suffolk coast, on 3 July 1992, a presumed immigrant.

Brown-line Bright-eye page 319
Mythimna conigera ([D. & S.])
Common. T   2192(10000)

Field characters FW 15-17mm. English name is derived from conspicuous, roughly tear-shaped white mark at base of small kidney-mark, and brown cross-lines and veins towards outer edge. Cross-line before

oval is V-shaped, and this combination is diagnostic. Markings hardly vary and ground-colour is either tawny or rusty brown.
Similar species None.
Flight season One generation. Late June-August. Comes to light and sugar, and feeds at flowers.
Life cycle Overwinters as a small larva, low down in the vegetation. Larva August-May, feeding at night. Pupates in an underground cocoon.
Larval foodplants Grasses, including Cock's-foot and Common Couch.
Habitat A wide range of grasslands, including woodland rides and edges, and rough grassland and gardens in urban areas.
Status & distribution Resident. Common. Throughout most of Great Britain. Local on Man. Widespread in Ireland. A few records from Orkney, where possibly resident, but not Shetland. One was recorded on Jersey in 1964.

Clay page 319
Mythimna ferrago (Fabr.)
Common. T   2193(10001)

Field characters FW 15-18mm. Thickset, with broad, rather plain forewing with a soft pastel texture. Small (sometimes very small) whitish tear-shaped or elliptical mark at base of kidney-mark. Forewing colour ranges from pinkish brown to dull sandy, light olive brown, or straw-coloured. Variation in markings is not great. Male has a broad black band on underside of abdomen, at the base.
Similar species White-point is similarly marked, with a comparable colour range, and male also has a black band on underside of abdomen. However, it is usually smaller with narrower forewing, and mark at base of kidney-mark is pure white, more conspicuous and round.
Flight season One generation. Late June-early August. Comes to light and sugar, and feeds at flowers.
Life cycle Overwinters as a small larva, low down in vegetation. Larva August-May, feeding at night. Pupation occurs in an underground cocoon.
Larval foodplants Grasses, especially Cock's-foot and meadow-grasses.
Habitat A wide range of open habitats, including gardens and wetlands; often numerous in open woodland.
Status & distribution Resident. Common. Throughout most of Britain, Man and Ireland, reaching north to Caithness, but not Orkney or Shetland. Widespread and abundant in the Channel Islands.

White-point page 319
Mythimna albipuncta ([D. & S.])
Immigrant; recent colonist.   2194(10002)

Field characters FW 14-17mm. Orange-brown forewing with prominent white spot. Hindwing smoky grey.
Similar species See Clay.

Flight season Mainly one resident generation. Immigrants arrive as two or more overlapping generations. Recorded May-November, but most frequent July-September. Comes to light and sugar; may be found on grass-heads after dark.
Life cycle Overwinters as a larva but rarely found in the wild, so the natural life cycle is not fully understood.
Larval foodplants Various grasses, including Common Couch and Cock's-foot.
Habitat Primarily coastal, often occurring on shingle beaches.
Status & distribution A regular immigrant, now thought to be established along parts of the south and south-east coasts of England. If widely confirmed it will merit Nationally Scarce B or Local status. Mostly recorded in south-east England but reported as far west as Scilly, occasionally being recorded inland in southern counties. Recorded on the east coast as far north as Yorkshire. Also recorded from Wales and southern Ireland but not Man. Widespread and frequent in the Channel Islands.

Delicate   page 319
Mythimna vitellina (Hb.)
Immigrant; resident Channel Islands.
                                2195(10003)

Field characters FW 12-14mm. Forewing quite pointed and rather angular. Three wavy cross-lines are often apparent, although these vary in prominence. Forewing coloration varies from pale buff to orange, cross-lines being least obvious on paler individuals. A kidney-mark and oval are also often visible, being slightly darker than rest of forewing, but again these are less prominent in some paler individuals. Very pale individuals are immigrants from hot, dry places; those which developed in the cooler climate of the British Isles and northern Europe are darker and orange.
Similar species The three wavy cross-lines distinguish this species from the wainscots.
Flight season Immigrants arrive as two or more overlapping generations. One or two generations in the Channel Islands, April-November (occasionally December), peaking August-October. Comes to light and sugar; may also be seen visiting Ivy flowers at or after dusk.
Life cycle Immigrants earlier in the season result in autumn progeny in some years. It is not known whether the species is able to overwinter, although this may happen occasionally in the extreme south-west of England.
Larval foodplants Various grasses, including Cock's-foot and Annual Meadow-grass.
Habitat Mainly grassy coastal areas for breeding, but occasional immigrant individuals have been captured far inland.
Status & distribution Regular immigrant, recorded annually in varying numbers. Abundant in some years, e.g. 1992 when over 7,000 were estimated, and there was much local breeding during the

summer. Most frequent in the south-west but also occurs regularly in other southern coastal areas of England and Wales, and occasionally inland. Much scarcer on the east coast. Also recorded from north-west England, Dumfries-shire, Man and southern Ireland. Widespread and frequent as resident and immigrant in the Channel Islands. Widely distributed in southern Europe and North Africa.

Striped Wainscot   page 319
Mythimna pudorina ([D. & S.])
Local. S,C   2196(10004)

Field characters FW 16-19mm. Unlike any other wainscot found in the British Isles. Forewing broad and rather rounded, softly marked, pale straw-coloured, streaked with pastel pink or pale brown and dusted with black, with no sign of cross-lines. The darker streaks, emphasised by scattered black scales, are most prominent along outer edge, through centre of wing and towards trailing edge. The fringes are pink. Slight variation in extent of streaking and pink tinge is sometimes absent. Hindwing grey-brown.
Similar species None.
Flight season One generation. June-July. Comes to light and sugar and feeds at flowers, especially of marshland grasses.
Life cycle Overwinters as a very small larva. Larva August-May. Feeds at night, usually close to the ground. Pupation occurs in a cocoon in leaf litter.
Larval foodplants Broadleaved grasses, including Common Reed, Purple Moor-grass and Reed Canary-grass.
Habitat Marshes, fens, boggy heathland and acid grassland.
Status & distribution Resident. Local. Widespread and quite well distributed in parts of southern England and East Anglia, and also occurring in south-west England, Wales, locally in the Midlands, north Lincolnshire, Yorkshire and south-west Ireland.

Southern Wainscot   page 319
Mythimna straminea (Treit.)
Local. S,C   2197(10005)

Field characters FW 14-18mm. Outer edge of forewing very straight compared with related species, and there is a more or less noticeable outward projection at tip. Ground-colour is soft light greyish straw, often tinged with light pinkish brown. A brown streak runs along central vein. Hindwing whitish, darkened along veins and slightly moderately dusted with grey, with a curved row of short blackish central dashes, sometimes faint. Undersides of forewing either clean pale straw or only slightly streaked or dusted with grey, especially near kidney-mark. There is generally a dark central spot on underside of hindwing, normally lacking in Common Wainscot, although this is not completely reliable.
Similar species Worn examples with more heavily dusted hindwing and faint dark dashes, and only a

slight projection at forewing tip can look very like Smoky Wainscot. However, that species is generally darker and less softly marked, and underside of forewing is extensively dusted and streaked with blackish scales. See also Common Wainscot, Mathew's Wainscot, Obscure Wainscot, Cosmopolitan and Reed Dagger.

Flight season One generation. July-August. Comes to light and feeds at sugar painted onto reeds and flowering grasses.

Life cycle Overwinters as a small larva. Larva August-May or early June. Feeds at night and hides in old reed stems or in leaf litter by day.

Larval foodplants Common Reed and Reed Canary-grass.

Habitat Marshes, fens, marshy riverbanks, and along canals and ditches.

Status & distribution Resident. Local. Widespread and fairly well distributed in southern and south-west England and East Anglia. More local in Wales, the Midlands, Cheshire, Yorkshire and Cumbria. Reported from scattered localities in Ireland but not from Man. Widespread and frequent in the Channel Islands.

Smoky Wainscot page 319

Mythimna impura (Hb.)

Common. T   2198(10006)

Field characters FW 14-18mm. Brown or black streak alongside whitish central vein of finely streaked, straw-coloured forewing, and smoky grey hindwing are the most conspicuous features. Forewing somewhat more rounded than similar species. Markings vary in intensity, and hindwing may be only lightly dusted and streaked with grey. Some examples, especially those from northern Britain, are smaller with darker hindwing. Underside of forewing is extensively dusted and streaked with blackish scales, sometimes covering most of wing apart from leading and outer edges.

Similar species See Southern Wainscot and Common Wainscot. Most of the closely-related wainscots have whitish hindwing.

Flight season Usually one generation. Late June-August. Occasionally a small second generation reported in southern England, September-October. Comes to light, often in large numbers, and feeds at sugar and flowers.

Life cycle Overwinters as a small larva, low down in the vegetation. Larva August-May or June, feeding at night. Pupates in an underground cocoon.

Larval foodplants A range of grasses, including Cock's-foot and Common Reed; also Hairy Wood-rush.

Habitat All types of grassland, including woodland rides. Particularly abundant in lowland grassland, including rough ground and urban gardens, and on sand-dunes in the north. Less frequent on moorland.

Status & distribution Resident. Common. Throughout Great Britain, Man and Ireland. Widespread and abundant in the Channel Islands.

Common Wainscot page 319

Mythimna pallens (L.)

Common. T   2199(10007)

Field characters & Similar species FW 14-17mm. Similar in markings and general form to Smoky and Southern Wainscots, but generally a paler, brighter straw-coloured or strongly reddish-brown moth, sometimes heavily streaked with brown. Forewing broadening more rapidly from a narrower base, more pointed with a more angled outer edge, but lacking a projection at tip. Blackish dots toward outer edge often absent. Hindwing usually whitish, sometimes slightly dusted with grey or less commonly extensively grey (usually on female), but rarely with blackish dashes. Examples with darkened forewing and smoky hindwing may also have extensive blackish streaks on underside of forewing. These are more frequent in the second generation (often later than usual flight season of Smoky Wainscot which tends to have more rounded forewing). See also Mathew's Wainscot.

Flight season Two generations in the southern half of England, June-July and August-October. From the Midlands northwards, one generation, July-August. Comes to light, sometimes in very large numbers, and feeds at sugar and flowers, especially grasses.

Life cycle Overwinters as a small larva, deep in the sward. Larva June-August and September-May in the south, August-June in the north.

Larval foodplants Various grasses, including Tufted Hair-grass, Annual Meadow-grass, Common Couch and Cock's-foot.

Habitat A wide range of dry and damp grasslands, including in urban areas, and often frequent in woodland rides.

Status & distribution Resident. Common. Throughout the whole of southern Britain, often in abundance, north to southern Scotland. Local in the rest of Scotland, north to Shetland. Widespread and abundant on Man, in Ireland and in the Channel Islands.

Mathew's Wainscot page 319

Mythimna favicolor (Barr.)

Nb. S,SE   2200(10008)

Field characters FW 16-18mm. A large proportion of individuals have a deep sandy-orange forewing which distinguishes them from all but occasional individuals of Common Wainscot, which is a very similar shape. However, there is also a straw-coloured form. Both forms generally have off-white hindwing with grey streaks, and lack pale veins in forewing.

Similar species Common Wainscots flying in June-July generally have clean white hindwing, and are slightly smaller with narrower forewing. Southern Wainscot differs from straw-coloured form of Mathew's Wainscot in having at least a weak brownish streak running along centre of forewing, while outer edge of wing has a slightly hooked tip but is otherwise very straight and square, rather than gently curved to trailing edge.

Flight season Normally one generation. Mid June-late July. Occasionally reported in September, suggesting a small and partial second generation in some years. Both sexes come frequently to light and sugar and visit the flowers of grasses and rushes, especially when sweet and sticky with the products of ergot fungus.

Life cycle Overwinters as a small larva. Larva August-late May. Feeds at night in mild weather. Pupates underground.

Larval foodplants Common Saltmarsh-grass and probably other grasses on saltmarshes. Has been reared on Cock's-foot and Annual Meadow-grass.

Habitat Coastal and estuarine saltmarshes. Occasionally individuals disperse or are blown inland.

Status & distribution Resident. Nationally Scarce B. First considered a distinct species in 1895 and recognised in the 1996 European checklist, although some authors regard it as a saltmarsh race of the Common Wainscot, in which the genitalia of the male are similar, and with which it has been found pairing and can interbreed. Found on the south and east coasts of England, where it is locally numerous in Dorset, Hampshire, West Sussex and the north-west coast of the Isle of Wight, and in coastal saltmarshes and estuaries from north Kent to Suffolk, with outlying records on the Norfolk coast (e.g. Cley Marshes and Horsey Warren) and on the south Kent coast at Greatstone and Dungeness.

Shore Wainscot   page 319
Mythimna litoralis (Curt.)
Nb. S,C,NE   2201(10021)

Field characters FW 15-18mm. A conspicuous white streak runs along centre of forewing from near thorax almost to outer edge. Hindwing brilliant white.

Similar species None.

Flight season Normally one generation. Late June-late August. Occasional smaller individuals of a partial second emergence in October. Comes readily to light, sometimes in numbers, and to sugar and flowering Marram.

Life cycle Overwinters as a small larva in sand. Larva August-late May. Feeds by night and hides in sand by day. Pupates in sand.

Larval foodplants Marram. Spring larvae have completed growth in captivity on Annual Meadow-grass, Mat-grass and Tufted Hair-grass.

Habitat Coastal sand-dunes and sandy beaches.

Status & distribution Resident. Nationally Scarce B. Recorded widely in suitable habitat all along the south coast of England, including Scilly, and extending up the coasts of England and Wales to Cumbria on the west and Northumberland on the east. In Scotland it appears to be extremely local; since 1980 apparently recorded only from the Kincardineshire coast and Dumfries & Galloway. Local and rare on Man. Recorded from scattered locations all around the coasts of Ireland, where

sometimes frequent. Locally frequent on Jersey, rare on Guernsey.

L-album Wainscot   page 319
Mythimna l-album (L.)
Nb; immigrant. S   2202(10022)

Field characters FW 15-16mm. White L-shape in centre of forewing is diagnostic. Rarely the L-shape is reduced to a dot (f. *o-album* Milman). Brownish-white hindwing with brown veins.

Similar species In Shoulder-striped Wainscot central vein of forewing is white to wing base, and an L-shape is not formed. Devonshire Wainscot has similarly coloured forewing but without the L-shape and with clean white hindwing. See also Obscure Wainscot.

Flight season Two generations. July and mid September-late October, occasionally November. Comes to light, sugar and flowers, including those of Ivy, as well as overripe blackberries.

Life cycle Overwinters as a first instar larva. Larva October-late May, with a second generation in August. Feeds at night. Pupates in a cocoon underground.

Larval foodplants Marram. Tall Fescue also suggested. Feeds on most common grasses in captivity, including Meadow Fescue, Cock's-foot and Annual Meadow-grass

Habitat Rough grassland by the sea, particularly near cliff edges.

Status & distribution Resident and immigrant. Nationally Scarce B. First recorded in Britain in 1901, in south Devon, but regarded as a rare immigrant until breeding was confirmed there in the 1930s. Now recorded annually along the south coast of England from Scilly and Cornwall to Dungeness, Kent. It probably breeds in all these counties but numbers no doubt continue to be supplemented by immigrants from mainland Europe. Stray singletons have been reported from central London, Berkshire, north Hampshire and Essex. Singletons recorded in 2000, 2001 and 2002 at Landguard, Suffolk. Widespread and frequent as a resident and immigrant in the Channel Islands.

White-speck   page 319
Mythimna unipuncta (Haw.)
Immigrant; probable transitory resident. S
                                                    2203(10035)

Field characters FW 18-21mm. Distinctly pointed and tapering forewing has dark apical streak and prominent white central dot, the latter sometimes part of a distinct white vein running to base of wing. Faint orange-outlined oval and kidney-mark. Ground-colour pale to dark sandy brown. Hindwing dark smoky brown.

Similar species The combination of forewing characteristics and dark hindwing distinguishes this species from other wainscots.

Flight season Has been recorded during every month of the year, although winter records are infrequent and generally coincide with southerly winds and milder temperatures. Most numerous August-October. Comes to light and sugar; may also be seen visiting Ivy flowers around dusk or later.

Life cycle Immigrants earlier in the season may result in late summer/autumn progeny in some years. It is possible that the species may occasionally survive the winter in the extreme south-west.

Larval foodplants Grasses, including Common Couch and Cock's-foot.

Habitat Grassy coastal areas.

Status & distribution Regular immigrant and probable transitory resident. Most frequent in southern coastal counties of England and Wales, particularly the south-west, and occasionally recorded inland. Recorded in hundreds in some years. Much scarcer on the east coast. Also recorded from Man, Scotland (including the Hebrides) and both northern and southern Ireland. A local resident and occasional immigrant in the Channel Islands. Probably resident for periods of years in Scilly and locally in south-west England. An American species which has colonised the Western Palearctic, and is found in southern Europe and North Africa.

Obscure Wainscot   page 319

Mythimna obsoleta (Hb.)

Local. S,EC,(WC)   2204(10010)

Field characters FW 15-18mm. Dark brown scales conspicuously emphasise white veins in centre of forewing, beyond which is a curved row of brown dots across wing. There is a small white central spot at the end of one of the major veins. Some individuals are much more heavily marked than others. Hindwing dirty whitish, slightly darkened near outer edges. Early start of flight period, from mid May rather than late June, also helps to distinguish this moth from related species.

Similar species Southern Wainscot has a straighter outer edge to forewing and usually an incomplete row of dots, less extensive dark scaling and whiter hindwing, on the underside of which is a conspicuous dark central spot usually lacking in Obscure Wainscot but occasionally present, especially in male. Dark scaling on forewing of Smoky Wainscot is more concentrated in a single stripe along main central vein, hindwing generally darker grey and there is a large dark area of grey on underside of forewing. Obscure Wainscot lacks dark forewing margin and shoulder-stripe of Shoulder-striped, Devonshire and L-album Wainscots.

Flight season One generation. Mid May-mid July. Comes frequently to light and sugar, and can be found after dark visiting the flowerheads of grasses to feed on sticky substances produced by ergot fungus.

Life cycle Overwinters as a fully grown larva, generally in a hollow, broken, but standing, dead stem of Common Reed or in fallen reed litter, sealed with silk, pupating in situ in the spring. Larva July-April.

Larval foodplants Common Reed.

Habitat Reedbeds, fens, marshes, riverside situations

including estuaries, and reedy margins of ponds and lakes.

Status & distribution Resident. Local. Searches of less accessible wetlands from the 1980s onwards with light-traps have revealed this species to be more widespread than previously thought. It is mainly a southern and eastern species, with many colonies along the south and east coasts from Dorset to Yorkshire, and inland populations northwards to the small Oxfordshire fens, widely in East Anglia and inland from the Thames and Humber estuaries. Scattered populations in Cornwall, Devon, Somerset and south Wales. Also reported from the Wirral and Cumbria. Recorded from the Channel Islands for the first time in 1999, as a singleton on Jersey.

Shoulder-striped Wainscot   page 319

Mythimna comma (L.)

Common. T   2205(10011)

Field characters FW 16-19mm. Very long, intensely black streak extending from forewing base, further black streaks reaching outer edge and broad whitish band along leading edge are diagnostic of this boldly striped, rather thickset wainscot. Central vein also prominent, whitish in colour. Ground-colour of forewing greyish brown or dull straw-coloured, varying little, and markings are very consistent, varying only slightly in intensity. Hindwing brown.

Similar species Devonshire Wainscot has a shorter streak at base of forewing, central vein not conspicuous, a curved row of black dots toward outer edge, has whitish hindwing, and is smaller. L-album Wainscot has a conspicuous short, thin white line in centre of forewing, and black streak at base is thin and shorter. It is also a smaller, more yellowish moth. See also Obscure Wainscot.

Flight season One generation. Late May-late July. Comes to light and sugar and feeds at flowers.

Life cycle Overwinters as a fully grown larva in an underground cocoon, in which it pupates in April or May. Larva feeds at night, July-September.

Larval foodplants Grasses, including Cock's-foot.

Habitat Most numerous in fens and marshes; also in other grassy places, including some gardens, and in damp woodland.

Status & distribution Resident. Common. Throughout southern Britain, including Scilly, north to southern Scotland, Man and Ireland. Further north, local on the eastern side of the Scottish mainland, to Easter Ross. Locally frequent in the Channel Islands.

Devonshire Wainscot   page 319

Mythimna putrescens (Hb.)

Na. SW   2206(10015)

Field characters FW 14-17mm. The only wainscot with the combination of heavy brown markings and shoulder-stripe on forewing but unmarked white hindwing. Some variation in intensity of forewing markings, with ground-colour tending to yellowish brown.

Similar species. L-album Wainscot is normally distinguished by white L-mark and has brown hindwing, as does Shoulder-striped Wainscot. See also Obscure Wainscot.

Flight season One generation. Mid July-early September. Flies from dusk, comes to light and sugar and has been recorded visiting flowers, frequently those of Wood Sage but also of Red Valerian and various maritime grasses.

Life cycle Overwinters as a larva, hatching by September. Continues feeding on mild nights throughout the winter, becoming fully grown by late January or February, when it burrows into the earth and forms a cocoon in which it rests until pupation in May.

Larval foodplants Unspecified grasses. Accepts Annual Meadow-grass and Cock's-foot in captivity.

Habitat Closely associated with cliffs and grassy places on the coast in the mildest parts of the south-west.

Status & distribution Resident. Nationally Scarce A. Restricted to south-west Britain. First discovered at Torquay, Devon, in 1859. Well established on the north and south coasts of Devon and Cornwall, Lundy and the south coast of Pembrokeshire. Occasionally recorded at Portland Bill, Dorset, on the coasts of Somerset and Carmarthenshire and on the Gower Peninsula of Glamorgan, but may not be continuously resident in these places. Does not appear to wander inland. Locally frequent in the Channel Islands.

2207 see Appendix

Cosmopolitan   page 319

Mythimna loreyi (Dup.)

Immigrant.   2208(10034)

Field characters FW 16-17mm. Prominent dark streak extends along middle of angular, somewhat pointed forewing, often merging with a dark wedge that extends inwards from outer part of wing. This combined darker area contrasts with paler leading edge. A small white spot is usually visible within the dark streak. Pearly white hindwing distinguishes this species from most similar wainscots.

Similar species Southern Wainscot is perhaps most likely source of confusion, but forewing usually slightly hooked at tip (unless worn), and hindwing at least slightly clouded with grey, not pearly, with a dark central spot on underside. White-speck has more pointed forewing and grey hindwing.

Flight season Two or more generations abroad, May-November, being most frequent between September-October. Comes to light and sugar; may also be seen visiting Ivy flowers at dusk or later.

Life cycle Immigrants earlier in the season may result in late summer/autumn progeny in some years.

Larval foodplants Grasses, including Cock's-foot.

Habitat Grassy coastal areas.

Status & distribution Scarce immigrant. Prior to 1975 fewer than 30 had been recorded but it has become more regular in recent years, the most recorded in a single year being over 400 in 1992. Numbers fluctuate greatly and it remains very rare in some years. Recorded from southern coastal counties of England and Wales, occasionally occurring inland. The majority of records come from south-west England, particularly Cornwall. Rare on the east coast but has been recorded as far north as Lincolnshire. Also recorded from Man and southern Ireland. A rare immigrant in the Channel Islands. Resident in southern Europe and North Africa.

Flame Wainscot   page 319

Mythimna flammea (Curt.)

Na. SE, S   2209(10017)

Field characters FW 14-18mm. Distinctive forewing shape, with curved leading edge, pointed wing tip and raked back outer edge is diagnostic. Flame-like black-and-pink streak in centre of forewing and pinkish tint more widely on forewing are more pronounced on some individuals than on others.

Similar species Silky Wainscot is smaller, with less pointed forewing and any central forewing streak is blackish, if present, never pinkish.

Flight season One generation. Mid May-early July. Comes readily to light but does not seem to feed at baits or flowers. Can be found at night on reed stems.

Life cycle Overwinters as a pupa, usually in a broken but standing hollow reed stem sealed with silk. Larva late July-September or even October. Hides in hollow stems by day, feeding at night.

Larval foodplants Common Reed.

Habitat Reedbeds, fens and marshes, preferring areas with scattered reeds rather than dense stands.

Status & distribution Resident and immigrant. Nationally Scarce A. Breeds widely but locally in East Anglia, south-east England and Dorset. Recorded on about 20 occasions as a suspected immigrant, along the south coast from Kent westwards to Dorset, including the Isle of Wight, and northwards to Essex and the London area, twice in Lincolnshire (in 1974 and 1993) and once on the Gower Peninsula, Glamorgan (in 1978). Breeding areas include Wicken and Chippenham Fens in Cambridgeshire (known since the mid 19th century), the Norfolk Broads, elsewhere in Norfolk and Suffolk at Strumpshaw and Surlingham Marshes and also at Redgrave and Lopham Fen, Stoke Ferry Fen, Roydon Common, the Thetford area, and in coastal marshes at Sea Palling Dunes and Cley. Noted at Fritton Lake and in the Walberswick/Minsmere/Thorpeness area of Suffolk since the 1950s. Discovered in a reedbed at Wye, Kent, in 1982 and established in the Winchelsea/St Leonards area of Sussex since at least the 1960s. Known from a site near Wareham, Dorset, since the 1930s and still present.

2210 see Appendix

Larva of Chamomile Shark.

Cuculliinae Sharks, shoulder-knots and allies

Mullein

Tawny Pinion

Red Sword-grass

Grey Chi

Wormwood page 320
Cucullia absinthii (L.)
Nb. S,C   2211(9183)

Field characters & Similar species FW 16-19mm. Bold black forewing markings distinguish this moth from Cudweed and Scarce Wormwood, which are also grey and similar in size. Black spots in kidney-mark and doubled, figure-of-eight-like oval are well defined, as are dashes along outer edge.

Flight season One generation. Mainly July, occasionally to mid August. Occasional at light, and reported at flowers of Red Valerian just after dusk; sometimes found by day at rest on fences.

Life cycle Overwinters as a pupa, in a tough cocoon of silk and earth, usually among surface debris but sometimes underground. Larva August-September. Rests by day and often basks among flowers of foodplant. This is the most productive stage at which to seek this species.

Larval foodplants The flowers and seedheads of

Wormwood; sometimes also Mugwort.

Habitat Wherever the foodplant grows, particularly in sunny, often sheltered situations, usually with bare, hard surfaces, from cliffs, cuttings and quarries to railway ballast, slagheaps and even among broken tarmac in car parks, dockyards and derelict airfields.

Status & distribution Resident. Nationally Scarce B. Until 1946 largely confined to coastal habitats in south-west Britain and isolated colonies in Suffolk. Invaded bombed urban sites and industrial wasteland in the Midlands, Essex and the London area in the late 1940s and 1950s and is still locally well established in these areas, although there are concerns that the tidying up and development of derelict land is removing breeding areas. There is also a concentration of records along the Magnesian limestone running down through south Yorkshire and Nottinghamshire. Scattered recent records of breeding elsewhere, including the coast of north Wales, the Chilterns and Portland, Dorset. Now rare in Devon and Cornwall. Older records extend north along the coast to Cumbria in the west and Norfolk in the east. Adults wander widely. In Ireland reported from Cos. Cork and Wexford. Rare on Jersey, where it was first recorded in 1995.

2212 see Appendix

Scarce Wormwood page 320
Cucullia artemisiae (Hufn.)
Rare immigrant; suspected import.   2213(9188)

Field characters FW 16-19mm. Forewing grey, tinged with brown. Cross-lines dull but distinct, as are kidney-mark and oval. Hindwing whitish with brownish border.

Similar species See Wormwood and Cudweed.

Flight season In mainland Europe, June-July.

Life cycle In mainland Europe, overwinters as a pupa underground. Larva late July-September.

Larval foodplants Mugwort and wormwoods.

Status & distribution Rare immigrant and possible import. On 4 September 1971 a larva was found on Mugwort at Nazeing, Essex, and subsequently reared and confirmed as a male of this species. The only other British or possibly British records are six individuals from the 19th century. Two adults were reported as found on a fence at Starcross, Devon, on 21 August 1885. At the time it was suggested they may have originated from imported pupae. Four others were reported in 1900 as having been found in different collections among rows of Wormwood, but without data. Recorded widely through western, central and south-eastern Europe and into Asia.

Chamomile Shark page 320
Cucullia chamomillae ([D. & S.])
Local. S,C,(N)   2214(9207)

Field characters FW 19-23mm. Like other members of this group, rests with wings closed tightly against body, with collar raised into a pointed projection, reminiscent of a shark's dorsal fin. Forewing long and narrow, strongly arched before tip, with outer edge strongly angled. Grey-brown, tinged and streaked to a varying degree with pale brown, grey and blackish, especially at outer edge. Female is generally darker. Fine blackish streaks near outer edge extend into the fringes. Hindwing grey in male, darker brownish grey in female.

Similar species See Shark.

Flight season One generation. April-May. Comes to light in small numbers and feeds at flowers. Occasionally found by day on posts and tree trunks.

Life cycle Overwinters, sometimes for more than one year, as a pupa underground in a strong cocoon. Larva late May-mid July. Feeds by day and night, and rests on the foodplant, on the flowers when smaller.

Larval foodplants The flowers of Scentless Mayweed, Chamomile, Corn Chamomile, Stinking Chamomile and Feverfew.

Habitat Open grassy places, often with disturbed ground, including arable field margins and some gardens, most frequently in calcareous areas.

Status & distribution Resident. Local. Quite well distributed and fairly frequent in southern Britain, including Scilly. Most densely distributed in south-east and central England north to Yorkshire and in low-lying areas near the coast elsewhere. Local and mainly coastal further north and in southern Scotland, mainly in the central belt, on Man and in Ireland. Widespread and frequent in the Channel Islands.

2215 see Appendix

Shark
page 320

Cucullia umbratica (L.)

Common. T
2216(9199)

Field characters & Similar species FW 22-26mm. Similar in shape, markings and resting posture to Chamomile Shark, but usually larger and greyer, and generally flies later in the season. Also, black streaks do not extend into fringes of forewing outer margin, there is a distinct pale brown streak running through the faint oval and kidney-mark and male has whitish hindwing with brown veins.

Flight season One generation. Late June-August. Comes to light and feeds at flowers such as Honeysuckle, Red Valerian and Rhododendron.

Life cycle Overwinters as a pupa underground in a strong cocoon. Larva July-early September. Feeds at night and hides under the lower leaves of the food-plant by day.

Larval foodplants The flowers and leaves of sow-thistles, wild lettuces, hawk's-beards and hawkweeds.

Habitat Usually rather open country, including urban gardens and rough ground, chalk and limestone grassland, marshes, coastal sand-dunes and shingle beaches.

Status & distribution Resident. Common. Well distributed and fairly frequent in England, Wales and parts of Ireland. Widespread but local in Scotland, including the Hebrides, and on Man. Recorded from

Larva of Star-wort.

Orkney, but status uncertain. Widespread and frequent in the Channel Islands.

Star-wort
page 320

Cucullia asteris ([D. & S.])

Nb. S,C
2217(9221)

Field characters FW 19-23mm. One of the larger sharks, with distinct oval and kidney-mark on contrasting reddish-brown and grey forewing.

Similar species Mullein flies earlier in year and lacks oval and kidney-mark.

Flight season One generation. Mid June-early August. Most records of adults are singletons from light-traps but the moth has been seen at dusk feeding on the wing at Honeysuckle, campions and introduced plants, including tobacco-plants, Red Valerian and evening-primroses, and has occasionally turned up at sugar.

Life cycle Overwinters as a pupa, in a tough earthen cocoon on the surface or just below ground. Larva late July-late August in woodland, until late September or even mid October on the coast. Feeds by day and basks in sunshine.

Larval foodplants & Habitat In coastal saltmarsh on the flowers and sometimes the leaves of Sea Aster, with occasional reports from Sea Wormwood; in woodland clearings and rides on the flowers of Goldenrod. Has been recorded in gardens on the flowers of Michaelmas-daisies and China Aster but in captivity will not feed on the naturalised Canadian Goldenrod.

Status & distribution Resident. Nationally Scarce B. Occurs mainly along the south and east coasts of England, from Hampshire and the Isle of Wight east-wards, with many records in the Thames Estuary and up the east coast to the Humber and Spurn Head, Yorkshire. Also present inland in woods, mainly in Dorset, Hampshire (where it has declined), Sussex and Kent. Recorded at various points along the Welsh coast from Pembrokeshire to Anglesey, and in several woodlands in south Wales. There are old records from Morecambe Bay, Lancashire. Larvae recorded near Bude, Cornwall, in 1984. Occasional adults light-trapped more widely, e.g. in Bentley Wood, south Wiltshire, in 1983, and at Nether Stoney, south Somerset, in 1984. The only record for the Channel Islands is of larvae on Guernsey in 1889.

Larva of Striped Lychnis.

Cudweed   page 320

Cucullia gnaphalii (Hb.)

ssp. *occidentalis* Bours.

Former resident; presumed extinct. SE

2218(9216)

Field characters & Similar species FW 17-19mm. Forewing grey-brown, with black trailing edge. Cross-lines faint or absent, except that beyond middle, which forms a scythed-shaped mark near trailing edge. Oval and kidney-mark distinct, marked inside with dark grey spots. An obvious black streak in trailing corner, and sometimes further streaks near outer edge. Scarce Wormwood has narrower forewing, with cross-lines distinct, trailing edge grey and no dark streak in trailing corner. See also Wormwood.

Flight season One generation. Late May-mid July. The adults were seldom seen except occasionally at light. Reported visiting flowers of Honeysuckle and Fragrant Orchid after dark.

Life cycle Overwinters as a pupa, in a tough earthen cocoon on the surface or just below ground. Larva late July-August. Feeds and basks in sunshine.

Larval foodplants The flowers and leaves of Goldenrod.

Habitat Woodland clearings and rides, the larvae requiring a very hot microclimate.

Status & distribution Former resident, now presumed extinct. In the British Isles only ever recorded from the extreme south-east of England, mainly Kent and Sussex, but with a few records from Surrey and Hampshire. Last recorded in Britain as a single larva on 11 August 1979 at Beckley Woods, on the East Sussex/Kent border.

Larva of Mullein.

Striped Lychnis   page 320

Shargacucullia lychnitis Ramb.

Na. S   2219(9232)

Field characters & Similar species FW 18-21mm. Similar in appearance and resting posture to Mullein, but on average smaller and lighter in colour. Central spot on underside of hindwing generally smaller and fainter than in Mullein, particularly in male, in which it is sometimes absent. Mullein flies earlier in year.

Flight season One generation. June-July. Occasional at light, otherwise rarely seen as an adult.

Life cycle Overwinters as a pupa, often for two winters and occasionally longer, in a tough earthen cocoon on the surface or just below ground. Larva mid July-early September. Feeds and basks among the flowerheads of the foodplant by day.

Larval foodplants Dark Mullein is the main foodplant. Also reported from White Mullein and has been found on ornamental mulleins in garden centres within the breeding range. Normally eats the flowers, but will resort to leaves if plant has gone to seed.

Habitat Verges and embankments, rough downland, fields that have recently been left fallow, and in woodland rides and clearings. Almost always in open, completely unshaded sites on calcareous soil.

Status & distribution Resident. Nationally Scarce A. Confined to southern England where it occurs very locally in Hampshire, Berkshire, Buckinghamshire, Oxfordshire and West Sussex. Formerly found in Dorset, Wiltshire, Gloucestershire, Surrey and East Anglia, but searches of these areas during and since the 1990s have all produced negative results. Adults recorded from Guernsey in 1971 and 1989.

Water Betony   page 320

Shargacucullia scrophulariae ([D. & S.])

Rare immigrant.   2220(9229)

Field characters & Similar species FW 18-22mm. Very similar to Mullein and Striped Lychnis, from which it can only be reliably distinguished by examination of the genitalia.

Flight season & Life cycle In mainland Europe overwinters as a pupa. Larva June-July. The adult flies during May-June.

Larval foodplants The flowers and seeds of figworts and mulleins.

Status & distribution Rare immigrant, although may be overlooked due to identification difficulties. There are two authenticated British records of single adults, both at Swanage, Dorset, on 12 June 1949 and 18 May 1994. In the 19th century, larvae found on figworts in East Anglia, Kent and other localities in southern England were sometimes reported as this species, but subsequent examination of specimens has usually revealed them to be Mullein or Striped Lychnis, even the widely reported specimens found and reared by the knowledgeable J.W. Tutt. The few 19th-century specimens confirmed as Water Betony are of unreliable origin. The species has been reported from most European countries.

Mullein
page 320
Shargacucullia verbasci (L.)
Common. S,C 2221(9233)

Field characters FW 19-24mm. Resembles a piece of dead reddish-brown plant stalk when at rest. Darker examples, with wider brown stripes, are generally females. Hindwing of male is greyish white with dark veins and a diffuse dark border, that of female either uniformly blackish grey or slightly paler near base. Fringes scalloped.
Similar species Starwort lacks scalloped fringes, middle of forewing is greyish rather than straw-coloured and oval and kidney-mark are distinct. See also Striped Lychnis and Water Betony.
Flight season One generation. Late April-May. Comes to light in small numbers, and feeds at flowers.
Life cycle Overwinters, sometimes for up to five years in captivity, as a pupa underground in a strong cocoon. Larva late May-July. Most often encountered as a larva, feeding by day and night.
Larval foodplants Wild and cultivated mulleins, Common and Water Figwort and buddleias, usually on the leaves.
Habitat Usually calcareous habitats, often with disturbed ground, including dry grassland and breck-land, recently cleared woodland and scrub, wood-land rides, roadside verges and ditches, marshes, shingle beaches and some parks and gardens.
Status & distribution Resident. Common. Well distributed in England from Scilly northwards and eastwards to south Cumbria, Co. Durham and East Anglia. More local in Wales, but reaches the Gower Peninsula, Glamorgan, and north Wales. In Ireland found locally in Co. Cork. Widespread and fairly frequent in the Channel Islands.

2222, 2222a see Appendix

Toadflax Brocade
page 320
Calophasia lunula (Hufn.)
RDB. SE 2223(9240)

Field characters FW 14-15mm. The banded fringe of broad forewing and three central white markings, including the tiny but conspicuous kidney-mark, are striking and diagnostic. Shows little variation.
Similar species None.
Flight season Two generations, the first in late May-June or even July, the second from July but usually August, although pupae may sometimes overwinter. Comes to light in small numbers, often soon after dark; otherwise seldom seen. Reported at flowers of Red Valerian.
Life cycle Overwinters as a pupa within a tough oval cocoon, sometimes among the drying seed-pods of the larval foodplant, which it resembles, but also found attached to stones, posts, walls and other objects. Larva late June-July, sometimes early August, with a second generation in late August-September. Feeds and rests among the flowerheads by day,

basking and growing quickly.
Larval foodplants A national survey in 1999 found most larvae on the introduced Purple Toadflax. Common Toadflax is also used regularly and larvae have been reported on Small Toadflax and Pale Toadflax.
Habitat Vegetated shingle beaches, usually where there has been ground disturbance and much bare shingle has been exposed. Also other open coastal situations where the foodplant grows surrounded by much bare ground. Occasionally breeds inland on verges and in gardens.
Status & distribution Resident and suspected immigrant. Red Data Book species. First confirmed in Britain as an adult at Shoreham, West Sussex, in 1939, and as a larva at Dungeness, Kent, in 1952, with further colonisation from the 1950s onwards. Larvae have been found since 1990 from Pagham Harbour, West Sussex, eastwards along the coast to Walmer and Sholden, east Kent. The 1999 survey confirmed breeding in nine 10km squares. Adults and larvae have occasionally been recorded inland from these sites but there appear to be no long-term inland populations. Adults have occasionally been recorded further west along the coast, including at Portland Bill, Dorset, in 1990, Southsea and Gosport, Hampshire, in 1992 and 1996 respectively, and Wareham, Dorset, in 1998. A single adult was recorded at Bradwell-on-Sea, Essex, in 1951. The moth is probably both arriving as an immigrant and wandering from the expanding breeding areas.

Antirrhinum Brocade
not illustrated
Calophasia platyptera (Esp.)
Suspected rare immigrant. 2224(9243)

Field characters & Similar species FW 12-15mm. Like Toadflax Brocade in shape, but slightly smaller, forewing narrower, grey with fine, rather than bold, streaking, no white oval or kidney-mark and cross-lines only apparent near centre of trailing edge, along with a dark blotch.
Status & distribution Suspected rare immigrant. The only known specimen captured in the British Isles is now in the Natural History Museum, London. Found while searching for shells near Brighton, Sussex, on 10 September 1896, a year in which very many immigrant moths were recorded. Resident around the Mediterranean and in southern Europe.

Minor Shoulder-knot
page 320
Brachylomia viminalis (Fabr.)
Common. T 2225(9642)

Field characters FW 13-15mm. The black streak at base of forewing, with a short diagonal black streak close by, along with grey colouring, are diagnostic. Forewing whitish grey through to blackish grey, sometimes marked with pinkish red along leading edge and around oval and kidney-mark. Antennae slightly feathered in male. The whitish grey f. *stricta*

285

Larva of **Sprawler**.

Hb. is most frequent. The dark grey f. *obscura* Stdgr. is frequent in the Midlands and northern England. Other rarer forms are f. *saliceti* Borkh., in which only the basal half of the forewing is dark grey, and f. *unicolor* Tutt, uniformly blackish.

Similar species Marbled, Rufous and Tawny Marbled Minors all lack basal streaks and emerge earlier in the year. See also Union Rustic.

Flight season One generation. July-August. Comes to light and sugar and feeds at flowers.

Life cycle Overwinters as an egg, laid on the twigs of the foodplant. Larva April-June, at first in a spun terminal shoot, later feeding openly at night, hiding between spun leaves by day. Pupates in leaf litter or just under the soil surface.

Larval foodplants Grey Willow; also other willows and Aspen.

Habitat Damp woodland, marshland, fens, heathland, river valleys, pond margins and some gardens.

Status & distribution Resident. Common. Quite well distributed throughout England, Wales and Scotland, including the Hebrides, and breeding locally in Orkney. Local on Man. Widespread but local in Ireland. Rare in the Channel Islands where it has been recorded from Jersey and Sark.

Beautiful Gothic   page 320
Leucochlaena oditis (Hb.)
RDB. S   2226(9628)

Field characters FW 14-16mm. The white lines like crazy paving, coupled with often golden oval and kidney-mark and the small size of the moth are diagnostic. Varies both in ground-colour and markings, from dark purplish forms in Cornwall to grey forms which are predominant at eastern end of range, although dark forms have also been noted here.

Similar species Bordered Gothic is superficially similar, but noticeably larger.

Flight season One generation. Late August-mid October. Adults rest on grass stems soon after dark and fly in numbers a couple of hours later. Frequent at light-traps in the breeding areas.

Life cycle Overwinters as a larva, hatching in October, feeding by night and growing slowly throughout the winter. Spins a cocoon in the soil in February but rests in it until late May or early June before forming a pupa.

Larval foodplants Various grasses. Reported from Common Couch and Annual Meadow-grass, eggs being laid on the seedheads.

Habitat Grassy cliffs and well-drained south-facing slopes by the sea, in areas where frosts are rare. Occasionally wanders 10-15km inland.

Status & distribution Resident. Red Data Book species. Confined in Britain to the western half of the south coast of England. Individuals recorded locally from Scilly, Cornwall, Devon, Dorset and the north and south coasts of the Isle of Wight. One recorded from near Bognor, West Sussex, on 21 October 1976, and Rye, Sussex, on 3 October 1999. Widespread and frequent in the Channel Islands.

Sprawler   page 320
Asteroscopus sphinx (Hufn.)
Common. S,C   2227(9320)

Field characters FW 17-22mm. Stout and very furry thorax, broad forewing, streaky pattern and flight period very late in the year make this an unmistakable moth. Antennae feathered in male. Minor variation in markings, but long black basal streak is a constant feature. In the normal form, forewing is light or cold brownish grey. The dark olive brown f. *fusca* Cock., first recorded in 1953 in the Chilterns, is now frequent in Hertfordshire, Buckinghamshire and Oxfordshire, and is increasing elsewhere.

Similar species None.

Flight season One generation. Late October-early December. Comes frequently to light, male usually from around midnight, female earlier. Does not feed.

Life cycle Overwinters as an egg, laid in small batches in a crevice on a tree trunk. Larva April-early June, most active at night. Pupates in a cocoon well below the soil surface.

Larval foodplants A wide range of broadleaved trees, including Pedunculate Oak, Hawthorn, Blackthorn, Hazel, Goat Willow, Small-leaved Elm and limes.

Habitat Broadleaved woodland and other well-wooded areas, including some gardens.

Status & distribution Resident. Common. Well distributed in the southern half of England, north to Lincolnshire, and in Wales. Local in northern England and in Ireland. The only records from the Channel Islands are from Jersey in 1903 and 1977.

Rannoch Sprawler   page 320
Brachionycha nubeculosa (Esp.)
RDB. N   2228(9323)

Field characters FW 20-24mm. A large, thickset moth with heavy black markings and a diagnostic white slit-like mark edged with black on trailing edge of large, slightly distorted kidney-mark, running along central vein of forewing. In the Aviemore area individuals vary from grey to blackish brown in ground-colour. Individuals from Rannoch and Glen Affric tend to be of the darker brownish form.

Similar species None.

Flight season One generation. March-mid April. Freshly emerged adults can be found by searching birch trunks by day, but this can take about six hours per moth on average. Both sexes come to light from about 10pm onwards. Recorded feeding at sap and sugar.

Life cycle Overwinters as a pupa underground, sometimes for more than one year – in captivity at least. Larva May-late June or early July. Occasionally beaten from lower branches of old birches by day.

Larval foodplants Birches, on mature trees. It is not clear whether there is a preference for Silver Birch or Downy Birch, or whether both are used, but the former predominates in the breeding area at Speyside and the latter at Rannoch. Captive larvae have reportedly shown little interest in eating leaves from small saplings of birch.

Habitat Long-established birch woodland and smaller groups of birch in which the trees are mature and the trunks are large in girth.

Status & distribution Resident. Red Data Book species. This moth occurs in four apparently discrete areas of the Scottish Highlands: the Loch Rannoch area, Perthshire, the Aviemore/upper Spey area, Inverness-shire, Glen Moriston and Glen Affric, Inverness-shire, and Braemar, Aberdeenshire, all of which have recent records. The area to the north of Fort William should be searched, as it has similar habitat.

Brindled Ochre   page 320

Dasypolia templi (Thunb.)

Local. N,C,SW   2229(9638)

Field characters FW 18-23mm. A stout and furry, rough-scaled moth. Forewing greenish brown, heavily dusted and marked with dull yellow and grey, or paler and predominantly yellowish brown. Paler and more yellowish examples tend to be males.

Similar species Usually unmistakable. Some forms of Northern Rustic have a similar forewing colour and pattern, but in most cases are noticeably silky and have dark grey hindwing with chalky white fringes.

Flight period One generation. Late August (in the north), September and October. Mating occurs in the autumn and only female overwinters, surviving as late as May. Comes to light, sometimes commonly, but does not feed.

Life cycle Overwinters as a female adult, in a rocky outcrop, drystone wall or outbuilding. Eggs are laid on the foodplant in the spring. Larva April-July or early August, at first inside the stems, later burrowing into the roots. Pupates just below the soil surface.

Larval foodplants Hogweed and Wild Angelica.

Habitat Mainly rough coastal grassland, cliffs and dune-slacks in the south; also upland grassland, moorland and marshes inland and on sand-dunes on the coast in northern Britain.

Status & distribution Resident. Local. Well distrib-uted in mainland Scotland, especially in the north and north-east where it is sometimes abundant, especially on the coast, and in Orkney and Shetland. Also westwards to the Hebrides. In northern England south to Derbyshire. Mainly coastal in Wales, Man, south-west England, and along the south coast to the Isle of Wight. Very local and mainly coastal in Ireland. Widespread and frequent on Jersey, occasional on Guernsey.

Feathered Brindle   page 321

Aporophyla australis (Boisd.)

ssp. *pascuea* (Humph. & Westw.)

Nb. S   2230(9647)

Field characters & Similar species FW 14-17mm. This moth's narrow forewing and squared shoulders resemble those of the shoulder-knots and pinions, none of which has white hindwing. Varies greatly in appearance from locality to locality. In general, individuals from Cornwall are heavily marked and dark, especially in central portion of forewing, the degree of contrast decreasing eastwards to Kent where the moths have light markings and pale ground-colour; but there are other local forms (such as all-grey forms on the Isle of Wight) rather than a single gradation. The dark brown melanic f. *ingenua* Freyer also occurs at low frequency. Grey forms patterned with black wedges, dashes and other spiky markings are distinctive. A constant feature is the black basal streak. See also Deep-brown Dart.

Flight season One generation. Late August-early October. Has been found at rest on grass stems and visiting Ivy flowers and sugar soon after dark. Comes well to light later in the night.

Life cycle Overwinters as a larva. Larva October-mid May. Feeds and grows slowly during the winter, before pupating under moss or in earth.

Larval foodplants Various low-growing plants, including Sea Campion, Common Sorrel, Bramble and Wood Sage; possibly also some grasses.

Habitat Shingle beaches, vegetated sand-dunes and soft-rock sea cliffs. Also on the south-facing slopes of the chalk downs that extend inland on the south coast of the Isle of Wight and on similar slopes on the South Downs, Sussex.

Status & distribution Resident. Nationally Scarce B. Mainly coastal, with colonies scattered along the south coast of England from Scilly and the extreme west of Cornwall to east Kent. Seems to avoid the Hampshire coast and the saltmarsh areas of north Kent and Essex, but extends northwards along the east coast as far as Norfolk. On the west coast, resident only on the north coast of west Cornwall and the south coast of Pembrokeshire, but one recorded from Llecryd, Cardiganshire, in 1980, and twice from Glamorgan. Recorded from south-east Ireland on the coasts of Cos. Waterford, Wexford and Wicklow, probably favouring areas warmed by the Gulf Stream. Widespread and frequent in the Channel Islands.

287

Deep-brown Dart — page 321

Aporophyla lutulenta ([D. & S.])

Common. S,C   2231(9649)

Field characters FW 15-18mm. A warm deep brownish-grey or blackish, fairly thickset moth. Forewing quite broad with leading edge straight or almost so and outer edge rather tapering to the tip. Markings vary in intensity and may be obscure. Often there is a broad darker central band. Hindwing in male white, sometimes with a central row of small blackish dots or short dashes; in the female, dark grey. Antennae of male slightly feathered.

Similar species See Northern Deep-brown Dart, which until fairly recently was regarded as a subspecies. The dark brown f. *ingenua* Freyer of Feathered Brindle, which occurs in Kent and Sussex, has narrower forewing and a black basal streak.

Flight period One generation. September-October. Comes to light and sugar, and feeds at flowers and overripe blackberries.

Life cycle Overwinters as a very small larva. Larva autumn-early June. Feeds at night and hides low down by day. Pupates underground.

Larval foodplants Apparently a range of woody and herbaceous plants and grasses, including Broad-leaved Dock and sorrels, and reportedly Broom, Blackthorn, Field Gromwell, Annual Meadow-grass and Tufted Hair-grass.

Habitat Open habitats, mainly on calcareous or light sandy soils but also clays, including permanent pasture, hay meadows, downland, heathland, coastal sand-dunes, rough grassland and some gardens. Also wide woodland rides.

Status & distribution Resident. Common. Well distributed in southern Britain south of a line from the Severn to the Humber, and including Scilly. Rare in the Channel Islands: singletons recorded on Guernsey in 1972 and Jersey in 1981.

Northern Deep-brown Dart — page 321

Aporophyla lueneburgensis (Freyer)

Common. N,WC   2231a(9650)

Field characters & Similar species FW 15-17mm. Very similar in shape and markings to Deep-brown Dart, but on average slightly smaller and seldom brownish. Forewing either uniformly dull blackish, or heavily dusted with cold grey and with a blackish central band. Black dots or dashes on hindwing of male usually evident, often well developed and sometimes joined to form a curved line. Antennae of male slightly feathered. The two species are largely separated geographically, but moths from the north and West Midlands and from south Wales should be examined carefully. See also Black Rustic.

Flight season One generation. Early August-mid September. Comes to light and sugar, and feeds at flowers.

Life cycle Overwinters as a small larva. Larva autumn-late May. Feeds at night and hides low down by day. Pupates underground.

Larval foodplants Various woody and herbaceous plants and grasses, including Heather, Bilberry and Common Bird's-foot-trefoil.

Habitat Moorland and rough grassy or rocky places, both on the coast and inland at low altitude.

Status & distribution Resident. Common. Well distributed and often fairly frequent in Scotland, including the Hebrides and Orkney, northern England, north Wales, Man and the north and west coasts of Ireland.

Black Rustic — page 321

Aporophyla nigra (Haw.)

Common. N,S,WC,(EC)   2232(9651)

Field characters FW 17-21mm. As the name suggests, this is a consistently glossy, deep black or brownish-black moth. Only conspicuous feature is white or creamy white outer edging of kidney-mark. Hindwing in male white, with narrow dark outer edges; in female grey, lighter near base. Antennae not visibly feathered in either sex.

Similar species Blackish examples of Deep-brown Dart and Northern Deep-brown Dart are smaller and never glossy, outer edge of kidney-mark is not strongly highlighted whitish and antennae of male are feathered.

Flight season One generation. September-October. Comes to light and sugar, and feeds at Ivy flowers and on overripe blackberries.

Life cycle Overwinters as a small larva. Larva October-May. Feeds at night and hides low down by day. Pupates underground.

Larval foodplants Various woody and herbaceous plants, including Tufted Hair-grass, Heather and clovers.

Habitat Open heathland, moorland, calcareous grassland, roadside verges and other rough grassy herb-rich places, including some gardens and woodland rides.

Status & distribution Resident. Common. Well distributed in most of Great Britain, except eastern England, East Anglia, parts of the Midlands, and north-east England, where it is local but increasing. Breeds in Orkney; possibly only a vagrant in Shetland. Widespread and frequent on Man, in Ireland and in the Channel Islands.

Golden-rod Brindle — page 321

Lithomoia solidaginis (Hb.)

Local. N,WC   2233(9655)

Field characters FW 18-21mm. When at rest on moorland vegetation, with wings folded around the body, and head end pointed slightly downwards, this moth closely resembles a piece of broken twig. When wings are spread, the narrow cold grey and whitish forewing is seen to be bluntly hooked. Kidney-mark is large and conspicuous and outermost cross-line is jagged in middle, with several elongated black arrowhead marks projecting inwards: this combination is diagnostic. Variation is only slight;

some examples have a distinct darker central band.
Similar species Sword-grass is superficially similar, and rests with wings tightly closed, but is larger, with a dark brown thorax.
Flight season One generation. August-September. Comes to light (in small numbers) and to sugar and flowers, especially of heathers and ragworts. Rests openly by day on vegetation, rocks, posts and often on barbed wire.
Life cycle Overwinters as an egg. Larva late April-July, resting on the foodplant. Pupates in a cocoon under moss or soil.
Larval foodplants Heather, Bilberry, Cowberry, Bearberry, Bog-myrtle, willows, birches and probably other moorland plants.
Habitat Moorland, upland scrub and open woodland.
Status & distribution Resident and occasional immigrant. Local. Well distributed in Scotland, including the Inner Hebrides and Orkney, northern England, the north Midlands south to Staffordshire, and north and central Wales. Recorded as an immigrant in the southern half of England in 1954 (at least 17 individuals), 1973, 1976 and 1983, most of which have been of the more uniformly grey f. *cinerascens Stdgr.*, resident in Germany.

2234, 2234a see Appendix

Tawny Pinion

page 321

Lithophane semibrunnea (Haw.)

Local. S   2235(9657)

Field characters FW 16-20mm. When at rest, resembles a piece of bark or broken twig. Forewing narrow, tawny brown, generally paler and straw-coloured towards leading edge. Key feature is solid blackish bar extending from near trailing corner inward along forewing, parallel with trailing edge. This is cut by a short, pale, flattened S-mark. Thorax has a crest in centre and shoulders are pointed, projecting forwards rather like a pair of ears. Variation is slight, mainly in ground-colour, which may be paler or greyish tinged.
Similar species See Pale Pinion.
Flight season One generation. October-November, reappearing March-May. Feeds after dark, in autumn on Ivy flowers and overripe blackberries, and in spring on sallow catkins. Also comes to sugar and in small numbers to light.
Life cycle Overwinters as an adult, probably under loose bark or in another sheltered situation. Mating occurs in spring. Larva May-July. Constructs a strong underground cocoon and pupates up to eight weeks later.
Larval foodplants Ash.
Habitat Open broadleaved woodland, parkland, some gardens, and marshy places.
Status & distribution Resident. Local. Well distributed in southern and south-east England, including East Anglia. More local in the south Midlands and south and central Wales. Seldom seen in numbers.

Recorded occasionally in the north and east Midlands and northern England. Rare in the Channel Islands.

Pale Pinion

page 321

Lithophane hepatica (Cl.)

Local. S,C   2236(9658*)

Field characters & Similar species FW 17-20mm. Quite similar to Tawny Pinion. Has same thoracic crests, but with slightly broader and usually paler forewing with a more curved leading edge. Diagnostic feature is lack of a black bar near trailing corner. Instead, there are two small brown elliptical marks. There may also be a brown or blackish bar, but it is placed more centrally, level with oval and kidney-mark. Some examples are extensively dark, especially towards trailing and outer edges, most frequently in western Britain and in Ireland. Hindwing brownish grey. See also Silver Cloud.
Flight season One generation. October-November, reappearing March-May. Feeds after dark, in autumn on Ivy flowers and overripe blackberries and in spring on sallow catkins. Also comes to sugar and in small numbers to light.
Life cycle Overwinters as an adult, probably under loose bark or in another sheltered situation. Mating occurs in spring. Larva May-July. Constructs a strong underground cocoon and pupates about a month later.
Larval foodplants Various trees and shrubs, including oaks, sallows, birches, Apple, Horse-chestnut, Bramble and Wild Privet. Also reported from herbaceous plants, although possibly only in captivity.
Habitat Broadleaved woodland and parkland.
Status & distribution Resident. Local. Thinly distributed and usually seen only in small numbers, in southern and south-west England, including Scilly, the south-west Midlands, Wales, Man and Ireland. Also occurs in south-east England and occasionally recorded from East Anglia, Lincolnshire and north-west England. Recorded once from Jersey in 1999.

Grey Shoulder-knot

page 321

Lithophane ornitopus (Hufn.)

ssp. *lactipennis* (Dadd)

Common. S,WC   2237(9660)

Field characters FW 17-19mm. Key feature is bold, black, curved antler-like mark at base of forewing, which is cold light grey, often marked with light brown in lower half of kidney-mark and along outermost cross-line. Shoulders slightly pointed with a central thoracic crest. Hardly varies, although some examples are slightly darker grey.
Similar species Grey Chi can be similar in size and colour, but lacks bold mark at base of forewing, having instead a bold black central mark. Forewing also broader and shoulders rounded.
Flight season One generation. September-

November, reappearing February-April, occasionally earlier. Feeds after dark, in autumn on Ivy flowers and overripe blackberries and in spring on sallow catkins. Comes to sugar and regularly to light. Can be found by day resting on tree trunks and fences, where it is often conspicuous.

Life cycle Overwinters as an adult, probably under loose bark or in another sheltered situation. Mating occurs in spring. Larva May-July. Constructs a strong underground cocoon and pupates about a month later.

Larval foodplants Pedunculate Oak; probably also Sessile Oak and possibly Turkey Oak.

Habitat Broadleaved woodland and parkland.

Status & distribution Resident. Common. Well distributed in southern and south-west England, East Anglia, the south and West Midlands and Wales. Occasionally recorded in northern England. Rare on Man. Widespread but local in Ireland.

Conformist
page 321

Lithophane furcifera furcifera (Hufn.)
Immigrant.   2238(9661)

ssp. *suffusa* Tutt
Presumed extinct.

Field characters FW 17-20mm. The pale immigrant ssp. *furcifera* has striking whitish shoulders and forewing base, edged with black, and a conspicuous orange kidney-mark on its mottled slaty-grey forewing. The resident ssp. *suffusa* is darker, without whitish wing base, as often are individuals reared in captivity. Both forms have a short thin black bar between kidney-mark and trailing edge of forewing. Outer end of bar is about level with centre of the kidney-mark, and bar veers inwards towards wing base, away from trailing edge.

Similar species See Nonconformist and *Lithophane consocia*.

Flight season One generation. Both presumed residents and suspected immigrants have been recorded in September-October and again in March-May, after hibernation. Both subspecies have been reported at light, sugar, Ivy flowers and sallow catkins.

Life cycle, Larval foodplants & Habitat In northern Europe, overwinters as an adult and larvae have been found April-June, mainly on Alder, although birches, sallows and poplars are also reported foodplants. No information on foodplants or habitats in Britain was ever published due to secrecy by the few reported to have found the moth. The eggs, larvae and pupae have probably never been found in the wild in Britain.

Status & distribution Ssp. *suffusa* Former resident. Presumed extinct (in 1987 Red Data Book) but some believe it could still be an overlooked resident. Discovered at Llantrisant, Glamorgan, in October 1859, when two individuals were captured on Ivy flowers, and apparently found regularly in the area up to the 1880s. Three specimens labelled 'Glamorgan' may have come from the Neath/Port Talbot area. Buckler (1869) records that one was

taken at sugar on 2 October 1869, in Monmouth, and that another had been taken a few days previously. A male was reported near Bigsweir, on the Gloucestershire bank of the River Wye, on 31 March 1907. The last was recorded at light near Cardiff, on 10 October 1959.

Ssp. *furcifera* Immigrant. About a dozen individuals were recorded as probable immigrants between about 1870 and 1946, all in England and mainly in the south-east, although the first was in Halifax, Yorkshire.

Nonconformist
page 321

Lithophane lamda (Fabr.)
Immigrant.   2239(9662)

Field characters & Similar species FW 17-20mm. Closely resembles Conformist but distinguished by a longer, thicker black bar running parallel to trailing edge of forewing, with outer end projecting just beyond kidney-mark, and lacks abdominal crests of Conformist. Black arrow near outer edge of forewing, pointing to wing base, weak or absent in Conformist. Ground-colour varies from light to dark grey or purplish grey. Forewing base generally pale, as in immigrant ssp. *furcifera* of Conformist.

Flight season One generation. All the British records are from September-October. In mainland Europe the moth hibernates and reappears in the spring. Comes to light, sugar and Ivy flowers in the autumn and sallow catkins in the spring.

Life cycle Overwinters as an adult. Larva May-July in mainland Europe, never found in Britain.

Larval foodplants Bog-myrtle, Bog Bilberry, Creeping Willow and poplars.

Habitat Mainly moorland in Europe.

Status & distribution Immigrant. Fourteen individuals reported between 1865 and 1938, all from south-east England, except for one at Ledbury, Herefordshire, in 1870. A number of the records were from north-west Kent, and it is possible that the species became temporarily established there. Not recorded in the British Isles since 1938 and never from the Channel Islands. Resident in Denmark and further north in Scandinavia. Rare and possibly not resident in Belgium and the Netherlands.

Blair's Shoulder-knot
page 321

Lithophane leautieri (Boisd.)

ssp. *hesperica* Bours.
Common. S,C   2240(9664)

Field characters FW 17-20mm. The narrow grey forewing with black streaks, notably a long, straight black one at base and others centrally, make this moth unlike any other flying in autumn. Kidney-mark often tinted with pinkish brown. Black streaks and other dark markings vary in intensity and some examples have a pink flush on hindwing, undersides of both fore- and hindwing and on abdomen.

Similar species None.

Flight season One generation. Late September-November. Comes regularly to light, but rarely to sugar and seldom seen by day.
Life cycle Overwinters as an egg, laid on the foliage of the foodplant. Larva March-July. Pupates underground.
Larval foodplants The flowers and young leaves of Monterey, Lawson's and Leyland Cypress; occasionally on Juniper.
Habitat Conifer plantations, parks, gardens and other places where the foodplants are found.
Status & distribution Resident – recent colonist. Common. First found in 1951 on the Isle of Wight and now well distributed and often abundant in southern and south-west England, south Wales, and the Midlands north to Yorkshire, where it is now numerous. Reached Cumbria by 1996, north Wales by 1997 and Scotland (Kirkcudbrightshire) by 2001. Well established on Man by 1997. Reported from Ireland (Wicklow) in. Widespread and frequent in the Channel Islands.

Red Sword-grass   page 321
Xylena vetusta (Hb.)
Local. N,W,(S)   2241(9670)

Field characters FW 24-29mm. Rests with wings creased and closed tightly around body, resembling a piece of wood. Diagnostic feature is contrast between the straw-coloured leading half of forewing, with orange-red tint, and the rich mahogany brown or blackish-brown trailing half, best appreciated when wings are unfolded. Less frequently the pale area is more extensive and reaches trailing edge, level with kidney-mark. One or two black sword-like streaks extend inward from outermost cross-line, the longest almost reaching the dark blotch beyond kidney-mark. Foot and lower part of hind leg dark red-brown.
Similar species On Sword-grass trailing half of forewing is grey or blackish grey and not sharply contrasting with leading half, and there is no reddish brown. Sword-like marks are more variable but are usually shorter, ending well short of dark area beyond kidney-mark.
Flight season One generation. September-November, reappearing March-late May, occasionally early June. Feeds after dark, in autumn on Ivy flowers and overripe blackberries and in spring on sallow catkins. Comes to sugar and light.
Life cycle Overwinters as an adult, probably under loose bark, or in a rocky outcrop or other sheltered situation. Mating occurs in spring. Larva May-July. Feeds openly by day and night. Pupates underground in a fragile cocoon.
Larval foodplants Woody and herbaceous plants, including Bog-myrtle, heathers, Yellow Iris, sedges and the flowerheads of Soft-rush and Compact Rush.
Habitat Moorland, rough upland pasture, boggy heathland, damp woodland and marshes.
Status & distribution Resident and possible immigrant. Local. Fairly well distributed and frequent in many parts of mainland Scotland and the Hebrides,

northern England, Wales, Man and Ireland. Regular suspected immigrant or possible resident in Orkney and Shetland. Local and rare as a resident in southern England, notably the New Forest, Hampshire. There is a wide scatter of recent records from other parts of southern England, and a few from the Midlands and East Anglia. Most of these are of singletons, presumed wanderers from further west or possibly international immigrants.

Sword-grass   page 321
Xylena exsoleta (L.)
Nb. N,C   2242(9671)

Field characters & Similar species FW 24-29mm. Rests, like Red Sword-grass, with wings creased and closed tightly around body, distinguishing them from most other noctuid moths. Lacks orange-red tint found in pale parts of forewing of Red Sword-grass, tending more to grey or straw-coloured. This colour difference is also evident on foot of hind leg, and can be used to identify worn individuals. See also Red Sword-grass for other distinguishing features, and Golden-rod Brindle.
Flight season One generation. September-October, reappearing in March-May. Feeds at Ivy flowers and overripe blackberries in autumn, and at sallow catkins and Blackthorn flowers in spring. Comes to sugar, more so in autumn than in spring. Comes readily to light.
Life cycle Overwinters as an adult, possibly in dense tussocks of grasses and rushes. Mating takes place after hibernation. Larva May-July. Feeds in warm sunshine as well as at night. Pupates in a cocoon among debris on the ground.
Larval foodplants Wild larvae reported from thistles, Creeping Cinquefoil, Common Restharrow, stonecrops, Groundsel, docks, Hop and Sugar Beet. Will accept other foodplants in captivity, including shrubs and trees such as Blackthorn, Bird Cherry and hawthorns.
Habitat Moorland, rough pasture and open woodland, mainly in uplands, but found as a larva in lowland woodland in Berkshire in 1929 and on a railway embankment in Buckinghamshire in 1938.
Status & distribution Resident and suspected immigrant or large-scale wanderer over Britain. Nationally Scarce B. The range has contracted northwards in recent decades. Regularly recorded, locally in numbers, at a scattering of sites throughout Scotland from the Firth of Forth northwards, including Orkney and Fair Isle, and undoubtedly breeding over a large area in this region. Also widely recorded, particularly in past decades, in north Wales and northern England. To the south of this the moth has been recorded only occasionally since 1980 and its breeding status is unclear; there are older records, including of larvae, scattered widely through southern England. Local and rare on Man. Scattered records through Ireland, more so near the east coast, but many are decades old. Recorded once from Jersey in 1913.

Early Grey   page 321
Xylocampa areola (Esp.)
Common. T   2243 (9676)

Field characters FW 15-18mm. Forewing ash grey, rough in texture and marbled with blackish grey. Oval and kidney-mark are pale, and there is an additional oval which is joined to the first, and also to kidney-mark in most cases. This pattern is diagnostic. Ground-colour varies, and some examples are quite dark. Others have a delicate pinkish flush, especially on fringes but sometimes extending across forewing.
Similar species Shears and Glaucous Shears can be superficially similar but lack extra oval and fly later in year.
Flight season One generation. March (occasionally February)-May. Comes to light, sometimes in numbers, often alighting and remaining on nearby trees or fences rather than entering a trap. Feeds at sallow catkins, but only rarely at sugar. Sometimes found by day on fences or trees.
Life cycle Overwinters as a pupa underground, in a strong cocoon. The egg is laid singly on a stem of the foodplant. Larva April-June. Feeds at night and rests along a woody stem by day.
Larval foodplants Wild and cultivated honeysuckles.
Habitat Broadleaved woodland, scrub, hedgerows and gardens.
Status & distribution Resident. Common. Very well distributed in England north to the Humber, in parts of northern England, in Wales, on Man and in Ireland. Local in western, northern and central mainland Scotland, and the Hebrides. Widespread and abundant in the Channel Islands.

Double-spot Brocade   not illustrated
Meganephria bimaculosa (L.)
Uncertain.   2244(9679)

Field characters FW 22-26mm. A rather large, distinctive noctuid. forewing broad and straw-coloured, with a large, bulbous kidney-mark (like that of Green-brindled Crescent) and curved leading edge. Hindwing dirty grey with two dark blotches, one fairly central and one near trailing edge.
Similar species None.
Status & distribution Uncertain. Unlikely as an immigrant, more probably an accidental import. A fairly frequent resident in parts of central and southern Europe; not known for migratory tendencies. The most recent record is of a slightly worn male taken at rest on a tree trunk in Leigh Woods, near Bristol, Somerset, in mid July 1949. There are two other specimens with British data: the first was also taken 'near Bristol', in July 1815; the second on Southsea Common, near Portsmouth, Hampshire, in 1892. Searches at Leigh Woods have produced no further specimens. The ports of Bristol and Portsmouth offer many opportunities for assisted immigration. The larval foodplants include elms and Blackthorn.

Green-brindled Crescent   page 321
Allophyes oxyacanthae (L.)
Common. T   2245(9682)

Field characters FW 17-20mm. There are two distinct forms of this unmistakable moth, although intermediates occur. The paler form has brown forewing, streaked and dusted to a variable extent with bright metallic green. F. *capucina* Mill. is dark brown or melanic, marked with tawny brown and without metallic green scales. Both forms have a white crescent-like mark close to forewing trailing edge beside second cross-line, and black basal streak and first cross-line together often form a mark like a loaded crossbow. F. *capucina* is unknown outside Great Britain. It is most frequent in industrial areas, such as London, the Midlands and northern England.
Similar species None.
Flight season One generation. September-November. Comes regularly to light and sugar. Often found after dark feeding at Ivy flowers, overripe blackberries and other fruit.
Life cycle Overwinters as an egg, laid singly on twigs of the foodplant. Larva April-June. Constructs a strong underground cocoon, pupating several weeks later.
Larval foodplants Hawthorn, Midland Hawthorn, Blackthorn, Crab Apple, Dog-rose, Plum, cotoneasters and (in the north) Rowan.
Habitat Broadleaved woodland, scrub, hedgerows and gardens.
Status & distribution Resident. Common. Well distributed and abundant throughout England, Wales, Man and parts of southern Scotland. Local in the rest of mainland Scotland, the Inner Hebrides and over much of Ireland. Widespread in the Channel Islands.

2246 see Appendix

Oak Rustic   page 322
Dryobota labecula (Esp.)
Suspected rare immigrant; Channel Islands resident
                               2246a(9692)

Field characters & Similar species FW 12-15mm. Late flight season and orange kidney-mark are good recognition characters for this medium-sized thickset noctuid. However, f. *albomacula* Culot, frequent on Guernsey, has a white kidney-mark and could be confused with forms of Common or Lesser Common Rustic. Small black basal streak on forewing is more conspicuous in Oak Rustic, which lacks black I-bar running parallel to centre of forewing trailing edge, has a more thickset thorax and flies later in the year.
Flight season One generation. October-December. Both sexes nocturnal and come to light, otherwise seldom seen.
Life cycle Overwinters as an egg. Larva slow-growing, April-September in mainland Europe.
Larval foodplants Evergreen Oak.
Habitat Recently recorded in gardens where it

evidently breeds on small stands of the larval food-plant in otherwise open hedgerows and fields. Also in larger stands on hillsides.

Status & distribution Resident in the Channel Islands, where it was first recorded on Jersey in 1991 and on Guernsey in 1995 and is now seen annually, widely and frequently. First recorded in the British Isles as a singleton at Freshwater, Isle of Wight, on 15 October 1999, only 15m from a row of Evergreen Oak, where a worn second individual was captured on 22 November 1999. Local breeding not confirmed but a likely colonist.

Merveille du Jour   page 322
Dichonia aprilina (L.)
Common. T   2247(9694)

Field characters FW 18-23mm. A beautifully and uniquely marked moth. Forewing broad with curved leading edge, light pastel green with black markings, many of which are edged with white. These may be fine and reduced, or more extensive, forming blotches or a central band. In extreme cases most of wing is black, but some green remains, including oval and kidney-mark.

Similar species Scarce Merveille du Jour is a similar shade of green but is slimmer, has distinct white streaks on forewing, a narrow black kidney-mark, and other black markings heaviest near base and tip of forewing, not centre, and flies much earlier in the year.

Flight season One generation. September-October. Comes to light and sugar, and feeds at Ivy flowers and overripe berries.

Life cycle Overwinters as an egg, laid singly or in small batches on branches or in bark crevices of the foodplant. Larva April-June. Feeds at first inside an opening bud, and when larger only at night, hiding in a bark crevice on the trunk by day. Constructs a strong underground cocoon close to the base of the tree, pupating several weeks later.

Larval foodplants The immature flowers and leaves of Pedunculate Oak; probably also Sessile Oak and possibly Turkey Oak.

Habitat Broadleaved woodland, parkland and hedgerows. Some gardens, but generally not in urban centres.

Status & distribution Resident. Common. Fairly well distributed and sometimes frequent throughout much of England and Wales. Local in mainland Scotland north to Sutherland, in the Inner Hebrides and on Man. Thinly distributed over most of Ireland, although the increase in recording activity in Northern Ireland in the last decade has revealed that it is quite well distributed there. Local in the Channel Islands but fairly frequent on Jersey.

Brindled Green   page 322
Dryobotodes eremita (Fabr.)
Common. T   2248(9699)

Field characters FW 15-17mm. Forewing dull green, greenish black or grey, either strongly variegated

with black, white and brown, or more obscurely marked. Diagnostic feature is small pale blotch in centre adjacent to oval, bordered with black along its rear and outer edges. This varies in shape, width, colour and intensity, but nearly always has a small projection at its trailing corner pointing towards outer edge of wing.

Similar species Shears has two projections on central blotch and is never green. Its main flight season is much earlier, although it can have a small second generation.

Flight season One generation. August-mid October. Comes regularly to light, sugar and overripe black-berries.

Life cycle Overwinters as an egg, laid in small batches on oak twigs. Larva April-June. Feeds at first inside a bud, later only at night, hiding by day in a spun terminal shoot. Pupates underground in a cocoon.

Larval foodplants The expanding buds and leaves of Pedunculate and probably Sessile Oak. Also found on Hazel under a canopy of Pedunculate Oak, and reared successfully on it. Reported from hawthorns.

Habitat Broadleaved woodland, parkland and some gardens, including suburban areas.

Status & distribution Resident. Common. Well distributed in the southern half of England and in Wales. Local in northern England, mainland Scotland north to Wester Ross and the Inner Hebrides. Local and rare on Man. Local in Ireland, but recently found quite widely in Northern Ireland. Rare in the Channel Islands, where it was first recorded from Guernsey in 2000 and from Jersey in 2002.

Beautiful Arches   page 322
Blepharita satura ([D. & S.])
Suspected rare immigrant; presumed extinct.
                                 2249(9738)

Field characters & Similar species FW 19-23mm. Most like an atypical Dark Arches or a very large Dark Brocade or Northern Arches. Dark Brocade and Northern Arches are smaller, with narrower forewing. Beautiful Arches has shorter, deeper forewing than Dark Arches, with large and diag-nostic patches of reddish brown on outer part contrasting with generally dark greyish-brown ground-colour. Thorax has a reddish crest. Outer cross-line and other forewing markings, including conspicuous large kidney-mark, are also reddish. Forewing has a black basal streak and central I-bar, like several related species.

Flight season One generation. July-October in main-land Europe.

Life cycle Overwinters as an egg. Larva May-June in mainland Europe.

Larval foodplants A wide range of plants reported in Europe, including Bramble, Honeysuckle, sallows, hawthorns, Blackthorn and Raspberry.

Habitat Uncertain. Open woodland and heathland in Denmark.

Status & distribution Possibly resident in the 19th

century but may have occured as an immigrant.. Some of the small number of records are misidentifications, others deliberate frauds, but a few appear genuine. Of the latter there are at least two, some years apart, from the mid 19th century: one from near Reading, Berkshire, the other from south Oxfordshire, both in areas that still have a wide range of species-rich habitats, including open woodland, heathland and fen. Two were reportedly taken at sugar by J.W. Tutt at Wicken Fen, Cambridgeshire, in 1891, and there is a previous record from the county at least 35 years earlier. In the 1920s two dealers reported specimens from Kent which have subsequently been dismissed. Two 19th-century specimens exist reportedly from Aberdeenshire, but these were dismissed at the time as improbable. Erroneously reported from Co. Wicklow, Ireland. Widespread throughout Europe.

Dark Brocade   page 322
Blepharita adusta (Esp.)
Common. T   2250(9741*)

Field characters FW 18-21mm. Forewing quite broad and rather pointed, pale brown, olive brown, dark brown sometimes tinged with reddish brown, or blackish brown. Darker examples have a paler dusting of greyish scales. A solid black bar usually joins second and third cross-lines, but this is sometimes thin and occasionally incomplete, failing to reach third line. There is a distinct wavy black basal streak. Outer edge of kidney-mark is whitish and pale outermost cross-line is jagged in middle, forming a distinct W.

Similar species Examples with an incomplete black bar are most likely to be confused with Cabbage Moth, which has a spine on each foreleg (tip of tibia) and chalky-white edging on kidney-mark, usually lacks a distinct basal streak and is generally greyer. Northern Arches and Exile are stouter, cross-lines are thicker, and outermost cross-line is less jagged and not does not make a well-defined W, or is barely discernible. Dusky Brocade has less pointed forewing and is greyer. Dark Brocade can be separated from Pale-shouldered Brocade and Cabbage Moth by its completely hairless eyes, and from all *Apamea* species by the distinctive long eyelashes.

Flight season One generation. Late May-early August. Comes to light and sugar and feeds at flowers.

Life cycle Overwinters as a fully grown larva underground in a cocoon, in which it pupates in April or May. Feeds June-September, mainly at night.

Larval foodplants Various woody and herbaceous plants, including Heather, Bog-myrtle, Alder, Bladder Campion and reportedly grasses. Readily accepts sallows and hawthorns in captivity.

Habitat In the south, heathland, chalk downland, fens, woodland and some gardens. Further north, moorland, upland grassland and sand-dunes.

Status & distribution Resident. Common. Quite

well distributed in most parts of England, Wales and Scotland, including Orkney and Shetland, on Man and in Ireland. More frequent in northern and uplands areas, where often abundant. Very local in south-west England. Has declined greatly in Hampshire since the 1960s.

Bedrule Brocade   page 322
Blepharita solieri (Boisd.)
Rare immigrant.   2250a(9744)

Field characters & Similar species FW 16-19mm. Resembles Dark Brocade but slightly smaller and more tawny brown, with paler hindwing, whitish in male with darker border, more generally dark brown in female; greyish white in Dark Brocade, which is usually a much darker moth.

Flight season One generation in mainland Europe. August-September. Comes to light.

Life cycle Overwinters as a larva, feeding from autumn to spring. Pupates underground.

Larval foodplants The roots and leaves of a wide range of herbaceous plants.

Habitat Open habitats, including in gardens and on farm crops.

Status & distribution Rare immigrant. Only one recorded in the British Isles, at Bedrule, near Denholm, Roxburghshire, on 29 August 1976. Resident mainly in south-eastern Europe and the Mediterranean islands, but has been recorded in Denmark. Sometimes a pest locally where resident.

Grey Chi   page 322
Antitype chi (L.)
Common. N,C,(S)   2254(9706)

Field characters FW 15-19mm. Black mark in centre of forewing, sometimes resembling the Greek letter χ (Chi), is diagnostic. It may also be anvil-shaped, or thickened to form a solid bar, or less often reduced. Forewing greyish white, cold light or dark grey, or greyish green (f. *olivacea* Steph. strongly marked, and f. *nigrescens* Tutt weakly marked). Hindwing whitish in male, grey in female. Greyish-green and dark grey forms are most frequent in the Midlands, northern England and parts of Scotland.

Similar species Grey Shoulder-knot may have the dark mark suggested. However, it has slightly narrower forewing with a long, bold, black antler-like streak at base.

Flight season One generation. August-September. Comes to light and sugar. Often found by day at rest on stone walls, on buildings near lights, on rocks and tree trunks.

Life cycle Overwinters as an egg. Larva April-June, feeding at night. Pupates underground in a strong cocoon.

Larval foodplants Few wild records but apparently docks and sorrels. Accepts sallows, hawthorns, Lilac, Red Currant and many other plants in captivity.

Habitat Moorland, upland grassland and other open grassy places, including parkland and gardens in urban areas.

Status & distribution. Resident. Common. Well distributed in the Midlands, Wales, northern England, mainland Scotland and the Hebrides. Local in south-west England and Wiltshire. Rare and probably vagrant in south-east, eastern and central southern England and East Anglia, but spreading eastwards. Local in Ireland but recently found in many sites in Northern Ireland. Local on Man. One reported from Jersey in the 1920s.

Flame Brocade
page 322

Trigonophora flammea (Esp.)

Immigrant; transitory resident.   2251(9716)

Field characters FW 20-23mm. A very distinctive species, the large whitish central kidney-mark with pointed extension being the most striking feature. Forewing otherwise purplish brown, tinged with a violet sheen, with several dark blocks and a light brownish outer band.

Similar species Two very similar species, *T. crassicornis* (Ob.) and *T. jodia* (H.-S.), occur in France. They have not yet been recorded as immigrants to Britain but could occur. *T. crassicornis* is paler, and antennae of male have long feathery extensions on both sides of central filament. *T. jodia* is noticeably smaller; antennae of male are only really feathered on one side, as in Flame Brocade, and hindwing of male whitish rather than brownish as in Flame Brocade.

Flight season One generation. September-early November. Comes to light, sugar and Ivy flowers.

Life cycle Overwinters as a small larva. Larva November-May. Pupates underground.

Larval foodplants Not confirmed in Britain. Reared initially on Lesser Celandine and buttercups, but seems to favour woody plants such as Blackthorn, privets and Broom in later stages of growth.

Habitat Sparse woodland, parkland, marshy ground and chalky slopes, usually within a few miles of the sea when resident in England. Usually searched for and reported where Ivy is abundant. Mainly coastal as an immigrant.

Status & distribution Scarce but regular immigrant and transitory resident in the British Isles; widespread and frequent resident in the Channel Islands. Resident, sometimes in numbers, along the base of the South Downs, from Arundel eastwards to Newhaven, Sussex, from its discovery in 1855 to about 1892, after which there were several hard winters and it was not seen again until 1919 and then 1946. As a suspected immigrant it has occurred on over 80 occasions along southern coastal counties between Devon and Kent, particularly in Dorset. In 2001 it was also recorded in Northamptonshire. Since 1990 records have been almost annual but breeding has not been proven. Resident from northern France and Spain to the Mediterranean and south-eastern Europe.

Large Ranunculus
page 322

Polymixis flavicincta ([D. & S.])

Local. S,EC   2252(9725)

Field characters FW 17-22mm. Quite a thickset moth, with broad, rough-textured, delicate pale greenish-grey forewing, usually with golden orange freckling, particularly along outermost cross-line and around kidney-mark. Some examples are whitish or darker greenish grey. Hindwing whitish or grey, with a distinct thick grey central line.

Similar species Black-banded is smaller and has narrower forewing with a blackish-grey central band, sometimes poorly defined. Hindwing without a thick central line, white in male, dark brownish grey in female. See also Feathered Ranunculus.

Flight season One generation. September-October. Comes to light and sugar, but only occasionally found feeding at flowers. Can be found by day at rest on walls, rocks and fences.

Life cycle Overwinters as an egg. Larva April-July. Feeds at night and hides low down by day. Pupates underground in a strong cocoon.

Larval foodplants The flowers and leaves of many wild and cultivated herbaceous plants, including several confirmed records from Dandelion in the wild; also Daisy, Michaelmas-daisies, Rosebay Willowherb, Red Valerian, cultivated mints, delphiniums and ragworts, and sometimes also on woody species such as currants and Plum.

Habitat Particularly gardens and disturbed ground in suburban areas, damp meadows, river valleys and coastal rough ground; sometimes heathland but more frequent in neutral and calcareous situations.

Status & distribution Resident. Local. Well distributed and fairly frequent in England south of a line from the Severn to the Wash, except in Hampshire and Kent, where very local. Recorded annually in small numbers from a scattering of sites in Lincolnshire and Yorkshire. Occasional records from Co. Durham and Northumberland. Occurs locally in south Wales, particularly the Gower Peninsula, Glamorgan. Rare or vagrant on Man, where recorded in 1974. Widespread and frequent in the Channel Islands.

Cameo
page 322

Polymixis gemmea (Treit.)

Suspected rare immigrant.   2252a(9734)

Field characters FW 16-20mm. Forewing olive brown with a greenish component, strongly variegated with white, showing little variation. Oval and kidney-mark large and white, with dark lines within, and a second oval below the first, equal in size to it.

Similar species White Spot is the only potential confusion species, but it is generally smaller, without a greenish tint and its white marks are less extensive, with a white central block rather than an extra oval.

Flight season One generation. July-September in mainland Europe.

Life cycle Overwinters as an egg. Larva April-June in

295

Larva of Black-banded.

mainland Europe. No evidence of breeding in Britain.
Larval foodplants Tufted Hair-grass, Timothy and probably other grasses.
Habitat Various open grassy situations.
Status & distribution Suspected rare immigrant. Recorded only once in the British Isles, at light in a garden at Cockpole Green, Berkshire, on 1 September 1979, at a time of much immigration activity. Widely distributed in central and northern Europe northwards to Finland, including northern France, but not a noted immigrant.

Black-banded   page 322
Polymixis xanthomista (Hb.)

ssp. *statices* (Gregs.)
Na. SW   2253(9721)

Field characters & Similar species FW 16-18mm. Likely to be confused with the larger and much more widespread Large Ranunculus, from which it is distinguished by more intense dark band crossing centre of forewing, passing between oval and kidney-mark, and by its smaller size and narrower forewing. Hindwing of male is white, that of female grey-brown. See also Feathered Ranunculus. Small Ranunculus is smaller, with a more chequered outer edge to forewing.
Flight season One generation. Mid August-September or early October. Comes to light, sometimes in fair numbers, and recorded at sugar.
Life cycle Overwinters as an egg. Larva March-early July, feeding by night. Pupates in a cocoon in a crevice or in soil under the foodplant.
Larval foodplants Mainly Thrift, eating the flowers and leaves. Also reported from the flowers of Sea Plantain, Sea Campion, Harebell and Kidney Vetch. Readily accepts sallow leaves in captivity.
Habitat Rocky coastlines, breeding usually on foodplants splashed at high tides, although adults are sometimes light-trapped further inland in scrubby areas.
Status & distribution Resident. Nationally Scarce A. A subspecies distinct from those in mainland Europe. Local on Scilly, the north and south coasts of Devon and Cornwall, and the Pembrokeshire coast including Skokholm Island, with a single known colony at

Craig-y-Gwbert, Cardiganshire. Recently discovered on Anglesey. Local on the south coast of Man. Also south-western Ireland, where recorded from Co. Cork.

2254 see below 2250a

Feathered Ranunculus   page 322
Polymixis lichenea lichenea (Hb.)
Local. S,C   2255(9724)

ssp. *scillonea* Rich.
Scilly

Field characters FW 15-18mm. Ssp. *lichenea* Forewing rather delicate greyish green, often dusted and freckled with whitish grey. Hindwing sometimes with a dark central line and with bold, black dashes around margin, and whitish in male, grey in female. Antennae feathered in male. Tends to be paler in calcareous areas in southern England, darker on rocky western coasts. Yellowish-marked forms occur in Devon and some from north Wales are strongly tinged with brown. Ssp. *scillonea* from Scilly has forewing darker green, often strongly freckled blackish, either with obscure markings apart from a distinct whitish kidney-mark, or with more extensive, strongly contrasting whitish markings.
Similar species Black-banded has a blackish-grey central band on forewing, sometimes weakly defined, often with orange freckling, antennae are not feathered in male and hindwing lacks a central cross-line, and has a narrow, more or less continuous dark line around outer edge.
Flight season One generation. Late August-early October. Comes to light, the male generally after midnight, and to sugar; feeds at Ivy flowers and overripe blackberries.
Life cycle Overwinters as a small larva, low down in the vegetation. Larva October-May. Feeds at night and is most frequently found in sheltered situations. Pupates underground in a strong cocoon.
Larval foodplants Various herbaceous plants, including Hound's-tongue, Sea Plantain, Thrift, Biting Stonecrop and Wild Cabbage.
Habitat Rocky and soft-rock coastal cliffs, sand-dunes, vegetated shingle, limestone and chalk slopes, sometimes slightly inland.
Status & distribution Ssp. *lichenea* Resident. Local. Mainly coastal. Well distributed along the south and west coasts of Britain from the Isle of Wight to south-west Scotland and Man. More local along the south and east coasts from Sussex to Yorkshire. Local inland in Kent, south Devon, north Wales, Cheshire, Staffordshire (not recently), Derbyshire (Dovedale and Matlock) and Warwickshire. Occurs locally around the coast of Ireland, recorded mainly from the east and south-west. Widespread and abundant in the Channel Islands. Ssp. *scillonea* is found in Scilly only.

Acronictinae Chestnuts, sallows and daggers

Chestnut

Centre-barred Sallow

Grey Dagger

Coronet

Satellite
page 323

Eupsilia transversa (Hufn.)

Common. T   2256(9596)

Field characters FW 17-20mm. Unmistakable. Diagnostic features are small kidney-mark on richly coloured forewing and the two small 'satellite' dots either side of it. These marks vary in colour from white or cream to orange or orange-brown. The satellites are sometimes a different colour to the kidney-mark and to one another and are occasionally hard to distinguish, but rarely absent. Forewing rich reddish brown, orange-brown or tawny brown, smooth with thick scalloped fringes, sometimes with a bluish or purplish sheen when fresh.

Similar species None.

Flight season One generation. Late September or October-late April. Comes regularly to light and sugar, and feeds at Ivy flowers and berries, including those of Guelder Rose.

Life cycle Overwinters as an adult, becoming active in mild weather. Larva April-June. Feeds at night and hides by day between spun leaves. Constructs an underground cocoon and pupates up to three months later.

Larval foodplants Omnivorous. At first the leaves of a variety of broadleaved trees and shrubs, including oaks, Blackthorn, Hawthorn, Hazel, Field Maple and elms. When larger, also preys on moth larvae of other species.

Habitat Broadleaved woodland, scrub, parkland, gardens, and moorland in the north.

Status & distribution Resident. Common. Widespread throughout England, Wales, Man and Ireland. More local in mainland Scotland north to Caithness, and in the Inner Hebrides and Orkney. Rare in the Channel Islands.

Orange Upperwing
page 323

Jodia croceago ([D. & S.])

RDB. S   2257(9598)

Field characters & Similar species FW 14-17mm. Pointed orange forewing contrasts with white hindwing. A dark band crosses centre of forewing and bends in a right-angle at base of the kidney-mark, beyond which is a row of blackish dots, and there are white dashes along leading edge, all of which distinguish Orange Upperwing from larger, more broadly-winged Orange Sallow. See also Blossom Underwing.

Flight season One generation. Early September-early November, flying again from February-mid May. Visits Ivy flowers, sallow catkins, sugar and light.

Life cycle Overwinters as an adult; occasional individuals have been beaten from the dry leaves retained by some oak trees over winter. Mating takes place in spring. Larva late April-mid July. Pupates in a slight cocoon just below the soil surface, the larva resting until August before pupation.

Larval foodplants The foliage of Pedunculate Oak and almost certainly Sessile Oak, which is the more frequent oak in the western sites. Young shoots in warm situations preferred, and coppiced oak provides such conditions.

Habitat Open oak woodland and scrub, oak coppice and oaks in hedgerows. In the mid 1970s, at Friday Street, about 30 wild larvae were found by day, mostly on oak foliage on branches virtually trailing the ground, from trunks about 30cm in diameter. All the oaks at this site keep their foliage in winter, not only the low saplings, and the site is a frost hollow.

Status & distribution Resident. Red Data Book species. This species is currently proving elusive, in spite of many searches. The last confirmed sighting was of six individuals between 15 October and 4 November 1994 in woodland between Cardigan and Aberystwyth, Cardiganshire, from which area singletons were also reported at Aber Magwyr on 4 May 1955, and near Llechryd in 1982. The best known localities were on the Surrey/West Sussex border, particularly at Friday Street/Abinger, where the moth was recorded in fair numbers up to 1977 but last seen as a singleton on 15 May 1983. Other recent reports are all of singletons, usually at light: in Cornwall on 4 May 1983; in Ashdown Forest, East Sussex, on 29 September 1984; in Pamber Forest, north Hampshire, on 15 April 1992 (unconfirmed); and at Bovey Tracey, near Newton Abbot, Devon, (where the moth had been seen annually from 1968 to the mid 1970s) on 8 October 1999 (unconfirmed). There are also unconfirmed single reports from Somerset and Shropshire since 1980. The historical distribution of the moth was always southern, but included Wiltshire, Oxfordshire and the West Midlands as well as the Isle of Wight.

297

Chestnut
page 323

Conistra vaccinii (L.)

Common. T
2258(9600)

Field characters FW 14-15mm. Outer edge of forewing rounded, readily distinguishing this from most other brown moths flying in autumn and early spring. Highly variable and can be very plain or strongly marbled. Ground-colour light or dark orange-brown, or a mixture of the two, or deep chestnut brown. Less frequent forms are heavily dusted and/or streaked with light brown or grey, or have grey- or black-edged cross-lines. More rarely, forewing is extensively blackish.

Similar species See Dark Chestnut. Red-headed Chestnut is larger, usually greyer and has two or three small black dots in kidney-mark.

Flight season One generation. Late September-May. Comes to light and sugar, and feeds at Ivy flowers, sallow catkins and overripe berries. In autumn usually found feeding, and more frequent at light in late winter and spring.

Life cycle Overwinters as an adult, becoming active in mild weather. Mating occurs in spring. Larva late April-June. Feeds at first on the leaves of trees, sometimes later on herbaceous plants, usually at night. Constructs a loose earthen underground cocoon, pupating up to two months later.

Larval foodplants Include oaks, elms, Blackthorn, Hawthorn, Downy Birch and docks.

Habitat Most frequent in broadleaved woodland; also in hedgerows, scrub and many gardens.

Status & distribution Resident. Common. Well distributed and frequent throughout mainland Britain, Man, Ireland, and the Inner Hebrides. Usually more numerous than the Dark Chestnut. Not recorded from Orkney or Shetland, or apparently Scilly. Widespread and frequent in the Channel Islands.

Dark Chestnut
page 323

Conistra ligula (Esp.)

Common. S,C,(N)
2259(9601)

Field characters FW 13-15mm. Forewing pointed or slightly hooked at tip; rather shiny, ground-colour usually dark chestnut brown, dark chocolate brown or blackish brown, less often paler chestnut brown. Sometimes there is a distinct light brown, grey or whitish-grey band near outer edge, and cross-lines of same colour.

Similar species Chestnut has generally paler, broader forewing with outer edge rounded and tip rather blunt. However, these characters vary slightly so care is needed.

Flight season One generation. October-February, occasionally March; male usually October-December or January. Comes to light in rather small numbers, also to sugar and Ivy flowers.

Life cycle Overwinters initially as an adult. Mates in December or January and eggs are laid in January or February. Larva April-June. Feeds at night, at first on leaves of trees, when larger on herbaceous plants.

Constructs a loose cocoon underground, pupating several weeks later.

Larval foodplants Include Blackthorn, Hawthorn, sallows, oaks, docks and Dandelion.

Habitat Woodland and more open country, including farmland. Also in some suburban gardens and urban areas, where sometimes more frequent than Chestnut.

Status & distribution Resident. Common. Well distributed and fairly frequent throughout most parts of England and Wales. Local in southern Scotland, with only scattered records further north, and only on the mainland. Rather local in Ireland, apparently mainly in the east, but recently found widely in Northern Ireland. Widespread and frequent in the Channel Islands.

Dotted Chestnut
page 323

Conistra rubiginea ([D. & S.])

Nb. SW,S
2260(9609)

Field characters FW 15-17mm. Heavy spotting and dotting over forewing distinguishes this moth from other chestnuts and sallows. Ground-colour varies from almost brick red to light chestnut orange. Hindwing brownish grey.

Similar species Chestnut has shorter forewing. Strongly patterned forms of Beaded Chestnut have a dark patch on leading edge of forewing near tip. In superficially similar Pale-lemon and Dusky-lemon Sallow hindwing is dirty white, not brownish grey.

Flight season One generation. October-November, flying again March-April. Comes to light before and after overwintering, and also to sugar and the flowers of Ivy, sallows and Blackthorn.

Life cycle Overwinters as an adult. Larva late April-mid June. Habits in the wild poorly known. One small larva was found by day near the terminal shoot of a low branch of Apple on 7 May 1983 in a garden in Lymington, Hampshire, where the adults occasionally visit a light-trap. Three freshly-emerged adults and two pupae were reported from within a hollow tree occupied by the ant *Lasius fuliginosus* at Thursley NNR, Surrey, in September 1997 and 1998, apparently unmolested by the ants. There has been speculation about interaction of this species with ants since the 19th century; the larva has protective hairs not present in others of the genus *Conistra*. The subject needs further study.

Larval foodplants Apple, including old fallen leaves. Also reared on Blackthorn, Plum and sallows. Accepts Dandelion and other low-growing plants. Possibly the larvae drop to the ground to feed when larger.

Habitat Woodland, wooded heathland and pastoral farmland with trees and thick hedgerows.

Status & distribution Resident. Nationally Scarce B. Central southern and south-west England and south Wales. Has expanded its distribution since 1990. Long established and most often recorded in the heathy parts of Surrey, West Sussex, Hampshire, south-east Dorset, Somerset, south Devon and southern Cornwall, but spread through

Gloucestershire during the 1990s, while also being noted in south Wiltshire, Oxfordshire and parts of Kent. Two were noted in Buckinghamshire in 2000, for the first time in 100 years. In 2002, recorded for the first time in Hertfordshire and Essex, in Glamorgan for the first time since before 1917, and in Warwickshire on 28 March 2003 for the first time since 1886.. Status in Ireland unclear. The only confirmed record is of one at Devil's Glen, Co. Wicklow, which could have crossed the Irish Sea.

Red-headed Chestnut
page 323

Conistra erythrocephala ([D. & S.])

Rare immigrant; transitory resident.   2261(9611)

Field characters FW 16mm. Diagnostic features of this moth, which initially looks like a slightly larger Chestnut, are two black dots within kidney-mark towards trailing edge and sometimes a third black dot just outside kidney-mark. Also, there is usually a dark wedge or dash on leading edge of forewing near tip. In many individuals, top of head is a lighter red than thorax. Ground-colour of forewing is often a uniform dull brown or grey, but may be reddish brown or purplish grey. Less frequently, forewing has patches of light and dark colours, usually reddish browns, lighter at the leading edge (f. *glabra* Hb.).

Similar species Forewing blunt, like Chestnut, not pointed like Dark Chestnut. Chestnut is smaller, with a single dark spot in kidney-mark, and head and thorax are the same colour.

Flight season One generation. Late September-November, reappearing March-April, although there is only one recent spring record in Britain. Has also been recorded in January on one occasion. Comes to sugar and light, and feeds at Ivy flowers.

Life cycle Overwinters as an adult. Eggs are laid in March. Larva April-June. In late June makes a cocoon underground, but does not pupate until August.

Larval foodplants Reportedly the young spring leaves of oaks, elms and Hornbeam initially, later feeding on the ground on plants such as Dandelion, plantains, bedstraws and violets.

Habitat Woodland and scrub.

Status & distribution Rare immigrant and transitory resident. Appears to have been established in woods in parts of East Sussex between 1847 and 1874, and again from 1913 to 1932. A series of records from near Canterbury, Kent, between 1866 and 1903 is clouded with uncertainty because dishonest insect traders were involved. Reported around a dozen times as a probable immigrant, mainly in south-east England but also at Portland, Dorset, on 3 November 1999. Recorded once on Jersey in 1996. Recorded from virtually every country in Europe and breeds just across the English Channel, in France.

Brick
page 323

Agrochola circellaris (Hufn.)

Common. T   2262(9566)

Field characters FW 14-19mm. Ground-colour of forewing is usually rather light reddish or brown, greyish- or pinkish-tinged, or darker. Trailing half of kidney-mark is blackish. Wavy dark grey or brown cross-lines and bands vary greatly in intensity; the outermost is broader, edged with reddish and light yellowish-brown lines. More boldly marked examples have dark veins. Hindwing grey with a broad brownish-white wedge along front edge.

Similar species Yellow-line Quaker is usually smaller with a narrow, almost straight outermost cross-line, notched near leading edge. See also Dusky-lemon Sallow and Pale-lemon Sallow.

Flight season One generation. September-early December in the south, from late August in the north. Comes regularly to light and sugar, and feeds at Ivy flowers, overripe berries and, in the north, at heather flowers.

Life cycle Overwinters as an egg, laid beside the buds of the foodplant. Larva April-June. Feeds inside a flower at first, later openly. Constructs an underground cocoon and pupates after about six weeks.

Larval foodplants Wych Elm, Aspen, poplars, sallows and Ash, at first on the flowers and maturing seeds, later on the leaves. Part-grown larvae have also been found and reared on the leaves of Midland Hawthorn under Aspen.

Habitat Broadleaved woodland, scrub, parkland and gardens.

Status & distribution Resident. Common. Well distributed and often frequent throughout most of England, Wales and Man. More local in Scotland, reaching the Hebrides and Orkney, and in Ireland. Widespread as occasional individuals in the Channel Islands.

Red-line Quaker
page 323

Agrochola lota (Cl.)

Common. T   2263(9569)

Field characters FW 15-18mm. Rather like a grey version of Yellow-line Quaker, but slightly larger with broader forewing. Outermost cross-line is reddish brown, edged yellowish, and is fairly straight apart from a small notch near leading edge. Variation is slight. Trailing half of kidney-mark is usually intensely black. Forewing usually slate grey, sometimes lighter. F. *rufa* Tutt is flushed with pinkish red and is most frequent in the north and west.

Similar species None.

Flight season One generation. September-mid November. Comes to light and sugar, and feeds at Ivy flowers and overripe berries.

Life cycle Overwinters as an egg, laid singly on the twigs of the foodplant. Larva April-early June. Feeds at first inside the flowers, later in a spun terminal shoot and finally hiding between spun leaves, coming out to feed at night. Constructs an underground cocoon and pupates about six weeks later.

Larval foodplants The catkins and leaves of large rough- and small smooth-leaved willows.

Habitat Woodland rides, scrub and hedgerows in open country; also river valleys, marshes, fens and

Larva of Southern Chestnut.

heathland. Often in suburban gardens.
Status & distribution Resident. Common. Well-distributed and frequent throughout most of Britain, Man and Ireland, including Scilly. More local in Scotland, and not recorded from Orkney or Shetland. Occasional in the Channel Islands.

Yellow-line Quaker

page 323

Agrochola macilenta (Hb.)

Common. T   2264(9571)

Field characters FW 14-16mm. This rather plainly marked moth is distinguished from other brownish autumn-flying species by the outermost cross-line, which is narrow and brown or reddish brown, edged yellowish and almost straight apart from a small notch near leading edge. Forewing usually light, rather milky brown or light yellowish brown, sometimes slightly reddish; less often distinctly yellowish or tinged with grey or pink. Trailing half of kidney-mark is often dark, sometimes intensely black, but in the frequent f. *obsoleta* Tutt, it matches ground-colour.
Similar species See Brick and Red-line Quaker.
Flight season One generation. September-November. Comes regularly to light and to sugar, and feeds at Ivy flowers and overripe berries.
Life cycle Overwinters as an egg, laid on branches of the foodplant. Larva April-June. Feeds at first in a spun terminal shoot, later on herbaceous plants. Constructs an underground cocoon and pupates several weeks later.
Larval foodplants Oaks, poplars, Beech, sallows, Hawthorn and herbaceous plants; also Heather on lowland heaths and in parts of northern Britain.
Habitat Broadleaved woodland, scrub, heathland, moorland and hedgerows in farmland. Often in suburban gardens.
Status & distribution Resident. Common. Well distributed and usually frequent throughout most of mainland Britain, Man and Ireland, reaching the north coast of Scotland and the Inner Hebrides. First recorded from Scilly in 1997. Occasional in the Channel Islands.

Southern Chestnut

page 323

Agrochola haematidea (Dup.)

RDB. S,SE   2264a(9572)

Field characters & Similar species FW 14-15mm.

Slightly smaller and with more pointed forewing than Beaded Chestnut. Distinguished from dark forms of the latter by deep reddish tint, and usually a dark, greyish or blackish shading along trailing edge of forewing, normally crossing wing beyond the weakly defined kidney-mark. Female usually smaller and darker than male.
Flight season One generation. End of September-mid November. The main flight time seems to begin about 30 minutes after dusk and to last only about 30-45 minutes. Both sexes come to light in numbers, sometimes dozens, and are also recorded at wine ropes.
Life cycle Overwinters as an egg, attached to the foodplant. Larva late April-early July. Feeds mainly by night and pupates underground about two months later.
Larval foodplants Mainly the flowers of Bell Heather. Has also been found on Cross-leaved Heath but not on Heather, even when the three grow intermingled. Does not thrive on Heather in captivity.
Habitat Extensive heathland on impoverished gravels and sand. In Sussex the foodplants are bushy, up to knee height in some places and not close cropped, and the site is rather dry. The New Forest sites are frequently dominated by Cross-leaved Heath, with hardly any Bell Heather, the ground is quite wet in places and the heaths grow thick and bushy, but not generally above calf height.
Status & distribution Resident, presumed to have been overlooked until recently. Red Data Book species. First discovered in Britain when five males came to light on 10 October 1990 at a heathland locality in West Sussex. Subsequent work has shown that the species is widely and well established on this site, but it has not been found elsewhere in Sussex. Many other heaths in southern and eastern England were searched following the original discovery. In October 1996 the moth was found in the New Forest, Hampshire, where it is now known to be quite widespread. It also occurs in the Herne area on the Hampshire/Dorset border. Recorded once from Jersey in 1997.

Flounced Chestnut

page 323

Agrochola helvola (L.)

Common. T   2265(9575)

Field characters FW 16-18mm. Diagnostic features are broad, pointed forewing, usually rather softly marked, with a wide dark reddish-brown or purplish-brown band at base and a slightly narrower one near outer margin. This pattern is constant, but intensity of markings varies, as does brown ground-colour, which may be tinged greenish or reddish. Hindwing smoky grey with pale fringe and a pale narrow band around outer margin, leading into a pale wedge along leading edge.
Similar species Beaded Chestnut has narrower forewing, kidney-mark and oval narrow, and hindwing entirely grey.

Flight season One generation. September-October. Comes to light and sugar, and feeds at Ivy flowers and particularly at overripe blackberries.

Life cycle Overwinters as an egg, laid on twigs or bark. Larva April-June, most active at night. Constructs an underground cocoon and pupates about eight weeks later.

Larval foodplants Broadleaved trees, including oaks, elms, birches and willows, and in the north Heather and Bilberry.

Habitat Mainly broadleaved woodland; also scrubby downland, heathland and moorland. Usually where Bramble is frequent, though possibly the moth is simply easiest to record where it is attracted to the overripe berries.

Status & distribution Resident. Common. Well distributed in many parts of southern Britain and sometimes abundant where it breeds; also wanders. More local in northern England, Man and mainland Scotland, reaching Caithness. Widespread but local in Ireland. Rare on Jersey.

Brown-spot Pinion   page 323
Agrochola litura (L.)
Common. T   2266(9586)

Field characters FW 14-17mm. Short diagonal dash near tip of forewing, marks along leading edge and partial cross-line near wing base, all intensely black, are diagnostic. Forewing reddish brown, less often dark purplish brown or greyish brown. In f. *rufa-pallida* Tutt, basal half, as far as obtusely angled narrow central band, is distinctly paler reddish brown, and in f. *borealis* Sp.-Schn. it is light greyish brown or whitish grey.

Similar species Beaded Chestnut lacks a short black cross-line near base of forewing, and marks along leading edge are dark brown, occasionally blackish but not intensely black and often weak. Kidney-mark is generally narrower, and oval smaller and often elongated.

Flight season One generation. Late August-October. Comes to light and sugar, and feeds at Ivy flowers and overripe blackberries.

Life cycle Overwinters as an egg. Larva April-early June, feeding at night. Constructs a strong underground cocoon and pupates about six weeks later.

Larval foodplants Herbaceous plants, including Meadowsweet, Common Sorrel and Bladder Campion. Also when larger on low-growing leaves of broadleaved trees such as oaks, sallows and hawthorns.

Habitat Broadleaved woodland, parkland, heathland, fens, scrub, hedgerows and gardens.

Status & distribution Resident. Common. Well distributed and often abundant throughout England, including Scilly, and in Wales. Local in southern and central Scotland, reaching Caithness and the Inner Hebrides. Rare on Man and in the Channel Islands, where it was recorded on Guernsey in 1964 and 1988.

Beaded Chestnut   page 323
Agrochola lychnidis ([D. & S.])
Common. S,C,(N)   2267(9565)

Field characters FW 15-18mm. Very variable, but not difficult to recognise. Forewing somewhat pointed, kidney-mark narrow. Oval generally dark, small and often elongated. Ground-colour most frequently chestnut brown or reddish brown, but can be brownish white, greyish yellow, light or dark greyish brown or blackish. There is usually a dark brown or blackish diagonal dash on leading edge near tip, and often several other weaker dark spots along leading edge, which itself is sometimes whitish (best seen from front). Some examples are very faintly marked, others have strong light or dark cross-lines or bands and pale veins.

Similar species See Brown-spot Pinion, Lunar Underwing, Southern Chestnut and Flounced Chestnut.

Flight season One generation. September-early November. Comes to light, sometimes in large numbers, and to sugar; feeds at Ivy flowers and over-ripe berries.

Life cycle Overwinters as an egg. Larva late March-June, feeding mainly at night. Forms a brittle cocoon underground, in which it pupates several weeks later.

Larval foodplants Various herbaceous plants, including buttercups, clovers and chickweeds. Also on grasses and when larger on broadleaved trees and shrubs, particularly Hawthorn.

Habitat Broadleaved woodland, scrub, hedgerows, grassland, heathland, gardens and many other situations.

Status & distribution Resident. Common. Frequent, but liable to large annual fluctuations in numbers. Well distributed from Scilly, throughout England and Wales to Northumberland, but few records from Cumbria. Local on Man. Rarely recorded in mainland Scotland. Widely distributed in Ireland. Widespread and frequent in the Channel Islands.

2268 see below 2313

Centre-barred Sallow   page 324
Atethmia centrago (Haw.)
Common. T   2269(9552)

Field characters FW 15-18mm. The broad, slightly hooked orange-yellow forewing of the normal form, with broad but incomplete pinkish-red or pinkish-brown central band. Kidney-mark and oval faintly defined or present in shape only. All markings vary somewhat in intensity, but general pattern and shape of cross-lines is constant. More uniformly orange, reddish and purplish forms are known, but these are rare in the wild.

Similar species None.

Flight season One generation. August-September. Comes regularly to light in small numbers, but rarely to sugar or flowers.

Life cycle Overwinters as an egg, laid in small batches on a twig or in a bark crevice. Larva early spring-early June. Lives at first inside an unopened bud, later hiding either in a crevice on the trunk or at the base of the tree, climbing very quickly just before dusk to feed during the night. Constructs an underground cocoon and pupates several weeks later.

Larval foodplants The unopened buds and flowers of mature Ash.

Habitat Broadleaved woodland and more open places with isolated Ash trees, including hedgerows, riverbanks and gardens.

Status & distribution Resident. Common. Well distributed throughout most of Great Britain, but more local in Scotland, reaching the Inner Hebrides, Inverness-shire and Morayshire. Widespread but somewhat local on Man and in Ireland. Local and occasional on Jersey, rare on Guernsey.

Lunar Underwing   page 324

Omphaloscelis lunosa (Haw.)

Common. T   2270(9591)

Field characters FW 14-17mm. The dark 'crescent moon' marking on hindwing is the diagnostic feature. Forewing quite pointed, but rounded at very tip. There is an outer row of small black spots, ending in a short diagonal black dash on leading edge, near tip. Very variable in ground-colour, from very light to very dark brownish grey, yellowish brown, reddish brown, dark brown or blackish. Veins are frequently pale, and some examples are distinctly banded. Hindwing usually whitish, with dark crescent in centre and a dark broken outer band. This can be reduced to two blotches, or be complete with extensive clouding.

Similar species Beaded Chestnut has uniformly grey hindwing, forewing is more sharply tipped and kidney-mark is generally narrower and more elbowed.

Flight season One generation. Late August-mid October. Comes frequently to light, and in smaller numbers to sugar, Ivy flowers and overripe blackberries. Can often be found at rest after dark, on grasses or fences.

Life cycle Overwinters as a small larva, low down among grass. Larva October-May. Feeds at night and hides low down by day.

Larval foodplants Grasses, including Annual Meadow-grass and Yorkshire-fog.

Habitat A range of grasslands, including damp pasture, parkland and downland, and gardens.

Status & distribution Resident. Common. Well distributed and frequent to abundant throughout England and Wales north to Yorkshire. More local further north in England and in southern Scotland, where mainly in the Borders and the central lowlands. Occurs northwards to Kincardineshire, Wester Ross and the Inner Hebrides. Widespread and abundant on Man, in Ireland and in the Channel Islands.

Orange Sallow   page 324

Xanthia citrago (L.)

Common. T   2271(9562)

Field characters FW 15-17mm. Broad, pointed, orange-yellow forewing is finely speckled with orange-red, less often with brown, and have veins the same colour. There are three complete orange-red or brown cross-lines, the central one thicker, fairly straight, diagonal and passing between oval and kidney-mark, touching the latter. This pattern is constant and diagnostic. There is slight variation in colour, with some examples dull orange, and in extent of speckling and intensity of dark cross-lines and veins.

Similar species See Orange Upperwing.

Flight season One generation. August-early October. Comes to light, wine ropes and sugar (especially if painted on lime leaves), and feeds at flowers, honeydew and overripe blackberries.

Life cycle Overwinters as an egg, laid on a twig of the foodplant. Larva late March-early June, feeding at night. At first hides by day between spun leaves and when larger at the base of the tree, climbing up at dusk to feed.

Larval foodplants Native and introduced limes. Also reported from Weeping Wych Elm.

Habitat Broadleaved woodland, parks, avenues and gardens.

Status & distribution Resident. Common. Widely distributed in mainland Great Britain, in many places where limes are numerous in rural and suburban situations, north to Easter Ross. One report from Man.

Barred Sallow   page 324

Xanthia aurago ([D. & S.])

Common. S,C,(N)   2272(9557)

Field characters FW 14-16mm. Forewing pinkish red or purplish brown, with a broad, wavy-edged central band, usually yellow or orange-yellow, and a small blotch at base and a thin wavy outer line both of same colour as central band. This pattern is very constant and diagnostic. Less frequently, central band is deep orange or reddish orange and ground-colour may be pale pinkish brown.

Similar species None.

Flight season One generation. September-early November. Comes to light and sugar, and feeds at Ivy flowers and overripe berries.

Life cycle Overwinters as an egg, laid on a twig of the foodplant. Larva April-early June, feeding mainly at night.

Larval foodplants Field Maple and Beech, at first on the buds and flowers, when larger on the leaves. Also recorded and reared on the leaves of Pedunculate Oak.

Habitat Broadleaved woodland, mature hedgerows, scrubby farmland, downland and some gardens. Usually on calcareous soils.

Status & distribution Resident. Common. Well

distributed, but seldom numerous, in south-east England and East Anglia. More local in south-west England, including Scilly, and in the Midlands, Wales and parts of northern England north to Cumbria. Scattered reports from Scotland. Local on Jersey and rare on Guernsey.

Pink-barred Sallow
page 324

Xanthia togata (Esp.)

Common. T   2273(9556)

Field characters FW 13-16mm. Deep red or pinkish-brown head and shoulders, contrasting with yellow thorax, readily distinguish this moth from other sallows. Slightly hooked forewing is bright orange-yellow, with deep pink or reddish-brown markings. 'Pink bar' is roughly diagonal band extending from leading edge to about halfway along trailing edge, its inner edge elbowed at kidney-mark, which is dark in trailing half. These features vary little; band is usually fairly solid, but sometimes consists of broken, scalloped lines.

Similar species Sallow has yellow or orange shoulders, and trailing half of kidney-mark is usually blackish.

Flight season One generation. September-October in the south, August-September in the north. Comes to light and sugar, and feeds at Ivy flowers and over-ripe blackberries.

Life cycle Overwinters as an egg, laid in short rows on twigs of the foodplant, close to a bud. Larva late March-early June. Feeds at first inside a catkin until it falls. Constructs an underground cocoon and pupates about six weeks later.

Larval foodplants The catkins of sallows and poplars; later on herbaceous plants such as docks.

Habitat Most frequent in broadleaved woodland, carr, marshes and fens but also occurs on heathland and other places where there are sallows and poplars, including gardens.

Status & distribution Resident. Common. Well distributed and frequent throughout most of Great Britain, Man and Ireland, including Orkney and Shetland. Local and occasional in the Channel Islands.

Sallow
page 324

Xanthia icteritia (Hufn.)

Common. T   2274(9559)

Field characters FW 14-17mm. Usually unmistak-able. Slightly hooked forewing is yellow or orange-yellow with reddish-brown, dark brown or pinkish markings and usually a black spot in trailing half of kidney-mark. There is huge variation in extent and intensity of markings. Most frequently, forewing is irregularly banded or extensively marbled. F. *flavescens* Esp. has almost pure yellow forewing with very faint orange cross-lines, a reddish-black spot in faint kidney-mark and a row of small dark spots near outer edge. F. *obsoleta* Tutt is similar but orange-yellow. Extreme examples of these forms, which occur regularly, are almost unmarked.

Similar species See Pink-barred Sallow, Dusky-lemon Sallow and Angle-striped Sallow.

Flight season One generation. September-October in the south, August-September in the north. Comes to light and sugar, and feeds at Ivy flowers and over-ripe blackberries.

Life cycle Overwinters as an egg, laid near buds of the foodplant. Larva late March-early June. Feeds inside catkins, at first on a twig and then on the ground after the catkins fall. Constructs an underground cocoon, pupating about six weeks later.

Larval foodplants The catkins of sallows and poplars; later on herbaceous plants such as docks.

Habitat Most frequent in broadleaved woodland, carr, marshes and fens, but also on heathland and moorland and in other places where there are sallows and poplars, including gardens.

Status & distribution Resident. Common. Well distributed and frequent throughout most of Great Britain, Man and Ireland, including Orkney and Shetland. Local and occasional in the Channel Islands.

Dusky-lemon Sallow
page 324

Xanthia gilvago ([D. & S.])

Local. S,C,(N)   2275(9560)

Field characters FW 15-18mm. Forewing not hooked, dull orange-yellow or orange-brown, vari-ably and irregularly banded, marked and clouded with blackish grey or less often dark brown. Dark markings may be reduced to narrow, broken cross-lines, while at the other extreme most of wing is clouded. Hindwing whitish, sometimes darker near trailing corner.

Similar species Variegated forms of Pale-lemon Sallow have slightly hooked forewing, as do darker forms of Sallow, which is also brighter orange-yellow. Some forms are superficially similar to Brick, which has grey hindwing with a brownish-white wedge at leading edge and several fine, unbroken cross-lines on forewing, the outer edged with reddish.

Flight season One generation. Late August-early October. Comes to light and sugar, and feeds at Ivy flowers and overripe blackberries.

Life cycle Overwinters as an egg, laid on the twigs of the foodplant. Larva April-early June. Feeds at first inside a flower bud and later more openly.

Larval foodplants The buds, ripening seeds and leaves usually of Wych Elm, but sometimes of English Elm.

Habitat Broadleaved woodland, hedgerows and parkland with elms: needs elms large enough to flower in abundance.

Status & distribution Resident. Local. Thinly distrib-uted throughout England, Wales and southern Scotland, along the east coast to Aberdeenshire. Local and rare on Man, where it was first recorded in 1989. Recorded once on Jersey, in 1962, and once on Guernsey in 1984.

303

304

Larva of Scarce Merveille du Jour.

Pale-lemon Sallow page 324

Xanthia ocellaris (Borkh.)
Na. SE   2276(9561)

Field characters FW 18-19mm. Forewing slightly hooked, and rather uniformly coloured in most frequent form, with clearly defined kidney-mark and outer cross-line. Less frequent f. *gilvescens* Worsley-Wood is more variegated. Hindwing whitish, darker near trailing corner.
Similar species Dusky-lemon Sallow and Brick have blunter forewing tip. Outermost cross-line of Brick is heavily edged with reddish and hindwing is grey with brownish wedges rather than whitish.
Flight season One generation. September-October. Attracted to overripe blackberries and other fruit, to sugar and also to the flowers of grasses and rushes. Comes to light in very small numbers, even when larvae are frequent nearby.
Life cycle Overwinters as an egg on a twig of the foodplant. Larva April-early June. Feeds mainly at night, and rests underground for about six weeks before pupating there.
Larval foodplants The catkins of Black-poplar and cultivars such as Lombardy-poplar, the larvae falling with the catkins to the ground and feeding on them until they disintegrate. Able to eat poplar leaves and also the foliage of docks and other low-growing vegetation below the trees.
Habitat Many low-lying open situations where the foodplants grow naturally or have been planted, including long-established commons, riversides and flood-plains, roadsides, windbreaks, parks and sports grounds.
Status & distribution Resident and suspected immigrant. Nationally Scarce A. Not found in Britain until 1893, in north-east Surrey, and seems unlikely to have been overlooked. In Surrey it occurs especially along the banks of the Thames, including suburban areas, and extends into north Kent, but is very local. Also locally distributed throughout East Anglia, with a concentration of records from the Breckland of Norfolk and Suffolk. Local in Essex, Cambridgeshire and Huntingdonshire and extending west into Bedfordshire, Buckinghamshire and Berkshire. Occasionally turns up outside this area, as at Wanlip Gravel Pit, Leicestershire, in 1987 and Melbury Down, Dorset, in 1994.

Scarce Merveille du Jour page 324

Moma alpium (Osb.)
RDB. S   2277(8772)

Field characters FW 17-20mm. Only large pale green, black and white noctuid flying in summer. Black markings on lichen-green forewing are largest near base and outer edge.
Similar species See Merveille du Jour (which flies in September-October).
Flight season One generation. Early June-mid July. Occasionally found at rest on oak trunks by day and seen feeding on aphid honeydew at night. Comes regularly to light and sugar, but not usually in large numbers.
Life cycle Overwinters as a pupa, in a cocoon on the ground among plant debris. Larva July-early September, occasionally beaten from foliage of large trees.
Larval foodplants Pedunculate Oak and probably also Sessile Oak. A single larva was beaten from coppiced Sweet Chestnut in West Sussex in 2002.
Habitat Oak woodland and scrubby oak. Usually but not always in large woods with mature oaks and those woodlands managed for tall trees. May occur in smaller copses in well-wooded areas.
Status & distribution Resident. Red Data Book species. Extremely southern in distribution, the majority of the localities being within 40km of the south coast of England. In woodlands in south Wiltshire, (e.g. Langley Wood, Redlynch, Whiteparish), Hampshire (including the New Forest and woods to the north and east), West Sussex (Emsworth and near Arundel), East Sussex (Beckley Wood) and Kent (Hamstreet NNR and the Orlestone Forest complex). There is a population in a single wood in south-east Cornwall, and another in the Great Torrington area of north Devon. Last seen in Essex in 1936 in a wood at Rettendon, which was clearfelled and replanted soon after.

Poplar Grey page 324

Acronicta megacephala ([D. & S.])
Common. T   2278(8780)

Field characters FW 17-20mm. Forewing quite broad, especially in female, and rather rounded. Ground-colour greyish white, heavily and coarsely dusted with black or blackish grey. A small area beyond kidney-mark is often pale. F. *nigra* Shaw is almost entirely blackish, often with the oval obliterated. Hindwing whitish in male, grey or greyish white in female, sometimes with grey banding towards outer edge; veins blackish grey, more strongly so in female.
Similar species Knot Grass has greyish-brown hindwing and a clear white spot near forewing trailing edge, two-thirds along from base; also it is usually smaller and more sharply marked. The dark f. *infuscata* Haw. of Sycamore lacks a lighter patch beyond kidney-mark.
Flight season Mainly one generation. Late May-early August. There is often a gap of two or three

weeks between the early and late individuals, suggesting a partial second generation, and reared wild-caught larvae sometimes produce adults in late summer. Comes regularly to light, sugar and flowers and is sometimes found at rest by day on tree trunks or fences.

Life cycle Overwinters as a pupa, in a flimsy cocoon under loose bark or in a suitable crevice. Larva July–September. Rests on a leaf in the shape of a question mark.

Larval foodplants Black-poplar, Aspen, White Poplar, Lombardy-poplar and other poplars; less frequently willows.

Habitat Woodland, fens, parkland, gardens and many other places where the foodplants occur.

Status & distribution Resident. Common. Well distributed and fairly frequent in England, Wales and the Channel Islands. Widely distributed but local in mainland Scotland, Skye and Ireland. Local and rare on Man.

Sycamore   page 324
Acronicta aceris (L.)
Local. S,EC   2279(8778)

Field characters FW 18-22mm. A pale, deeply S-curved line of pale blocks across outer part of forewing is obvious, even on dark individuals. Forewing broad, rather narrower in male; usually cold light grey, finely dusted with dark grey and slightly freckled with brownish grey, especially along outer edge of S-shaped cross-line. There is usually a long, wavy, branched black streak at forewing base. Hindwing whitish in male, greyish white in female, with dark veins. F. *infuscata* Haw. is darker grey. First found in London in late 19th century and rare until the 1950s, this form (and forms approaching it) now predominates in the London area and has occurred elsewhere.

Similar species See Poplar Grey, Sweet Gale Moth.

Flight season One generation. Mid June–early August. Comes to light, sugar and flowers and is sometimes found at rest by day on tree trunks or fences.

Life cycle Overwinters, sometimes more than once, as a pupa in a double-layered cocoon in a bark crevice or among moss or leaf litter. Larva July–September.

Larval foodplants Sycamore, Field Maple, cultivated maples and Horse-chestnut; also reported from oaks, birches, Plum, roses, London Plane and Laburnum.

Habitat Most frequent in urban areas, in parkland and gardens, where the non-native Horse-chestnut is often apparently the main foodplant. Also in woodland and scrub. Breeds on small saplings as well as mature trees.

Status & distribution Resident. Local. Well distributed and fairly frequent in south-east and central southern England and East Anglia. Local in south-west England, south-west Wales, the east Midlands, south Yorkshire and Cheshire. Widespread and frequent on Jersey, rare on Guernsey, Alderney and Sark.

Larva of Sycamore.

Miller   page 324
Acronicta leporina (L.)
Common. T   2280(8779)

Field characters FW 16-21mm. Fine, rather sparse black markings and quite pointed, grey-dusted or white forewing diagnostic. Most noticeable and consistent feature is a black crescent which forms the inner edge of faint kidney-mark. There is a short black streak at base, an arrowhead mark nearby, and outer cross-line is thickened towards trailing edge, sometimes forming a short dagger mark. Female is generally larger, with broader forewing. The whitish-grey f. *grisea* Cochrane is most frequent in most of Great Britain and Ireland. A pure white form predominates in parts of Scotland, and the dark grey f. *melanocephala* Mansbridge occurs regularly in the Midlands and northern England and occasionally elsewhere.

Similar species None.

Flight season One generation. Late May–early August. Comes to light, sugar and flowers.

Life cycle Overwinters as a pupa, burrowing into rotten wood. Larva July–early October.

Larval foodplants Usually Downy and Silver Birch and Alder, but also Grey Willow, and recorded on Aspen, Black-poplar and oaks.

Habitat Broadleaved woodland, heathland, moorland, fens and, increasingly, urban areas, especially where the main foodplants have been planted.

Status & distribution Resident. Well distributed and fairly frequent in England and Wales. Local in mainland Scotland, the Inner Hebrides, Man and Ireland. Rare on Jersey and Guernsey.

Alder Moth   page 324
Acronicta alni (L.)
Local. S,C   2281(8774)

Field characters FW 16-19mm. Uniquely marked. Blackish clouding on forewing, covering all or most of trailing half and extending to leading edge through and around kidney-mark, is diagnostic. There is a thick black bar at base and a long, thick black dagger mark from trailing corner. Only minor variation in markings, but blackish clouding varies somewhat in extent, sometimes covering most of wing. In f. *suffusa* Tutt, ground-colour is darker brownish grey. This form comprises up to half the population in

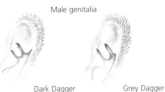
Male genitalia

Dark Dagger   Grey Dagger

306

Larva of Alder Moth.

the London area and occurs in other urban centres.
Similar species None.
Flight season One generation. May-June. Comes to light and occasionally to sugar.
Life cycle Overwinters as a pupa, burrowing into rotten wood. Larva June-August. Rests on the upper side of a leaf.
Larval foodplants A range of broadleaved trees, including Downy Birch, Alder, Goat Willow, oaks and elms.
Habitat Broadleaved woodland and scrub, often on poorly drained ground.
Status & distribution Resident. Local. Rather thinly distributed, but often locally frequent at light, throughout England and Wales, and recorded from south-west Scotland and Man. Widely distributed but local in Ireland.

2282 see Appendix

Larva of Dark Dagger.

Larva of Grey Dagger.

Dark Dagger   page 325
Acronicta tridens ([D. & S.],)
Common. S,C,(N)   2283(8776)

Field characters & Similar species FW 17-20mm. See Grey Dagger, which is virtually identical. The two are clearly distinguished from all other species by the clear black markings on grey forewing, including a long dagger mark near trailing corner and a long, straight, branched streak at base, and black edging between pale kidney-mark and oval. This pattern varies only in minor detail. Forewing sometimes slightly tinged brownish, or pink (f. *rosea* Tutt). See Grey Dagger for further identification details.
Flight season Mainly one generation. Mid May-July. Sometimes individuals of a partial second generation occur in September-October. Comes regularly to light, less often to sugar and flowers.
Life cycle Overwinters as a pupa, in a cocoon spun under loose bark or in a crevice in wood. Larva July-October.
Larval foodplants A range of broadleaved trees and shrubs, including Hawthorn, Blackthorn, roses and cotoneasters, Goat Willow and oaks, with a preference for species of the rose family.
Habitat A wide range of habitats, particularly woodland and fens, but also suburban gardens.
Status & distribution Resident. Common. Well distributed in most of southern Britain. Local in northern England and very local in mainland Scotland. Widespread and frequent in the Channel Islands.

Grey Dagger   page 325
Acronicta psi (L.)
Common. T   2284(8777)

Field characters & Similar species FW 17-20mm. Virtually identical in colour and wing pattern to Dark Dagger and impossible to distinguish with certainty in the field. There are trends within each species, but some examples do not conform, and inspection of the genitalia is necessary for confirmation. With male this is quick and easy (see illustration) and, with practice, it is possible to select a few likely males of each species in order to confirm which species are present at a site without man-handling or killing large numbers for examination. Dark, protruding structure near base of the claspers has three sharp teeth in Dark Dagger, whereas Grey Dagger has only two, shaped to form a pincer. Female Grey Dagger has a simply-shaped sperm receptacle visible on dissection, while Dark Dagger has an appendix where the duct enters the receptacle (for techniques, see Cribb *et al.* 1972). Dark Dagger tends to have slightly shinier forewing, which in male is often comparatively narrow, and male hindwing usually pure white, without dark veins or dusting. Male Dark Dagger tends to have a narrower thorax than Grey Dagger. Both the very lightest and darkest individuals tend to be Grey Dagger, especially warm, dark grey examples (f. *suffusa* Tutt).

Flight season Mainly one generation. Mid May-August, sometimes with individuals of a partial second generation in September-October. Comes regularly to light, sugar and flowers.

Life cycle Overwinters as a pupa in a silk cocoon under loose bark, in a crevice or in rotten wood. Larva late July-early October when one generation, July-early September and September-early November when two generations.

Larval foodplants A wide range of broadleaved trees and shrubs, including Blackthorn, hawthorns, Apple, birches, limes, elms and Rowan.

Habitat Most habitats, particularly woodland, hedgerows and gardens, and scrub in many situations, including heathland, calcareous grassland and fens.

Status & distribution Resident. Well distributed and frequent throughout England (including Scilly), Wales, Man, Ireland and the Channel Islands. Widely distributed in the lowlands of mainland Scotland, and in the Hebrides.

Marsh Dagger page 325

Acronicta strigosa ([D. & S.])
Rare immigrant; former resident.   2285(8781)

Field characters FW 13-15mm. Three heavy black bars along trailing edge of forewings, where they meet at rest, almost run into a single line and are diagnostic of this small dagger moth.

Similar species None.

Flight season One generation. Late June-early July. Comes to sugar and light. Occasionally found on tree trunks by day.

Life cycle Overwinters as a pupa, sometimes in rotten wood. Larva August-early September.

Larval foodplants Hawthorns and occasionally Blackthorn.

Habitat Mature hawthorn scrub and overgrown hedgerows in damp locations, including river valleys, the edges of fens and marshes, rough pasture and field margins.

Status & distribution Former resident, now probably extinct. A male suspected immigrant was captured at light at Rye Harbour nature reserve, East Sussex, on 22 July 1996. Formerly recorded locally in Huntingdonshire and Cambridgeshire, but last seen there in 1933. Light-traps have been operated frequently in recent decades in many of the places in which the moth was previously found, including Monk's Wood, Wicken Fen, Fulbourn, Mepal and Chatteris, with negative results. There were also scattered colonies in the Severn Valley near Gloucester and Tewkesbury, where the last records are two seen in July 1905. Two were reported at Castlemorton, Worcestershire, in July 1904.

Light Knot Grass page 325

Acronicta menyanthidis menyanthidis (Esp.)
Local. N,W,EC   2286(8782)
ssp. *scotica* Tutt
Local. N

Field characters FW 16-20mm. Ssp. *menyanthidis* Quite thickset, with rather broad, rounded, grey forewing with blackish markings, the most conspicuous of which are kidney-mark and cross-lines, the outermost being pale-edged. Oval very small. Some examples are diffusely banded and clouded with dark grey, and in f. *suffusa* Tutt, which occurs in northern England and very locally in Norfolk, the ground-colour is blackish grey.

Ssp. *scotica* Generally larger than ssp. *menyanthidis*, and generally with more strongly-marked, paler forewing and more brownish hindwing.

Similar species See Scarce Dagger.

Flight season One generation. Late May-mid July. Comes to light, sugar and flowers and rests by day on rocks and posts.

Life cycle Overwinters as a pupa, in a cocoon among leaf litter. Larva June-September.

Larval foodplants Mainly low-growing woody plants, including Bog-myrtle, Heather, Bilberry and sallows; also Bogbean.

Habitat Moorland, bogs and heathland, especially the damper parts.

Status & distribution Resident. Local. Ssp. *menyanthidis* is well distributed in England from Staffordshire and north Lincolnshire northwards, and in north Wales and south-east Scotland. Local in south Wales and Ireland, and very local in Norfolk and on Man. Ssp. *scotica* is well distributed in mainland Scotland (except the south-east) and the Hebrides.

Scarce Dagger page 325

Acronicta auricoma ([D. & S.])
Rare immigrant; former resident.   2287(8783)

Field characters & Similar species FW 16-17mm. Similar to darker forms of Light Knot Grass, but slimmer and distinguished by larger oval on forewing, with a black central spot. Knot Grass lacks outer black dagger mark and has a conspicuous white spot two-thirds of the way along trailing edge of forewing.

Flight season Two generations. May-early June and mid July-August. Comes to sugar and light and rests by day on tree trunks.

Life cycle Overwinters as a pupa, in a cocoon on the foodplant or in leaf litter. Larva June-early July and September.

Larval foodplants Oaks; also reported from wild Raspberry. Accepts birches, Bramble and Bilberry in captivity.

Habitat Lowland oak woodland. In coastal habitats as suspected immigrant.

Status & distribution Rare immigrant and former resident, now presumed extinct. Well established in

307

Larva of Knot Grass.

308

parts of Surrey, East Sussex and east Kent from the early 19th century but in decline by the 1870s. Continued to be found occasionally, including larvae, until the First World War. Since then recorded as single adults, presumed immigrants, at light on about 15 occasions from the 1930s to the present, scattered widely over Hampshire, the Isle of Wight, Sussex and Kent, including coastal sites such as Folkestone and Dungeness, Kent. One was recorded on Guernsey in 1995. Widely distributed and locally frequent in western Europe.

Sweet Gale Moth   page 325
Acronicta euphorbiae ([D. & S.])
ssp. *myricae* Guen.
Na. N   2288(8784)

Field characters & Similar species FW 14-16mm. Lacks strong black markings at base of forewing present in most daggers, and also lacks white spot near trailing corner of forewing which is so conspicuous in Knot Grass. Forewing markings are most like those of Sycamore, which is much larger. Hindwing white in male, grey in female.
Flight season Mainly one generation. Late April-early June, but often not until late May. In Ireland a second generation occurs in July-August. Rests by day on rocks, stone walls and posts. Visits flowers after dusk and comes to sugar and light.
Life cycle Overwinters as a pupa in a cocoon on the ground, attached to rocks or in crevices in dry-stone walls; reported to require humid conditions. Larva July-September, with a second generation September-October in Ireland.
Larval foodplants & Habitat In moorland habitats on Bog-myrtle, Heather and probably other moorland plants. In the Inner Hebrides larvae have been found on birches and sallows, including Creeping Willow and Eared Willow. Has also been found on roadsides in farmland near the coast in east Aberdeenshire, away from Heather, feeding on Ribwort Plantain. Sea Plantain, Common Sorrel, Meadowsweet, Bramble and Common Ragwort are other reported foodplants. Sea Campion is a confirmed foodplant in Ireland.
Status & distribution Resident. Nationally Scarce A. The majority of records are from the central Highlands of Scotland, but those from eastern

Aberdeenshire, Sutherland, Argyll, Coll and Galloway indicate that the species is much more widespread. Reported from Shetland, but not in recent decades, and not from Orkney. Occurs on the west coast of Ireland, widely in the Burren, Co. Clare, locally to the south-east in Cos. Kerry and Cork, further north in Cos. Galway and Sligo, and has been reported from Co. Antrim.

Knot Grass   page 325
Acronicta rumicis (L.)
Common. T   2289(8787)

Field characters FW 16-20mm. A rather small but distinct chalky-white spot (sometimes two) near trailing edge of forewing, about two-thirds along from base, and usually a distinct but broken white cross-line near outer margin are the diagnostic features of this dagger. Forewing grey with a grainy texture, irregularly dusted and indistinctly marked with blackish. Amount of blackish clouding variable. In f. *salicis* Curt. ground-colour is sooty. Hindwing greyish brown.
Similar species Scarce Dagger has a dagger mark near trailing corner and a distinct basal streak, and although a whitish spot may be present near trailing edge it is no brighter than the other markings. See also Poplar Grey, Sweet Gale Moth and Coronet.
Flight season Two generations in southern Britain, May-June and August-early September. One generation from the Midlands northwards, May-July. Comes to light, sugar and flowers.
Life cycle Overwinters as a pupa, in a cocoon among leaf litter. Larva June-September, and also September-October in the south.
Larval foodplants Herbaceous and woody plants, including Broad-leaved Dock, Common Sorrel, plantains, Water Mint, Bramble, Hop, Hawthorn, Burnet Rose and sallows.
Habitat Most open habitats, including gardens, grassland, heathland, wetlands and some woodlands.
Status & distribution. Resident. Common. Well distributed and fairly frequent throughout most of England, Man, Ireland and the Channel Islands. Less frequent and mainly lowland in Scotland. Not recorded from Orkney or Shetland.

Reed Dagger   page 325
Simyra albovenosa (Goeze)
Nb. SE   2290(8793)

Field characters & Similar species FW 16-20mm. Easily mistaken for a wainscot such as Southern, Striped or Large Wainscot, but pure white hindwing distinguishes Reed Dagger from all wainscots with similar forewing appearance.
Flight season Two generations, though the second may be only partial. May-July and August-early September. Hides by day among reed litter. Flies from dusk and comes to light, sometimes in large numbers, but does not seem to feed.

Life cycle Overwinters as a pupa, in a cocoon among living reed foliage or debris on or near the ground. Larva June-early August and late August-September, feeding mainly by night.

Larval foodplants Mainly Common Reed. Occasional wild larvae have been observed feeding on Yellow Loosestrife, Water Dock, Greater Tussock-sedge and Great Fen-sedge, and in each case have been reared to adult on these. Also reported from Grey Willow, Whorl-grass and Tufted-sedge.

Habitat Among reeds in various wetland habitats near the coast, inland marshes, and fens in the Breckland area, and in both neglected and commer-cially harvested reed-beds.

Status & distribution Resident and suspected immi-grant. Nationally Scarce B. Largely confined to East Anglia, particularly the Norfolk Broads and the Southwold/Walberswick area of the Suffolk coast. Breeding populations also known from Howlands Marsh and other marshes near the coast in Essex, where it seems to be increasing and spreading southwards, the north Kent marshes and the Dungeness area, Kent. Probably survives at Freshwater, Isle of Wight, where one was recorded in 1992. Probably now lost from the Huntingdonshire fens. Occasional individuals have been reported on or near the coast in Sussex, Hampshire, Dorset and south Devon. There are records from Spurn, Yorkshire, where the moth was first recorded on 3 August 1970, with eight more up to the most recent on 19 July 1996, all now consid-ered to have been immigrants.

Coronet   page 325
Craniophora ligustri ([D. & S.])
Local. T   2291(8789)

Field characters FW 17-19mm. Quite distinct from other members of the group, with smooth texture and (normally) fine white marbling on forewing and thorax, forming a patch beyond kidney-mark said to resemble a crown. Ground-colour of forewing appears blackish, but on closer inspection is found to be a subtle pattern of brownish purple and dark olive green, with numerous black cross-lines and blotches. Sometimes black is more extensive. In f. *coronula* Haw. white markings are reduced or completely absent, but crown is usually still apparent in purplish green. This form is most frequent in the Midlands but has been recorded from the London area and more widely.

Similar species Dark forms of Poplar Grey and Knot-grass usually have longer, more pointed forewing, with a rough texture.

Flight season One generation. June-July. Comes regularly to light and sugar.

Life cycle Overwinters as a pupa, in a strong cocoon, usually under moss on a tree trunk. Larva July-September.

Larval foodplants Ash and Wild Privet. Also recorded from Alder and Hazel.

Habitat Woodland, scrub on calcareous grassland,

and fens, mountain streamsides and open hillsides with well-spaced Ash trees.

Status & distribution Resident. Local. Quite well distributed and locally frequent in southern and south-west England and Wales. Local in East Anglia, the Midlands, northern England, and southern, central and western Scotland, north to Ross and Cromarty. Very local in Ireland, mainly in the west. Widespread and frequent on Jersey, occasional on Guernsey.

Bryophilinae

Tree-lichen Beauty   Marbled Beauty

Tree-lichen Beauty   page 325
Cryphia algae (Fabr.)
Immigrant.   2292(8801)

Field characters FW 10-13mm. Variable. Most frequent form is easily recognised by bright lichen-green band near base of forewing, sometimes extending to base, rest of forewing being generally dark and not marbled. F. *calligrapha* Borkh. has the green replaced by yellow, others are brownish. Area between two main cross-lines and near trailing edge is generally darker than rest of wing. Kidney-mark and oval indistinct.

Similar species Small forms of Marbled Green usually have more chequered forewing, with dark spots along leading edge, and paler hindwing.

Flight season One generation in mainland Europe. July-September, but the majority of British records have been during August. Comes to light.

Life cycle Overwinters as a larva among lichens. Larva September-June in mainland Europe.

Larval foodplants Lichens on trees and probably other substrates. No confirmation of breeding in the British Isles.

Habitat Most British records are from coastal situa-tions, but also recorded inland in gardens.

Status & distribution Immigrant. Until 1991 only three reported, two from Disley, Cheshire, in July 1859, and one from Hastings, East Sussex, in 1873. In 1991 singletons were captured in Hampshire and West Sussex, since when over 40 have been recorded, spread over a number of years and all from south-east England, mainly Kent but west to Dorset and north to Hertfordshire. In 2002 five were recorded in one garden in Kent, suggesting the possibility of local breeding. First recorded on Guernsey in 1990 and noted in subsequent years. Recorded from Jersey in 1995. Widespread and fairly frequent in western Europe.

Marbled Beauty page 325
Cryphia domestica (Hufn.)
Common. T 2293(8816)

Field characters & Similar species FW 12-14mm. Diagnostic feature of the delicately marbled, rather narrow and somewhat tapered forewing is a cross-line before the oval, which extends fully from leading to trailing edge, unlike that of Marbled Green. Outer edge of forewing is curved and strongly angled and tips are rounded. Ground-colour is greyish or greenish white, with pastel green, greyish-green or dull orange marbling, or less often extensively green (f. *suffusa* Tutt). Most examples are well marked, but sometimes marbling is reduced. See also Marbled Green.

Flight season One generation. July-August. Comes frequently to light and also to sugar and flowers, and often rests by day on walls.

Life cycle Overwinters as a small larva, among the foodplant. Larva September-May or early June. Feeds at night and hides in a silken retreat, in which it pupates.

Larval foodplants Lichens growing on rocks, walls, roofs and trees.

Habitat Often associated with old buildings and frequent in urban areas, but also in open country, orchards, calcareous woodland and coastal cliffs, particularly where there are stone walls, rocks, gravestones, old hedge-banks or lichen-covered trees.

Status & distribution Resident. Common. Well distributed and often frequent throughout southern Britain, north to southern Scotland. Very local and mainly coastal in eastern mainland Scotland north to Morayshire. Widespread and frequent on Man, in the east of Ireland and in the Channel Islands.

Marbled Grey page 325
Cryphia raptricula ([D. & S.])
Immigrant. 2294(8810)

Field characters FW 12-14mm. Longer, narrower forewing than in closely-related species, usually dark grey. Sometimes pale grey with well-defined markings, but immigrants tend to have dark charcoal forewing. A paler grey crescent-like outer cross-line is usually apparent on forewing, sometimes enclosing a light grey patch. Hindwing dirty brownish white.

Similar species None.

Flight season One generation in northern Europe. July-August, occasionally late June. Comes to light.

Life cycle Overwinters as a larva among lichens. Larva September-June in northern Europe. Reported to bask in sunshine, but not yet found in Britain.

Larval foodplants Lichens such as *Sticta pulmonacea* on walls, rocks and tree trunks.

Habitat Open habitats.

Status & distribution Immigrant. First recorded in the British Isles on 12 August 1953 at Arundel, Sussex. About 15 individuals have been recorded subsequently, mostly since 1990 and mainly from coastal situations in south-east Kent, but also from Hampshire. Apparently expanding its distribution in mainland Europe and now fairly frequent in Belgium, the Netherlands and parts of France as well as the more distant European countries.

Marbled Green page 325
Cryphia muralis muralis (Forst.)
Local. S 2295(8818)

Field characters & Similar species FW 12-15mm. Distinguished from Marbled Beauty by cross-line before oval on forewing, which fails to reach trailing edge. Instead, basal cross-line curves around to almost meet it, sometimes forming a pale blotch shaped like a clover leaf. Usually larger than Marbled Beauty, with broader forewing; outer edge straighter and more nearly at a right-angle to trailing edge. Ground-colour greenish white, pastel green, bright lichen-green or olive green. Black cross-lines vary from strong to faint. See also Tree-lichen Beauty.

F. *impar* Warr. has forewing greyish brown or greyish green, coarsely and irregularly dusted and blotched blackish. Markings obscure, cross-lines rather faint, the second often with an incomplete dark band or block on its outer edge.

F. *westroppi* Cock. & Will. is smaller on average, with rather indistinct markings and extremely variable. A very dark grey-brown form, f. *castanea* Cock. & Will., occurs occasionally.

Flight season One generation. July-August. Comes to light, sugar and flowers and rests by day on walls, roofs and rocks.

Life cycle Overwinters as a small larva among the foodplant. Larva September-early June. Feeds at night and hides in a silken retreat, in which it pupates.

Larval foodplants Lichens such as *Xanthoria* and *Caloplaca* species growing on walls, rocks and occasionally trees.

Habitat Rocky places by the sea; also inland in towns and open country on calcareous soils, especially where there are stone walls.

Status & distribution Ssp. *muralis* Resident. Local. Well distributed and fairly frequent along the south and south-western coasts of England and Wales from Pembrokeshire to Kent; also Scilly and the Channel Islands. Locally frequent in Gloucestershire and west Oxfordshire. F. *impar* is considered an urban colour form, which sometimes predominates locally and has been reported from Cambridge and Gloucester. Various other colour forms occuring at low frequency in populations of f. *muralis* have also been named. F. *westroppi* is local on the south and west coasts of Ireland.

Noctuidae (Noctuinae) Darts, yellow underwings and clays pages 238-241

Square-spot Dart
Euxoa obelisca grisea

White-line Dart
Euxoa tritici

311

White-line Dart
Euxoa tritici

Garden Dart
Euxoa nigricans

Coast Dart
Euxoa cursoria

Light Feathered Rustic
Agrotis cinerea

Archer's Dart
Agrotis vestigialis

Turnip Moth
Agrotis segetum

Wood's Dart
Agrotis graslini

Noctuidae (Noctuinae) Darts, yellow underwings and clays pages 241-245

———————————— Heart and Club ————————————
Agrotis clavis

———— Heart and Dart ————
Agrotis exclamationis

———— Heart and Dart ————
Agrotis exclamationis

———— Crescent Dart ————
Agrotis trux lunigera

———— Dark Sword-grass ————
Agrotis ipsilon

♂ ♀ ♂ ♀

———— Spalding's Dart ————
Agrotis herzogi

———— Shuttle-shaped Dart ————
Agrotis puta puta   Agrotis puta insula

———————————— Sand Dart ————————————
Agrotis ripae

Great Dart
Agrotis crassa

The Flame
Axylia putris

♂

♀

Portland Moth
Actebia praecox

Black Collar
Ochropleura
flammatra

Flame Shoulder
Ochropleura
plecta

Radford's Flame
Shoulder
Ochropleura
leucogaster

Eversmann's Rustic
Actebia fennica

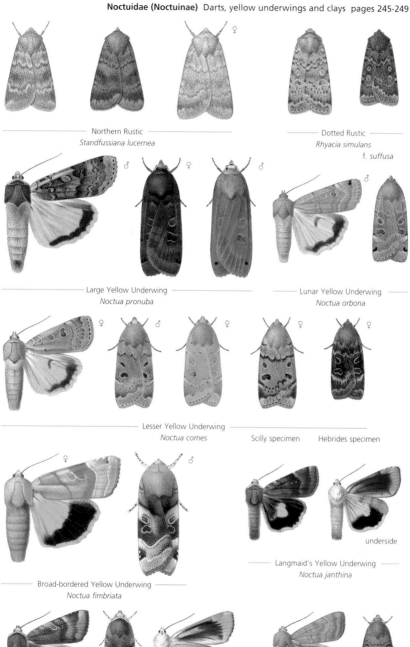

♀

313

Northern Rustic
Standfussiana lucernea

Dotted Rustic
Rhyacia simulans
f. *suffusa*

♂

♀ ♂ ♂

Large Yellow Underwing
Noctua pronuba

Lunar Yellow Underwing
Noctua orbona

♀ ♂ ♀ ♀ ♀

Lesser Yellow Underwing
Noctua comes

Scilly specimen   Hebrides specimen

♀ ♂

underside

Langmaid's Yellow Underwing
Noctua janthina

Broad-bordered Yellow Underwing
Noctua fimbriata

underside

Lesser Broad-bordered Yellow Underwing
Noctua janthe

Least Yellow Underwing
Noctua interjecta caliginosa

Noctuidae (Noctuinae) Darts, yellow underwings and clays pages 249-253

Stout Dart
Spaelotis ravida

Double Dart
Graphiphora augur

Rosy Marsh Moth
Coenophila subrosea

Cousin German
Protolampra sobrina

Autumnal Rustic
Eugnorisma glareosa

Plain Clay
Eugnorisma depuncta

True Lover's Knot
Lycophotia porphyrea

Pearly Underwing
Peridroma saucia

Ingrailed Clay
Diarsia mendica mendica

Ingrailed Clay
Diarsia mendica mendica

D. m. thulei

2nd generation

Scottish specimen

Barred Chestnut
Diarsia dahlii

Purple Clay
Diarsia brunnea

Small Square-spot
Diarsia rubi

——— Fen Square-spot ——— ———————————— Northern Dart ————————————
Diarsia florida *Xestia alpicola alpina* Cumbrian specimen

Setaceous Hebrew Triple-spotted Double ——— Ashworth's ———
Character Clay Square-spot Rustic
Xestia c-nigrum *Xestia ditrapezium* *Xestia triangulum* *Xestia ashworthii*

——— Dotted Clay ——— Square-spotted Clay ——— Neglected Rustic ——— Six-striped Rustic
Xestia baja *Xestia rhomboidea* *Xestia castanea* *Xestia sexstrigata*

——————— Square-spot Rustic ——————— ——— Heath Rustic ———
Xestia xanthographa *Xestia agathina agathina*

Gothic ——— Great Brocade ——— Green Arches
Naenia typica *Eurois occulta* *Anaplectoides prasina*

——— Red Chestnut ——— White-marked
Cerastis rubricosa *Cerastis leucographa*

Noctuidae (Hadeninae) Brocades, quakers and leaf-eating wainscots pages 259-265

hindwings

Beautiful Yellow
Underwing
Anarta myrtilli

Small Dark Yellow
Underwing
Anarta cordigera

Broad-bordered White
Underwing
Anarta melanopa

——————— Nutmeg ———————
Discestra trifolii

——————— Shears ———————
Hada plebeja

Pale Shining
Brown
Polia bombycina

——————— Silvery Arches ———————
Polia trimaculosa

——————— Grey Arches ———————
Polia nebulosa

Feathered Ear	White Colon	——————— Bordered Gothic———————		Cabbage Moth	Dot Moth
Pachetra sagittigera	*Sideridis*	*Heliophobus*	*Heliophobus*	*Mamestra*	*Melanchra*
britannica	*albicolon*	*reticulata marginosa*	*reticulata hibernica*	*brassicae*	*persicariae*

——————— Broom Moth ———————
Melanchra pisi

Beautiful Brocade
Lacanobia contigua

Light Brocade
Lacanobia w-latinum

———— Pale-shouldered Brocade ————
Lacanobia thalassina

———— Dog's Tooth ————
Lacanobia suasa

Bright-line Brown-eye
Lacanobia oleracea

Glaucous Shears
Papestra biren

Broad-barred White
Hecatera bicolorata

Small Ranunculus
Hecatera dysodea

Campion
Hadena rivularis

———— Tawny Shears ————
Hadena perplexa perplexa

———————— Tawny Shears ————————
Hadena perplexa perplexa

Pod Lover
Hadena perplexa capsophila

Viper's Bugloss
Hadena irregularis

———— Barrett's Marbled Coronet ————
Hadena luteago barrettii

Varied Coronet
Hadena compta

———— Marbled Coronet ————
Hadena confusa

White Spot
Hadena albimacula

Lychnis
Hadena bicruris

———— Grey ————
Hadena caesia mananii

———————— Silurian ————————
Eriopygodes imbecilla

———— Antler Moth ————
Cerapteryx graminis

Hedge Rustic
Tholera cespitis

Feathered Gothic
Tholera decimalis

———— Pine Beauty ————
Panolis flammea

Noctuidae (Hadeninae) Brocades, quakers and leaf-eating wainscots pages 272-275

——————— Silver Cloud ———————
Egira conspicillaris

——————— Small Quaker ———————
Orthosia cruda

Essex specimen

——— Blossom Underwing ———
Orthosia miniosa

——————— Northern Drab ———————
Orthosia opima

♂

——— Lead-coloured Drab ———
Orthosia populeti

——————— Powdered Quaker ———————
Orthosia gracilis

♂

——————— Common Quaker ———————
Orthosia cerasi

——— Clouded Drab ———
Orthosia incerta

——————— Clouded Drab ———————
Orthosia incerta

——— Twin-spotted Quaker ———
Orthosia munda

Twin-spotted Quaker
Orthosia munda

——————— Hebrew Character ———————
Orthosia gothica

318

Noctuidae (Hadeninae) Brocades, quakers and leaf-eating wainscots pages 276-281

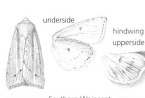

Double Line
Mythimna turca

Brown-line Bright-eye
Mythimna conigera

Clay
Mythimna ferrago

White-point
Mythimna albipuncta

———————— Delicate ————————
Mythimna vitellina

Striped Wainscot
Mythimna pudorina

———— Southern Wainscot ————
Mythimna straminea

———— Smoky Wainscot ————
Mythimna impura

underside

hindwing
upperside

underside

hindwing
upperside

———————— Common Wainscot ————————
Mythimna pallens

———— Mathew's Wainscot ————
Mythimna favicolor

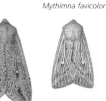

Shore Wainscot
Mythimna litoralis

L-album Wainscot
Mythimna l-album

———— White-speck ————
Mythimna unipuncta

Obscure Wainscot
Mythimna obsoleta

Shoulder-striped
Wainscot
Mythimna comma

Devonshire Wainscot
Mythimna putrescens

Cosmopolitan
Mythimna loreyi

Flame Wainscot
Mythimna flammea

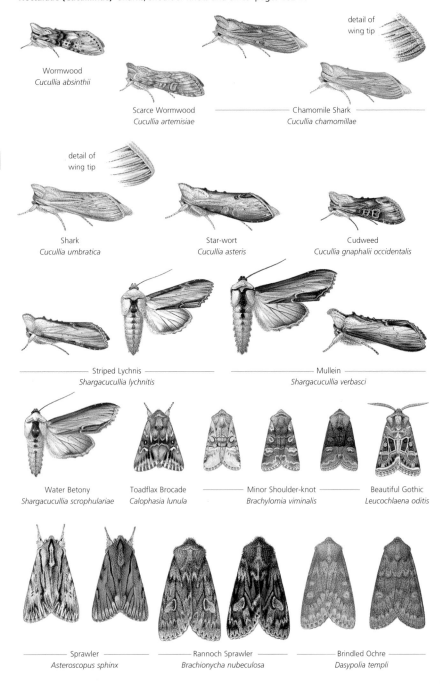

detail of
wing tip

Wormwood
Cucullia absinthii

Scarce Wormwood
Cucullia artemisiae

Chamomile Shark
Cucullia chamomillae

320

detail of
wing tip

Shark
Cucullia umbratica

Star-wort
Cucullia asteris

Cudweed
Cucullia gnaphalii occidentalis

Striped Lychnis
Shargacucullia lychnitis

Mullein
Shargacucullia verbasci

Water Betony
Shargacucullia scrophulariae

Toadflax Brocade
Calophasia lunula

Minor Shoulder-knot
Brachylomia viminalis

Beautiful Gothic
Leucochlaena oditis

Sprawler
Asteroscopus sphinx

Rannoch Sprawler
Brachionycha nubeculosa

Brindled Ochre
Dasypolia templi

——— Feathered Brindle ———
Aporophyla australis pascuea

Deep-brown Dart
Aporophyla lutulenta

——— Northern Deep-brown Dart ———
Aporophyla lueneburgensis

Black Rustic
Aporophyla nigra

Golden-rod Brindle
Lithomoia solidaginis

Tawny Pinion
Lithophane semibrunnea

Pale Pinion
Lithophane hepatica

Grey Shoulder-knot
Lithophane ornitopus lactipennis

Lithophane consocia
(p. 413)

——————— Conformist ———————
Lithophane furcifera suffusa   *Lithophane furcifera furcifera*

Nonconformist
Lithophane lamda

Blair's Shoulder-knot
Lithophane leautieri hesperica

Red Sword-grass
Xylena vetusta

Sword-grass
Xylena exsoleta

——— Early Grey ———
Xylocampa areola

——— Green-brindled Crescent ———
Allophyes oxyacanthae

———————————— Oak Rustic ————————————
Dryobota labecula   f. *albomacula*

Merveille du Jour ——— Brindled Green ——— Beautiful Arches ——— Dark Brocade ———
Dichonia aprilina   *Dryobotodes eremita*   *Blepharita satura*   *Blepharita adusta*

Dark Brocade   Bedrule Brocade
Blepharita adusta   *Blepharita solieri*

———————————— Grey Chi ————————————
Antitype chi

Flame Brocade ——— Large Ranunculus ——— Cameo
Trigonophora flammea   *Polymixis flavicincta*   *Polymixis gemmea*

——— Black-banded ———   ——— Feathered Ranunculus ———
Polymixis xanthomista statices   *Polymixis lichenea lichenea*   *P.l. scillonea*

Satellite
Eupsilia transversa

Orange Upperwing
Jodia croceago

Chestnut
Conistra vaccinii

Dark Chestnut
Conistra ligula

Dotted Chestnut
Conistra rubiginea

Red-headed Chestnut
Conistra erythrocephala

Brick
Agrochola circellaris

Red-line Quaker
Agrochola lota

Yellow-line Quaker
Agrochola macilenta

Southern Chestnut
Agrochola haematidea

Flounced Chestnut
Agrochola helvola

Brown-spot Pinion
Agrochola litura
f. *rufa-pallida*

Beaded Chestnut
Agrochola lychnidis

——— Centre-barred Sallow ———
Atethmia centrago

——————————— Lunar Underwing ———————————
Omphaloscelis lunosa

Orange Sallow ——— Barred Sallow ——— Pink-barred Sallow ——— Sallow ———
Xanthia citrago   *Xanthia aurago*   *Xanthia togata*   *Xanthia icteritia*

——— Dusky-lemon Sallow ——— ——— Pale-lemon Sallow ———
Xanthia gilvago   *Xanthia ocellaris*

Scarce Merveille
du Jour
Moma alpium

——— Poplar Grey ———
Acronicta megacephala

——— Sycamore ———
Acronicta aceris
f. *infuscata*

——————— Miller ———————
Acronicta leporina
f. *grisea*   f. *melanocephala*

——— Alder Moth ———
Acronicta alni
f. *suffusa*

———— Dark Dagger ————
Acronicta tridens

Grey Dagger
Acronicta psi

Marsh Dagger
Acronicta strigosa

———— Light Knot Grass ————
Acronicta menyanthidis menyanthidis

Acronicta menyanthidis scotica

Scarce Dagger
Acronicta auricoma

Sweet Gale Moth
Acronicta euphorbiae myricae

———— Knot Grass ————
Acronicta rumicis
f. *salicis*

Reed Dagger
Simyra albovenosa

———— Coronet ————
Craniophora ligustri
f. *coronula*

——— Tree-lichen Beauty ———
Cryphia algae

————— Marbled Beauty —————
Cryphia domestica

Marbled Grey
Cryphia raptricula

——— Marbled Green ———
Cryphia muralis muralis

——— Marbled Green ———
Cryphia muralis muralis   f. *impar*

Noctuidae (Amphipyrinae) Arches, brindles, minors, rustics and allies pages 339-344

underside of hindwing

underside of hindwing

Copper Underwing
Amphipyra pyramidea

Svensson's Copper Underwing
Amphipyra berbera svenssoni

Mouse Moth
Amphipyra tragopoginis

Bird's Wing
Dypterygia scabriuscula

Old Lady
Mormo maura

♂ ♀

Brown Rustic
Rusina ferruginea

Guernsey Underwing
Polyphaenis sericata

Straw Underwing
Thalpophila matura

Orache Moth
Trachea atriplicis

Small Angle Shades
Euplexia lucipara

Angle Shades
Phlogophora meticulosa

Purple Cloud
Actinotia polyodon

Pale-shouldered Cloud
Actinotia hyperici

Latin
Callopistria juventina

Double Kidney
Ipimorpha retusa

Olive
Ipimorpha subtusa

Angle-striped Sallow
Enargia paleacea

Noctuidae (Amphipyrinae) Arches, brindles, minors, rustics and allies pages 344-348

——————— Suspected ——————— ——————— Dingy Shears ———————
Parastichtis suspecta *Parastichtis ypsillon*

Lesser-spotted
Pinion White-spotted Pinion
——————— Heart Moth ——————— *Cosmia affinis* *Cosmia diffinis*
Dicycla oo

———————————————— Dun-bar ————————————————
Cosmia trapezina f. *badiofasciata*

——————— Lunar-spotted Pinion ——————— Saxon
Cosmia pyralina *Hyppa rectilinea*

——————— Dark Arches ——————— Light Arches Reddish Light Arches
Apamea monoglypha f. *aethiops* *Apamea lithoxylaea* *Apamea sublustris*

Northern Arches ——————— Exile ——————— ——————— Crescent Striped ———————
Apamea zeta assimilis *Apamea zeta marmorata* *Apamea oblonga*

327

──── Clouded-bordered Brindle ────
Apamea crenata

Clouded Brindle
Apamea epomidion

Scarce Brindle
Apamea lateritia

Confused
Apamea furva britannica

328

──── Dusky Brocade ────
Apamea remissa

Small Clouded Brindle
Apamea unanimis

──── Large Nutmeg ────
Apamea anceps

Rustic Shoulder-knot
Apamea sordens

Slender Brindle
Apamea scolopacina

──── Double Lobed ────
Apamea ophiogramma

Union Rustic
Eremobina pabulatricula

──────── Marbled Minor ────────
Oligia strigilis

──── Rufous Minor ────
Oligia versicolor

──── Tawny Marbled Minor ────
Oligia latruncula   Burren specimen

── Middle-barred Minor ──
Oligia fasciuncula
f. *pallida*

──────────── Cloaked Minor ────────────
f. *bicoloria*   *Mesoligia furuncula*   f. *latistriata*

──────── Rosy Minor ────────
Mesoligia literosa   f. *aethalodes*

Common Rustic
Mesapamea secalis

♂ ♀

Least Minor
Photedes captiuncula expolita

Lesser Common Rustic
Mesapamea didyma

Small Dotted Buff
Photedes minima

Morris's Wainscot
*Chortodes morrisii
morrisii*

Bond's Wainscot
*Chortodes morrisii
bondii*

Concolorous
*Chortodes
extrema*

Lyme Grass
Chortodes elymi

Mere Wainscot
Chortodes fluxa

Small Wainscot
Chortodes pygmina

Fenn's Wainscot
*Chortodes
brevilinea*

Dusky Sallow
Eremobia ochroleuca

Flounced Rustic
Luperina testacea

Sandhill Rustic

*Luperina nickerlii
demuthi*

*Luperina nickerlii
leechi*

*Luperina nickerlii
gueneei*

*Luperina nickerlii
knilli*

Noctuidae (Amphipyrinae) Arches, brindles, minors, rustics and allies pages 359-363

——— Dumeril's Rustic ———
Luperina dumerilii

Scarce Arches
Luperina zollikoferi

——— Large Ear ———
Amphipoea lucens

——— Saltern Ear ———
Amphipoea fucosa paludis

——— Crinan Ear ———
Amphipoea crinanensis

——— Ear Moth ———
Amphipoea oculea

Rosy Rustic
Hydraecia micacea

Butterbur
Hydraecia petasitis

Marsh Mallow Moth
*Hydraecia osseola
hucherardi*

Frosted
Orange
Gortyna flavago

Fisher's Estuarine
Moth
*Gortyna borelii
lunata*

Burren Green
*Calamia tridens
occidentalis*

Haworth's Minor
Celaena haworthii

——— Crescent ———
*Celaena leucostigma
leucostigma*

*Celaena leucostigma
scotica*

Twin-spotted Wainscot
Archanara geminipuncta

f. *fraterna*

Bulrush Wainscot
Nonagria typhae

Brown-veined Wainscot
Archanara dissoluta

f. *arundineta*

White-mantled Wainscot
Archanara neurica

Webb's Wainscot
Archanara sparganii

Rush Wainscot
Archanara algae

Blair's Wainscot
Sedina buettneri

Fen Wainscot
Arenostola phragmitidis
f. *rufescens*

Large Wainscot
Rhizedra lutosa

Brighton Wainscot
Oria musculosa

Small Rufous
Coenobia rufa

Treble Lines
Charanyca trigrammica

——————————— Uncertain ———————————   ——————————— Rustic ———————————
Hoplodrina alsines   *Hoplodrina blanda*

332

Powdered Rustic   ————— Vine's Rustic —————   Small Mottled Willow   Dark Mottled Willow
Hoplodrina   *Hoplodrina ambigua*   *Spodoptera exigua*   Mediterranean   *Spodoptera cilium*
superstes   Brocade
Spodoptera littoralis

——— Mottled Rustic ———   Lorimer's Rustic   ——— Pale Mottled Willow ———
Caradrina morpheus   *Paradrina flavirena*   *Paradrina clavipalpis*

♂   ♀

——————————— Silky Wainscot ———————————   ——— Marsh Moth ———   Porter's Rustic
Chilodes maritimus   *Athetis pallustris*   *Proxenus hospes*
f. *nigristriata*   f. *wismariensis*   f. *bipunctata*

♂   ♀   ♂   ♀

——— Reddish Buff ———   ——— Anomalous ———   Rosy Marbled   Small Yellow
Acosmetia caliginosa   *Stilbia anomala*   *Elaphria venustula*   Underwing
Panemeria
tenebrata

Plain Golden Y
Autographa jota

Gold Spangle
Autographa bractea

Stephens' Gem
Megalographa biloba

Scarce Silver Y
*Syngrapha
interrogationis*

Essex Y
Cornutiplusia circumflexa

Dark Spectacle
*Abrostola
triplasia*

Spectacle
Abrostola tripartita
f. *plumbea*

head-on view
showing
'spectacles'

Clifden Nonpareil
Catocala fraxini

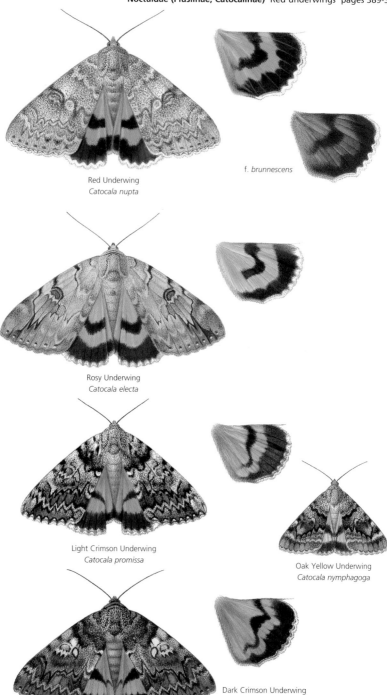

336

f. *brunnescens*

Red Underwing
Catocala nupta

Rosy Underwing
Catocala electa

Light Crimson Underwing
Catocala promissa

Oak Yellow Underwing
Catocala nymphagoga

Dark Crimson Underwing
Catocala sponsa

Lunar Double-stripe
Minucia lunaris

Passenger
Dysgonia algira

Geometrician
Prodotis stolida

Mother Shipton
Callistege mi

———— Burnet Companion ————
Euclidia glyphica

hindwing

Alchymist
Catephia alchymista

Four-spotted
Tyta luctuosa

Blackneck
Lygephila pastinum

Scarce Blackneck
Lygephila craccae

f. *fusca*

—— Levant Blackneck ——
Tathorhynchus exsiccata

Herald
Scoliopteryx libatrix

———— Small Purple-barred ————
Phytometra viridaria

Lesser Belle
Colobochyla salicalis

Beautiful Hook-tip
Laspeyria flexula

Straw Dot
Rivula sericealis

Waved Black
Parascotia fuliginaria

♂
 ♀

2nd generation

——————— Beautiful Snout ———————
Hypena crassalis

——————— Snout ———————
Hypena proboscidalis

——————— Bloxworth Snout ———————
Hypena obsitalis

Paignton Snout
Hypena obesalis

——————— Buttoned Snout ———————
Hypena rostralis
f. *unicolor*

White-line Snout
Schrankia taenialis

——————— Pinion-streaked Snout ———————
Schrankia costaestrigalis

Marsh Oblique-barred
Hypenodes humidalis

Common Fan-foot
Pechipogo strigilata

Plumed Fan-foot
Pechipogo plumigeralis

Fan-foot
Zanclognatha tarsipennalis

Jubilee Fan-foot
Zanclognatha lunalis

Dusky Fan-foot
Zanclognatha zelleralis

Shaded Fan-foot
Herminia tarsicrinalis

Small Fan-foot
Herminia grisealis

Dotted Fan-foot
Macrochilo cribrumalis

Clay Fan-foot
Paracolax tristalis

Olive Crescent
Trisateles emortualis

Amphipyrinae Arches, brindles, minors, rustics and allies

Larva of Svensson's Copper Underwing (above) and Copper Underwing (below).

Dark Arches   Marbled Minor   Ear Moth

Fen Wainscot   Uncertain

2296 see below 2467

Copper Underwing   page 326
Amphipyra pyramidea (L.)
Common. S,C,(N)   2297(9307)

Field characters & Similar species FW 21-26mm. The two British species of copper underwing are very similar. The most reliable way to separate them is to examine the underside of the hindwing. This can be done on an anaesthetised live moth (see Introduction for further details). On Copper Underwing, copper colour is limited to outer third, and ends abruptly at dark cross-band, and basal two-thirds is largely straw-coloured, apart from grey-brown speckled streak along leading edge, making a sharply contrasting effect. On Svensson's, copper continues towards base in trailing half, and grey-brown speckling is more extensive, so that basal third is either not or only slightly paler. On upperside, forewing markings of Copper Underwing are generally brighter and more sharply defined than in Svensson's, which looks duller by comparison, especially in torchlight. On forewing of both species, cross-line before middle is very jagged, and forms two distinct V-marks in trailing half. In Copper Underwing, the points of these are usually roughly level, but in Svensson's, V nearer trailing edge usually protrudes further out. However, this character should not be used on its own to separate the species. A dark brown form, still with pale markings, seems to occur only in Copper Underwing.

Flight season One generation. Late July-early October. Comes very readily to tree sap, sugar and wine ropes, and in reasonable numbers to light. Sometimes found by day hiding in groups, often accompanied by Svensson's Copper Underwing, in hollows in tree trunks or behind bark, in empty oil drums, pheasant feeders and in outbuildings.

Life cycle Overwinters as an egg. Larva mid April-early June. Pupates underground.

Larval foodplants Hawthorn, Midland Hawthorn, Blackthorn, Crab Apple, Hazel, Honeysuckle and Downy Birch. Reported also from a wide range of other broadleaved trees and shrubs, including Wild and Garden Privet. Seems to prefer low-growing and understorey shrubs to mature trees.

Habitat Most abundant in woodland, but occurs in open scrub, hedgerows, urban plantings, gardens and parks.

Status & distribution Resident. Common. Widely and well distributed throughout England and Wales northwards to Yorkshire, although rare in this county. There are records of occasional individuals northwards into southern Scotland. Local on Man. Quite widespread and well distributed in Northern Ireland, with widely scattered records from the Republic. Widespread and frequent in the Channel Islands.

Svensson's Copper Underwing   p.326
Amphipyra berbera Rungs
ssp. *svennsoni* Fletch.
Common. S,C   2298(9308)

Field characters & Similar species FW 21-26mm. See Copper Underwing.

Flight season One generation. Late July-mid September. Comes very readily to tree sap, sugar and wine ropes, and in reasonable numbers to light. Roosting habits as for Copper Underwing.

Life cycle Overwinters as an egg. Larva mid April-late May. Pupates underground.

Larval foodplants Sometimes frequent in the canopy of Pedunculate Oak; also reported from limes, Hornbeam, willows and even Rhododendron. Much less frequent than Copper Underwing on shrubs and coppice regrowth, at least in some sites studied in southern England.

Habitat Most abundant in woodland, but occurs in open scrub, hedgerows, urban plantings, gardens and parks.

Status & distribution Resident. Common. Widely and well distributed in England and Wales north to

Yorkshire, where it has become more frequent in recent years and outnumbers Copper Underwing. Less well distributed than Copper Underwing in south Wales. Only confirmed from Ireland (Co. Clare) in the late 1990s, where it is apparently much scarcer than Copper Underwing. Local, with few records, on Man. Rare in the Channel Islands.

Mouse Moth
page 326

Amphipyra tragopoginis (Cl.)

Common. T   2299(9311)

Field characters FW 16-18mm. The English name of this drab-coloured but unmistakable moth is highly appropriate: forewing is mousy brown and the moth often runs rapidly, mouse-like, towards cover when exposed to light. Forewing shiny when fresh, almost plain apart from a small dark oval and kidney-mark, the latter represented by two small dark spots. Ground-colour varies somewhat, and sometimes a dark outer cross-band is discernible with a paler area beyond it.
Flight season One generation. July-September, with stragglers into October. Comes regularly to light, sugar and flowers, and can be found by day roosting under bark and in outbuildings, sometimes in numbers.
Life cycle Overwinters as an egg. Larva April-June. Feeds at night and hides low down on the foodplant by day. Pupates in a cocoon at or just below ground.
Larval foodplants Leaves and sometimes flowers of a wide range of wild and cultivated herbaceous plants, including Salad Burnet, teasels, Mugwort, Fennel and Californian Poppy; also sallows and hawthorns.
Habitat A wide range, including gardens, woodland, sand-dunes, moorland and fens.
Status & distribution Resident. Common. Well distributed and frequent throughout England, Wales and lowland Scotland, Scilly, Man, the Hebrides and Ireland. Local and occasional in the Channel Islands.

Old Lady
page 326

Mormo maura (L.)

Local. T   2300(9490)

Field characters FW 30-36mm. An unmistakable, large, dark brown moth with very broad forewing. Varies little in general forewing pattern, but more so in colour and intensity of markings. Some examples are more uniformly dull brown. F. *virgata* Tutt has brighter, pale brown markings, sometimes pink-tinged, and a broad, darker central band. Undersides of fore- and hindwings have broad fawn borders, easily seen on moths at wine ropes.
Similar species None.
Flight season One generation. July-September. Comes to light in very small numbers, but sometimes lingers briefly around traps, without approaching closely. Comes to sugar in much greater numbers, and also to aphid honeydew and sap oozing from damaged trees. Can be found roosting in outbuildings, birds' nests or other suitable shelters by day.

Life cycle Overwinters as a small larva, low down in the vegetation. Larva September-May. Feeds at night and hides in leaf litter or in the ground by day. Pupates in a cocoon, which has been found behind bark, among Ivy, in crevices in walls and in loose earth.
Larval foodplants In autumn on herbaceous plants, including chickweeds and docks. In spring usually on woody plants, including Ivy, Hawthorn, birches and spindles, but has also been found on Water Dock in the drier part of a reedbed.
Habitat Riverbanks, marshes, gardens, hedgerows, scrub and woodland.
Status & distribution Resident. Local. Very well distributed throughout south-east England. Widely and fairly well distributed throughout much of England and Wales, southern Scotland, Man, Ireland and the Channel Islands. Local elsewhere on the Scottish mainland, recorded northwards to east Inverness-shire and Banffshire.

Bird's Wing
page 326

Dypterygia scabriuscula (L.)

Local. SE,WC   2301(9481)

Field characters FW 16mm. Diagnostic feature of this unmistakable dark chocolate-brown moth is a conspicuous, streaky, wavy-edged pale brown patch, pinched in middle, which cuts across trailing corners of forewings and resembles the wings of a bird. Forewing varies only very slightly in colour and detail of markings.
Similar species None.
Flight season Mainly one generation, late May-July. Occasionally a small second generation in southern England, August-September. Comes to light and sugar.
Life cycle Overwinters as a pupa underground. Larva late June-August, with occasional second generation in September.
Larval foodplants Docks, sorrels, Knotgrass and probably others.
Habitat Broadleaved woodland, parks, heathland and scrubby areas.
Status & distribution Resident. Local. Well distributed in south-east and central southern England, East Anglia and the north-west Midlands. Very local in south-west England, west Wales, the Midlands and northern England. Widespread and frequent on Jersey, rare on Guernsey.

Brown Rustic
page 326

Rusina ferruginea (Esp.)

Common. T   2302(9483)

Field characters FW M 16-18mm, F 14-16mm. Despite its rather drab colour and often obscure markings, not usually a difficult moth to recognise. Male has strongly-feathered antennae and quite broad brown or dark brown forewing, with outer edge roughly at right angles to trailing edge. There are five or six small whitish dots along leading edge, the largest at ends of the two irregular, fine, dark brown

or blackish complete cross-lines. Female is smaller with narrower, more round-tipped forewing, has unfeathered antennae and is generally less strongly marked.
Similar species Male is distinctive, but female can be puzzling at first. It could be confused with female Square-spot Rustic, which usually flies later in year and lacks whitish spots along leading edge of forewing.
Flight season One generation. June-July. Comes to light, the male frequently, and to sugar and flowers.
Life cycle Overwinters as a larva, almost fully grown. Larva August-May. Feeds at night and hides in leaf litter by day. Pupates in an underground cocoon.
Larval foodplants A wide range of herbaceous plants, including vetches, plantains, docks and bistorts.
Habitat Most numerous in broadleaved woodland, but regular in suburban gardens and in many other open habitats, including calcareous grassland, heathland and moorland.
Status & distribution Resident. Common. Well distributed and frequent throughout most of mainland Britain, the Inner Hebrides, Man and Ireland. Widespread but occasional on Jersey, rare on Guernsey and Alderney.

Guernsey Underwing · page 326
Polyphaenis sericata (Esp.)
Channel Islands · 2302a(9492)

Field characters FW 17-20mm. Combination of greenish forewing and orange hindwing with broad dark brown borders is diagnostic among the noctuids. Extent of whitish cross-lines and black markings on forewing varies.
Similar species See Orache Moth.
Flight season One generation. Mid June-mid August.
Life cycle Overwinters as a larva, hatching in autumn and pupating about May.
Larval foodplants Honeysuckle; also reported from oaks.
Habitat Sheltered coastal valleys.
Status & distribution Resident in the Channel Islands. Recorded from Guernsey in the 1870s, then not until 1986. First recorded on Jersey in 1989. Now locally frequent on both islands. In Europe mainly southern, central and south-eastern.

Straw Underwing · page 326
Thalpophila matura (Hufn.)
Common. S,C,(N) · 2303(9496)

Field characters FW 17-20mm. Pale straw-yellow hindwing with brown borders, together with broad, dark forewing, white outer cross-line and thickset build, are diagnostic. General forewing pattern varies in detail; sometimes a solid blackish bar joins central cross-lines. Forewing greyish brown, brown or dark brown, sometimes marked with reddish brown or dusted with white. In north-east England, forewing is often dull and obscurely marked and hindwing is

dusted blackish. In western Ireland forewing is more brightly marked, particularly with reddish brown. In the rare f. *trescoensis* Rich., known only from Scilly, kidney-mark and outer cross-line are straw yellow.
Similar species Hedge Rustic is superficially similar at rest, but hindwing whitish, not straw-coloured.
Flight season One generation. Late July-August. Comes to light, sugar and flowers, including Common Ragwort and Marram.
Life cycle Overwinters as a small larva. Larva September-early May. Feeds through winter at night, hiding low down by day. Pupates in an underground chamber.
Larval foodplants Grasses, including Annual Meadow-grass, Mat-grass and Silver Hair-grass.
Habitat Gardens, parks and most open habitats, including calcareous grassland, moorland and sand-dunes; also woodland rides and glades.
Status & distribution Resident. Common. Well distributed in most of southern mainland Britain, including Scilly, but very local in south-west England. Local and mainly coastal in northern England and Scotland, including the Inner Hebrides. Local on Man and in Ireland. Widespread and frequent in the Channel Islands.

341

Orache Moth · page 326
Trachea atriplicis (L.)
Rare immigrant; former resident; resident
Channel Islands · 2304(9501)

Field characters FW 20-22mm. Thick; oblique pinkish-white forked streak in centre of green-tinged forewing is diagnostic. Some individuals are almost fluorescent green. Large oval and kidney-mark partly outlined in white. Hindwing dull brown, darker near edges.
Similar species Guernsey Underwing lacks oblique central forewing streak.
Flight season One generation. June-early July. Immigrants also recorded in August. Attracted to sugar and light.
Life cycle Overwinters as a pupa in a tough cocoon underground. Larva July-September.
Larval foodplants Oraches, goosefoots, Knotgrass and other low plants.
Habitat Fens, damp meadows and marshes. Immigrants mainly on the coast, occasionally inland.
Status & distribution Rare immigrant and extinct British resident; resident in Channel Islands. During the 19th century, resident in the fens of Huntingdonshire and Cambridgeshire, and in Norfolk, Suffolk, Essex and Hertfordshire. Last seen in 1915. Since 1984, recorded as a suspected immigrant just over a dozen times, mainly in south-east England, but also in Cheshire, Dorset and Devon. First recorded in the Channel Islands in 1984. Now resident on Guernsey (probably a recent colonisation, numbers increasing). Widespread and abundant on Jersey and recorded from Alderney and Sark. Recorded from almost every country in Europe, and frequent just across the English Channel.

Noctuidae (Amphipyrinae) Arches, brindles, minors, rustics and allies

Small Angle Shades page 326
Euplexia lucipara (L.)
Common. T   2305(9503)

Field characters FW 14-17mm. Unmistakable. Shares an unusual resting posture with Angle Shades. When fully at rest, sits with forewings creased and held horizontally about 5mm from the surface, with leading edge folded under and front end pointing slightly downwards. In this position it closely resembles a dead leaf. Most conspicuous feature is golden yellow kidney-mark. Forewing varies little in pattern; area beyond dark central band is either pale brown or pinkish brown, except for an area beyond kidney-mark which is usually distinctly golden. On some examples basal area is also pinkish.
Similar species None.
Flight season Mainly one generation, June-July. Occasionally a small second generation in September, particularly in southern England. Comes to light, sugar, honeydew and flowers. Usually rests under cover by day but occasionally exposed, although highly cryptic.
Life cycle Overwinters as a pupa underground. Larva July-September, occasionally later. Feeds at night, resting by day under a leaf of the foodplant or in plant debris.
Larval foodplants A wide range of herbaceous and woody plants, but particularly frequent on Bracken, Male-fern and other ferns. Also reported from Ivy buds, Foxglove, willowherbs, nettles, mallows, currants, birches, sallows and oaks.
Habitat Gardens, parks, woodland, heathland and moorland.
Status & distribution Resident. Common. Well distributed and fairly frequent throughout most of Great Britain, Man and Ireland, except Shetland; rare on Orkney. Widespread and frequent in the Channel Islands.

Angle Shades page 326
Phlogophora meticulosa (L.)
Common. T   2306(9505)

Field characters FW 21-25mm. Unmistakable. Rests like Small Angle Shades, but with creases and folds deeper. When fresh, most examples are olive green and pinkish brown, but these colours are inclined to fade. Pattern is very constant, but pale straw area beyond central band is variable in extent. In the uncommon f. *suffusa* War., the olive green is replaced by reddish brown and central cross-band is rusty brown or reddish.
Similar species None.
Flight season Recorded all year round, but mainly May-October, probably in two generations. A small peak occurs May-June and a larger one August-October, when immigrants arrive, sometimes in large numbers. Comes to light, and feeds at sugar and flowers, including those of Common Reed and other grasses. Frequently seen by day, resting openly on walls, fences or vegetation.

Life cycle Overwinters as a larva, feeding in mild weather. Larva all year round. Usually pupates in a cocoon just under the soil, but will use soft mortar in a wall if no suitable ground is readily available.
Larval foodplants A wide range of wild and culti-vated herbaceous and woody plants, including Common Nettle, Hop, Red Valerian, Broad-leaved Dock, Bramble, Hazel, birches and oaks. Very frequent on Barberry.
Habitat Ubiquitous. Frequent in gardens, hedgerows, fens and woodland.
Status & distribution Resident and immigrant. Common. Well distributed and frequent throughout most of Britain, Man and Ireland. Scarce and possibly not resident in some northern parts of Scotland but recorded north to Orkney and Shetland. Widespread and abundant in the Channel Islands.

Purple Cloud page 326
Actinotia polyodon (Cl.)
Immigrant.   2097(9515)

Field characters FW 13-15mm. Striking forewing markings and purplish tint on brown ground-colour are diagnostic. Conspicuous features are ear-shaped kidney-mark, two pale bars and thin black streak at base of forewing, and pale area with zigzag edges near wing tip. Hindwing brownish.
Similar species Latin has a pale violet band running across outer part of forewing and a conspicuous whitish curved cross-line either side of kidney-mark.
Flight season One generation in northern Europe, May-June, with a second generation in August further south. Comes to light and sugar. In mainland Europe often seen visiting flowers. Most British records have occurred in May-June, but two were in August.
Life cycle Overwinters as a pupa underground. Larva June-August in northern Europe. No evidence of breeding in the British Isles.
Larval foodplants The flowers, seeds and leaves of St John's-worts.
Habitat Disturbed open ground.
Status & distribution Immigrant. Recorded about 20 times in the British Isles, mainly on the coast, particularly in Norfolk, where the first British record was in June 1839, but also in Essex and along the south coast from Hampshire to Kent. Recorded six times during the 1990s, all at light. Recorded throughout mainland Europe; resident just across the English Channel in France, Belgium and Denmark.

Pale-shouldered Cloud page 326
Actinotia hyperici ([D. & S.])
Rare immigrant.   2097a(9518*)

Field characters FW 12-16mm. Quite distinctive. Forewing grey with faint brown blotches, especially just beyond kidney-mark. A long, thick, black basal streak and a large whitish patch in leading half of basal area are diagnostic. Shows little variation.
Similar species None.

342

Flight season Two generations in northern Europe, May-June and August; three generations in the Mediterranean, with adults recorded from April to October. Comes to light.

Life cycle Overwinters as a pupa underground. Larva unrecorded in Britain. Most likely to be found here in July-August after immigrant adults of the first generation or September-October after those of the second.

Larval foodplants Perforate St John's-wort and other St John's-worts.

Habitat Rough, open disturbed ground.

Status & distribution Rare immigrant. Recorded twice only in the British Isles to date, at light at Dungeness, Kent, on 20 August 1996, and at Landguard Point, near Felixstowe, Suffolk, on 6 May 2003. The typical form is widespread in central and southern parts of France and Germany, through the Mediterranean eastwards to at least Turkey, Iraq and Iran. It is known to be expanding its range north-westwards in Europe and has been found breeding in Belgium during the 1990s following the first record there in 1987. The bluish-grey ssp. *svendseri* Fibiger occurs in parts of Scandinavia.

Berber   not illustrated
Pseudenargia ulicis (Stdgr.)
Suspected rare immigrant.   2307(9534)

Field characters & Similar species FW 17-19mm. Resembles Dun-bar in shape of cross-lines, but larger and forewing light or dark grey-brown (like larger version of Olive) or reddish-brown, more pointed and leading edge almost straight.

Status & distribution Suspected rare immigrant. The only individual recorded in the British Isles was captured at sugar near Brockenhurst, Hampshire, on 16 August 1935. In Europe recorded only from Spain, Portugal and the extreme south of France, feeding on Gorse. Also found on the Mediterranean coast of Africa.

Latin   page 326
Callopistria juventina (Stoll)
Rare immigrant.   2308(9520)

Field characters FW 15-16mm. An intricately marked and distinctive species. Conspicuous features include cream veins running along forewing, pale pinkish-violet cross-band near outer edge, cream mark at tip extending into a jagged line, and cream-edged kidney-mark.

Similar species See Purple Cloud.

Flight season One generation in mainland Europe, June-July.

Life cycle Overwinters as a fully grown larva and pupates in spring. Larva August-spring.

Larval foodplants Bracken.

Status & distribution Rare immigrant. Four records, all at light: Sussex, 16 May 1959; Kent, 27 July 1962; Guernsey, 29 July 1995; and Dorset, 7 July 2001. Abroad it occurs in central and southern Europe.

2309, 2310 see Appendix

Double Kidney   page 326
Ipimorpha retusa (L.)
Local. S,C   2311(9527)

Field characters FW 13-15mm. Pale-outlined oval is elongated, quite large and often kidney-shaped, hence the English name. Rather dark olive-brown broadish forewing is distinctly hooked and often dusted with grey and tinged with pink. Cross-lines are fine and pale, roughly parallel, that before middle slightly curved and that beyond middle almost straight or slightly bent; there are darker bands on their outer edges with a further dark band running through kidney-mark. This fairly simple pattern shows only minor variation.

Similar species See Olive.

Flight season One generation. Late July-early September. Comes to light, sugar, honeydew and flowers, usually in small numbers.

Life cycle Overwinters as an egg, laid on the food-plant. Larva early April-late May. Lives inside a shelter of spun leaves. Pupates in an underground cocoon.

Larval foodplants Sallows, willows and Black-poplar.

Habitat Damp woodland, fens, riverbanks and marshes.

Status & distribution Resident. Local. Mainly in southern and south-west England and Wales, where it is quite well distributed but seldom numerous. Very local through the Midlands and East Anglia to Lancashire and Yorkshire. Local and rare on Man.

Olive   page 326
Ipimorpha subtusa ([D. & S.])
Local. S,C,(N)   2312(9528)

Field characters & Similar species FW 14-16mm. Similar in general pattern and colour to Double Kidney but generally larger, with paler olive-brown forewing, never pinkish tinged. Most importantly, forewing is not or only slightly hooked, and cross-lines are not parallel but converge slightly towards trailing edge, with that before middle angled so that it is furthest from body at trailing edge and that beyond middle curved. Any banding is diffuse. Variation in colour and markings is slight.

Flight season One generation. Late July-early September. Comes to light in small numbers and to sugar and honeydew.

Life cycle Overwinters as an egg, laid on the food-plant. Larva April-May. Feeds in leaves spun together, usually quite high up on the tree. Pupates in an underground cocoon.

Larval foodplants Aspen and other poplars.

Habitat Broadleaved woodland, shelterbelts, marshes, lakesides and gravel-pits, parks and gardens.

Status & distribution Resident. Local. Widely but somewhat thinly distributed in England, Wales and southern Scotland. Rare in Ireland, but recorded from

343

Cos. Kildare, Fermanagh, Tyrone, Armagh and Antrim. Rare in the Channel Islands.

Angle-striped Sallow   page 326
Enargia paleacea (Esp.)
Nb; suspected immigrant. C,N   2313(9531)

Field characters & Similar species FW 17-20mm. A variable moth. Strongly-marked individuals have a conspicuous elbowed cross-line before middle of forewing which distinguishes them from the smaller Dun-bar (which has this cross-line straight and very oblique) and all the sallows except Orange Sallow, which lacks a dark kidney mark and angle and cross-line before middle is elbowed closer to leading edge. In weakly-marked individuals there is hardly any trace of cross-lines or kidney-mark, although the latter may contain a dark spot. Such forms could be confused with f. *flavescens* Esp. of Sallow, but are larger, with more yellowish hindwing.
Flight season One generation. Residents mainly August-mid September, but suspected immigrants sometimes in July. Both sexes come readily to sugar, and the male particularly to light, sometimes in large numbers. Has been recorded feeding at the flowers of Heather.
Life cycle Overwinters as an egg on the foodplant. Larva late April-mid June, hides between spun young leaves by day, feeding at night. Pupates underground.
Larval foodplants The young leaves of Silver Birch and Downy Birch, usually on mature trees. Also reported from Aspen in Yorkshire and elsewhere.
Habitat Woodland with mature birch, both in low-lying and upland areas, and lowland heathland with mature birch trees. Strongly associated with large sites with a long continuity of birch, but has also colonised new sites.
Status & distribution Resident and suspected immigrant. Nationally Scarce B. A predominantly northern species in Britain, which has increased its range eastwards in England over the last 150 years. Widespread along the Spey Valley and the Great Glen in Scotland, extending north to the coasts of Inverness-shire, Morayshire and Banffshire; also recorded from the Dee Valley and in the Rannoch area of Perthshire. There is a large gap in distribution to the south. The few records from Northumberland are considered immigrants. The moth is distributed in a broad belt south-west to north-east from the Welsh Marches, through the Midlands to Lincolnshire and central and eastern Yorkshire, within which it is widely recorded and sometimes very numerous. It is regarded as an immigrant or vagrant south of a line from the Severn to the Wash, where widely scattered singletons have been recorded, often accompanied by known immigrants from eastern Europe such as the Great Brocade; these specimens are often paler than the residents. There were about 80 such records up to 2000. Recorded once from Jersey in 1982.

Suspected   page 327
Parastichtis suspecta (Hb.)
Local. T   2268(9536)

Field characters FW 14-16mm. Quite slender and fairly distinctive, although variable. Forewing narrow at base, but rather broad and slightly pointed; rather plain greyish brown, reddish brown or purplish brown, or a mixture of these, or variegated with brownish yellow. Cross-line beyond middle finely scalloped or represented by tiny black dots or dashes. Oval and kidney-mark as ground-colour or paler, with pale outlines. Variegated and richly marked forms predominate in northern and western Britain.
Similar species Worn examples of the plain grey-brown form could be mistaken for Common Rustic or Lesser Common Rustic, which have blunt-tipped forewing and kidney-mark usually narrower.
Flight season One generation. July-August. Comes to light in small numbers, and to sugar and flowers, notably of ragworts.
Life cycle Overwinters as an egg. Larva April-early June. Feeds at first within a spun terminal shoot, later between folded leaves. Pupates in an underground cocoon.
Larval foodplants Birches and probably sallows.
Habitat Fens, carr, woodland, heathland and moorland with birch scrub.
Status & distribution. Resident and immigrant. Local. Fairly well distributed in southern and south-east England, East Anglia and from north Wales and the Midlands north to Ross-shire. Very local elsewhere in southern mainland Britain. Immigrant in Orkney, probably from mainland Europe, since only plain forms occur here. Local in Ireland, from Co. Kerry to Co. Armagh.

Dingy Shears   page 327
Parastichtis ypsillon ([D. & S.])
Local. S,C,(N)   2314(9537)

Field characters FW 15-19mm. Diagnostic features are the rather plain, light or dark, soft greyish-brown or warm grey forewing, the blackish blotches between oval and kidney-mark and on both sides of oval, and the usually gently curved leading edge. Tooth-like mark in centre of forewing is variable in size and shape, and oval and kidney-mark may be joined.
Similar species F. *dissimilis* Knoch of Dog's Tooth has a white outermost cross-line, deeply jagged in middle, forming a distinct W.
Flight season One generation. Late June-early August. Comes regularly to light and sugar, usually in small numbers.
Life cycle Overwinters as an egg. Larva April-early June. Feeds at first inside a catkin, later at night, hiding under loose bark or in leaf litter by day. Pupates in a cocoon under bark or on the soil surface.
Larval foodplants The leaves and catkins of

willows, sallows and poplars.
Habitat Damp woodland, marshes, fens and river-banks.
Status & distribution Resident. Local. Well distributed in southern and eastern England, including Scilly. More local in northern England, Wales and Man and very local in mainland Scotland, reaching the north coast. Rare in the Channel Islands.

Heart Moth
page 327
Dicycla oo (L.)
RDB. S   2315(9544)

Field characters FW 15-17mm. Kidney-mark is often a perfect heart-shape. Both this, the oval, the lines on outer edge and fringe of golden-yellow and reddish forewing are boldly outlined in reddish. Extent of greyish shading in central part of forewing varies considerably, and in widespread but infrequent f. *renago* Haw. it covers most of the wing.
Similar species None.
Flight season One generation. Late June-mid July. Comes to sugar, often well before dark. Comes fairly readily to light, usually after midnight, and the weather does not have to be unusually warm as sometimes believed.
Life cycle Overwinters as an egg, probably on oak twigs in the canopy of mature trees. Larva mid April-early June, between leaves strongly spun together. Beating for larvae is seldom successful, even at night, although occasionally they have been obtained from branches within reach of the ground. Pupates in a fragile cocoon just below ground.
Larval foodplants The young and expanding leaves of mature and over-mature Pedunculate Oak.
Habitat Woodland, lightly wooded commons and parkland with widely spaced mature Pedunculate Oaks, usually with other lower vegetation providing some shelter. At Leigh, Surrey, occurs in farmland with oaks growing in and around the fields. Soil types range from heavy clay to lighter heath-like conditions.
Status & distribution Resident. Red Data Book species. Very local and southern, and apparently prone to many years of great scarcity at some of its sites. Now occurs in numbers only in the Ashtead/Epsom area of Surrey, and in Windsor Great Park and its environs, Berkshire. Reported from various other localities in Surrey, but neither regular nor numerous at these. Still present in Salcey Forest, Northamptonshire, but has been lost from woodlands in Oxfordshire and Buckinghamshire owing to felling of old oaks. Recent records suggest other small populations may persist elsewhere. Three were seen at Wellington Country Park, Berkshire, in 1986, and one was recorded about 20km to the west, at Burghfield Common, Berkshire, on 26 June 1992. On 12 July 1994 a fresh adult was light-trapped at West Wickham, north-west Kent, a historic locality with records from 1896 and 1897 – the first record for Kent since 1919. Recorded in the Hampshire part of Pamber Forest on 1 and 17 July 1993, and also

Larva of White-spotted Pinion.

formerly reported in the New Forest. Survived in the Ongar/Stondon Massey area of Essex into the 1970s.

Lesser-spotted Pinion
page 327
Cosmia affinis (L.)
Local. S,(C)   2316(9548)

Field characters & Similar species FW 12-16mm. Small size of white markings at leading edge of reddish-brown forewing, which are only a slight broadening of the thin, angled cross-lines, distinguishes this species from White-spotted Pinion. Lunar-spotted Pinion has a better developed half-moon shape near tip of forewing, generally tinged pinkish and purple. Hindwing of Lesser-spotted Pinion is almost black with off-white edges, in contrast to those of White-spotted and Lunar-spotted Pinions which are usually pale brown. All three species pull forewings in tightly to the side of the body when fully at rest.
Flight season One generation. Mid July-late August. Comes to light from early in the night, sometimes in fair numbers, and to sugar.
Life cycle Overwinters as an egg. Larva late April-mid June. Pupates in a cocoon among old leaves.
Larval foodplants English Elm, Small-leaved Elm and Wych Elm; also probably other elms.
Habitat Quite frequent in some elm woods and shelterbelts; also in hedgerows and other open sites, including some where Wych Elm is the only elm present.
Status & distribution Resident. Local. Widely and quite well distributed in Wales and England northwards to south Yorkshire, with occasional records from Cumbria. Over most of its range it has survived the major outbreaks of Dutch Elm Disease which killed off large elms in the 1970s and 1980s. Widespread and frequent in the Channel Islands.

White-spotted Pinion
page 327
Cosmia diffinis (L.)
pRDB. S,(C)   2317(9546)

Field characters & Similar species FW 14-16mm. Distinguished from Lesser-spotted and Lunar-spotted Pinions by its much larger and bolder, pure white markings on leading edge of forewing. These are especially obvious in ultraviolet light.

Flight season One generation. Late July-late August, rarely to mid September, but peak numbers are in early August. Male comes readily to light, arriving from about 10.30pm onwards. Female is much less frequent at light.

Life cycle Overwinters as an egg, probably on the foodplant. Larva April-mid June. Pupates in a cocoon between spun leaves or (reportedly) on bark.

Larval foodplants Formerly recorded both from English Elm and Wych Elm. The elms in the Huntingdonshire breeding sites have been identified as Small-leaved Elm and English Elm, and some are growing in single-species plantations. Many have reached full height, with much epicormic growth.

Habitat Elms growing in woodland, copses, plantations and shelterbelts. The larvae are reportedly more frequent on epicormic foliage, i.e. the shoots growing direct from the trunk. There is no evidence yet of breeding in low elm regrowth in hedges without large trees.

Status & distribution Resident. Proposed Red Data Book species. Formerly Nationally Scarce A. Until Dutch Elm Disease from the 1970s onwards, this moth was widely distributed in England and Wales north to the Mersey, with a more northerly population on the limestone in south Cumbria. During the 1990s it was seen annually and dependably only in a group of woodlands in Huntingdonshire and Cambridgeshire, with occasional scattered records elsewhere, suggesting a few isolated populations survived. Populations were re-found in 2002 in Essex and Bedfordshire.

Dun-bar   page 327
Cosmia trapezina (L.)
Common. T   2318(9550)

Field characters FW 13-16mm. Variable in colour, but easily recognised by the shape of central cross-lines on forewing; that before middle is very oblique and that beyond middle is curved or angled. Often, the central band thus formed is a different shade. Most frequently forewing is a shade of brown and central band is darker brown, but there are greyish and reddish forms and occasionally the central band is black (f. *badiofasciata* Teich). Kidney-mark usually obvious.

Similar species See Angle-striped Sallow.

Flight season One generation. Mid July-mid September. Comes readily to light, sugar and aphid honeydew, and recorded at flowers such as Hemp-agrimony and ragworts.

Life cycle Overwinters as an egg. Larva April-late June. Pupates in a cocoon in plant debris on the ground.

Larval foodplants The larvae have been beaten from most broadleaved trees and shrubs, particularly large larvae which feed on larvae of other moth species as well as leaves. Frequent on Pedunculate Oak, elms, birches, Blackthorn, hawthorns, Hazel, willows, Aspen and Field Maple, but also recorded from less abundant species such as Wild Service-tree.

Habitat Most situations with trees or shrubs, including gardens and hedgerows, but most abundant in woodland.

Status & distribution Resident. Common. Much the most widespread and frequent of the four *Cosmia* species in the British Isles. Very widely and well distributed in England, Wales and lowland Scotland. Recorded from Orkney and Shetland. Local on Man. The only *Cosmia* species recorded in Ireland, where it seems to be more frequent in the east. Widespread and frequent in the Channel Islands.

Lunar-spotted Pinion   page 327
Cosmia pyralina ([D. & S.])
Local. S,(C)   2319(9549)

Field characters FW 13-16mm. A half-moon-shaped marking near forewing tip gives this moth its common name, but the marking is more like a rose petal, frequently marked with pink and mauve as well as much white. Forewing otherwise deep brownish pink, usually with hardly a trace of white elsewhere, and has a curved leading edge. Hindwing pale brown, or sometimes darker, but never blackish.

Similar species Lesser-spotted Pinion has almost black hindwing, and white cross-lines on narrower, browner forewing, which usually has a rather straighter leading edge.

Flight season One generation. Early July-late August. Comes to light, sugar and aphid honeydew.

Life cycle Overwinters as an egg. Larva April-mid June. Pupates in a cocoon among plant debris.

Larval foodplants Blackthorn, hawthorns, Apple, Bullace, and elms including English Elm, Small-leaved Elm and Wych Elm.

Habitat Hedgerows, scrub, woodland, parks and occasionally gardens.

Status & distribution Resident. Local. Well distributed in southern, central and eastern England north to the Humber, with a few records from south Yorkshire. Less well distributed in south-west England and the West Midlands but reaches Cornwall and south Wales, with a few records north to Anglesey and Lancashire. Rare in the Channel Islands.

Saxon   page 327
Hyppa rectilinea (Esp.)
Nb. N   2320(9508)

Field characters FW 16-19mm. Fairly easily recognised, and rather invariable. Pale area at base of forewing extends round both sides of thick, black basal bar, cross-line before middle is very jagged in trailing half, and oval is small and compressed. Striking black central bar is also a consistent feature.

Similar species Light Brocade is somewhat similar, but paler patch at base of forewing is in leading half only, cross-line before middle is less jagged in trailing half, and oval is larger and rounded.

Flight season One generation. Late May-June. Sometimes found at rest on tree trunks and posts,

346

reportedly visits Raspberry flowers regularly, and comes readily to sugar and light, sometimes in numbers.

Life cycle Overwinters as a larva. Hatches in July and feeds until October, then forms a silk-lined chamber just below ground, in which it pupates in spring.

Larval foodplants A range of woody plants, including sallows, Bramble, Raspberry, Bearberry, Bilberry and Cowberry.

Habitat Light scrub and fringes of trees by streams and rivers in moorland; also upland marshes, open woodland and recently-established plantations.

Status & distribution Resident. Nationally Scarce B. Recorded from widely scattered localities over much of northern and central mainland Scotland and Mull, also occurring locally in the Southern Uplands, the Borders, Cumbria and Northumberland. Several recorded in Yorkshire in the late 19th century but not since. In Ireland apparently in the south-west only, where it has been found regularly in the Killarney district of Co. Kerry (e.g. Torc Wood) for many years.

Dark Arches   page 327
Apamea monoglypha (Hufn.)
Common. T   2321(9748)

Field characters FW 19-26mm. Quite variable in colour, but easily recognised. Forewing rather pointed, most frequently greyish brown, but can also be pale greyish straw, dark brown or blackish. Large and usually conspicuous oval and kidney-mark and a W-mark near outer edge are constant characters. Another useful diagnostic feature is a dark V-mark on either side of thorax, present even in dark examples. F. *infuscata* White is blackish with the markings conspicuous and f. *aethiops* Stdgr. is similar but with the markings obscured. This dark form predominates in parts of northern Britain. A rather small, warm brown form lacking in contrast occurs in Shetland.

Similar species See Northern Arches and Crescent Striped.

Flight season Usually one generation, June-August. Sometimes a partial second generation in the south, September-November. Comes to light, often in abundance, and to sugar and flowers, where it usually rests with wings horizontal and quivering.

Life cycle Overwinters as a larva in a chamber among grass roots. Larva August-June. Feeds when small on flowers and seeds, later on roots and stem-bases from within its chamber. Pupates under-ground.

Larval foodplants Grasses, including Common Couch and Cock's-foot. Egg-laying observed in the wild into leaf-sheaths of Tufted Hair-grass.

Habitat Ubiquitous. In gardens, all types of grass-land, arable land, hedgerows and verges, woodland, marshes, heathland and high moorland.

Status & distribution Resident. Common. Very well distributed and usually abundant throughout Great Britain, Man, Ireland and the Channel Islands.

Light Arches   page 327
Apamea lithoxylaea ([D. & S.])
Common. T   2322(9752)

Field characters FW 18-23mm. Forewing rather pointed, light reddish straw, finely marked with darker streaks and dots. Diagnostic characters are short, dark, roughly scythe-shaped mark near centre of wing, thickened in middle, and two diffuse brownish wedges on outer edge. Cross-line beyond middle is curved and represented by fine blackish dots. Variation slight.

Similar species See Reddish Light Arches.

Flight season One generation. Late June-early August. Comes regularly to light, sometimes in quite large numbers, and to sugar and flowers.

Life cycle Overwinters as a larva, probably at the base of the foodplant, on or below the ground. Larva August-June. Pupates underground.

Larval foodplants Initially the flowers and seeds and later the stem-bases of grasses, including Annual Meadow-grass.

Habitat A wide range of grassy places, including gardens, calcareous grassland and woodland rides.

Status & distribution Resident. Common. Widespread and frequent throughout most of Great Britain, Man, Ireland, and the Channel Islands, but not recorded from Shetland.

Reddish Light Arches   page 327
Apamea sublustris (Esp.)
Local. S,C   2323(9753)

Field characters & Similar species FW 18-21mm. Quite similar to Light Arches, but generally darker with slightly shorter, broader and less pointed forewing. Diagnostic markings are clearly defined reddish-brown wedges on outer edge, and instead of a centrally placed scythe-shaped mark, a shorter, evenly thickened solid brown bar. Pattern is quite constant, but ground-colour varies from whitish to reddish straw. See also Pale Shining Brown.

Flight season One generation. June-July. Comes to light from dusk, sometimes in numbers, and to sugar.

Life cycle Early stages apparently unknown in the wild, but probably overwinters close to the ground as a larva, like closely related species, and feeds until June, pupating underground. Hatches in August in captivity.

Larval foodplants In captivity, at first the flowers and seeds of unspecified grasses, and later the roots.

Habitat Chalk and limestone grassland, breckland, well vegetated sand-dunes and shingle.

Status & distribution Resident. Local. Fairly well distributed and locally frequent in central southern and south-east England. Local in Cambridgeshire and in East Anglia, mainly in Breckland. Very local in south-west England, the Midlands, northern England, Wales and Ireland.

347

Northern Arches
page 327

Apamea zeta (Treit.)

ssp. *assimilis* (Doubl.)

Na. N   2324(9761)

Exile
page 327

ssp. *marmorata* (Zett.)

Shetland

Field characters & Similar species

Northern Arches: FW 17-19mm. Key feature is broad, deep-scaled shaggy thorax, alongside which legs look spindly because not especially furry. About the size of Dusky Brocade and not as big as Dark Arches, with less pointed forewing. These are broad and blunt, not relatively narrow like those of Dark Brocade. Both Dusky and Dark Brocades have a sharply defined double crest of scales on thorax, absent in Northern Arches. Forewing colours and patterning variable: usually dark brown, even blackish, but sometimes paler brown and more variegated, but indistinctly marked, although kidney-mark is generally paler. Lighter brownish forms usually have a pinkish tinge, especially to cross-lines, which distinguishes them from Confused and Dusky Brocade. Outer edge of kidney-mark in Dark Brocade has three points, not two. Some varieties closely resemble Exile.

Exile: FW 19-20mm. Tends to be larger, more strongly marked and less reddish than Northern Arches, although some of the latter collected from mainland Scotland are almost indistinguishable. Ground-colour varies considerably, from honey-coloured on Unst to blackish on the mainland of Shetland.

Flight season One generation. Northern Arches: July-early August, less frequently to late August. Comes readily to sugar and light. Exile: Mid July-August.

Life cycle Overwinters as a larva, possibly over more than one winter. Larva September-May or June. Pupates underground.

Larval foodplants Not confirmed in the wild. Assumed to be the lower stems and roots of grasses which occur in its habitats, as with all the other *Apamea* species found in the British Isles, possibly starting development on the flowers and seeds. Has been reared successfully on Purple Moor-grass.

Habitat Northern Arches: Peaty moorland and upland grassland (from c.200m to over 1000m). Exile: Peaty moorland and grassland, often close to sea level.

Status & distribution Resident. Northern Arches: Nationally Scarce A, but probably more widespread than records suggest. Considered an endemic subspecies to mainland Scotland, Orkney and Arran; widespread but local, mainly in the Highlands and other upland areas of northern and western Scotland. One was caught at light by Belling Burn, on the north bank of Kielder Reservoir, Northumberland, on 13 July 1992, probably the first record of the moth in England. Exile: Within the British Isles occurs in Shetland only, hence the name Exile, and is locally frequent here. Also well distributed in Norway and Sweden. One was recorded on Fair Isle in 1987.

Crescent Striped
page 327

Apamea oblonga (Haw.)

Nb. S,C   2325(9765)

Field characters FW 18-21mm. Forewing quite broad, with leading edge nearly straight and tip rather blunt; pale to dark grey-brown with a smooth, silky texture. Kidney-mark partly outlined in creamy white. Outermost cross-line forms a distinct W and a solid dark bar joins central cross-lines. Most frequent form is faintly marked, but f. *abjecta* Hb. is strongly marked.

Similar species Dark Arches is larger, has more pointed forewing, lacks white outline on kidney-mark, and has V-marks on thorax. Dusky Brocade is smaller with a more curved leading edge. Confused has a similar combination of features, but is also smaller. All lack silky texture of Crescent Striped. Large Nutmeg has narrower, more pointed, warmer brown, mottled forewing. See also White Colon.

Flight season One generation. Late June-early August. Visits flowers of Marram, thistles, Sea Campion and rushes, from dusk. Comes readily to sugar and light, sometimes in numbers.

Life cycle Overwinters as a larva. Larva late summer-late May or June. Hides by day in tunnels among roots or under stones, feeding at night and not climbing stems. Pupates in an underground chamber.

Larval foodplants The roots and stem-bases of grasses, including Common and Reflexed Saltmarsh-grass, Bulbous Meadow-grass and Red Fescue.

Habitat Saltmarshes, estuaries, mudflats, coastal grazing marshes, especially by ditches, brackish marshes, dune-slacks, the Norfolk Broads, and fens.

Status & distribution Resident. Nationally Scarce B. Almost exclusively coastal, with occasional wanderers inland; also an infrequent resident in the fens of East Anglia. Widely recorded up the east coast of England north to Northumberland, but particularly the marshes of north Kent and Essex, the Thames Estuary, the Wash and the Humber. Very local on the south coast, mainly around the Solent and the Isle of Wight, but regularly recorded at Dungeness, Kent. Very local on the west coasts of England and Wales, mainly around the Severn, the Mersey and north to Morecambe Bay, Lancashire. Also reported from south-west Scotland. Some inland records are undoubtedly misidentifications, although one recorded from Potteric Carr, South Yorkshire, on 6 August 1982 is genuine. Thinly-scattered records on the east coast of Ireland, from Co. Waterford north to Co. Antrim. Recorded once from Guernsey in 1989.

Clouded-bordered Brindle
page 328

Apamea crenata (Hufn.)

Common. T   2326(9755)

Field characters FW 18-22mm. Variable, with two distinct colour forms. In one, forewing is light yellowish brown, tinged with red or grey, often inclining to greyish white, especially along trailing edge. Key features are two well-defined reddish-brown wedges projecting from outer edge, some-times joined by a thin brown band. Wedge beyond kidney-mark is often double-pointed, and that near trailing edge is usually longer and narrower. There is another long brown pointed wedge at base of trailing edge. The second colour form, f. *combusta* Haw., is rather plain reddish brown to mahogany, with the oval and kidney-mark pale-outlined but all other markings faint. Similar blackish-brown or blackish-red forms without pale markings are known, but are rare. Intermediates between the two main forms occasionally occur.

Similar species See Clouded Brindle and Scarce Brindle.

Flight season One generation. Late May-July. Comes frequently to light, sugar and flowers, and is often seen flying fairly low over grassland at dusk.

Life cycle Overwinters as a larva close to the ground. Larva August-April. Feeds at first among flowerheads of foodplant, later feeding on the leaves and hiding at ground level by day. Pupates in a loose cell among roots.

Larval foodplants Grasses, including Cock's-foot.

Habitat Gardens, all types of grassland, fens, moorland and woodland rides.

Status & distribution Resident. Common. Throughout Great Britain, Man and Ireland. Local on Jersey, rare on Guernsey.

Clouded Brindle
page 328

Apamea epomidion (Haw.)

Common. S,C,(N)   2327(9756)

Field characters & Similar species FW 17-20mm. Extensive dark brown or reddish-brown brindling on forewing of some examples is distinctive (f. *lipara* Tams), but some are mainly pale, and relatively plain. Lighter parts of forewing vary from yellowish brown or fawn to reddish. A pale, wavy cross-line near outer edge has two short, ill-defined dark wedges projecting inwards from it. There are two short, thick, dark streaks at forewing base and one along trailing edge. Oval and basal side of kidney-mark heavily outlined with dark brown.

Similar species Pale examples can superficially resemble Clouded-bordered Brindle, which lacks pale cross-line in dark area along outer edge and has dark outer wedges well-defined, usually only one basal streak or wedge (along trailing edge) and oval and basal side of kidney-mark not darkly outlined.

Flight season One generation. June-July. Comes to light in small numbers and to sugar and flowers.

Life cycle Overwinters as a larva, probably close to the ground. Larva August-early March. Feeds at night except when small, hiding at ground level by day. Pupates in a cocoon on the soil surface.

Larval foodplants Grasses, including Cock's-foot and Tufted Hair-grass, feeding at first on the seeds and later on the leaves.

Habitat Broadleaved woodland and long-established scrub, including some gardens and parkland.

Status & distribution Resident. Common. Fairly well distributed and locally fairly frequent in England and Wales. Local in southern and western Scotland and in Ireland. Rare on Man and Jersey, occasional on Guernsey.

Scarce Brindle
page 328

Apamea lateritia (Hufn.)

Immigrant.   2328(9758)

Field characters FW 19-24mm. Forewing rather plain, reddish brown, light yellowish brown, dull brown, grey-brown, or even blackish. Outer part of kidney-mark normally outlined in white, even in dark examples. Oval less conspicuous. Cross-line of small black spots beyond kidney-mark. Usually small whitish spots along leading edge.

Similar species The reddish-brown f. *combusta* of the Clouded-bordered Brindle is smaller, with a conspicuous pale oval near kidney-mark and pale bases to the narrower, more pointed forewing. Pale Shining Brown has reddish-brown forewing but has shiny texture, broad reddish outermost cross-line, conspicuous pale oval and kidney-mark and lacks spotting on leading edge.

Flight season One generation. As suspected immigrants in July-August, but June-August in mainland Europe. Comes to light.

Life cycle Overwinters as a larva, feeding September-May.

Larval foodplants The roots of various grasses, such as Sheep's-fescue, Tufted Hair-grass and Wavy Hair-grass.

Habitat Possibly established briefly in gardens and allotments at Dovercourt, Essex, but unconfirmed.

Status & distribution Immigrant. Twelve published British records, the first about 1887 at Porthkerry, Glamorgan, the second not until 17 July 1972 in south London, with another the following night in Bexley, Kent. Six records from Dovercourt, Essex, between 1985 and 1990 may have been the result of temporary establishment. The only others are from Spurn, on the Yorkshire coast, on 17 July 1991, Norwick, Shetland, on 11 and 12 August 1995 and Landguard, Suffolk, on 4 July 2000. Resident in most European countries. The predominantly easterly distribution of the British records and meteorological backtracking for the two from Shetland in 1995 suggest a northern European origin.

350

Confused
page 328

Apamea furva ([D. & S.])

ssp. *britannica* Cock.

Local. N,W,S
2329(9759)

Field characters FW 16-19mm. Forewing dull, mousy brown, leading edge straight or slightly curved towards tip. Markings fine, dainty and rather indistinct, but outline of kidney-mark and wavy outermost cross-line are usually whitish. There is a tuft of long scales near base of trailing edge, forming a slight projection, and two dark narrow outer bands on underside of forewing. A local form, distinctly greyer, occurs in the Burren, Co. Clare.

Similar species Easily confused with the very variable f. *obscura* of Dusky Brocade. This lacks a scale tuft near base of trailing edge, and also has generally broader forewing with a more curved leading edge, usually with an element of richer brown and with only one dark band on underside. See also Crescent Striped and Nutmeg.

Flight season One generation. July-September. Comes to light and sugar.

Life cycle Overwinters as a larva underground. Larva September-June. Hides underground by day and pupates in the soil without a cocoon.

Larval foodplants The roots and lower stems of grasses, including Rough Meadow-grass and Wood Meadow-grass.

Habitat Rocky coasts and mountain moorland; also very locally on sand-dunes.

Status & distribution Resident. Local. Locally frequent in Wales, the north and West Midlands, northern England and Scotland, including the Hebrides, Orkney and Shetland. Very local in south-west England and near Dover and Folkestone, Kent. Widely distributed but local in Ireland. Rare on Man and in the Channel Islands.

Dusky Brocade
page 328

Apamea remissa (Hb.)

Common. T
2330(9766)

Field characters & Similar species FW 17-19mm Very variable. Forewing quite broad, leading edge arched towards tip. Colour ranges from brownish grey, usually marbled with slightly richer brown and with inconspicuous markings (f. *obscura* Haw.), or with stronger markings, including a distinct central black bar and two basal streaks (f. *submissa* Treit.) to greyish brown with striking paler, sometimes sandy, markings.

Similar species See Confused, Crescent Striped, White Colon, Dark Brocade and Large Nutmeg. F. *submissa* can superficially resemble Light Brocade, which is noticeably greyer, or Pale-shouldered Brocade, which has a whiter W-mark; both have hairy eyes.

Flight season One generation. June-July. Comes regularly to light, and to sugar and flowers.

Life cycle Overwinters as a larva close to the ground. Larva August-April. Feeds at night except when small, hiding at ground level by day. Pupates underground.

Larval foodplants Grasses, including Reed Canary-grass and Common Couch, feeding at first on the flowers and seeds and later on the leaves.

Habitat A range of grassy places, including gardens, damp pasture, drier calcareous grassland, hedgerows and open woodland.

Status & distribution Resident. Common. Well distributed and often numerous throughout Great Britain, Man and Ireland. Widespread in small numbers in the Channel Islands.

Small Clouded Brindle
page 328

Apamea unanimis (Hb.)

Common. S,C,(N)
2331(9767)

Field characters FW 15-17mm. The small size and kidney-mark always outlined in white, more noticeably so along outer edge, are the most obvious features. Forewing pale or dark brown, reddish brown or olive brown, variably marbled with paler or darker markings. Two basal streaks, one placed centrally and one along trailing edge.

Similar species Resembles some forms of the extremely variable Common Rustic and Lesser Common Rustic, which have blunter forewing, usually lacking a centrally-placed basal streak, and crescent-shaped mark on hindwing smaller and narrower, especially noticeable on underside. Common Rustics emerge from early July, by which time Small Clouded Brindles are usually in worn condition.

Flight season One generation. Late May-early July. Comes to light, sugar and flowers, particularly those of rushes.

Life cycle Overwinters as a fully grown larva among leaf litter or in other sheltered places. Larva July-March or April. Pupates among leaf litter or inside a dead plant stem.

Larval foodplants Grasses, including Reed Canary-grass and Wavy Hair-grass.

Habitat Marshes, fens, margins of ponds and lakes, damp grassland and damp open woodland.

Status & distribution Resident. Common. Well distributed and fairly frequent in England and Wales. Local in Scotland north to Aberdeenshire and the Outer Hebrides, on Man and in northern parts of Ireland. Rare in the Channel Islands.

2332 see below 2336

Large Nutmeg
page 328

Apamea anceps ([D. & S.])

Local. S,C
2333(9770)

Field characters FW 16-21mm. Forewing often rather pointed, but varying somewhat in shape and width, pale straw to sandy brown, or greyish brown, with sandy marbling or panels, particularly near outer edge. Oval and kidney-mark usually distinct and often outlined whitish. There are two very fine dark cross-lines, the first jagged and the second scalloped, and two darker blunt wedges along outer margin. Rather variable in size.

Similar species Dark examples somewhat resemble

Dusky Brocade (f. *obscura* Haw.), which lacks sandy marbling. See also Rustic Shoulder-knot, Crescent Striped and Pale Shining Brown.

Flight season One generation. June-July. Comes regularly to light, and to sugar and flowers.

Life cycle Overwinters as a larva close to the ground. Larva August-April. Feeds at night, hiding by day in a silken cell. Pupates underground.

Larval foodplants Grasses, including Cock's-foot, Common Couch and cereal crops, initially feeding on the flowers and seeds and later on the leaves.

Habitat Usually dry calcareous grassland, including pasture, arable farmland, some gardens, and woodland rides and edges. Occasionally in habitats on more poorly drained clays.

Status & distribution Resident. Local. Well distributed and locally abundant, particularly on well-drained farmland, in south-east and central southern England. Local in south-west England, Wales, the Midlands and northern England. Rare on Man. One reported from Jersey in 1979.

Rustic Shoulder-knot   page 328
Apamea sordens (Hufn.)

Common. T   2334(9771)

Field characters & Similar species FW 16-19mm. Combination of black and slightly branched basal streak on broad and rather plain, quite pointed sandy-brown or greyish-brown forewing is diagnostic. Oval and kidney-mark distinct, the latter often outlined whitish. Forewing sometimes with a reddish tinge. Darker forms predominate in north and west. There is little variation in markings but basal streak is sometimes greatly reduced.

Similar species Large Nutmeg has more marbled forewing, which may also have a basal streak, but this is brown, indistinct and not branched. Dusky Brocade is greyer and less plain.

Flight season One generation. May-July. Comes to light, sugar and flowers.

Life cycle Overwinters as a larva close to the ground. Larva July-March. Pupates in a strong cocoon on or just below the ground.

Larval foodplants Grasses, including Cock's-foot, Common Couch and cereal crops, initially feeding on the seeds and later the leaves.

Habitat A wide range of grasslands, arable farmland, woodland rides and many gardens, including in urban areas.

Status & distribution Resident. Common. Well distributed and often abundant throughout Great Britain, Man and Ireland, but rare in Orkney and doubtfully recorded from Shetland. Widespread in small numbers in the Channel Islands.

Slender Brindle   page 328
Apamea scolopacina (Esp.)

Common. S,C   2335(9774)

Field characters FW 14-17mm. Quite distinctive. Forewing pale straw-coloured or orange-brown with

dark outer edge, kidney-mark strongly outlined in white, with adjacent dark brown patch. A central chocolate-brown spot on thorax and trailing edge of forewing is very obvious at rest. Forewing fairly broad, with a rather curved leading edge and two very fine black scalloped cross-lines, the outer more distinct. These markings show little variation.

Similar species None.

Flight season One generation. Late June-mid August. Comes to light, sugar and flowers.

Life cycle Overwinters as a larva close to the ground. Larva August-May. Pupates in an underground cocoon.

Larval foodplants Woodland grasses, including Wood Melick, Wood Meadow-grass and False Brome, and wood-rushes, feeding at first inside the stems and later on the leaves and flowers.

Habitat Chiefly woodland with grassy rides and clearings, but sometimes more open country.

Status & distribution Resident. Common. Quite well distributed in central southern, south-east and south-west England, Wales and the Midlands, north to Yorkshire, Cumbria and Dumfries & Galloway. Rather local in eastern England, from Cambridgeshire north to Yorkshire, and including East Anglia. Rare on Man. Discovered in Ireland in 1999 at Rostrevor Forest, Co. Down. Local and occasional in the Channel Islands.

Double Lobed   page 328
Apamea ophiogramma (Esp.)

Common. T   2336(9775)

Field characters FW 13-16mm. The smallest and slimmest species of the genus, and rather strikingly and uniquely marked. Forewing rather narrow, sandy, pale or dull reddish brown. A large, roughly triangular reddish-brown or dark brown blotch extends along leading edge almost to tip and into central area, surrounding pale kidney-mark, and culminating in a dark bar. The lower edge of this blotch is variably edged with white. A melanic form occurs, as illustrated, in which forewing is mainly dark brown, but the large, dark, double-lobed blotch at leading edge remains visible.

Similar species None.

Flight period One generation. Late June-August. Comes to light, sugar and flowers.

Life cycle Overwinters as a larva inside a stem of the foodplant. Larva August-early June. Pupates in a cocoon on the ground or in leaf litter.

Larval foodplants Reed Canary-grass, Reed Sweet-grass and cultivated Pampas-grass, feeding inside the stems and burrowing downwards.

Habitat Fens, marshes, riverbanks and lake margins, water-meadows and damp woodland. Also in gardens where it breeds on cultivated Reed Canary-grass and Pampas-grass.

Status & distribution Resident. Common. Quite well distributed throughout England, Wales, Man, and southern Scotland locally north to Aberdeenshire and Ireland. Rare on Jersey.

351

Clasper short, roughly triangular

Tawny Marbled Minor

Clasper long, almost straight

Marbled Minor

Ventral view
(hairs from left-hand valve removed)

Clasper quite long, distinctly bent

Rufous Minor

Detail of cucullus

Genitalia of male *Oligia* species.

Union Rustic page 328
Eremobina pabulatricula (Brahm)
Former resident; extinct. 2332(9778)

Field characters & Similar species A whitish-grey moth, rather like a pale form of Minor Shoulder-knot, but with an additional dark bar in centre of forewing near trailing edge and more pointed forewing.
Flight season One generation. Mid July-mid August. Comes to sugar before dusk, and also to light. Recorded at rest on oak trunks by day.
Life cycle Overwinters as a larva. Larva about September-late May or June.
Larval foodplants Unknown in the British Isles. Reported from woodland grasses in mainland Europe.
Habitat Grassy places in woodland.
Status & distribution Extinct former resident. Most of the records are from Yorkshire and the east Midlands, where the moth was sometimes frequent. Some 116 were captured in Wharncliffe Wood, Yorkshire, in 1888, and about 60 were seen near Lincoln in early August 1916. The moth was last seen in these areas in 1919. There are also a few older scattered single records from Glamorgan, Shropshire, Leicestershire, Norfolk, Suffolk, Cheshire and Cumbria. Specimens were collected in Scotland, near Paisley, Renfrewshire, until 1902. The last British record is from Bushey Heath, Hertfordshire, in 1935.

Marbled Minor page 328
Oligia strigilis (L.)
Common. T 2337(9780)

Field characters & Similar species FW 11-13mm. Highly variable and only separable with certainty from comparably variable Rufous Minor and Tawny Marbled Minor by differences in genitalia, a simple operation with males. Brightly-marked examples of all three species are usually characterised by a solid black bar between central cross-lines of forewing and a broad paler band beyond, but a large proportion of most populations are blackish, obscurely-marked melanics. However, some characters are helpful in selecting probable examples of each species for detailed examination. Large examples with outer band chalky white, beyond middle cross-line well defined, black and scalloped beyond kidney-mark, and an orange tuft at rear end of thorax, are likely to be Marbled Minors. Outer band can also be greyish white, light brown, reddish brown, dark brown or even absent, as may be black central bar. Equally variable throughout its range. See also Rosy Minor.
Flight season One generation. Late May-July. Comes regularly to light, sugar and honeydew.
Life cycle Overwinters as a larva. Larva August-May. Feeds inside a stem, moving to new ones as it grows. Pupates among the roots of the foodplant.
Larval foodplants Grasses, including Cock's-foot, Common Couch and Reed Canary-grass.
Habitat A wide range of grassy places, including gardens, grassland on most types of soil, woodland rides and marshes.
Status & distribution Resident. Common. Well distributed and frequent throughout mainland Britain, Scilly, Man, and the Channel Islands, although less frequent in Scotland. Apparently rather local in Ireland, more so than Tawny Marbled Minor.

Rufous Minor page 328
Oligia versicolor (Borkh.)
Local. S,C,(N) 2338(9781)

Field characters & Similar species FW 11-12mm. See Marbled Minor. Medium-sized, well-marked examples with bright, conspicuous pale brown oval and kidney-mark are likely to be Rufous Minors. These are often marbled with reddish brown, and have one or more reddish-brown tufts on thorax and a greyish-white outer band. Note that there is a form of Tawny Marbled Minor in which forewing is extensively tinged with deep reddish brown. See also Rosy Minor.
Flight season One generation. June-July. Comes to light and sugar.
Life cycle Overwinters as a larva. Larva August-spring. In captivity feeds inside a stem, moving to new ones as it grows. Pupates in a flimsy cocoon among the roots of the foodplant.
Larval foodplants As yet, unknown in the wild. In captivity, the insides of the stems of grasses.

Habitat Woodland, heathland, coastal cliffs and many other grassy places. Much less likely to be found in urban areas (except London) than Marbled or Tawny Marbled Minor.

Status & distribution Resident. Local. Probably under-recorded, but apparently somewhat thinly distributed throughout England, Wales and southern Scotland. Apparently very local in Ireland and only confirmed from Cos. Tyrone, Clare, Galway and Kerry. Confirmed on Man but status uncertain. Widespread and frequent in the Channel Islands.

Tawny Marbled Minor
page 328

Oligia latruncula ([D. & S.])

Common. S,C,(N)   2339(9782)

Field characters & Similar species FW 11-13mm. See Marbled Minor. Small, blackish examples with a brown, often coppery outer or central band and no reddish or orange tufts on thorax are likely to be Tawny Marbled Minors. The whitish-banded form is more rare, except in Ireland where it is frequent, although examples with a light brown band tinged whitish occur elsewhere but are relatively infrequent. See also Rosy Minor.

Flight season One generation. Late May-late July, or early August in northern Britain. Comes regularly to light, and to sugar.

Life cycle Overwinters as a larva. Larva August-April or May. Feeds inside a stem, moving to new ones as it grows. Pupates in a flimsy cocoon among the roots of the foodplant.

Larval foodplants Grasses, including Cock's-foot.

Habitat A wide range of grasslands, including woodland rides and gardens.

Status & distribution Resident. Common. Well distributed throughout England, Wales, Scilly, southern Scotland, Man, Ireland and the Channel Islands. Local further north in mainland Scotland, to Inverness-shire.

Middle-barred Minor
page 328

Oligia fasciuncula (Haw.)

Common. T   2340(9784)

Field characters FW 10-12mm. A small, quite thickset and distinctive noctuid. Diagnostic feature is a dark central bar along forewing, between central cross-lines, edged at each end with white, most strongly on its outer edge. Two main colour forms: orange-brown and pale greyish brown (f. *pallida* Tutt). Variation is relatively slight, but in north-east England dull greyish-brown forms occur, and in northern Britain the moth generally tends to be smaller and darker.

Similar species Female Small Dotted Buff is slimmer. See also Cloaked Minor and Least Minor.

Flight season One generation. June-July, or early August in northern Britain. Comes to light, sugar and flowers.

Life cycle Overwinters as a larva. Larva August-May. Feeds at night, hiding by day inside a leaf-sheath.

Pupates in a cocoon near the ground.

Larval foodplants Grasses, particularly Tufted Hair-grass.

Habitat Damp grassland, marshes, fens, woodland edges, rides and clearings; also regularly in gardens.

Status & distribution Resident. Common. Well distributed and fairly frequent throughout Great Britain, Man, Ireland and the Channel Islands.

Cloaked Minor
page 328

Mesoligia furuncula ([D. & S.])

Common. T   2341(9786)

353

Field characters & Similar species FW 10-12mm. More slender than the other minors, with narrower forewing. Extremely variable. In distinctive f. *bicoloria* Vill., basal half of forewing is brown, contrasting sharply with broad white outer half and thereby forming a 'cloak' when moth is at rest. Other less contrasting forms occur, often with a short dark central bar, somewhat resembling Rosy Minor, but not pinkish brown. See also Least Minor and female Small Dotted Buff. F. *reticulata* Tutt is brownish with a whitish kidney-mark and obscurely marbled with greyish white and shades of brown. These and almost unmarked brown, dark brown or dull straw-coloured forms, with outer edge darker, occur quite frequently. Plain, light straw-coloured forms occur on sand-dunes in western Ireland and also in Northumberland, where f. *latistriata* Hoff. & Knud. occurs in addition, also pale with a long blackish streak near trailing edge. These pale forms are somewhat like Small Wainscot, which is stouter, usually with a central dark streak on forewing.

Flight season One generation. Late July-early September. Comes to light, sugar and flowers, especially of Marram and ragworts. Male flies low over the ground late in the day, especially around sunset.

Life cycle Overwinters as a larva. Larva August-early June. Feeds inside stems, then eats out a chamber at base of foodplant, in which it pupates.

Larval foodplants Grasses, including Sheep's-fescue, Tufted Hair-grass and False Oat-grass.

Habitat Typically in open, well-drained grassland on light soils, usually with a short sward, especially coastal sand-dunes and cliffs, chalk downland and some gardens.

Status & distribution Resident. Common. Well distributed in southern Britain, including Scilly, and the Channel Islands. Local and more coastal in northern England, mainland Scotland, the Inner Hebrides, Man and Ireland.

Rosy Minor
page 328

Mesoligia literosa (Haw.)

Common. T   2342(9787)

Field characters & Similar species FW 10-13mm. Mixture of pinkish or reddish brown and grey is diagnostic in most cases. Ground-colour sometimes fawnish. Central cross-lines are strongly bowed towards one another near centre and consequently dark bar joining them is short. In the London area and elsewhere in southern England, the Midlands and northern England, rather dark, poorly-marked forms are frequent, along with brownish-black f. *aethalodes* Rich. A very pale form occurs on the Sussex coast and particularly bright forms occur in western Ireland. Marbled, Rufous and Tawny Marbled Minors are similar in build, but central cross-lines are further apart, so that any dark central bar is longer; they also emerge earlier in the year. See also Cloaked Minor.

Flight season One generation. Mid July-late August. Comes to light, sugar and flowers, especially of ragworts and Marram.

Life cycle Overwinters as a larva. Larva September-early June. Feeds at first on roots, then inside a stem. Pupates in a thin cocoon in soil or leaf litter.

Larval foodplants Various grasses, including Lyme-grass, Marram, Cock's-foot, and also cereal crops and sedges.

Habitat Various open calcareous habitats, including grassland, fens, scrub, gardens, coastal cliffs and sand-dunes.

Status & distribution Resident. Common. Most abundant in coastal situations but well distributed inland in calcareous areas, and at lower densities elsewhere, in mainland Britain, the Inner Hebrides, Man and Ireland. Local and occasional on Jersey, rare on Guernsey.

Common Rustic

page 329

Mesapamea secalis (L.)

Common. T   2343(9789)

Field characters FW 12-16mm. Extremely variable, but with two consistent features. Forewing is blunt-tipped and outer edge is rounded and not sharply angled. Kidney-mark is always discernible and at least partly outlined with white, sometimes largely white or creamy white, usually with roughly concentric markings. Ground-colour can be almost any shade of yellowish brown, greyish brown, reddish brown, blackish brown or black, and be either uniform or patchy. Cross-lines vary in strength and central ones may be joined by a blackish bar. One distinctive form, usually without blackish bar, is largely yellowish brown, with dark brown along leading edge and around oval and kidney-mark. Occasionally there is a broad, darker central cross-band.

Similar species See Lesser Common Rustic and Remm's Rustic, separable only by examination of genitalia, and Small Clouded Brindle. Crescent and the ear moths all have sharp-tipped forewing. See also Oak Rustic.

Flight season One generation. July-August. Comes to light, sometimes in large numbers, and to sugar and flowers, especially of grasses, buddleias and ragworts.

Life cycle Overwinters as a larva. Larva September-May. Feeds inside a stem, moving to new ones as it grows. Pupates in a cocoon underground.

Larval foodplants Grasses, including Cock's-foot, Tall Fescue, Tufted Hair-grass and cereal crops; also Hairy Wood-rush.

Habitat A wide range of grasslands and grassy places, including gardens, farmland, heathland, calcareous grassland and woodland.

Status & distribution Resident. Common. Well distributed and generally abundant throughout England, lowland Scotland and Wales, Man, Ireland and the Channel Islands.

Lesser Common Rustic

page 329

Mesapamea didyma (Esp.)

Common. T   2343a(9790)

Field characters & Similar species FW 11-16mm. Almost identical to Common Rustic, with a comparable range of variation, and only separable by examination of genitalia. Slightly smaller on average. Black examples with kidney-mark chalky white are almost invariably Lesser Common Rustic. See also Remm's Rustic and Small Clouded Brindle. Crescent and the ear moths all have sharp-tipped forewing.

Flight season One generation. July-August. Comes to light, sugar and flowers.

Life cycle Overwinters as a larva. Larva September-May. Feeds inside a stem, moving to new ones as it grows. Pupates in an underground cocoon.

Larval foodplants Grasses, including Cock's-foot and fescues.

Habitat A wide range of grasslands and grassy places, including gardens.

Status & distribution Resident. Common. Only recently recognised as a species, so knowledge of its distribution is very incomplete. Indications are that it occurs throughout most of Great Britain, Man and Ireland. Confirmed from the Channel Islands, where the distinctive black form is widespread.

Remm's Rustic

not illustrated

Mesapamea remmi Rézb.-Res.

Local. S,C,?N   2343b(9791)

Field characters & Similar species FW 11-16mm. Remm's Rustic is listed as a distinct species in both the British and European checklists, but some authorities are doubtful of its validity and the authors of some recent works have opted not to include it. It was described on the basis of slight differences in genitalia and is otherwise indistinguishable from Common Rustic and Lesser Common Rustic. This account is provided for consistency with the British list.

Flight season, Life cycle & Larval foodplants Assumed to be similar to the Common Rustic.

Habitat Individuals conforming to the genitalia descriptions have been recorded in gardens and other open habitats.

Status & distribution Resident. Overlooked, if distinct. Distribution largely unknown. Individuals matching the genitalia descriptions have been confirmed from southern England (e.g. Weyhill,

Hampshire, August 1984 and July 1985). Appears to be very scarce compared with Common and Lesser Common Rustics, leading to speculation that it may be only an occasional naturally occurring hybrid or variant. One author reported just three individuals in a sample of 600 *Mesapamea,* and many other moth-trappers have failed to find any.

Least Minor page 329
Photedes captiuncula (Treit.)

ssp. *expolita* (Stt.)
RDB. C   2344(9794)

ssp. *tincta* (Kane)
Ireland

Field characters & Similar species FW 7-9mm. Smaller and more slender than all other noctuid species. The larger male is distinguished from small forms of Cloaked Minor by trailing half of outer edge of darker central cross-band, which is straighter, and often strongly edged with white, and broader forewing. The Irish ssp. *tincta* Kane is redder and brighter in colour than the English ssp. *expolita* Stt., with stronger white edging to central band, sometimes extending into leading half. These cross-lines are more pronounced in female of both subspecies.
Flight season One generation. Mid June-early August. Male flies about wildly and erratically in sunny weather, usually between noon and 4pm, diving deep down among grass to rest, from which it is often disturbed at the slightest touch of the vegetation. Less active in dull weather. Comes to light.
Life cycle Overwinters as a part-grown larva in the sward. Larva August-late May. Pupates in a flimsy cocoon on the ground.
Larval foodplants Glaucous Sedge and possibly other sedges.
Habitat Open limestone grassland. Present in rough fields, usually on south-facing hills and dales near the coast, and grassy coastal cliff-tops.
Status & distribution Resident. Red Data Book species. Ssp. *expolita* is virtually confined to the carboniferous limestone formations in the extreme south of Cumbria (the Arnside/Beetham area north to Warton, near Kendal), and to the same formation in the Malham/Grassington area at the western edge of north Yorkshire and on the coast of Northumberland. Also occurs on the coast of Co. Durham on the Magnesian limestone from Blackhall Rocks to Beacon Point, just north of Hartlepool. There is an inland colony in Cassop Vale, Co. Durham, some 12km from the coast due west of Blackhall Rocks, also on Magnesian limestone. There are pre-1980 records from the Druridge Bay/Morpeth area of Northumberland on Westphalian coal measures. Records from outside these parts of Britain generally prove to be misidentifications, but odd individuals may turn up some distance from colonies. Ssp. *tincta* occurs in the Burren area of Cos. Clare and Galway and in similar habitat in Co. Mayo, and is locally frequent.

Small Dotted Buff page 329
Photedes minima (Haw.)
Common. T   2345(9795)

Field characters FW 11-14mm. Slender, with whitish-straw or yellowish-straw forewing, sometimes tinged with reddish brown. Forewing broad and rather plain in male, with leading edge gently curved. Central cross-lines very fine, blackish brown, scalloped or represented by a series of dots. There is a roughly triangular brown blotch on leading edge near tip, sometimes extended as a dark outer cross-band. This combination is diagnostic. Female is much smaller, with narrower forewing, either similarly marked to male or with a darker central band, most apparent towards trailing edge, and distinct whitish edging on cross-lines.
Similar species Female can resemble some forms of Cloaked Minor, but leading edge of forewing is less curved and central cross-lines are closer together towards trailing edge. See also Middle-barred Minor.
Flight season One generation. Late June-early August. Comes to light, the male more frequently, and occasionally to sugar. At dusk, male flies slowly over grassland, and female rests on grass stems.
Life cycle Overwinters as a larva. Larva August-early June. Feeds inside a stem, hollowing out the base. Pupates in an underground cocoon.
Larval foodplants Tufted Hair-grass.
Habitat Poorly drained grassland, including woodland rides and marshes. Occasional in some gardens.
Status & distribution Resident. Common. Well distributed and frequent throughout most of Great Britain, Man and Ireland. Recorded from Shetland but unclear if resident. Local and occasional on Jersey, rare on Guernsey.

Morris's Wainscot page 329
Chortodes morrisii morrisii (Dale)
RDB. SW   2346(9878)

Bond's Wainscot page 329
ssp. *bondii* (Knaggs)
RDB; probably extinct. SE

Field characters & Similar species FW 12-14mm. Morris's Wainscot has larger, whiter forewing than Concolorous, with leading edge distinctly curved. There is a curved outer cross-line of black dots on some individuals. Hindwing white, tinged grey-brown at edges. Bond's Wainscot is slightly larger and more brownish, usually with a line of heavier black spots on forewing and browner hindwing with white fringes.
Flight season One generation. Late June-mid July. Male flies from dusk. Both sexes rest on stems of the foodplant after dark, sometimes in numbers. Comes to light and sugar.
Life cycle Overwinters as a larva within a stem of the foodplant. Larva August-late May. Feeds inside the stems, and usually pupates among shoots at the base.

355

Larval foodplants Tall Fescue.

Habitat Grassy south-facing slopes and terraces of undercliff by the sea. Frequent landslips in the occupied sites create large areas of bare calcareous ground and wet flushes, maintaining the early successional habitat and suitable microclimate for colonisation by the foodplant.

Status & distribution Resident. Probably extinct. Red Data Book species. Morris's Wainscot occurs very locally but in numbers along about 25km of the south coast of England, from Black Ven and the Spittles, Charmouth, Dorset, to Sidmouth, Devon. In 1995 a colony was discovered below Thorncombe Beacon, Dorset. This is several kilometres east of the known colonies and it is possible the moth may be found at other points in between. Also recorded from Portland, Dorset, but not recently. Bond's Wainscot was a distinct form in Kent, known only from a short stretch of rough grass on a chalk cliff overlying Gault clay, with seepages and landslips of varying degrees of stability and plant colonisation, between Folkestone Leas and the beach. Not seen here since the 1970s, and feared extinct.

Concolorous   page 329

Chortodes extrema (Hb.)

RDB. SE,(EC)   2347(9874)

Field characters & Similar species FW 11-13mm. Similar size and shape to Mere Wainscot, pale examples of which have a grey spot in lower half of kidney-mark, whereas kidney-mark of Concolorous lacks this and is very faint or absent. Also, in Concolorous hindwing is grey and curved row of faint black dots across outer portion of pale straw or whitish forewing is usually stronger. Small Wainscot flies later in the year, and has narrower forewing, usually with darker streaks. See also Morris's and Bond's Wainscots, which are larger.

Flight season One generation. Mid May-mid July. Sometimes found among foodplant but mostly seen at light, flying from dusk, also late at night and just before dawn, usually in small numbers.

Life cycle Overwinters as a part-grown larva in a stem of the foodplant, near the base. Larva late June-May. Enters a stem on hatching and feeds in several stems before pupating in a tough cocoon among leaves at the base of the plant.

Larval foodplants Purple Small-reed and Wood Small-reed. Only Wood Small-reed is present at some of the ancient woodland sites. At Woodwalton Fen the moth is more numerous among Purple Small-reed, which is more of a fenland plant, although both species are present.

Habitat The drier parts of fens, without standing water or dominant Common Reed, and marshy open areas and clearings within lowland ancient woodland on heavy soils.

Status & distribution Resident and suspected immigrant. Red Data Book species. Occurs very locally in Huntingdonshire (Woodwalton Fen, Holme Fen and Monks Wood), Northamptonshire (Castor Hanglands,

Bedford Purlieus, Salcey Forest and other woodlands into Buckinghamshire), in two limewoods near Bardney in central Lincolnshire, and at Ketton Quarries and Luffenham Heath in Leicestershire. Occasional individuals, assumed to be wanderers, recorded in nearby areas. Others, assumed to be immigrants, recorded very occasionally on the coast of south-east England, from Thorpeness, Suffolk, on 12 June 1966 (2) and 2 August 1974, and Bradwell-on-Sea, Essex on 14 June 1980 and 30 June 1986, to Eastbourne, Sussex, in 1957, with several on the Dungeness/Greatstone part of the Kent coast.

Lyme Grass   page 329

Chortodes elymi (Treit.)

Nb. E   2348(9880)

Field characters FW 15-18mm. Slender, rather blunt or rounded forewing and clean white hindwing distinguish this moth from other wainscots which might be found at the same time in the same habitat. Forewings of some individuals are heavily marked with dark brown, others are almost plain fawn.

Similar species Obscure Wainscot has more pointed, slightly broader forewing and dirty white hindwing.

Flight season One generation. Mid June-early August. Comes readily to light from dusk, and sometimes seen in hundreds at rest on the foodplant after dark.

Life cycle Believed to overwinter as a small larva within the foodplant, the eggs probably hatching in August. Lives and feeds within the lower part of the stem, below the level of the sand. Large larvae are regularly found in April and May, and pupate in early June at the base of the plant.

Larval foodplants Lyme-grass.

Habitat Coastal sand-dunes and dune-slacks, wandering into saltmarsh and other adjacent habitats.

Status & distribution Resident. Nationally Scarce B. Confined to the east coast and a single site on the south coast (Camber Sands, East Sussex, where it is believed to have been introduced with the foodplant). Two individuals were noted in 1992 (30 June, 8 August) at Dungeness, 14km east of Camber, the first records for Kent. On the east coast it is known to occur locally in the Hamford Water area of Essex, which it colonised around 1975, the Thorpeness/Minsmere/Aldeburgh area of Suffolk, and sandy stretches of the coasts of Norfolk, Lincolnshire, Yorkshire, Durham, Northumberland, Fifeshire, Angus and Kincardineshire, northwards to the sands near Findhorn on the Morayshire/Nairnshire coast.

Mere Wainscot   page 329

Chortodes fluxa (Hb.)

Nb. EC,S   2349(9875)

Field characters & Similar species FW 12-15mm. Rather plain, with cross-lines faint, or represented by tiny black dots. Kidney-mark has grey spot in trailing half. Forewing varies in colour from creamy white to sandy or reddish brown. Hindwing whitish or pale grey. Small Wainscot usually has dark streaks (although it can be quite plain), kidney-mark is absent or barely suggested, forewing is narrower, and it emerges at least a fortnight later. See also Concolorous, which is much more localised and has a small but conspicuous row of black dots on forewing.

Flight season One generation. July-mid August. Flies from dusk. Often seen on the wing where numerous. Comes readily to light, and sometimes to sugar and wine ropes.

Life cycle Overwinters as a part-grown larva in a stem of the foodplant. Larva September-June. Feeds within lower part of stem. Pupates in a tough cocoon among foodplant debris.

Larval foodplants Wood Small-reed.

Habitat Woodland rides, clearings and plantations, usually ancient woodlands on poorly drained soils. Also the drier parts of various wetland habitats, both coastal and inland, including fens, marshes, reedbeds, broads and ditch-banks in old or partially reclaimed wetland sites.

Status & distribution Resident and suspected immigrant. Nationally Scarce B. The main distribution is in a belt from the heavy clay soils of Oxfordshire and Buckinghamshire, north-eastwards through the east Midlands and into both the Breckland and Broads of East Anglia, with additional scattered colonies in the West Midlands, Lincolnshire and Yorkshire. There are also records from many places along the east and south coasts of England north to the Humber and west to Devon. Certainly resident in some coastal reedbeds and other suitable coastal habitat, e.g. Walberswick, Suffolk, near Sandwich, Kent, Browndown Marsh, Hampshire, and Pagham Harbour, West Sussex, although other records appear to be of wandering individuals or immigrants. A population was discovered in 1980 in a wood near Portskewett, Monmouthshire, the first locality for the moth in Wales.

Small Wainscot   page 329
Chortodes pygmina (Haw.)
Common. T   2350(9876)

Field characters FW 10-14mm. Small and quite thickset. Forewing light straw, pinkish straw, orange-brown, pinkish brown or reddish brown, or rarely smoky brown. There is usually a dark grey or brown central streak, with further streaks radiating out towards outer edge, and a faint, gently curved row of dark dots. No other discernible markings. Occasionally streaks and dots are very faint or even absent, or forewing is heavily streaked and dusted with dark scales. Hindwing grey with whitish fringe.

Similar species Concolorous also flies earlier in year. See also Cloaked Minor, Mere Wainscot and Porter's Rustic.

Flight season One generation. August-September. Flies at dusk and again later in the night, when it comes to light and rests on the larval foodplant. Does not feed.

Life cycle Overwinters as a larva. Larva September-early July. Feeds within stems. Pupates in a cocoon in hollow stems or among debris of plants, including foodplant.

Larval foodplants Sedges, including Lesser Pond-sedge, Glaucous Sedge and cottongrasses; also Reed Meadow-grass, other grasses and possibly rushes.

Habitat Most abundant in fens, marshes, boggy moorland and damp woodland, but also along ditches in other habitats and sometimes in gardens.

Status & distribution Resident. Common. Well distributed in suitable habitat throughout Great Britain, Man, Ireland and the Channel Islands.

Fenn's Wainscot   page 329
Chortodes brevilinea (Fenn)
RDB. E   2351(9881)

Field characters FW 14-17mm. The rather broad, square-ended, sandy brown forewing, speckled and dusted with blackish, and with cross-lines represented by black dots, make this quite a distinctive wainscot. Some individuals have a short dark basal streak, but f. *sinelinea* Farn lacks this.

Similar species Brown-veined Wainscot is smaller, and has more rounded forewing and a distinct kidney-mark. Webb's and Rush Wainscots are larger, with slightly hooked, usually plainer forewing, and Webb's has black dots along outer edge. None of these has a black basal streak.

Flight season One generation. Mid July-mid August. Flies from dusk, visiting flowering grasses and aphid honeydew on reeds and sallows. Comes to sugar, and often in numbers to light.

Life cycle Overwinters as an egg, laid on a standing reed or in reed litter. Larva April-mid June. Feeds in the upper parts of stems and later on the leaves, not burrowing down into the roots. Pupates in a cocoon among plant debris.

Larval foodplants Common Reed.

Habitat Reedbeds, preferring the drier areas. The greatest population densities are often where areas of reeds are cut every couple of years or are growing rather sparsely.

Status & distribution Resident. Red Data Book species. Recorded only from the Norfolk Broads, where it occurs widely, and reedbeds on and near the Suffolk coast from about Dunwich north to Benacre. Has colonised newly-created habitat in the Minsmere area.

Dusky Sallow   page 329
Eremobia ochroleuca ([D. & S.])
Common. S,EC   2352(9797)

Field characters FW 14-16mm. Unmistakable. Forewing variegated tawny or olive brown and straw, with a broad, dark, whitish-edged central band, pinched in middle. Shade of brown on forewing varies slightly but markings are very consistent. Fringes chequered. Hindwing dusky grey with darker borders.

357

Larva of Flounced Rustic.

Similar species See Viper's Bugloss.
Flight season One generation. Late July-early September. Comes to light, sugar and flowers. Often seen by day at rest on flowers, especially of knapweeds, sometimes actively feeding in hot weather.
Life cycle Overwinters as an egg. Larva late April-early July. Active by day and night. Pupates underground in a cocoon.
Larval foodplants The flowers and seeds of grasses, including Cock's-foot, False Oat-grass, Common Couch and sometimes cereal crops.
Habitat Grassland and grassy places, especially but not exclusively on calcareous soils or shingle. Has colonised or been moved with limestone chippings used to build up woodland rides, roads and embankments.
Status & distribution Resident. Common. Well distributed in central southern England, the south Midlands, south-east England, East Anglia and eastern England north to Yorkshire. Very local in south-west England and south Wales. Recorded once from Jersey in 1998, and once from Man in 1996.

Flounced Rustic   page 329
Luperina testacea ([D. & S.])
Common. T   2353(9801)

Field characters FW 14-18mm. Rather thickset and variable in size and forewing breadth. Forewing usually coarse-textured but very variable in colour, being dull straw, light or dark brown, often dusted with grey, or blackish brown. Sometimes a solid dark bar joins central cross-lines. Other markings vary in detail and intensity, but basic pattern is the same. Hindwing white or brownish white, occasionally grey.
Similar species Sandhill Rustic is coastal and has kidney-mark edged with white and hindwing generally pure silky white, rarely brownish at edges, except in ssp. *demuthi*. See also rare Dumeril's Rustic, immigrants of which are generally smaller and paler, with less freckling and more distinct markings.
Flight season One generation. August-September. Comes to light, often in numbers, and rests on grasses at night, but does not feed.
Life cycle Overwinters as a larva. Larva September-June. Lives in the soil among the roots of the foodplant, where it also pupates.
Larval foodplants The roots and stem-bases of

grasses, including Common Couch, fescues and sometimes cereal crops.
Habitat A wide range of grassy places, arable fields and woodland rides, but most abundant on light calcareous soils, including coastal sand-dunes and cliffs.
Status & distribution Resident. Common. Well distributed and often abundant throughout England, including Scilly, Wales, southern Scotland, Man, Ireland and the Channel Islands. Local elsewhere in mainland Scotland, the Hebrides and Orkney.

Sandhill Rustic   page 329
Luperina nickerlii (Freyer)
ssp. *demuthi* Goater & Skinner
Na. SE   2354(9803)
ssp. *leechi* Goater
RDB. SW
ssp. *gueneei* Doubl.
RDB. WC
ssp. *knilli* Bours.
Ireland

Field characters FW 15-18mm. In all four subspecies oval is very small and round and may be hard to see, kidney-mark is usually outlined with white and hindwing is generally silky white. Ssp. *leechi* is a consistent silvery white with a darker grey central band and other markings on forewing. Ssp. *knilli*, by contrast, has forewing almost uniformly brown. Forewing of ssp. *gueneei* finely marked with shades of light brown. Ssp. *demuthi* is the most variable, forewing ranging from predominantly straw-coloured to sandy red or dark brown, while hindwing may have brownish edges.
Similar species Flounced Rustic has a larger oval, a rougher texture to forewing, and plainer, dirtier brownish-white hindwing, especially at edge. See also Dumeril's Rustic.
Flight season One generation. Late July-late September, but peak numbers late August, especially for ssp. *leechi*. Male in particular comes readily to light, especially after dark, while female can be found after dark at rest on stems of the foodplant.
Life cycle Overwinters as a part-grown larva within the foodplant. Larva September-early July. Pupates in a flimsy cocoon in tussocks of the foodplant or loose in sand.
Larval foodplants Sand Couch in north Wales and Cornwall, Common Saltmarsh-grass, Borrer's Saltmarsh-grass, Bulbous Meadow-grass and other saltmarsh-grasses in Essex and Kent, and probably Sand Couch or Red Fescue in Ireland.
Habitat All four subspecies are restricted to coastal situations and can survive salt-water inundation or spray. The habitats are predominantly sandy beaches in north Wales and north-west England, a sparsely vegetated coastal sand-bar in Cornwall, the drier parts of saltmarshes in south-east England and grassy coastal cliffs in Ireland.

Status & distribution Resident. Ssp. *demuthi* is Nationally Scarce A, the others merit Red Data Book status. Ssp. *gueneei* has a very large population at Newborough Warren, Anglesey, and occurs locally along the coast of north Wales to Point of Ayr, Flintshire, and on the Cheshire and Lancashire coast, particularly around St Annes-on-Sea and Formby. Ssp. *demuthi* was not recognised until 1973, and not named until 1995, but occurs in numbers from Faversham and the Isle of Sheppey, Kent, through the Thames Estuary, and at many places on the Essex coast north to Aldeburgh, Suffolk. Ssp. *leechi* is known only from one sandy shingle beach in south Cornwall, where it was discovered in 1974. Ssp. *knilli* occurs along the south coast of the Dingle Peninsula, Co. Kerry, where it was discovered in 1962. Singletons recorded at Bude, Cornwall, on 6 August 1990 (not of the Cornish race) and inland at Farringdon, north Hampshire, on 22 September 1950 indicate occasional dispersal.

Dumeril's Rustic   page 330
Luperina dumerilii (Dup.)
Immigrant.   2355(9810)

Field characters & Similar species FW 11-16mm. Very variable. Forewing frequently yellowish or straw-coloured with a broad, pale, plain outer band and distinct central kidney-mark, oval and bar. As such, easily recognised. Plain forms also distinguished from related species by their finer markings and pale central veins on forewing. Reddish-brown and grey-brown forms also occur, but seldom reach Britain. All forms distinguished from Flounced Rustic and Sandhill Rustic by obliquely elongated oval.

Flight season One generation. The majority of British records have been at light in September, but has occurred in August.

Life cycle In mainland Europe overwinters as a larva, feeding from autumn to spring. Immature stages unknown in Britain.

Larval foodplants Roots of grasses.

Habitat As an immigrant, recorded from open coastal situations.

Status & distribution Immigrant. About 35 British records. Recorded at various places along the south coast of England, from Cornwall to Kent, including the Isle of Wight, and twice inland, in Hertfordshire. One each on Jersey in 1997 and on Guernsey in 1999. In Europe, mainly Mediterranean and south-eastern.

Scarce Arches   page 330
Luperina zollikoferi (Freyer)
Immigrant.   2356(9812)

Field characters FW 18-25mm. A large pale fawn noctuid. Indistinct kidney-mark often darker towards trailing edge. Dark scales form an obscure central line from kidney-mark towards base of wing. F. *internigrata* Warr. has forewing dusted with blackish scales, interrupted by light veins and a light band on outer part of wing.

Similar species Bulrush Wainscot has broader, more rounded forewing, with kidney-mark indistinct and not darker in trailing half, and a series of small black arrowhead marks near outer edge. Large Wainscot has more pointed forewing and kidney-mark is absent or very faint. See also pale forms of Dark Arches.

Flight season One generation. August-October. Most British records in September. Comes to light and sugar.

Life cycle Breeding unknown in the British Isles; life cycle poorly known in the rest of Europe.

Larval foodplants Meadow-rues and Great Fen-sedge are reported foodplants in mainland Europe.

Habitat As an immigrant, recorded predominantly from open sites.

Status & distribution Immigrant. Seventeen records between 1867 and 1996, with eight in 1934. Recorded from Devon, Sussex, Kent, Norfolk, Yorkshire, Angus and Aberdeenshire. The mainly eastern distribution of records probably reflects the source, because the moth breeds mostly in eastern Europe, although it has occurred north to Iceland.

Large Ear   page 330
Amphipoea lucens (Freyer)
Local. SW,WC,N   2357(9831)

Field characters & Similar species FW 14-17mm. The four species of ear moth are very similar in appearance and range of variation, and where all four occur together they are reliably distinguishable only by examination of genitalia (see *AES Guide* for details of genitalia differences). They have up to six fine, dark, wavy cross-lines of varying intensity which distinguish them from Crescent. See also Common Rustic. Within the group, Large and Saltern Ear both tend to be larger than Ear Moth and Crinan Ear. The genitalia of male Large and Saltern Ear are extremely similar, and some populations of Large Ear in western Scotland and Ireland have a proportion of moths with intermediate genitalia, possibly indicating hybridisation. Here, it is necessary to examine a number of individuals to establish the nature of the resident population. No underside characters have been found completely reliable for distinguishing the four species, but moths with strong bands on under-side of fore- and hindwing are likely to be Large Ear.

Male genitalia The clasper has two arms, one much longer than the other, as on Saltern Ear, but on cucullus, two rows of spines do not overlap.

Flight season One generation. August-September. Comes to light and flowers, notably of Heather and rushes.

Life cycle Overwinters as an egg. Larva May-July. Feeds at first inside lower stems, and later among roots. Pupates on the ground in leaf litter.

Larval foodplants Purple Moor-grass and Common Cottongrass.

Habitat Wet acid moorland and marshes.

Status & distribution Resident. Local. South-west England, Wales, the north Midlands, northern

England, Man, mainland Scotland, the Hebrides and Orkney. Widespread in Ireland. Often abundant where resident. Singletons recorded from Jersey in 1986 and Alderney in 1961.

Saltern Ear
page 330

Amphipoea fucosa (Freyer)

ssp. *paludis* (Tutt)

Local. S,C,NW   2358(9829)

Field characters & Similar species FW 14-16mm. The most likely species of ear moth in coastal districts of southern Britain, although Ear Moth may also be present in numbers. Typical examples can be distinguished from Ear Moth by compressed crescent-like kidney-mark and normally longer, narrower forewing, which is olive brown, pale brown, or less commonly pale reddish brown. However, variation is considerable and it is necessary to examine genitalia of a number of moths to appreciate the differences fully. The possibility of vagrant or even immigrant Large Ear or Crinan Ear in southern Britain should not be discounted. See also Large Ear.
Male genitalia The clasper has two arms, one much longer than the other, as on Large Ear, but on cucullus, inner row of spines overlaps outer row by over half the length of outer row.
Flight season One generation. August-September. Comes to light, sugar and flowers.
Life cycle Overwinters as an egg. Larva May-July. Pupates underground. Rarely seen in the wild.
Larval foodplants In captivity, the stems and roots of grasses.
Habitat Saltmarshes, sand-dunes and wet moorland.
Status & distribution Resident. Local. In suitable habitat around the coasts of England and Wales, from the Humber to Morecambe Bay. Probable vagrants from the strong populations of the lower Thames marshes are fairly regular in the London area and occasional further west in the Thames Valley, to Oxfordshire. Local on the east and west coasts of Scotland, including the Outer Hebrides, and possibly hybridises with Large Ear in parts of the west, and also in Ireland. Local and rare in the Channel Islands.

Crinan Ear
page 330

Amphipoea crinanensis (Burr.)

Local. W,C,N   2359(9832)

Field characters & Similar species FW 13-15mm. Virtually indistinguishable from Ear Moth in shape and markings, but on average slightly larger and usually with orange kidney-mark and oval. Genitalia are distinct, and should always be checked. An unlikely species in southern and eastern Britain. See also Large Ear and Saltern Ear.
Male genitalia The clasper is a serrated dome-like structure, with no arms.
Flight season One generation. August-September. Comes to light, and to flowers, including those of ragworts and Heather, sometimes by day.
Life cycle Overwinters as an egg. Larva May-July.

Pupation site not known, but probably as for Large Ear.
Larval foodplants Apparently unknown in the wild, but has been reared in captivity on Yellow Iris.
Habitat Moorland, agriculturally unimproved damp pasture, coastal grassland, vegetated sand-dunes and dune-slacks.
Status & distribution Resident. Local. Widespread in Ireland, where it is the most frequent of the four species, mainland Scotland, the Inner Hebrides, north-west England, Northumberland, including Lindisfarne, and west Wales.

Ear Moth
page 330

Amphipoea oculea (L.)

Common. T   2360(9828)

Field characters FW 12-15mm. Forewing quite broad, usually slightly pointed as often in Saltern Ear, with outer margin slightly concave below tip. Ground-colour reddish olive brown, olive brown or dark olive brown. Kidney-mark conspicuous, rounded, white or orange.
Male genitalia The clasper has two arms of roughly the same length.
Similar species See Crinan Ear, Saltern Ear and Large Ear. Ear Moth is the most likely species inland in southern Britain.
Flight season One generation. Late July-September. Comes to light, sugar and flowers, the latter sometimes by day.
Life cycle Overwinters as an egg. Larva April-June. Rarely encountered in the wild. Pupates in an underground cell.
Larval foodplants The insides of the lower stems and roots of grasses, including Annual Meadowgrass and Tufted Hair-grass; also Butterbur.
Habitat Less restricted to damp habitats than the other ear moths. Sometimes recorded in gardens, but more frequently in unimproved grassland, woodland rides, marshes, moorland and saltmarshes.
Status & distribution Resident. Common. In suitable habitat, often at low density, throughout much of Great Britain, Man and Ireland. Recorded from Orkney and Shetland. Local and rare in the Channel Islands.

Rosy Rustic
page 330

Hydraecia micacea (Esp.)

Common. T   2361(9834)

Field characters FW 14-21mm. Fairly unmistakable, but varies considerably in size, with some females particularly large and dark, especially in northern Britain. Quite pointed forewing usually pinkish brown, smooth and rather velvety in texture when fresh, and generally darker between central crosslines; the outer of which is diagonal, gently curved or straight then sharply bent just before leading edge. Ground-colour pale to dark pinkish brown, purplish brown or rarely dull brown. Intensity of pink flush varies from quite bright, especially in pale moths, to

360

dull and very faint in dark examples.

Similar species Butterbur is normally substantially larger and is dull brown, never pinkish. Outermost cross-line is more jagged, usually forming a distinct but shallow W in centre, and leading edge is usually more curved.

Flight season One generation. August-October, occasionally late July or November. Comes regularly to light, occasionally to sugar and flowers.

Life cycle Overwinters as an egg. Larva late April-early August. Feeds at first in the stem of the food-plant and then later into the roots. Pupates underground, without a cocoon.

Larval foodplants A range of low-growing plants, including Broad-leaved Dock, Ribwort Plantain, Field Woundwort, sea-lavenders, Potato, cultivated straw-berries, Hop, Lesser Burdock, and reportedly horse-tails and Yellow Iris.

Habitat A wide range, including gardens, disturbed weedy places, hedgerow bases, pasture, fens, marshes and woodland rides.

Status & distribution Resident. Common. Well distributed throughout Great Britain, Man, Ireland and the Channel Islands.

Butterbur
page 330

Hydraecia petasitis Doubl.

Local. S,C,N
2362(9837)

Field characters & Similar species FW 19-23mm. Similar to Rosy Rustic, with broad dark central band on pointed forewing, but is brown rather than pinkish in colour and up to almost twice the size. Notably larger than most dark female Rosy Rustics, which are sometimes mistaken for this species. See under that species for further differences.

Flight season One generation. August-early September. Most easily found by searching patches of Butterbur soon after dark with a bright light: can be seen flying over the plants and settling on or disappearing under the large leaves. Also comes to light-traps placed in or very close to stands of the foodplant. Seldom caught far from the foodplant.

Life cycle Overwinters as an egg on the remains of the foodplant. Larva April-mid July. Mines the stem and then the roots of the foodplant, pupating in the earth among the roots, or in a chamber in a root open to the surrounding soil.

Larval foodplants Butterbur.

Habitat Riverbanks, ditches, roadsides, damp fields and marshes, occurring both where the plant grows in the open and under the shade of trees.

Status & distribution Resident. Local. The majority of recent records are from the Wirral and the Humber northwards through northern England to the Scottish borders, but it also occurs in river valleys and floodplains in central southern England, with a thin scatter of records from the West Midlands, east-wards through Hertfordshire and in East Anglia. There are pre-1980 records from the Thames Valley/London area and elsewhere in south-east England, where the moth could still persist at low

density, and very old records from south Wales. Recorded on Man but not since the 19th century when pupae were found.

Marsh Mallow Moth
page 330

Hydraecia osseola (Stdgr.)

ssp. *hucherardi* Mab.

RDB. SE
2363(9839)

Field characters FW 18-20mm. Unmistakable. Straw-coloured forewing usually has a darker reddish-brown kidney-mark and outer cross-band, but these may be faint. Hindwing off-white.

Similar species None.

Flight season One generation. Late August-early October, but peaking late August-early September. Flies from dusk, mainly low down around the food-plant. Mating pairs can be found at rest near the ground soon after dusk. Comes just after dark to light-traps placed by or in stands of the foodplant, and occasionally wanders greater distances.

Life cycle Overwinters as an egg on the foodplant or adjacent litter. Larva May-late July. Feeds in the stems and roots. Pupates underground, attached to a root.

Larval foodplants Marsh-mallow.

Habitat Both foodplant and moth favour open, damp low-lying saline places near the sea, the banks of brackish rivers, and ditch-banks and marshy places in the associated grazing levels.

Status & distribution Resident. Red Data Book species. First discovered in Great Britain in 1951. Only two breeding areas are known – the Romney Marsh/Rye area on the East Sussex/Kent border, and the banks of the Medway between Maidstone and Rochester, Kent. The two populations are about 40km apart. Stands of the foodplant at Minsmere, Suffolk, and on the Gower Peninsula, Glamorgan, have been investigated without success.

Frosted Orange
page 330

Gortyna flavago ([D. & S.])

Common. T
2364(9841)

Field characters FW 16-19mm. The wide, striking golden-yellow central cross-band, oval and kidney-mark on broad, sharp-tipped greyish-brown forewing are diagnostic. Also a golden band along outer edge, often rather faint except at wing tip, and a golden blotch at base. Variation is slight.

Similar species See Fisher's Estuarine Moth.

Flight season One generation. Late August-October. Comes to light, usually in small numbers, and rests on the foodplant at night.

Life cycle Overwinters as an egg. Larva April-August. Feeds inside the lower part of a stem, where it also pupates, head upwards.

Larval foodplants Robust herbaceous plants, partic-ularly thistles, burdocks and Foxglove. Other recorded hosts include ragworts, Hemp-agrimony, mulleins and figworts.

Habitat Rough grassland, woodland rides and

Larva of Fisher's Estuarine Moth.

362

edges, disturbed weedy places, ditch-banks, fens, marshes and some gardens.
Status & distribution Resident. Common. Well distributed throughout England, including Scilly, Wales, and southern, central and north-east mainland Scotland. Local on Man, in Ireland and in the Channel Islands.

Fisher's Estuarine Moth page 330

Gortyna borelii (Pierr.)

ssp. *lunata* Freyer

RDB (Protected species). SE   2365(9845)

Field characters & Similar species FW 21-24mm. Superficially like Frosted Orange, but noticeably larger. Inner edge of broad dark outer border of forewing, facing kidney-mark, is finely scalloped, unlike Frosted Orange in which it is plain. The oval and kidney-mark are white, while those of Frosted Orange are yellow.
Flight season One generation. Early September-late October. Male sometimes seen from dusk, perching on stems before taking flight just before midnight. Female can be found resting or crawling about while egg-laying throughout the night. Does not appear to visit flowers or sugar, but both sexes come to light in small numbers.
Life cycle Overwinters as an egg, usually between a stem and leaf-sheath of Sea Couch, False Oat-grass or other grasses near the foodplant rather than on it. Larva early May-late August. Feeds within stems and roots before pupating in a tunnel that breaks out of a root into the earth.
Larval foodplants Hog's Fennel.
Habitat In Essex, on marshy open ground, fields and dyke-banks which are so low-lying they are in danger of being inundated by sea water if sea walls are breached. (Salt-water inundation can kill Hog's Fennel.) In Kent, on a steep grassy slope by shingle without any likelihood of inundation. The moth and its larvae are most numerous in the less dense stands of foodplant growing among tall grasses.
Status & distribution Resident. Red Data Book species. First recognised in Britain in 1968, although the *Victoria County History for Essex* (1903), refers to a large pale form of the Frosted Orange which might have been this species. Thought to be confined to several places in the Walton-on-the-Naze Backwaters

area of Hamford Water, north Essex, until 2001, when a second resident British population was confirmed, in Kent. A singleton, presumed vagrant, was taken at Dovercourt, on the Essex coast, in 1996.

Burren Green page 330

Calamia tridens (Hufn.)

ssp. *occidentalis* Cock.

Ireland   2366(9848)

Field characters FW 17-18mm. The uniformly green thorax and forewing, without any cross-stripes, are diagnostic. Hindwing off-white.
Similar species None.
Flight season One generation. Late July-August. Freshly-emerged adults can be found at rest on grass stems, drying their wings, from an hour after dark. Others fly from dusk and come to light-traps and car headlights.
Life cycle Overwinters as an egg. Larva April-late June. Pupates among the roots of the foodplant.
Larval foodplants Probably Blue Moor-grass: eats the stems and roots of this and other grasses in captivity.
Habitat Open grassland and sheltered fissures in the limestone formations of the Burren.
Status & distribution Resident. Ireland only. In the British Isles, known only from the Burren area, Co. Clare and Co. Galway, where it was first discovered in 1949 and is widespread and fairly frequent. Best known from Black Head to Ballyvaughan on the coast of Galway Bay, it occurs also on Fanore Strand and up to 30km inland.

Haworth's Minor page 330

Celaena haworthii (Curt.)

Local. C,N,(S)   2367(9856)

Field characters FW 10-14mm. Fairly unmistakable. Forewing blunt, rather square-ended, reddish brown (sometimes pinkish) or dark purplish brown. Kidney-mark whitish and conspicuous, with two whitish streaks extending from it towards outer edge, and sometimes towards base. This combination is diagnostic. Worn examples may appear greyish. Individuals from southern England are, on average, larger, and those from the Norfolk Broads are more brightly marked.
Similar species Crescent (f. *fibrosa*) has pale streaks extending from kidney-mark, but is usually larger, with more pointed forewing, has a clear-cut, pale outer cross-band and rarely flies by day.
Flight season One generation. August-September. Comes to light, sugar and flowers such as ragworts. Male also flies on sunny afternoons, and again just before dusk.
Life cycle Overwinters as an egg. Larva April-July. Feeds inside stems, changing to new ones as it grows. Pupates in a cocoon formed close to the ground.
Larval foodplants Common Cottongrass. In some southern localities where this plant is absent, probably rushes and club-rushes, which are recorded

foodplants abroad.

Habitat Boggy acid moorland, fens and marshes.

Status & distribution Resident. Local. Very local in the East Anglian fens, Hampshire (Itchen and Test Valleys), south-west England, south Wales, most of the Midlands and eastern England. Fairly well distributed in north Wales, the north Midlands, northern England, Man and Scotland, including the Hebrides, Orkney and Shetland. Local in Ireland. Recorded once on Jersey in 1984.

Crescent   page 330

Celaena leucostigma leucostigma (Hb.)
Local. T   2368(9857)

ssp. *scotica* Cock.
Local. N

Field characters FW 14-17mm. In ssp. *leucostigma*, forewing dark chocolate brown or reddish brown, somewhat pointed. Kidney-mark rather narrow and crescent-like, chalky white or pale buff. There are two forms, with intermediates. One is quite plain, apart from the kidney-mark and a wavy blackish band along outer edge. F. *fibrosa* Hb. has a pale brown diagonal outer band with straight inner edge, and kidney-mark has one or more fine whitish lines extending from it along the veins. Ssp. *scotica* is smaller and darker than ssp. *leucostigma* and is more brightly marked. Irish individuals are also dark, but are as large as those from southern Britain.

Similar species Ear moths have several fine, dark, wavy cross-lines. See also Haworth's Minor, Common Rustic and Lesser Common Rustic.

Flight season One generation. Late July-September. Comes to light, sometimes in fair numbers, and to sugar and flowers, including those of Common Reed and rushes.

Life cycle Overwinters as an egg. Larva March-July. Feeds inside leaves, stems and roots of the foodplant. Pupates in a flimsy cocoon in leaf litter.

Larval foodplants Yellow Iris and Great Fen-sedge. Ssp. *scotica* has been observed laying eggs on Purple Moor-grass.

Habitat Fens, reedbeds, marshy ground, carr and boggy moorland.

Status & distribution Resident and suspected immigrant. Local. Ssp. *leucostigma* occurs in suitable habitat throughout England, Wales, Man, southern Scotland and Ireland, and occasionally in Orkney and Shetland as a suspected immigrant. Local and occasional in the Channel Islands. Ssp. *scotica* occurs in the northern half of mainland Scotland and the Hebrides.

Bulrush Wainscot   page 331

Nonagria typhae (Thunb.)
Common. T   2369(9859)

Field characters FW 20-24mm. Large, with broad, rather blunt-tipped forewing with small, blackish dashes or crescents along outer edge and (usually) fine arrowheads near them, distinguishing it from

Larva of Bulrush Wainscot (pupa below).

other wainscots. Male is light reddish brown, sometimes darker. Female is light straw-coloured or darker greyish straw-coloured. F. *fraterna* Treit. is dark brown or blackish, with indistinct markings.

Similar species Large Wainscot has narrower, more pointed forewing without dark marks along outer edge. Webb's Wainscot is smaller, and trailing half of kidney-mark is thickly ringed with blackish, and small blackish dots along outer edge of forewing. See also Scarce Arches.

Flight season One generation. Late July-late September. Comes to light, sometimes far from breeding sites (usually female). Does not feed.

Life cycle Overwinters as an egg. Larva April-early August. Feeds inside stems, at first in the upper parts, then lower, moving to new stems as it grows, and leaving very obvious exits and entrances. Pupates in the final foodplant, or in a dead stem.

Larval foodplants Bulrush, and less often Lesser Bulrush.

Habitat Margins of ponds, lakes and ditches, fens, marshes and estuaries. Highly dispersive, rapidly colonising even small patches of foodplant.

Status & distribution Resident. Common. Fairly well distributed in suitable habitat throughout England, Wales and Man. Local in southern, south-west, central and north-east Scotland, in Ireland and in the Channel Islands.

Twin-spotted Wainscot   page 331

Archanara geminipuncta (Haw.)
Local. S,EC   2370(9864)

Field characters FW 11-16mm. Forewing quite broad, ground-colour light brown, reddish brown, greyish brown, dark brown or blackish. Markings rather plain, with any noticeable dark streaks restricted to base, closest to leading edge. Kidney-mark very narrow, often divided into twin spots, either chalky white with dark edging or entirely dark, sometimes faint.

Similar species Dark form of Brown-veined Wainscot is slimmer, kidney-mark is dark but usually broader and white-edged or less often entirely dark, and forewing narrower near base. Small dark Rush Wainscot has richer brown, sharper-tipped forewing, kidney-mark is wider, never white, and there is usually a dark central streak.

Flight season One generation. Early August-mid September. Flies at dusk among the larval foodplant and is often frequent where it occurs, but only comes to light in small numbers. Does not feed.
Life cycle Overwinters as an egg. Larva May-July. Feeds inside stems, changing to new ones as it grows. Pupates low down in a sturdy stem of the foodplant, head upwards.
Larval foodplants Common Reed.
Habitat Extensive reedbeds and small patches of reeds in ditches, ponds, riversides and fens, with highest population densities in unmanaged reedbeds. Often wanders into other habitats without reeds, including gardens.
Status & distribution Resident. Local. Fairly well distributed and sometimes abundant in suitable habitat in southern England, East Anglia and eastern England, south Wales and the Channel Islands. In Ireland, known only from Co. Cork.

Brown-veined Wainscot   page 331
Archanara dissoluta (Treit.)
Local. S,C   2371(9866)

Field characters FW 12-15mm. Female tends to be paler, greyer and plainer than male. Forewing quite broad in male, with blunt tip; narrower and more pointed in female. One diagnostic feature of most frequent form (f. *arundineta* Schmidt) is thick, diffuse brown streak emanating centrally from base of dull straw-coloured or reddish straw-coloured, grey- and black-dusted forewing. This is restricted to base in female, but in male extends to outer edge, broadening as it does so. Kidney-mark outlined with white, most strongly in blackish trailing half, less often narrow and entirely dark. Hindwing grey or whitish grey, with a central spot on underside of both forewing and hindwing. A less frequent form is plain dark brown or blackish brown.
Similar species White-mantled Wainscot is usually slimmer, has a white band on collar and lacks central spots on the underside of wings. Male is similar in shape to that of Webb's Wainscot, which is larger, usually paler, and lacks white edging on kidney-mark. See also Twin-spotted Wainscot, Silky Wainscot and Fenn's Wainscot.
Flight season One generation. Comes to light, and occasionally to sugar.
Life cycle Overwinters as an egg. Larva April-early July. Feeds inside stems, changing to new ones as it grows. Pupates a few centimetres from the ground in a sturdy stem of the foodplant, head downwards.
Larval foodplants Common Reed.
Habitat Reedbeds and ditches. Adults sometimes wander into other habitats, including gardens.
Status & distribution Resident. Local. Southern England, East Anglia, eastern England, the Channel Islands, south Wales, the Midlands, south Yorkshire, Lancashire and north Wales. Locally frequent in the Channel Islands.

White-mantled Wainscot   page 331
Archanara neurica (Hb.)
RDB. SE   2372(9865)

Field characters & Similar species FW 12-13mm. English name refers to diagnostic white edges of the shoulder flaps on thorax. Usually three whitish dots near vein running through centre of forewing. Brown-veined Wainscot has a central spot on underside of both forewing and hindwing, absent in White-mantled Wainscot, which is also a slighter insect. A blackish form became frequent in the 1920s and 1930s in the now lost Sussex population but is seldom seen elsewhere. Reddish f. *rufescens* Edelsten is more frequent.
Flight season One generation. July-early August. Comes to light, sometimes in numbers, otherwise seldom seen.
Life cycle Overwinters as an egg on an old reed stem. Larva late April-late June. Feeds in stems, usually about half-way up. Pupates head down in an old dry reed stem, not a green one.
Larval foodplants Common Reed.
Habitat Edges of reedbeds and reed-lined ditches on or near the coast, with abundant dead stems. Frequently cut or burned sites are thought to be unsuitable.
Status & distribution Resident. Red Data Book species. Currently known only from a 15km stretch of coastal reedbeds in Suffolk, from Thorpeness to Southwold, the sites in between including Sizewell and the Minsmere/Walberswick area. Discovered in Great Britain in 1908 on Pevensey Marshes, near Eastbourne, Sussex, where it survived until its habitat was destroyed during the Second World War. Singletons were recorded nearby in 1952 and 1953 but no resident population has been re-found.

Webb's Wainscot   page 331
Archanara sparganii (Esp.)
Nb. S,SE,SW   2373(9867)

Field characters FW 15-18mm. Both sexes normally have a very pale but faint kidney-mark on blunt forewing, most obvious where the dark central streak runs through it. The extent of the streaking is quite variable, usually crossing a curved row of black spots. There is a second row of black spots along outer edge. Ground-colour plain and uniform across forewing, varying from orange to cream. Hindwing often streaked. Tip of abdomen projects conspicuously beyond wings at rest.
Similar species The rarer Rush Wainscot is smaller on average, and lacks black spots on outer edge of forewing. See also Bulrush Wainscot, which is more freckled with dark spots.
Flight season One generation. August-early October. Comes to light. Often wanders from breeding sites.
Life cycle Overwinters as an egg, attached to a leaf of the foodplant. Larva May-mid August. Pupates head upwards by a prepared window in a stem,

particularly of Bulrush.

Larval foodplants Bulrush, Lesser Bulrush, Yellow Iris, Common Club-rush and Branched Bur-reed. Bulrush is frequently the only foodplant present at breeding sites.

Habitat Breeding areas have included small patches of Bulrush by ponds in woodland, but open habitats are more usual, such as mixed growth of the above plants in ponds, ditches, fens, marshes, estuaries and flooded gravel-pits. Most colonies are at or near the coast, but are not necessarily in brackish or saline habitat.

Status & distribution Resident. Nationally Scarce B. First reported in Britain in 1879 in south-east Kent. Now recorded all along the south and east coasts of England, from Cornwall and Scilly to the Norfolk Broads, and from the north coast of Somerset and the south coast of Wales, including Skomer. Established on the Wash in Lincolnshire. Since 1980, recorded increasingly widely inland, in Essex, Kent, Sussex, Oxfordshire and Hampshire. In Ireland recorded locally in Co. Cork. Local and occasional in the Channel Islands.

Rush Wainscot
page 331
Archanara algae (Esp.)

RDB. SE,EC   2374(9868)

Field characters & Similar species FW 14-18mm. Orange-brown forewing of most males distinguish them from other large wainscots. Both sexes differ from Webb's Wainscot in lacking black spots along very edge of forewing. Irish individuals from the Burren are more heavily marked than English specimens, male being shaded with grey and black scales, and forewing markings on female being more striking.

Flight season One generation. August-September. Flies from dusk and sometimes seen at rest on stems after dark. Comes to light, sometimes in good numbers within breeding habitat, particularly male.

Life cycle Overwinters as an egg on the foodplant. Larva late May-early August. Pupates head upwards, usually in dead standing stems.

Larval foodplants Bulrush, Lesser Bulrush, Common Club-rush and Yellow Iris.

Habitat Stands of emergent plants at the edges of broads, freshwater lakes and water-filled gravel workings. Records suggest the moth wanders and this may explain the colonisation of recent man-made habitat.

Status & distribution Resident. Red Data Book species. Occurs very locally in five main areas: the Norfolk Broads; the Breckland wetlands near Brandon, west of Thetford Forest on the Suffolk/Norfolk border; lakeside habitats on both sides of the Sussex/Surrey border; near Rye, East Sussex; and at Burton Gravel Pits near Lincoln, where it was discovered in 1974. Also recorded since 1980 from a single locality in Nottinghamshire. Resident temporarily at Dungeness, Kent, in 1952-1954, but no recent evidence of a population. There are a few

records of singletons scattered along the south and east coasts from Dorset and Hampshire to Essex, so there may be overlooked populations. In Ireland recorded from lakes in the Connemara district of Cos. Galway and Kildare, the Burren, Co. Clare, and in lakeside habitats at Crom Estate, Co. Fermanagh, where discovered in 2000. One recorded on Guernsey in 1998.

Large Wainscot
page 331
Rhizedra lutosa (Hb.)

Common. T   2375(9814)

Field characters FW 16-23mm. Very variable in size. Forewing pointed, or even slightly hooked, light greyish straw or reddish straw, less often brownish grey, lightly or (less often) heavily dusted and streaked with black. There is an outer series of fine dark dots, occasionally forming a curved, jagged cross-line. Hindwing whitish, lightly or (less often) heavily dusted with grey, usually with a central row of dark dashes.

Similar species Blair's Wainscot is smaller, forewing even more pointed and hindwing smoky, with pale streaks and borders. Rush Wainscot has uniformly grey hindwing with a thin dark central band, stronger on underside. See also Bulrush Wainscot and Scarce Arches.

Flight season One generation. August-October. Flies briefly at dusk and again later in the night, when it comes to light, sometimes far from breeding sites (usually female). Feeds at flowers and occasionally at sugar.

Life cycle Overwinters as an egg. Larva April-late July. Feeds inside roots and stem bases. Pupates among the roots of the foodplant.

Larval foodplants Common Reed.

Habitat Reedbeds and reedy ditches, breeding in the drier parts and margins, not where there is permanent standing water. Only in small numbers where reedbeds are burned after winter cutting.

Status & distribution Resident. Common. Fairly well distributed in suitable habitat throughout England, including Scilly, Wales, Man, Ireland and the Channel Islands. Local in mainland Scotland, the Inner Hebrides, Orkney and Shetland.

Blair's Wainscot
page 331
Sedina buettneri (Her.)

RDB. S   2376(9870)

Field characters & Similar species FW 12-14mm. Forewing much more pointed than those of any other wainscot of similar size, and flight season later than most. Streaky dark grey hindwing distinguishes Blair's Wainscot from small forms of Large Wainscot.

Flight season One generation. Late September-mid October. Flies from dusk and can be found moving among dense stands of sedges after dark. Comes readily to light-traps placed in the breeding areas, but rarely captured away from this habitat.

Life cycle Overwinters as an egg, laid in rows on

leaves of the foodplant. Larva late April-August. Feeds within stems of young shoots. Pupates near ground level, within a stem of the foodplant.
Larval foodplants Lesser Pond-sedge.
Habitat Sedge-beds in river systems and marshes.
Status & distribution Resident and suspected immigrant. Red Data Book species. Several apparently long-established populations discovered in sites on rivers in Dorset from October 1996 onwards. First discovered in the British Isles in September 1945 in Freshwater Marsh, Isle of Wight, where recorded, sometimes in large numbers, annually until 1951-52 when the marsh was drained, cut and burned, after which the moth was never seen here again. Between 1952 and 1996 the following single-tons were recorded and have been regarded as suspected immigrants from mainland Europe: 14 October 1966, Playden, near Rye, East Sussex; 30 September 1985, Walberton, West Sussex; 2 October 1987, Lydd, Kent; 12 October 1991, Dungeness, Kent; 16 October 1994, Frinton-on-Sea, Essex.

Fen Wainscot   page 331
Arenostola phragmitidis (Hb.)
Local. S,EC,(WC)   2377(9872)

Field characters FW 14-16mm. Unmistakable. Smooth, rather slender moth, forewing quite broad, light or dull greyish straw-coloured or light reddish brown (f. *rufescens* Tutt), and unmarked, but darker towards outer margin, with coffee-coloured fringes. Hindwing grey with whitish fringes.
Similar species None.
Flight season One generation. July-August. Flies at dusk and later comes to light, sometimes in numbers, and to flowering grasses.
Life cycle Overwinters as an egg. Larva April-late June. Feeds inside stems, changing to new ones as it grows. Pupates on the ground among leaf litter.
Larval foodplants Common Reed.
Habitat Reedbeds. Inclined to wander into other habitats, including gardens.
Status & distribution Resident. Local. In southern England from Dorset to Kent, most frequent on or near the coast, but extending locally inland as far as Oxfordshire. Well distributed in East Anglia, Cambridgeshire, Lincolnshire and south Yorkshire. Local in the Midlands, north Wales, Lancashire and Cumbria. Local and rare in the Channel Islands.

Brighton Wainscot   page 331
Oria musculosa (Hb.)
pRDB. S   2378(9885)

Field characters FW 12-16mm. Two broad whitish-fawn stripes running through rather angular, sandy brown or fawn forewing are diagnostic. These stripes are present, but less striking, in pale and worn individuals.
Similar species None.
Flight season One generation. Late July-mid

August. Has been disturbed in large numbers by day during cereal harvesting, and seen flying and resting on stems from dusk. Comes readily to light.
Life cycle Overwinters as an egg attached to grasses or standing cereals. Larva late April-mid June. Pupates in the ground below the foodplant.
Larval foodplants Various grasses, later moving on to winter wheat, summer rye, oats or barley, feeding initially within the stems, then moving to the ears to eat the unripe grains.
Habitat Arable farmland, particularly fields of wheat and oats and their grassy margins, verges and hedge bases, the latter probably important as overwintering sites.
Status & distribution Resident and probable immigrant. Proposed Red Data Book species, formerly Nationally Scarce A. In the past, widely recorded in central southern England north to Northamptonshire, but in steep decline in recent decades. Now proving difficult to locate in any numbers in its last strong-holds in Wiltshire and north Hampshire, although a few individuals have been recorded since 2000. Some records are of unusually small, pale adults early in July before the main flight period, often near the south coast or away from the breeding habitat, suggesting immigration.

Small Rufous   page 331
Coenobia rufa (Haw.)
Local S,C,(N)   2379(9890)

Field characters & Similar species FW 10-12mm. Not unlike Small Wainscot in size, colour and markings, but body much slimmer and with more rounded, less pointed forewing. Forewing has a narrow, diffuse central streak, and further streaks radiating out to outer edge, and is finely and variably dusted with light and dark grey. An often indistinct, curved outer cross-line is represented by blackish dots. Ground-colour light straw white, pinkish straw, pinkish brown, reddish brown or smoky brown. Hindwing usually whitish, sometimes grey, with a central cross-line or row of dots. Forewing somewhat narrower in female.
Flight season One generation. July-August. Flies in the hour before dusk, and occasionally comes to light later in the night.
Life cycle Overwinters as a small larva. Larva September-May. Feeds inside stems, changing to new ones as it grows. Pupates low down in an old stem of the foodplant.
Larval foodplants Jointed Rush, Sharp-flowered Rush and Soft-rush.
Habitat Fens, marshes, poorly-drained pasture and bogs, breeding in the drier parts.
Status & distribution Resident. Local. Quite well distributed in suitable habitat in southern and south-west England, East Anglia and Jersey. Local in eastern England, the Midlands, Wales, northern England, southern Scotland, Ireland and on Guernsey. One record from Man, in 1895.

Treble Lines
page 331

Charanyca trigrammica (Hufn.)

Common. S,C   2380(9456)

Field characters FW 15-17mm. Quite thickset, with fairly broad and rather pointed forewing. Three fine, fairly straight dark cross-lines; otherwise plain. This pattern is diagnostic. Ground-colour pale (sometimes darker) rather milky greyish brown, or orange-brown. Some examples have dark shading outside central cross-line, less often extending to outer edge. The infrequent but regular f. *obscura* Tutt is dark greyish brown, with dark inner and outer cross-lines edged paler.

Similar species See also Double Line.

Flight season One generation. May-early July.

Life cycle Overwinters as a small larva. Larva June-April. Feeds at night at ground level, hiding in the soil by day. Pupates underground.

Larval foodplants A range of herbaceous plants, including knapweeds, Greater Plantain and Dandelion.

Habitat Many open situations, including some gardens, grassland, grassy heathland, hedgerows, verges, sand-dunes, open woodland and rides.

Status & distribution Resident. Common. Well distributed and often locally numerous in most of England (local in the north), Wales, Man and Ireland. Locally frequent in the Channel Islands.

Uncertain
page 332

Hoplodrina alsines (Brahm)

Common. T   2381(9449*)

Field characters FW 14-16mm. Forewing rather blunt-tipped. Rich brown or tawny-brown, generally darker in female and shinier, sometimes dusted with grey, especially along cross-lines, that before middle being wavy and that beyond middle finely scalloped. Oval and kidney-mark slightly darker than ground-colour, with pale outlines: oval fairly small, kidney-mark fairly narrow, straight or slightly bent. A dark, rather narrow cross-band, sometimes indistinct, runs through kidney-mark. Hindwing in male dirty brownish grey, darker and more uniformly grey in female.

Similar species See Rustic, which usually has rather plain cold grey or grey-brown forewing. See also Mottled Rustic and Vine's Rustic, which have much whiter hindwings. See also the rare immigrant Powdered Rustic.

Flight season Usually one generation, mid June-mid August. Occasionally a small second generation in late autumn.

Life cycle Overwinters as a larva. Larva July-April. Pupates in a strong cocoon underground.

Larval foodplants A range of herbaceous plants, including chickweeds, docks, dead-nettles and Primrose.

Habitat Most lowland habitats, from woodlands and open meadows to gardens, including urban areas.

Status & distribution Resident. Common. Well distributed and often abundant throughout England, including Scilly, Wales, Man and the Channel Islands. Local in mainland Scotland and Ireland.

Rustic
page 332

Hoplodrina blanda ([D. & S.])

Common. T   2382(9450)

Field characters & Similar species FW 13-16mm. The similarity between this species and Uncertain has long been a source of confusion (hence English name of latter!), but there are several differences that can be used, with care, to identify most examples. Rustic is more variable in colour, and usually greyer. Forewing pale to dark greyish brown through to sooty brown, heavily dusted with grey, or almost blackish. Usually blander, with fine cross-lines and central band usually faint, and cross-line beyond middle usually reduced to a series of dots. Forewing may be smoother and shinier than worn examples of Uncertain, which emerges earlier, but not compared with fresh ones, especially the darker females, so this often quoted character can be misleading. Hindwing greyish white to uniformly grey, browner in Uncertain. Worn Uncertains tend to retain cross-lines, whereas Rustic appears more washed out. However, some moths show characters of both species, and in these cases the genitalia should be examined for confirmation. See also Vine's Rustic, Mottled Rustic and the rare immigrant Powdered Rustic.

Flight season Usually one generation, late June-mid August. Starts emerging about two weeks later than Uncertain and is often rare at sites where Uncertain is frequent. Occasionally a partial second generation in southern England in October. Comes to light, sugar and flowers.

Life cycle Overwinters as a larva. Larva July-April. Pupates in a strong cocoon underground.

Larval foodplants A wide range of broad-leaved herbaceous plants, including chickweeds, docks and plantains.

Habitat Most lowland habitats, including urban areas.

Status & distribution Resident. Common. Widely distributed throughout most of England, Wales, Man, Ireland and the Channel Islands, but more local and less frequent than Uncertain over much of this range. Local in mainland Scotland, mainly in the south and on the east and west coasts, and in the Hebrides.

Powdered Rustic
page 332

Hoplodrina superstes (Ochs.)

Rare immigrant.   2383(9451)

Field characters FW 13-15mm. Forewing is a lighter brown, tinged with grey, than related moths, with brown speckling and outer cross-line of black dots. Oval and kidney-marks light-edged, large and distinct.

Similar species Vine's Rustic has greyer, narrower forewing with a more angled tip, a less speckled appearance and whiter hindwing. Inner line of dots on forewing is less distinct in Vine's Rustic. Middle sections of male antennae in Powdered Rustic have short projections, the length being only half the diameter of the shaft, whereas in Vine's Rustic these are almost equal to the diameter of the shaft. This is best seen under a microscope. Uncertain and Rustic are also very similar, although Uncertain is browner, with darker hindwing, and Rustic has brown hindwing margin.

Flight season Single generation. June-August.

Life cycle, Larval foodplants & Habitat Breeding not confirmed in Britain. In mainland Europe overwinters as a larva, feeding September-April or May on Dandelion, plantains and other herbs, pupating in loose earth. Favours warm, open, well-drained sites, including gardens.

Status & distribution Rare immigrant. Seven reportedly British records, all on or near the south or south-east coasts of England, the last in 1945, when two males were captured at Honiton Clyst, south Devon, on 9 and 11 June. The others are two from Deal, Kent, in July 1886, and singletons at Brentwood, Essex, on 18 August 1890, Dawlish, Devon, in August 1901 and Torcross, Devon, in 1902. Reported from Guernsey in 1893 as abundant, but not recorded since! One on Alderney in 1899. There is an unconfirmed 20th-century record of a singleton from Jersey. Widely recorded in central and southern Europe.

Vine's Rustic   page 332

Hoplodrina ambigua ([D. & S.])

Common. S,(C)   2384(9454)

Field characters & Similar species FW 13-15mm. Forewing pale to dark brownish grey with pale grey dusting, or silvery grey, and almost straight leading edge. Markings similar to Rustic and Uncertain, but with central band usually faint and kidney-mark and oval larger and more rounded. Hindwing whitish with a faint pearly sheen, often with a narrow grey outer band, especially on examples with darker forewings. Some individuals, especially darker ones, closely resemble Rustic, which is a little larger, with broader and slightly blunter forewing and less whitish hindwing. Has also been mistaken for Common Quaker, which has a more rounded, brownish forewing.

Flight season Two generations. May-July and August-September, the second more numerous. Comes frequently to light, and to sugar and flowers.

Life cycle Overwinters as a larva. Larva September-April and May-August. Pupates in a cocoon underground.

Larval foodplants A wide range of herbaceous plants, including docks, Dandelion, Prickly Lettuce and Primrose.

Habitat Grassland, heathland, woodland rides and weedy places, including gardens.

Status & distribution Resident and suspected immigrant. Common. Regarded as an immigrant in 19th and early 20th centuries. Temporarily established along the south coast, it then spread rapidly in the 1940s and is now well distributed in southern

England (including Scilly) and East Anglia, colonising Lincolnshire and Yorkshire, with scattered records elsewhere in mainland Britain north to southern Scotland, on Man and in the south of Ireland. Widespread and abundant in the Channel Islands.

Small Mottled Willow   page 332

Spodoptera exigua (Hb.)

Immigrant; resident Channel Islands.

                                           2385(9460)

Field characters & Similar species FW 13-14mm. Small and dull brown, but has a distinctive resting position with its narrow forewings wrapped around the body, rather than held flat. This helps distinguish it from Pale Mottled Willow and the rare immigrant Dark Mottled Willow. Small Mottled Willow usually has pale pink or orange oval and kidney-mark. Pale Mottled Willow has much broader forewing, with four conspicuous black dots along leading edge, and at least part of kidney-mark is dark brown. Dark Mottled Willow also has slightly broader forewings and holds them more horizontally.

Flight season Recorded in all seasons, but chiefly occurs June-October. Winter and early spring records are scarce but always possible during periods of mild weather and southerly winds. Comes to light and may be seen visiting buddleias and Ivy flowers. Also recorded at honeydew and disturbed by day.

Life cycle In the British Isles successful breeding as yet unconfirmed, but likely. Larvae expected within one month of arrival of immigrants, producing adults before autumn, based on observations in captivity.

Larval foodplants A wide range of plants accepted, including Dandelion, Groundsel, docks and Common Restharrow.

Status & distribution Immigrant. Recorded annually in recent years. Occasionally has years of abundance, when hundreds are reported. Possibly early immigrants sometimes produce offspring during the summer, but the weather is too cool and wet for breeding in most years. Although most frequently recorded along the south coasts of England and Wales, also widely reported over southern England with inland records not unusual. Less frequent on the east coast of England. Also recorded in northwest England, Man, Ireland and north to the Hebrides. A local resident in and occasional immigrant to the Channel Islands. Distributed worldwide and a pest species in some regions. Numerous in much of Europe.

Mediterranean Brocade   page 332
(African Cotton Leafworm)

Spodoptera littoralis (Boisd.)

Suspected rare immigrant; import.   2386(9462)

Field characters FW 14-19mm. Fairly distinctive. Male has diagonal cream flash through oval; in female cream colour is restricted to central veins. Forewing rather narrow, brown, often with a violet tint. Hindwing very white, with a faint brown line just inside fringe.

Similar species Far Eastern Brocade (or Asian Cotton Leafworm) *Spodoptera litura* (Fabr.), thus far recorded only as an import. Bordered Gothic has more extensive cream venation and cross-lines.

Flight season Immigrants recorded in June, September and October. Several generations in tropical and subtropical regions.

Larval foodplants A wide range of plants abroad. Often a pest on vegetables, fruits, flowers and other crops, including Potato, Tomato, Cabbage, beans, Peanut, Maize and Banana, with which it is occasionally imported.

Status & distribution Suspected rare immigrant and import. In 1963 imported with cut chrysanthemums from the Canary Islands and became a greenhouse pest. Has occurred about six times in England as a suspected immigrant, the first in 1960 on the north Norfolk coast near Cromer, and the others on or near the coasts of Dorset, Hampshire and Suffolk, with one in Berkshire. Twice found on Guernsey, in 1963 and 1999, on imported plants. Breeds widely in Africa and Mediterranean Europe, with adults reaching central and northern Europe.

2386a, 2386b see Appendix

Dark Mottled Willow
page 332

Spodoptera cilium (Guen.)

Rare immigrant. 2386c(9461)

Field characters & Similar species FW 13mm. Similar to Pale Mottled Willow, but instead of a tawny outer cross-band there is a grey-brown blotch in centre of inner edge of pale outer cross-line, and kidney-mark lacks white spots. Male is brown, with dark kidney-mark quite conspicuous. Female is darker and grey, with markings more obscure. Examination of genitalia may be necessary for confirmation. See also Small Mottled Willow and Clancy's Rustic.

Larval foodplants & Habitat Various grasses. In Africa, larvae often numerous in short swards such as regrowth after fire or on closely-mown lawns and golf courses.

Status & distribution Rare immigrant. First recorded in the British Isles on 29 September 1990 at Coverack, Cornwall. Eight additional British records to 1998, all of which have been caught at light in Cornwall and Dorset, during late September and October. Primarily an African species, sometimes reaching pest status there. Also occurs in the Canaries and parts of southern Spain and France.

Mottled Rustic
page 332

Caradrina morpheus (Hufn.)

Common. T 2387(9417)

Field characters & Similar species FW 13-16mm. Kidney-mark and oval broad, dark and blurred, without any crisp lighter edging. Otherwise markings somewhat similar to Uncertain, Rustic and Vine's Rustic. Forewing brown or dark brown, rapidly

broadening in male, slightly narrower and shorter in female. Leading edge slightly curved. Forewing has a distinct silky texture when fresh. Inner margin of outer forewing band is well defined and smooth. Hindwing whiter than Uncertain and Rustic.

Flight season Usually one generation, June-mid August. Sometimes a partial second generation in southern England in October. Comes frequently to light, less often to sugar and flowers.

Life cycle Overwinters as a fully grown larva in a cocoon underground, in which it pupates in the spring. Feeds at night July-November, hiding at ground level by day.

Larval foodplants A wide range of herbaceous plants, including Common Nettle, docks, goosefoots, teasels and Hedge Bedstraw; also Hop and Goat Willow.

Habitat Most lowland situations, including gardens, farmland, grassland, heathland, scrub, woodland and many coastal habitats.

Status & distribution Resident. Common. Well distributed and frequent to abundant throughout England, including Scilly, lowland Wales, Man and the Channel Islands. Local in lowland eastern Scotland, with some records from the west coast, including the Hebrides. Similar distribution in Ireland.

Clancy's Rustic
not illustrated

Platyperigea kadenii (Frey.)

Rare immigrant. 2387a(9424)

Field characters & Similar species FW 13-15mm. At first glance resembles a Pale Mottled Willow, but ground-colour is pale grey when fresh, and band along outer edge of forewing is also pale (dark grey in Pale Mottled Willow). Outer brown band is restricted to leading half of forewing, away from leading edge, and is dull brown rather than tawny, oval is very small, dark and easily lost, kidney-mark lacks white spots and cross-lines are weak. Hindwing whitish, with very little dark shading on veins. Likely to require dissection of genitalia to distinguish from the several similar species in this group resident in mainland Europe, which may have been overlooked in the past. These include *Platyperigea proxima* (Ramb.), which has a more westerly distribution than Clancy's Rustic, and Lorimer's Rustic, also grey and weakly marked, but with a larger oval and white spots on kidney-mark, and rests with wings wrapped around body.

Status & distribution Rare immigrant. One British record. An individual was captured in a light-trap in a garden at New Romney, Kent, on 3 October 2002, and reported as this book was in preparation. Resident mainly in southern Europe, but also recorded from parts of central Europe, including Poland, the Czech Republic and Slovakia.

Lorimer's Rustic
page 332

Paradrina flavirena (Guen.)

Suspected rare immigrant. 2388(9436)

Field characters & Similar species FW 13-15mm. Very similar to Pale Mottled Willow, but distinguished by its resting posture, in which wings are wrapped tightly around abdomen. Grey, rather weakly marked, and with outer area of forewing either not or only slightly darker. Hindwing thinly edged with grey. In spite of resting posture, confirmation of immigrants by genitalia examination is required. See also Clancy's Rustic.

Status & distribution Suspected rare immigrant. Recorded once in the British Isles: a male in a light-trap at Totteridge, Hertfordshire, on 8 October 1967, a night when other more familiar immigrant moths were recorded widely in southern England. The specimen is f. *noctivaga* Bellier, which is resident in south-west France but occurs widely throughout southern Europe, feeding on broadleaved herbs.

Pale Mottled Willow
page 332

Paradrina clavipalpis (Scop.)

Common. T 2389(9433)

Field characters FW 12-15mm. Rather slim with quite narrow, pale to dark brownish-grey forewing and 3-4 small black dots along leading edge. Kidney-mark darker, rather small and narrow, and variably edged with small white spots. There is a narrow, pale-edged, tawny-brown band near outer edge, and a darker grey band along it, sometimes extending inwards. Hindwing white or greyish white with a slight pearly sheen, and a narrow grey outer band, its colour extending inwards along the veins.

Similar species Vine's Rustic and some Rustics are similar in size and coloration, but are stouter and lack white spots on kidney-mark, black dots on leading edge and dark outer edge. See also Small Mottled Willow, Dark Mottled Willow, Lorimer's Rustic, Clancy's Rustic and Porter's Rustic.

Flight season Probably two generations, mainly May-July and late August-October, but occurs February-November. Comes to light, sometimes in numbers, and to sugar and flowers.

Life cycle Overwinters as a larva underground in a cocoon, in which it pupates in spring. Larva September-spring and through summer.

Larval foodplants Grass seeds, including cereal grains, both growing and stored after harvest. Also recorded on seeds of plantains and Garden Pea.

Habitat Grassland, farmland (especially around farm buildings) and urban gardens. Also formerly recorded in coal mines, living on the fodder of pit ponies.

Status & distribution Resident and suspected immigrant. Common. Well distributed and frequent throughout most of England, Wales, lowland Scotland, Man, Ireland (where more local) and the Channel Islands. Unusually large numbers sometimes recorded on nights coincident with arrivals of known immigrant species.

African
not illustrated

Perigea capensis (Guen.)

Suspected rare immigrant. 2390(9335)

Field characters FW 12-17mm. A dull brownish broad-winged moth about the size of Marbled Clover, with a distinctive, rather complex and ornate whitish kidney-mark.

Similar species None in the British Isles.

Status & distribution Suspected rare immigrant. One record from the British Isles, captured in a light-trap at Bodinnick on the south coast of Cornwall, on 3 May 1958, at the start of a big influx of immigrant moths, including Striped Hawk-moth and large numbers of Silver Y. Occurs widely and abundantly throughout Africa. Denmark is the only other country in Europe where it has been recorded.

Silky Wainscot
page 332

Chilodes maritimus (Tausch.)

Local. S,C 2391(9471)

Field characters FW 13-15mm. Slender build and narrow, light greyish-straw forewing, with leading edge curved and outer edge quite angular with pointed tip, and silky white hindwing are diagnostic. Most frequent form rather plain, delicately streaked with grey and very finely dusted with black towards leading edge. F. *nigristriata* Stdgr. is black between veins in leading half of forewing. F. *bipunctata* Haw. has blackish oval and kidney-mark and a short, thin blackish streak at base. F. *wismariensis* Schmidt has a long, thick blackish streak from base. These strongly-marked forms are regular in small numbers at some sites.

Similar species The micro-moths *Chilo phragmitella* (Hb.) and *Calamotropha paludella* (Hb.) are superficially similar, but have very long palps. Female Brown-veined Wainscot can be somewhat similar, but darker with greyish hindwing, and outer edge of forewing curved.

Flight season One generation. Mid June-mid August. Flies weakly among reeds from dusk onwards and comes to light.

Life cycle Overwinters as a larva. Larva August-April. Lives inside dead stems of the foodplant that have been broken, or tunnelled by other larvae. Pupation site apparently unknown, probably within broken reed stems. Possibly once reared from a cigar-gall.

Larval foodplants Omnivorous. Living and dead invertebrates and the inner tissues of dead Common Reed stems. In captivity will eat animal fat.

Habitat Reedbeds, especially drier areas where plant debris is allowed to remain. Frequently wanders into other habitats.

Status & distribution Resident. Local. Southern and eastern England, East Anglia, Yorkshire, south Wales and southern Scotland. In Ireland recorded from Co. Cork. In the Channel Islands local and frequent on Jersey, rare on Guernsey.

Marsh Moth
page 332
Athetis pallustris (Hb.)
RDB. EC
2392(9476)

Field characters FW M 15-16mm, F 9-11mm. Rather distinctive when seen alive. Male has a conspicuous light build and flappy flight as it arrives at light. Kidney-mark and compressed oval small, but usually dark and apparent. Forewing slender and rounded. Ground-colour of male forewing varies from fawn to grey. Female is smaller with reduced, rounded, darker brown forewing with very bowed leading edge, and usually scuttles like a beetle rather than flying.

Similar species Pale Mottled Willow has more dark spots on forewing. Uncertain, Rustic and related species are more robust, with larger kidney-marks.

Flight season One generation. Late May-June. Male comes readily to light and one has been reported at sugar. Female has been reported several times flying in late afternoon in hot weather, but is otherwise rarely seen, except occasionally crawling under sheets used with light-traps, or by searching for freshly-emerged individuals.

Life cycle Overwinters as a fully grown larva on or near the ground. Larva June-April, feeding until October or later.

Larval foodplants Ribwort Plantain confirmed in Lincolnshire. Apparently Meadowsweet in the East Anglian fens. Probably also other low-growing plants.

Habitat The main Lincolnshire site is a flat, open, marshy meadow on sandy soil, sometimes cut for hay, with an average sward height of only about 10cm when the moth is flying, with abundant herbs, especially Ribwort Plantain, just inland of sand-dunes and generally without standing water at any time in the year. Former inland sites are fens and marshy fields, in which the drier parts with sparser vegetation were favoured.

Status & distribution Resident. Red Data Book species. Currently known from the Lincolnshire coast only, where it still breeds in one or possibly two sites. Recorded in two inland sites in Lincolnshire in the 1970s. Collected for many years at Chippenham and Wicken Fens, Cambridgeshire, and Woodwalton and Holme Fens, Huntingdonshire, but not seen at any of these sites since the 1960s. Others reported from Stoke Ferry Fen, Norfolk, in 1964 and 1966; near Norwich in 1869; on the outskirts of a wood near Carlisle, Cumbria, where two females 'were netted' on 30 May 1896 and 12 June 1897 and other adults shortly thereafter; and at Compton's Wood/Stockton-in-the-Forest, near York, prior to 1855. There is also a single female specimen recorded as having been taken flying by day at Ringwood, Hampshire, in 1870.

Porter's Rustic
page 332
Proxenus hospes (Frey.)
Rare immigrant.
2392a(9478)

Field characters FW 11-13mm. A rather drab and easily overlooked species. Forewing rather narrow,

Larva of Marsh Moth.

dull brown with indistinct markings, including kidney-mark and oval in centre of forewing, but these may be barely discernible. A reddish streak often extends along centre of forewing. Hindwing white, with a narrow light brown line along outer edge.

Similar species Perhaps most likely to be confused with Small Wainscot, from which it differs in the way in which it holds its wings flat rather than tent-like over the body. Pale Mottled Willow has several dark spots along leading edge of forewing.

Flight season Two generations in southern Europe. May-June and late August-September.

Larval foodplants The larva has not been recorded in Britain. In mainland Europe it feeds on various herbaceous plants, including plantains.

Status & distribution Rare immigrant. Singletons recorded from Kynance Cove, Cornwall, on 26 August 1978, and from Scilly on 14 September 1993, 31 August 1998, 5 September 2000 and 11 October 2001. All records have been at light. Mainly southern in Europe, but individuals have been reported from Denmark.

Reddish Buff
page 332
Acosmetia caliginosa (Hb.)
RDB (Protected species). S
2393(9405)

Field characters FW M 13-15mm, F 9-12mm. Ground-colour varies from brick red, through pinkish buff to greyish with pink, but is never yellow. Intensity of markings varies but normally two cross-lines and various dots can be seen. The only noctuid of slight build with the above characteristics. Female much smaller than male and has narrower wings.

Similar species Small Dotted Buff is not dissimilar in flight and outline, but is a yellower moth when seen at rest in daylight.

Flight season One generation. Mid May-late June, occasional individuals recorded to mid July. Sometimes the male, and rarely the female, flies up when disturbed from vegetation by day, particularly in late afternoon. Male comes to light from soon after dark, arriving throughout the night: the best catches are obtained by operating all night. Female rare at light, occurring mainly towards the end of the flight season when they have laid most of their eggs. In captivity they spend much time walking about

Larva of Reddish Buff.

below the leaves of Saw-wort plants, laying eggs. Both sexes bask on the upper surfaces of leaves in the early morning sunshine.

Life cycle Overwinters as a pupa underground. Larva July-early August. Feeds mainly at night, resting on the undersides of leaves of the foodplant by day.

Larval foodplants Saw-wort.

Habitat Open heath-like vegetation, where the larval foodplant grows abundantly, and in unshaded conditions. Previous reports from woodland rides and clearings were from sites where conifer plantations had been established on the original open habitat and the moth was in decline.

Status & distribution Resident. Red Data Book species. Confined to a single British locality consisting of two adjacent fragments of once more extensive open habitat in the west of the Isle of Wight. Formerly occurred in at least three nearby sites, now conifer plantations, where it was last seen in the 1950s, 1979 and 1987 respectively. Occurred at several places in the New Forest, Hampshire, in the 19th century, and in a wood and wood-pasture situation near Fareham, Hampshire, where it was discovered in 1931 and survived until 1961. These former records cover at least five 10km squares. In addition, one was taken in a light-trap at Freshwater, Isle of Wight, in 1956.

Anomalous
page 332

Stilbia anomala (Haw.)

Local (S),SW,W,N   2394(9407)

Field characters FW 13-17mm. Unmistakable. Rather slender, forewing smooth and silky when fresh, narrow at base with straight leading edge, broadening rapidly in male. Ground-colour slate grey, consistently blackish between oval and kidney-mark and generally paler towards trailing edge. Female has narrower blackish-grey forewing with faint markings. Male varies in degree of contrast.

Similar species Slim build and forewing shape, especially of male, are somewhat suggestive of some of the snouts, but these all have very long palps.

Flight season One generation. August-September. Male flies at dusk and both sexes sit on low vegetation after dark. Male comes regularly to light, female less frequently.

Life cycle Overwinters as a larva. Larva October-

April. Pupates underground in a cocoon, after lying dormant within it for several weeks.

Larval foodplants Wavy Hair-grass and Tufted Hair-grass.

Habitat Moorland, grassy uplands, lowland heathland and some coastal grasslands, including dune-slacks.

Status & distribution Resident. Local. Local in Hampshire, Dorset, Wiltshire, the Breckland of East Anglia, and the Midlands. Well distributed in southwest England, Wales, Man, northern England, mainland Scotland, the Hebrides and Orkney. Local in Ireland, mainly on the north and west coasts. Considered an occasional immigrant in the Channel Islands.

2395 see below 2396

Rosy Marbled
page 332

Elaphria venustula Hb.

Nb. SE   2396(9396)

Field characters FW 10-11mm. A rosy pink stripe runs parallel to leading edge of pinkish-white forewing. The small, dark central block and roughly triangular brown blotches on trailing and outer edges are also diagnostic.

Similar species The pyralid moth *Scoparia pyralella* ([D. & S.]) often flies with Rosy Marbled and superficially resembles it, especially in flight, but has slenderer forewing, and although colours may be similar, details of wing pattern do not match, and Rosy Marbled holds its wings in a more tent-like position at rest, which distinguishes it from many micro-moths.

Flight season One generation. Late May-mid July. Sometimes disturbed from vegetation by day. Both sexes fly from just before dusk and male especially comes to light after dark.

Life cycle Overwinters as a pupa, in a cocoon on or below the ground among roots. Larva late June-August.

Larval foodplants Probably the flowers of Tormentil and Creeping Cinquefoil, although not confirmed recently. In captivity also reared successfully on the flowers of Silverweed, Bramble, roses, Garden Strawberry and Field Bindweed.

Habitat Mainly dry open woodland on warm acid soils, particularly where Bracken grows; also heathland, roadside verges and other open places with Tormentil and similar flora.

Status & distribution Resident. Nationally Scarce B. Occurs mainly in south-east England, where it is widely distributed and recorded on a frequent basis from Kent, through Sussex and Surrey, west into Hampshire and north as far as Berkshire, south Oxfordshire, Buckinghamshire and Essex. Appears to be extending its range eastwards and northwards in Kent, or at least is wandering over these areas, and has advanced westwards in Hampshire, where it is now frequently recorded in the New Forest. Recorded on the Isle of Wight at Freshwater on 13 June 1992, and at Binstead on 19 June 1998. There are several long-established colonies on the Suffolk coast. Seems also to have become established in the Breckland since the late 1970s or early 1980s. Records of singletons further from the core distribution, presumed to be wanderers, include Steeple Ashton, south Wiltshire on 8 June 1982, Baston Fen, Lincolnshire on 14 June 1986, south Worcestershire on 26 June 1986 and Lundy Island, Devon, also in 1986.

Stiriinae

Goldwing   not illustrated
Synthymia fixa (Fabr.)
Rare immigrant.   2395(9350)

Field characters & Similar species FW 15-18mm. Somewhat like Burnet Companion in shape and appearance, but larger and distinguished by conspicuous yellowish kidney-mark and oval on grey-green forewing and orange-yellow, broadly brown-bordered hindwing.
Status & distribution Rare immigrant. One British record of this mainly day-flying species. A singleton, recorded as collected at Start Point lighthouse, south Devon in 1937, is now in the Natural History Museum, London. In Europe, recorded mainly in the extreme south around the Mediterranean.

Small Yellow Underwing   page 332
Panemeria tenebrata (Scop.)
Local. S,C   2397(9338)

Field characters FW 8-10mm. Unlike any other British or Irish macro-moth. Combination of size, dark brown forewing dusted with grey, and black hindwing with a broad yellow band is unique. Shows little variation, but some examples have slightly reddish forewing.
Similar species *Pyrausta aurata* (Scop.), a frequent day-flying micro-moth, has blackish hindwing with a narrow yellow band. Forewing dull brown when worn, but is narrower and has at least one orange-yellow spot.
Flight season One generation. May-early June. Flies in sunshine and feeds at flowers, often with hindwings exposed. Mating pairs sometimes seen in sward in late afternoon.
Life cycle Overwinters as a pupa, in a cocoon underground. Larva June-July.
Larval foodplants The seed capsules of Common Mouse-ear and Field Mouse-ear.
Habitat Flower-rich grassland, including haymeadows, calcareous grassland, roadside verges and soft-rock sea-cliffs.
Status & distribution Resident. Local. Thinly distributed throughout much of England, Wales, south-east Scotland and south-west Ireland. Easily overlooked owing to small size and non-appearance in light-traps. Recorded only once on Man, in 1903.

Heliothinae

Bordered Sallow   Marbled Clover

Pease Blossom   page 333
Periphanes delphinii (L.)
Possible immigrant; import; possible former
resident   2398(9378)

Field characters FW 14-15mm. Beautiful purplish-pink shading on forewing and sinuous cross-lines are diagnostic.
Similar species None.
Flight season One generation. The dates of the few purported British records range from early April to June. In mainland Europe, mainly May-June, often flying by day.
Life cycle Overwinters as a pupa underground. Larva July-August.
Larval foodplants Reportedly Monk's-hood and the related naturalised Larkspur.
Habitat Said to have been caught on Hampstead Heath, London, in gardens in London and Hampshire, and at various coastal sites.
Status & distribution Possibly an extinct resident, a rare immigrant or a deliberate or accidental import. About 20 individuals have been reported, all prior to 1900. Contemporary accounts indicate that dead specimens or livestock were definitely being imported from southern Europe for collections from at least the early 19th century. Thought to be British by Haworth (1802), and also by Stephens (1829) who reported that few native specimens were known. Records of individuals apparently captured wild include a wing found in a spider's web at Bulstrode, Buckinghamshire, prior to 1794, one in a Chelsea garden before 1802 and several from Windsor, Berkshire, in June about 1815. The subsequent reports are mainly from the London area (possibly garden imports) or the south coast of England (possibly immigrants), the last being from Dover, Kent, in 1893.

Bordered Sallow   page 333
Pyrrhia umbra (Hufn.)
Local. S,C,NE   2399(9372)

Field characters FW 16-19mm. Unmistakable. Quite thickset. Forewing with leading edge straight and clearly defined, invariable markings. Ground-colour orange or orange-yellow (less often orange-brown) from base to the sharply diagonal, slightly curved cross-line beyond kidney-mark; pinkish brown beyond this line, including fringes. This sharp demar-

373

cation is diagnostic and is always present, although degree of contrast varies somewhat. Hindwing yellowish white with a broad, blackish outer band and usually a large, dark, rather blurred crescent-mark.

Similar species None.

Flight season One generation. June-July. Comes to sugar, and also to light in small numbers, and feeds at flowers at dusk.

Life cycle Overwinters as a pupa, just beneath the soil surface. Larva July-August, most active at night.

Larval foodplants Frequently the flowers, seeds and shoots of Common and Spiny Restharrow, but also those of Henbane and Sea Sandwort, as well as the leaves of Hazel, oaks and willows.

Habitat Calcareous grassland, coastal sand-dunes and shingle. Less often open woodland, in which larvae have been found on low regrowth of coppiced Hazel and oak.

Status & distribution Resident. Local. Quite well distributed in southern Britain, but largely coastal north of the Midlands and in Wales and Man. Local in Scotland, mainly on the east coast north to Ross-shire, and in Ireland. In the Channel Islands recorded only from Alderney, where it is local and occasional.

Scarce Bordered Straw (Old World Bollworm)

page 333

Helicoverpa armigera (Hb.)

Immigrant.   2400(9370)

Field characters & Similar species FW 16-19mm. A variable species, forewing ranging from dark purplish brown through to pale sandy shades. Forewing markings hardly discernible on some individuals but very prominent in some paler forms. Hindwing has broad black border. Bordered Straw has a prominent, dark, roughly triangular mark adjacent to kidney-mark, and a small but distinct black dot at trailing corner. Some paler individuals of Scarce Bordered Straw have been mistaken for Eastern Bordered Straw, which also has a black dot at trailing corner, has three small black dots on outer edge of forewing near tip, and a distinct inward kink near centre of outermost cross-line. Forewing of Scarce Bordered Straw often appears broader than that of the other two species.

Flight season Continuous generations in subtropical regions. Has been recorded throughout the year, but winter records are rare. Most frequent in late summer and early autumn, particularly September-October. Comes to light and sugar, also visiting flowers by day or at dusk.

Life cycle Larvae rarely found in the wild in the British Isles.

Larval foodplants Has been found in the wild on Scarlet Geranium and Yellow-rattle. Recorded from many cultivated plants elsewhere in the world, including Cotton, Maize, Tomato and carnations.

Habitat Mainly seen on coasts but also occurs inland, particularly during years of abundance.

Status & distribution Immigrant. Occurs almost annually in varying numbers: over 300 were recorded in 1996. Most frequently noted in southern England and Wales, particularly south-west England, but has occurred as far north as Shetland and occasionally on Man, in Ireland and in the Channel Islands. Larvae frequently imported with vegetables and flowers. Resident in southern Europe and North Africa, where sometimes a pest.

Marbled Clover

page 333

Heliothis viriplaca (Hufn.)

RDB; suspected immigrant. S,EC   2401(9364)

Field characters & Similar species FW 13-15mm. Distinguished from Shoulder-striped Clover by absence of dark shoulder-stripe on base of forewing, and less angled inner edge to dark band across forewing. Intensity of colour and markings variable.

Flight season One main generation, mid June-July, with a partial second generation at the end of July-August in early seasons. Flies rapidly in sunshine, darting from place to place and visiting flowers, including Viper's-bugloss, clovers and many others. Also comes to light.

Life cycle Overwinters as a pupa, in a flimsy cocoon on or below the ground. Larva July-September, sometimes with a partial second generation into October.

Larval foodplants The flowers and unripe seed-heads of many unrelated plants, including Restharrow, Common Toadflax, White Campion, Bladder Campion, Chicory, Wild Carrot, Smooth Hawk's-beard, Red Clover, Sticky Groundsel and various scabiouses, hawkweeds and knapweeds.

Habitat Breeds mainly in open breckland, flowery chalk downland, sand or shingle beaches, marginal and set-aside farmland, wide flowery rides and large temporary clearings in breckland plantations, other disturbed calcareous ground, and sometimes fields of clover and Lucerne. Singletons have been light-trapped in many open situations, including gardens.

Status & distribution Resident and suspected immigrant. Red Data Book species. Often occurs with influxes of known immigrant species and well known as an immigrant elsewhere in Europe. As a long-term resident, the main breeding areas are the Breckland of Norfolk and Suffolk and the Suffolk coast, especially between Thorpeness and Aldeburgh. Also breeds locally in Wiltshire and possibly intermittently in north Hampshire. In previous decades bred more widely, e.g. at Dungeness, Kent (from the 1930s to the 1950s). Such coastal colonies are probably temporary estab-lishments resulting from immigration. There is a wide scatter of records of singletons, usually from light-traps, in southern and eastern England, which may be immigrants or wanderers from British popu-lations, and localised breeding may occur inland as a consequence. Recorded once in the Channel Islands, a singleton on Guernsey in 1949.

Shoulder-striped Clover
page 333

Heliothis maritima (Grasl.)

ssp. *warneckei* Bours.
RDB. S   2402(9365)

ssp. *bulgarica* (Draudt)
Rare immigrant.

Field characters & Similar species FW 13-17mm.
Dark shoulder-stripe at base of forewing and more
angled inner edge of dark band across forewing
distinguish this moth from Marbled Clover, which is
much less likely to be found on acid heathland.
British populations of Shoulder-striped Clover are the
endemic ssp. *warneckei*. A single female, determined
by Boursin as ssp. *bulgarica*, was captured in a
lucerne field at St Nicholas-at-Wade on the Isle of
Thanet, Kent, on 20 August 1947, flying with immigrant Clouded Yellow butterflies. It was presumed an
immigrant. This race, which lacks a distinct basal
streak, is a resident of Bulgaria and Yugoslavia.
Flight season One generation. Late June-July.
Apparently no partial second emergence, unlike
Marbled Clover. Flies fast in sunshine and visits the
flowers of heathers and heaths, favouring plants on
south-facing slopes above boggy and bare ground.
Also comes to light.
Life cycle Overwinters as a pupa in a flimsy cocoon on
or below the ground. Larva August-early September,
sometimes until late September. Feeds at night.
Larval foodplants Mainly the flowers of Cross-
leaved Heath, but also recorded from Heather and
the seedheads of Bog Asphodel.
Habitat Large tracts of damp, acid heathland where
Cross-leaved Heath is abundant, in contrast to the
calcareous sites favoured by Marbled Clover.
Status & distribution Resident. Red Data Book
species. Very local in Dorset (Wareham and Studland
Heaths), Hampshire (some of the New Forest heaths)
and Surrey (e.g. Thursley and Chobham Commons).
Also recorded from a small section of heathland on
the Lizard NNR at Goonhilly Downs, and just north of
Erisey Barton, Cornwall, but the last definite sighting
was in 1981. A rather worn adult was reported from
Porthleven, Cornwall, on 23 July 1984, and the moth
has also been reported from Haldon Moor, Devon.
Note: when researching old records this species was
not recognised as distinct from Marbled Clover until
the late 1930s. Some of the literature up to the
1980s continued to confuse the two species.

Bordered Straw
page 333

Heliothis peltigera ([D. & S.])
Immigrant.   2403(9367)

Field characters FW 16-19mm. Distinct, grey
kidney-mark, with a diffuse, sometimes faint brown
blotch between it and leading edge, along with a
darker outer band, further darkened at leading edge
to form a roughly triangular blotch, are diagnostic. A
smaller dark mark is also usually visible along leading
edge nearer to base and there is a small, bold black

dot at trailing corner. Ground-colour is strongly
affected by the temperatures experienced by early
stages. Thus, primary immigrants early in the season
from hot climates are straw-yellow and their
offspring are darker, yellow-brown. Hindwing has a
thick dark brown or blackish band along outer edge,
often with a white blotch within it.
Similar species See Scarce Bordered Straw (where
differences with Eastern Bordered Straw are also
described). Worn individuals in particular are sometimes confused with Eastern Bordered Straw.
Flight season Has been recorded in every season,
but winter records are rare; most frequent June-
August. Comes to light and sugar; also flies at dusk
and during sunshine, visiting flowers and laying eggs.
Life cycle Larvae occur in some years, occasionally in
abundance, June-October. A late summer/autumn
generation may result from eggs laid early in the
season, but the species is unlikely to survive winter in
the British Isles.
Larval foodplants The flowers of Common
Restharrow, Ploughman's-spikenard, Scentless
Mayweed, Sticky Groundsel and garden marigolds.
Habitat Primarily coastal, but also occurs inland.
Status & distribution Immigrant. Recorded in most
years. Occurs primarily in southern England and Wales,
but recorded north to Shetland, and also from Man
and Ireland. Exceptionally large numbers occurred in
1996, with widespread breeding in the south. An
occasional immigrant in the Channel Islands. Resident
in mainland Europe and North Africa.

Eastern Bordered Straw
page 333

Heliothis nubigera (H.-S.)
Rare immigrant.   2404(9368)

Field characters & Similar species FW 16-20mm.
Has at least three bold, black dots along outer edge
of forewing, while Bordered Straw has a bold dot at
trailing corner only, and these dots are rather faint in
Scarce Bordered Straw.
Larval foodplants Various wild and cultivated
plants, including chrysanthemums and Tomato.
Status & distribution Rare immigrant. Five British
records: Sheringham, Norfolk, 28 May and 3 June
1958; Iwerne Minster, Dorset, 9 May 1958; Swanage,
Dorset, 14 May 1992; and Thorverton, Devon, 5
January 1999. Mainly an eastern Mediterranean
species but also resident on the Canary Islands.

Spotted Clover
page 333

Schinia scutosa ([D. & S.])
Immigrant.   2405(9358)

Field characters FW 15-16mm. Distinctive
chequered brown and white appearance, with
noticeable whitish veins, large brown kidney-mark,
basal block and other patches on whitish forewing.
Hindwing white, with brown border and central
spot.
Similar species None.
Flight season Two generations in mainland Europe.

375

As an immigrant, recorded May-September but most frequently June-August. Most records from the British Isles are of moths flying around flowers by day or at dusk, occasionally at light.

Life cycle In mainland Europe, overwinters as a pupa underground, with larva June-July and August-September. Larvae not recorded in the British Isles.

Larval foodplants Field Wormwood and goosefoots.

Habitat Usually seen on the coast, but has occurred inland.

Status & distribution Immigrant. Erratic appearance. Around 60 were recorded in the British Isles between 1835 and 2002. Some records are of a number of moths, including more than 30 seen between Bude and Boscastle, Cornwall, on 30 May 1943, with a large influx of Striped Hawk-moths. Recorded from Cornwall, Devon, Somerset, the Isle of Wight, Surrey, Kent, Cambridgeshire, Suffolk, Norfolk, Lincolnshire, Yorkshire, Cumbria, Aberdeenshire, Inverness-shire, Man and Co. Donegal. Most records are from eastern England, particularly East Anglia. Distribution includes central, eastern and southern Europe, as well as North Africa and much of Asia.

2406 see Appendix

Eustrotiinae

Purple Marbled

Marbled White Spot

Silver Hook

Purple Marbled   page 333
Eublemma ostrina (Hb.)
Immigrant.   2407(9140)

Field characters FW 8-9mm. Purple streaks in outer part of small, brownish, pointed forewing are diagnostic when present. In f. *carthami* H.-S. forewing is almost white, with pale brown markings and no purple streaks.

Similar species See Small Marbled.

Flight season At least two generations in mainland Europe. As an immigrant, recorded March-early November, but more usually May-October. May be disturbed by day or seen flying in sunshine. Comes to light and sugar.

Life cycle No evidence of overwintering in the British Isles. Larvae found occasionally in July-August, the progeny of spring immigrants. Pupates in or on flowers of the foodplant.

Larval foodplants The flowers and seedheads of various thistles, particularly Carline Thistle.

Habitat Open and disturbed ground.

Status & distribution Immigrant. There have been over 100 records of the adult in the British Isles, the largest yearly total being 36 in 1992; larvae and

pupae have also been found in some years, particularly during the 1990s. Mainly recorded from the southern coastal counties of England, particularly south-west England. Occasionally occurs inland in southern England. Also recorded from south Wales, north-west England, southern Scotland and the Republic of Ireland. A species mainly of southern Europe and North Africa.

Small Marbled   page 333
Eublemma parva (Hb.)
Immigrant.   2408(9142)

Field characters FW 7-8mm. Very small and easily overlooked as a micro-moth, with a conspicuous, fairly straight brown and white central line across yellowish-white forewing. Cross-line beyond middle (or outer edge of central band) is in form of a question-mark. Usually has darker brown shading towards tip of forewing. Hindwing whitish.

Similar species Purple Marbled is larger, lacks central line and usually (but not always) has distinctive purple streaks. Marsh Oblique-barred is browner, with oblique stripes. See also Scarce Marbled.

Flight season Two or more generations abroad. As an immigrant, recorded March-October. Most records from the British Isles at light.

Life cycle No evidence of overwintering in the British Isles. Larva July-September in the British Isles, producing late-season adults. Pupates in a cocoon attached to flowers of the foodplant.

Larval foodplants The flowers of Common Fleabane and Ploughman's-spikenard.

Habitat Open and disturbed habitats.

Status & distribution Immigrant. Over 150 adults have been recorded in the British Isles, the record year being 1953 when over 40 were noted; larvae have also been reported on several occasions. Mainly recorded from the southern coastal counties of England but occasionally inland. Also recorded from northern England, Man, southern Scotland, the Republic of Ireland and the Channel Islands, where two were found on Guernsey in 1998. Resident in central and southern Europe and North Africa.

Scarce Marbled   not ilustrated
Eublemma minutata (Fabr.)
Suspected rare immigrant.   2409(9134)

Field characters & Similar species FW 7-8mm. Somewhat similar to Small Marbled, but cross-line beyond middle of forewing has a distinct V-shaped central kink and is otherwise straight.

Status & distribution Suspected rare immigrant. A singleton was captured in a cornfield near the cliffs at Freshwater, Isle of Wight, in June 1872, a year in which immigrants were numerous. There is another specimen, labelled 'Freshwater, 1868' in the Natural History Museum, London, and Barrett mentions that two were recorded in 1873. This predominantly southern European species has populations in central France, western Germany and Denmark.

Marbled White Spot
page 333

Protodeltote pygarga (Hufn.)

Common. S,C   2410(9114)

Field characters FW 11-12mm. Diagnostic feature is distinct whitish patch toward trailing corner of blackish-grey and brown forewing. This patch does not reach leading edge, and is usually marked with grey along its outer margin. It varies in width and in the uncommon f. *albilinea* Haw. is reduced to white edging on outside of outermost cross-line. Variation otherwise slight.
Similar species Pretty Marbled is similar in size, shape and colour, but forewing extensively marbled with white, both towards outer edge and near base.
Flight season One generation. Late May-July. Rests on tree trunks and fences by day, and flies when disturbed. Comes to light regularly and occasionally to sugar.
Life cycle Overwinters as a pupa in a cocoon just below ground. Larva July-September. Feeds mainly at night.
Larval foodplants Grasses. Recorded from Purple Moor-grass and False Brome, but probably also uses others, such as Tufted Hair-grass.
Habitat Woodland, grassy heathland and moorland, most frequently on acid and neutral soils.
Status & distribution Resident. Common. Well distributed and fairly frequent in the southern half of England. Local in the Midlands, Lincolnshire, Yorkshire and Wales. Very local in Ireland, mainly in the south-west but also recorded from Co. Down. In the Channel Islands, widespread and often seen on Jersey, rare on Guernsey.

Pretty Marbled
page 333

Deltote deceptoria (Scop.)

Immigrant; transitory resident.   2411(9116)

Field characters & Similar species FW 12-13mm. Superficially resembles Marbled White Spot but has white patches at base of forewing as well as near outer edge. Oval and kidney-mark white in outline against black central band. Hindwing greyish white, with brown borders.
Flight season One generation in mainland Europe, late April-mid July. British records May-June, mostly at light, but one caught by day.
Life cycle In mainland Europe, overwinters as a pupa. Breeding unconfirmed in the British Isles.
Larval foodplants Grasses, especially Timothy and cat's-tails.
Habitat British records mainly from woodland and open coastal habitats.
Status & distribution Immigrant and probable transitory resident. There were 18 British records between 1948 and 1998. Recorded from Kent, Sussex, Surrey, Hampshire, Gloucestershire and Norfolk. These records include a cluster from the Hamstreet/Orlestone woodlands, Kent, between 1948 and 1956, which suggest a resident population may have been established temporarily. Widely

distributed in central Europe, and thought to be expanding its range.

Silver Hook
page 333

Deltote uncula (Cl.)

Local. S,C,NW   2412(9117)

Field characters FW 11-12mm. Unmistakable. Slender, with a unique, invariable pattern. Diagnostic feature is a creamy-white streak running close to leading edge of olive-brown forewing, from which the oblique white kidney-mark forms a hook-like projection. Ground-colour varies somewhat in shade. There are grey streaks along leading and trailing edges which may be pink-tinged.
Similar species None.
Flight season One generation. Late May-early July. Occasional adults in August may be a partial second generation. Flies by day when disturbed, and from dusk onwards. Comes to light, usually in small numbers.
Life cycle Overwinters as a pupa, in a strong cocoon underground. Larva July-September.
Larval foodplants Grasses and sedges, including Tufted Hair-grass and Wood-sedge.
Habitat Fens, marshes, boggy heathland and high moorland. Sometimes wanders into other habitats.
Status & distribution Resident. Local. In suitable habitat in southern England, Wales, East Anglia, eastern and northern England, south-west and western Scotland, Man and Ireland.

Silver Barred
page 333

Deltote bankiana (Fabr.)

RDB; suspected immigrant. SE   2413(9118)

Field characters FW 10-12mm. The two parallel slanting silvery-white bars on forewing of this small brown moth are diagnostic. Irish individuals tend to be slightly larger and redder than English specimens.
Similar species None.
Flight season Mainly one generation, early May-late July, with occasional individuals, possibly of a partial second generation, in mid August. Easily disturbed by day, flying up from low swards, and active from dusk, coming to light.
Life cycle Overwinters as a pupa, in a cocoon low in the sward. Larva June-August. Can be swept at night.
Larval foodplants Reported from Purple Moor-grass (with which it is strongly associated across the English Channel) and Smooth Meadow-grass, but accepts Annual Meadow-grass in captivity.
Habitat Fens, marshes and peat bogs. Suspected transitory resident on a patch of damp grassland below chalk downs. May prefer rides and other annually cut areas to tall fen swards.
Status & distribution Resident and suspected immigrant. Red Data Book species. As a long-term breeding resident, confined in Britain to Chippenham and Wicken Fens in Cambridgeshire. Present more widely in the wetlands of Huntingdonshire,

Cambridgeshire and Norfolk in the 19th century, prior to drainage operations. Seems to have colonised a small coastal marsh near Sandwich, Kent, from about 1980, as a result of immigration. A second colony appears to have been established temporarily at the foot of downland at Dover, Kent, in 1993, when the moth was regularly seen in double figures over a fortnight in June, but this has not persisted. Elsewhere there have been numerous records of singletons, presumed immigrants, mainly at coastal sites in the south-east and east (Kent, Sussex, Essex, Suffolk and Norfolk) and on dates ranging from May to August, mostly at light-traps. A singleton reached Huntington, Yorkshire, on 8 June 1992. In Ireland a long-term resident of peat bogs, occurring widely in Co. Kerry and from Glengariff, Co. Cork, but not recorded outside the south-west.

Acontiinae

Spotted Sulphur   Pale Shoulder

Spotted Sulphur
page 333

Emmelia trabealis (Scop.)

Presumed extinct.   2414(9097)

Field characters FW 10-11mm. Intricate pattern of dark chocolate spots and stripes running along yellowish-cream forewing of this delicate moth, and its small size, are diagnostic. Hindwing brown with white margins.

Similar species None, but could be mistaken for a micro-moth.

Flight season One generation. Mid June-early July, occasionally August. Easily disturbed and flushed by day near the larval foodplant, especially in dry, sunny weather. Flies naturally in late afternoon. Sometimes captured after dark in light-traps.

Life cycle Overwinters as a pupa, among grass stems near the ground. Larva July and September.

Larval foodplants Field Bindweed.

Habitat Lightly-vegetated open ground in the Breckland, including sandy heaths, fallow fields, other disturbed land, banks and verges.

Status & distribution Former resident and suspected immigrant, now presumed extinct in the British Isles. First recorded as occasional captures in Kent from 1782 onwards, with one at light at Swanage, Dorset, on 20 August 1947. Discovered breeding in the Breckland in 1847 and recorded at various sites there until the early 1950s. Survived in a single plot planted with asparagus near Mildenhall, Suffolk, where it was last seen in Britain on 25 June

1960. The decline and extinction of this species have been attributed to ecological changes resulting from large-scale afforestation and agricultural intensification in the Breckland.

Pale Shoulder
page 333

Acontia lucida (Hufn.)

Immigrant; resident Jersey.   2415(9100)

Field characters & Similar species FW 12-15mm. Resembles Four-spotted but distinguished by large white or greyish-white patches at base of forewing – the 'pale shoulders'. Hindwing off-white in centre, with broad blackish borders.

Flight season Two generations in mainland Europe, May-June and July-August. As an immigrant, recorded June-August, mainly August. Visits flowers in sunshine and comes to light.

Life cycle In mainland Europe, overwinters as a pupa just below ground. Larva June-July and August-September.

Larval foodplants Reported from Ground-ivy, Field Bindweed, Common Mallow, Dwarf Mallow and Marsh-mallow.

Habitat Hot, dry, open flowery places.

Status & distribution Immigrant. Approximately 15 were reported from south-east England during the 19th century, as suspected immigrants. No further records until 1994 when singletons were trapped at West Bexington, Dorset, and Dymchurch, Kent, both on 5 August. Another five have been recorded in the British Isles up to 2001, from Scilly, Devon, Hampshire and Sussex, and including another at West Bexington. Possibly now breeding on Jersey, where first recorded as three in 1995 and two in 1998. First seen on Guernsey in 2001. Its range includes central and southern Europe and North Africa.

2416, 2417 see Appendix

Eariadinae

Cream-bordered   Spiny Bollworm   Egyptian
Green Pea   Bollworm

Cream-bordered Green Pea
page 333

Earias clorana (L.)

Nb. S,EC   2418(10456)

Field characters & Similar species FW 10-12mm. White leading edge of forewing, white hindwing and resting posture with wings held close to sides of body, distinguish this species from the much more widespread and abundant micro-moth Green Oak

Tortrix *Tortrix viridana* L. (see pp. 12-13), which is flatter at rest and has grey, not white hindwing. Occasional individuals of Cream-bordered Green Pea are brownish green with brown wing fringes (f. *flavimargo* Joann.), and have been mistaken for Spiny Bollworm.

Flight season Usually one generation, late May-July. Occasionally a partial second generation, August onwards. Rests among foliage by day, flying from dusk. Can be netted around the foodplant and comes well to light and to sugar, sometimes in numbers.

Life cycle Overwinters as a pupa, in a tough boat-shaped cocoon often constructed on the bark of a twig or stem of the foodplant. Larva late June-August, sometimes with a partial second generation in September-October.

Larval foodplants The terminal shoots of sallows and willows, possibly favouring Osier but even recorded near ground level on Creeping Willow.

Habitat The Norfolk Broads, fens, marshes, sallow carr and damp woodland (especially in East Anglia), and the flood-plains and valleys of major rivers such as the Humber, Thames and latterly the Severn; also damp heathland in Dorset and vegetated shingle at Dungeness, Kent. Breeding recently suspected in well-established gardens or along nearby ditches and amenity plantings of native trees and shrubs in the east Midlands.

Status & distribution Resident and possibly occasional immigrant. Nationally Scarce B. Widely and well distrib-uted from Kent north to Thorne Moor and the Humber, Yorkshire, where it may be expanding its distribution. Also well distributed, although local, west to Buckinghamshire and the east Midlands, and along the south coast to Cornwall, where it is now a suspected new resident on the Lizard, following a series of records during the 1990s. Singletons, suspected wanderers, have been recorded westwards into Wales, where the first was taken at Usk, Monmouthshire, on 20 June 1983. Probably now breeding in the Severn Vale and estuary. First discovered in Ireland in 1914 in the Coomarkane Valley, near Glengariff, Co. Cork, which still appears to be the only known Irish locality. Singletons of f. *flavimargo* were light-trapped at St Austell, Cornwall, on 12 June 1992 and Freshwater, Isle of Wight, on 25 June 1992 and may have been immi-grants. Local but frequent in the Channel Islands.

Spiny Bollworm   page 333
Earias biplaga (Walk.)
Rare immigrant/import.   2419(-)

Field characters & Similar species FW 11-12mm. One form has a large purplish-brown blotch centrally on trailing edge of green or yellowish forewing, and these merge when at rest, making it quite distinctive. Forewing has faint cross-lines and brown fringes. The form without the blotch is some-what similar to the rare form of Cream-bordered Green Pea with brown fringes, but this has forewing more pointed, lacks cross-lines and has a curved leading edge with a distinct white stripe along it. Green form of Egyptian Bollworm has narrower

forewing and fringes are not brown.

Status & distribution Suspected accidental import or rare immigrant. Recorded three times in Britain as singletons in light-traps: a male in perfect condition on 17 July 1964 at Buckingham Palace Gardens, London, following the visit of a delegation from East Africa; another on 23 July 1982 at Lymington, Hampshire; and a third on 11 September 1999 with a small influx of other immigrant moths at Dungeness, Kent. The immature stages have been found in imported produce at British airports. Not recorded elsewhere in Europe. Resident in sub-Saharan Africa where it is sometimes a pest on Cotton.

Egyptian Bollworm   page 333
Earias insulana (Boisd.)
Suspected rare immigrant; import.   2420(10460)

Field characters & Similar species FW 10-11mm. Forewing narrower and less pointed than that of Cream-bordered Green Pea, and without a broad white stripe along leading edge. Either green or brownish green, with darker green cross-lines, often V-shaped. Fringes in green form are green. See also Spiny Bollworm.

Status & distribution Suspected rare immigrant and import. One was light-trapped at Brockenhurst, Hampshire, on 8 October 1967, when scarce immi-grants were recorded elsewhere in England. Another was discovered as an unlabelled set specimen in a series of Green Oak Tortrix: it had been collected some time in 1962 in southern England, possibly Devon. Singletons recorded at Portland, Dorset on 24 Augsut 1999, and at Stoke Bishop, Gloucestershire on 27 July 2001. The immature stages have been found in imported produce at British airports. Resident in Africa, Asia and Australia and recorded in Mediterranean Europe.

2420a see Appendix

Chloephorinae

Green Silver-lines   Oak Nycteoline

Scarce Silver-lines   page 333
Bena bicolorana (Fuess.)
Local. S,C   2421(10449)

Field characters FW 19-23mm. Unmistakable. Rather slender green thorax, with broad, bright green forewing crossed by two thin, parallel diagonal yellowish-white lines; leading edge curved and yellowish white. Hindwing white. Antennae, palps and front legs salmon pink. Hardly any variation, but very occasionally one of the cross-lines is absent.

Similar species None.

Flight season One generation. Late June-July. Comes to light regularly and to sugar.

Life cycle Overwinters as a small larva on or near a bud of the foodplant. Larva August-May. Pupates in a tough, boat-shaped cocoon on the underside of a leaf of the foodplant.

Larval foodplants The buds and leaves of Pedunculate Oak and probably other oaks; also recorded on Downy Birch and Silver Birch.

Habitat Broadleaved woodland and parkland.

Status & distribution Resident. Local. Well distributed and fairly frequent south of the Humber in England and in Wales. More local in northern England, occurring north to Yorkshire, where it has increased its distribution since 1980, and Cumbria.

Green Silver-lines page 333

Pseudoips prasinana (L.)

ssp. *britannica* Warr.

Common. T   2422(10451)

Field characters FW 16-19mm. Unmistakable. Forewing green, usually with three roughly parallel diagonal white cross-lines, the first sharply angled at leading edge, and sometimes a white central band. Head and thorax are green, antennae are orange or pink and palps and front legs are pink. Male has bright green forewing, with bright pink or pinkish-brown fringes and yellowish-white hindwing. Female is slightly slimmer, with broader, lighter green forewing with green or greenish-white fringes and white hindwing.

Similar species None.

Flight season One generation. May-July, with occasional individuals in August-September, possibly of a second generation. Comes to light, sometimes in moderate numbers.

Life cycle Overwinters as a pupa, in a tough boat-shaped cocoon either on the underside of a leaf of the foodplant or in a bark crevice. Larva July-September.

Larval foodplants Broadleaved trees, usually oaks, Downy Birch, Silver Birch or Beech, but sometimes Hazel and occasionally Sweet Chestnut, Aspen and elms.

Habitat Mainly woodland, but sometimes seen in garden light-traps some distance from woodland.

Status & distribution Resident. Common. Fairly well distributed and quite frequent over much of England and Wales north to Co. Durham. More local and confined to the lowlands in Northumberland, Cumbria and southern Scotland, including Mull. Local on Man and in Ireland. Widespread but occasional in the Channel Islands.

Oak Nycteoline page 333

Nycteola revayana (Scop.)

Local. T   2423(10441)

Field characters FW 11-13mm. Very variable, and examination of genitalia may be required for definite identification. Forewing narrow, leading edge steeply arched or shouldered at base, then straight or slightly concave. Markings very variable: slate grey, or a mixture of grey, brown, or blackish, or less frequently pale grey, often finely marbled and with dark wavy cross-lines or a cross-band; more rarely, a broad tawny band along leading edge and a long, branched blackish central streak from base. Paler examples may have one or more black spots and a brown or blackish roughly triangular blotch midway along leading edge. Hindwing grey.

Similar species Sallow Nycteoline is larger and has white head and palps. The extremely variable *Acleris cristana* ([D. & S.]) and *A. hastiana* (L.) (family Tortricidae, micro-moths) are slimmer and usually smaller. *A. hastiana* has much shorter palps and *A. cristana* has a tuft of raised scales in centre of forewing. See also Eastern Nycteoline.

Flight season Probably two generations in southern England, where freshly emerged moths occur from early July, and in Scilly. Elsewhere, one generation, August-May or early June. Occasionally comes to light, sugar, Ivy flowers and sallow catkins. Best located by beating lower branches of oaks or dense Hazel understorey in the evenings in October.

Life cycle Overwinters as an adult, among dead leaves accumulated in epicormic growth on oaks, and also in conifers. Larva May-July and also recorded in September. Pupates in a tough, boat-shaped cocoon formed on the underside of a leaf of the foodplant.

Larval foodplants Pedunculate Oak and probably Sessile Oak.

Habitat Broadleaved woodland and parkland.

Status & distribution Resident. Local. Quite well distributed, usually in small numbers but sometimes abundantly, in southern England from the south-west, including Scilly, to East Anglia. Local in Wales, the Midlands, eastern and northern England, mainland Scotland north to Ross-shire, on Man and in Ireland. Widespread but occasional in the Channel Islands.

Eastern Nycteoline not illustrated

Nycteola asiatica (Krulikovsky)

Suspected rare immigrant.   2423a(10444)

Field characters & Similar species FW 11-13mm. Similar to some forms of Oak Nycteoline, but distinguished by base of forewing leading edge, which is much less steeply-arched. Forewing also generally broader, glossy grey, with fine, dark, wavy central cross-lines. Central spot reddish brown or dark brown, often within a blotch of same colour, which may extend to leading edge or form a diffuse cross-band.

Flight season One generation in northern Europe, August-May. Two generations further south, June-July and September-May.
Life cycle Overwinters as an adult. Larva May-July where one generation, May-June and July-August where two. Pupates in cocoon attached to the food-plant.
Larval foodplants Poplars and sallows in mainland Europe.
Habitat Found in an open coastal site.
Status & distribution Suspected rare immigrant. One record. A single male was captured in a light-trap at Kew Villa, Kilnsea, Spurn, south-east Yorkshire, on 11 September 2002, in the company of three species of confirmed immigrant moths. Widely reported in mainland Europe, from Spain and Greece to Scandinavia.

2424 see Appendix

Grey Square   page 333
Pardasena virgulana (Mab.)
Suspected import.   2424a(-)

Field characters & Similar species FW 8-12mm. Somewhat like Oak Nycteoline, but with forewing broader and leading edge curved, not concave. Markings variable, but forewing predominantly grey. Fine blackish cross-lines often present, the basal one slightly curved and central ones wavy, often with a dark central bar. Hindwing white, sometimes grey-brown around outer edge.
Status & distribution Suspected accidental import. Recorded only once in the British Isles. A female in good condition was captured in a light-trap on the edge of Hamford Water near Thorpe-le-Soken, Essex, on 27 September 1992. The trap site is near the ports of Harwich and Felixstowe so transport on a ship is suspected. Larvae have been imported into Britain on okra from Cyprus and on peas from East Africa. Does not occur naturally in Europe but widespread in Africa.

Pantheinae

Nut-tree Tussock

Nut-tree Tussock   page 334
Colocasia coryli (L.)
Common. T   2425(10372)

Field characters FW 14-17mm. A thickset furry moth; forewing broad, rounded and usually predominantly dark brown in basal half (although grey at very base), contrasting with light grey or pale brown

in outer half. Male has feathered antennae.
F. *medionigra* Vorbrodt is light grey (white in parts of northern Scotland), with basal area very dark. In f. *avellana* Huene, basal patch is faint or occasionally absent. F. *melanotica* Haverkampf is dark brownish grey or blackish: this form occurs in southern England, most frequently in Buckinghamshire, Oxfordshire and Hertfordshire.
Similar species None.
Flight season Two generations in southern Britain, late April-mid June and late July-early September. One generation in northern England and Scotland, late May-early July. Male flies from dusk and comes frequently to light; the rather sedentary female does so only rarely.
Life cycle Overwinters as a pupa, in a cocoon formed either among leaf litter, under moss or at the base of a tree. Larva late May-early July and September-early October in the south, late June-September in the north. Feeds at night and hides between spun leaves by day.
Larval foodplants Most frequently Hazel and Downy Birch, but also Silver Birch, Beech, oaks, Field Maple, Hornbeam and other broadleaved trees.
Habitat Broadleaved woodland.
Status & distribution Resident. Common. In suitable habitat, often in numbers, throughout much of mainland Britain, Arran, the Inner Hebrides and Ireland. Discovered on Man in 2000. Rare in the Channel Islands, where three were reported on Jersey in 1999, with previous records from 1924.

2426 see Appendix

Brother   not illustrated
Raphia frater Grote
Suspected import.   2427(-)

Field characters & Similar species Somewhat like the Knot Grass in size and appearance. Hindwing pure white, with a conspicuous black spot on trailing edge.
Larval foodplants In North America, birches, alders, cottonwoods, poplars and willows.
Status & distribution Uncertain: probably an accidental import. The only British record is of one captured in a light-trap at Rothamsted Experimental Station, Hertfordshire, on 3 July 1949. It had never been recorded in Europe before and there were no influxes of unusual immigrant moths around this date. Its origin remains a mystery. A widespread and frequent species in North America.

Plusiinae
Silver and gold Ys
and brasses

Gold Spot   Silver Y

Golden Twin-spot   page 334
Chrysodeixis chalcites (Esp.)
Immigrant; import.   2428(9088)

Field characters & Similar species FW 15-18mm.
Male has black tufts on underside of abdomen at tip,
which distinguishes it from male Tunbridge Wells
Gem. Both sexes lack the distinct, dark, elbowed
crescent-mark in sheen at forewing tip, which is a
distinguishing feature of Tunbridge Wells Gem; in
Golden Twin-spot it is weak and curved. Golden
sheen of both species separates them from related
ones. Golden Twin-spot has a black spot midway
along outer fringe of forewing, which is usually
much more prominent than in related species. See
also Tunbridge Wells Gem.
Flight season Several generations abroad. Recorded
as an immigrant July-November, but mainly August-
October. Mostly seen at light but also reported
visiting flowers of Ivy and Red Valerian after dusk.
Adults occasionally emerge indoors from larvae
imported with cut plants and other produce.
Life cycle No evidence of successful overwintering in
the British Isles. A larva was found on the leaves of
Tomato in Essex in September 1984.
Larval foodplants Sage, Viper's-bugloss, chrysan-
themums, Celery, Tobacco and other plants.
Status & distribution Immigrant and occasional
import. Over 120 records, mainly from the coasts of
south-east and south-west England, the first in 1943.
More records in the 1990s than in any previous decade.
Also recorded from Merionethshire, Glamorgan,
Berkshire, Hertfordshire, Norfolk, Lincolnshire, Yorkshire,
Perthshire and Inverness-shire. Resident in southern
Europe, North Africa and the Canary Islands. In some
parts of Europe it can be a greenhouse pest. As an
immigrant, recorded north to Denmark.

Tunbridge Wells Gem   page 334
Chrysodeixis acuta (Walk.)
Rare immigrant.   2429(9089)

Field characters & Similar species FW 14-18mm.
Male has very obvious large fawn brushes 5mm in
length down each side of abdomen, best viewed
from below, and lacks black tufts on underside of tip
of abdomen seen in male Golden Twin-spot. Both

sexes have a distinctly elbowed crescent-mark in
sheen near forewing tip, which looks black at certain
angles to the light; elbow points towards outer edge.
In Golden Twin-spot, sheen mark is weak and curved.
Differences in forewing size, shape and colouring are
not reliable features for determination because they
vary, depending on the temperatures experienced by
the early stages. See also Golden Twin-Spot.
Flight season Recorded in May and September-
November, but mainly during October.
Life cycle No evidence of breeding in the British
Isles. Several generations in North Africa.
Larval foodplants Thorn-apple, Tomato, Tobacco,
Banana, *Canna* lilies and many other plants where
resident.
Status & distribution Rare immigrant. Since the
first British record at Tunbridge Wells, Kent, in May
1870, there have been a further nine records,
including six in October 1995. Recorded from
Cornwall, Dorset, Hampshire, the Isle of Wight,
Surrey, Kent and Yorkshire. The only other record for
mainland Europe appears to be from Brittany in
September 1991. The known range includes North
Africa, the Canary Islands and parts of the Oriental
and Australian regions. The records from 1995 were
accompanied by other rare immigrants, such as
Crimson Speckled, Dark Mottled Willow, Silver-
striped Hawk-moth and Golden Twin-spot.
Meteorological backtracking suggests the source was
North Africa.

Scar Bank Gem   page 334
Ctenoplusia limbirena (Guen.)
Immigrant.   2430(9086)

Field characters & Similar species FW 15-18mm.
Resembles Silver Y and Ni Moth but differs in having a
small violet, lilac, pinkish or red-brown ellipse, or tear-
drop shape, by middle of outer edge of forewing.
Forewing more ornate than Silver Y and lacks contrasting pale grey patches. Ground-colour varies from
medium brown to almost black. Purplish tinge frequent.
Flight season Recorded June-October but mostly
September, always at light.
Life cycle No evidence of breeding in the British Isles.
Larval foodplants In Africa, recorded from Sage,
mulleins, Potato, Tobacco and other plants.
Status & distribution Immigrant. Fourteen British
records. First recorded in Britain on 13 September
1947 at Swanage, Dorset. Subsequently reported
from Scilly, Cornwall, Dorset, Hampshire, the Isle of
Wight, Berkshire and Essex. Recorded once on Jersey
in 1997. Resident in much of Africa, the Canary
Islands and Madeira. Has also reached Denmark as
an immigrant.

Accent Gem   page 334
Ctenoplusia accentifera (Lefeb.)
Suspected rare immigrant.   2431(9085)

Field characters & Similar species FW 11-14mm.
Quite distinctive, and much smaller than most exam-

ples of related species. Forewing reddish brown or darker greyish brown. Diagnostic features are roughly sock-shaped central mark, strongly outlined in gold on outer edge, a black bar near base of trailing edge and a small black wedge or arrowhead mark placed centrally near outer edge.
Status & distribution Suspected rare immigrant. One British record. A rather worn individual was captured in a light-trap at Halstead, Kent, on 10 September 1969, during a period in which many other immigrant moths were recorded. Widespread in Africa. Frequent and probably a transitory resident on the Mediterranean coasts of France and Spain.

Larva of Burnished Brass.

383

Ni Moth page 334
Trichoplusia ni (Hb.)
Immigrant. 2432(9081)

Field characters & Similar species FW 15-17mm. Resembles much more frequent Silver Y but has more ornately-marked, light brown forewing. The central silver mark is usually broken in two, forming an 'n' and a detached tail. Lacks a pale grey patch towards tip of forewing, but usually has a white spot in trailing corner. Some individuals of Silver Y are as small and have a similar mauvish tinge. See also Scar Bank Gem.
Flight season Recorded in almost every month of the year, but more usually May-October, and most frequently in August. Mostly seen at light but sometimes visits flowers at dusk or by day.
Life cycle No firm evidence of successful overwintering in the British Isles. A few larvae produced by spring immigrants have been found in August.
Larval foodplants Recorded once from each of Sea Rocket, marigolds and the flowers of a hawkweed. Has also been found on Tomato in greenhouses and known to accept many cultivated plants.
Habitat Occasionally breeds in coastal situations.
Status & distribution Immigrant. Not seen every year, but occasionally appears in numbers. The year of greatest abundance was 1996, with 140 individuals. Mainly recorded from the south coast of England; less frequently on the east coast, with occasional records inland, as far north as Cumbria. Also recorded from north and south Wales and the Republic of Ireland. Singletons recorded on Man in 1998, on Guernsey in 1996 and 2001 and on Jersey in 2002. Importation of larvae to Guernsey was confirmed in 1996. Resident in southern Europe and North Africa.

Streaked Plusia page 334
Trichoplusia vittata (Wall.)
Suspected rare immigrant. 2432a(9082)

Field characters & Similar species FW 15-18mm. Forewing grey as in Silver Y, but not metallic and with a long, creamy-coloured central streak.
Status & distribution Suspected rare immigrant. One British record. A single male was captured in a light-trap at Rye Harbour Nature Reserve, East Sussex, on 31 July 1995. Not previously recorded from Europe. Widespread in Africa.

Slender Burnished Brass page 334
Thysanoplusia orichalcea (Fabr.)
Immigrant; import. 2433(9078)

Field characters & Similar species FW 17-20mm. Resembles Burnished Brass but has narrower forewing, distinguished by shape of brassy yellow area, which tapers to a point towards base. This varies little and is diagnostic. Individuals from hot dry regions are paler brown than those from cooler climates.
Flight season As an immigrant, usually recorded mid August-mid October, but also in June and November. Mainly recorded at light-traps, but also visits flowers. Several generations abroad.
Life cycle No evidence of breeding in the British Isles. Larvae occasionally imported with chrysanthemums.
Larval foodplants A wide range of low-growing plants where resident, including members of the daisy and cabbage families.
Status & distribution Immigrant and occasional import. About 90 have been recorded in the British Isles. The first British record is from Dover, Kent, in 1820, with another around the same time in the London area. The next records are from 1943 onwards, since when it has been recorded every few years, with a maximum of 10 in 1969. Most records are from the southern coastal counties of England, but also seen in Glamorgan, Gloucestershire, Warwickshire, Oxfordshire, Bedfordshire, Surrey and Norfolk, as well as Northern Ireland and the Republic of Ireland. A rare immigrant in the Channel Islands, where recorded on Jersey and Guernsey in 1998 and on Guernsey again in 2001. Resident in much of Africa, and possibly on Malta and around the Mediterranean, where adults are seen in most months of the year.

Burnished Brass page 334
Diachrysia chrysitis (L.)
Common. T 2434(9045)

Field characters FW 16-19mm. Broad, hooked forewing with bold, shiny metallic, brassy yellow or brassy greenish-yellow pattern is unmistakable. There are two forms, both frequent. In f. *aurea* Huene the broad brown central cross-band is entire. In f. *juncta* Tutt it is broken into two blotches. Moths of the

Larva of Scarce Burnished Brass.

second generation are usually smaller.
Similar species See Slender Burnished Brass.
Flight season One main generation, June-July. A partial second generation in southern Britain, August-September and occasionally individuals in November. Flies at dusk, when it feeds at flowers, including those of Red Valerian, buddleias and Honeysuckle, and later in the night comes regularly to light.
Life cycle Overwinters as a small larva, near the ground among vegetation. Larva July-May or June, feeding at night and hiding low down on the food-plant by day. In the south, may become fully grown in August. Pupates in a loose cocoon formed on the underside of a leaf of the foodplant.
Larval foodplants Most frequently Common Nettle, but also other herbaceous plants, including White Dead-nettle, Wild Marjoram, Lesser Burdock and Spear Thistle.
Habitat Gardens, hedgerows, ditch-banks, marshes, fens, wood edges and other rough swards.
Status & distribution Resident. Common. Well distributed and fairly frequent throughout mainland Britain, Scilly, Man, the Hebrides, Orkney, Ireland and the Channel Islands.

Scarce Burnished Brass   page 334
Diachrysia chryson (Esp.)
Na. S,WC   2435(9049)

Field characters FW 20-24mm. Reddish-brown forewing has a single brassy golden patch, near wing tip, bisected by a thin wavy brown line.
Similar species Gold Spangle has a single, more triangular, silvery gold, patch, near centre of forewing.
Flight season One generation. July-August. Occasionally flies in sunshine. Recorded visiting flowers after dark, including those of Meadowsweet, Honeysuckle and the larval foodplant. Comes to light but apparently not to sugar.
Life cycle Overwinters as a larva among the stems of the foodplant and other rank vegetation. Larva late August-late May or early June. Pupates in a whitish oval cocoon spun under or near a leaf of the food-plant.
Larval foodplants Hemp-agrimony. Larvae are seemingly more frequent on plants growing in the shade of trees and shrubs rather than in the open.

Habitat River valleys, canal banks, and associated marshes, fens and damp open woodland; also coastal undercliffs in Pembrokeshire and formerly in Kent.
Status & distribution Resident. Nationally Scarce A. Found locally in southern England and Wales, breeding in the valleys of the Test and Itchen in Hampshire and the Kennet in Berkshire, the Oxfordshire/Berkshire group of fens, including Cothill Fen, and College Pond Fen north-east of Oxford. Also breeds in a number of localities on and near the coast in Pembrokeshire and west Glamorgan, and in Cardiganshire near New Quay and along the banks of the Afon Teifi, near Llechryd. A number of singletons, presumed wanderers, have been recorded away from these sites. Formerly known from Chippenham and Wicken Fens, Cambridgeshire, and also reported from Kent, Devon, Dorset and Gloucestershire in the 19th century and from certain riverbanks in Norfolk until the 1950s.

2435a see Appendix

Dewick's Plusia   page 334
Macdunnoughia confusa (Steph.)
Immigrant.   2436(9051)

Field characters FW 12-17mm. Easily recognised by metallic silver dog-leg mark in centre of forewing, consisting of a thick central bar with a thin silver line extending to trailing edge. Area of forewing between this mark and trailing edge is generally a rich bronze or orange colour, rest of wing appearing plainer brown by comparison.
Similar species Golden Twin-spot may have the two metallic spots merged, and along with Tunbridge Wells Gem may be confused with Dewick's Plusia, but the usually more variegated and golden appearance of the former species' forewings should prevent confusion. Gold Spangle has a larger, more golden and more triangular forewing mark.
Flight season Recorded in May and July-October, although most records are August-October. The majority of British records have been at light, although moths have also been found at rest. In mainland Europe sometimes seen flying by day.
Larval foodplants Common Nettle, Yarrow, mayweeds, Chamomile, wormwoods and other herbaceous plants.
Status & distribution Immigrant. Around 50 British records, mainly from coastal counties of southern England, particularly south-east England. Recorded north to Cumbria, Orkney and Shetland, and has occurred inland. Recorded on a number of occasions from the Channel Islands, the first in 1991. Widely distributed in Europe and thought to be expanding its range.

Golden Plusia   page 334
Polychrysia moneta (Fabr.)
Common. S,C,(N)   2437(9036)

Field characters FW 17-20mm. Combination of fine

pattern on broad golden-yellow forewing, large kidney-mark outlined in silvery white, and large fan-like scale tufts on thorax is diagnostic. Pattern is very constant, but intensity of gold colour varies: some examples are paler and greyer, others darker and browner. Very rare f. *maculata* Lempke has brown forewing with large black spots near outer edge.
Similar species None.
Flight season Usually one generation, late June-early August. Sometimes a partial second generation in southern England, in September.
Life cycle Overwinters as a very small larva. Larva August-June. Lives in a web when small, and later rests on the underside of a leaf. In the south, some feed up rapidly and become fully grown in late August or September. Pupates in a yellow cocoon formed under a leaf of the foodplant.
Larval foodplants The leaves, flower buds and unripe seeds of cultivated delphiniums and Larkspur; in captivity reared on Wormwood and Mugwort.
Habitat Mainly gardens and parks, but wanders into other habitats.
Status & distribution Resident. Common. Recent colonist since the late 19th century, following a northward expansion of its range in mainland Europe. It spread rapidly over most of mainland Britain, reaching Inverness-shire and Aberdeenshire by the 1950s. It then retreated south and is now infrequent in northern Britain and less frequent, although still well distributed, in the southern half. Rare on Man. Recorded in Ireland from Cos. Dublin and Armagh. One recorded on Alderney in 1961.

Purple-shaded Gem
page 334
Euchalcia variabilis (Pill.)
Probable import.   2438(9027)

Field characters & Similar species FW 17-19mm. Similar size and shape as Golden Plusia but distinguished by two belts of pink on forewing, much less distinct central marks and smooth cross-lines.
Status & distribution Probably an accidental or deliberate import. Two possibly authentic records from the British Isles and one improbable report; resident mainly in mountainous areas of mainland Europe. Placed on the British list in 1809 on the basis of a specimen allegedly collected in Wales. Stephens in 1829 refers to a number taken by day over 20 years previously on Salisbury Plain, Wiltshire. The problems with this record are that the larval foodplants (French Meadow-rue and Monk's-hood) are absent from the Plain and that if an immigration producing a number in this area had occurred, others would surely have been reported elsewhere. The last record from the British Isles was in August 1887, an adult feeding at Bramble flowers at Castle Kevin, Co. Wicklow. The most likely origin of the British and Irish records of this spectacular moth is as a deliberate import or an accidental importation with alpine plants.

Gold Spot
page 334
Plusia festucae (L.)
Common. T   2439(9053)

Field characters FW 14-19mm. Forewing reddish brown or rich brown, with golden yellow blotches dusted with brown. Two central silvery white blotches, occasionally joined, are the most conspicuous features. These vary in shape, but outermost is always smaller and elliptical or tear-shaped. There are three small golden yellow blotches between dark veins near wing tip, the smallest at tip, next to an elongated silvery white mark which usually tapers to a point away from outer edge. Sometimes the third blotch is also silvery. Fine brown cross-lines unclear in places, notably between the two sets of silvery marks.
Similar species See Lempke's Gold Spot.
Flight season Two generations in southern Britain (and occasionally in northern England), June-July and late August-September. One generation elsewhere, late June-mid August. Flies from dusk, when it feeds at flowers, including those of Red Valerian, buddleias and Water Mint.
Life cycle Overwinters as a small larva. Larva September-May, also July-August in southern Britain. Pupates in a transparent white cocoon spun vertically between the leaves or stems of rushes, where it somewhat resembles the egg cocoon of a spider.
Larval foodplants Tufted-sedge, Glaucous Sedge and other sedges; also Yellow Iris, Branched Bur-reed and Water-plantain. In captivity reared on grasses, Grey Willow and Common Nettle.
Habitat A range of mostly damp places, including ditch-banks, canals and rivers, fens, marshes, woodland rides, heathland, moorland and upland pasture.
Status & distribution Resident. Common. Quite well distributed and fairly frequent in suitable habitat throughout Great Britain, Man, Ireland and the Channel Islands.

Lempke's Gold Spot
page 334
Plusia putnami (Grote)
ssp. *gracilis* (Lempke)
Local. C,(N,S)   2440(9054)

Field characters & Similar species FW 14-15mm. Very similar to Gold Spot, but slightly smaller on average, with forewing usually orange-brown. Fine brown cross-lines are distinct, notably between central marks and series of blotches near tip. Elongated silvery mark near tip ends fairly bluntly at cross-line, not in a point as in Gold Spot. Outermost of the two central silvery blotches is smaller and more rounded than in Gold Spot. However, both species vary in colour and Gold Spot in particular is quite variable in detail of markings, with some individuals showing characters of Lempke's Gold Spot. Therefore if there is any doubt, genitalia should be examined for confirmation.
Flight season One generation. July-August. Flies at dusk, when it feeds at flowers, including those of

comfreys. Comes to light.
Life cycle Overwinters as a small larva. Larva
August-May. Pupates in a cocoon spun among the
foodplant.
Larval foodplants Wood Small-reed, Purple Small-
reed, Yorkshire-fog and probably other grasses.
Habitat Fens, marshes and other damp open places,
including upland pasture.
Status & distribution Resident. Local. Frequent in
the East Anglian fens, and very thinly scattered in
southern England and Wales. Well distributed in
northern England and southern Scotland and locally
north to Aberdeenshire. Confirmed from various sites
on Man, and from Cos. Cork and Kerry.

Silver Y   page 334
Autographa gamma (L.)
Immigrant. T   2441(9056)

Field characters FW 13-21mm. Moths with a
conspicuous unbroken metallic silver Y-mark and
metallic sheen on forewing marbled brown and grey,
sometimes purplish-tinged, are most likely to be this
species. Size and shade of forewing vary greatly. Pale
f. *pallida* Tutt results from a hot climate, and spring
immigrants are often of this form. The small
f. *gammina* Stdgr. are thought to be the result of star-
vation in the larval stage, while dark examples reflect
growth in cooler climates such as the British Isles. The
rare f. *nigricans* Spul. is black. In all forms, the Y-mark
is obvious, but very rarely is broken (f. *bipartita*
Orstadius) or greatly enlarged (f. *gartneri* Skåla).
Similar species See Ni Moth, with which small individuals are easily confused. Y-mark is generally
broken in two in other related species. Plain Golden
Y and Beautiful Golden Y are generally redder.
Scarce Silver Y is blacker and more ornate. See also
Scar Bank Gem, Essex Y and Dewick's Plusia, which
are rare immigrants.
Flight season Several generations. Recorded during
every month of the year but most frequently May-
September. Winter records are uncommon and
generally coincide with mild southerly winds.
Frequently seen flying in abundance during sunny
weather, usually visiting flowers. Comes to light,
sometimes in large numbers. Often has a well-
defined feeding flight at around sunset, well before
most other moths.
Life cycle Winter survival is probably rare, but larvae
have occasionally been found in February, in
Bedfordshire and Yorkshire, after hard frosts. Larva
any time from spring to autumn, initially resulting
from immigrant adults, later from further influxes
supplemented by one or more locally bred generations.
Larval foodplants Many low-growing wild and
cultivated plants, from bedstraws, clovers and
Common Nettle to crops such as Garden Pea,
Cabbage and Runner Bean, on which it is sometimes
a pest.
Habitat Adults invade most habitats, coastal and far
inland, including gardens, in search of nectar. Tends

to breed on plants in unshaded situations, but this
includes wide woodland rides.
Status & distribution Immigrant. Breeds every
summer. Numbers vary annually but never less than
frequent and sometimes hugely abundant, especially at the coast. Recorded throughout Great
Britain north to Fair Isle, and on Man, in Ireland and
the Channel Islands. Widespread and usually abundant throughout Europe and parts of Africa and
Asia.

Beautiful Golden Y   page 334
Autographa pulchrina (Haw.)
Common. T   2442(9059)

Field characters FW 17-20mm. When fresh, this
moth really lives up to its name. Forewing dark
reddish brown or purplish brown, extensively
marbled with pink or light purplish brown, with a
metallic grey-green blotch near outer edge towards
trailing corner. A key feature is kidney-mark, sharply
pinched and finely edged in gold. Central golden
Y-mark is in fact very variable, and usually split into a
V and an oval spot, but is sometimes complete
(f. *percontatrix* Aurivillius). Occasionally it is reduced
to a small dot, and very rarely expanded to form a
large wedge (f. *gloriosa* Cock.).
Similar species See Plain Golden Y.
Flight season One generation. Late May-late July in
southern Britain, late June-August or early
September in the north. Feeds at flowers at dusk and
comes frequently to light.
Life cycle Overwinters as a small larva among leaf
litter. Larva July or August-May. Feeds mainly at
night, hiding low down on the foodplant by day.
Pupates in a cocoon formed in a folded leaf of the
foodplant.
Larval foodplants Herbaceous plants, including
Common Nettle, Hedge Woundwort, Common
Ragwort and Wood Avens; also Honeysuckle.
Habitat A wide range of upland and lowland habi-
tats, including woodland, hedgerows, gardens,
scrubby pasture, moorland and heathland. More
frequent on acid soils but also occurs on calcareous
grassland.
Status & distribution Resident. Common. Well
distributed and fairly frequent throughout Great
Britain, Man and Ireland. More numerous in northern
Britain. Rare in the Channel Islands.

Plain Golden Y   page 335
Autographa jota (L.)
Common. T   2443(9061)

Field characters & Similar species FW 17-21mm.
Similar to Beautiful Golden Y but slightly larger on
average. Key differences are lighter, redder forewing
(although a duller, brown form occurs infrequently),
more uniformly coloured and less ornate, and
kidney-mark not gold-edged and therefore indistinct
or absent. Forewing dark to light reddish brown,
rather softly marbled with pink or pinkish brown.

386

Golden Y-mark usually broken, but sometimes complete (f. *percontationis* Ochs.). Infrequently, it is reduced to a small dot (f. *inscripta* Esp.) and very rarely expanded to form a large wedge.

Flight season One generation. Mid June-early August in southern Britain, mid July-August in the north. Feeds at flowers at dusk and comes regularly to light.

Life cycle Overwinters as a small larva among leaf litter. Larva August-May or June. Feeds mainly at night, hiding low down on the foodplant by day. Pupates in a cocoon formed on the underside of a leaf of the foodplant.

Larval foodplants Herbaceous plants, including Common Nettle, White and Red Dead-nettles, and reportedly Hogweed; also Honeysuckle. In captivity, other woody plants including Hawthorn and sallows.

Habitat A wide range of habitats, including woodland, downland, hedgerows and gardens. Usually more frequent than Beautiful Golden Y in suburban gardens and urban areas, but less frequent on acid soils.

Status & distribution Resident. Common. Well distributed and fairly frequent throughout most of Great Britain, Man and Ireland, but local in the northern half of Scotland. Occasionally recorded from Orkney. Rare in the Channel Islands.

Gold Spangle   page 335
Autographa bractea ([D. & S.])
Common. W,N,(S)   2444(9062)

Field characters FW 18-21mm. The large central metallic golden mark, like a bent triangle, on rather plain, dark reddish-brown forewing clouded with dull pinkish brown and sometimes greyish brown is a diagnostic combination. Little variation, although golden mark varies slightly in shape.

Similar species Scarce Burnished Brass has metallic patch near tip of forewing, and is restricted to southern Britain.

Flight season One generation. Early July-early August. Feeds at flowers at dusk and comes to light, usually in small numbers. Sometimes flies by day.

Life cycle Overwinters as a small larva. Larva August-May or early June. Pupates in a cocoon formed under a leaf of the foodplant.

Larval foodplants A wide range of herbaceous plants, including Common Nettle, White Dead-nettle and Ground-ivy; also Bilberry and Honeysuckle.

Habitat Moorland, upland pasture, woodland rides and edges, hedgerows and gardens.

Status & distribution Resident and suspected immigrant. Common. Well distributed and fairly frequent in the north Midlands and West Midlands, Wales, northern England, Man, Scotland (except Shetland) and Ireland. The southerly extent of its distribution fluctuates periodically. In the first half of the 20th century it became rare south of Cumbria, then during the 1970s it became frequent as far south as Gloucestershire and Warwickshire; now rarer in these counties again. Possible immigrants, or wanderers

from the north, are occasionally recorded in East Anglia and eastern, southern and south-west England.

Stephens' Gem   page 335
Megalographa biloba (Steph.)
Suspected rare immigrant.   2445(-)

Field characters & Similar species FW 15-18mm. Resembles Silver Y in size and wing shape, but distinguished from all related species by unmistakable large double-lobed silver marking in centre of forewing.

Status & distribution Suspected rare immigrant. Described in 1830 and included as British on the basis of a specimen found in a collection, the origin of which was unknown. This abundant North American species, which is sometimes a pest on Cabbages, Garden Lettuce, clovers and Tobacco in the USA and is known as the Bilobed Looper, has been recorded twice subsequently in the British Isles as a believable transatlantic immigrant, three times as either an import or possibly the progeny of an undetected earlier immigration, and once, on 9 July 2002 in Scilly, where all three possibilities are equally likely. The first was taken in very worn condition at light on 19 July 1954 at Trawscoed, Cardiganshire, after prolonged transatlantic winds; the second in good condition at light on 1 October 1958 at Maidencombe, Devon. The second arrived when seven species of North American birds were reported in Britain, after an unusually prolonged westerly airstream. Three were reported in 2001, two on Guernsey in garden light-traps 6km apart, on 13 and 17 August, and one on 27 October at Sparsholt, Hampshire; but weather conditions at the time were not suggestive of unassisted transatlantic crossing. One recorded on 9 July 2002, St Marys, Scilly. Importation with produce, possibly with carnations from Colombia, has been suggested. Not recorded as an immigrant elsewhere in Europe.

2446 see Appendix

Scarce Silver Y   page 335
Syngrapha interrogationis (L.)
Local. C,N   2447(9074)

Field characters FW 15-18mm. Forewing blackish, extensively marbled and clouded with light, silvery grey (sometimes darker grey or mauve-tinged) and with a central silver mark. This combination is diagnostic. Central mark is irregular and extremely variable, usually split into a V and an oval, but sometimes forming a Y or a meandering blotch, or thin and reduced. Most immigrant examples are small, marked with dull grey and have paler hindwing, which is brown with a darker border.

Similar species Ni Moth is brownish grey, marbled with brown, and central silver mark is duller and less irregular.

Flight season One generation. Late June-mid August. Immigrants occur in late July and August.

387

Feeds at flowers from dusk and comes to light. Sometimes active by day, flying in sunshine or flushed from Heather.

Life cycle Overwinters as a small larva. Larva late July-early June. Rests on the foodplant. Pupates in a white cocoon formed on the foodplant.

Larval foodplants Heather, Bilberry and Bog Bilberry.

Habitat Moorland.

Status & distribution Resident and occasional immigrant. Local. Fairly frequent in suitable habitat in the north Midlands, Wales, northern England, mainland Scotland and Ireland. A few records from Devon and Cornwall but no evidence of breeding, despite there being extensive moorland in that area. Immigrants have occurred in south-east and central southern England, East Anglia, Lincolnshire, Orkney and Shetland, occasionally as small influxes, with up to 14 recorded in a year, often as part of a larger migration elsewhere in north-west Europe.

Essex Y   page 335

Cornutiplusia circumflexa (L.)

Suspected rare immigrant.   2448(9068)

Field characters & Similar species FW 16-21mm. Similar to Silver Y, but forewing less metallic, with more ornate markings. Central silver mark is broad, rather like an oblique, distorted U. Forewing often tinged with lilac or violet when fresh. Hindwing brown with darker borders and chequered fringe, as in Silver Y.

Flight season Several generations per year, and often active by day where resident abroad.

Life cycle & Larval foodplants No record of breeding in the British Isles. Reported elsewhere on Potato, Garden Pea, members of the cabbage family and other low-growing plants.

Status & distribution Suspected rare immigrant. The only recent record is of one at a light-trap at Sway, Hampshire, on 29 July 1979, at the same time as a large influx of Silver Y in Sussex and a Spurge Hawk-moth in Essex. The only other likely British record is of one captured in Essex prior to 1807, although other specimens were present in British collections at this time. Widely resident in Africa, the Canary Islands and Madeira. Also recorded from the Mediterranean and south-east Europe, and has reached Finland as an immigrant.

Dark Spectacle   page 335

Abrostola triplasia (L.)

Common. W,(T)   2449(9093)

Field characters & Similar species FW 14-18mm. Similar in pattern to Spectacle, but differs in several respects. Ground-colour is brownish black, base of forewing is dull straw or reddish brown and crosslines are edged with reddish brown. There is also a diffuse dull straw-coloured blotch beyond kidney-mark, and trailing corner blotch and outer cross-line are straw-grey (whitish in Spectacle). Oval and

kidney-mark comparatively faint.

Flight season In most regions, one main generation, June-July, with an occasional and partial second generation in southern England and a regular one in south-west England late August-September. Flies from dusk and feeds at flowers, including those of Red Valerian. Comes to light in small numbers.

Life cycle Overwinters as a pupa, in a cocoon in a folded leaf of the foodplant. Larva July-September, and again in October-November in south-west England. Rests on the foodplant and is active by day and night.

Larval foodplants Common Nettle and Hop.

Habitat A wide range of habitats, often acidic, including rocky river valleys, marshes, hedgerows and gardens.

Status & distribution Resident. Common. More numerous in western Britain: well distributed in south-west England, Wales, north-west England, Man and Ireland. Recorded from all other parts of England, including Scilly, but rather local and generally infrequent. Very local in mainland Scotland and the Inner Hebrides. Widespread and frequent in the Channel Islands. Some records may refer to Spectacle owing to confusion resulting from changes in scientific name.

Spectacle   page 335

Abrostola tripartita (Hufn.)

Common. T   2450(9091)

Field characters FW 15-17mm. Named after the grey shape, like a pair of spectacles or flying goggles, visible on thorax when viewed from front. Fur on top of thorax is piled up into a turret. Forewing grey, sometimes tinged with lilac or pink. A broad blackish central band encloses the large, blackish-outlined oval and kidney-mark. Oval is larger than kidney-mark and is fused with a second central oval. General pattern varies little, but whitish markings vary in extent and are absent in f. *plumbea* Cock., which is warm dark grey and is frequent in many parts of England.

Similar species See Dark Spectacle.

Flight season In most regions one generation, late May-mid July. In southern England, a partial (or occasionally full) second generation, late July-early September. Flies from dusk. Feeds at flowers, including those of Red Valerian and cultivated Sage, and comes to light regularly.

Life cycle Overwinters as a pupa, formed among plant debris or low down, behind bark. Larva July-September, again in October-November in the south.

Larval foodplants Common Nettle.

Habitat Gardens, hedgerows, ditches, rough pasture, fens, woodland edges and disturbed ground.

Status & distribution Resident. Common. Well distributed and fairly frequent throughout most of Great Britain, Man and Ireland, but not recorded from Shetland. Widespread and frequent on Jersey, occasional on Guernsey.

Catocalinae

Red Underwing

Clifden Nonpareil
page 335

Catocala fraxini (L.)

Immigrant; transitory resident. 2451(8873)

Field characters FW 41-48mm. Very large grey forewing and broad violet-blue curved band across black hindwing make this species unmistakable. Key features at rest, when hindwings are covered, include a conspicuous, dark, zigzagged cross-line beyond middle, a small pale blotch between prominent dark kidney-mark and trailing edge, and an undulating inner cross-line. Hindwing has broad white fringe.

Similar species Larger and greyer than all the red and crimson underwings when seen at rest.

Flight season One generation. Mid August-mid October, but usually seen during September. Recorded by day at rest on tree trunks and walls, at least once in a mist-net set for birds, and flying inland from the sea. Strongly attracted to sugar at dusk. Comes to light in small numbers.

Life cycle Overwinters as an egg on the foodplant. Larva late April-July, feeding at night. Pupates in a silken cocoon spun between leaves or among leaf litter.

Larval foodplants Mainly Aspen, but recorded on other poplars in mainland Europe.

Habitat Broadleaved woodland.

Status & distribution Immigrant and transitory resident. Resident between 1935 and 1964 in woodland at Orlestone Forest near Hamstreet, Kent, and in the Norfolk Broads in the early 1930s. As an immigrant, recorded annually in small numbers in recent years, but in less than half the years between 1850 and 1935, despite the widespread use of sugar at that time. Often associated with the arrival of Camberwell Beauty butterflies, Great Brocade moths, and in 1995 Barred Warblers, and predominantly recorded on the south-east and east coast of Britain, north to Shetland. This all suggests that the main source of immigrants is eastern Europe, Scandinavia or Siberia. The most recorded in a single year was about 20 in 1976 but this was exceptional. Recorded once from Man, in 1912, and has reached Ireland. A very rare

immigrant in the Channel Islands. Widespread in Denmark, Scandinavia and central Europe but occurs westwards to Spain.

Red Underwing
page 336

Catocala nupta (L.)

Common. S,C 2452(8874)

Field characters FW 33-40mm. Very large, with grey forewing crossed by irregular jagged lines and bands and rather obscurely marbled with brownish grey. Hindwing red, with bold black border and central band and white scalloped fringe. Underside of fore- and hindwings black with bold white bands, which show up strikingly in flight. Rare f. *cockaynei* Lorimer (= f. *nigra* Cock.) has black forewing, and has occurred in Hertfordshire and Middlesex on four occasions. An even rarer form, f. *brunnescens* Warr. (= f. *nigra* Lempke), in which the hindwing is dark brown and black, was recorded at Orpington, Kent in 1971.

Similar species See Rosy Underwing and French Underwing.

Flight season One generation. Early August-October. Comes to light in small numbers, less so early in the flight season, and often ignores light-traps; more frequent at sugar. Sometimes found at rest on walls by day. Has been observed feeding at flowers of buddleias in afternoon sunshine, and is easily disturbed, when it flies vigorously.

Life cycle Overwinters as an egg, laid in a bark crevice on the main trunk of the foodplant. Larva May-July. Feeds at night, hiding by day under loose bark or in a crevice. Pupates in a cocoon, formed either in a bark crevice or among plant debris.

Larval foodplants Black-poplar, White Poplar, Aspen, other poplars, mature Crack-willow, White Willow and other willows.

Habitat Woodland, parkland, scrub, carr, riverbanks and gardens.

Status & distribution Resident. Common. Well distributed in central southern and south-east England, East Anglia, Lincolnshire, the Midlands and east Wales. Local in south-west England, west Wales, northern England to Cumbria, and on Man. Recorded in Scilly, and once in Ireland, in Cork in 1906. Widespread and frequent in the Channel Islands.

Rosy Underwing
page 336

Catocala electa (View.)

Rare immigrant. 2453(8883)

Field characters & Similar species FW 33-39mm. Similar to Red Underwing, but forewing paler, greyer and smoother-looking. Outer jagged cross-line dark and much more noticeable, projecting strongly towards outer edge in leading half of wing. Red on hindwing tends to rosy pink.

Flight season One generation. July-September in mainland Europe. All immigrants to Britain recorded in September. Comes to sugar, and in small numbers

389

Noctuidae (Catocalinae)

Larva of Dark Crimson Underwing.

to light.
Life cycle No evidence of breeding in the British Isles. Larva May-June elsewhere.
Larval foodplants Willows and poplars.
Status & distribution Rare immigrant. Six reported British records: Sussex, 1875; Dorset and Essex, 1892; Hertfordshire, 1927; London, undated; and most recently from Portland, Dorset on 11 September 1993. Recorded in the Channel Islands for the first time in 2002, with six individuals on Jersey and two on Guernsey. Resident in central and southern Europe.

French Red Underwing   not illustrated
Catocala elocata (Esp.)
Rare immigrant (Jersey).   2453a(8883)

Field characters & Similar species FW 39-43mm. Very similar to Red Underwing but with less distinct forewing markings, and often slightly larger. Diagnostic feature is dark central cross-band on hindwing, which is gently curved, of even thickness in leading half and gradually tapering in trailing half. In Red Underwing, this band is strongly elbowed and pinched in leading half.
Status & distribution Rare immigrant. A single record, from Jersey in 1903, is accepted by the Jersey moth recorder. A report from Dungeness, Kent, in August 1996 was an error. Resident and fairly frequent in central and southern Europe.

Light Crimson Underwing   page 336
Catocala promissa ([D. & S.])
RDB. S   2454(8882)

Field characters & Similar species FW 26-32mm. Most reliable single character is shape of wavy black band on crimson hindwing: it is much straighter than in any of the related underwing moths, but this can be hard to see in live individuals without handling them. Dark Crimson Underwing is larger, with darker and more uniformly coloured forewing, but this may also have patches of whitish scales, especially near kidney-mark. Size difference is more obvious when both species are seen at rest together (e.g. at sugar), and forewing of Light Crimson Underwing has a distinctly more whitish-grey appearance.
Flight season One generation. Mid July-early

September. Both sexes come to light, but more readily and in larger numbers to sugar, wine ropes and sap oozing from trees, sometimes arriving well before dusk. Occasionally seen flying around the oak canopy in afternoon sunshine.
Life cycle Overwinters as an egg attached to an oak twig, probably high up in the canopy. Larva late April-late May or early June. Feeds at first on the flowers and leaf buds. Later it eats the foliage, feeding at night and growing rapidly. Pupates in a cocoon between leaves or on the trunk, thus never needing to leave the oak canopy throughout the life cycle.
Larval foodplants Pedunculate Oak and possibly Sessile Oak.
Habitat Large tracts of mature oak woodland.
Status & distribution Resident and possible immigrant. Red Data Book species. Now almost confined to large oakwoods in the New Forest, Hampshire, where it remains widespread, and to Langley Wood and woodlands near Redlynch and Whiteparish, in south Wiltshire. Lost since the 1940s and 1950s from other woodlands in Hampshire, Sussex and Kent and from Hell Coppice/Bernwood Forest on the Oxfordshire/Buckinghamshire border, coincident with large-scale clear-felling of mature oaks. Has been reported as a suspected immigrant or wanderer away from the usual habitat on a number of occasions, usually near the south coast from Dorset to Kent, e.g. singletons at Arne, Dorset, in 1978; at Highcliffe, Hampshire, on 4 August 1982; and several times from the Isle of Wight, including at Westhill, Shanklin, on 12 September 1979 and 14 August 1982. The moth was apparently more widespread in the 19th century, with records of resident populations north to Gloucestershire, Huntingdonshire and Cambridgeshire, and reports from Monmouthshire and Suffolk.

Dark Crimson Underwing   page 336
Catocala sponsa (L.)
RDB. S   2455(8871)

Field characters & Similar species FW 29-34mm. Wavy black stripe across crimson hindwing is contorted into a deep W-shape. See the smaller and paler Light Crimson Underwing for other characters and comparisons.
Flight season One generation. Late July-early September, occasionally October, especially as a suspected immigrant. Comes to light, but more readily and in larger numbers to sugar, wine ropes and oozing tree sap, sometimes arriving well before dusk. Has been confirmed recently flying in daylight at least two hours before dusk, investigating sap runs and sugar patches.
Life cycle Overwinters as an egg on the foodplant. Larva April-early June. Feeds by night, initially on flowers and buds, then on the expanding foliage, resting on twigs and in grooves in the trunk bark by day. Pupates in a cocoon spun between leaves.
Larval foodplants Pedunculate Oak and possibly

390

Sessile Oak.
Habitat Large tracts of mature oak woodland.
Status & distribution Resident and suspected immigrant. Red Data Book species. Breeding is now confined to large oakwoods in the New Forest, Hampshire, where it was still widespread in 1995. Appears to fluctuate greatly in numbers, with occasional good years. Occasional singletons have been reported from Devon to Essex, usually in open sites near the coast, and these are probably immigrants. Formerly bred outside the New Forest: it used to be recorded regularly, sometimes in numbers, in the Weald of Kent, and there are records from the Orlestone Forest complex in Kent up to 1969, and from other woods in the county into the early 1950s. Possibly resident in Sussex at one time, but probably not since the middle of the 19th century. Also old reports of former populations as far afield as Warwickshire, Buckinghamshire, Suffolk and Essex.

Oak Yellow Underwing   page 336
Catocala nymphagoga (Esp.)
Suspected rare immigrant.   2455a(8888)

Field characters & Similar species FW17-21mm. Like a miniature Crimson Underwing, but with yellow hindwing. Forewing broad and mottled with various shades of brown. The most abundant of several European *Catocala* species with yellow hindwing, distinguished from the others by the right-angled bend in the black central hindwing stripe. This stripe, visible even with wings only partly open, distinguishes Oak Yellow Underwing from Lesser Yellow Underwing and related species.
Flight season In mainland Europe, July-August.
Life cycle Larva March-June, in mainland Europe.
Larval foodplants In mainland Europe, various species of oak.
Status & distribution Suspected rare immigrant. The only two individuals recorded in Britain prior to 2002 were taken within three days of each other, in Rothamsted light-traps at Tregaron, Cardiganshire, on 28 July 1982, and at Denny Lodge, New Forest, Hampshire, on 31 July 1982. A third was recorded in central London on 4 September 2002. Resident in central and southern Europe.

Lunar Double-stripe   page 337
Minucia lunaris ([D. & S.])
Immigrant; transitory resident.   2456(8897)

Field characters FW 23-26mm. Diagnostic features are two thin, slightly wavy, cream cross-lines and dark brown, sometimes crescent-shaped, kidney-mark. Oval reduced to a black spot. Forewing warm brown to grey, with darker brown shading, especially towards outer edge, rarely almost black. Hindwing pale brown with a golden sheen, with slightly darker central band.
Similar species See Double Line, but this is smaller, reddish-brown with dark cross-lines and a whitish kidney-mark.

Flight season One generation. Mid May-late June in Britain, but from April in southern Europe. Easily flushed by day from dry leaf litter. Comes readily to sugar and light.
Life cycle Overwinters as a pupa, in a cocoon among leaf litter. Larva early July-mid August, but no British records since the 1950s.
Larval foodplants Pedunculate Oak, apparently preferring the young shoots of coppice stools or warm places near the ground. Fairly frequent on Evergreen Oak in southern Europe.
Habitat Young oak coppice regrowth in open woodland.
Status & distribution Immigrant and transitory resident. First recorded in 1832 at Lowestoft, Suffolk, followed by at least ten reliable 19th-century records, six of which were in Sussex from 1873 to 1880, suggesting possible local establishment. There was confirmed establishment from 1942 to 1958 in woodlands near Hamstreet, Kent, and in the early to mid 1950s near Laughton, Sussex. About 20 additional suspected immigrant individuals were recorded in the 20th century, including at least seven in the 1990s, mainly from the coast of south-east England but also from Cheshire, Co. Kerry and possibly Perthshire. One recorded on Guernsey in 1998. Resident in central and southern Europe.

Trent Double-stripe   not illustrated
Clytie illunaris (Hb.)
Import/rare immigrant.   2457(8899)

Field characters & Similar species FW 18-20mm. Roughly the same size and shape as Passenger, with forewing rather broad, but milky-brown to creamy buff in colour. Has a jagged, chocolate-brown outer cross-line or series of arrowhead marks; other cross-lines fine and brown. Kidney-mark small, pale and divided in two.
Status & distribution Accidental import or rare immigrant. Recorded only once in the British Isles: a single larva found feeding at night on the foliage of wild Horse-radish beside the River Trent at Amcotts, near Scunthorpe, Lincolnshire, in June 1964. It was reared to an adult which emerged on 25 August 1964. In mainland Europe, resident chiefly in the Mediterranean area, extending into Portugal, Egypt and eastwards into Asia, with reported foodplants including Bog-myrtle and Tamarisk.

2458, 2459 see Appendix

Passenger   page 337
Dysgonia algira (L.)
Immigrant.   2460(8904)

Field characters FW 17-23mm. Its wide delta shape and the broad, waisted, pale grey-brown or pinkish-grey band across dark brown forewing distinguish this from all other moths on the British list. Ground-colour varies from medium to dark brown, sometimes with a purplish tinge. There is a conspicuous

Noctuidae (Catocalinae)

Larva of Mother Shipton.

392

pair of dark brown spots at forewing tip. Hindwing with narrow oblique off-white central stripe.
Similar species See Geometrician.
Flight season In southern Europe, two generations, April-May and July-September. All British records August-September. Sometimes disturbed by day. Comes to light.
Life cycle In southern Europe overwinters as a pupa. Larva June-October. No evidence of breeding in the British Isles.
Larval foodplants In Europe reported from many plants, including Pomegranate, Castor-oil-plant, Pellitory-of-the-wall, Bramble, and possibly willows and Blackthorn.
Status & distribution Immigrant. About 10 British records, the first near Dover, Kent, in August 1967, others subsequently in Dorset, Kent and Essex, at light. Recorded twice on Jersey in 1960 and once in 1992. Resident in southern Europe, most of Africa and in the Canary Islands.

Geometrician   page 337
Prodotis stolida (Fabr.)
Rare immigrant.   2461(8909)

Field characters FW 14-16mm. Forewing dark brown, crossed by a straight cream and brown inner band and a thinner wavy white and red-brown outer band. Hindwing dark brown with a white fringe, a rather straight white central stripe and a white spot in trailing corner.
Similar species Somewhat similar Passenger is larger, with a much broader, waisted central band across forewing and no white spot on hindwing. Note that there are other similar species in Africa which may yet arrive as immigrants.
Flight season Two generations in mainland Europe, May-June and August-September. Both British records September. Comes to sugar and readily to light.
Life cycle In southern Europe overwinters as a pupa. Larva June-October. No evidence of breeding in the British Isles.
Larval foodplants In southern Europe, recorded from Bramble and oaks as well as various plant species absent from the British Isles.
Status & distribution Rare immigrant. Two British records: one in fine condition at sugar among

Bramble near Dartmouth, Devon, on 23 September 1903, and one at light at Crowborough, Sussex, on 30 September 1990. Resident in southern Europe and much of Africa, where it is locally frequent. As an immigrant recorded north to Finland on several occasions.

Mother Shipton   page 337
Callistege mi (Cl.)
Common. S,C,(N)   2462(8967)

Field characters FW 13-16mm. When viewed across the body, the large, irregular cream-edged dark brown blotch in centre of forewings of this unmistakable moth resembles a caricature of an old hag in profile, with conspicuous eye and hooked nose. It was therefore named after Old Mother Shipton, a 16th-century Yorkshire witch. Forewing dusted and marked with greyish yellow. Variation in colour and in detail of markings very slight.
Similar species None.
Flight season One generation. Early May-early July. Flies only in sunshine and is easily disturbed, flying short distances. Visits flowers of Oxeye Daisy, Red Clover and other plants.
Life cycle Overwinters as a pupa, in a cocoon formed among grass blades or just beneath the ground. Larva late June-early September. Most active at night, resting on the foodplant or along a grass stem by day.
Larval foodplants White Clover, Red Clover, Hare's-foot Clover, Black Medick, Lucerne and Common Bird's-foot-trefoil. Also confirmed feeding on Cock's-foot and other grasses, on which it has been reared.
Habitat A range of open, grassy places, including downland, heathland, low moorland, flower-rich hay-meadows, woodland rides, verges and embankments.
Status & distribution Resident. Common. Fairly well distributed and quite frequent in England, Wales and Ireland. Local in Scotland north to Ross-shire. Local and rare on Man and in the Channel Islands.

Burnet Companion   page 337
Euclidia glyphica (L.)
Common. S,C   2463(8969)

Field characters FW 13-15mm. Forewing warm dark greyish brown, sometimes tinged with lilac, with two dark brown cross-bands (occasionally absent), and a dark blotch near tip. Basal half of hindwing dark brown, outer half largely orange-yellow, with dark veins and a dark band. No other species has this combination of markings. There is only slight variation. Often settles with hindwings partly exposed. Undersides of wings are orange-yellow, with dark brown markings, and it therefore looks very different in flight.
Similar species See Goldwing.
Flight season One generation. Mid May-early July. Flies by day, in sunshine or warm overcast weather. Easily disturbed, flying only short distances.

Life cycle Overwinters as a pupa, in a cocoon formed among plant debris. Larva late June-late August. Feeds at night, resting by day stretched out along a stem of the foodplant.

Larval foodplants White Clover, Red Clover, Common Bird's-foot-trefoil, Black Medick, Lucerne, Tufted Vetch and probably other trefoils and vetches.

Habitat Dry or damp grassland, usually on calcareous soils, including downland, flower-rich hay-meadows, woodland rides, verges and embankments.

Status & distribution Resident. Common. Fairly well distributed and quite frequent in the southern half of England. Local in Wales, northern England, Man, southern Scotland and Ireland. Local and rare in the Channel Islands.

Ophiderinae

Blackneck   Herald

Alchymist   page 337

Catephia alchymista ([D. & S.])

Immigrant.   2464(8956)

Field characters FW 19-21mm. A black, medium-sized noctuid with broad forewing and a striking large white basal patch on hindwing, like no other British moth. Sections of hindwing fringes also white. Forewing marked with light brown, especially in trailing corner.

Similar species None in the British Isles, but several in Africa which might arrive as immigrants in the future.

Flight season Two generations in southern Europe, the second partial; one generation in northern France and Belgium. British records mainly June-July but also August-September. Majority of records at sugar, but comes to light and has been found at rest by day on a tree trunk.

Life cycle In Europe overwinters as a pupa, in a cocoon on the ground. Larva July-August and possibly later.

Larval foodplants Reportedly, mainly small free-standing oaks. Also recorded on Evergreen Oak and on elms.

Habitat Open woodland and scrub.

Status & distribution Immigrant. Fifteen adults and two larvae have been reported in the British Isles. The first record was at sugar on 13 September 1858 at Bembridge, Isle of Wight; the most recent, also at sugar, was at Middleton-on-Sea, Sussex, on 3 July 1963. Other records are from Kent and Essex, all near the coast, and one from Shropshire. The two larvae, reported from Abbots Wood, Sussex, on 5 July 1894, may not be genuine. Resident in northern France and Belgium, but more frequent in central and southern Europe.

Four-spotted   page 337

Tyta luctuosa ([D. & S.])

Na; suspected immigrant. S,C,E   2465(8965)

Field characters FW 12-13mm. The large, white spots, one centrally in each brownish-black forewing, combined with the white band on hindwing which looks like a spot when moth alights with wings half open, are diagnostic.

Similar species Pale Shoulder has whitish or greyish-white base to forewing.

Flight season Two generations on the Isle of Portland, Dorset, mid May-late June and late July-late August, occasionally to mid September, the second generation being more numerous. Elsewhere the first generation is protracted, mid May-early July, with only a partial, often small, second generation late July-late August. Very rarely adults have been seen at the end of April, for example, in 2003. Flies on sunny days, male patrolling, female staying closer to the ground and often basking. Visits flowers for nectar, including those of Field Bindweed, Oxeye Daisy, clovers and others. Also flies after dark and comes to light, usually as singletons but often in large numbers at Portland.

Life cycle Overwinters as a pupa. Larva late June-August, and again in September. Feeds by night, hiding on the lower stems of the foodplant by day.

Larval foodplants Field Bindweed. Wild larvae have been found eating young leaves from the first instar onwards, although some authors have reported a preference for the flowers.

Habitat Hot, well-drained open sites, often on south-facing slopes and with thin soils and sparse or collapsed vegetation, including unimproved calcareous grassland, field margins, commons, breckland, embankments and derelict ground.

Status & distribution Resident and suspected immigrant. Nationally Scarce A. Formerly widespread and fairly frequent in England south of the Wash, but now much decreased and very local. The two largest populations are near Portland Bill, Dorset, and along the main east coast railway line and associated land between Peterborough and Helpston, Northamptonshire, with other records, often associated with railway lines, elsewhere in Northamptonshire, Leicestershire, Lincolnshire and Oxfordshire. There is at least one colony in Bedfordshire, and one or more in Essex and Somerset. Colonies in Nottinghamshire and Surrey have recently died out. Now very rare or absent from the Breckland of East Anglia. Singletons still recorded sporadically throughout the former range, particularly in south-east England, some probably from undiscovered colonies, others suspected immigrants such as at Dymchurch, Kent, on 10 July 1999, the first Kent record since 1967. One was photographed in a field near St Mary's College, Durham, on 12 June 1994. In the Channel Islands recorded only from Jersey, where two were reported in 1903 and one in 1995.

2465a see Appendix

Blackneck   page 337
Lygephila pastinum (Treit.)
Local. S,C   2466(8932)

Field characters FW 18-21mm. Body rather slender, with ample wings. Top of head and collar are dark brown, often appearing blackish to naked eye. Forewing light pastel grey, sometimes darker, with very fine wavy brown pencilling. Dark brown, rather narrow kidney-mark has one or two spots beside it, and oval is reduced to a dot. Little variation.
Similar species Scarce Blackneck is stouter and has narrower, darker forewing, often with pale veins, sometimes very finely flecked, but not pencilled. There are three or four dark brown spots along leading edge, and narrow blackish kidney-mark is broken along its outer edge.
Flight season One generation. Mid June-mid July. Easily disturbed by day, feeds at flowers at dusk, and comes to light. Can be seen on the wing soon after dusk by sweeping meadows with the beam of a bright light.
Life cycle Overwinters as a small larva. Larva August-late May. Feeds at night, resting low down on the foodplant by day. Pupates in a cocoon, usually formed on or just beneath the ground.
Larval foodplants Tufted Vetch; also recorded on Marsh Pea and Wild Liquorice.
Habitat Damp pasture, water-meadows, hay-meadows, fens, marshland, dry calcareous grassland, damp woodland rides and wood edges.
Status & distribution Resident. Local. Fairly well distributed and locally quite frequent in most southern parts of England, including the south Midlands. Local in south-west England, Wales, the north Midlands, Lincolnshire and Yorkshire.

Scarce Blackneck   page 337
Lygephila craccae ([D. & S.])
RDB. SW   2467(8934)

Field characters & Similar species FW 18-20mm. Four dark dots on leading edge of forewing, and absence of small dark spots beyond kidney-mark distinguish Scarce Blackneck from Blackneck. Both have distinctive blackish-brown head and collar. See also under Blackneck.
Flight season One generation. Mid July-mid August, sometimes a week or so earlier or later. Adults sometimes disturbed by day from among the larval foodplant, especially in hot weather, and seen flying gently around it soon after dark, when they also visit flowers such as Wood Sage, Goldenrod, Hemp-agri-

mony and Red Valerian. Comes to light and sugar.
Life cycle Overwinters as an egg. Larva May-early July, but sometimes fully grown by late June. Feeds by night. Pupates in a cocoon among plant debris on the ground.
Larval foodplants Wood Vetch; also accepts other vetches and vetchlings in captivity, so possibly not restricted to one species in the wild.
Habitat Rocky coastlines and rather steep coastal cliffs, occurring particularly on landslip sites; landslips create fresh areas of open ground for the moth and its larval foodplant to colonise, and it appears to specialise in exploiting these unstable zones.
Status & distribution Resident and possible immigrant. Red Data Book species. Known only from a few sites on the north coasts of Cornwall and Devon, where the historical records span over 100km of coastline, and a single site on the coast of Somerset. A very worn individual thought to be this species was reported from Kynance Cove on the Lizard, Cornwall, on 15 October 1985, but was not kept for confirmation. As this date is two months after the end of the normal flight period in Britain, and as the main larval foodplant is not known from the area, immigration is suspected.

Levant Blackneck   page 337
Tathorhynchus exsiccata (Led.)
Rare immigrant.   2296(8938)

Field characters FW 13-18mm. Hardly resembles the more familiar Blackneck. Forewing narrow and rather blunt, grey-brown with black streak at base and another between small and indistinct, pale oval and kidney-mark. Whitish zigzagged outer cross-line not always conspicuous. Hindwing has broad, dark grey-brown border.
Similar species Might be confused with some forms of Silky Wainscot, which has more pointed forewing.
Flight season British records in February, March, June, September and November. Comes to light.
Life cycle At least two generations in Africa. No evidence of breeding in the British Isles.
Larval foodplants Poorly known. Reported on Lucerne and Tree Indigo, and may feed on other members of the pea family.
Status & distribution Rare immigrant. Ten British records, the first three in 1952, from widely separated locations: Maidencombe, Devon, on 20 March, Farringdon, Hampshire, on 21 March and Ashford, Kent, date not precisely recorded. Subsequently recorded from Cornwall (September 1954), Gloucestershire (1 June 1955) and Sussex (three on 2 June 1955). Three were caught at Martyr Worthy, Hampshire, on 2 and 3 February 1967. The most recent record was in Cornwall on 22 November 1981. Resident in Africa, the Canary Islands and the Middle East; resident or regular immigrant in Mediterranean Europe.

2468 see Appendix

Herald
page 337

Scoliopteryx libatrix (L.)

Common. T
2469(8984)

Field characters FW 19-23mm. Unmistakable. Quite thickset, with broad, strongly-hooked light to dark greyish-brown forewing, tinged pink or purple, with outer edge deeply indented and scalloped, and with white cross-lines. Variation in markings is slight, mainly in extent of orange blotches near base and in centre of forewing. Male has feathered antennae.
Similar species None.
Flight season One generation in most places, August-November and March-June after hibernation. Emerges from July in southern England, with a second generation from September. Most often found feeding after dark, often for long periods night after night, at flowers, including those of Ivy, on overripe berries and at sugar. Also comes to light in small numbers.
Life cycle Overwinters as an adult, in a sheltered location such as an outbuilding or cave, sometimes in numbers. Larva May-July and again in August in the south. Pupates in a cocoon spun between two leaves, often near the end of a twig.
Larval foodplants Willows, Aspen and other poplars.
Habitat Open broadleaved woodland, hedgerows, scrub, fens, heathland, parkland, gardens and other places where the foodplants occur.
Status & distribution Resident. Common. Well distributed and fairly throughout England (including Scilly), Wales, Man, Ireland and the Channel Islands. Local in Scotland, but recorded from most lowland parts, including the Hebrides, Orkney and Shetland.

Small Purple-barred
page 337

Phytometra viridaria (Cl.)

Local. T
2470(9006)

Field characters FW 9-11mm. Quite distinctive but with two frequent forms, both having dull olive-brown forewing and hindwing. F. *aenea* (Hb.) has magenta or pinkish-purple cross-bands towards and along outer edge of forewing, with a pale outer cross-line, and sometimes a magenta band around outer edge of hindwing. F. *fusca* Tutt lacks the magenta bands; the less frequent f. *lunghali* Nordström is similar, but with a darker outer band on forewing and hindwing.
Similar species Plain examples of the day-flying micro-moth *Pyrausta despicata* (Scop.) have narrower forewing with discernible oval and kidney-mark, and a thin but distinct pale central band on hindwing.
Flight season One generation. Late May-July, or August in southern England, which may indicate a partial second generation. Flies mainly in sunshine, but sometimes after dark when it comes to light.
Life cycle Overwinters as a pupa, in a strong cocoon formed among plant debris. Larva late June-early September. Rests on the foodplant.
Larval foodplants Common Milkwort and Heath

Milkwort; also reported from Lousewort.
Habitat Calcareous grassland, heathland, moorland, woodland rides and coastal sand-dunes.
Status & distribution Resident. Local. Fairly well distributed, usually in small numbers, in central southern and south-east England and in Wales and Ireland. Local in the rest of mainland Britain, Man and the Inner Hebrides. Local and rare in the Channel Islands.

Angled Gem
not illustrated

Anomis sabulifera (Guen.)

Import/rare immigrant.
2471(-)

Field characters FW 15-19mm. Forewing shape is distinctive, the outer edge projecting noticeably midway along its length. Markings variable; some examples are fairly plain, but others have strong, dark cross-lines and bands. Kidney-mark has two dark brown spots. Ground-colour varies from yellowish fawn to reddish brown.
Similar species Beautiful Hook-tip has outer edge of forewing similar, but is grey, and much smaller and slimmer.
Status & distribution Suspected accidental import but possibly a rare immigrant. Only one British record, one caught at sugar in an orchard at Goudhurst, Kent, in September 1935. Not recorded elsewhere in Europe. Widespread and frequent in Africa and parts of Asia, eastwards to Japan and Australia. Widely known as the Brown Cotton Moth and sometimes a pest on Cotton.

Rivulinae

Beautiful Hook-tip

Straw Dot

Lesser Belle
page 337

Colobochyla salicalis ([D. & S.])

Rare immigrant; former resident.
2472(9018)

Field characters FW 13-15mm. A grey delta-shaped moth. Forewing pointed, with three diagnostic red cross-lines lightly edged with yellow, the outermost of which curves to meet wing tip.
Similar species Beautiful Hook-tip has notched forewing with only two cross-lines, and these are sharply angled near leading edge.
Flight season One generation. End May-mid July. Recorded once as a presumed immigrant in mid August; one possible example of a second emergence has been noted in mid September. Easily disturbed by day from among the larval foodplant.

Noctuidae (Rivulinae)

Comes to light from dusk onwards.
Life cycle Overwinters as a pupa, in a tough cocoon of silk and chewed bark on the foodplant. Larva July-early August.
Larval foodplants Aspen, favouring the tenderest foliage on low regrowth 1-3m tall.
Habitat Clearings and the edges of open rides in often damp woodland on heavy soils.
Status & distribution Former resident, presumed extinct, and rare suspected immigrant. No resident population seen since 1977. Recorded in Surrey at Dulwich in 1858 and at Haslemere, where several were captured from 1862 to 1866. Seen near Petersfield, on the borders of Hampshire and Sussex, in 1877, the only record for these two counties. Thereafter known to be resident only at Orlestone Forest, Hamstreet, Kent, where it was discovered in 1932 and last noted in 1977. Singletons, presumed immigrants, recorded at light-traps at Maidencombe, near Torquay, south Devon, on 14 August 1965, and Eccles-on-Sea, Norfolk, on 23 June 1998.

Beautiful Hook-tip   page 337
Laspeyria flexula ([D. & S.])
Local. S,WC   2473(8975)

Field characters FW 13-15mm. Quite slender, with warm greyish-brown, often lilac-tinted forewing, rusty brown towards outer edge, with strongly-hooked tips and with outer edge coming to a blunt central point. There are two small dark central dots and two fine, fairly straight, dark-edged yellowish-brown cross-lines, angled at leading edge, with another on hindwing. This pattern and wing shape are constant and diagnostic.
Similar species The unrelated Scalloped Hook-tip is superficially similar, but has outer edge of forewing irregularly scalloped, only one central dot, cross-lines darker than ground-colour, and hindwing paler without a cross-line. See also Lesser Belle.
Flight season One generation. Late June-early August. Flies from dusk and comes to light in small numbers.
Life cycle Overwinters as a small larva. Larva August-late May, most active at night. Pupates in a tough cocoon, formed on a twig or branch.
Larval foodplants Lichens growing on the twigs and branches of broadleaved and coniferous trees.
Habitat Woodland, parkland, scrub, hedgerows, old orchards and some mature gardens.
Status & distribution Resident. Local. Well distributed and locally fairly frequent in southern England, north to Lincolnshire, the south Midlands and the southern half of Wales. Recorded in Yorkshire in 1997 for the first time in 120 years. Local and occasional on Jersey, rare on Guernsey.

Straw Dot   page 337
Rivula sericealis (Scop.)
Common. T   2474(9008)

Field characters FW 13-15mm. Unmistakable. Dark kidney-mark appears brown, but under a lens is purple and black. Forewing usually straw yellow, fading to pale straw when worn, with outer edge and fringe brown. Less often yellowish brown or entirely light brown, most frequently in second generation. Variation in pattern is slight.
Similar species None.
Flight season One main generation, June-July. A smaller second generation in southern Britain, August-September. Easily disturbed during the day; flies from dusk and comes to light.
Life cycle Overwinters as a small larva. Larva August-May and again in July in the south. Pupates in a cocoon formed between grass blades.
Larval foodplants Grasses, including False Brome, Tor-grass and Purple Moor-grass.
Habitat Mainly in tall, usually damp grassland, marshes, fens, heathland, moorland and the wetter rides in woodland.
Status & distribution Resident and suspected immigrant. Common. Well distributed and frequent in southern Britain, on Man and in Ireland. Local and predominantly western in northern England and Scotland, including the Inner Hebrides. Recorded in Orkney and on the east coast of England as a possible immigrant. Widespread and frequent in the Channel Islands.

Waved Black   page 337
Parascotia fuliginaria (L.)
Nb; suspected immigrant. S   2475(9016)

Field characters FW 11-14 mm. The charcoal colour, white or cream spotting and weak cross-lines are distinctive. Rests with wings widely spread and pressed flat against a tree trunk or wall, like a small geometrid moth. When worn it can develop a broad beige band on outer part of forewing.
Similar species None specifically, but often mistaken for a small and unidentifiable geometrid.
Flight season Usually one generation, June-July. Occasional, sometimes small, individuals in September, after hot summers, suggest a partial second emergence, as often happens in captivity. Sometimes flushed out by day; flies from dusk, visiting sugar and coming to light, usually soon after dark.
Life cycle Overwinters as a small larva. Larva August-mid June. Pupates on or near the larval food, on the underside of which larvae can be found day and night.
Larval foodplants The earliest records were from slime moulds growing on rotting wood in docks and cellars in London. The main food is fungi growing on rotting trees, particularly birches and pines, including bracket fungi such as *Coriolus versicolor, Hirschioporus abietina, Piptoporus betulinus* (these three most frequently), *Phaeolus schweinitzii, Paxillus panuoides, Stereum hirsutum, Daldinia concentrica* and *Botryobasidium* spp. The lichen *Cladonia fimbriata* is also eaten. The food must be in moist condition.
Habitat Damp or boggy woodland, especially in old stands of birch; also on wooded heathland. Reported occasionally in rural and suburban gardens, to which

it is sometimes imported with firewood. Shelter and high humidity are important.

Status & distribution Resident and suspected immigrant. Nationally Scarce B. Two main centres of distribution, with the moth increasing its range in recent decades. The largest collection of records is centred on Surrey and extends into West Sussex, Kent, Hampshire (including the New Forest), Wiltshire, Berkshire, Oxfordshire, Buckinghamshire, Middlesex and Hertfordshire. The second is centred on Worcestershire, extending into Herefordshire, Shropshire and Staffordshire. There are also scattered post-1980 records from other counties south-west as far as Gloucestershire, Somerset, Dorset and Devon, east to Essex and Norfolk, and north as far as Lincolnshire, Yorkshire and, in 2002, Nottinghamshire. One recorded at Whitchurch, Cardiff, in August 1992. Has occurred as a suspected immigrant near the coast in south-east England a number of times, including at New Romney, Kent, on 6 July 1999.

2475a see Appendix

Hypeninae
Snouts

Beautiful Snout   Snout

Beautiful Snout
page 338

Hypena crassalis (Fabr.)

Local. S,WC   2476(9002)

Field characters FW 14-16mm. Large dark blotch covering most of broad, sharp-tipped forewing is diagnostic. In male, blotch is dark chocolate brown and outer third and trailing edge of forewing are predominantly grey, with variable brown and white markings. In female, blotch is paler, and outer third and trailing edge are predominantly whitish, except along outer margin and at tip.

Similar species None.

Flight season One generation. Late May-early August, depending on altitude. Flies from dusk and comes to light and occasionally to sugar. Rests by day on tree trunks or among the foodplant and is easily disturbed.

Life cycle Overwinters as a pupa, formed among plant debris or just under the ground. Larva mid July-late September.

Larval foodplants Bilberry. Reports from Cross-

leaved Heath and Bell Heather require confirmation. At some known localities, for example in Kent, Bilberry is absent, and the foodplant there is apparently unknown.

Habitat Usually open woodland, also moorland and heathland. Occasional singletons, presumed wanderers, are recorded away from breeding areas.

Status & distribution Resident. Local. Fairly frequent in suitable habitat in south-west England, Hampshire, Berkshire, Surrey and Kent, the West Midlands, Wales and south Cumbria. Populations were discovered in Derbyshire and Yorkshire in 2001. Recorded at least twice from the Isle of Wight but possibly not resident. In Ireland in Cos. Kerry, Cork, Mayo and Wicklow. In the Channel Islands the only record is of one on Guernsey in 1983.

Snout
page 338

Hypena proboscidalis (L.)

Common. T   2477(8994)

Field characters FW 15-19mm. Easily recognised by its slender body, broad, slightly hooked forewing with clear dark brown cross-lines and very long, upturned palps or 'snout'. Varies in colour from brown to dull greyish brown or dark purplish brown. Examples of the second generation are considerably smaller and often darker.

Similar species Bloxworth Snout and Paignton Snout lack clear brown cross-lines. Buttoned Snout has much narrower forewing with a curved leading edge.

Flight season Two generations in southern Britain, June-early August and late August-mid October. One generation from the Midlands northwards and in Ireland, June-August. Rests by day among the foodplant or other vegetation and is easily disturbed. Flies at dusk over the foodplant, feeds at flowers and occasionally at sugar, and comes frequently to light.

Life cycle Overwinters as a larva. Larva August-May and again July-August in the south. Feeds at night and hides between spun leaves of the foodplant by day. Pupates in a cocoon formed among leaves of the foodplant.

Larval foodplants Common Nettle.

Habitat Woodland, scrub, hedgerows, gardens, rough fields, riverbanks, wetlands and a wide range of other places where the foodplant occurs.

Status & distribution Resident. Common. Well distributed and frequent to abundant throughout most of Britain, Man and Ireland, but absent from Shetland and the Outer Hebrides. Widespread and abundant in the Channel Islands.

Bloxworth Snout
page 338

Hypena obsitalis (Hb.)

RDB. SW   2478(8997)

Field characters FW 15-17mm. There are two forms of this moth, both with irregular cross-line beyond middle. The form with a dark central patch in a lighter brown forewing is distinctive, and occurs in

Larva of Buttoned Snout.

398

both sexes. Another form is almost uniformly dark brown with only faint markings on forewing.

Similar species In small, second-generation Snout, cross-line beyond middle is solid, and slightly curved or bent, but not irregular, and hindwing is paler. See Paignton Snout, which is larger.

Flight season Two generations, the first flying in September-October and again after hibernation in May-June, and another late July-mid August. Flies around the larval foodplant after dark; recorded visiting the flowers of Ivy and Traveller's-joy, and occasionally comes to sugar and light.

Life cycle Overwinters as an adult (first generation only), when it is sometimes found in unheated outbuildings. Larva June-July and August-September. Pupates in a cocoon among the foodplant.

Larval foodplants Pellitory-of-the-wall.

Habitat On south-facing cliffs, rough ground above and below such cliffs, and beside adjacent footpaths and walls where the foodplants are sheltered.

Status & distribution Resident and immigrant. Red Data Book species. A new colonist. First recorded as a single suspected immigrant at Bloxworth, Dorset, on 21 September 1884. Recorded about ten more times on or near the south coast of England from Scilly to Kent, before a colony was discovered on 2 August 1990 on a cliff path in the Torbay area of Devon. Larvae have now been found along the coast as far west as Boscastle, Cornwall, and as far east as Purbeck, Dorset. Records of occasional singletons from the Lizard, Cornwall, (where the foodplant is plentiful) also suggest local breeding. Several records elsewhere in the south-west since 1990 may be of local wanderers rather than international immigrants. Established since the 1960s on the Channel Islands, where it is widespread and frequent. Recorded in Ireland only once, as a suspected immigrant, at Ummera, Co. Cork, on 5 October 1936.

Paignton Snout   page 338

Hypena obesalis (Treit.)

Rare immigrant.   2479(8996)

Field characters FW 18-22mm. Quite distinctive. Forewing pointed, marbled with dark brown and paler, yellowish brown; leading half generally darker, especially centrally. Cross-lines rather indistinct.

Similar species Of related species only Snout is as large, but has forewing broader, plainer and slightly hooked, with a distinct smooth cross-line beyond middle. Bloxworth Snout is smaller, with less pointed forewing.

Flight season One generation in central Europe, August-June. British records August-October. Comes to Ivy flowers, sugar and light.

Life cycle In central Europe overwinters as an adult, probably in caves, hollow trees and elsewhere. Larva June-July. No evidence of breeding in the British Isles.

Larval foodplants Common Nettle.

Status & distribution Rare immigrant. Four British records: a male, at Paignton, Devon, on 5 October 1908, mistakenly identified as Bloxworth Snout and not recognised until re-examined in 1946; a male at Chobham, Surrey, on 14 September 1969; a female at Charlecote, Warwickshire, on 26 August 1973; and a male at Timsbury, Somerset, on 21 September 2002, the last three individuals light-trapped during influxes of immigrant moths to Britain. Resident in central, eastern and southern Europe.

Buttoned Snout   page 338

Hypena rostralis (L.)

Nb. S   2480(8995)

Field characters & Similar species FW 13-15mm. Well-marked individuals have a diagnostic marking resembling a button-hole in centre of forewing, and basal half of forewing is sometimes darker than outer half. Sometimes there are also white markings. One striking and fairly regular form has a broad, pale band along leading edge and pale streaks towards outer edge. However, both sexes also have the predominantly uniform brown f. *unicolor* Tutt. Narrow forewing separates Buttoned Snout from other snouts, and very large 'snout' formed by palps separates it from the various fan-foots.

Flight season One generation. August-early October and again after hibernation, late April-mid June, although occasionally seen as early as late March. Comes to light sources, including lighted porches, but light-traps can fail to detect it even where larvae are numerous. Also recorded at Ivy flowers, overripe blackberries and sugar.

Life cycle Overwinters as an adult, when sometimes found in unheated outbuildings, cellars, garages etc. Natural hibernation sites include caves, hollow trees and probably the shelter of Ivy. Larva July, but in some years from early June and as late as mid August. Pupates in a cocoon under a leaf of the foodplant, usually from mid July onwards.

Larval foodplants Hop, including the garden cultivar Golden Hop.

Habitat Favours large, dense stands of Hop, often in sunny locations, and in proximity to suitable overwintering sites. Hops sprawling over outbuildings and across the ground are ideal, but larvae occur in hedgerows, woodland margins, clearings, along ditches and in scrub, frequently in river valleys.

Status & distribution Resident. Nationally Scarce B. Formerly widely recorded in southern Britain south of a line between south Wales and Lincolnshire. Appeared to have declined since the late 1940s, but recent surveys of larvae have revealed it to be well distributed and locally frequent in parts of its range, such as the low-lying areas of Oxfordshire near the Thames, elsewhere in the Thames basin, parts of Surrey, valleys in the Chilterns, and parts of Northamptonshire, Cambridgeshire and Essex. Other records are scattered along the course of the Waveney/Little Ouse in East Anglia, along the south coast of England, in Kent and around the Bristol Channel/Severn Estuary and the estuaries of the Stour and Blackwater in Essex. Reported further north in the 19th century, including from Yorkshire and southern Scotland. Apparently recorded once from Man, in 1902. Local and rare on Jersey.

Black Snout — not illustrated
Plathypena scabra (Fabr.)
Probable import. 2481(-)

Field characters Raised scales beyond kidney-mark distinguish this species from the other snouts recorded in the British Isles.
Similar species Initially misidentified as a black form of Buttoned Snout.
Status & distribution Probable accidental import. There is only one British record of this species, which is abundant throughout much of eastern North America and is sometimes a pest on legumes and strawberries. A single male was captured on 31 August 1956 in a light-trap in a garden at Lee, north-west Kent. The trap site is 5km from the London docks and most likely the individual was imported with produce.

Strepsimaninae

White-line Snout   Pinion-streaked Snout   Marsh Oblique-barred

White-line Snout — page 338
Schrankia taenialis (Hb.)
Nb. S 2482(8868)

Field characters FW 9-11mm. A rather straight white line, with black on inner side, crosses outer part of forewing from trailing edge. Central black mark is not connected to this line. Shows only minor variation.
Similar species See Pinion-streaked Snout, Marsh Oblique-barred and Autumnal Snout.
Flight season Mainly one generation, early July-mid August, but occasional adults of a partial second generation have been recorded September-October. Adults reared in captivity from eggs (see below) were

White-line Snout   Autumnal Snout

Pinion-streaked Snout   Marsh Oblique-barred

Details of Strepsimaninae forewing markings.

produced in the autumn, probably as a consequence of warm conditions in confinement. Comes to flowers, sugar and light, and is sometimes netted at dusk.
Life cycle As yet unknown. By analogy with related species, probably overwinters as a part-grown larva. The pupae are suspended from grass stalks and other objects near the ground.
Larval foodplants Unknown: the larva has not been found in the wild. Reared from eggs once in recent years in Britain, initially on a mixture of lettuce and the flowers of Cross-leaved Heath, Bell Heather and Wild Thyme, later on sliced immature runner beans. Flowers of Hogweed have also been accepted and, in mainland Europe, the fresh flowers of Heather.
Habitat Open moorland, conifer plantations and damp broadleaved woodland. Has been found in numbers in sunken lanes with shady hedgebanks in Devon and Pembrokeshire. Found in both acid and calcareous areas.
Status & distribution Resident. Nationally Scarce B. Very much a southern species with a western bias to its distribution in Britain. Most of the post-1980 records are concentrated in south Cornwall, Devon and Somerset, with another concentration in east Dorset, Hampshire, the Isle of Wight and the Surrey heaths. There is a further cluster of records around the Bristol Channel and Severn and Wye valleys, with a thin scatter of records in south Wales and south-east England, apparently declining in the latter. There are a few older records extending to the Wirral, Cheshire, and the Humber. Discovered in Ireland on 2 July 2000, when one was light-trapped at Crom Estate, Co. Fermanagh.

Autumnal Snout — not illustrated
Schrankia intermedialis Reid
Rare probable hybrid. SE 2483(8867)

Field characters & Similar species FW 9-10mm. Key forewing markings are intermediate between those of White-line Snout and Pinion-streaked Snout. Central black forewing mark is not connected to outer cross-line, which has a sharp bend in it like that of Pinion-streaked Snout but is well-defined as in White-line Snout.
Flight season All six records are from late September-October; White-line Snout and Pinion-

streaked Snout have a partial emergence at this time, but their main flight season is July-August. Has been netted at dusk and recorded at light.

Life cycle & Larval foodplants As yet unknown.

Habitat Damp woodland on heavy soil.

Status & distribution Resident. Would merit Red Data Book status if considered a distinct species – only six specimens known. However, now thought by Reid and others to be a rare, naturally occurring hybrid between the resident White-line Snout and Pinion-streaked Snout, both of which occur in the three localities from which Autumnal Snout has been reported. Single males were taken at light in Broxbourne Woods, Hertfordshire, on 21 and 22 October 1971, but none was seen in subsequent searches of the site until one male was netted at dusk on 1 October 1982; a male was also found just over 3km from the original site on 4 October 1973, in a damp copse at Bayfordbury, Hertfordshire. The most recent specimens are two singletons taken in a Rothamsted light-trap at Fagg's Wood, Warehorne, Kent, on 23 September 1988 and 21 September 1992. Only these two specimens have been recorded at the Fagg's Wood site, even though by 1992 the trap had been operated in the same site every night for over five years. Not reported outside Britain.

Pinion-streaked Snout　　　　page 338

Schrankia costaestrigalis (Steph.)

Local. S,C,(NW)　　　　　2484(8866)

Field characters FW 9-11mm. Small, slender and easily mistaken for a pyralid or other micro-moth, especially since it sits with front end raised. Forewing narrow, dull straw-coloured or brown. A thick, dark streak obscures kidney-mark and reaches faint outer cross-line, and there is often a pale diagonal streak from tip. However, markings may be faint, and whole forewing almost uniform brown apart from cross-lines.

Similar species White-line Snout has broader forewing, with kidney-mark clear, small and dark; there is sometimes a short streak running through it, but this rarely reaches outer cross-line, which is distinct and edged whitish on the outside, especially towards trailing edge.

Flight season One main generation, late June-mid August. A partial second generation in southern England, late August-mid October. Flies from dusk, when it feeds at flowers and comes to sugar. Also comes to light, usually in small numbers.

Life cycle Unknown: the early stages have not been found in the wild.

Larval foodplants Unknown in the wild. In captivity eats lettuce leaves, flowers of Heather, Wild Marjoram, Wild Thyme and mints, and damp, withered sallow leaves.

Habitat Damp woodland, fens, wet meadows, boggy heathland, raised bogs, riversides and other marshy areas.

Status & distribution Resident. Local. Fairly well distributed and quite frequent, but often overlooked, in suitable habitat throughout southern Britain, including Wales, Scilly and the Channel Islands. Local in northern England, western Scotland, on Man and in Ireland.

Marsh Oblique-barred　　　　page 338

Hypenodes humidalis Doubl.

Nb. T　　　　　　　　　2485(8863)

Field characters & Similar species FW 6-8mm. Easily confused with micro-moths because of its small size and appearance. Examine small moths in suitable habitat for the two diagnostic dark, oblique cross-lines on forewing, outer one extending to wing tip. White-line Snout is somewhat similar, but larger and outer dark cross-line does not reach wing tip.

Flight season Mainly one generation in late June-late August, depending on latitude. Occasionally a partial second generation in September. Best searched for by netting in the late afternoon, or at dusk when it is sometimes seen on the wing in numbers. Comes to sugar and light, sometimes in abundance.

Life cycle Largely unknown. Overwinters as either a larva (most likely) or a pupa. Pupates in a pendulous cocoon suspended from a plant stem near the ground.

Larval foodplants Unknown: the larva has not been found in the wild. Reported to have been reared on Cross-leaved Heath and, in mainland Europe, on *Sphagnum* moss and Marsh Cinquefoil. At one British breeding site the only plants present, in addition to those above, are Heather and Purple Moor-grass.

Habitat Boggy moorland, heathland, bogs, swamps, fens, marshes and water-meadows, including small sites of only 1-2ha.

Status & distribution Resident. Nationally Scarce B. Easily overlooked. Has a scattered distribution up the west side of Britain from Devon and the turf moors of north Somerset, through the boggy moorland of western Wales, the raised bogs of Shropshire and Cumbria, and on moorland in Scotland from the southern uplands to Argyllshire, in Flanders Moss in west Perthshire and north to the Moray Firth. Occurs widely on the heaths of east Dorset, Hampshire and Surrey and extends to a small number of sites in Sussex, where it is still fairly frequent. Other sites in this area are river marshes and water-meadows such as in the Itchen Valley in Hampshire. Recorded at Cothill Fen, Oxfordshire, and at Dersingham Bog and other sites near the Norfolk coast, including the Ant marshes and Catfield Fen, although it appears to be rare or local in the Broads generally. In Ireland locally frequent in Cos. Kerry, Cork and Clare; found in Northern Ireland at Peatlands Park, Co. Armagh, on 21 July 1998 and subsequently at Monmurray and the Crom Estate, Co. Fermanagh.

2486, 2487 see Appendix

Herminiinae
Fan-foots

Fan-foot   Small Fan-foot   Dotted Fan-foot

Common Fan-foot   page 338
Pechipogo strigilata (L.)
Na. S   2488(8852)

Field characters & Similar species FW 14-16mm.
Individuals recorded after early July, except in very
late years, are generally not Common Fan-foot.
Forewing whitish fawn or greyish fawn, dusted with
grey and with slightly diffuse brown cross-lines, the
outermost pale-edged, reaching leading edge close
to tip. Kidney-mark narrow and rather faint.
Hindwing whitish. All similar species are deeper,
richer brown, have cross-lines better defined and
hindwing grey-brown. Fan-foot is much more widespread and is actually the 'common' species.
Flight season One generation. Generally late May-
June, occasionally to early July, but very rarely late
July when the Fan-foot is well on the wing. Easily
flushed by day from shrubs and coppice regrowth.
Flies from dusk. Comes to light in small numbers,
more so if the light-trap is placed near understorey
plants.
Life cycle Overwinters as an almost fully grown
larva, among leaves withered on the branch or fallen
on the ground. Larva July-April. Pupates in a flimsy
cocoon among leaf litter or possibly on a trunk.
Larval foodplants Pedunculate Oak, particularly on
damaged branches with withering leaves. In
captivity, will feed at first on fresh young leaves but
later prefers older, withered and even mouldy leaves.
It is possible that leaves of other species such as
Hazel are also eaten, but this needs confirmation.
Habitat Usually found in fairly open ancient woodland, with mature trees and plenty of low bushy
growth, but may be found surviving in more overgrown conditions. Probably benefits from rotational
coppicing. Usually on heavy soils. May benefit from
higher humidity within plant cover.
Status & distribution Resident. Nationally Scarce A.
A much declined species. There are post-1980
records from a few woodlands scattered through the
former range, which included most of central and
southern England south of the Humber and parts of
Wales. Locations of surviving colonies include the
Cannop area of the Forest of Dean, Gloucestershire;
Wyre Forest, Shropshire/Worcestershire; Bernwood
Forest on the Oxfordshire/Buckinghamshire border;
woods in south Wiltshire such as Langley and Bentley

Woods; Pamber Forest and at least two other sites in
north Hampshire; Parkhurst Forest, Isle of Wight; and
various sites in Northamptonshire, Huntingdonshire
and Cambridgeshire. Very local in East Sussex and
possibly in south-east Kent, although recent reports
from Kent are mainly from July and thus probably
erroneous. In Ireland, reported, probably in error,
from Cos. Down (not recently), Dublin, Kerry and
Clare – these records are likely to refer to Fan-foot.

Plumed Fan-foot   page 338
Pechipogo plumigeralis (Hb.)
Rare immigrant; probable resident.   2488a(8853)

401

Field characters & Similar species FW 13-15mm. A
warm reddish-brown, quite large fan-foot with
pointed forewing. Conspicuous pale, dark-edged
outermost cross-line and broad kidney-mark distinguish it from most others except Dusky Fan-foot.
Differs from latter in that ground-colour is more
uniform and smooth forewing lines and markings
narrower; kidney-mark is larger and cross-line
passing round it is fine, and rather jagged in leading
half. Male antennae distinctly feathered.
Flight season Probably one generation in Britain.
July-August. Comes to light.
Life cycle Overwinters as a larva. Larva August-May
or June but produces a second generation in
captivity, if kept warm. Probably pupates on the
ground among plant debris.
Larval foodplants Unknown in Britain. In mainland
Europe, roses, Broom, Ivy and probably other plants.
In captivity, also accepts withered leaves of Bramble,
Hawthorn and Dandelion.
Habitat The site at Rye is a linear strip of gardens,
with bare shingle on one side and scrubby areas
nearby.
Status & distribution Rare immigrant and probable
resident. First recorded in Britain on 12 October
1995 at Greatstone, Kent (a female), with a male at
the same site on 20 July 1999, and singletons nearby
on 8 August 1996 at New Romney and 9 August
1997 at Dungeness, all at light. Three were light-
trapped at Rye Harbour Nature Reserve, Sussex, in
1996, followed by one in 1997, two in 1998 and
others subsequently, suggesting a local population
has been established. Resident in central and
southern Europe and northern Africa.

Fan-foot   page 338
Zanclognatha tarsipennalis (Treit.)
Common. T   2489(8858)

Field characters FW 13-16mm. Forewing brown,
with three dark brown cross-lines, the innermost
gently curved and slightly wavy, second shaped like a
question mark and outer almost straight, meeting
leading edge away from tip. There is a fine dark
central crescent-mark, and a row of very fine dashes
along outer edge. In male, antennae have a small
bulge roughly in middle. These last two characters
are best seen with a hand-lens. A yellowish-brown

form has been found in western Scotland and southern Ireland.

Similar species Common Fan-foot has similar markings, but has grey-brown forewing and whitish hindwing. Shaded Fan-foot is slightly smaller and has a straighter first cross-line, a diffuse dark central crossband, a continuous fine dark line along outer edge and no central bulge in male antennae. See also Small Fan-foot and Jubilee Fan-foot.

Flight season Mainly one generation. June-early August. Occasional, usually small, individuals are recorded in late summer and autumn, probably representing a partial second generation. Flies from dusk and comes to light and sugar. Often disturbed by day.

Life cycle Overwinters as a fully grown larva. Larva late July-April. Feeds until October, when it forms a slight cocoon among plant debris, in which it pupates in the spring.

Larval foodplants Withered leaves, including those of oaks and Beech on the ground or on fallen or damaged branches, and of Bramble.

Habitat Broadleaved woodland and other places with substantial cover, such as hedgerows and gardens.

Status & distribution Resident. Common. Well distributed and frequent throughout southern Britain, north to Lancashire and Yorkshire, and in Ireland. Local further north in England, on Man and in southern Scotland, with a scatter of records north to the Moray Firth. Widespread and frequent in the Channel Islands.

Jubilee Fan-foot
page 338

Zanclognatha lunalis (Scop.)

Rare immigrant. 2490(8856)

Field characters & Similar species FW 14-17mm. Slightly larger than Fan-foot, with a bolder and more strongly arched central crescent-mark on forewing than any other British fan-foot. Forewing light brown to red-brown, often with a purplish tinge. Central cross-line finely scalloped (smooth or slightly irregular in Fan-foot) but less so than in Dusky Fan-foot, which is a darker, rougher-looking moth, distinguished by conspicuous pale outer cross-line. See also Shaded Fan-foot.

Flight season In northern Europe one generation, June-August. British records July-August. Comes to light.

Life cycle In Europe, overwinters as a larva. Larva August-April or May. Probably pupates on the ground. No evidence of breeding in the British Isles.

Larval foodplants In Europe, reported to feed on withered and dead leaves of many broadleaved plants.

Status & distribution Rare immigrant. Two British records. The first was light-trapped in a garden at Dorney Reach, Buckinghamshire, during late August 1976. As the species is not a noted immigrant there was speculation that a resident population might exist. A second individual has since been light-trapped, on 4 July 2001, at Durlston Country Park,

Swanage, Dorset, a much-trapped site for intercepting immigrant moths, from which the species would surely have been recorded previously if resident there. Widespread in western Europe, from Portugal to southern Sweden, but local and infrequent from Belgium northwards.

Dusky Fan-foot
page 338

Zanclognatha zelleralis (Wocke)

Rare immigrant. 2491a(8857)

Field characters FW 14-17mm. Generally looks rougher and darker than other British fan-foots, and is distinguished by broad kidney-mark, a conspicuous broad, pale, outer cross-line across fore- and hindwings and a stronger, more finely scalloped central cross-line on forewing than any other fan-foot. Markings more intense than those of other fan-foots, and a prominent dark brown spot on trailing edge of hindwing near abdomen is particularly diagnostic. Also distinguished from all except Plumed Fan-foot by thickened kidney-mark.

Similar species See Plumed Fan-foot, Jubilee Fan-foot and Shaded Fan-foot.

Flight season In central Europe one generation, June-July. Comes to light.

Life cycle In central Europe, overwinters as a larva. Larva August-May. Pupates among plant debris. No evidence of breeding in the British Isles.

Larval foodplants In mainland Europe, the withered leaves of many low-growing plants.

Status & distribution Rare immigrant. Recorded once in the British Isles: one was captured in a light-trap at Stackpole, Pembrokeshire, in late July 1982. Widespread in central and southern Europe.

Shaded Fan-foot
page 338

Herminia tarsicrinalis (Knoch)

RDB. SE 2491(8858)

Field characters & Similar species FW 12-14mm. Similar to Fan-foot, but slightly smaller and distinguished by distinct (although rather diffuse) brown central cross-band, running through, or just before, the narrow, curved kidney-mark. See also Small Fan-foot.

Flight season One generation. Late June-July. Prone to a partial second generation in captivity and in southern Europe. Seldom seen except at light. Traps should be placed within Bramble thickets as it seems to be very sedentary. Comes to light from dusk to about midnight.

Life cycle Overwinters as a nearly fully grown larva, probably in leaf litter below Bramble. Larva late July or August-May. Pupates in a cocoon among Bramble debris.

Larval foodplants Larvae have not been found in the wild, but captive larvae selected withered and even mouldy leaves of Bramble.

Habitat Bramble thickets and dense Bramble ground-cover, both among oaks and birches in ancient woodland and in more open scrubby places.

Status & distribution Resident. Red Data Book species. Recorded very locally from Norfolk, Suffolk and Essex. Unknown in Britain until 11 July 1965 when a male was captured between Thorpeness and Aldeburgh on the Suffolk coast, with a second on 27 June 1967 between Aldeburgh and Woodbridge. At first considered to be a casual immigrant: no more were seen until a light-trapping survey in 1982 produced over 20, mostly worn males, on 10 July on lightly-wooded common land near the sites of the first captures. Since recorded from four 10km squares on the Suffolk coast, including Minsmere RSPB reserve. In July 1989 it was discovered 20km further inland in woodland just north of Harleston, Norfolk. Others have since been recorded in north Essex at Riddles Wood and Stour and Copperas Woods. Likely to prove more widespread as targeted searches continue. One, a presumed immigrant, was reported from Dungeness, Kent, on 18 June 2000. Recorded from the Channel Islands for the first time in 2002, a singleton on Jersey.

Larva of Small Fan-foot.

Small Fan-foot
page 338

Herminia grisealis ([D. & S.])

Common. T   2492(8846)

Field characters & Similar species FW 11-13mm. Similar to Fan-foot, but distinguished from this and all other related species by its smaller size and crucially by third cross-line, which is curved and extends to forewing tip. Forewing markings generally sharper than those of Fan-foot.
Flight season One generation. Early June-late August. Sometimes disturbed by day from bushes and low branches. Flies from dusk, feeding at flowers and sugar, and comes to light, sometimes in fair numbers.
Life cycle Overwinters as a pupa, in a cocoon formed in a bark crevice or among plant debris. Larva July-October.
Larval foodplants Healthy and withered leaves of a range of trees, including Pedunculate Oak, Downy Birch, Alder, Hazel, Hawthorn, and Bird Cherry, on the tree or on the ground, and of Bramble and Traveller's-joy.
Habitat Broadleaved woodland, scrub, hedgerows and gardens.
Status & distribution Resident. Common. Well distributed and frequent throughout most of England, including Scilly, Wales, Man, southern Scotland and Ireland. Local further north in mainland Scotland, reaching Ross-shire. Widespread and frequent in the Channel Islands.

Dotted Fan-foot
page 338

Macrochilo cribrumalis (Hb.)

Nb. SE   2493(8843)

Field characters & Similar species FW 13-14mm. Easily distinguished from other fan-foots and snouts by whitish-fawn coloration and two rows of black

dots rather than cross-lines on forewing.
Flight season One generation. Mid June-August. Sometimes disturbed from the sward by day; flies from just before dusk. Comes to light, sometimes in fair numbers, and is often seen resting on sedges, grasses and other low plants after dark.
Life cycle Overwinters as a part-grown larva in tussocks of vegetation. Larva July-May. Pupates in a cocoon at ground level among plant debris.
Larval foodplants Reported to feed on Wood-sedge, Hairy Wood-rush and Field Wood-rush, living in the stems but eating the leaves as well.
Habitat Sedge-beds and other habitats where the foodplants are frequent, including fens, bogs and other peaty areas, marshes and ditch-banks, in both calcareous and acid situations, favouring open areas, but also present within light carr.
Status & distribution Resident. Nationally Scarce B. Largely confined to East Anglia and marshes through Essex south to the Thames Estuary, with a few colonies in Kent (mainly the north Kent marshes and near Sandwich), East Sussex (Pevensey Levels and nearby), and Hampshire (Emer Bog and possibly in the Lower Test valley). Local in Hertfordshire, where it is resident at Sawbridgeworth Marsh Nature Reserve in the Stort valley and at Rye Meads in the Lea valley. In Lincolnshire there are recent records from Messingham Heath. The main centres in East Anglia are the Norfolk Broads and the wetlands on the Cambridgeshire/Norfolk/Suffolk borders, including strong populations at Chippenham Fen NNR and Redgrave and Lopham Fen. There is a strong outlying colony at Woodwalton Fen NNR in Huntingdonshire. There are also populations on the Suffolk coast in the Minsmere/Walberswick area and further south. In Essex, it appears to have extended its range and has now been reported from over a dozen sites, mainly along the coast. There are 19th-century reports from Surrey, Somerset and Dorset.

Clay Fan-foot
page 338

Paracolax tristalis (Fabr.)

Na; immigrant. SE   2494(8839)

Field characters FW 14-16mm. Warm sandy colour of fore- and hindwings distinguishes this moth from all other fan-foots.

Similar species In Olive Crescent, cross-lines are lighter, not darker, than ground-colour. The micro-moth *Ebulea crocealis* (Hb.) has a passing resemblance in colour and markings of forewing. It is easily distinguished by its white hindwing and its smaller size, but has nevertheless been reported as Clay Fan-foot in the Midlands and elsewhere.

Flight season One generation. Late June-early August, with peak numbers in mid-late July. Flies up readily from low vegetation by day if disturbed and makes short flights, usually settling on the underside of a leaf. Also flies at dusk and later, and comes in small numbers to sugar and to light.

Life cycle Overwinters as a small larva, in spun leaves on the ground, and pupates in similar situations. Larva August-early June.

Larval foodplants Oaks and possibly other broadleaved trees or shrubs such as hawthorns or Hazel. Larvae have been beaten from unspecified oaks in autumn, although they are usually stated to feed mainly on moist fallen oak leaves on the ground, perhaps also eating herbaceous plants when completing their growth.

Habitat Broadleaved woodland, favouring sunny but sheltered areas where trees have been felled or coppiced and regrowth has begun. The glades occupied in one Sussex woodland tend to be individually of less than 1ha but linked together, with regrowth of Sweet Chestnut stools. Occurs on soil types ranging from heavy Wealden Clay to gault and chalk.

Status & distribution Resident, also wanderer or immigrant. Nationally Scarce A. Apparently contracting in distribution. Confined to south-east England, where it occurs very locally but sometimes in numbers in a few woodlands in Kent, Sussex and Surrey. There are a number of records from Essex, but not seen since 1976, despite subsequent searches. A single male was taken at a Rothamsted light-trap at Alice Holt, north-east Hampshire, on 11 August 1971, but no more have turned up at this site, in spite of daily light-trapping. Another example was light-trapped at the Warren LNR near Hawkley, Hampshire, on 16 July 1995, near recently-coppiced Beech. Four individuals were light-trapped between 1992 and 2002 on the Kent coast in the Dungeness/Greatstone area, suggesting immigration. Singletons were previously recorded at the Clarendon Estate, Wiltshire, on 24 June 1938 and Swanage, Dorset, on 28 July 1948. Two on Guernsey in 1898 appear to be the only records for the Channel Islands.

Olive Crescent

page 338

Trisateles emortualis ([D. & S.])

RDB; suspected immigrant. SE   2495(9169)

Field characters & Similar species FW 14mm. Cross-lines on fore- and hindwings are lighter than ground-colour, rather yellowish, distinguishing Olive Crescent from Clay Fan-foot and related species, in which cross-lines are darker than ground-colour. Ground-colour varies from light fawn to sandy brown.

Flight season One generation. Late June-mid July in Buckinghamshire, but in the cold summer of 1974 seen in Essex as late as 24 August. Seldom seen except at light-traps on warm nights.

Life cycle Overwinters as a pupa, in a cocoon between dead leaves among leaf litter on the ground. Larva July-October.

Larval foodplants Oaks, Beech, and possibly other trees such as Sweet Chestnut. Wild larvae have been beaten from withered oak foliage on damaged branches, and in the autumn from dry Beech leaves on twigs. When subsequently reared in captivity, seems to prefer oak leaves that have fallen the same year to older leaves or those of Beech.

Habitat Mature woodland containing oaks and sometimes Beech, seeming to favour places where there are trees with damaged branches and wilting leaves, such as the edges of rides and clearings, wind-thrown stands and where trees are rubbing together.

Status & distribution Resident and suspected immigrant. Red Data Book species. Recorded almost annually, sometimes in double figures, in two woods near the coast in north Essex, where it was discovered in 1974. Found in a small group of woodlands in the Chilterns, Buckinghamshire, on 12 July 1962, when five adults were captured. Recorded there at various times later in the 1960s, as adults and larvae, but has become difficult to locate in recent years. Previous records from this area, reported as Stonor, in mid July 1859 and again in 1910, suggest it has been a long-term resident here. The other British records, of which there are about 20, are almost exclusively from sites on the south and east coasts, from the first time the species was recorded in Britain, at Brighton, Sussex, on 18 June 1858, to Ventnor, Isle of Wight, in July 1939, Dorset, on 5 and 18 July 2001, in Kent, including three at different sites in 2001, and at Bradwell-on-Sea, Essex, on 27 June 1970 and 9 June 1993. These records suggest immigration from mainland Europe. One was captured on Guernsey on 23 August 1984.

Appendix
Species doubtfully recorded in Great Britain and Ireland, or recorded as probable imports only

The following are included on the British checklist and been given serial numbers by Bradley (2000), but are obvious imports or dubious records. Moths are constantly arriving in the British Isles accidentally with imported produce, other materials and products, and on the vehicles which transport them, including species not mentioned in the list. The authors do not see the point of including any of these as British. These brief accounts are provided so the reader has the facts.

Great Peacock Moth
Saturnia pyri ([D. & S.])
Rare immigrant/suspected import.   1643a(6793)

Field characters At least twice the size of Emperor Moth. Both sexes not unlike female Emperor Moth in colour and markings, although darker.
Status & distribution Recorded only as a possible very rare immigrant, on 24 May 1984 at 6.30am, a male close to the M27 motorway at Swaythling, Southampton, Hampshire. Quite possibly an accidental cross-Channel import. This large, eyed, southern European species is sometimes bred in captivity, from which escapes or releases might occur, possibly explaining one found by a ten-year-old boy at Fairfield, Buxton, Derbyshire, (reported in *The Daily Telegraph* of 13 September 1967). Resident in central and southern Europe, particularly around the Mediterranean, including north Africa, and extending eastwards across the Caucasus to the Near East, the larvae feeding on the foliage of a wide range of woody plants, including various fruit trees.

Blackberry Looper
Chlorochlamys chloroleucaria (Guen.)
Suspected import.   1671(-)

Field characters Similar to Small Grass Emerald but slightly smaller and distinguished by two well-defined, rather straight white cross-lines on fore- and hindwing.
Status & distribution Suspected import. A frequent and well distributed moth throughout eastern North America, where it feeds on Bramble and the flowers of various members of the daisy family. Inclusion on the British list is based solely on an individual present in the Stephens collection from the early 19th century, now in the Natural History Museum, London.

Streaked Wave
Scopula virgulata ([D. & S.])
Doubtfully British.   1685(8043)

Status & distribution Doubtfully British. Two individuals of this central and southern European species were allegedly captured in Gravesend, Kent, during 1870. The precise location is not known. Some previous authorities discount these records through lack of convincing evidence.

Middle Lace Border
Scopula decorata ([D. & S.])
Doubtfully British.   1686(8051)

Status & distribution Doubtfully British. British records of this widespread European species cannot be traced and confirmed.

Large Lace Border
Scopula limboundata (Haw.)
Doubtfully British.   1695(-)

Status & distribution Doubtfully British. A single unconfirmed record of this North American species from about 1820 was admitted to the British list of 1828.

Strange Wave
Idaea laevigata (Scop.)
Suspected import.   1700(8111)

Status & distribution Suspected import. Four larvae of this central and southern European species were discovered among coconut fibre at Durham, in 1927, and were successfully reared on shrivelled leaves of Dandelion and willows.

Rusty Wave   page 133
Idaea inquinata (Scop.)
Suspected import.   1703(8134)

Field characters & Similar species A small, distinctive wave, all wings mottled with rusty reddish brown, often in the form of bands but sometimes more broken. Somewhat like Weaver's Wave but smaller and more reddish brown.
Status & distribution Suspected import. All records clearly associated with imported dried herbs and plants, the larval foodplants. Found a number of times in the late 19th century, mainly in central London, the first in Bloomsbury Street in 1856. Others, most revealingly, in a herbalist's shop in Holbourn in June 1868, and also in shops in other streets in subsequent years. Two captured in the basement of a museum in Tring, Hertfordshire, where it was believed introduced with plant-derived packing materials. In the late 20th century found associated with dried decorative flowers, in which the larvae may have been imported. Widespread in central and southern Europe and the Mediterranean coast of Africa.

Purple-barred Yellow

Lythria purpuraria (L.)
Doubtfully British. 1717(8221)

Status & distribution Doubtfully British. Unconfirmed 19th-century records, chief of which are two males reportedly disturbed from Broom 'not far from the city of Perth' on 18 June 1861, and two from Stockton Forest, near York, about 1870. This striking purple and yellow day-flying moth of open dry habitats is unlikely to be overlooked, yet there were no records during the 20th century. Widespread and frequent in mainland Europe.

Cumbrian Umber

Horisme aquata (Hb.)
Doubtfully British. 1783(8409)

Field characters & Similar species FW 14mm. Like a slightly smaller, paler version of Small Waved Umber, with straighter cross-lines on forewing and abdomen pale grey rather than dark brown.
Status & distribution Doubtfully British. In 1882, five specimens were located in a collection in Cumbria (but not necessarily captured there) as pale forms of the Small Waved Umber, which is not found there. Four additional specimens have subsequently been located in old British collections. Only one has data. It is labelled 'Sherwood Forest'. In mainland Europe, recorded from Pasque-flower and accepts the related Traveller's-joy, neither of which occur in such northern localities.

Light Magpie

Abraxas pantaria (L.)
Doubtfully British. 1886(7525*)

Status & distribution Doubtfully British. An unconfirmed record from 1885, but there appears to be no confirmed British record of this largely Mediterranean species. It should be dropped from the British list.

Dingy Angle

Macaria bicolorata (Fabr.)

ssp. *praeatomata* (Haw.)
Doubtfully British. 1892(-)

Status & distribution Doubtfully British. No British record in the last 200 years. A widespread and frequent moth in much of North America, where the larvae feed on pines. Somewhat like Dusky Peacock in appearance and habits.

White Spot

Hypagyrtis unipunctata (Haw.)
Doubtfully British. 1898(-)

Status & distribution Probable deliberate import. No British record for over 200 years and probably never taken in Britain. Included in British list by Haworth in the early 19th century. An abundant species of North America, where it is known as the One-spotted Variant, and feeds on many tree species.

Bordered Chequer

Nematocampa limbata (Haw.)
Doubtfully British. 1900(-)

Status & distribution Probable deliberate import. No British record for over 200 years and probably never taken in Britain. Included in British list by Haworth in early 19th century. A local and infrequent species of North America, where it is known as the Horned Spanworm Moth, and feeds on many broadleaved tree species.

Clouded August Thorn page 148

Ennomos quercaria (Hb.)
Doubtfully British. 1916(7637)

Field characters & Similar species Similar to September Thorn in size, resting posture and appearance, but paler, more whitish, with two cross-lines on forewing converging less closely at trailing edge.
Status & distribution Doubtfully British. Records unconfirmed. Reported in the 19th century and again in Essex in 1992. A local species of mainly southern Europe.

Ennomos subsignaria (Hb.)
Suspected import. 1916a

Status & distribution Suspected import. Recorded as a single pupa at Covent Garden Market, London, on 26 April 1984 among Asparagus imported from Florida. The adult emerged on 2 May 1984 and is preserved in the Natural History Museum, London. A North American species clearly imported with produce.

Pink-spotted Hawkmoth

Agrius cingulata (Fabr.)
Suspected import. 1971(-)

Field characters & Similar species FW c50mm. Resembles Convolvulus Hawkmoth, from which it can be distinguished by fawn shoulder patches on base of forewing, a wavy grey band across central portion of forewing, pink bands on hindwing and fawn patches on body in front of first black band on abdomen.
Status & distribution Suspected import. This American moth, also known as the Sweet Potato Hornworm, was imported to Britain in 1778 and 1826 with shipments of Sweet Potato from North America, and has also been recorded on ships off the French coast. It is frequent in the tropics and sub-tropics of the Americas, and has recently established itself in the Cape Verde Islands west of Senegal, West Africa. It occurs as a migrant north to Canada and south to Patagonia, and may land on ships destined for Europe. It is just possible this moth may reach the British Isles unassisted, and it is worth looking out for it among Convolvulus Hawkmoths in the autumn. Larval foodplants Sweet Potato, Pawpaw and Jimsonweed.

Five-spotted Hawkmoth

Manduca quinquemaculatus (Haw.)

Suspected import.   1974

Field characters FW c55mm. Resembles Convolvulus Hawkmoth but has yellow bars on abdomen and hindwing is crossed by three clearly-defined, very zigzag brown lines and a broad outer band.

Status & distribution Suspected import with shipments of food. First described by Haworth in 1803 as English based on a specimen which probably arrived with imports. Reported from Chelsea, Hull and Leeds in the 19th century. Larva, known as the Tomato Hornworm, feeds on Tomato, Potato and Tobacco plants.

Tomato Sphinx

Manduca sexta (Johan.)

Suspected import.   1975

Field characters FW c57mm. Forewing has white spots at regular intervals along outer edge. The black line running through wing near these is very wavy, not relatively straight as in Five-spotted Hawkmoth. Has yellow bars on abdomen, as in the latter, but brown bands on hindwing are not zigzagged.

Status & distribution Suspected import. A pair was reportedly taken by a Mr Thompson on 28 August 1796 at West Cowes, Isle of Wight, and found their way into Curtis's collection. This moth of the Americas has been recorded from Canada to Chile, Argentina and Uruguay, Cuba and many of the Caribbean islands. It is considered a pest species in the central part of its range. Larva, known as the Tobacco Hornworm, feeds on Tomato, Potato and Tobacco plants and other Solanaceae.

Rustic Sphinx

Manduca rustica (Fabr.)

Suspected import.   1975a

Field characters Striking two-tone forewing with dark brown blocks on a whitish background crossed by many fine blackish-brown zigzag lines. Three pairs of yellow spots on abdomen.

Status & distribution Suspected import. Recorded once in the British Isles, as a live adult in the Aberdeen docks of eastern Scotland in 1983. Its natural range is from Uruguay to Vancouver and as strays further north. Also present in the West Indies. Larva feeds on Bignonia, Fringe-tree, Jasmine and various members of the Forget-me-not and Vervain families.

Wild Cherry Sphinx

Sphinx drupiferarum Smith in Abbot 1797

Rare immigrant/suspected import.   1977

Field characters Similar in appearance to Privet Hawkmoth but pink coloration on hindwing and abdomen of the latter is replaced by greyish-white,

as is the brown on forewing. The moth is generally darker.

Status & distribution Rare immigrant or suspected import. A single individual of unknown origin was captured in a light-trap on 21 May 1965 at Weston-super-Mare, Somerset. A North American species which has been recorded from the southern USA and California, north to Nova Scotia and British Colombia in Canada. Larva feeds on Apple, Plum, Wild Cherry, Hackberry and Lilac.

Mediterranean Hawkmoth

Hyles nicaea (Prunn.)

Suspected import/immigrant.   1988(6856)

Field characters Closely resembles Spurge Hawkmoth. Large spot on inner edge of hindwing is pinkish in Mediterranean Hawkmoth and creamy white in Spurge Hawkmoth.

Status & distribution Suspected import or immigrant. The inclusion of this species on the British list rests solely on a published report of two almost full-grown larvae said to have been found feeding on Common Toadflax on the South Devon coast at Thurlestone, near the mouth of the Avon, on 20 August 1954. Both reportedly produced adults that emerged on 12 July 1955. This moth is not normally migratory, and the usual larval foodplants are herbaceous species of Spurge. Pittaway (1993) considers records from Toadflax erroneous and Skinner (1984 & 1998) decided not to include the species as recorded in Britain. Newman (1965) ventured that a female moth might have been transported on a ship from Spain. The moth breeds on the Mediterranean coasts of North Africa and southern Europe and eastwards through Turkey to India and China.

Seathorn Hawkmoth

Hyles hippophaes (Esp.)

Dubious rare immigrant/import.   1989(6859)

Field characters Closely resembles Spurge Hawkmoth, from which it is distinguished by colour of broad stripe across centre of hindwing, which is grey, not fawn or white.

Status & distribution Dubious rare immigrant or import. Inclusion of this species on the British list is based solely on the following statement from Barrett in 1895, 'Dr Mason possesses from the collection of the late Mr E. Brown, a specimen of *D. hippophaes*, Esp., a local species in southern and eastern Europe, labelled "Devonshire"'. The moth has three disjunct populations in southern Europe, the nearest of which is the Mediterranean coast of France, from which it is known to wander considerable distances. The main larval foodplant in this area is Sea Buckthorn, which grows on coastal dunes and shingle beaches as in the British Isles, but also along riverbeds in mountainous areas. Also breeds on the related Oleaster, an introduction from Turkey now established over much of southern Europe. This is the main foodplant of the population in the Aegean region.

Local Long-tailed Satin
Trichocercus sparshalli (Curt.)
Suspected import. 2023

Status & distribution Suspected import. Included on the British list on the basis of a single individual said to have been captured near Horning, Norfolk in 1829. An Australian species most unlikely to have reached Britain unassisted.

Isabelline Tiger
Pyrrharctia isabella (Smith)
Accidental introduction. 2065

Field characters FW 25mm. Resembles a large Buff Ermine but more elongate spotted forewing.
Status & distribution Accidental introduction. Larvae reported and reared to adult at Carnforth, Lancashire, for several years to 1906. In the late 1960s, some larvae arrived in Edinburgh with consignments of American oak imported for building beer barrels, and three adults were reared for confirmation. Resident in North America where it is frequent throughout.

Halysidota moeschleri Roths.
Rare immigrant/suspected import. 2066

Field characters FW 23mm. Resembles a large Buff Ermine but more elongate patterned forewing.
Status & distribution Rare transatlantic immigrant or suspected import. A single male of this West Indian species was captured in a light trap at Charlton Kings, Cheltenham, Gloucestershire, on 19 July 1961. Larva feeds on a wide range of broadleaved trees.

Great Leopard
Hypercompe scribonia (Stoll)
Suspected import. 2069a

Field characters FW 40mm. A large, whitish moth with several rows of open black spots or rings across forewing.
Status & distribution Suspected import. Originally reported as *Ecpantheria deflorata* Fabr. and added to the British List on the basis of a larva imported in 1969 with American Oak from the USA. In 1994 an adult was found at rest by a light on the outside wall of a warehouse at Aberdeen docks about three days after the warehouse had handled a shipment of crates from Dallas, Texas, USA. The moth is widespread in central and eastern USA and was most likely imported accidentally to the UK with the crates.

Handmaid
Dysauxes ancilla (L.)
Rrare immigrant/import. 2071(10521)

Field characters FW 12mm. Forewing slender, light brown, with three whitish transparent spots near wing tip. Hindwing deep yellow with a brown border

in female, brown to transparent in male.
Status & distribution Suspected rare immigrant or import. One example, reportedly captured near Worthing, Sussex, was exhibited at a meeting of the Entomological Society in 1867. Resident mainly in central, eastern and south-east Europe where it is local, but also recorded from Denmark and Belgium.

Ctenuchidae (Euchromiinae)

The following neotropical members of the Euchromiinae have been placed on the British list but they were all clearly imported. Probably other species of this group have been imported but do not appear on the British list. These moths are like the Syntominae in shape, usually with clear patches in the wings and metallic-coloured bands on the abdomen.

Basker
Euchromia lethe (Fabr.)
Import, with bananas from West Indies 2072

Antichloris viridis (Druce)
Import, with bananas from West Indies 2073

Docker
Antichloris caca (Hb.)
Import, S. American species. 2074

Banana Stowaway
Antichloris eriphia (Fabr.)
Import, S. American species. 1981-85, 1997, 2001 2074a

Gregson's Dart
Agrotis spinifera (Hb.)
Doubtfully British. 2086

Field characters & Similar species Similar to brown forms of Archer's Dart but compressed circular spot is often obliterated by a pale streak along leading edge of forewing. Forewing has a large, sharp dark brown streak in trailing half, projecting from near kidney-mark towards thorax.
Status & distribution Doubtfully British. Recorded once only. An example was reportedly captured on Man in 1869, flying in afternoon sunshine with Archer's Darts, of which it was originally thought to be an unusual example. A specimen, allegedly this one, was confirmed at the time as this species but there has been subsequent doubt as to its origin. Widespread and frequent in Africa and parts of southern Europe.

Gothic Dart
Feltia subgothica (Haw.)
Doubtfully British. 2095

Field characters Broad blackish-brown forewing

with a conspicuous pale streak running from thorax to oval. Also an area of pale shading between kidney-mark and trailing edge of forewing.

Status & distribution Doubtfully recorded in the British Isles. In 1809, Haworth described the species for the first time from a specimen said to have been taken in England. A specimen of this species, reported to have been captured with some others near Barnstable, north Devon, prior to 1829, still exists in the Natural History Museum, London. Stephens' *Systematic Catalogue of British Insects* refers to this specimen and states that others had been recorded near London and in Norfolk. Not reported again in Britain. A North American cut-worm, which feeds on tobacco and many other low-growing plants.

Tawny Shoulder
Feltia subterranea (Fabr.)
Doubtfully British. 2096

Status & distribution Doubtfully British. Probably either imported or a misidentification. Another North American moth which is treated as British in Stephens' *Systematic Catalogue of British Insects* but was never reported in the British Isles again. According to Stephens, 'one was taken nearly 30 years ago and later destroyed; one in June 1817, near West Ham; and one near Cork in June 1826, now in the cabinet of Mr Stone.' At the time, it was referred to as *Agrotis annexa* Treit. J W Tutt, writing in 1891, attributed these records to small forms of Dark Swordgrass.

Kidney-spotted Minor
Lacinipolia renigera (Steph.)
Doubtfully British. 2146

Field characters & Similar species Although related to Shears, this is somewhat like a dark form of Garden Dart in size and appearance, with a more conspicuous whitish kidney-mark and three well-defined wavy whitish cross-lines on forewing, and more variation in ground-colour.

Status & distribution Doubtfully British. Stephens described and named the species in 1829 based on three specimens said to have been taken near London many years previously. Note that Stephens also listed as British another moth with a similar scientific name, a relative of the Flame Shoulder called *Ochropleura renigera*, but his specimens were later found to be a form of the Northern Rustic, which he had misidentified. Widespread and abundant in North America, where it is known as the Bristly Cutworm moth, feeding on the leaves of many crops, from apple trees to cabbages.

Spanish Moth
Xanthopastis timais (Cramer)
Doubtfully British.. 2179a

Field characters & Similar species A very striking moth, with pink- and black-spotted forewing and a woolly black thorax, likely to be mistaken for a tiger moth.

Status & distribution Doubtfully British. A single specimen without data was found in a collection of insects said to have been taken in the London area. It was exhibited at a meeting of the South London Entomological & Natural History Society on 22 May 1946, and was presumed imported with produce. A resident of the New World, occurring from Argentina to the southern USA and as a vagrant north to New York, feeding on Figs and various other plants.

Kew Arches
Brithys crini ssp. *pancratii* (Cyr.)
Suspected import. 2180

Field characters & Similar species A dark, charcoal-coloured moth with pure white hindwing. Outer part of narrow forewing is tinted with reddish brown.

Status & distribution Suspected import. In October 1933, 24 larvae found in Kew Gardens feeding on an edging plant *Zephyranthes candida*, and were reared successfully. The plant is a native of South America, where the moth does not occur, and had not been recently imported to Kew. The moth is resident on the Mediterranean coast and occurs inland in southern Europe. Most probably it arrived in a consignment of other plants.

Mythimna commoides (Guen.)
Doubtfully British. 2207

Field characters & Similar species Resembles Shoulder-striped Wainscot.

Status & distribution Probable import or hoax. The only British record is of four individuals stated as having been captured 'in a spot bordering on Romney Marsh, during the first week of August 1873'. A North American species.

Maori
Graphania dives (Philp.)
Suspected import. 2210

Field characters & Similar species Similar in size and shape to Silver Cloud. Forewing buff brown, hindwing grey.

Status & distribution Suspected import. Recorded once in the British Isles. One captured alive on Spurn Head, on the Yorkshire coast, on a warm afternoon in July 1950. The most likely means of arrival is as an escape from a passing ship. Resident in New Zealand.

Green Silver-spangled Shark
Cucullia argentea (Hufn.)
Doubtfully British. 2212

Field characters Forewing greenish with a number of large silver blocks, unlike any other species.

Status & distribution Doubtfully British. Two speci-

409

mens of this widespread European species have been claimed as captured in the British Isles. Stephens, in 1829, reports that the only one he knew of had been caught about 20 years earlier 'near Dedingstone, by Mr Shelton - Dr Leach'. The specimen is now in the Natural History Museum, London. There is nowhere today called Dedingstone, and it is not even clear to which county the record refers. A second specimen was discovered in 1977 in a row of Green Silver-lines in the collection of J S Greenhill, labelled 'Kent, 7/1932' in Greenhill's handwriting. While Kent is particularly well placed to receive immigrant moths, it has also been the base for several dubious traders who have sold imported specimens as British at inflated prices.

Lettuce Shark

Cucullia lactucae ([D. & S.])
Doubtfully British.   2215

Field characters & Similar species Easily confused with Shark, but distinguished from it by two black zigzag lines across centre of forewing.
Status & distribution Very doubtfully recorded in the British Isles, but widespread in mainland Europe, including Scandinavia. Haworth and Stephens record it as frequent around London in the early 19th century, but Stephens' description appears to refer to forms of the Shark. A specimen collected by A Sidgwick is labelled 'bred, Oxford District, June 3, 1900', but his diary records that he was in Switzerland in August 1899, which is a good time and place to find the caterpillar, which he probably then reared in Oxford. This loose approach to labelling was common at the time. An adult was reported at light at Stone, Buckinghamshire, on 21 July 1965, but was not retained so it cannot be confirmed that it was not a form of the Shark.

False Water Betony

Shargacucullia prenanthis Boisd.
Doubtfully British.   2222

Status & distribution Doubtfully British. No confirmed British record. This moth was illustrated in the first volume of *British moths and their transformations* by Humphreys & Westwood (1843) based on two dark specimens in Stephens' collection, but Stephens did not include them as British in his own work. The inclusion by Humphreys & Westwood is therefore probably a mistake. There are no other records.

Shargacullia caninae Ramb.
Doubtfully British.   2222a

Status & distribution Doubtfully British. No confirmed British record. The only basis for including this species on the British list is that four larvae which William Buckler obtained to illustrate the Water Betony for his *Larvae of British butterflies and moths* are, from the illustrations, clearly those of *Cucullia caninae*. The larvae may have been found

near Tuddenham, Suffolk, in 1827, according to Barrett (1900) in *Lepidoptera of the British Isles*.

Ash Shoulder-knot

Scotochrosta pulla ([D. & S.])
Doubtfully British.   2234

Status & distribution Doubtfully British. Most likely a fraud. Stephens in 1829 refers to one said to have been captured at Woodside, near Epping, Essex, in 1817. The dealer, Mr Plastead, sold specimens of other 'rarities' obtained from mainland Europe as British, alleging they were from Epping Forest about this date, so this record is highly dubious.

Fawn Sallow

Copipanolis styracis (Guen.)
Suspected import.   2234a

Field characters & Similar species Somewhat resembles a fawn version of December Moth.
Status & distribution Suspected import. The authors are mystified as to why this species has been included on the British list. A single, slightly worn female of this moth was found alive among Asparagus imported from Florida at New Covent Garden, London, on 22 February 1980. The moth is widespread and frequent in eastern North America, where it is known as the Fawn Sallow.

Green-brindled Dot

Valeria oleagina ([D. & S.])
Doubtfully British.   2246

Field characters & Similar species Forewing a striking mix of green and brown shades, with a conspicuous white kidney-mark. Similar in size to Green-brindled Crescent.
Status & distribution Doubtfully British. Almost certainly this species has not been found in the wild in the British Isles, and definitely not since 1830. It was added to the British list by Donovan, who reports capturing an individual flying at dusk along hedges near Fishguard, Pembrokeshire, in July 1800. However, the moth flies only in March and April elsewhere in Europe, so this record appears to be in error. Other alleged British specimens are associated with the unreliable dealer Plastead, who appears to have supplied Stevens and probably fabricated details of capture.

Large Dagger

Acronicta cuspis (Hb.)
Doubtfully British.   2282

Field characters & Similar species Larger than Grey Dagger and Dark Dagger, with noticeably longer and heavier dagger marking and black shoulder streak on forewing.
Status & distribution Doubtfully British. Not reliably recorded in the British Isles. The only report is from Stephens in 1829, who thought a specimen collected

near Dulwich, London, a few years earlier might have been this species, but he was not sure.

Callopistria latreillei (Dup.)
Doubtfully British. 2309

Status & distribution Doubtfully British. No confirmed record. Included on the British list on the basis of a single specimen labelled 'bred August 7, 1856, John Hunter, Warings colln.', but nothing is known of the origin of the larva. Resident around the Mediterranean, Spain, Portugal and south-eastern Europe.

Cumberland Gem
Eucarta amethystina (Hb.)
Doubtfully British. 2310

Status & distribution Doubtfully British. No confirmed record. Included on the British list on the basis of a statement in Meyrick's *Revised handbook of the British Lepidoptera* (1928), which reads simply 'Cumberland, once, probably a casual immigrant'. No specimen or further details have been traced.

Asian Cotton Leafworm
Spodoptera litura (Fabr.)
Suspected import. 2386a

Field characters & Similar species See Mediterranean Brocade (2386).
Status & distribution Suspected import. The species was only recognised as distinct from Mediterranean Brocade in 1963, and is now known to be Far Eastern, with no resident populations west of Iran and Oman. First recorded in the British Isles as larvae in 1978 at Manchester, on unnamed aquatic plants imported from Singapore. Has not been recorded except with imported produce, and is extremely unlikely to reach Britain unassisted.

Southern Army Worm
Spodoptera eridania (Stoll)
Suspected import. 2386b

Status & distribution Suspected import. First recorded in the British Isles at Clacton-on-Sea, Essex, in a plant nursery, as larvae in 1977.

Scarce Meal-moth
Schinia rivulosa (Guen.)
Doubtfully British. 2406

Field characters About the size of Marbled Clover, with a striking greyish hour-glass shape across the chocolate forewing.
Status & distribution Doubtfully British. This North American species, known in the USA at the Ragweed Flower Moth, was described by Haworth (1809) as inhabiting England, based on a single specimen known to him, which he named *Crambus marginatus*. There is no evidence it occurred in the British Isles.

Nun
Acontia aprica (Hb.)
Doubtfully British. 2416

Field characters A striking black and white moth about the size of Pale Mottled Willow, with two diagnostic black blotches on leading edge of forewing.
Status & distribution Doubtfully British. Probably an accidental or deliberate import, recorded once only. A North American species, known there as the Exposed Bird-dropping Moth and associated with Hollyhocks. Haworth (in 1809) knew of one specimen in a British collection and said it was very rare in England. Stephens (in 1829) adds that this sole British specimen had been captured in England nearly 50 years previously, around 1780, by Mr Tinley, who was known to have maintained a personal museum.

Brixton Beauty
Acontia nitidula (Fabr.)
Doubtfully British. 2417

Status & distribution Doubtfully British. Probably a deliberate import, with one dubious record only. Stephens (in 1829) states 'said to have been taken by Mr Plastead at Brixton, in Surrey, about the middle of September'. What was probably the same specimen was illustrated by Sowerby in 1805. Plastead claimed a number of species from different parts of the world as great rarities captured in Britain, and is now considered an unreliable source of information. An Asiatic species never subsequently recorded anywhere in Europe.

Earias vittella (Fabr.)
Suspected import. 2420a

Field characters & Similar species Like Cream-bordered Green Pea but leading and trailing parts of forewing are broadly marked with yellow.
Status & distribution Suspected import. Recorded in Britain only as airport interceptions of the immature stages with produce. First recorded in 1976 on Okra pods imported from India. Does not occur naturally in Europe.

Sallow Nycteoline page 333
Nycteola degenerana (Hb.)
Rare immigrant/suspected import. 2424(10443)

Field characters & Similar species FW 12-13mm. Resembles Oak Nycteoline in shape, but slightly larger with forewing broader and head and palps white. Forewing with a complex pattern, usually strongly variegated with well-defined white or greenish-white markings.
Status & distribution Uncertain: possibly an immigrant or suspected import with timber. Reported three times in the British Isles, although details are vague and unconfirmed. One individual is now in the Natural History Museum, London. It is in very fresh

condition and is labelled 'New Forest, 1905, E Morris', with no further details as to the circumstances of its origin. Sheldon referred in 1922 to this and two additional specimens captured earlier, one of which was believed to have been taken at Chattenden, Kent, in the 19th century, but gave no more information about this or the other individual. Widespread in Europe, where larva feeds on willows.

Marbled Tuffet
Charadra deridens (Guen.)
Suspected import.   2426

Field characters A pale grey moth with wavy black marbling on forewing, slightly larger than Nut-tree Tussock.
Status & distribution Suspected deliberate import. The only 'British' record is of a male captured in a light-trap by C H Hards in his garden at Plumstead, Kent, on 24 May 1952. The moth may have been an escape from insects he imported from the USA. Widespread and frequent in eastern North America, the larvae feeding on a wide range of broadleaved trees.

Soybean Looper
Pseudoplusia includens (Walk.)
Suspected import.   2435a

Field characters & Similar species Resembles a small Silver Y but the silver mark is broken in two and surrounded by a light purplish tint.
Status & distribution Suspected import. A single individual of this abundant North American species, which feeds on many low-growing plants, was found rather battered but alive at Covent Garden Market, London, on 20 December 1978, in a box of Asparagus imported from Florida.

Double-spotted Spangle
Autographa bimaculata (Steph.)
Doubtfully British.   2446

Field characters & Similar species Resembles Silver Y and Golden Twin-spot, but distinguished by shape of metallic markings in centre of forewing. In Double-spotted Spangle the inner of the two silvery or golden spots is shaped like a G on the left forewing (mirror image on right forewing).
Status & distribution Doubtfully British. Included on the British list by Stephens in 1830 on the basis of a single specimen, without data, in a British collection. There have been no reports of this species occurring in the wild in the British Isles or elsewhere in Europe subsequently. An abundant species in the North America and parts of Canada, where it is known as the Two-spotted Looper Moth.

Double-barred
Caenurgina crassiuscula (Haw.)
Suspected import.   2458

Field characters & Similar species Very much like Burnet Companion in size, appearance and habits but outer edge of dark band across forewing is straight rather than indented in the middle.
Status & distribution Suspected import. Reported twice only in the British Isles. Stephens (in 1829) recorded that he knew of two specimens found in Britain, 'one in Mr Swainson's collection, the other in my own: the latter captured about three years' since in the north of England'. Haworth used Swainson's specimen when he formally described the species in 1809, stating that he examined it 'many years ago', so this first one was presumably captured in the late 18th century. An abundant North American day-flying species, where it is known as the Clover Looper Moth.

Triple-barred
Mocis trifasciata (Steph.)
Doubtfully British.   2459

Field characters Unlike any resident British species. A broad-winged brown moth, usually with two rather straight lines across forewing, widely placed either side of a fairly well-defined kidney-mark.
Status & distribution Doubtfully British. Described by Stephens in 1830 from a specimen said to have been captured by the Rev W Kirby at Barham. Nothing more is known about the origin of this specimen, nor even whether Barham refers to that in Kent, Suffolk or Huntingdonshire. Frequent in clover fields in North America.

Diphthera festiva (Fabr.)
Suspected import.   2465a

Field characters & Similar species Forewing of this amazing moth is bright yellow, boldly marked with black and metallic blue spots and shapes, including three parallel rows of dots, as if painted on. Quite unlike any European moth. Slightly larger than Herald; known in North America as the Hieroglyphic Moth.
Status & distribution Suspected import.The only report from Britain is of one stated to have been found at Union Dock, Limehouse, London, on 19 September 1867. The moth was apparently fluttering its wings and crawling, in perfect condition, as if newly emerged from a pupa. The port had been visited by ships from all over the world. A resident mainly of Central America, but breeds northwards to South Carolina. Occasionally found as a vagrant to Michigan. Recorded on Sweet Potato and Pecan, among others.

Great Kidney
Synedoida grandirena (Haw.)
Suspected import.   2468

Field characters & Similar species Somewhat like Passenger. A striking species, with black and white hindwing.
Status & distribution Accidental or deliberate import. One, in poor condition, was reported in 1809 as from Bristol some years earlier, and was added to the British list, but the owner of the specimen expressed doubts

about the circumstances of capture. A widespread and locally frequent resident of eastern North America, where it is known as the Figure-Seven Moth.

Orodesma apicina (H.-S.)
Suspected import.   2475a

Status & distribution Suspected import. A female of this Central and South American species was captured on the banks of the Leeds and Liverpool Canal near Chorley, south Lancashire, and subsequently reported in the *Entomologists' Weekly Intelligencer* (9: 31) in 1861, under the name *Pandesma opassina* Guen. Doubleday wrote that he had a male of the same species taken near London and considered an import. No other records.

Waved Tabby
Idia aemula (Hb.)
Doubtfully British.   2486

Field characters & Similar species Somewhat like the Large Tabby in size and shape, but greyish with a conspicuous yellowish kidney-mark on forewing.

Status & distribution Doubtfully British. No confirmed British record. Stephens included this North American species in *Illustrations of British Entomology* (1834) and knew of two specimens. He described the moth as very rare. There is no evidence they were collected in Britain and none have been reported subsequently.

Twin-striped Tabby
Idia lubricalis (Geyer)
Doubtfully British.   2487

Field characters & Similar species Somewhat like the British Large Tabby (*Aglossa pinguinalis*, Pyralidae) in size and shape, but with glossy black forewing with two jagged, whitish cross-lines.

Status & distribution Doubtfully British. No confirmed British record. Stephens included this species in *Illustrations of British Entomology* (1834) and knew of two specimens, but not their origin. There is no evidence they were collected in Britain and none have been reported subsequently. A plentiful species in eastern North America.

Stop Press – Recent records

Lithophane consocia   page 321
Supected rare immigrant.   2238a(9663)

Field characters & Similar species FW 18-20mm. Very similar to ssp. *fucifera* of Conformist, and any suspected specimen of either should be retained for confimation. Ground-colour of forewing dark grey and general appearance usually more contrasting, with darker speckling and often stronger whitish variegation (cleaner, more slaty-grey in Conformist). Nonconformist has a much thicker black bar in central area of forewing.

Flight season One generation. September-November and March-May after hibernation.

Larval foodplants Alder, birches and Hazel.

Status & distribution Suspected rare immigrant. A noctuid moth, originally thought to be an example of the continental ssp. *furcifera* of the Conformist, was caught in an actinic light-trap in Hampstead, London, on 21 September 2001. It was retained, and recently has been positively identified as *Lithophane consocia*. Mainly found in northern and eastern Europe, including France, Denmark, Poland and Russia. The wind was light northerly when the Hampstead moth was caught, suggesting that it was an immigrant.

Authors' names which have been abbreviated in the descriptions

For an explanation of their use, see page 14.

Barrett	Barr.	Mabille	Mab.
Bastelberger	Bast.	Metcalfe	Metc.
Boheman	Boh.	Millière	Mill.
Boisduval	Boisd.	Müller	Müll.
Borkhausen	Borkh.	Newman	Newm.
Boursin	Bours.	Oberthür	Ob.
Brünnich	Brünn.	Ochsenheimer	Ochs.
Bytinski-Satz	Byt.-Salz	Osbeck	Osb.
Clerk	Cl.	Pallas	Pall.
Cockayne & Williams	Cock. & Will.	Philpott	Philp.
Cockayne	Cock.	Piller	Pill.
Cockerell	Cockll.	Prunner, de	Prunn.
Curtis, W. Parkinson	W.P. Curt.	Rambur	Ramb.
Curtis, W.	Curt.	Rezbanyai-Reser	Rézb.-Res.
DeGeer	DeG.	Richardson	Rich.
Dennis & Schiffermüller	D.& S.	Rothschild	Roths.
Donovan	Don.	Rottemburg	Rott.
Doubleday	Doubl.	Rowland-Brown	Rowl.-Br.
Duponchel	Dup.	Scharfenberg	Scharf.
Esper	Esp.	Scheven	Schev.
Eversmann, von	Eversm.	Schrank	Schr.
Fabricius	Fabr.	Schreber	Schreb.
Fletcher	Fletch.	Scopoli	Scop.
Forster	Forst.	Sheldon	Sheld.
Fuessly	Fuessl.	Sparre-Schneider	Sp.-Schn.
Graslin	Grasl.	Spuler	Spul.
Gregson	Gregs.	Stainton	Stt.
Guenée	Guen.	Staudinger	Stdgr.
Harrison	Harr.	Stephens	Steph.
Haworth	Haw.	Tauscher	Tausch.
Hering	Her.	Thunberg	Thunb.
Herrich-Schäffer	H.-S.	Treitschke	Treit.
Hohenwarth	Hohen.	Tremewan	Trem.
Hübner	Hb.	Turner	Turn.
Hufnagel	Hufn.	Verity	Ver.
Humphreys &		Vieweg	View.
Westwood	Humph. & Westw.	Villers	Vill.
Joannis, de	Joann.	Walker	Walk.
Jordan	Jord.	Warren	Warr.
La Harpe	La Harpe, de	Werneburg	Werneb.
Laspeyres	Lasp.	Wnukoqaky	Wnuk.
Lederer	Led.	Wollaston	Woll.
Lefebvre	Lefeb.	Zeller	Zell.
Linnaeus	L.	Zincken	Zinck.

Scientific names of plants

These are larval and nectar plants mentioned in the text.
Nomenclature follows Stace (1997)

Alder *Alnus glutinosa*
Alison, Golden *Allyssum saxatile*
Almond *Prunus dulcis*
Angelica, Wild *Angelica sylvestris*
Apple *Malus domestica*
Apple, Crab *Malus sylvestris*
Archangel, Yellow *Lamiastrum galeobdolon*
Ash *Fraxinus excelsior*
Aspen *Populus tremula*
Asphodel, Bog *Narthecium ossifragum*
Aster, Sea *Aster tripolium*
Aven, Wood *Geum urbanum*
Azalea, Trailing *Loiseleuria procumbens*

Balsam, Indian *Impatiens glandulifera*
Balsam, Orange *Impatiens capensis*
Balsam, Small *Impatiens parviflora*
Balsam, Touch-me-not *Impatiens noli-tangere*
Barberry *Berberis vulgaris*
Barberry, Mrs Wilson's *Berberis wilsoniae*
Barberry, Thunberg's *Berberis thunbergii*
Bartsia, Red *Odontites vernus*
Bearberry *Arctostaphylos uva-ursi*
Bedstraw, Fen *Galium uliginosum*
Bedstraw, Heath *Galium saxatilis*
Bedstraw, Hedge *Galium mollugo*
Bedstraw, Lady's *Galium verum*
Bedstraw, Marsh *Galium palustre*
Bedstraw, Northern *Galium boreale*
Beech *Fagus sylvatica*
Beet *Beta vulgaris*
Beet, Sea *Beta maritima*
Bellflower, Clustered *Campanula glomerata*
Bellflower, Giant *Campanula latifolia*
Bellflower, Nettle-leaved *Campanula trachelium*
Bent, Bristle *Agrostis curtisii*
Bent, Common *Agrostis capillaris*
Bilberry *Vaccinium myrtillus*
Bilberry, Bog *Vaccinium uliginosum*
Bindweed, Field *Convolvulus arvensis*
Bindweed, Hedge *Calystegia sepium*
Bindweed, Sea *Calystegia soldanella*
Birch, Downy *Betula pubescens*
Birch, Silver *Betula pendula*
Bird's-foot-trefoil, Common *Lotus corniculatus*
Bird's-foot-trefoil, Greater *Lotus uliginosus*
Bitter-vetch *Lathyrus linifolius*
Black Medick *Medicago lupulina*
Black-bindweed *Fallopia convolvulus*
Black-poplar *Populus nigra*
Blackthorn *Prunus spinosa*
Bluebell *Hyacinthoides non-scripta*
Bog-myrtle *Myrica gale*
Bog-rosemary *Andromeda polifolia*

Bracken *Pteridium aquilinum*
Bramble *Rubus fruiticosus* agg.
Brome, False *Brachypodium sylvaticum*
Broom *Cytisus scoparius*
Buckthorn *Rhamnus cathartica*
Buckthorn, Alder *Frangula alnus*
Bullace *Prunus insitia*
Bulrush *Typha latifolia*
Bulrush, Lesser *Typha angustifolia*
Burnet, Salad *Sanguisorba minor*
Burnet-saxifrage *Pimpinella saxifraga*
Bur-reed, Branched *Sparganium erectum*
Butterbur *Petasites hybridus*
Buttercup, Meadow *Ranunculus acris*

Cabbage *Brassica oleracea*
Californian Poppy *Eschscholzia california*
Campion, Bladder *Silene vulgaris*
Campion, Red *Silene dioica*
Campion, Sea *Silene uniflora*
Campion, White *Silene latifolia*
Canary-grass, Reed *Phalaris arundinacea*
Carrot, Wild *Daucus carota*
Castor-oil-plant *Ricinus communis*
Catchfly, Nottingham *Silene nutans*
Catchfly, Spanish *Silene otites*
Cedar of Lebanon *Cedrus libani*
Celandine, Lesser *Ranunculus ficaria*
Chamomile *Chamaemelum nobile*
Chamomile, Corn *Anthemis arvensis*
Chamomile, Stinking *Anthemis cotula*
Cherry Plum *Prunus cerasifera*
Cherry, Bird *Prunus padus*
Cherry, Wild *Prunus avium*
Chestnut, Sweet *Castanea sativa*
Chickweed, Common *Stellaria media*
Chicory *Cichorium intybus*
Cinquefoil, Creeping *Potentilla reptans*
Cleavers *Galium aparine*
Clover, Hare's-foot *Trifolium arvense*
Clover, Red *Trifolium pratense*
Clover, White *Trifolium repens*
Club-rush, Common *Schoenoplectus lacustris*
Cock's-foot *Dactylis glomeratus*
Colt's-foot *Tussilago farfara*
Comfrey, Common *Symphytum officinale*
Corn Spurry *Spergula arvensis*
Cottongrass, Common *Eriophorum angustifolium*
Couch *Elytrigia repens*
Couch, Sand *Elytrigia juncea*
Cowberry *Vaccinium vitis-idaea*
Cowslip *Primula veris*
Cow-wheat, Common *Melampyrum pratense*
Crack-willow *Salix fragilis*

Cranberry *Vaccinium oxycoccos*
Crane's-bill, Shining *Geranium lucidum*
Crowberry *Empetrum nigrum*
Currant, Black *Ribes nigrum*
Currant, Red *Ribes rubrum*
Cypress, Lawson's *Chamaecyparis lawsoniana*
Cypress, Leyland x *Cupressocyparis leylandii*
Cypress, Monterey *Cupressus macrocarpa*

Dandelion *Taraxacum* spp.
Dead-nettle, Red *Lamium purpureum*
Dead-nettle, White *Lamium album*
Dewberry *Rubus* sect. *Caesii*
Dock, Broad-leaved *Rumex obtusifolius*
Dock, Curled *Rumex crispus*
Dock, Water *Rumex hydrolapathum*
Dog's Mercury *Mercurialis perennis*
Dog-rose *Rosa canina*
Dog-violet, Common *Viola riviniana*
Dogwood *Cornus sanguinea*

Elder *Sambucus nigra*
Elm, English *Ulmus procera*
Elm, Small-leaved *Ulmus minor*
Elm, Wych *Ulmus glabra*
Enchanter's-nightshade *Circaea lutetiana*
Evening-primrose, Common *Oenothera biennis*
Everlasting, Mountain *Antennaria dioica*
Eyebright *Euphrasia* spp.

Fat-hen *Chenopodium album*
Fennel, Hog's *Peucedanum officinale*
Fen-sedge, Great *Cladium mariscus*
Fescue, Meadow *Festuca pratensis*
Fescue, Red *Festuca rubra*
Fescue, Tall *Festuca arundinacea*
Feverfew *Tanacetum parthenium*
Figwort, Common *Schrophularia nodosa*
Figwort, Water *Schrophularia auriculata*
Fir, Douglas *Pseudotsuga menziesii*
Fir, Giant *Abies grandis*
Fir, Noble *Abies procera*
Fir, Silver *Abies alba*
Flax, Fairy *Linum catharticum*
Fleabane, Common *Pulicaria dysenterica*
Flixweed *Descurainia sophia*
Foxglove *Digitalis purpurea*

Garlic Mustard *Alliaria petiolata*
Geranium, Scarlet *Pelargonium x hybridum*
Goldenrod *Solidago virgaurea*
Goldenrod, Canadian *Solidago canadensis*
Golden-samphire *Inula crithmoides*
Gooseberry *Ribes uva-crispa*

Scientific names of plants

Goosefoot, Red *Chenopodium rubrum*
Gorse *Ulex europaeus*
Grape-vine *Vitis vinifera*
Greenweed, Dyer's *Genista tinctoria*
Gromwell, Field *Lithospermum arvense*
Ground-elder *Aegopodium podagraria*
Ground-ivy *Glechoma hederacea*
Groundsel *Senecio vulgaris*
Groundsel, Sticky *Senecio viscosus*
Guelder-rose *Viburnum opulus*

Hair-grass, Early *Aira praecox*
Hair-grass, Silver *Aira caryophyllea*
Hair-grass, Tufted *Deschampsia cespitosa*
Hair-grass, Wavy *Deschampsia flexuosa*
Harebell *Campanula rotundifolia*
Hawk's-beard, Smooth *Crepis capillaris*
Hawk's-head, Tuberous *Aetheorhiza bulbosa*
Hawthorn, Common *Crataegus monogyna*
Hawthorn, Midland *Crataegus laevigata*
Hazel *Corylus avellana*
Heath, Cross-leaved *Erica tetralix*
Heather *Calluna vulgaris*
Heather, Bell *Erica cinerea*
Hemlock-spruce, Western *Tsuga heterophylla*
Hemp-agrinomy *Eupatorium cannabinum*
Hemp-nettle, Common *Galeopsis tetrahit*
Henbane *Hyoscyamus niger*
Hogweed *Heracleum sphondylium*
Holly *Ilex aquifolium*
Hollyhock *Alcea rosea*
Honeysuckle *Lonicera periclymenum*
Hop *Humulus lupulus*
Horehound, Black *Ballota nigra*
Hornbeam *Carpinus betulus*
Horse-chestnut *Aesculus hippocastanum*
Horse-radish *Armoracia rusticana*
Hound's-tongue *Cynoglossum officinale*

Iris, Yellow *Iris pseudacorus*
Ivy *Hedera helix*

Jasmine, Winter *Jasminum nudiflorum*
Juniper, Common *Juniperus communis*

Knapweed, Common *Centaurea nigra*
Knapweed, Greater *Centaurea scabiosa*
Knotgrass *Polygonum aviculare*

Laburnum *Laburnum anagyroides*
Larch, European *Larix decidua*
Larkspur *Consolida ajacis*
Lettuce, Great *Lactua virosa*
Lettuce, Prickly *Lactuca serriola*
Lilac *Syringa vulgaris*
Lime, Large-leaved *Tilia platyphyllos*
Lime, Small-leaved *Tilia cordata*
Liquorice, Wild *Astragalus glycyphyllos*
Lombardy-poplar *Populus* 'Italica'
Loosestrife, Yellow *Lysimachia vulgaris*
Lousewort *Pedicularis sylvatica*
Lucerne *Medicago sativa*

Lupin, Tree *Laburnum arboreus*
Lyme-grass *Leymus arenarius*

Madder, Wild *Rubia peregrina*
Male-fern *Dryopteris filix-mas*
Mallow, Common *Malva sylvestris*
Mallow, Dwarf *Malva neglecta*
Maple, Field *Acer campestre*
Marigold *Tagetes* spp.
Marjoram, Wild *Origanum vulgare*
Marram *Ammophila arenaria*
Marsh-mallow *Althaea officinalis*
Mat-grass *Nardus stricta*
Mayweed, Scentless *Tripleurospermum inodorum*
Meadow-grass, Annual *Poa annua*
Meadow-grass, Bulbous *Poa bulbosa*
Meadow-grass, Rough *Poa trivialis*
Meadow-grass, Smooth *Poa pratensis*
Meadow-grass, Wood *Poa nemoralis*
Meadow-rue, Common *Thalictrum flavum*
Meadow-rue, Lesser *Thalictrum minus*
Meadowsweet *Filipendula ulmaria*
Medick, Black *Medicago lupulina*
Melick, Wood *Mica uniflora*
Michaelmas-daisy *Aster* spp.
Milkwort, Common *Polygala vulgaris*
Milkwort, Heath *Polygala serpyllifolia*
Mint, Garden *Mentha* spp.
Monk's-hood *Aconitum napellus*
Moor-grass, Blue *Sesleria caerulea*
Moor-grass, Purple *Molinia caerulea*
Mouse-ear, Common *Cerastium fontanum*
Mouse-ear, Field *Cerastium arvense*
Mouse-ear, Sticky *Cerastium glomeratum*
Mouse-ear-hawkweed *Pilosella officinarum*
Mugwort *Artemisia vulgaris*
Mullein, Dark *Verbascum nigrum*
Mullein, White *Verbascum lychnitis*

Navelwort *Umbilicus rupestris*
Nettle, Common *Urtica dioica*
Nightshade, Deadly *Atropa belladonna*

Oak, Evergreen (Holm) *Quercus ilex*
Oak, Pedunculate *Quercus robur*
Oak, Sessile *Quercus petraea*
Oak, Turkey *Quercus cerris*
Oat-grass, False *Arrhenatherum elatus*
Orache, Common *Atriplex patula*
Orache, Grass-leaved *Atriplex littoralis*
Osier *Salix viminalis*
Oxlip *Primula elatior*

Pampas-grass *Cortaderia selloana*
Parsley, Cow *Anthriscus sylvestris*
Pea, Garden *Pisum sativum*
Pea, Marsh *Lathyrus palustris*
Pear *Pyrus communis*
Pellitory-of-the-wall *Parietaria judaica*
Periwinkle, Lesser *Vinca minor*
Petty Whin *Genista anglica*

Pignut *Conopodium majus*
Pine, Corsican *Pinus nigra laricio*
Pine, Lodgepole *Pinus contorta*
Pine, Maritime *Pinus pinaster*
Pine, Scots *Pinus sylvestris*
Plane, London *Platanus* x *hispanica*
Plantain, Buck's-horn *Plantago coronopus*
Plantain, Greater *Plantago major*
Plantain, Ribwort *Plantago lanceolata*
Plantain, Sea *Plantago maritima*
Ploughman's-spikenard *Inula conyzae*
Plum *Prunus domestica*
Pond-sedge, Lesser *Carex acutiformis*
Poplar, White *Populus alba*
Primrose *Primula vulgaris*
Privet, Garden *Ligustrum ovalifolium*
Privet, Wild *Ligustrum vulgare*
Purple-loosestrife *Lythrum salicaria*

Ragged-Robin *Lychnis flos-cuculi*
Ragwort, Common *Senecio jacobaea*
Ragwort, Hoary *Senecio erucifolius*
Rape *Brassica napus*
Raspberry *Rubus idaeus*
Red-cedar, Japanese *Cryptomeria japonica*
Red-cedar, Western *Thuja plicata*
Redshank *Persicaria maculosa*
Reed, Common *Phragmites australis*
Restharrow, Common *Ononis repens*
Restharrow, Spiny *Ononis spinosa*
Rhododendron *Rhododendron ponticum*
Rocket, Sea *Cakile maritima*
Rock-rose, Common *Helianthemum nummularium*
Rose, Burnet *Rosa pimpinellifolia*
Roseroot *Sedum rosea*
Rowan *Sorbus aucuparia*
Rush, Compact *Juncus conglomeratus*
Rush, Jointed *Juncus articulatus*
Rush, Sharp-flowered *Juncus acutiflorus*

Sage *Salvia officinalis*
Sage, Wood *Teucrium scorodonia*
Sainfoin *Onobrychis viciifolia*
Saltmarsh-grass, Borrer's *Puccinellia fasciculata*
Saltmarsh-grass, Common *Puccinellia maritima*
Saltmarsh-grass, Reflexed *Puccinellia distans*
Saltwort, Prickly *Salsola kali*
Sandwort, Sea *Honckenya peploides*
Saw-wort *Serratula tinctoria*
Saxifrage, Mossy *Saxifraga hynoides*
Saxifrage, Purple *Saxifraga oppositifolia*
Scabious, Devil's-bit *Succisa pratensis*
Scabious, Field *Knautia arvensis*
Scabious, Small *Scabiosa columbaria*
Sea-blite, Annual *Suaeda maritima*
Sea-buckthorn *Hippophae rhamnoides*
Sea-holly *Eryngium maritimum*
Sea-lavender, Common *Limonium vulgare*
Sea-milkwort *Glaux maritima*

Sea-purslane *Atriplex portulacoides*
Sea-spurry, Rock *Spergularia rupicola*
Sedge, Glaucous *Carex flacca*
Selfheal *Prunella vulgaris*
Service-tree *Sorbus torminalis*
Sheep's-bit *Jasione montana*
Sheep's-fescue *Festuca ovina*
Shepherd's-purse *Capsella bursa-pastoris*
Silverweed *Potentilla anserina*
Small-reed, Purple *Calamagrostis canescens*
Small-reed, Wood *Calamagrostis epigejos*
Snapdragon *Antirrhinum majus*
Sneezewort *Anthemis ptarmica*
Snowberry *Symphoricarpos albus*
Soapwort *Saponaria officinalis*
Soft-grass, Creeping *Holcus mollis*
Soft-rush *Juncus effusus*
Sorrel, Common *Rumex acetosa*
Sorrel, Sheep's *Rumex acetosella*
Southernwood *Artemisia abrotanum*
Speedwell, Germander *Veronica chamaedrys*
Spindle *Euonymus europaeus*
Spindle, Evergreen *Euonymus japonicus*
Spruce, Norway *Picea abies*
Spruce, Sitka *Picea sitchensis*
Spurge, Sea *Euphorbia paralias*
Spurge, Wood *Euphorbia amygdaloides*
Spurry, Sand *Spergularia rubra*
St John's-wort, Perforate *Hypericum perforatum*
Stitchwort, Greater *Stellaria holostea*
Stitchwort, Lesser *Stellaria graminea*
Stonecrop, Biting *Sedum acre*
Stonecrop, English *Sedum anglicum*
Strawberry, Garden *Fragaria* x *ananassa*
Strawberry, Wild *Fragaria vesca*
Strawberry-tree *Arbutus unedo*

Swede *Brassica napus rapifera*
Sweet-grass, Reed *Glyceria maxima*
Sweet-William *Dianthus barbatus*
Sycamore *Acer pseudoplatanus*

Tamarisk *Tamarix gallica*
Tare, Smooth *Vicia tetrasperma*
Thistle, Carline *Carlina vulgaris*
Thistle, Creeping *Cirsium arvense*
Thistle, Spear *Cirsium vulgare*
Thorn-apple *Datura stramonium*
Thrift *Armeria maritima*
Thyme, Wild *Thymus polytrichus*
Timothy *Phleum pratense*
Toadflax, Common *Linaria vulgaris*
Toadflax, Ivy-leaved *Cymbalaria muralis*
Toadflax, Pale *Linaria repens*
Toadflax, Purple *Linaria purpurea*
Tormentil *Potentilla erecta*
Traveller's-joy *Clematis vitalba*
Treacle-mustard *Erysimum cheiranthoides*
Tree-mallow *Lavateria arborea*
Trefoil, Hop *Trifolium campestre*
Tufted-sedge *Carex elata*
Turnip *Brassica rapa*
Tussock-sedge, Greater *Carex paniculata*

Valerian, Common *Valeriana officinalis*
Valerian, Red *Centranthus ruber*
Vetch, Bush *Vicia sepium*
Vetch, Horseshoe *Hippocrepis comosa*
Vetch, Kidney *Anthyllis vulneraria*
Vetch, Tufted *Vicia cracca*
Vetchling, Meadow *Lathyrus pratensis*
Viper's-bugloss *Echium vulgare*
Virginia-creeper *Parthenocissus quinquefolia*

Wallflower *Erysimum cheiri*
Water-plantain *Alisma plantago-aquatica*
Wayfaring Tree *Viburnum lantana*
Whorl-grass *Catabrosa aquatica*
Willow, Creeping *Salix repens*
Willow, Downy *Salix lapponum*
Willow, Eared *Salix aurita*
Willow (Sallow), Goat *Salix caprea*
Willow (Sallow), Grey *Salix cinerea*
Willow, White *Salix alba*
Willowherb, Broad-leaved *Epilobium montanum*
Willowherb, Great *Epilobium hirsutum*
Willowherb, Rosebay *Chamerion angustifolium*
Willowherb, Square-stalked *Epilobium tetragonum*
Woodruff *Galium odoratum*
Wood-rush, Field *Luzula campestris*
Wood-rush, Hairy *Luzula pilosa*
Wood-sedge *Carex sylvatica*
Wormwood *Artemisia absinthium*
Wormwood, Field *Artemisia campestris*
Wormwood, Sea *Seriphidium maritimum*
Woundwort, Hedge *Stachys sylvatica*

Yarrow *Achillea millefolium*
Yellow-rattle *Rhinanthus minor*
Yew *Taxus baccata*
Yorkshire-fog *Holcus lanatus*

Further reading

Allan, P B M 1947 *A moth-hunter's gossip*. Watkins & Doncaster, London

Allan, P B M 1949 (reprinted 1979) *Larval foodplants*. Watkins & Doncaster, Hawkhurst

Beirne, B 1952 *British pyralid and plume moths*. Warne, London

Bradley, J 2000 *Checklist of Lepidoptera recorded from the British Isles*. (2nd ed.) D Bradley, Fordingbridge

Cribb, P W 1972 *An amateur's guide to the study of the genitalia of Lepidoptera. Leaflet 34*. Amateur Entomologists' Society, Feltham, Middlesex

Dickson, R 1992 *A lepidopterists' handbook. Amateur Entomologist 13*. Amateur Entomologists' Society, Feltham, Middlesex

Emmet, A M 1991 *The scientific names of the British Lepidoptera – their history and meaning*. Harley Books, Essex

Friedrich, E *Breeding butterflies and moths – a practical guide to British and European species*. Harley Books, Essex

Fry, R, & Waring, P 2001 *A guide to moth traps and their use. Amateur Entomologist 24*. (2nd ed.) Amateur Entomologists' Society, London

Goater, B, 1986 *British pyralid moths*. Harley Books, Essex

Haggett, G M 1981 *Larvae of the British Lepidoptera not figured by Buckler*. British Entomological & Natural History Society, London

Heath, J, Cooke, R, Skelton, M J, & Reid, J, 1969-1972 Lepidoptera distribution maps scheme guide to the critical species. In: *AES Pamphlet 12. A Golden Jubilee reprint (1985)*. Amateur Entomologists' Society, Hanworth, Middlesex

Heath, J, & Emmet, A M and others 1976 *The moths and butterflies of Great Britain and Ireland*. Vols. 1, 2, 7, 9 & 10. Harley Books, Essex

Karsholt, O, & Razowski, J 1996 *The Lepidoptera of Europe – A distributional checklist*. Apollo, Stenstrup

Leverton, R, 2001 *Enjoying moths*. Poyser, London

Macleod, R D 1959 *Key to the names of British butterflies and moths*. Pitman, London

Majerus, M 2002 *Moths*. New Naturalist Series. HarperCollins

Marren, P 1998 The English names of moths. *British Wildlife* 10: 29-38

Newman, E 1869 *An illustrated history of the British butterflies and moths*. Allen, London

Newman, L W, & Leeds, H A 1913 *Textbook of British butterflies and moths*. Gibbs & Bamforth, St Albans

Parsons, M, Green, D, & Waring, P 2001 A brief review of Butterfly Conservation's Action for Threatened Moths Project (1999 & 2000). *Atropos* 13: 25-29

Porter, J 1997 *The colour identification guide to caterpillars of the British Isles*. Viking, London

Riley, A M, & Prior, G 2003 *British and Irish Pug Moths – a guide to their identification*. Harley Books, Essex

Salmon, M A 2000 *The Aurelian legacy. British butterflies and their collectors*. Harley Books, Essex

Scoble, M J 1992 *The Lepidoptera – form, function and diversity*. Oxford University Press, Oxford

Shirt, D B (ed.) 1987 *British Red Data Books 2. Insects*. Nature Conservancy Council, Peterborough

Skinner, B 1998 *The colour identification guide to moths of the British Isles*. Viking, London

South, R 1961 *The moths of the British Isles*. 2 volumes. Warne, London

Stace, C 1997 *New flora of the British Isles*. (2nd ed.) Cambridge University Press, Cambridge

Tams, W H T 1941 Some British moths reviewed. In: *AES Pamphlet 12*. A Golden Jubilee reprint (1985). Amateur Entomologists' Society, Hanworth, Middlesex

Tutt, J W 1994 *Practical hints for the field lepidopterist. Amateur Entomologist 23*. Facsimile reprint. Amateur Entomologists' Society, Orpington, Kent

UK Biodiversity Group 1999 *Tranche 2 Action Plans Volume IV – Invertebrates*. English Nature, Peterborough

Waring, P 1989-present Wildlife reports – Moths. *British Wildlife* (every issue)

Waring, P Conserving Britain's rarest moths. *British Wildlife* 1: 226-284

Waring, P 1994 *National Moth Conservation Project*. News Bulletin 5. Butterfly Conservation, Dunstable

Waring, P 1999a The national recording network for the rarer British macro-moths. *Atropos* 6: 19-27

Waring, P 1999b *National Moth Conservation Project*. News Bulletin 10. Butterfly Conservation, Dedham, Colchester

Waring, P (in press) *A review of the nationally scarce and threatened macro-moths of Great Britain*. Joint Nature Conservation Committee, Peterborough

Young, M R 1997 *The natural history of moths*. Poyser, London

National journals and magazines

Atropos – 36 Tinker Lane, Meltham, Holmfirth, West Yorkshire HD9 4EX (www.atropos.info)

British Wildlife – British Wildlife Publishing, Lower Barn, Rooks Farm, Rotherwick, Hook, Hampshire RG27 9BG (www.britishwildlife.com)

Entomologist's Gazette – c/o The Editor, Pentreath, 6 Carlyon Road, Playing Place, Truro, Cornwall TR3 6EU (email: wgt.pentreath@talk21.com)

Entomologist's Record – The Editor, 14 West Road, Bishops Stortford, Hertfordshire CM23 3QP (email: colinwplant@ntlworld.com)

Index of English names

Bold numbers refer to colour plates and photographs

Index of English names

421

Index of English names

422

423

Index of English names

Index of scientific names

Bold numbers refer to colour plates and photographs

425

Index of scientific names

Index of scientific names

429

Index of scientific names

Publisher's note

This guide was inspired by a chance conversation with Richard Lewington many years ago, when he expressed a wish to paint all the larger British moths in their natural resting postures. Bringing in Paul Waring and then Martin Townsend to the project has brought many new perspectives to the concept of a 'field guide' to moths. We hope that this new approach will prove successful. We would like to thank Richard, Paul and Martin and all those who kindly gave their advice, assistance and guidance. As with all guides, we are always keen to receive readers' comments.

Andrew and Anne Branson
British Wildlife Publishing

Acknowledgements

The authors would like to thank warmly the following individuals and organisations for their invaluable help in preparing this guide: Oxford University Museum of Natural History for their generous permission to borrow specimens, provision of access to the Hope collections, use of computer facilities and general encouragement (particularly George McGavin, Darren Mann, James Hogan and John Ismay); Natural History Museum, London, for access to the national collection and comments on difficult and rare species (particularly Martin Honey and David Carter); Biological Records Centre, CEH, Monks Wood (particularly Nick Greatorex-Davies, Henry Arnold and Paul Harding); British Entomological & Natural History Society (particularly Peter Chandler, and many others for discussions and data over the years); Butterfly Conservation (particularly Mark Parsons and David Green); Joint Nature Conservation Committee (particularly Ian McLean and Deborah Procter); National Scarce Moth Recording Network (all county recorders and contributors); Peterborough Museum (Julia Habershaw), Insect Survey, IACR Rothamsted, Harpenden (Ian Woiwod); Mark Tunmore (assistance with accounts of immigrant noctuid moths); Colin Plant (for reading through the manuscript); Royal Entomological Society (library); David Redhead (forewing measuring); Rich Austin (Guernsey); David Barbour and Keith Bland (Scotland); Gordon Craine (Isle of Man); Roger Hayward and Norman Hall (additional forewing measurements); Roger Long (Jersey); Bernard Skinner (for comments on the text, particularly on immigrant species, and loan of specimens); John and Mike Bradley (nomenclature); and David Brown, Anthony Dobson, Andrew Foster, Reg Fry, Gerry Haggett, Roy Leverton, Adrian Riley, Gerry Tremewan, all for commenting on sections of the text.

All photographs supplied by Paul Waring, except Common Swift (page 21) kindly supplied by Jim Porter.

This guide could not have been written without all the moth literature that has preceded it, from the standard textbooks, particularly Bernard Skinner's excellent *Colour Identification Guide to Moths*, to the many articles in the specialist entomological journals, the county moth lists and the moth group newsletters. It incorporates tips shared by lepidopterists past and present, and discussions from many field excursions.

Richard Lewington would like to thank the following for the assistance they gave him during the preparation of the artwork: in particular, Jim Porter and George McGavin, also Dave Green, Mark Parsons, Tim Crafer, David Brown, Roy Leverton, Robert Thompson, Mike Wilkins, Michael Chinery, Sean Clancy, B Banson, Paul Pugh, Adrian Riley, Peter Chandler (BENHS), David Wilson, Barry Goater, Martin Harvey, John & Judy Geeson, Adrian Spalding, Gerry Tremewan, John Chainey, Bernard Skinner, Reg Bell, Michael Taylor, Jon Clifton, David Carter, Norman Hall and David Wedd.